NEW YORK

How to use this book

The main text provides a survey of the city's cultural history from its founding by the Dutch as Nieuw Amsterdam and then as the English New York in 1664 to the present time. It is illustrated with paintings, sculpture, buildings and general views.

The map (pp. 246-47) shows the principal landmarks museums and historic buildings, using symbols and colours for quick reference.

To find a museum or gallery turn to Appendix I, which lists them alphabetically, with their address, opening times and a note on their scope and contents. The larger collections are sub-divided into departments. Page numbers indicate where these are mentioned or illustrated in the text.

To find a historic building or landmark turn to Appendix II, which gives a similar alphabetical list of important buildings, churches, skyscrapers, bridges, etc.

For information on artists—painters, sculptors, architects, etc. — turn to Appendix III. Here are listed those who contributed to the cultural greatness of New York and whose works are now to be seen there. Each entry consists of a biographical note, details of where the artist's works are located, and references to the main text where they are mentioned or illustrated.

World Cultural Guides

NEW YORK

Dore Ashton

150 illustrations
in colour and black and white

special photography
by Mario Carrieri

Holt, Rinehart and Winston
New York • Chicago • San Francisco

'It is the first time that men have projected
all their strength and labour into the sky -
a whole city in the free air of the sky.
Good God, what disorder, what impetuosity!
What perfection already, what promises!'

Edward Le Corbusier
When the Cathedrals were White
Harcourt Brace Jovanovich, Inc, 1947.

The World Cultural Guides
have been devised and produced by
Park and Roche Establishment, Schaan.

Copyright 1972 in London, England, by Park and Roche Establishment, Schaan.
All rights reserved, including the right to reproduce
this book or portions thereof in any form.
Published simultaneously in Canada by Holt, Rinehart
and Winston of Canada, Limited.
Library of Congress Catalog Card Number: 70-155541
First Edition

ISBN: 0-03-088048-3

Printed and bound in Italy by Amilcare Pizzi S.p.A.

Contents

Jacket illustration: The Solomon R. Guggenheim Museum.

End-paper illustration: Manhattan at night.

Significant dates
in the history of New York

1626	Manhattan Island purchased from the Indians by Dutch settlers.
1664	Nieuw Amsterdam surrenders to the British and is renamed New York.
1766	St Paul's Chapel designed in style of James Gibbs by Thomas McBean.
1776	Declaration of Independence.
1783	Federal Government established in New York.
1789	George Washington inaugurated as president in New York, the new capital.
1799	St Mark's-in-the-Bouwerie Church, Georgian style, architect Ithiel Town.
1811	City Council draws up rectangular grid plan.
1820s-30s	Greek Revival architecture in vogue.
1840s	Gothic, Romanesque, Egyptian Revival styles popular.
1846	Trinity Church, architect Richard Upjohn.
1846	Grace Church, architect James Renwick Jr., Both in Gothic Revival style.
1857	Haughwout Building, architect John P. Gaynor, first with cast-iron pre-fabricated curtain wall panels.
1858	Central Park design competition won by Olmsted & Vaux.
1858-79	St Patrick's Cathedral, Gothic Revival style, architect James Renwick Jr.
1861-5	Civil War. Abraham Lincoln president. Hundreds of commercial buildings completed.
1870-83	Brooklyn Bridge, designed and built, engineer A.J. Roebling and son.
1880	Metropolitan Museum, founded 1870, opened in Central Park.
1884	Dakota Apartments, first luxury apartment house, architect Henry J. Hardenberg.
1898	Bayard Building, radical solution to skyscraper problem, architect Louis H. Sullivan.
1906	J.P. Morgan Library, architects McKim, Mead & White.
1908	Ashcan School exhibit stirs controversy.
1911	New York Public Library opens, style of French chateau, architects Carrère & Hastings.

1913	Armory Show. Many new forms of European art shown for the first time in US.
1913	Flatiron Building, architect Daniel Burnham.
1913	Woolworth Building, architect Cass Gilbert.
1917	USA enters World War I.
1929	Wall Street stock market crash.
1930-1	Empire State Building erected, 102 storeys, architects Shreve, Lamb and Harmon.
1931	George Washington Bridge completed, architect Cass Gilbert, engineer O. H. Ammann.
1931-47	Rockefeller Center complex designed and built.
1932	Museum of City of New York, architect Joseph Freedlander.
1933-45	Franklin D. Roosevelt president. Government-sponsored art schemes launched.
1935	Frick Residence (1914) renovated as art museum by John Russell Pope.
1938	The Cloisters opened in Fort Tryon Park.
1939	Bronx-Whitestone Bridge, Aymar Embury II, architect, engineer, O. H. Ammann.
1939	Museum of Modern Art housed in new building, architects Philip Goodwin and Edward D. Stone.
1941	USA enters World War II.
1947-53	United Nations complex designed and built, by international team of architects, chairman Wallace K. Harrison.
1952	Lever House causes sensation with glass structure and use of space, architects Skidmore, Owings & Merrill.
1958	Seagram Building with refined metal curtain wall structure, architects Mies van der Rohe, Philip Johnson, Kahn and Jacobs.
1959	Guggenheim Museum erected, with revolutionary spiral structure, architect Frank Lloyd Wright.
1962-8	Lincoln Center for the Performing Arts built.
1966	Whitney Museum housed in new building, architects Marcel Breuer and Hamilton Smith.
1967	Ford Foundation, architects Kevin Roche and John Dinkeloo.

Founding of the City

In a city where from one day to the next, literally, a venerable land-mark can disappear, it is not surprising that there is almost nothing left to remind us of the original Dutch settlement in New York. A sprinkling of Dutch street names, a few images of the old West India company governors, some portraits of prosperous burghers, and the painstaking reconstructions of history in the Museum of the City of New York — this is about all that is left for reference. Except for the narrow streets of lower Manhattan, which recall the early replicas of Dutch prototypes in Europe, the heritage of Nieuw Netherlands is largely received through history books.

From its beginning in the early 1600s, Nieuw Netherlands was a purely commercial undertaking. The original plans of the Dutch West India Corporation paid little heed to the cultural development of a colony. The sole aim was profit—profit through trade which was facilitated by the ideal harbour situation of Manhattan Island. From the outset, there was a tendency for this new settlement to absorb a population which could help the Corporation in its aim to exploit the trade outpost to the fullest extent. The history of those early days is turbulent enough; frequent bitter exchanges took place between members of the new settlement and the company overseers, including the last powerful governor, Peter Stuyvesant. Whatever the quarrels may have been, they were rarely based on cultural aspirations.

The salient mercantile motives that persisted throughout New York's history are reflected in early historical documents. Approximately one year after the first permanent settlers had arrived, Pieter Jansen Schagen, a deputy of the States-General in The Hague, wrote, on November 5, 1626, of the purchase of Manhattan 'from the wild men for the value of sixty guilders' and reported on the prosperity of the settlers. His ship had returned to Holland with a cargo of hundreds of skins—otter, mink and beaver—which he records with evident satisfaction.

The trappers who made these record hauls were not skilled craftsmen and their homes, as described by travellers of the time, were mere hovels. The more prosperous members of the settlement managed to reproduce the habitats they had enjoyed in Holland by copying Dutch urban architecture, bringing art and artifacts from the home country. The majority of these early Dutch city houses had disappeared by 1776, following a devastating fire.

The first settlers, aside from the merchant and patroon class, must have been exceptionally heterogeneous and unusually poor. The art historian, Alan Gowans, writes: 'For their heterogeneity we have plenty of evidence: the well-known remark of Father Jorgues, in 1644, about

◁
Famous tribute to the American ethos, the Statue of Liberty,
by Frédéric Bartholdi, erected 1886; over 300 feet high.

9

hearing eighteen different languages spoken in Manhattan; records of
Walloons and French in Albany, of twenty-three Jews come to New
Amsterdam from Brazil; Peter Stuyvesant's description of Nieuw Netherlands as "peopled by the scrapings of nationalities", and so on.'
For all its mixed population, New Amsterdam must to some degree
have looked like Amsterdam itself, particularly in the lowest reaches
of Manhattan where both the fort and the trading companies were
located. Judging by the rapid growth of the settlement (120 houses

*Plan of New Amsterdam by Castello, based on Jacques Cortelyou's
drawing of 1660, New York Public Library.*

in 1656, 300 in 1660), the original farms, or 'bouweries', were used at an early stage for land speculation—a practice that has always flourished shamelessly in New York. Commenting on the Castello Plan, based on a drawing of 1660 by Jacques Cortelyou who had been asked by the burghers to survey and prepare a plan of the city, John A. Kouwenhoven notes, 'The reason for the survey was that the city fathers were hard pressed to find house sites for newcomers to the growing city, largely because "many spaces and large lots had not been built

upon, their owners preferring to use them as gardens or orchards while waiting for land values to rise." The plan was sent by Stuyvesant to the directors in Amsterdam who remarked that 'too great spaces are as yet without buildings.'

By the time the British had taken New Amsterdam in 1664 and renamed it New York, a fairly dense lower section of the island was urbanized. The city house in seventeenth- and eighteenth-century America is summarized by Gowans as 'salmon, yellow, red and purple brick set off by glazed tiles and headers laid in geometric patterns, with tall narrow gables fronting the street, edged in steps or mousetooth designs, decorated with iron "beam anchors" wrought into ornamental patterns, numbers or letters and finials in the forms of balls, urns and weather vanes.' He also points out that by the time the last vestiges of the old patroon system were abolished in 1846, stepped-gabled brick houses had practically vanished.

English-style architecture rapidly supplanted urban Dutch building after 1664 and even the old farmhouses were modified. There are almost no authentic remains around New York although the guide books dutifully note those of exceeding age, at least by New York standards. One is the modest farm house known as the Pieter Claessen Wyckoff House in Brooklyn, in which the transplanted Dutch country house can be seen almost as it originally must have been. More impressive is the Dyckman House. It is the only eighteenth-century house remaining in Manhattan which reflects the style of the wealthier provincial farmers in the seventeenth century, having a broadly sloped gambrel roof, a very high basement, fieldstone walls below and wood above, and a kitchen typical of the period.

Those who lived in these country estates, or in the neatly laid out lower regions of New York, and who had prospered, were by all accounts keenly aware of the need for wealth-proving artifacts. They imported china, silver and other luxuries from Europe, and lined their walls with paintings, which were mostly early seventeenth-century Dutch portraits or occasionally landscapes. There is no record of any exceptional works, although good, workmanlike portraits reflecting the competence of the painting industry in the mother country can be seen in the New-York Historical Society's collection. If, as might be assumed from the volume of china and silver that has survived, there were also paintings and drawings in quantity in New Amsterdam, the legacy that has been passed down is meagre indeed. New Yorkers have always had wilfully short memories, and little desire to conserve.

British New York in the eighteenth century developed quickly, and was marked by the extraordinary bustle that travellers since the seventeenth century have found peculiar to the city. When William Burgis engraved *A South Prospect of the Flourishing City of New York c.* 1717, there were numerous solid bourgeois houses of a Dutch cast in lower Manhattan, and further uptown the new Renaissance architecture favoured by the English. There were many churches; numerous shops; new docks and warehouses, and a burgeoning thirst for culture. By the middle of the eighteenth century, there were grand, fashionable houses in which portraits, frequently by anonymous local artists, boasted of the illustrious, or at least wealthy lineage of their owners. Burgis himself seems to have been patronized by the well-to-do merchants whose children he taught painting and drawing.

In both the visual arts and architecture, the city deferred to British precedent wherever possible. The architecture known as Georgian in England, based on Renaissance and classical styles, was faithfully

Dyckman House, c. 1783, the only remaining Manhattan farm house.

imitated in urban New York. Unfortunately, the city's history is fraught with spectacular fires, which, coupled with the New Yorkers' exceptional urge to destroy and rebuild, has left almost no authentic eighteenth-century Georgian town houses, and only a scattering of roughly restored suburban houses. From old engravings, however, it is possible to reconstruct a vision of the prosperous neighbourhoods of lower New York, with their rows of brick houses, simple in proportions, with elegant doorways, well-proportioned plain windows, and lightly accented columns and pilasters in modified classical order.

Those who financed the building of churches and public buildings sought always to echo English precedents. The conservative counsel of Sir Christopher Wren was well heeded. 'An Architect', he wrote, 'ought to be jealous of Novelties, in which Fancy blinds the Judgment... That which is commendable now for Novelty, will not be a new Invention to Posterity, when his Works are often imitated, and when it is unknown which was the Original; but the Glory of that which is good of itself is eternal.'

The best of the eighteenth-century churches were inspired by English examples. In the case of St Paul's Chapel, 1766, Thomas McBean, a pupil of James Gibbs, evokes the church style of Sir Christopher Wren. It appears that McBean had studied Gibbs's St Martin-in-the-Fields in London and he achieved a close approximation with his then-fashionable Trinity parish church downtown. Ada Louise

St Paul's Chapel, 1766, the only
pre-Revolution religious
structure in New York. George
Washington worshipped here.
(Left) exterior and
(above) interior.

Huxtable, the distinguished art critic, regards St Paul's as having a handsome exterior, with its fluted Ionic columns, and a particularly fine interior where 'fluted columns on bases, engaged against the galleries, support a barrel-vaulted ceiling, with narrow vaults above the galleries ending in consoles on the window wall. Columns and pilasters are elaborately, exquisitely Corinthian, with architrave sections above them. The chancel wall has a superb Palladian window, as well as clear glass side windows, through which light floods the church and illuminates the cream-and-gold pulpit topped by a sounding board...'

The other outstanding eighteenth-century Georgian church, St Mark's-in-the-Bouwerie, is of a later period (1799) and has been greatly modified. Far simpler both in its fieldstone construction and its details, St Mark's is nevertheless one of the most beautiful survivors of its period. 'Like its prototype,' writes Mrs. Huxtable, 'it has two tiers of round arched windows, but only a simple pediment on its entrance façade', but it lacks the sophisticated refinements of belt course, balustrade, keystones and quoins. Since the church was originally built the additions of an attractive steeple, designed by Ithiel Town in 1828, and a cast-iron portico in 1858, both congenial to the original architecture, have made St Mark's corner one of the city's landmarks.

Those who worshipped at these churches came primarily from among the 'moneyed aristocracy' whose material aspirations had been well rewarded through the mercantile efficiency of New York. Towards the middle of the century, they appear to have become rivals of Bostonians and Philadelphians for the services of the few outstanding portrait painters so far to have emerged in America. The painter was still not much more than a keeper of physiognomic records—a point noted with some acrimony by several eighteenth-century American painters—but he found New York an increasingly active market. Among the intelligentsia of New York, there were patrons of considerable distinction in the years just before the Revolution, some of whom befriended and subsidized young artists in their studies. When the distinguished American portraitist, John Singleton Copley, came down from Boston in 1771, he found a list of subscribers that kept him busy for more than six months. Moreover, as he wrote to a friend, 'the Gentry of this place distinguish very well, so I must slight nothing.'

One of his patrons was Samuel Verplanck, who must have been typical of the gentry to whom he referred. Verplanck, a fifth-generation American who was a member of the first graduating class of King's College, was sent to Amsterdam for training in banking, and returned to New York in 1763. Active in civic affairs, he was a founding member of the New York Chamber of Commerce, and appears to have been a Whig sympathizer. The political divisions of the period were a source of considerable difficulty to painters who found their patrons politically exigent and often on opposite sides of the crisis which was brewing. Copley wrote to Benjamin West in 1770 that the artist should remain apolitical since political struggles 'were neither pleasing to an artist or advantageous to the Arts itself', thus initiating one of the conflicting themes of American aesthetic history.

New York boasted no local artist of comparable distinction during the years immediately preceding the Revolution. The painter was an

▷

Built around 1680, the Billopp or Conference House is a fine colonial example of American modifications.

*(Above) Voorlezer House, 1695,
served as school and church to
Dutch colonials.*

*(Right) Lefferts Homestead,
1777-83, late Dutch colonial house.*

P. 20/21
*St Mark's-in-the-Bouwerie,
originally a small chapel, became
this Georgian style church in 1799.*

artisan and technician, often trained as a sign or house painter, and
was not expected to indulge in the kind of profound aesthetic theoriz-
ing that characterized England during the same period. Few of the
gentry really believed that there could be an American art of the calibre
of European precedents. Proof lies in the fact that nearly every singularly gifted native-born painter was urged to go abroad to cultivate
his talent.

The same was true of the architect who, during the eighteenth century,
was either a gentleman of general culture with an aptitude for architecture, such as Thomas Jefferson, or a craftsman (mason or
carpenter) with lofty ambitions. In Jefferson's case, there was never
any question of an American vernacular in architecture. In Nîmes
he had been smitten by the Maison Carrée. 'Here I am, Madam,' he
wrote to the Comtesse de Tessé, 'gazing whole hours at the Maison
Carrée, like a lover at his mistress.' Jefferson's enthusiasm for antiquity succeeded his early liking for Palladio but both remained firmly
ensconced in high European traditions, even in his own brilliant
adaptation. As the painter, John Trumbull, complained in his memoirs,
published in 1841, Jefferson betrayed an extravagant regard for
French customs and for French artists of a revolutionary stripe in
particular. His Francophile interests were partly the result of the political situation of his time; partly, too, they reflected his admiration
for the expansive planning of the great French cities.

There was little hope that New York could profit from Jefferson's
large vision. Already in the immediate post-Revolutionary War period,
speculators were busy filling up the city's lots, including those razed
during the war. Most of lower Manhattan, much of the lower East
Side and even Greenwich Village was occupied by a rapidly growing
population, which increased from 33,000 in 1790 to some 60,000 in
1800. Travellers remarked on the density of the population, the

stench of the streets in the poorer quarters, and the general air of confusion induced by the multifarious activities of industrious New Yorkers. Nevertheless, the establishment of the Federal government in New York, following the end of hostilities, did result in several monumental architectural projects and plans to change the character of the city.

The first ambitious plans for the new capital were drawn up by Major Pierre Charles L'Enfant, at the urging of President Washington. Major L'Enfant had been a volunteer in the Continental Army and was first called upon to design a huge pavilion for a banquet in 1788 celebrating the Constitution. His next commission was to redesign the city hall for use by the Federal government. The architectural historian Talbot Hamlin regards L'Enfant's plans as the 'first attempt at an "American order" in a modified Doric, with the American stars decorating the necking of the capitals and the triglyphs of the frieze eloquent of this ideal.' According to Kouwenhoven, it was not the stars and eagles employed as decorative elements that suggested an American departure from French and English prototypes, but rather the monumentality and simplicity that prefigured the classic revival sponsored by Jefferson. The new regime, inaugurated when Washington took the oath of office on the open portico of the city hall with its sculptured gable, was consciously to employ the principles of uncomplicated classicism that characterizes the Federal style.

Several country mansions built during the last years of the eighteenth century still remain in New York, showing varying degrees of accommodation to the new architectural ideals. The present home of New York City's mayors was either built or restored by Archibald Gracie in 1799. It preserves an English colonial flavour in its white frame structure, although it has a Federal fanlight doorway. The Morris-Jumel Mansion, like Gracie Mansion, has an unclear history.

19

*Morris-Jumel Mansion, a Georgian colonial house of 1765,
once General Washington's headquarters.*

It was built by a loyalist, Roger Morris, who fled America in 1775,
and was used subsequently as headquarters for Washington, then
for the British, and later as a tavern. By the time Jumel bought it in
1810, it needed restoration. Its present predominantly Georgian
character was probably the result of extensive nineteenth-century
modifications to the original. Mrs Huxtable points out that the wide
boards and wooden corner quoins of the exterior are eighteenth-
century characteristics, but that the giant order of the elaborate,
pedimented two-storey colonnade is more typically nineteenth-century. These two houses, and the stables of the Abigail Adams Smith
House, now occupied by the Colonial Dames of America, are the
meagre remnants of the great country houses that burgeoned throughout the early Federal period.

Traditionally New York had the polyglot foundation which permitted
a high degree of tolerance for ideas coming from many external
sources. The vivid architectural expansion of the first few decades
of the nineteenth century was in large measure due to the energetic
absorption of ideas from overseas which were emphatically turned
to the cultural advantage of America. An outstanding example was
the design for New York's present City Hall. 'The most radical
prophecy of what was to follow appeared in the competition for the
New York City Hall in 1802,' writes Hamlin, 'and was largely due
to the appearance on the scene of a man foreign to the English
tradition—Joseph François Mangin.' Mangin, a French refugee, working with a local architect John McComb, Jr. who, like his father
before him, had begun as a mason, produced the winning design

*Gracie Mansion, built in 1799, is now the residence
of New York City's mayors.*

for the City Hall, 'and with this the entire English tradition received
its deathblow.'

This is an overstatement since the Federal style did carry over some
of the English refinements in detail—for example, those which Mc-
Comb had worked out for the City Hall. Yet it departed from the
Georgian manner, according to Hugh Morrison, with 'the giant portico; the almost universal "Federal doorway" with its narrow flanking sidelights and an embracing elliptical fanlight; the projecting
curved or polygonal bay on an exterior wall; the balustrade or
parapet placed over the eaves rather than higher up on the roof; the
graceful spiral stairway of the front hall; and most of all the fragile
and attenuated but very rich ornament executed in carved wood or
moulded plaster...' An American vernacular was clearly established in
the earliest years of the nineteenth century.

The City after the Revolution

How New York changed during its spectacular years of growth from
the founding of the Republic to the outbreak of the War of 1812
was described by foreign visitors with fair frequency. In 1797 the
Duke de la Rochefoucauld-Liancourt reported that the city contained
upwards of 50,000 inhabitants, and that no less than 450 new houses
had been built in the year. 'The town had formerly been built
without any regular plan, whence everywhere almost, except what
has been rebuilt in consequence of the fire, the streets are small and

crooked; the footpaths where there are any, narrow, and interrupted by the stair from the houses, which makes walking them extremely inconvenient. Some good brick houses are situated in these narrow streets, but in general the houses are mean, small, and low, built of wood, and a great many of them yet bear the marks of Dutch taste... There is not in any city of the world a finer street than Broadway... Most part of the houses are of brick and a number of them extremely handsome...'

By 1807 John Lambert, a British travelling business man, could report that 'New York has rapidly improved within the last twenty years; and land which then sold in that city for fifty dollars is now worth $1,500... In the vicinity of the Battery, and for some distance up the Broadway, they are nearly all private houses, and occupied by the principal merchants and gentry of New York; after which the Broadway is lined with large commodious shops of every description... There are several extensive book stores, print-shops, music shops...'

He also noted the existence of a public library, several public reading-rooms and a museum, and that it had become the fashion in New York to attend lectures. Most commentators, however, even Lambert himself who seemed among the best disposed to see New York's virtues, ranked the city rather low on a cultural scale, attributing its dearth of high calibre art to an exclusive concern with commerce.

For all that, the more prosperous elements of the community did show taste and aesthetic judgment in the new houses built during the first two decades of the century. Very few of these remain intact in Manhattan, but the smaller house, developed in those years, remained a basic model for many of the later houses that survive. Hamlin has described the peculiarities of the New York type as 'usually twenty or twenty-five feet wide and but two rooms deep, with the stairs at the side light from the rear windows, and with a colonnaded porch in the back yard leading to the privy... Two or three storeys high, these houses usually had low-pitched roofs with delicate and beautiful dormer windows; in the deeper houses gambrel-type roofs were frequent. The main floor was raised considerably above street level, and the steps leading up to it had delicate iron railings. The door, at one side to the front, was often the only touch of richness to relieve the simplicity of the rest...'

A fine example of the early Federal brick house is the Stuyvesant-Fish building, once the country home of Peter Stuyvesant's descendant, Nicholas Stuyvesant. Built as a country house in 1803-4, it was surrounded by gardens. The generous façade fully illustrates characteristics peculiar to New York. Houses on West 10th Street, or on Charlton Street, bear many of the features described by Hamlin and typify the building that persisted well into the late 1820s. They were houses largely designed by craftsmen, sometimes in rows, several intended for speculative sales. Those in Greenwich Village, built in the 1820s, probably resulted in handsome profits for their builders since many residents of lower Manhattan sought urgently to escape the recurring epidemics of yellow fever in the densely populated

◁
Van Cortlandt Manor, built in 1748, Georgian colonial style, formerly a country house.

P. 26/27
City Hall, the elegant stairwell. Completed 1812, it was restored by Grosvenor Atterbury and is one of the city's most beautiful buildings.

Metropolitan Museum of Art.
Portrait of Luman Reed, *1785-1836, by Asher B. Durand.*
Bequest of Mary Fuller Wilson, 1963.

(Right) The Oxbow (the Connecticut river near Northampton),
1846, by Thomas Cole.
Bequest of Mrs Russell Sage, 1908.

older sections of the city. Both Greenwich Village and the easterly portions of the Bowery were probably settled as a result of such epidemics as well as the almost incredible number of devastating fires that plagued New York, from the Revolutionary period on.

The plans for neighbourhoods were rigidly fixed when, in 1807, the city council decided to organize its population of 83,530. The appointed commissioners were empowered 'to lay out the leading streets and great avenues... of a width not less than sixty feet, and in general, to lay out said streets, roads, and public squares, of such ample width as they may deem sufficient to secure a free and abundant circulation of air...' Anthony Bailey, in *New York, N.Y.* (American Heritage), writes that the commissioners 'started in 1807, the year Robert Fulton's steamboat sped to Albany (at four miles per hour) and finished in 1811 the year the Erie Canal was authorized.' In the course of their deliberations, they considered that a city is composed principally of the habitations of men, and that straight-sided, right-angled houses are the cheapest to build, and 'when, therefore, the price of land is so uncommonly great, it seems proper to admit the principles of economy to greater influence...' The surveyor to the group maintained that the usefulness of the plan lay in the way it facilitated 'buying, selling and improving of real estate.'

With this goal in mind, the commission was able to complete the devastation of Manhattan Island's natural beauties—its hills, wooded areas and ponds—and pave the way for the kind of fortune accruing from speculation in real estate that made John Jacob Astor a millionaire. Bailey quotes him as having said on his deathbed that if he had known then what he knew now, he would have bought every foot of land on Manhattan. As it was, others like him proceeded to do just that, and the harsh, rectangularly patterned city plan was then, and is still, an inducement to unconscionable real estate practices.

Some of the citizens who kept a shrewd eye on real estate and stock exchange activity soon perceived the moral advantages of patronizing the arts. In the years before the boom in the 1830s, New York saw a steady rise in demand for the cultivation of the fine arts. Under constant fire from Bostonians, Philadelphians and Europeans for the materialism of their city, the more prosperous merchants sought to compensate with their activities as men of civic conscience and general culture. With their aid, the American Academy of the Fine Arts was founded in 1802 and plaster casts of classical sculpture were imported for the benefit of the students. Years later, the conservative director of the academy, John Trumbull, was to admonish the students for their ingratitude to the 'gentlemen' who so thoughtfully set up and attempted to control the institution.

The gentlemen patrons of the arts in those early days were incurably addicted to portrait painting. No one could make his way in the commerce of art who could not strike off a competent likeness—a fact which artists were still lamenting many decades after. Nevertheless, little by little, New York was acquiring a corps of active professional artists who found patronage. Art supply stores were

being set up where artists could exhibit their wares in the business district, and there were art dealers such as 'Old Paff' who imported 'golden toned' old masters, most of them spurious, to sell to the new aspirants to culture.

Culturally inclined business men often sought the company of the artistic community which, toward the 1820s, included not only several accomplished painters, such as Thomas Cole, Samuel F. B. Morse, Henry Inman and Asher B. Durand, but their friends among the writers, poets and architects. There was the beginning of a sophisticated bohemian tradition that survived in New York in the little circle of Knickerbocker artists and intellectuals, about whom James Fenimore Cooper wrote. Accounts of artists' lives during this period often mention the 'eccentric' painter John Wesley Jarvis, who drank, whored, told witty stories, kept a successful atelier going with

Portrait of Peter Stuyvesant, *painted from life by an unknown artist.*
Courtesy of the New-York Historical Society.

◁

The Stuyvesant-Fish House, 1804, a fine example of early Federal style.

effective assistants, and was often left out of evening plans that included the ladies because of his bad reputation. Jarvis, like his fellow painters, of necessity, limited himself to portraits. His pupil Henry Inman, after his own great success as a portraitist, told the critic Charles E. Lester: 'The business of a few generations of artists in this country, as in all others, is to prepare the way for their successors; for the time will come when the rage for portraits will give way to higher and purer taste.'

The time was too far off in the opinion of many of Inman's younger contemporaries. Neil Harris describes their situation thus: 'American artists were caught, in the early years of the century, between two roles, bearing the worst part of each; they still carried the marks of the manual worker, occasionally acting as salesmen and entrepreneurs, yet lacked the aura of steady respectability which was the most valuable property of honest tradesmen. They aspired to the free life of the great creator and the status of gentlemen, yet the artist image had not yet been hammered out in a society which continued to see frivolity or idleness in their dreams of glory...'

Samuel F. B. Morse was particularly sensitive to the harsh paradoxes of his situation, complaining frequently of the demands made upon his artist's conscience, and the adoration of money prevalent in New York. Like Rembrandt Peale who said that he refused to 'Worship the God of this country—Money', Morse tried to live up to the lofty ideals he had imbibed during his student years in England. As a way of combatting the wrongs he and his colleagues felt to be perpetuated by the 'gentlemen' supporting the American Academy, he proposed and founded the National Academy of Design in 1826, which was run by its own members. In this way and by providing progressive

Allegorical landscape showing New York University, Washington Square, *1836, by Samuel F. B. Morse.*
Courtesy of the New-York Historical Society.

artistic instruction, as well as having artist-run and artist-juried exhibitions, the young painters and sculptors hoped to avoid the psychological indenture to arrogant patrons characteristic of the first two decades of the century. Their experiment proved to be ineffective, for American artists continued to be largely dependent on the patronage of wealthy and exigent patrons, as are many still today.

The architects were similarly beset with the problems raised by their uncertain status in the early years of the nineteenth century. Often they were regarded merely as designers, subservient to both the contractors whom they served and the clients who employed the contractors. In some of the most elegant town houses of the 1820s, the architect's name was not known. Architectural historians have had to make attributions in many significant cases based on guesswork. The builders still followed the old American practice of

consulting style books. Several of the most important architects during the first years of the Greek Revival movement became known primarily through their builders' guides.

The passion for Greek Revival that swept the United States during the 1820s and 1830s has been attributed to various social and political forces. Gowans feels that it reflected a revulsion against the Jeffersonian aristocratic concept of Roman republicanism popularly associated with money and privilege. Others have pointed to the development of the archaeological sciences in Europe, where accurate drawings of Greek antiquities were being engraved and sent to the United States; to interest in the Greek War of Independence, partly popularized by Lord Byron through his poetry; and to the new Jacksonian enthusiasm for popular democracy, which found its prototype in Athens. The rage for Greek Revival which, when carried to excess, drew the scorn of knowing intellectuals, was clearly an extenuation of the continuing struggle to establish an 'American style.' In the best hands, Greek Revival was no mere slavish copying of Greek prototypes but rather a sober adaptation of principles of simplicity. Henry Latrobe, who was critical of Jefferson's devotion to the correct imitation of classic prototypes, advocated 'firmness, commodity and delight' in modern buildings—traits which appeared in the specific New York modifications of Greek styles. With the generalizing Greek classicism established as a prevailing mode, the architectural profession developed rapidly. Just as the Greek Revival was capturing the imagination of Americans all over the Eastern seaboard, the names of specific architects began to emerge and, before long, completely overshadowed the old builder-contractor tradition.

A significant name was that of Martin Thompson, whose design for

Fluted columns on a classic house at 56 West 10th Street.

the Bank of the United States on Wall Street, which later became the US Assay Office (now the North Wing of the Metropolitan Museum), probably greatly influenced his contemporaries. 'This building,' writes Hamlin, 'commissioned as early as 1822, is a polished and knowing piece of dignified classic work, well detailed and beautifully executed. In the breadth of its proportions it shows that freedom from rigidly conventional classic proportions—a quality that may have been a result of ignorance but is often the cause of great and characteristic charm—which is frequently typical of American Classic Revival work.' Thompson is also credited with the design of many town houses, most probably those on Washington Square North.

When Ithiel Town came to New York in 1826, after having made a fortune as the designer of a truss for bridges, he took Thompson into partnership, founding one of the first thoroughly professional architectural firms. Town's 'architectural rooms' were filled with his outstanding collection of architectural and art books, and with many engravings. He attracted a circle of enlightened patrons, artists and writers, many of whom used his office as a gathering place. When the National Academy of Design was founded, first as the New York Drawing Association at the home of Samuel Morse, Ithiel Town was one of a group that included some of New York's most gifted artists.

In 1829, the brilliant architectural draughtsman Alexander Jackson Davis joined the firm, bringing with him an established reputation as an 'architectural composer' and a meticulous executant of city scenes and landscapes. Davis moved in painterly circles, and seems to have provided many of the plans for buildings undertaken by the firm. Of his own work, Colonnade Row or La Grange Terrace, begun in 1833, is perhaps the best example extant in New York.

The remains of Colonnade Row, originally nine houses, now only four, indicate Davis's awareness of the importance of visual cohesion in urban design. At the time of its completion in 1836, New Yorkers were astounded by its munificence, and the most perceptive among them understood the importance of the unifying colonnade of Greek columns running the whole length of the group. These houses, occupied by extremely wealthy clients, among them Astors and Vanderbilts, were intended by Davis to have pergolas and gardens on the roof. Instead, the present group have awkward additions, which provide extra living accommodation.

Other architects were very busy in the late 1820s and the 1830s. There is some evidence that, after the disastrous fire of 1835, the local firms were unable to handle the great number of commissions available. Among them was Minard Lafever whose three books, published between 1829 and 1835, are thought to have been the sources of countless Greek Revival variations in New York. Lafever's own work in Greek Revival is hard to identify. He was probably a contractor's designer for many years before he began his major work in the 1840s on Gothic Revival churches. But many of his concepts, according to Talbot Hamlin, are visible in the interiors and much of the detail of the Old Merchant's House (the Seabury-Treadwell House).

The advancing professionalism of architects was soon to be formalized. In 1857, the first professional organization, called the American Institution of Architects, was founded by, among others, Alexander Davis, Isaiah Rogers, Ithiel Town, Minard Lafever, Thomas U. Walter and Asher Benjamin. One of the many by-products of the new professionalism was the intense discussion of theory that now took place on a broad scale. Criticism, originating with the talented architect himself, was to bring in a new era in the 1840s—an era branded eclectic by many scholars, but nonetheless released from the uniformity imposed by the widespread popular vision of Greek Revival.

Metamorphoses in the 1830s and 1840s

In New York City, there was an increase in architectural diversity with every year of the city's rapid expansion. Philip Hone, a Whig mayor of New York and a merchant who retired at forty-one with a fortune to be spent on cultural pursuits, kept a diary liberally sprinkled with observations concerning the precipitate changes in his city. On May 9, 1831, he notes that 'the city is now undergoing its usual annual metamorphosis; many stores and houses are being pulled down, and others altered, to make every inch of ground productive to its utmost extent.' In 1835, he wryly notes that 'the rise of lots in the upper part of the city goes on without interruption from any cause, foreign or domestic.' (Prices were, at the time, extraordinarily high. A house on Second Avenue and St Mark's Place had just been sold for $35,000.) In other reminiscences of the day, indeed as early

▷

Mansions facing Washington Square park, where some date back to the 1830s, celebrated in the memoirs of Henry James and Edith Wharton.

Colonnade Row (or La Grange Terrace), designed in 1836
by Alexander Jackson Davis, once a complex of nine houses, remarkable
for the use of Corinthian columns to bind the rhythms of individual houses.

as 1779, there are frequent references to 'modernizing' or 'modern improvements'. A French agent wrote to Governor Clinton that year offering a group of Dutch paintings for sale, which he described as 'pictures painted in oyl, on boards in black ebony frames highly polished, of these kinds the Dutch settlers brought a great many with their other furniture... I pikt them up in New York in garrets, where they had been confined as unfashionable when that city was modernized.'

The conscious impulse to modernize was accompanied by a growing awareness of American culture as 'modern' and necessarily different from its European counterpart. The wealthy travellers who had stocked their houses with second-rate European old masters were supplanted in New York's cultural circles by a new group of patrons who turned to indigenous modern painters. Typically, these men had begun by buying the imported wares of dealers such as Paff. Through their extended commercial activities, they sometimes came into contact with the upper circles of a burgeoning bohemia. Toward the 1830s, it became quite fashionable for the merchants to cultivate the society of artists. The story of Luman Reed, one of

New York's first great sponsors of the idea of modern art, illustrates the rapid change in cultural mores.

Reed started his career in commerce as a clerk in a country store in upstate New York. At the age of twenty-eight, he became a partner in a wholesale grocery house in New York City and, because of the opening of the Erie Canal, made a fortune. He built a mansion in lower Manhattan which he stocked with Paff's dubious old masters which were very shortly disposed of in favour of contemporary American paintings. He made his first important purchases at the 1834 exhibition of the National Academy, and spent the next two years providing remarkable patronage for artists like Asher Durand, Thomas Cole, William S. Mount and George Flagg. He built a gallery on to his Greenwich Street house which was open to the public once a week. The nucleus of his collection was later bought by a group of merchant-patrons whom he had inspired, and made into the New York Gallery of Fine Arts.

In encouraging a few of the painters who had turned to landscape as a specifically American genre, Luman Reed and other patrons genuinely contributed to an upsurge of local activity. The swift acknowledgment of Thomas Cole, who had come to America from England in 1825 at the age of seventeen and, within a couple of years, found his place in New York, was a substantial beginning for an American school of painting. Cole's natural interest in the wild landscapes he found in the New World was further stimulated by the contemporary literature of Washington Irving, James Fenimore Cooper and William Cullen Bryant. His romantic temperament, so apparent in the panoramic landscapes with which he first made his name, found confirmation in the works of his literary friends. His great admirer Bryant wrote of the delight in contemplating Cole's pictures which 'carried the eye over scenes of wild grandeur peculiar to our country, over our aerial mountain-tops, with their mighty growth of forests never touched by the axe, along the banks of streams never deformed by culture, and into the depths of skies bright with the hues of our own climate; skies such as few but Cole could ever paint, and through the transparent abysses of which it seemed that you might send an arrow out of sight.'

Bryant was equally enthusiastic over the work of Asher Durand who had been inspired by Cole, but whose temperament was less flamboyant. When he painted the well-known 'Kindred Spirits', now in the New York Public Library, Durand showed Cole and Bryant staidly engaged in conversation in a wilderness of trees and gorges. Durand singled out the features of both nature and man with painstaking detail. His more sober approach to painting, with a meticulous and often cramped technique, and a conception which was limited to a fairly direct transcription of what he saw, was to prove highly popular with collectors.

Another friend of Cole's, William Sidney Mount, developed the genre tradition with specific reference to his own locale, nearby Long Island. Mount's ability to structure a composition, and to alter or even ignore principles he had learned through study of the European genre painters, brought him into prominence along with his landscape-painting friends of the Hudson River School. Mount's intense desire to retain his originality and what he called his 'nationality' kept him from making the usual voyage to Europe, and aligned him with the newly born nationalist aspirations of painters and patrons alike.

Men like Reed and Philip Hone were generous in their support, and often sent artists abroad. Nevertheless, the artists' situation vis-à-vis their patrons was no happier than it had ever been. For all the generous prices these merchant-princes were ready to pay, they were not willing to cede complete authority to the artist. Cole, for instance, was given highly specific instructions by a Baltimore patron in 1826. He was told that he should show deer or cattle drinking or a canoe with Indians paddling, and that scenes from Fenimore Cooper's most recent novel should be introduced 'to give animation and interest to the whole.'

No doubt the fortunes of the artists waxed and waned as New York went through recurrent economic crises. One of the most severe, that of 1837, was widely attributed to the unsound practice of speculation in real estate which had always beset New York. Michel

▷

Friends' Meeting House facing Stuyvesant Park, with St George's Church in the background, an example of brick colonial simplicity carried over into the mid-19th century.

P. 42/43
Gramercy Park, sole survivor of
an era when owners of facing
farm houses had exclusive rights to
the park keys.

▷

Litchfield Mansion, 1857, built by
A. J. Davis, showing a strong
Italianate penchant, but the corncob
capitals place it squarely
in the American tradition.

P. 46/47
St Patrick's Cathedral, 1858-79
by James Renwick, Jr., adaptation
of French-Gothic style.

Richard Upjohn's Trinity Church, 1846, an example of modified Gothic Revival, somehow resisting encroachment by the huge-scale office buildings.

Chevalier wrote in 1835, 'Everybody is speculating, and everything has become an object of speculation.' He added that the whole of Manhattan was laid out in building lots and, according to him, enough had been sold to accommodate a population of two million. Several commentators have suggested that the rage for speculation was carried over in the newly acquired habit among the wealthier merchants of forming art collections.

Such limitless speculation left little room for the kind of civic planning that would result in spacious, beautifully ornamented public places. When de Tocqueville arrived in New York in the early 1830s, he wrote immediately to his mother of his disappointment in not finding the church spires, civic buildings and monuments that make a city more than a suburb. There had been a few exceptions. Samuel Ruggles had bought up a number of lots in order to set them aside for Gramercy Park, still one of the few elegant private parks in New York. Union Square had been enlarged in 1832, and was considered a fashionable place to stroll at mid-century. A few public buildings of distinction were visible in lower Manhattan. Gathering places such as the celebrated Niblo's Gardens, which opened in 1830 and functioned until 1846 in the original building, combined large meeting and exhibition halls with smaller theatre areas and refreshment pavilions. By European standards, New York was architecturally not impressive.

By the beginning of the 1840s, the physical appearance of New York City was characterized by what critics have called eclecticism, or confusion. John Burchard and Albert Bush-Brown suggest what it was like to walk the streets of New York:

'At Hudson Park, there was a serene moment in the contemplation of John McComb's dignified St John's Church of 1803-1807, but nearby the Infant School Society met in a ramshackle basement. Wall Street clearly revealed a society in transition; plain brick houses alternated with Greek temples, occupied by banks or the Mercantile. Exchange, and here too, were drab houses for insurance companies and newspapers. At the Fulton Street Market in 1821, one might walk along cobblestoned streets, past arcaded stalls, only to pick a way among barrels, casks, wheelbarrows, hucksters' wagons and horses toward the tower of an undistinguished church... at the North River he would meet a jumbled assemblage of utilitarian brick buildings forming an iron foundry where locomotive parts were made. Or one might visit Henry Brevoort's Ionic-porticoed three-storey brownstone at Fifth and Ninth, designed by Alexander Jackson Davis. All its interior spaces, from the library and parlour to the entrance with its curved stair, announced a New Yorker of taste and distinction, yet not far away at the headquarters of the Fourteenth Ward on Broadway in 1840 the presidential campaign of William Henry Harrison was conducted from a synthetic log cabin fitted chiefly with hard cider. It would be easy to wonder which was the true America and perplexity might mount when one compared Roger's Mercantile Exchange of 1836-42 and its giant Ionic portico and the large Pantheonic dome with Barnum's Museum on Broadway, its upper face covered with a giant billboard showing the picture of a menacing serpent...'

Included in this general confusion must have been the rarely mentioned slums of the time. During the period between 1815 and 1845, the population had risen from 100,000 to 371,000. Many waves of immigration from Europe had swelled the ranks of the labouring forces. In the mid '20s, James Fenimore Cooper learned that in less than one year some 22,000 Irish immigrants had arrived, and remarked on the 'extraordinary medley' of New York's people. Many immigrants, and many of the local black population, lived in conditions of extreme squalor, which Charles Dickens noted on his first trip to New York. There were already signs of serious friction in the depressed groups, as the frequent reports of 'mob' activity testify. The skilled workers, encouraged by the Jacksonian attitude toward the man whose labour would never produce the kind of sudden wealth the speculators knew, were trying, as early as 1829, to organize themselves and, as the Workingmen's Party, polled thirty percent of the vote that year. They called for equal and universal education, and a fair division of property—demands regarded by most educated people as preposterous. Diarists such as George Templeton Strong and Philip Hone were clearly alarmed by the growing demands of the working classes and the sentiments of the abolitionists who were then agitating, also by the growing cosmopolitanism of the population. With trading, manufacturing and stock exchange dealing recovering from recent crises, New York, in the mid-'40s, began a fanciful conquest of all the architectural styles in history. Lewis Mumford, discussing American architecture between 1820 and the Civil War, said it was 'a collection of tags, thrown at random against a building... In elevation and interior treatment, these ante-bellum buildings were all what-nots. Souvenirs of architecture, their forms dimly recall the monuments of the past without in any sense taking their place.'

Other critics have been less severe in their evaluation of the eclecticism that overtook America in the 1840s, but nearly all commentators agree that the fine proportions and craftsmanship of the Federal and Greek Revival period were greatly diminished as the vogue for Gothic, Romanesque and even Egyptian styles overtook the builders. The history of architecture in New York City at that moment was naturally somewhat restricted by the gridiron plan. Very few of the Gothic extravagances that appeared in country estates could be seen in New York. Whatever there was seems to have been largely inspired by the example set by Alexander Jackson Davis who had designed a new building for New York University on Washington Square as early as 1833. This building, demolished at the end of the century, was a sanctuary for Samuel Morse, who invented his telegraph there, and for countless later New York artists who had studios there. When first completed, it was admired as one of the few distinguished 'modern' public buildings. Not many others were to be undertaken, however, and the Gothic Revival was largely marked by the erection of churches.

The first masterly Gothic Revival church was designed by James Renwick, Jr. at Broadway and 10th Street. Grace Church opened its doors in 1846 and quickly became one of the most fashionable Episcopalian churches in the city. Renwick's only experience when he undertook the planning of Grace Church had been as an engineer. By assiduously studying books on English style, he was able to capture the elegant detail of high Gothic and the use of marble, without losing an intimately adjusted scale suitable to the site. His imaginative variations on Gothic elevation are far more exciting in this first structure than in his later St Patrick's Cathedral, where a European is likely to flinch at the awkward adaptation of the European original.

The other church of the 1840s which caused the local gentry considerable excitement and was admired by them from its early building stages is Trinity Church. It was designed by Richard Upjohn who had come to America from England as a young man. Upjohn made his way as a draughtsman and architect in upstate New York, Maine and Massachusetts before coming to New York. He had a reputation as a devout Episcopalian and held that 'the object is not to surprise with novelties in church architecture, but to make what is to be made truly ecclesiastical—a temple of solemnities...' His Trinity Church does not, indeed, surprise with novelties, and it is very sober in design, but, as many contemporaries understood, Upjohn had not merely copied a Gothic prototype. He had created a genuine work of architecture marked by his own sensibility, especially the

▷

Grace Church (detail), 1846, by James Renwick, Jr., Gothic Revival structure in an area fashionable in the mid-19th century.

lofty spire that once dominated the skyline of lower New York. Dissident voices such as that of Edgar Allan Poe were few. Poe called Trinity 'a very showy building' and 'a very good object for the Wall Street brokers to contemplate' but thought its general aspect poor. His reaction to the Gothic Revival, which he thought 'incongruous', was echoed by many other intellectuals who were mounting their critical assault on the American weakness for the picturesque and eclectic.

In discussing the romantic eclecticism of the period, there is scarcely a writer who does not quote Nathaniel Hawthorne's lament in his preface to *The Marble Faun*. Hawthorne maintained that 'no author, without a trial, can conceive of the difficulty of writing a romance about a country where there is no shadow, no antiquity, no mystery, no picturesque and gloomy wrong, nor anything but a commonplace prosperity, in broad and simple daylight, as is happily the case with my dear native land.'

Citizens of bustling New York were increasingly aware of their commonplace prosperity. Many of them were haunted with a newborn nostalgia for the mysteries and solaces of the countryside, and beyond it the virgin wilds of America that were, even then, fast becoming populous. Inspired by the wilderness literature of James Fenimore Cooper and Washington Irving, whom the indefatigable journalist-poet, William Cullen Bryant, had so assiduously defended in the '20s, the gentry of New York yearned romantically—as they still do—for the open spaces and clean air of ideal nature. It became fashionable to complain about the dirt, the rush, the noise of industry, the dense population of cities. Asher B. Durand called New York 'this miserable little pen enclosing 250,000 human animals or more.'

By the 1830s a preoccupation with nature and the Wordsworthian glorification of the country cottage dominated the thoughts of the culturally inclined in New York. Landscape artists were becoming as successful as portrait painters and, for more than three decades, the romantic landscape, tempered by characteristic American concern for realistic detail, was the fashionable genre.

A growing concern with a national identity can be discerned in the work of the landscape painter, Thomas Cole, whose New York career began in the 1820s and who set a precedent for a long history of rationalizations in American painting that continue through the present. Like painters before him and after, he sought to make a virtue of America's lack of cultural history. 'All nature here is new to art, no Tivolis, Ternis, Mont Blancs, Plynlimons, hackneyed and worn by the daily pencils of hundreds; but primeval forests, virgin lakes and waterfalls.'

On the other hand, Cole was caught in the peculiar American dilemma between the real and the ideal, as the art critic Barbara Novak points out. The rich idealism that had nourished the English landscapist, fed by the Coleridgean conception of imaginative power, was most congenial to his temperament. But the practical needs of the merchant classes could never go far enough to meet him. 'I am not the painter I should have been had there been a higher taste', he wrote towards the end of his life. 'Instead of working according to the dictates of feeling and imagination, I have painted to please others in order to exist...' Novak remarks that Cole 'felt a pull

▷

Trinity Church seen through the downtown canyons of Wall Street.

52

1846 buildings by Alexander Jackson Davis, facing Gramercy Park.

between the public preference for specific views—which would transcend, nonetheless, "mere mechanical imitation"—and his heroic principles and philosophic ambitions...'

Durand, who was inspired by Cole, was temperamentally less inclined to the poetic fervours that characterized the early Romantic movement in both Europe and the United States. He could understand the requirement of specificity imposed by the city dwellers who bought his windows to the wilderness. Those New Yorkers were

breeding in themselves a pride of place, and an American sensibility suitable to their new, rudimentary capitalist environment. Durand's tart American response to his European tour in 1840 could probably stand for the attitudes of most New York painters actively engaged in selling their works.

'I can now look with admiration and wonder on the beauty and sublimity of the scenes before me; I can look with gratification and advantage on the great works of art, as I have done in England

An almost Palladian mode in a cast-iron building at 801 Broadway.

(Left) The Haughwout Building, 1857, by J.P. Gaynor. Its design is taken from Sansovino's library in Venice.

and on the Continent, and still expect to do in Italy; yet when all this looking and studying and admiring shall have an end, I am free to confess that I shall enjoy a sight of the signboards in the streets of New York more than all the pictures in Europe; and for real and unalloyed enjoyment of scenery, the rocks, trees and green meadows of Hoboken will have a charm that all Switzerland cannot boast.'

With the New Yorkers' appetite for unspoiled nature already stimulated by the painting and literature of the '20s and '30s, it is not surprising that the Gothic Revival and all other revival styles, could make such astonishing progress. Critics have variously bestowed the credit for the strong psychological turn away from Greek modes, but one man, Andrew Jackson Downing, is always mentioned as having had immense influence.

Downing was an upstate landscape architect who found extraordinary success with the publication of his first book on landscape gardening in 1841, and who became a celebrity with his second book on cottage architecture in 1842. In the course of little more than a decade (he died in a steamboat disaster in 1852), Downing had reached into the parlours of innumerable prospering urban dwellers, convincing them of the essential morality of country living; of the necessity of 'smiling lawns and tasteful cottages'. His utopian visions were indebted to English taste, and its Bostonian Transcendentalist counterpart, but much of what he offered his eager readers was practical advice. He knew how to deal with specifics, and seemed to understand that his deeper philosophical insights would have to be expressed within the social scheme. Those insights were similar to those proffered by the landscapists, particularly Cole. He maintained that 'every outward material form is a symbol or expression of something which is not *matter*, and which, rightly understood, gives us the key to the power with which that form immediately and without reflection, acts upon the sense of beauty.'

In order to act tastefully on every man's sense of beauty, Downing prescribed many possibilities, some of which were enthusiastically put in practice by his friend, Alexander Jackson Davis. Grecian, Moorish, Italian, high Gothic and Tudor Gothic plans poured from his draughting table in the '40s and '50s. Vernacular 'carpenter Gothic' houses appeared in great profusion in all Manhattan suburbs. A few of these remain in Staten Island, the Bronx, and Brooklyn; that on Gates Avenue, Brooklyn, might well have been compiled by a builder after consulting Davis's plans in Downing's books.

The clients in New York rich enough to own a cosy country cottage in the wilds of Brooklyn or up along the Hudson's shores were in many cases concerned with other buildings in the city. Business premises, warehouses, small manufactories and retail stores on a grand scale were appearing ceaselessly in the '40s and '50s. The same man who could indulge his wife with a Gothic fantasy in the country would look to a rational and functional model for his place of business in the city.

Mid-century Rationalism

Rationalism had not been lost in the great vogue for the picturesque. Downing had some highly practical suggestions for the builder of the country cottage, and not even he sanctioned the inappropriate adaptation of European luxury models. 'In all architecture', he wrote, 'adaptation to the end in view is important'. Much more sternly, the sculptor Horatio Greenough wrote of the end in view when he chastised Americans for their readiness to over-indulge in the picturesque. Greenough's writings do not appear to have affected many architects in his day, but they impressed Emerson and a group of intellectuals who disliked the eclectic abuses rampant in the mid-1900s.

Greenough, like Emerson and the great English romantics, was an organicist, stressing the importance of nature's internal function in producing the outer forms. Goethe, Shelley, Coleridge and a host of others shared a reverence for natural organic activity. Greenough advocated an architecture that would be as respectful of the laws of nature as natural forms themselves; an architecture stripped of the superficial lath and plaster imitation that seemed typical of the new Gothic Revival. He asked the architect to observe the economy, functional intricacy and absolute adaptation to its end of the skeletons of animals and the hulls of ships. 'Instead of forcing the functions of every sort of building into one general form, adopting an outward shape for the sake of the eye or of association, without reference to the inner distribution. Let us begin from the heart as a nucleus and work outward.'

This spareness and utility of functional forms demanded by Greenough were not realized in private urban houses and suburban villas, but rather in the industrial buildings making use of new technologies.

▷

Fire-watch tower in cast-iron by James Bogardus, Mount Morris Park.

Throughout the 1840s there were constant references in periodicals to new building methods, more efficient tools and labour-saving inventions. The 'mechanic' was achieving a new status as he entered the building field with his scientific efficiency proposals. Engineering mechanics such as James Bogardus, rather than well-known architects, were called in to design warehouses. Bogardus was a watchmaker, engraver, inventor and developer of technology. He is credited by some writers with the invention of the pre-fabricated building; by others with the development of cast-iron skeletons which could engender the non-bearing curtain wall that came to be the hallmark of modern architecture. Although Bogardus was only one of several competitors in the field of cast-iron construction, his patent-office description of his method in 1850 is still the best definition of the technique. Among other important features, he pointed out that

Statue of Peter Cooper, 1897,
by Augustus St-Gaudens,
in Cooper Square.

(Below) the Great Hall
of Cooper Union, 1859.

New York Public Library, 1911. French Renaissance style with portico of Corinthian columns and triumphal arches.

'such a building may be erected with extraordinary facility, and at all seasons of the year... As fast as the pieces can be handled they may be adjusted and secured by the most ignorant workman.' It follows, he went on, that 'a building, once erected, may be taken to pieces with the same facility and dispatch without injuring or destroying any of its parts, and then re-erected elsewhere...'.

Such utility apparently caused the gentlemen architects considerable pain. Members of the newly formed American Institute of Architects had one of their stormiest sessions when a young member, Henry Van Brunt, delivered a paper in 1859 in defence of cast-iron. His call for an architecture of 'strict mechanical obedience' was hardly adaptable for the architect busily engaged in capturing mansion commissions from the nouveaux riches.

Despite the disdain of most of the better known architects, cast-iron proved to be one of the most important boons to building in the city. In the years between Bogardus's first complete cast-iron buildings, the Edgar Laing Stores at Washington and Murray Streets, and the last decade of the century, literally miles of cast-iron fronted business buildings were erected below 23rd Street.

The flexibility of the milled parts inspired considerable fantasy in the designers of these buildings. Details borrowed from the new Italian vogue, from venerable Palladian precedents; from Gothic and Baroque, appeared frequently on their faces. But the boast of Bogardus that his structure would save space, since the thick brick columns could be eliminated, assured a certain elegance. The very large window areas, and the rhythmic designs of their often pillared sequences imposed certain felicities of style that might not have been the case in stone or brick buildings.

One of the buildings most often cited for its beauty is the famous Haughwout Building designed by John P. Gaynor and fabricated in the factory of Bogardus's chief rival, Daniel Badger, in 1857. It is considered by students of cast-iron architecture to be a masterpiece. Turpin Bannister, the distinguished architect, praises the way Gaynor echoes Palladio in the bay motif of a window arch on a small order between piers with engaged Corinthian columns, while Ada Louise Huxtable regards it as an admirable forerunner of modern architecture. This building is supposedly the first commercial building to have had a passenger elevator which functioned properly and, as such, would have been the direct forerunner of the next phase in commercial building, the skyscraper.

The undeniable merit of lightness and interchangeability that metal structures possess was expressed in various new designs. Bogardus's own fire-watch towers, of which one remains intact in Mount Morris Park, were beautiful, elegantly wrought, functional structures. The yearning for lightness had existed for a long time, but its sensational expression in the famous Crystal Palace in London in 1851 fired the American imagination. Joseph Paxton's system of small prefabricated units leading to the enormous, airy, greenhouse-like palace of glass astonished contemporary viewers. In no time reproductions were finding their way to remote corners of Europe and America. Within a year, New Yorkers saw the erection of their own Crystal Palace designed by George Carstenson and Charles Geldemeister. Unfortunately, it met the fate of many cast-iron buildings that had boasted fireproof status, and, in 1858, it burned to the ground in only fifteen minutes. Still, it left New Yorkers with an inextinguishable memory of glass and metal magic.

Such confections, while greatly admired for fairs, or for department stores and warehouses, were not considered appropriate to significant public buildings. These were more likely to be built in marble and brownstone, still appreciated for their solid permanence. William Chambers, a publisher from Edinburgh on a tour of the United States, described New York in 1853 as a great emporium of commerce. His description of Broadway, which had once upon a time been a fashionable promenade and residential district of small-frame dwellings and three-storey brick buildings, is of the splendours of 'high and handsome buildings, of brown sandstone or brick, with several of white marble and granite.' The largest portion of Broadway was now occupied by luxurious hotels, elegant department stores and places of public entertainment such as P. T. Barnum's theatre 'covered with great gaudy paintings'. This theatre was described by a young Englishwoman in 1854 as a 'gaudy building, denoted by huge paintings, multitudes of flags, and a very noisy band. The museum contains many objects of real interest, particularly to the naturalist and geologist, intermingled with a great deal that is spurious and contemptible.' The note of obstreperous advertising was to be increasingly remarked by visitors to the city, who practically never failed to notice the unusual number of signboards and displays, designed to stimulate the increasing masses of consumers.

For all that, ever since the depression of 1837, an undercurrent of serious interest in the elevation of public education was noted by travellers. In the 1840s and 1850s, many civic-minded patrons found means to enrich the public intellect. William Chambers duly notes that in New York, 'the means of social improvement, through the agency of public libraries, lectures and reading-rooms are exceedingly conspicuous. One of the most munificent of these institutions is the recently opened Astor Library... I went to see this library and found that it consisted of a splendid collection of 100,000 volumes, a large proportion of which were works in the best European editions, properly classified, with every suitable accommodation for literary study.'

This library is one of the fortunate edifices in New York City, having been restored for public use by architect Giorgio Cavaglieri in 1967 as the New York Shakespeare Festival Theatre. The grand Italianate lines of its central portion have been carefully preserved, demonstrating how well the Italian Revival architects could adapt to the peculiarities of New York.

Another distinctive building begun around the same time is the Cooper Union for the Advancement of Science and Art. A product of the reformist enthusiasm that swept through Jacksonian America in the 1830s and 1840s, the Cooper Union was unique in its time and, in many ways, remains so. Peter Cooper who, in 1808, began modestly as an apprentice mechanic without any education, had worked his way up from a small grocery store to ownership in factory enterprises. He was an inventor of some note, the first in America to build an adequate steam locomotive, and several other machines that were patented and put into use. His scheme for the Cooper Union was fixed in his mind already in the 1830s, and much of his subsequent industry was devoted to accumulating funds for its realization. Aside from its handsome Italianate exterior, the Cooper building is graced with a distinctive interior—spacious, amazingly varied in design, and functional. The Great Hall in its basement was one of the important lecture halls in its day, and was the scene of a key Lincoln address in 1860. In structure, it was the forerunner of the steel-frame building, since Peter Cooper developed a way to use, as structural members, the railroad beams he manufactured in his mill. Cooper's interest in sponsoring what he considered a polytechnical school, as well as a centre for the fine arts, found expression in the large, light areas he designed. By providing tuition-free courses in both day and night sessions, Cooper achieved his aim: an institution that would serve the countless poor youths of New York who otherwise would not have been able to develop their latent talents.

Good works in the public interest were rarities during those pre-Civil War boom years. William Cullen Bryant, the lively editor of the Evening Post, saw the overcrowded, unsanitary, ruthlessly exploited poor neighbourhoods in the 1840s as a potential menace to the whole city. He and a few others began to call for a halt to the mindless real estate expansion that the grid plan of 1811 had done so much to foster. In 1844, he noted that 'Commerce is devouring inch by inch the coast of the island, and if we would rescue any part of it for health and recreation it must be done now.' His campaign was joined by other intellectuals and social reformers, among them the landscape architect Andrew Jackson Downing. By the early 1850s, the notion of a large park for New York was firmly fixed in the

▷

Central Park, looking south towards 59th street, and on pp. 66-67, with the late afternoon sun shining through the trees on to the lake.

P. 68/69
Brooklyn Bridge, opened in 1883, one of the world's most notable suspension bridges in the 19th century.

public mind, and, in 1858, a board of commissioners and an advisory committee, which included Washington Irving, was established.

On Irving's recommendation, Frederick Law Olmsted, an amateur landscapist and a writer who had contributed to Downing's popular magazine, *The Horticulturist*, was engaged as superintendent in charge of clearing the huge area. Shortly after, he was approached by Downing's collaborator, the English-born architect Calvert Vaux, who suggested that they jointly submit a plan in the competition for the design of the park. With similar aesthetic and sociological aspirations, these men had absorbed the idealism that guided the civic-minded philosophers of the Boston school. Vaux was fond of quoting Emerson, particular the celebrated essay on self-reliance. Olmsted was highly sensitive to the idea of a public environment that would enhance the 'perceptive faculties' of a democratic society. Olmsted

The tennis house in Prospect Park, Brooklyn. In the romantic, picturesque English tradition, this park was designed 1867-72.

conceived of the park as 'a democratic development of the highest significance and on the success of which, in my opinion, much of the progress of art and esthetic culture in this country is dependent.'

Still cleaving to the romantic school's notion of irregularity as the superior expression of natural beauty, Olmsted and Vaux plotted the park down to the last detail. Olmsted's view was that 'a park is a single work of art, and as such subject to the primary law of every work of art, namely, that it shall be framed upon a single, noble motive, to which the design of all its parts, in some more or less subtle way, shall be confluent and helpful.' He noted that 'every foot of the park's surface, every tree and bush, as well as every arch, roadway and walk, has been fixed where it is with a *purpose.*'

In completing their visionary scheme for New York, Olmsted and Vaux contributed the first effective environmental scheme. The

critic, Albert Fein, credits them with the establishment of what he calls 'the park-complex, an environmental ideal.' Of great importance is the feature introducing four transverse roads below the surface of the park, enabling traffic to cross Manhattan without interfering with the recreational uses of the park. He notes that the designers made separate provisions for three forms of movement within the park itself (vehicular, equestrian and pedestrian) and that such attention to public safety was a revolutionary development.

The park was New York's last great undertaking before the Civil War. The dirt, noise and smoke that had depressed visitors in the late '50s was cancelled out in the boundless beauty of Central Park. 'Conceived in contrast to the deflowered landscape and the muddled city, the park alone re-created the traditions of civilization', wrote Lewis Mumford in *Sticks and Stones,* while architecture was 'sullen, grim, gauche and unstable'. There were, of course, architects who could use Gothic, Romanesque and even Moorish motifs discreetly, and who could produce handsome well-proportioned houses, theatres, churches and commercial buildings. Among those active immediately before the Civil War were important Europeans who had settled in New York like Leopold Eidlitz, Dietlef Lienau, Frederick Diaper, Calvert Vaux, Richard Upjohn, and European-influenced Americans such as Richard Morris Hunt. But for all their taste and good background as professionals, they could not succeed in countering the vulgar eclecticism that accompanied New York's sensational growth in wealth and population.

During the last years before the Civil War, the roster of artists in New York was greatly enlarged due to the increasing support they found in the merchant classes. While the moneyed aristocracy of long standing tended to import their treasures from Europe, the merchants, many of whom had started as grocers' clerks or mechanics, proved to be active enthusiasts for contemporary art. Neil Harris uses the membership of the Century Club, where artists and patrons often met in the 1840s and 1850s, as a barometer. He mentions that the original list of members showed ten artists, ten merchants, four authors, three men of leisure, three physicians and two lawyers, and suggests that the energetic response of these merchants to the needs of the local artists helped to make New York the true aesthetic centre of the United States.

The thriving bohemia of the artists' world proved attractive and it tended to be centralized in a few districts of the city. One of the most important centres was the West 10th Street Studio Building, designed by young Richard Morris Hunt, recently back from his studies at the Ecole des Beaux Arts in Paris. An ideally designed building, the three-storey brick studio enclave was a tremendous success. Right down to the day of its destruction in the 1950s, the building served artists to perfection. There was a large communal exhibition room on the ground floor, and all the studios were large and well lit.

In the absence of vigorous commercial galleries, the artists themselves received their patrons, performing their required roles, and helped to define the nature of American art for their eager listeners. There,

◁
The Administration building in the Brooklyn Botanic Gardens.

P. 74/75
Brooklyn Bridge, whose graceful sweep and strong lines have inspired poets and painters alike to paeans of praise.

The American Museum of Natural History, a sturdy remnant of the stone age of the 'brown decades'.

Frederick Edwin Church filled his studio with trophies from his South American painting trips; Emanuel Leutze gave sumptuous dinners; and receptions were held, drawing well-known artists such as East-man Johnson, Daniel Huntington, J. F. Kensett and Asher B. Durand. Those same cosmopolitan artists who held forth in the 10th Street Studio Building were, for the most part, carrying out the imperatives set by such Hudson River School leaders as Asher B. Durand

himself, whose influential letters on landscape painting had been recently published. Church brought back dramatic but rather bombastic views of exotic wilderness from South America. Far more profound were the studies made by John Kensett whose paintings of Maine and New Hampshire show a more sophisticated sense of contrast and selection of detail than any of the older landscapists. Still younger men such as Winslow Homer, who had come to New York

and settled in the New York University building, were busy establishing careers in the field of illustration—a field that was to support American painters for many years to come. Journals such as *Harper's Weekly* helped to create an audience for depictions of American life. Both the sweetness of rural pleasures and the vastness of the land beyond the cities became urgently required anodynes as the pre-war years drew to a close, heralding the full implications of the Industrial Revolution.

Civil War and Paradoxical Prosperity

The Civil War hit New York at first only mildly. New York's businessmen were notoriously reluctant to allow a breach with their good customers in the South. Abolitionists had not been thoroughly successful in rousing the 'empire city' which, as many critical commentators noted, was more devoted to profit-making activities and worldly pleasures than to matters of principle. Yet, when the first attack at Fort Sumter was reported, there were wild rallies to the Union cause; great mass meetings in Union Square; tremendous musters of volunteers, and a general carnival atmosphere only conceivable in a city that had known no serious wars since the American Revolution.

For many residents of New York, the carnival persisted, for the war years from 1861 to 1865 saw the value of property and goods nearly double. Quick fortunes were made by countless speculators in war material. Small manufacturers doubled and tripled their businesses, taking advantage of all the new tools put at their disposal by the rapid development of technology. Railroads and banks prospered, and the Stock Exchange, despite early fears of the business men, flourished. The Civil War, in its great upheaval, changed American society above all in the urban centres. New York was scarcely recognizable to visitors who had known it in the 1850s. Far from having halted its normal activities, New York accelerated them. Hundreds of raw commercial buildings were completed during the war, and many great mansions sprang up on Fifth Avenue. Mark Twain's 'Gilded Age' came upon New York even before the cessation of hostilities.

Not all construction was in the realm of what Thorstein Veblen would later call 'conspicuous consumption'. The growth of the city had inevitably changed its social structure, pushing the middle-income residents into neighbouring suburbs. Visitors to New York during the decade of the Civil War increasingly remarked on the residential division which was now reduced to the very rich and the very poor. The famous Five Points downtown district was overcrowded with Negroes and immigrants who lived in squalid conditions while the war profiteers lined the avenues with their new, rather ostentatious dwellings. Others sought fresh air and more modest housing in boroughs such as Brooklyn. In 1867, Olmsted & Vaux began work on Prospect Park in Brooklyn, a masterpiece of planning. Sometime later, a great engineering feat was undertaken by John Roebling.

The Brooklyn Bridge, which provided New Yorkers with ceaseless dramatic episodes, from the death of its designer to the collapse of his son, Washington A. Roebling, who had heroically supervised its construction, was greatly to contribute to both business and residential expansion. Mumford called it a testimony to the swift progress of physical science. 'The strong lines of the bridge, and the beautiful

◁
A typical loft building in the downtown area.

curve described by its suspended cables, were derived from an elegant formula in mathematical physics—the catenary curve... All that the age had just cause for pride in—its advances in science, its skill in handling iron, its personal heroism in the face of dangerous industrial processes, its willingness to attempt the untried and the impossible—came to a head in the Brooklyn Bridge.' Mumford's appreciation is echoed by countless others, among them Walt Whitman in his paean to Manhattan, Hart Crane, and the painter Joseph Stella. For all of these creators, the Brooklyn Bridge symbolized the best of cosmopolitan genius; the prime strength of American enterprise. Its sweeping lines and soaring towers inspired them to think with pride of the tremendous energy that drove industrial America to ever greater engineering undertakings, signalling a new social order. Roebling himself had predicted that 'this structure will forever testify to the energy, enterprise and wealth of that community which shall secure its erection.'

Although some houses of distinction appeared in New York City during the 1860s and 1870s, the eclecticism of the new patronage was the predominant trait. The critic James Jackson Jarves in his book *The Art Idea*, published in 1864, ruefully urged his compatriots to face the fact that if they were annihilated tomorrow, nothing would be learned of America from its architecture, which he felt displayed only plagiarism and superficiality, and disregarded the fundamental law of art which demands the harmonious relationship. Like many intellectuals Jarves referred to ocean-clippers, river-steamers and industrial machines as the best exemplars of American invention and enterprise. Jarves could certainly not have found enthusiastic praise for local New York mannerisms. Yet, within the Victorian revivalism, there were several architects of merit, who were able to produce perfectly decent, sometimes even distinguished buildings. The National Arts Club on Gramercy Park and the Museum of Natural History are examples of a modified Gothic endowed by their creators with originality and utility, while the Jefferson Courthouse, recently restored, bespeaks the heady fantasies in which architects would indulge during the 1870s.

As many critics have conceded, the 1870s and 1880s were dominated by one architect, Henry Hobson Richardson. Keenly aware of the frivolous and transitory character of American architecture, Richardson sought to educate himself thoroughly in matters of structure. In Europe he absorbed the lessons of the modern methods employed by architects along with the aesthetic lessons implicit in the works of the past. Richardson's feelings were obviously most deeply stirred by the great stone prodigies of the Romanesque period. When he came back to the United States to carve out his great reputation, it began with what he called 'a free rendering of the French Romanesque' in Trinity Church, Boston. His later elaboration of a Romanesque mode was expressed in countless suburban railroad stations and libraries, in which he carefully built solid, simple stone exteriors.

Richardson's love for great blocks of stone made his employment somewhat impracticable in New York City, perhaps, for there is no surviving monument by him to remind us of his powerful sense of design.

▷

*McKim, Mead & White's stately Morgan Library, designed 1906.
to house a famous collection of mss from 6th-16th centuries.*

But his influence is, to this day, highly visible in the numerous works of his contemporary admirers working in those plush years. Perhaps the most distinguished adaptations of Richardsonian principles remain the numerous business buildings in which the Romanesque austerity of rhythmic arches, sharply defined, make for an impression of simple monumentality. A frequently praised building is Babb, Cook & Willard's former deVinne Press Building, now called simply 399 Lafayette Street, still one of the most imposing commercial structures in downtown New York.

Mansions and chateaux for millionaires were not the only structures

The Racquet and Tennis Club, 1918, one of McKim, Mead & White's most effective Italianate adaptations, from the terrace of the Seagram Building.

that profited from the post-war prosperity. New York was building the newly fashionable apartment houses to replace the individual dwelling, and to offer a new solution to the chronic New York housing shortage. For years a great many newly married couples had had to resort to boarding house accommodations, but the apartment, introduced by Richard Morris Hunt in 1869, brought a whole new concept of urban life. Many wealthy families sought housing in such enormous structures as the Dakota Apartments by Henry J. Hardenbergh. The Dakota, a very fashionable address still, was built overlooking Central Park, with a central courtyard, reminiscent of the

Villard Houses, 1886 and (right) the University Club, 1899, in the Italian Renaissance style, both built by the firm of McKim, Mead & White.

luxurious spaces found in Parisian mansions. Although it somewhat resembled a Bavarian castle, the Dakota had a great many original features that made it the model for many subsequent upper-class apartment buildings.

Besides apartment houses, many new hotels were erected which boasted modern plumbing, elevator service and lofty vistas. One of the few remaining hotels of the period, the Chelsea Hotel on West 23rd Street, was built originally as a cooperative apartment house and converted into a hotel only in 1905. The building, by Hubert, Pirsson & Company, is still one of the attractive elements of this street, although it has no particular style. Its façade is covered with lacy ironwork balconies, an unusual and enlivening feature of the period.

Beyond the fashionable quarters where spacious apartments were springing up in the 1880s, there were even larger districts housing the working classes in tenements. 'As early as 1835 the multiple-family tenement had been introduced in New York as a means of producing congestion, raising the ground-rents, and satisfying in the worst possible way the need of the new immigrants for housing', Mumford wrote angrily in *Sticks and Stones*. He indicts the architectural profession for permitting the worst features of tenement-house construction to be standardized in the so-called dumbell tenement, designed in 1879. The dumbell tenements, some of which survive to this day in the lower East Side district of Manhattan, in the Bronx and in Brooklyn, were to be the source of agitation on the part of reformers for several succeeding generations. Their unwieldly structures, shaped roughly like dumbells, allowed only

*Statue of George Washington by J.Q.A. Ward (1883)
at the Federal Hall National Memorial, and (right)
looking from behind the statue at the New York Stock Exchange.*

inches of air to penetrate the narrow interiors. The initial problem—
—that of housing New York's labouring force in high density—has
never been adequately solved.

The chief architects of the day did not concern themselves with com-
petitions for well-designed tenements. In fact, Richardson's star pupils,
McKim, Mead & White, commenced their careers outside the urban
limits altogether, designing large country houses for families whose
wealth was drawn from the metropolis. They had formed their partnership in 1879. Charles Follen McKim, who had studied at the Ecole
des Beaux-Arts, had spent a profitable time in Richardson's office,
while William Rutherford Mead, his first partner, had worked in the
office of Russell Sturgis, a Gothic Revival specialist. Stanford White,
who joined them in 1879, was another of Richardson's protégés. Together, this trio of worldly and gifted architects produced much of the
pomp and some of the glory of late nineteenth-century New York
architecture.

Wayne Andrews has given an amusing account of the origins of the
trio's first major work in the city in his *Architecture in America*: 'A
revolution in American architecture occurred on the evening of March
26, 1883, when Mr and Mrs W. K. Vanderbilt gave their never-to-be-
forgotten ball in their new and noble chateau by Richard Morris
Hunt... The chateau, now destroyed, proved that a millionaire could
be superbly housed in a French Renaissance design.'

Such a challenge could not be ignored, and McKim, Mead & White met
it by designing in 1886 a complex of five adjoining mansions for railroad financier Henry Villard and four of his friends. With strong
reminiscences of Italian palazzos implicit in its courtyard, its stone-
work, its fenestration and interiors, the Villard mansion complex, at
Madison Avenue and 50th Street, was considered a masterpiece of taste
and splendour in its day, and certainly helped to make the firm

virtually the sole agent for the promotion of Renaissance-style buildings in New York. The rage for Italian palazzos continued into the early twentieth century, and not a few of New York's more satisfying buildings are still these sumptuous relics of the Gilded Age. Although the firm was able to modify its designs, so that certain of their buildings are classified as neo-Georgian (as is the Harvard Club in some books) or Roman Eclectic (as is Columbia University's Low Library), it was basically their abiding love for the grandeur of Renaissance Florence and Rome that inspired most of McKim, Mead & White's best work, and also some of their worst.

The new regard for the treasures of Europe was not limited to the adaptation of European architecture. The patrons who wanted to inhabit a French chateau or an Italian palazzo on Fifth Avenue wished also to stock it with appropriate imports from European capitals. The post-Civil War era saw a marked decrease in interest in the painting and sculpture of local New York artists. Oliver Larkin notes that when department store magnate A.T. Stewart's collection was auctioned in 1887, a painting by the once immensely successful Frank E. Church went for $7,050 while Meissonier's *1807* was sold for $66,000. In the same year, Rosa Bonheur's *Horse Fair* was bought for $55,000 while the native painter, Albert Ryder, received between $250 and $500 for his work, if indeed he could sell it at all.

Artists themselves shared their patrons' new enthusiasm for the super-iorities of European culture. Already in the late 1860s the pattern of foreign studies was established, several young painters going to Munich to absorb Wilhelm Leibl's realism, tinged with the brushwork and dark tones of Frans Hals, and others going to Paris, to learn the tricks of the fashionable salon painters. When they returned to New York, they struggled to introduce their new approach, derived from Europe, to patrons who preferred to travel to Europe themselves, and who no longer had the civic conscience of a Luman Reed.

Theirs was a different breed of civic pride, which led them away from the intimacies of New York's bohemia to the grand world of international travel, cross-Atlantic communications, and the amassing of art and artifacts on a scale previously unknown to New Yorkers. As Thorstein Veblen was to point out not long after in his *Theory of the Leisure Class,* post-Civil War society, with its 'Captains of Industry', was acquisitive by definition. 'Habituation to war entails a body of predatory habits of thought, whereby clannishness in some measure replaces the sense of solidarity and a sense of invidious distinction supplants the impulse to equitable, everyday servicibility... The generation that follows a season of war is apt to witness a rehabilitation of the element of status.' Such a generation, Veblen maintained, established rituals and institutions to flatter their status seeking.

Status on a national level made its appearance in the rush, after the Civil War, to commemorate its glories and, in a few rare instances, its horrors. Comfortable citizens felt it their duty to turn away from the classic motifs of the usual Roman model, imported from expatriate artists in Italy, toward the new national statuary of local heroes. In New York City the academician John Quincy Adams Ward fulfilled numerous orders for standing or equestrian monuments, most often of living heroes. His statue of George Washington, completed in 1883 for the

▷

Metropolitan Museum of Art, façade of central building, a grandiose conception in Roman style by Richard Morris Hunt, completed 1902.

site where the president took his first oath of office (now Federal Hall
National Memorial), was an exception. It was greatly admired at the
time for the sweep of the military cloak, and the lifted hand, which, as
one commentator wrote, is a 'simple gesture which betokens authority
guided by moderation and intelligence.' Ward's other important work
in New York is his portrait of Henry Ward Beecher, the abolitionist
minister, a realistic study on a base designed by Richard Morris Hunt
now standing in Cadman Plaza in Brooklyn.

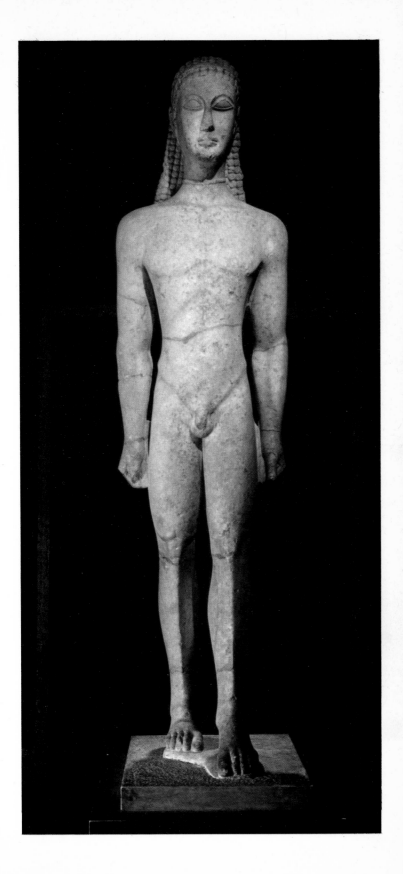

The Harvesters, c. *1528-30-1969, by Pieter Bruegel the elder.*
Metropolitan Museum of Art. Rogers Fund, 1919.

The other New York sculptor participating in the new campaign for
public statuary was Augustus Saint-Gaudens. Born in Ireland but
reared in New York, Saint-Gaudens began his apprenticeship to a cameo
cutter at the age of thirteen, and studied drawing at night in the newly
founded Cooper Union. He pursued his studies at the Ecole des Beaux
Arts in Paris and later in Rome, returning to New York in 1874. In
1878 he received the commission for a monument to Admiral Farragut
which was to be one of his masterpieces. The Admiral, who stands

to this day in Madison Square at 23rd Street and Fifth Avenue, is seen in a quiet, rather grim stance, astride an impressive pedestal designed by Stanford White, and bearing delicate low reliefs. The majesty of this monument is unfortunately unmatched in New York City, although Saint-Gaudens created several other monuments of quality, including the portrait of Peter Cooper in Cooper Square and the equestrian statue of General Sherman on the northern side of Grand Army Plaza at 60th Street and Fifth Avenue. Ward and Saint-Gaudens

Metropolitan Museum of Art.
(Above) the Blumenthal Patio.

(Right) Mr and Mrs Isaac Newton Phelps Stokes, *1897,*
by John Singer Sargent. Bequest of Edith Minturn Phelps Stokes, 1938.

(Below) Madame Charpentier and her children, *1878, by Renoir.*
Catharine Lorillard Wolfe Fund, 1907.

were both superior to most of the busy statuary-producers who were zestfully filling Eastern cities with their boastful, grandiloquent public sculptures.

In some measure, the so-called old aristocracy resisted these displays of status. They too had turned away significantly from the new generations of artists, seeking their visual pleasures abroad. It was, in fact, in Paris's Bois de Boulogne that the foundation of a great museum of art was proposed by a group of celebrating Americans who later pushed through the foundation of the Metropolitan Museum of Art.

The situation of American art during that period immediately after the war was ideally summarized by the writer Henry Theodore Tuckerman in 1867. Discerning an advance in public art taste, he could point to a score of eminent and original landscape painters who had achieved high reputations, and noticed that collections of pictures had become a 'new social attraction'. He said that exhibitions of works of art were now lucrative and popular; studio buildings and art shops were appearing; artists' receptions were held; Americans painting abroad were establishing reputations. In view of what he thought to be the 'enhanced intellectual resources' of the American people, he felt the time had come to establish a permanent gallery of art.

The men who undertook to organize New York's permanent gallery were still from the old pre-war society that had learned to appreciate the importance of a native visual culture. When the first committee was set up, it included publisher George P. Putnam as chairman; the very popular landscape painter John Kensett; sculptor J.Q.A. Ward; another landscape painter, Worthington Whittredge; a portrait painter, George A. Baker, and a collector and art dealer, Samuel P. Avery. This committee was abetted in its efforts by the powerful crusader and journalist William Cullen Bryant. Bryant, extending his conviction which had led him to defend the establishment of Central Park as a panacea for social ills, now proposed that the organization of a great collection of the art of all time would help to stem the rising tide of social unrest: 'It is in the labyrinths of such mighty and crowded populations that crime finds its most seductive and fatal snares', he told some 300 important listeners at the Union League Club in 1869, 'and sin is pampered and festers and spreads its contagion... Its is important that we should encounter the temptations to vice in this great and too rapidly growing capital by attractive entertainment of an innocent and improving character.'

While Bryant may have considered the development of a great historical collection as an innocent entertainment, others saw it as a fitting display of the 'empire city's worldwide power. The Policy Committee itself, in 1870, projected nothing less than a 'more or less complete collection of objects illustrative of the History of Art from the earliest beginnings to the present time,' and included 'all the aims, whether industrial, educational, or recreative, which can give value to such an institution.' It is interesting to note that the artists initially involved in planning the Metropolitan repeatedly urged their associates to make provision for the acquisition and display of American contemporary art. They sensed already in 1870 the coming vogue for exotic culture, and were prepared to fight back. The note of caution appears in Henry James's assessment of New York's cultural possibilities in the 1870s: 'Acquisition—

◁

The Woolworth Building. Cass Gilbert's 1913 skyscraper, soon to be dwarfed by the World Trade Center tower, in the rear.

it need be on the highest terms—may, during the years to come, bask here as in a climate it has never before enjoyed. There was money in the air, ever so much money—that was, grossly expressed, the sense of things—for *all* the most exquisite except creation, which was to be off the scene altogether.'

Despite depressions and complicated arrangements with the city, the Metropolitan Museum was opened in 1870 in a former dancing academy, its temporary quarters. After a second move to 14th Street, plans for a new building were consolidated. It was to be designed by Central Park's architect, Calvert Vaux, and J. Wrey Mould, and it opened its doors in 1880—New York's first permanent grand-scale museum. Leo Lerman, art connoisseur, describes the building as 'that single, stark, cathedral-like edifice on the Deer Park land, a big, gambrel-roofed, lavishly skylighted, gas-lighted, chimney-studded, ruddy-stone structure whose glittering windows were surmounted by decorations of stone slabs like gigantic raised eyebrows.' It was a fine extension of the grand dreams its founders had realized, which was very soon to prove inadequate to the collection that came pouring into its exhibition halls. In 1888 Theodore Weston added a southwest wing and façade, and, in 1895, Richard Hunt completed his central portion facing Fifth Avenue. Hunt's plans for the huge central section recall the significance of the Chicago Exposition, of which he was one of the active designers.

The long story of enlargements and improvements for the Metropolitan Museum is not yet over. In 1970, there was a new design for the entry stairs and a huge front plaza was developed, incorporating two 160-foot long fountains which, in their wall-like configuration, echo the classic lines of the main façade. Plans to install the Temple of Dendur in a glazed structure and the Lehman Collection in a new wing to be carved out of parkland are still being contested by community leaders and park enthusiasts. The Metropolitan, however, will undoubtedly find a way to extend its traditional imperial domain.

Fin-de-Siècle

The World's Colombian Exposition of 1893 represented to many Americans the crowning moment of the nineteenth century. Every consideration was given to the complete expression of America's technological efficiency, its tremendous financial growth in the post-Civil War era, and its desire to surpass the culture of the old world, which at last America could regard as rival rather than progenitor. The exposition was planned in great haste, the chief organizer being the Chicago architect Daniel H. Burnham. A measure of the esteem the Empire City had generated in the rest of America is indicated by the fact that Burnham called the three most prominent architectural firms in New York to his aid. They were McKim, Mead & White; Richard M. Hunt; and George B. Post. On plans laid out by New York's Olmsted, these architects, together with their counterparts from Boston, Chicago and Kansas City, planned the extravagant Court of Honour that was to inspire so much controversial discussion. In 1891, Hunt spoke of what he and his colleagues intended when they decided against the iron and glass fair solutions that had preceded them in Europe.

Hunt's own contribution, the Administration building, was, as fellow architect Henry Van Brunt described it, a civic temple based upon the model of the domical cathedrals of the Renaissance. It set the tone for the whole court, which as Van Brunt pointed out, contained façades

Seated Madonna and Child, c. 1630. *Austrian with Bohemian influence.*
Lindenwood, partially painted and gilded.
Metropolitan Museum of Art. Cloisters Collection.

far exceeding in dimensions those of any other ancient or modern architectural group, with their 'monumental colonnaded pavilions, their sculptured enrichments, their statuary, domes and towers...'

Such splendours in lath and plaster as these white monuments at the Fair were critically viewed by Louis Sullivan. He, and a few other discerning intellectuals, saw only the pernicious effects of the new rage for the classical. 'Thus did the virus of a culture, snobbish and alien to the land, perform its work of disintegration; and thus ever works the pallid academic mind, denying the real, exalting the fictitious and the false, incapable of adjusting itself to the flow of living things... The damage wrought by the World's Fair will last for half a century from this date, if not longer.'

Those who viewed Hunt's new Metropolitan Museum in 1895 hardly saw it as an alien element in New York. Its stately design inspired feelings of great pride in its very grandeur; its reference to Roman might; its stony solemnity bespeaking the solid resources that brought it into existence. For the next two decades, New York would see an epidemic of massive, eclectic, classically oriented public buildings, clubs and private mansions produced by Hunt, McKim, Mead & White, Ernest

Flagg, Carrère & Hastings, and a host of lesser devotees of classic and Renaissance examples. Sullivan's prediction appeared, to a very small minority of architectural critics, as only too accurate. It was to be a long time before the pretentions of classic grandeur would give way to a truly modern architecture.

When Lewis Mumford referred to *fin-de-siècle* America, he called it the age of the Imperial Façade; an age in which industry shifted to finance, and in which 'architecture came to dwell in the stock exchanges, the banks, the shops, and the clubs of the metropolis.' Delusions of Roman Imperial grandeur appeared everywhere, and particularly in such imposing piles as Grand Central and the old Pennsylvania railroad stations. (Unfortunately, McKim, Mead & White's masterful station has been totally ravaged.) The imperial façade was further abetted in its conquest of American sensibilities by the development of the steelcage construction which, in Mumford's eyes, placed a premium upon the mask. Mumford's judgment would certainly seem confirmed by the early history of skyscrapers, in which the practical lessons of Bogardus and the other 'iron-mongers' were largely ignored. There are many scholarly studies of the skyscraper, usually taking one of two positions: either that the skyscraper was a natural development of certain technological processes, or that the skyscraper represented the social and political aspirations of its owners. In both cases, numerous early examples are put forward and studied individually, but in reality, the skyscraper phenomenon is best understood in terms of ensembles of tall buildings. New Yorkers were very early aware of the natural importance of the skyline. From the eighteenth century on, topographers rendered the changing aspect of the skyline of lower Manhattan, and by the mid-nineteenth century, there were already critical laments concerning the dark canyons of Wall Street, and the dangers of exceedingly high business buildings in close proximity. Henry James in the 1870s had complained about the downtown skyscrapers as 'extravagant pins in a cushion already overplanted... They are not all of marble, I believe, by any means, even if some may be, but they are impudently new and still more impudently "novel"—this in common with many other terrible things in America—and they are triumphant payers of dividends...' And George Templeton Strong shuddered as he remarked in his journals about these hideous nightmares of buildings that shut out the sky.

But others noted the upward thrusting colossus of Manhattan with pride, and read in its expansion the history of the consolidation of power and wealth. When the steeple of Trinity Church was dwarfed by its business neighbours, most visitors saw only the spectacular symbolic meaning of all this piled up activity and did not worry too much about the less enchanting loss of light, air and breathing space. Mumford claims that in its social context the skyscraper encouraged our characteristic American weakness, 'our love of abstract magnitude, our interest in land gambling, our desire for conspicuous waste.'

At the same time, Mumford does not lose sight of the positive aspects of the new skyscraper mania. The development of the steel-framed structure, as it took place in both Chicago and New York, is of cardinal importance to American architecture. It was through the rationalization of building—those technological possibilities offered by rolled steel, the invention of the elevator, and various ventilation and heating innovations—that a new aesthetic appeared. Many critics feel that its birthplace was Chicago, and that it came about partly as a result of the great Chicago fire in 1871. Unquestionably, the theory and practice of designing tall buildings found its soundest exponents in such men as

Monument to Admiral Farragut, *1880,*
by Augustus St-Gaudens in Madison Square.

Daniel Burnham, John Wellborn Root, William Le Baron Jenny, and
Louis Sullivan. Sullivan is still the best source for understanding the
ideas with which the more advanced architects of the period were
grappling.

In his *Autobiography of an Idea* Sullivan wrote of the tremendous
importance of the steel frame. He 'felt at once that the new form of engineering was revolutionary, demanding an equally revolutionary architectural mode. That masonry construction, in so far as tall buildings
were concerned, was a thing of the past, to be forgotten, that the
mind might be free to face and solve new problems in new functional
forms. That the old ideas of superimposition must give way before
the sense of vertical continuity.' His romantic view of the new possibility of the many-storeyed building is often quoted: 'It must be tall,
every inch of it tall. The force and power of altitude must be in it,
the glory and pride of exaltation must be in it. It must be every inch
a proud and soaring thing, rising in sheer exultation from bottom to top;
it is a unit without a single dissenting line...'

Unfortunately Sullivan was given little opportunity to express his
theories in New York, whose only Sullivan building, the Bayard, or
Condict Building, is not his most impressive, yet it was considered
a radical solution to the skyscraper problem in its time. The most
discerning critic of the period, Montgomery Schuyler, discussed the
building in an article in *Architectural Record*, for January and March
of 1899, shortly after the building was completed. 'The actual structure is left, or rather, is helped to tell its own story... Neither the
analogy of the column, nor any other tradition or convention, is allowed

The Bayard (Condict) Building,
1898, by Louis H. Sullivan,
his only New York structure
(left), and (above)
the portal, a detail.

103

to interfere with the task of clothing the steel frame in as expressive forms as may be. There is no attempt to simulate the breadth and massiveness proper to masonry in a frame of metal that is merely wrapped in masonry for its own protection...'

According to Schuyler, such important buildings of the period as Ernest Flagg's two Singer buildings, George Post's Union Trust Building and later, Cass Gilbert's Woolworth Building always stress the importance of the frame, and the architect's obligation to think of appropriate ways to express it. His insistence that the frame should be manifest could not find full expression until the winds of the International Style reached American shores more than twenty years later.

The admiration of most spectators went to the Richardson echoes of stone solidity to be found in Daniel Burnham's Flatiron Building. Constructed on a triangular site in rusticated limestone, the Flatiron

Grand Central Station, completed 1920, last of the huge scale termini.

Building was for years one of the most admired buildings in the city, its Italianate lines finding favour with those who had not yet understood the potentially new aesthetic in the skyscraper form. Even such modestly adventurous modern departures as Robert D. Kohn's Evening Post Building, with its *art nouveau* overtones, were passed over in favour of the imposing stone masks that generally fronted the run-of-the-mill business buildings erected during the first years of the twentieth century.

While there was a large economic expansion in the so-called gay '90s which, like most other decades, had a financial panic and a slow recovery and, while building continued unabated through booms and busts, the cultural life of the city was not notably enhanced. In fact, for artists and writers seeking to establish rapport with their countrymen, circumstances seemed far less propitious than they had during the more

The Evening Post Building, 1906,
a rare example of art nouveau
influence.

(Right) The Plaza Hotel, 1907,
from Central Park, gracious vestige
of Edwardian elegance.

primitive pre-Civil War era. Already at the turn of the century the familiar figure of the wandering American artist was in many cases turned into the expatriate American artist—an expatriate who harboured considerable bitterness that the promise of industrial America did not apply to him. Those who remained to fight the battles sponsored by a rising social consciousness were most often artists who, by inclination and tradition, could identify with Yankee realism. They were reformist in terms of the content of their work, and if they were visual artists, they largely came out of the newspaper illustration tradition. It was a period when Theodore Dreiser and Upton Sinclair could find eager readers. The painters who could be sent as reporters during the Spanish American War in 1898 were able to survive, but those who were keen to explore the vanguard idioms they learned in Paris found almost no moral or economic support.

Artists and Collectors at the Turn of the Century

The legacy of the nineteenth century to the painter at the beginning of the twentieth was embedded in the genteel tradition, which turned the eyes of the millionaires away from the local product unless it could, in some way, flatter their notions of elegance. Neil Harris has pointed out that the growth of private fortunes, far from helping the indigenous young American artist, harmed him: 'Greater reliance on art importers and collecting for fashion replaced the earlier search for local talent and the excitement of personal discovery. The reflected glory of accepted masterpieces was more attractive than the uncertainty of unknowns. Business men and financiers borrowed the fame of established artists for moral and social support. This reversed the older dependency relationship, when young artists had leaned on merchants for social status. Patrons of the gilded age aroused the contempt of satirists and art lovers who condemned their vulgar extravagances and crude taste.'
Rebellion was stirring in the ranks, however. By the end of the century a generation of reformers were busily attacking the institutions, particularly the National Academy of Art, which inhibited the growth of art life in America. The organization of new art schools, such as the Educational Alliance in New York's Lower East Side, reflected their dissatisfaction with the patronage system evolved after the Civil War. Together with the concern for social reform a new interest in sponsoring the native arts of New York developed, particularly that art which addressed itself to the specific life and colour of the city.
John I. H. Baur, the noted art critic, accurately stated the situation between 1900 and the First World War when he wrote: 'Early in the twentieth century American artists made two profoundly important discoveries—one, that American life held rich material for the painter, which had not yet been explored; the other, that art could be built out of pure form and color alone.' The situation has not changed since. Those who discovered the necessity of engaging in American life in order to express it included a band of newspaper illustrators from Philadelphia who migrated to New York and eventually came to be known as the painters of the Ashcan School. Their most vivid spokesman was Robert Henri who inspired others such as William Glackens,

▷
The Flatiron Building by D.H. Burnham.
In 1902 New Yorkers were enthralled by its triangular shape.

George Luks and Everett Shinn, and lastly Stuart Davis, with his indefatigable praise of life itself as the source of artistic inspiration. Henri opened a school in New York in 1907 which became the gathering place of bohemians and aesthetic rebels emerging from this illustration tradition. Stuart Davis, a student there from 1910 to 1913, recalled the Henri School as radical and revolutionary in its methods. 'All the usual art school routine was repudiated... We were encouraged to make sketches of everyday life in the streets, the theatre, the restaurant and everywhere else.'

When Henri's friends were rejected by the National Academy, he organized the exhibition in 1908 at the Macbeth Gallery, which won for them the scornful title of the Ashcan School. Their recourse to the racier districts of the city, and their lusty interest in the seamy side of life was a direct affront to the hypocritical genteel taste of the time. Much of the obloquy their show brought upon them was based far more on the subject matter of their paintings, than on their quality as works of art. In fact, as works of art, most of the Ashcan School products fell far short of standards acceptable to the European vanguard.

This was being discovered by one young painter after another in the years before the First World War. Those whose inclinations were not stimulated by the realism of the Ashcan School found little to keep them in America. As Marsden Hartley, another artist who struggled to get to Europe for years before Stieglitz helped him, noted, 'they want Americans to be *American* and yet they offer little or no spiritual sustenance for their growth and welfare.'

He, like John Marin, Arthur Dove, Max Weber and many others, found what little spiritual sustenance there was, and some physical sustenance, in the circle of Alfred Stieglitz. Stieglitz had returned to New York from Germany where he had studied in 1890. He immediately began photographing what reformer Jacob Riis had described in his important work *How the Other Half Lives,* as well as the more beautiful aspects of city life. He also began his lifelong campaign for the acceptance of originality in photography or the other visual arts. By 1903 he had founded his important journal, *Camera Notes,* later called *Camera Work,* and by 1907 he had opened an exhibition room. In that room, at 291 Fifth Avenue, Stieglitz showed a remarkable series of exhibitions that included Picasso and Matisse as well as such young Americans as Marin, Hartley, Dove and Alfred Maurer.

The existence of the Stieglitz circle was of inestimable importance in the development of the first *avant-garde* in America. Stieglitz gathered together the few intellectuals capable of gauging the quality in the new work, and the few wealthy patrons who could provide a means of subsistence to his artists. In his publication he promoted a lively exchange between Europe and the United States, keeping his young artists informed of the latest excitement in the arts, and thrusting forward the advanced ideas so vital to modern art.

For both Stieglitz's circle, and the artists of Henri's circle, there was the common bond of antipathy to provincialism and institutionalized art. It was this shared bohemianism which enabled a force of widely disparate artists to band together long enough to set the conditions which made it possible to stage the celebrated Armory Show in 1913. This show, organized by the Association of American Painters and Sculptors, was consciously intended to strike a blow at the genteel tradition, and at the prevalent American indifference to what in those years was generally called the 'new spirit.' As the painter Arthur B. Davies said

Lower Manhattan (composing derived from tip of Woolworth),
1922, by John Marin. Museum of Modern Art.
Acquired through the Lillie P. Bliss Bequest, purchase.

at the opening of the exhibition: 'The members of this association have
shown you that American artists—young American artists, that is—do
not dread, and have no need to dread, the ideas or the culture of Europe.
They believe that in the domain of art, only the best should rule.'
More than 1,200 American and foreign works of art were gathered
together, including examples of the most advanced European painters
and sculptors, among them: Bonnard, Brancusi, Braque, Cézanne, Degas,
Delaunay, Duchamp, Duchamp-Villon, Dufy, Gauguin, Van Gogh,
Kandinsky, Monet, Matisse, Picasso, Renoir, Toulouse-Lautrec and
Vuillard.

The furore caused by the Armory Show is legendary, as is the profound
effect it was to have on the young artists, who, like Stuart Davis, could
say that it was the greatest single experience in their artistic life.
Armed now with the new idioms coming from Europe, the American
painters, and a very few sculptors, sought to shape a modern art that
was supra-national and free of inhibition.

The city, being even then the epitome of modern life, played its part.
A number of the young painters who were not sympathetic to the
realism of the Ashcan School tried, nonetheless, to record their strong
feelings about the Empire City, and to reveal its modern beauties.
John Marin's first significant watercolours dwelt on New York City
motifs, including its waterfronts, skyscrapers and bridges. He spoke
of seeing 'great forces at work, great movements; the large buildings and
the small buildings; the warring of the great and the small; influences
of one mass on another greater or smaller mass... each subject in some
degree to the other's power... I can hear the sound of their strife and
there is great music being played.' Even in the Woolworth Building,
of which Marin did a whole series of watercolours, there was for him
great music being played; while Brooklyn Bridge epitomized the feelings of Joseph Stella. He had been one of the early wanderers in

Europe and had returned to America filled with the exuberant spirit of the Italian Futurists. His contradictory emotions concerning New York, which basically frightened and repelled him, found full expression in paintings depicting the 'battle of lights' on Coney Island, and of Brooklyn Bridge, which he saw as an apotheosis of the machine age—a beautiful, frightening, 'superb assertion of power.'

These painterly allusions to the city as the dynamic symbol of modern existence were, as Stella, in his rather exalted literary style, pointed out, machine-age offspring. The long history of American concern with technological improvement provided the natural background for an accepting attitude toward modernism at least insofar as it reflected the power of its industries.

Founding of the Great Collections

But some great financiers continued to lust after the masterpieces of the European past, and as the twentieth century began, they accelerated their efforts to garner all that was esteemed by the experts. J.P. Morgan was known to every impoverished prince, every dealer, and every private collector in Europe. His power as the head of the Metropolitan Museum was unparalleled, as the British connoisseur, Roger Fry, was to discover. In his late years, Morgan, with what Fry called his 'strawberry nose,' managed to ferret out vast collections, many formed by other men, which he often bestowed on the Metropolitan Museum. His interest in modern art was certainly negligible, as Fry found out when he acquired Renoir's *Madame Charpentier and her children* for the Metropolitan and nearly lost his job. (Fry's year in residence in New York, and association with Morgan and the Metropolitan was brief—a matter of a few more years as European adviser.) For all his rapacious acquisitiveness, and the way he swallowed entire collections in a single visit to a dealer, Morgan seemed to have a discerning spirit that was most active in his main area of collecting, that of rare manuscripts and books. His early acquisition of an autographed manuscript was almost accidental, but it led him to amass one of the most extraordinary private collections in the world. When he saw that his old brownstone house would not accommodate his library, he commissioned Charles McKim to design a fitting Renaissance home for his treasure. McKim seemed to relish the commission, planning a sober one-storey structure in more or less sixteenth-century Italian style. His ambitions for the building led him to lament to Morgan that its marble blocks could not be fitted in the classical Greek method without mortar. Morgan bluntly asked how much it would cost, McKim stated an enormous figure, and Morgan replied, 'Go ahead.' The present building is certainly one of the rarest and purest of McKim's imperial dreams. It houses not only the vast collection of manuscripts from the sixth to the sixteenth century, but also many singular examples of early printing. Morgan left funds for maintenance and acquisition when the library was made a public institution after his death. The professional

▷

The campanile of the Cloisters.

P. 114/115

The Campin altarpiece: The Annunciation *(central panel) by Robert Campin.*
Metropolitan Museum of Art.
Cloisters Collection, purchase.

Virgin enthroned
French (Autun Region)
1st half 12th century.
French walnut. 4'5" high.
Metropolitan Museum of Art,
Cloisters Collection, purchase.

(Right) The Gothic chapel
in the Cloisters with
13th-century tomb effigy.

staff has conscientiously followed his predilections, acquiring rare illuminated books, such as the section of the *Book of Hours* made for
Catherine of Cleves, and occasional rare prints and drawings. The scope
of the Morgan Library's collections, renowned especially for medieval
and Renaissance manuscripts, brings scholars from all over the world.
The other great private collection in New York City, housed in its
own museum, was formed by Henry Clay Frick, a coal and steel baron
from Pittsburgh whose rags-to-riches story excited the imagination of

Philip IV of Spain, *1644, by Velázquez, Frick Collection.*

◁
Arcades and garden of the St Guilhem Cloister, at the Cloisters.

many. Born on a farm, and scantily educated, Frick made his first million while in his twenties. At the age of thirty, he went abroad with Andrew Mellon, the future donor of the National Gallery in Washington,
where he was apparently impressed by the calibre of old private
collections. His initial purchases followed French *fin-de-siècle* taste but,
by the turn of the century, Frick was after the biggest game, competing
with other millionaires for the acknowledged masterpieces of Europe.
In this he had the advice of leading experts, including Roger Fry who also on several occasions acted as Frick's agent in Europe. Between the
turn of the century and the outbreak of World War I (and in spite of
the panic of 1907), Frick acquired a number of indisputable masterpieces
including Rembrandt's *Self Portrait,* El Greco's *Purification of the Temple,* Holbein's *Sir Thomas More* and Velazquez's *Philip IV of Spain.*
In 1914, Frick began the construction of his new residence in New
York, selected specifically for its beneficial climate for paintings.
Pittsburgh was too smoky. He chose the architectural firm of Carrere

& Hastings, very active at that time in designing both French chateau-like mansions and huge public buildings such as the New York Public Library. Thomas Hastings designed a graceful residence which would at the same time house, in museum conditions, the great collection. To this day, the Frick Collection is one of the most pleasing havens in the city, calm, dignified and filled with extraordinary visual delights, though never on an overwhelming scale. Visitors can rest in a large enclosed court, where there are regular concerts, or they can move through the rooms that remain very much the way they were when Frick was alive. They can experience the pleasures of the celebrated Fragonard room with the series of four paintings, *The Progress of Love* (rejected by Mme du Barry after they were installed in her house in Louveciennes), and the several subsequent panels that Fragonard painted after removing his works to his native city of Grasse. Or, if they are scholars, they can use the library, which is an exceptionally rich collection of important art books.

The third important public collection, the Cloisters, was made possible by John D. Rockefeller, Jr. Originally, the Cloisters had been a collection of medieval and Gothic fragments assembled by the sculptor George Grey Barnard, whose enthusiasm for the 'spirit of Gothic' led him into one of the most audacious collecting adventures ever recorded.

Over a short period, Barnard managed to acquire sections from four significant Romanesque or Gothic monasteries. One of these, Saint-Michel-de-Cuxa, founded in 878, was considered to be among the most important Benedictine abbeys of its time. These he managed to ship, stone by stone, to New York shortly before the French government passed stringent laws to prevent further pillage of national treasures. In 1914 Barnard opened his own version of a cloister museum, and John D. Rockefeller was so impressed that he bought no fewer than one hundred medieval objects from Barnard. In 1925 Barnard offered his museum to the Metropolitan for $700,000, and Rockefeller put up enough money to purchase and maintain the collection. By 1926 it was apparent that the collection was outgrowing its housing, and in 1927 Rockefeller renewed an offer of fifty-six acres of hilltop land overlooking the Hudson to the city with the proviso that four acres be set aside for a new museum.

In 1930 the city accepted, and Charles Collens was engaged to design the museum. It went through many stages of planning before reaching its discreetly medieval form at the time of its public opening in 1938. A carefully maintained site in Fort Tryon Park makes it one of the outstanding natural settings in New York City, constantly visited by residents seeking an intimation of the eloquence of medieval Europe. Aside from the cloisters, the museum houses an excellent collection of medieval art and artifacts. Most celebrated are the Unicorn Tapestries, a series of six tapestries and the fragment of another, which, despite frequent reproduction, never fail to astonish on direct encounter with their vibrancy of colour and sophistication of design. Amongst paintings and sculptures of the period, the Robert Campin Annunciation altar-piece deserves to be signalled as a brilliant example of early Flemish realism subordinated to an extremely sophisticated pictorial space.

The men who amassed European treasures were often unappreciated by many young artists, writers and architects. For them, few patrons

◁
The Empire State Building,
not so long ago the highest building in the world.

The metallic spire of the Chrysler Building.

The McGraw-Hill Building with horizontal blue-green façade, was one of the first skyscrapers to show the effects of the International Style in 1931.

▷

The dome of St Bartholomew's with the General Electric tower behind.

of an enlightened turn of mind existed in New York, and few among them were in the millionaire class. There was one very wealthy patroness, Gertrude Vanderbilt Whitney, whose means were used to keep alive indigenous artists. A sculptor herself, Mrs Whitney settled into Macdougal Alley in Greenwich Village in 1907. Her studio soon became a focal point for progressive activity in the arts. She early supported the efforts of rebellious young contemporaries, among them The Eight, and was one of the supporters of the artists organizing the Armory Show. In 1914 she opened the building at 8 West 8th Street as a gallery, calling it the Whitney Studio, where many significant young artists got their start. The prototypes of the Whitney Annuals were presented there, as were a number of one-man shows. In 1930, Mrs Whitney founded the Whitney Museum of Modern Art and had the firm of Noel & Miller remodel the buildings at 8, 10 and 12 West 8th Street into a very elegant and welcoming museum which opened in 1931. At the time hers was probably the largest collection of contemporary American art, and by 1949, when the Whitney made its first move, it could no longer be contained on 8th Street. (The building was happily saved, at least temporarily, from the speculators when the New York Studio School, an independent art school, installed itself there in the late 1960s.) Although sophisticated patrons of modern art during the 1920s were sparse, it is true that between the Armory Show and the outbreak of the war, a rudimentary artistic bohemia existed in which occasional

Edward Durrell Stone's
General Motors Building,
with its white marble vertical lines
and sunken plaza, broke into
the stately elegance of Grand Army
Plaza when it appeared in 1968.

(Right) The Corning Glass
Building, with its sparkling green
glass walls. The plaza pool and
Josef Albers' relief in the
lobby attracts leisurely visitors.

wealthy patrons appeared. Celebrated artists who came from Europe, like Marcel Duchamp, Jules Pascin, Man Ray and Francis Picabia were warmly received by such people as Walter Arensberg, John Quinn and Katherine Dreier. Broadway was already crammed with billboards, flashing lights, all-night movies and sandwich bars, but in the narrow, picturesque streets of Greenwich Village, they could still find small restaurants and cafés that reminded them of their Left Bank origins in Paris. New York had its allure, and many visiting refugees from the First World War appreciated it a lot more than its local denizens.

Between the Wars

But the post-war atmosphere discouraged the few expatriates who returned to New York during the 1920s in the hope of finding roots again. The turbulent, airless, noisy metropolis was, as always, being torn down and rebuilt at a rapid pace. Land values soared, making office buildings of the highest density desirable to investing financiers. A number of office buildings of gigantic proportions had already blotted out the light of many districts when back in 1916 the city established a new building code which required a set-back building system based on the width of the street. But once the set-back reached twenty-five percent of the site, the builders were free to add as many storeys as they liked. The resulting buildings, sometimes characterized as wedding cakes, were rarely designed to be beautiful, but only profitable and big. William Van Alen's Chrysler Building (1929-32) is 67 storeys high while Shreve, Lamb & Harmon's Empire State Building (1930-31) has 102 storeys. The impracticality of such giganticism was soon visible when the Empire State had, and probably still has, renting difficulties. Few distinguished office buildings appeared during the '20s and '30s, and those—like Raymond Hood's Daily News Building and his American Radiator Building—which were decently designed, and sensitive to site as well as air and light problems, could scarcely be called masterworks.

Yet, as Le Corbusier noted in *When The Cathedrals Were White* (based on observations made during his 1936 sojourn), New York was destined to be a vertical city, and as such was still in the making. Le Corbusier responded to the inhuman aspects of city environment with some horror, but he also saw the powerful potentials. He reported that he was 'offended by this blow at legitimate human hopes' found in the slums and business district, but that 'a proper plan can make New York the city par excellence of modern times.'

His alternate exhilaration and scorn were apparent in his various remarks about the skyscraper as it then existed in New York. They were not constructed with serious and wise intention, he wrote. 'The skyscraper as *proclamation* won. Here the skyscraper is not an element in city planning but a banner in the sky, a fireworks rocket, an aigrette in the coiffure of a name henceforth listed in the financial Almanach de Gotha.' The obvious material motivation of most office buildings, and their indifference to principles of light, air and ground space enraged Le Corbusier. But, on the other hand, he could exclaim: 'It is the first time that men have projected all their strength and labour into the sky—a whole city in the free air of the sky. Good God, what disorder,

▷

The towering climax of Rockefeller Centre.

128

what impetuosity! What perfection already, what promises! What unity in a molecular state, grid-iron street plan, office on top of office, clear crystallization. It is sublime and atrocious...'

What he recommended to astonished listeners was that the skyscrapers be made bigger still, but with the great difference that the area of free ground at its base be correspondingly larger and that walls be replaced with films of glass. He said that the normal form for a skyscraper would be vertical, plumb, without set-backs or slopes, unlike most of those of the New York skyline. At that time, there were almost no examples that could be cited which even moderately fulfilled Le Corbusier's recommendations, although Raymond Hood's McGraw-Hill Building (with Godley & Fouilhoux), designed in 1931, was praised for its lightness and the absence of romantically applied verticalism.

Without question, the most important commercial undertaking in the years between the wars was to be Rockefeller Center. Its genesis, painstakingly traced by Winston Weisman, is of interest not only to the

The skating rink in the heart of Rockefeller Center.

historian, but to the sociologist and urbanist as well. What proved to be an instructive prototype in urban design was originally conceived in 1926 not as a complex but as a new building to replace New York's Metropolitan Opera House. Then, as now, the Metropolitan Opera, supported largely by wealthy patrons, was faced with the problem of economics. New York City, like other American cities, has little to offer its artistic populace in terms of financial support. There are no state opera companies or repertory theatres in America. Consequently, when the chairmen of the Metropolitan's board first called in architects Joseph Urban and Benjamin Wister Morris, they requested plans for both a new opera house and an office building which would bring in revenue. Several plans for different sites were submitted but none seemed likely to produce the revenues necessary to warrant erecting a new opera house.

From the beginning, Morris had envisioned a plaza. When a new site owned by Columbia University on Fifth Avenue at 48th and 49th

Midtown Manhattan, a panoramic sweep looking downtown.

Streets was proposed, Morris visualized four large units arranged around a central plaza, the opera house and several other revenue-producing units—a plan that was the germ of the present Rockefeller Center. The only problem was, as Weisman writes, that 'despite the elaborate development given the revenue units, the plan was apparently neither entirely self-sustaining nor operative.' Since the chief problem was the open space, the architects realized that the plaza would have to be subsidized by a donor, who materialized in the form of John D. Rockefeller, Jr.

Work began on plans in 1929 with the object of providing a site for the Metropolitan Opera House, 'and to assure appropriate and artistic environment, ample and convenient approaches, circulation, and a dignity and harmony of architectural composition in the development of the land surrounding the Opera.'

At this stage, the opera house was still uppermost in the thoughts of the developers, but already the shadows of commerce threatened the project. The Metropolitan, faced with tremendous costs incurred on the leasehold, became alarmed. With what appears to be unseemly haste, the rest of the corporation read them out of the scheme altogether, announcing to its architectural board that 'from now on this Square would be based upon a commercial center as beautiful as possible consistent with the maximum income that could be developed.'

Given these imperatives, the team of architects, which included L. Andrew Reinhard, Henry Hofmeister, with Henry Wiley Corbett, Benjamin Morris and Raymond Hood as consultants, wrestled with numerous schemes, all designed to meet the difficult conditions of cost-and-return planning. In 1930, a plan coming close to the present scheme was signed by Reinhard & Hofmeister; Corbett, Harrison & MacMurray; Raymond Hood, Godley & Fouilhoux. By 1935, the basic design of Rockefeller Center was established. Ten buildings had been completed, and plans for the rest were on the board. The intricate demands of new tenants and large corporations must have been very taxing for the architects, although that story has not been told. Weisman implies it, however, in the summary to his essay: 'After fourteen years of planning and building the Rockefeller Center scheme evolved. Fourteen buildings of various sizes and shapes tied together with a dollar sign. This was architecture based on the laws of economics not on the canons of proportion...'

As Le Corbusier had said, 'What promises!' Although the saga of Rockefeller Center's planning bespeaks the problems of American culture, it also indicates the value of a certain largeness of vision. Finally, Rockefeller Center has been much admired and used as a model for other urban commercial ensembles. The American Institute of Architects' Guide calls the seventeen-acre cluster, with its 10,000 square feet of rentable space, the most successful effort at high-density urban design in the nation. 'The 13 buildings constructed up through 1947 have a uniform vertical wall treatment of gray Indiana limestone that identifies them as a group.' It praises the promenade from Fifth Avenue between 49th and 50th Streets through which one can pass 'between low buildings, with a series of planting beds and fountains stepping down the center; it descends a whole floor from the avenue to the edge of the skating rink that is the focus of the whole complex.' The guide comments on the complex of terraces around the rink, decorated with flags and the *Prometheus* fountain by Paul Manship, which are revealed gradually, and through which the viewer passes, then only seeing the 850-foot RCA tower, its height emphasized by the vertically striped walls.

With about two of some twelve acres devoted to landscaped open space, Rockefeller Center is an unprecedented achievement of the between-the-wars period. Its use of a private street, of underground concourses, large parking facilities within the complex and considerable pedestrian thoroughfare, marked it and brought considerable critical attention. Even Le Corbusier who, no doubt, would have objected to the stone slab concepts, found admiration for the way Rockefeller Center deployed its vertical traffic. 'It is rational, logically conceived, biologically normal, harmonious in its four functional elements: halls for entrance and division of crowds, grouped shafts for vertical circulation (elevators), corridors (internal streets), regular offices.'

The grandeur of this commercial adventure could not be found in other architectural enterprises in New York. The period between the wars was not marked for its hospitality to the original genius of the individual architect. Both Sullivan and his student Frank Lloyd Wright who, by 1910, had already been acknowledged in Europe, were treated with brutal indifference until Sullivan's death. Wright was to exclaim in 1940: 'They killed Sullivan and they nearly killed me.'

At about the same time the Opera had hoped to find new quarters, there were other cultural stirrings which were to have significant consequences for the physical and spiritual life of New York City. A number of young ambitious architects were bridling under the constraints placed by American commerce upon the development of a distinguished architecture. They looked increasingly toward Europe, where the modern idioms in architecture had long been accepted. They eschewed native mercantilism and chauvinism in favour of the new spirit of internationalism.

In this they were joined by the young art historian, Alfred H. Barr, Jr. whose interest in all aspects of advanced twentieth-century art made him a natural candidate for the organization of a permanent museum of modern art in New York City. Ever since the Armory Show a sprinkling of wealthy collectors had appeared to buy the Cézannes, Gauguins, Matisses and Van Goghs which Stieglitz and others brought to their attention. Among them were the wives of several very wealthy men. They were well aware of the great gap in New York's public collections which, as Alfred H. Barr, Jr. pointed out early in 1929, owned not a single Van Gogh painting. Barr, who was among the first generation of students to be trained in museum practice, was charged by Lillie P. Bliss, Mrs Cornelius Sullivan and Abby Aldrich Rockefeller, with organizing a new Museum of Modern Art which would be temporarily housed in six rooms in the Heckscher Building at 730 Fifth Avenue. The first exhibition of works by Cézanne, Gauguin, Seurat and Van Gogh was visited by 47,000 people

The Daily News Building, one of the most successful skyscrapers of the 1930s.

during its first month in 1929. Barr's determination to make the small venture into a permanent and incomparable museum was evident in the speed with which he moved to start a collection.

The first work was acquired during the month of the first exhibition —a bronze torso by Maillol. A few months later, the first painting entered the collection: Edward Hopper's *House by the Railroad* of 1925. Two years after she helped found the Musum of Modern Art, and became its vice-president, Miss Bliss died, bequeathing a large part of her own rich collection to the museum. She had begun her perceptive collecting during the Armory Show, when her friend Arthur B. Davies apparently counselled her to buy five important paintings, two Degas, two Redons, and a Renoir. She also then purchased her first Cézanne painting, the cornerstone of her group of twenty-six works by this artist. The exceptional quality of the works bequeathed to the museum provisionally in 1931, and formally in 1934, gave Alfred Barr the broad indispensable base for the permanent collection.

Although Cézanne, Van Gogh, Redon and Gauguin would hardly have been considered 'modern' in Europe where half-a-dozen vanguard movements of the twentieth century had long since made them seem like old masters, for New York these artists were considered sufficiently unknown to alarm part of the public and start brisk controversies over the role of a modern museum. Barr's idea was to 'establish a collection of the immediate ancestors of the modern movement and the most important living masters' and to 'help people enjoy, understand and use the visual arts of our time.' His loan exhibitions were carefully organized to display the most vivid international developments in all the arts. By 1932, he had started several departments, among them the first photography department in any museum with Edward Steichen as its guiding inspiration. His interest in motion pictures, industrial arts of all kinds, theatre design, prints and drawings led to a series of epoch-making exhibitions during the years immediately following the museum's inception. The crash of 1929 delayed fulfilment of the larger dream of a permanent building with a flowering collection, but it did not deter the enthusiasts around Barr from staging a series of unprecedented exhibitions in their then modest quarters on West 53rd Street on the site of the present museum.

One of the indisputably consequential shows was the famous 1932 exhibition of modern architecture inaugurating the Museum's Department of Architecture. In 1931, Barr requested Henry-Russell Hitchcock, an accomplished young architectural historian and critic, and Philip Johnson, a young scholar who had recently accompanied Hitchcock on a grand tour of modern architecture in Europe, to compile an exhibition which would present for the first time in New York the most progressive works of international architecture. Hitchcock and Johnson also were preparing what was to be the most important modern primer, *The International Style : Architecture Since 1922*, which appeared around the same time.

The consequences of this exhibition with its important documentation were inestimable. All the disparate views that had sustained the cost-and-return principle of the skyscraper boom were effectively attacked. The indignation of the men guiding the Museum of Modern Art's architectural programme was apparent in their statements. Barr himself, in his introduction to the catalogue, commented first on the importance of expositions and exhibitions in changing the character of American architecture, usually for the worse. Clearly, he hoped this exhibition would bring an end to what he called the confusion of the forty preceding years. His particular ire was directed against a society which ignored its native geniuses—Sullivan and Wright—and encouraged the decorative modernism of the skyscraper to mask its lack of aesthetic and environmental integrity. With youthful ardour, Barr exclaimed in his preface to Hitchcock and Johnson's book: 'American skyscraper architects with cynical good humor have been willing to label their capricious façade ornament "functional"—"one function of the building is to please the client." We are asked to take seriously the architectural taste of real estate speculators, renting agents, and mortgage brokers!'

Barr and his associates looked to European pioneers, whose philosophies embraced certain social considerations, to enlighten the American public. Accordingly, photographs and models of works by Le Corbusier, J.J.P. Oud, Gropius, Mies van der Rohe and Frank Lloyd Wright (included as an isolated native genius) were emphasized, and attention was given to a few experimental Americans, among them the firm of Hood, Howe & Lescaze, and the German-born Richard Neutra. Through this stunning exhibition with its catalogue, a full

Pines and rocks, c. 1904, by Paul Cézanne.
Museum of Modern Art. Lillie P. Bliss Collection.

length book and the widespread response in the press and professional journals, the Museum of Modern Art took the lead in re-educating both public and patron. Many of the qualities most admired by Barr and his associates were to be realized years later in the extensive rebuilding of Park Avenue.

Those qualities, as he and Hitchcock admitted even at the time, were primarily derived from functional principles. Barr described the International Style in terms of its distinguished aesthetic principles: emphasis on volume—space enclosed by planes or surfaces—rather than on mass and solidity; regularity rather than symmetry; dependence upon the intrinsic elegance of materials and fine proportions instead of exterior ornament. Very gingerly he and others confronted the various contradictions that plague the modern tradition. Hitchcock and Johnson carefully noted that distinguished Europeans such as Siegfried Giedion and the architect Hannes Meyer could combat the

(Above) The starry night, *1889, by Vincent Van Gogh.*

(Below) Les Demoiselles d'Avignon, *1907, by Picasso.*

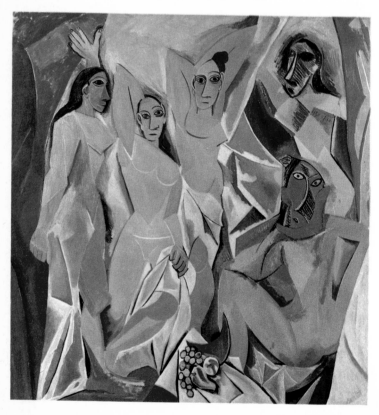

Color Planes in Oval, *1914?, by Mondrian. Museum of Modern Art.*

trend of aestheticism, preferring to see architecture in terms of economic and social problems. They pointed out that the counterparts to
the stringent functionalists of Europe, who were primarily concerned
with collective problems, are, in the United States, the architects and
critics who regard architecture as a merely subordinate technic of industrial civilization' and who are first and last practical builders. The
authors propose, instead, a respect for the generalizing tendencies of
the Style, without a proportionate loss of respect for individual variations. The same dilemma hidden in the words of these authors in 1932
haunts the contemporary architect today.

The American vanguard theorists were not insensitive to the needs of
a mass society, as Barr indicated when he inserted an important article by Lewis Mumford in the exhibition's catalogue. Because one
of the tenets of the Style was its attack on verticality, associated
with false dreams of Gothic grandeur, many of the exhibits were of
individual houses, such as Le Corbusier's villas, and Wright's work

for individual patrons. Where there were examples of factories, schools or city-block developments, they were invariably horizontal, and often in small cities or towns. Yet the acute problems of New York City were not directly confronted in this first attempt to rationalize the chaos of American building.

But, as Barr and the others understood very well, the crash of 1929 and the Depression which followed made it imperative that slum conditions in major cities be dealt with. City planning, always at a shocking minimum in New York City, had to be introduced along with the principles of the International Style. Mumford recommended comprehensive planning, mass production, limited profits and, above all, state subvention as the prerequisites for a new architectural order in housing. His article was undoubtedly informed by the harsh facts of the two preceding years when the national income and industrial production were down by fifty percent and nearly half the working population in the large cities was unemployed.

Less than two years later, New York saw the establishment of a housing authority, charged with developing plans for mass low-cost housing. Under Roosevelt's New Deal the US Housing Authority was founded, and the Civil Works Administration set up which provided jobs for the unemployed, often in the form of construction work on public housing, post-offices and schools. Still, for all the fervent advocacy of

◁
The beautiful bird revealing the unknown to a pair of lovers, 1941, by Joan Miró. Museum of Modern Art. Acquired through the Lillie P. Bliss Bequest.

Blue Poles, 1952, by Jackson Pollock. Ben Heller Collection.

Lewis Mumford, and his friends Henry Wright and Clarence Stein, there was not a single public housing project in New York to which the Museum of Modern Art, in the exhibition of 1932, could point with pride. For reasons that continue to harass American culture, the gifted and imaginative architect rarely finds himself in a position to realize his projects on a large public scale. Such projects, often subsidized in New York by large businesses such as insurance companies—and not for altruistic motives—almost invariably fall to the builders whose prime concern is to fit the largest number of people into the smallest amount of space legally permissible. The few projects in which three- or four-storey buildings were emphasized during the 1930s were decent by hygienic standards perhaps, but hardly aspired to the stylistic grace of their European counterparts.

Owh! in San Pão, *1951, by Stuart Davis. Whitney Museum of American Art.*

◁
Number 10, *1950, by Mark Rothko. Museum of Modern Art.*
Gift of Philip Johnson.

The very few buildings of any distinction privately constructed between the wars included Harrison & Fouilhoux's luxury Rockefeller Apartments of 1936, which consisted of two elegantly designed buildings with curved bays set back-to-back around an interior garden; architect William Lescaze's private house at 211 West 48th Street, built in 1934, startling New Yorkers of the period with its modern use of glass brick in rectilinear, flush patterns; and Joseph Urban's New School for Social Research of 1930, still imposing with its façade of closely rhymed horizontal spandrels alternating with continuous strip windows. Its earliest decor consisted of a room of frescoes by José Clemente Orozco which, from their first unveiling, never ceased to arouse controversy.

One of the last distinguished buildings for public use to be privately constructed before the Second World War was the new edifice to house the Museum of Modern Art on the site of its former townhouse at 11 West 53rd Street. Designed by Philip L. Goodwin and Edward

Big red, *1953, by Sam Francis. Museum of Modern Art.*
Gift of Mr and Mrs David Rockefeller.

Durrell Stone, and erected in 1939, the building was faithful to the
principles of horizontality stressed a few years before in the great international exhibition. Its external façade, still eloquent with its large
expanse of glass, its discreet strips of offices above, and its open roof con-
crete-slab design offering circular openings to the sky.
The entire building reflected the vision of the museum's organizers
ten years before. Provisions were made for a wide range of activities,
from the daily exhibition of important films in the 500-seat theatre
in the basement (where the auditorium with comfortable plush chairs,
non-parallel walls and excellent acoustics, is still one of the most

satisfying in New York) to the installation of temporary exhibitions, and consideration for other needs of visitors such as eating and strolling in the open air sculpture garden.

One of the most important contributions to museum architecture was the extreme flexibility of the building. Areas were designed as free spaces which could be divided with temporary partitions, according to the exhibition. To this day, this original section of the museum is a highly workable plant on the second and third floors where important selections from the permanent collection are shown. Since the building was first erected, the museum has undergone several expansions and modifications. In 1952, Philip Johnson redesigned the garden, making a formal sculpture court and a grand stairway leading to an upper terrace which provides an unexpectedly exciting view of both the museum's court and the surrounding high-rise buildings of the rapidly expanding neighbourhood. Johnson also completed additional gallery spaces in 1964 following the same loft principle of the original building, but using dark smoked glass and steel grids in relief for the façade.

By the outbreak of the Second World War, the Museum of Modern Art had proved to be a cultural centre of unprecedented vitality. There was then no modern museum in the world that could match its records of a decade of some 125 special exhibitions in the fields of painting, sculpture, architecture, industrial design and film history, and more than a million and a half visitors. Its extraordinary collection of paintings and sculptures was already probably the most comprehensive of its kind in the world, and included a number of works of historical importance, among them Picasso's *Demoiselles d'Avignon*, acquired in 1939.

The Depression had obviously curtailed urban building, but it did serve to awaken citizens to possibilities of federal and state responsibilities. There was a flourishing programme of highway and bridge building during the 1930s, and New York saw the completion of two exceptionally beautiful bridges during the '30s, both supervised by the rather remarkable engineer, O.H. Ammann. The George Washington Bridge, completed in 1931, was considered by Le Corbusier to be the most beautiful in the world. 'Made of cables and steel beams, it gleams in the sky like a reverse arch. It is blessed... When your car moves along, the two towers rise so high that it brings you happiness; their structure is so pure, so resolute, so regular that here, finally, steel architecture seems to laugh. The car reaches an unexpectedly wide apron; the second tower is very far away; innumerable vertical cables gleaming against the sky, are suspended from the magisterial curve which swings down and then up...' Le Corbusier's delight in the 600-foot high towers was possible largely because when these were constructed in their steel framework, some wise city official decided to restrain the architects from adding the envisioned carved masonry.

The second elegant bridge to gain worldwide admiration was the Bronx-Whitestone Bridge completed in 1939. Even more simple in its tower design, the gossamer lightness of its long lines was widely praised when it opened. Unfortunately, after the collapse of a suspension bridge based on the Bronx-Whitestone, its refined lines suffered revision when safety considerations forced the authorities to add trusses and storm stays.

Access to these and other bridges was developed in the new parkway systems of the 1930s. Clover-leaf and pretzel patterns of cross-highway circulation were worked out in adjoining Queens and Brooklyn, and in the elaborate development of the Henry Hudson Parkway, following the Hudson River down from the George Washington Bridge to the top of Manhattan. New York was considered a leading influence in the development of parkways, and sophisticated traffic patterning on its incoming and outgoing motor arteries but, as Giedion pointed out, it could not solve the problems of the interior city.

For all that, the model for establishing relationships between riverside arteries and inner neighbourhoods remains Carl Schurz Park, astride the Franklin Delano Roosevelt Drive. The drive, designed by Harvey Stevenson and Cameron Clark, is certainly one of the most agreeable arteries in New York. It takes motorists on the lower tier along the very edge of the East River, from which they can glimpse colourful river traffic, the various islands in the river, and several bridges. Above, between 84th Street and 90th Street, Carl Schurz Park extends from East End Avenue to the very edge of the river, its plantings on the roof of the freeway, and easy access for residents of Sutton and Beekman Place, and neighbourhood visitors, who have merely to stroll to the end of their streets to find greenery and a water vista of great visual excitement and beauty.

Lower down on the F.D.R. Drive, the citizens are far less eager to make use of narrow strips of parkland because the freeway is a prohibitive barrier. Imaginative planning would bring the residential sections of the city close to the waterfront and reclaim the wasted beauty of any waterscape. Then the problems of the interior city would be mitigated by the uses of both the freeways and waterways.

The look of the inner city, its very life, was sharply altered by the Depression. Even with little new building, the character of the city changed. People began to notice the grimness of its gridiron regularity, the unspeakable conditions of New York's vast slums, greatly amplified by the high rate of unemployment. The cultural life of the city was naturally curtailed by the absence of money. It was a quiet time, yet there was much fermenting. Downtown, clustered around Union Square, or in the vicinity of West 8th Street, or in the West 20s, the Chelsea district, there were cheap small industrial lofts for rent which New York's painters and sculptors began to convert into studios. Lke many others, the artists were living in near starvation conditions until the Federal Arts Project got under way soon after Roosevelt's election. Arshile Gorky, who rented a loft four flights up at 36 Union Square, described the period as the bleakest, most spirit-crushing time in his life (his wife reports), and spoke with bitterness of the paralyzing poverty he endured. But even he had moments of exhilaration when fellow artists, in the same deprived situation, would visit his loft, or go downstairs to a Fourth Avenue coffee shop to discuss the exciting art issues of the day. To get to the shop they would pass Union Square, first laid out in the 1830s as public gardens for the more privileged residents, but later to become famous as the Hyde Park of New York. There, during the Depression, Gorky would see large groups of fervently gesticulating men, discussing the situation, and listening to radical orators proposing remedies. Once again, Union Square fulfills this function, and today the unemployed, the young and disaffected still cluster to hear speakers or have discussions.

The artists would most often gather in all-night cafeterias—Stewart's on 23rd Street and Seventh Avenue, on 14th Street, or on Sheridan Square. The meetings and discussions at Stewart's are often seen as being the genesis of an artistic community which came to be known as the

Union Square, before the Civil War a quiet residential park, later a centre for soap-box orators, still a gathering place for political debate.

New York School. The sculptor David Smith would speak nostalgically of a Greenwich Village restaurant, famous for its credit-granting proprietress, Romany Marie, where such future celebrities as Willem de Kooning, Arshile Gorky, and Frederick Kiesler talked long into the night.

In a famous memoir of the period, Edwin Denby, America's most distinguished dance critic and an early patron of Willem de Kooning, describes late nights at Stewart's and when the cafeteria closed in the early morning, going back to de Kooning's loft in the West 20s for more talk. He remembers also, walking at night with de Kooning in the Chelsea district, 'and his pointing out to me on the pavement the dispersed compositions—spots and cracks and bits of wrappers and reflections of neon light—neon signs were few then... At the time we all talked a great deal about scale in New York, and about the difference of instinctive scale in signs, painted color, clothes, gestures, everyday expressions between Europe and America.'

When a great many artists finally got on the rolls of the Works Progress Administration, meetings and discussions became even more frequent. This Federal project was set up in 1935 in a remarkably

147

flexible fashion, capable of harbouring easel painters, who often worked at home in their own lofts and reported weekly, and painters who
wanted to have the experience they admired in the Mexicans, of
painting murals for the public at large. The battle between modern
abstract art and social realism was constantly before them. Jackson
Pollock was one of the project's mural enthusiasts, having watched
Orozco complete a mural, and many others stood by and watched
(and some assisted) when Diego Rivera painted murals for the radical
New Workers' School. Some, including Pollock, were known to
have participated in the Union Square workshop, briefly led by
David Alfaro Siqueiros in 1936, which was devoted to the development
of experimental techniques in mural painting. In such workshops, artists
had unusual opportunities to develop large-scale ideas, especially when
preparing the huge floats that in those days accompanied the May Day
parades from Union Square.

Many artists' groups sprang up during the Depression in collective efforts
to protect their livelihoods, or to protect their aesthetic integrity.
American Abstract Artists, the only group with the avowed purpose
of preserving the great modern European tradition, was formed in
1936 to combat the increasing tendency of the public, officials
and even some artists to revive the old American illustration tradition,
the so-called 'American Scene Painting'. The founding group included
Ibram Lassaw, the sculptor, Balcomb Greene, Harry Holtzman (who
later induced Mondrian to show with the group), George L.K. Morris

The Museum of Modern Art sculpture garden.

and Ilya Bolotowsky. Later the annual exhibitions became important events and boasted works by many of the important European emigrés, and a number of Americans who would subsequently be considered major artists. These exhibitions continued into the 1950s and kept alive the small vanguard movement.

Some of the initial anger was directed against the institutions that were presumably on their side. Although the Museum of Modern Art was steadily acquiring European masterworks, even of the most advanced abstract or constructivist modes, and although in 1936 it had opened its epoch-making 'Cubism and Abstract Art' and in 1938 an important exhibition on the Bauhaus, members of the American Abstract Artists felt that the museum had neglected the most recent European developments, and certainly their own developments. Not even Alexander Calder, one of the first American abstract artists to gain international fame for his mobile sculptures, was singled out for a large exhibition until 1943. This was understandable since, as it became more involved with the social consequences of the Depression, the museum tried to present trends in mural art, social satire and indigenous realism which seemed to dominate the period. It had also shown the products of the WPA in an effort to encourage what most people regarded as a healthy government subvention of the arts. When the American Abstract Artists picketed the museum in 1940 and issued a broadsheet designed by Ad Reinhardt the era was literally at an end. It was the eve of America's entry into the Second World War.

Trends in the War Years

The two decades of education by the few institutions specializing in modern art, however, had made their impress and there were signs of a coming upsurge in creative work. One of those institutions was not quite an institution, but a whimsical person called the Baroness Hilla Rebay who was helping her patron, John Simon Guggenheim, form a collection of modern art. The Baroness from time to time held small public showings of her growing collection which already by 1936 included a great many capital works by Kandinsky, and works by Gris, Picasso, Seurat, Chagall, Gleizes and others. In 1939, the Baroness took a town house not far from the Museum of Modern Art, on East 54th Street, in which she housed about half of the 726 works in the collection at that time. Her opening exhibition was ridiculed by the press, not only because of its emphasis on what she insisted on calling non-objective art, but also because of its bizarre installation in thickly carpeted and draped rooms where spiritual music was continuously piped in. Nevertheless, the exhibitions of the Guggenheim Collection, in which the works of Kandinsky, Klee and many others rarely seen in New York could be studied, were to prove very important in the lives of young artists during the next few years.

Those years—the war years—saw a tremendous upswing in the economy. Employment was naturally increased by the necessities of war manufacture. The effect on New York City's cultural life was marked. Museums engaged energetically in wartime projects, such as posters for the Office of War Information, travelling exhibitions, and art centres for veterans. The Museum of Modern Art undertook contracts with the government for war films, and the Metropolitan kept a sharp lookout for works of art depicting the war. The presence of numerous public information agencies in New York brought many intellectuals and artists from other cities. The atmosphere was calculated to stimulate activity in the arts and New York for the first time saw its ballets, operas and theatres fully attended.

Artists saw a rising interest in their work. Peggy Guggenheim had established her Art of This Century Gallery, with its eccentric and revolutionary interior by the architect Frederick Kiesler. There such artists as Jackson Pollock, Robert Motherwell and William Baziotes had their first chance to exhibit, and there they would meet the distinguished European artists such as André Breton, André Masson, Max Ernst and others who had sought refuge in New York.

Thus during the 1940s American artists, who had long suffered the indifference of their society, began to sense a shift in attitude. Release from the social and political climate of the 1930s, coupled with a profound feeling of depression engendered by the war, left them with a paradoxical sense of freedom. One by one, the painters who would later be called Abstract Expressionists, or more narrowly, the New York School, began to realize their own imaginative liberty.

Rapid changes occurred in the work of those artists who had already established themselves among their peers as the legitimate avant-garde. Arshile Gorky, who had served a long apprenticeship to European models, among them Picasso and Miró, started to fuse a delicate linear abstract mode with what André Breton was later to call 'biomorphic'

▷

Building, formerly a guest house for the Museum of Modern Art, designed by Philip Johnson.

imagery. His paint began to appear in thin washes, often with rills of freely flowing, quasi-accidental effects, and his colour became heightened, recalling the expressionist phase of Kandinsky. Between 1945 and his death in 1948, Gorky exhibited each year at the Julien Levy Gallery, gaining increasing attention in the press.

His friend Willem de Kooning was meanwhile developing a group of black and white enamel abstractions, in which the organic interweave of curvilinear forms stressed the ambiguity of his spaces. These bold departures from his earlier semi-figurative style were celebrated among his colleagues several years before his first one-man exhibition at the Egan Gallery in 1948. Not only his peers, but also museum curators and serious art critics were ready to concede de Kooning's extraordinary power, and rank him as a central figure in a new movement.

Pollock, who had had an exceptionally successful first one-man show at Peggy Guggenheim's gallery in 1947, and whose expressionist symbolism was already marked by the passion that would, in 1947, lead him to experiment with unprecedented means, was the first of the bohemian vanguard artists to enter the public domain as a celebrity. Once he began his great adventure with the so-called 'drip' paintings —those finely webbed, linear skeins of expansive spaces—he became a controversial painter of wide acclaim. Through the vigorous support of such critics as James Johnson Sweeney and Clement Greenberg, Pollock reached into the consciousness of Americans who had never before been deeply concerned with paintings—the educated middle classes, long interested in music and literature, had scarcely noticed the visual arts in their own milieu.

The endeavour to establish a new vision of abstract painting was not limited to those in the New York School. In 1944, Mark Tobey, then a Seattle resident, exhibited his own linear abstractions, which, though small in scale and intimate in vision, represented a similar rebellion against traditional modern sources. Clyfford Still, who had quietly worked out a new way of dealing with lateral space in San Francisco, came East to show New York his densely painted, crackling abstractions in 1944. His interest in the symbols found in Mexican and American Indian works had paralleled the interest of several painters of the New York group who had begun to work with primitive imagery in the early 1940s.

These artists found a valid spokesman in the person of Barnett Newman. Newman, in those days more of an intellectual companion than a fellow painter, stimulated discussions on the deepest sources of creativity, and urged his friends to consider the pure psychic expressions in primitive art. Adolph Gottlieb often discussed painting with Newman in the early 1940s when he was developing his vocabulary of esoteric symbols enclosed in a compartmented, grid-like container. Mark Rothko, who in the mid-1940s was painting softened visions of marinelike, dream landscapes (as was William Baziotes at that time), entered these conversations, declaring the prime importance of immemorial sources, above all the ancient myths. By 1947, he had also eliminated suggestions of readable imagery and had begun his great ascent to the pure, illuminated surfaces that were to become so important to the 1950s.

Younger, but with precocious talent, Robert Motherwell also spurred the artists towards an articulation of a new aesthetic. Motherwell

The George Washington Bridge, much admired by architects as well as engineers. ▷

Single form, *1962-63,*
by Barbara Hepworth in front of the United Nations Secretariat.

had come from the West Coast to study in New York and had met the European surrealists during the early war years. His association with the dynamic young Chilean, Matta Echaurren, led him to explore Mexico in 1941, and to return to New York brimming with fresh ideas. His activities as a writer, organizer of discussions, and editor helped to amplify the ideas of the painters who, by 1950, were already referred to as Abstract Expressionists, or the New York School.

Once the 'ice was broken', as de Kooning put it, many artists began to appear in exhibitions and museum travelling shows with distinctive new work. Bradley Walker Tomlin, once a lyrical cubist, came forward with calligraphic abstractions in the late 1940s; Hans Hofmann, long a revered teacher, exhibited his exuberant paintings for the first time in New York; and Franz Kline gained immediate renown in his first exhibition in 1950, with his intense black and white canvases. Philip Guston, another figurative painter, also moved into prominence with his first abstract expressionist paintings—delicate, wandering compositions in pinks and oranges that veered away from the strongly tectonic composition he had formerly favoured.

As the 1950s got under way, these painters, and others such as Jack Tworkov, James Brooks, Esteban Vicente and Theodoros Stamos, coalesced in the public consciousness as the first American vanguard 'school' to achieve international renown. The years of isolation forced upon Americans by the Second World War had served to change their lives. The intellectual and artistic life of the city grew more vivid as the war grew more threatening. Artists were able to form a loosely organized entity within the natural cultural life, and so realize their great longing for acknowledgment from their society, New York was finally becoming cosmopolitan in the full sense.

The physical character of the city had changed little during the war years, except that the need for housing grew ever more urgent. With returning veterans and a new influx of the war young seeking their fortunes in the big city, there was considerable pressure on the political forces to undertake large housing schemes. The great confusion on the federal level, resulting from the controls established in the 1930s and their transformation into wartime controls, was the subject for most editorials between 1945 and 1950 in the architectural and building journals. There was a clear will, at least on the part of those with the power to realize their wishes, to escape from the limitations of federal control. Means were sought to take advantage of new veterans' legislation. The results were too often traditional: a good yield for the proprietors in terms of dense housing and many rents; a grim compromise for tenants, occupying such slabs as the Stuyvesant development between 14th and 20th Streets along the East River, completed in 1947.

Post-War Architecture

All the lessons implicit in Le Corbusier's dream of the radiant city, with its vertically efficient and beautiful skyscrapers and its broadly landscaped ground spaces, seemed to have been lost on the builders of New York. They had, ever since the 1930s in fact, learned that the slab, per se, is an effective way to introduce light and ventilation, but they had learned very little more. Although the Regional Plan of New York committee had already, in 1931, strongly recommended that all high-rise buildings be planned with ample ground spaces, and that the city be enhanced with plazas, and had warned about the tremendous dangers of unrestricted density, no one seemed inclined to pay much heed. The housing projects that were begun in the immediate post-war years were almost consistently lamentable and lacking in space.

On the other hand, commercial building construction, little by little, had begun to show signs of reading Le Corbusier's lessons well. In 1952, Hitchcock and Johnson could write that by the late 1940s, the slab concept for office buildings had been widely accepted, and was indeed 'almost platitudinous', while Lewis Mumford, always scornful of the superficial adaptation of the glass curtain wall was calling the International Style skyscraper a cliché.

The most important test case of 'The Style' in the immediate post-war years was embodied in the creation of the United Nations, and the attendant publicity brought the discussion of architectural aesthetics for the first time into the popular press.

The great controversy over the plans must certainly have encouraged the younger architects then preparing careers in New York City. For once the modern principles to which they were committed were proposed unhesitatingly by a distinguished panel of world architects as the only possible foundation for the new palace of world peace. The unhappy lessons of the aftermath of the First World War, when Le Corbusier's plans for the League of Nations structure were ignominiously scrapped, were not to be repeated.

From the beginning, many knowledgeable critics considered that the site (donated by John D. Rockefeller, Jr.) of about eighteen acres of land bounded by the East River Drive and spreading from 42nd

*Lever House tower
and (right) a detail.*

The Manufacturer's Hanover Trust Operations Center, 1969.

Street and First Avenue to 48th Street, was unsuitable for an organization representing the entire world, which was bound to expand greatly. The problems of planning for such a site, and planning by team, were certainly unprecedented. At the head of the team was Wallace Kirkman Harrison, whose experience at Rockefeller Center, would, it was presumed, stand him in good stead. His own view of the project made clear the intention in 1947: 'Building is a matter of stone on stone and steel on steel, air conditioning and elevators that run. The layman thinks that all we have to do is come in with a beautiful sketch, and out of that everything is going to function. Just the opposite is true. These UN buildings can only grow out of requirements, now and of five or ten years hence. They must have stateliness and dignity. But the question is, are we building some phony Greek temple for a Greek god, or are we building to accommodate human beings in a complex civilization?' Although such colleagues on the team as Brazil's Oscar Niemeyer hoped for a more exalted original conception, to stress the tremendous political importance of the organization, the final scheme presented for ratification was dominated by the austere and absolutely functional Secretariat building. It was, to a large degree, pretty much as Le Corbusier had said it should be: a meeting centre with office buildings efficient to the last detail.

The Secretariat building, which influenced commercial building for years after its completion, was greatly admired by those who saw in its mirror-like sheath a poetic metaphor for the synthesis of nature and metropolis, reflected in constantly moving patterns on the west façade. Those who approach the city from Kennedy airport are often moved by the slim tower lifting up from the East River and catching the river's flickering light. Or, at night, as one approaches the vast array of Manhattan's lights, the isolated elegance of the UN building cannot fail to please.

Less pleasing, at least to many architectural experts, is the scale and interior of the Secretariat. Mumford complained that the tall prismatic slab reduced the other two buildings to insignificance, and Ada Louise Huxtable in *Four Walking Tours of Modern Architecture* criticizes the 39-storey Secretariat for the poor handling of corners, columns and detailing of the marble ends. She also objects to the confusing nature of the lobby, with its multiplicity of inadequately related details. Like Mumford, she sees the glass walls on the east and west sides of the building as highly impractical in terms of airconditioning and heat control, but points out that had the building been turned, the rest of the site would have been in shadow for most of the day.

The General Assembly building to the north with its horizontal curving lines was conceived as a fitting free form that could play against the severity of the slab. There was apparently a fair amount of contention in the planning, and economic setbacks that made of it considerably less than its original Le Corbusier conception. Housing a 65 by 115 foot auditorium, decorated by Fernand Léger, the building on a busy day has the considerable merit of seeming very much alive, although somewhat chaotic in its design. The great north lobby is cluttered with a great many distracting details, but it is still impressive with its 75-foot high ceiling.

The third construction of the ensemble, the Conference building, is visible only from the East River side, and is a four-storey oblong housing the chambers for the Security, Trusteeship, and Economic and Social councils; restaurants, lounges and meeting halls. Much of the interior was designed by Sweden's Sven Markelius with considerable taste, but not enough to offset the impression of soulless group planning and generally unsatisfactory space allocation.

The sculpture and painting at the UN, mostly donated by member countries, is scattered rather cavalierly throughout the ensemble. The exception is Barbara Hepworth's *Single Form,* a bronze sculpture standing some 21 feet high. Flanked as it is by the reflecting surface of the tower and two lower but weighty structures, the circular pool within which the bronze is placed demanding the kind of simple profiled form Miss Hepworth created for the site. Not only does the lightly scored bronze surface catch the shifting light of the sun as it rakes the plaza, but through its single 'eye' at its crest, relays a vibrating series of illuminations bounced off the glass. At night, properly lit, the sculpture is not only attractive in itself, but also serves as a module, enhancing the architecture around it and revealing grace in the buildings.

The example of the Secretariat, for all its inadequacies, suggested the modern possibilities of prestige in architecture to many corporations during the years to come. The first, and still one of the most satisfying, luxurious glass-sheathed building to sacrifice density for elegance was the Lever House by Skidmore, Owings & Merrill, with Gordon Bunshaft as chief designer. Begun in 1950, the building opened for business two years later, and quickly became almost as popular for visiting tourists as the UN complex. In persuading the client to forego the most profitable system of getting revenue from a building, the architects were able to institute several ideas of design that were to influence many later clients. The chief merit of the elegant blue-green glass tower is that it stands free in a generous space, achieved ingeniously by the designers who used only a quarter of the legally permitted airspace. Since the main structure is set back 100 feet from the south building line and 40 feet from the north, the tower is, to this day, one of the best illuminated buildings in New York. Only 60 feet wide, it has light on three sides and, as Mumford noted in *The New Yorker* in 1952, even the least-favoured workers on the premises may enjoy a psychological lift by raising their eyes to the skyscraper.

For Mumford, whose formative years were during those of the great idealogical battle, the consideration of the least-favoured worker was of utmost importance. His years of sharp critical writing summarized the faults and gross injustices in the organization of American society, and warned consistently against specific hazards such as urban overcrowding and the totally uncontrolled proliferation of motorized traffic without concomitant planning. The voice of Mumford and a few others persisted throughout the '30s, '40s and '50s but, for the most part, they were blithely ignored by the great corporate interests which were engaged in building not only their own commercial plants, but even some of the essential housing in the large cities.

There was, during the 1950s, a general acceptance of the modern style, which made for some very elegant individual buildings, both private and commercial; a brisk rise in prosperity and a comparable rise in luxury consumption which called for modern shops; some considerable patronage which financed the building of the new Guggenheim Museum; some lavish spending to produce prestige architecture, as in the case of the Seagram Building; a demand for new and well-appointed, modern banks, and a steadily increasing interest in placing works of art in the context of the new architecture.

Midtown Manhattan saw the rehabilitation of several private townhouses in the International Style, two of which were designed by Philip Johnson. The first was designed in 1950 during what Henry-Russell Hitchcock called his 'Miesian' period as a guest house for the Museum of Modern Art at 242 East 52nd Street. Johnson took the original stable and gutted it. He made a severe façade of brick, steel and glass behind which he designed an interior divided by a reflecting pool and graced by glass walls.

Nine years later, Johnson completed the transformation of two brownstone houses into a museum, Asia House, using slightly modified principles, but still very much in the classic International Style idiom. This museum, one of the most appealing and serene in the city, has a rather conventional glass façade in tinted grey with its steel rectilinear members painted white, while the interior is sober and restrained, perfectly adapted to the temporary exhibitions of Oriental art staged by the resident Asia Society.

One of the most impressive such projects then—and still today—is

▷

Seagram Building (1958) by Mies van der Rohe and Philip Johnson

P. 162/163
Secretariat building of the United Nations complex (1947-53).

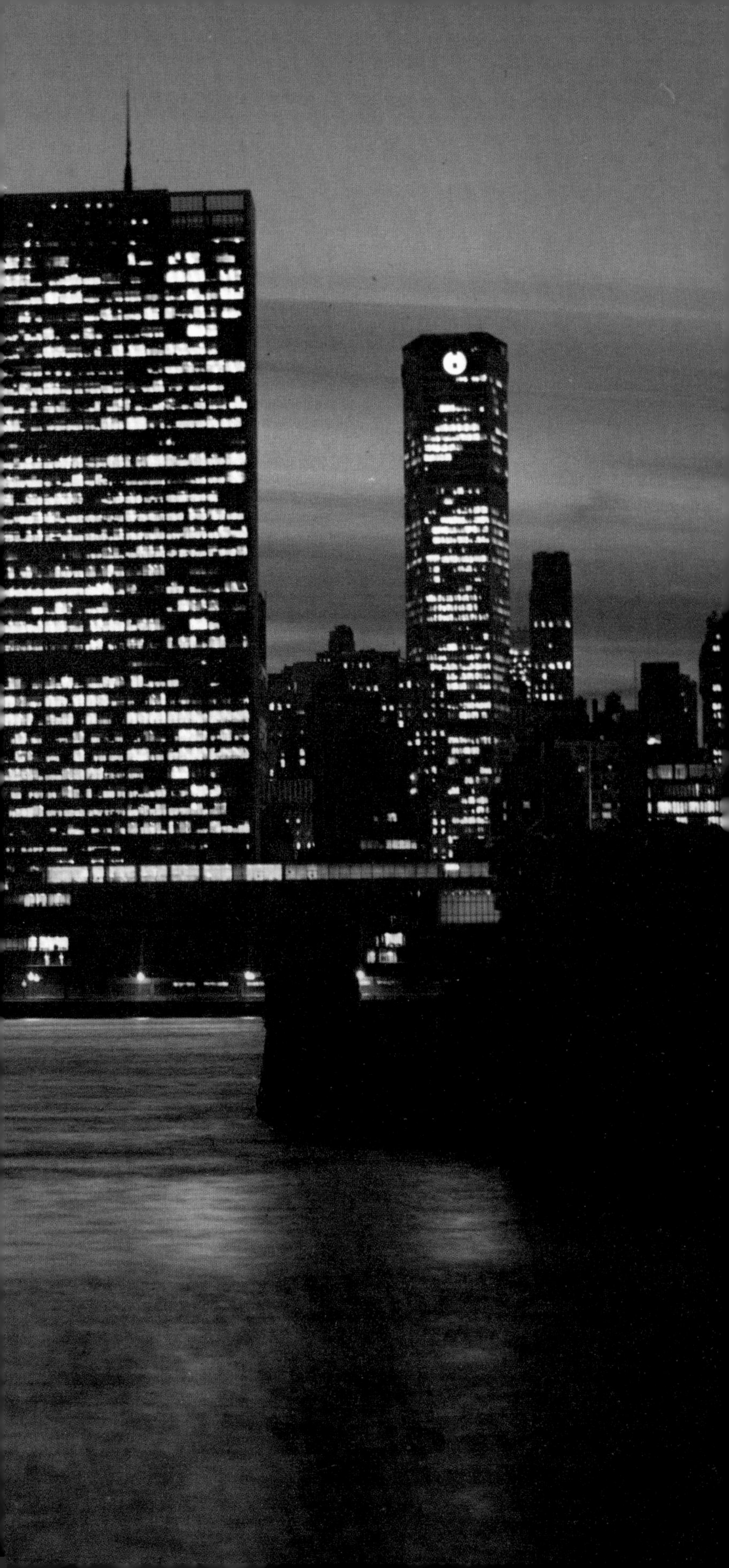

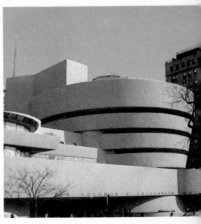

The Guggenheim Museum (1959),
Frank Lloyd Wright's brilliant
building, notable for its
spiral structure (above)
and (left) the skylight.

Improvisation 28, *1912, by Wassily Kandinsky*
Solomon R. Guggenheim Museum.

Manhattan House on 66th Street and Third Avenue, completed in
1951 by Skidmore, Owings & Merrill, and Meyer & Whittlesey. This
was constructed by the New York Life Insurance Company as an
'upper-middle income' dwelling which, in New York, is to say a
luxury dwelling. Restricted to a six percent return on its investment,
the insurance company authorized the architects to be generous with
open space. The result is an attractive block-long building, set well
back from the street, with pleasant landscaping and a rather festive
air. The AIA Guide has described it as the closest to the blocks of

Le Corbusier which New York has aesthetically to offer. The subtle
decision to choose pale grey glazed brick and white-painted steel windows by itself raised this block substantially above its coarse new
neighbours' 'white glazed brick and pasty aluminium sash'. The
writer obviously takes objection to the widespread use of a material
that was in great demand during the 1950s—aluminium. Some of
New York's worst visual catastrophes are faced with pre-fabricated
aluminium, a material that is particularly practical and particularly
ugly in the urban context. Others only look flimsy and cheap, as do

Painting No. 5, 1914-15, by Marsden Hartley.
Whitney Museum of American Art.

the Third Avenue neighbours of Manhattan House to which the
writer objects.

Third Avenue was the site of much tearing down and rebuilding
during the 1950s, once the elevated railway, the famous Third Avenue
'El', had been removed. The rush to fill it up with luxury housing
and office buildings has resulted in considerable diversity of style and
character of architecture, and a lamentable lack of general planning.
One of the more adventurous undertakings on Third Avenue was
an office block at 711 Third Avenue, designed by William Lescaze in
1956 with the initial understanding that it would incorporate works
by living artists. The building, rather clumsy with its massive ground
structure of white and beige brick surmounted by a blue tower, has
a stainless steel vestibule wall which is carried outside and wrapped
around the first column. For this wall, Lescaze commissioned an
abstract stainless steel sculpture by Jose de Rivera. For the interior
elevator bank, he commissioned Hans Hofmann to design a mosaic
mural some 60-70 feet high. By seeking collaboration in the early
planning stages, Lescaze blazed the trail for other architects who
began more actively to collaborate with artists in the designing of
commercial buildings.

Such ideas were less difficult to promote in the field of ecclesiastical architecture, revived in the postwar period with tremendous advances. In New York City, the young firm of Kelly & Gruzen asked the painter Adolph Gottlieb to co-operate with ther on the chapter house for the Park Avenue Synagogue in 1955. The resulting design with its sheer stained-glass wall, discreet structural planning (reducing structure lines to minimal thickness and eliminating spandrels), and its air of spirituality helped considerably to alleviate the heavy air of the surrounding architecture. The building is illuminated by night and floats resplendently.

Aside from the building of churches and synagogues, as well as offices, banks were being erected all over the city, some of which were destined to incorporate works by living artists. The major achievement of the 1950s was undoubtedly the Manufacturers Trust at Fifth Avenue and 43rd Street, by Skidmore, Owings & Merrill. With Gordon Bunshaft in charge of design, it was a radical conception with its thoroughly exposed mechanism. The glass curtain wall envelops five floors of banking activity, all totally visible from the street. The impression of complete transparency is accentuated by means of the cantilevered mezzanine floor which stops eight feet away from the wall. Perhaps its most beautiful sculptural particular is the elegant steel vault placed on the main floor and visible even from a fast-passing taxi. The architects did, however, use more specific sculptural detail when they commissioned a 70-foot high metal screen wall by Harry Bertoia for the mezzanine floor.

The two outstanding architectural events in the 1950s, both in terms of aesthetics and architectural history, were the commissions given to the great masters, Frank Lloyd Wright and Mies van der Rohe, to construct buildings in New York. Both of these tremendously influential pioneers had been consulted by building colleagues in New York, but neither had ever completed a major work in New York. In the case of Mies, his style had become canonized by hundreds of adapters long before the master himself ever had a chance to demonstrate its merits. Wright had had a chance only in 1955 to design a Mercedes Benz showroom at Park Avenue and 56th Street, but even its spiral ramp could not successfully demonstrate Wright's genius.

The Seagram Building was marked from its earliest conception by the intelligence and largesse of its patrons. The avowed intention was to allow Mies to contribute an architectural masterpiece to New York's rapidly changing Park Avenue. No expense was to be spared to get the finest design and the finest materials. Both Mies and his associate, Philip Johnson, were given the rare opportunity of indulging their love for expensive materials, such as the bronze used for the mullions and spandrels, and the greenish marble facing its spine.

When the building was completed in 1958 it was almost immediately acknowledged as the key work, the culmination perhaps, of the International Style in New York. It fulfilled all the aesthetic canons defined nearly thirty years before during the Museum of Modern Art's didactic campaign: it emphasized volume and not mass; it stressed structural regularity, and eschewed ornament in favour of elegant materials and technical perfection.

Writing at the time the Seagram Building opened to the public, Arthur Drexler the critic and curator pointed out that it was the only skyscraper to be organized in terms of bi-lateral symmetry, still keeping distinctly different front, back and sides. Mies's courage in putting his tower well back from the street, in complete and aristocratic isolation and old-fashioned frontality, was greatly admired by the many critics who had tired of International Style clichés. As Drexler remarks, Mies's building, like the Racquet and Tennis Club opposite, is 'classically and hierarchically composed'.

The 38-storey tower is all the more awesome when approached frontally, across the broad pink granite plaza, with its two severe rectangular pools, its reserved and simple fountains. From the level of the plaza, which is often called a podium by critics who admire Mies's idea of a three-step lift from the ordinary sidewalk, the straight bronze mullions which appear to begin with the very columns of the lobby, seem to fly upward at vertiginous speed to the crest of the tower. The beauty of Mies's building, as Drexler suggests, is that the whole is more than the sum of its parts.

The plaza is too austere to attract idlers, but the marble hedge at either side is usually peopled with office personnel at lunch hour. On a hot summer's day, the small spray of the fountains and the slight shade of the rather spiky willow trees seems a blessing to many. Unfortunately, no permanent sculpture has ever passed muster on the plaza. The most successful experiment was a temporary exhibition of a gigantic Olmec head on the plaza, its great stone volume performing in a perfectly complementary way to the weightless volumes of the tower and the dry expansiveness of the granite court. In one of the wings on 53rd Street, Philip Johnson has designed the two-roomed Four Seasons Restaurant which houses a pair of brass constructions hanging from the ceiling by sculptor Richard Lippold, and the famous backdrop for 'Le Tricorne' ballet painted by Picasso in 1929. An earlier commission to Mark Rothko for murals for an executive dining room ran into difficulties, and those murals are now part of the Rothko bequest to the Tate Gallery in London.

A brief sortie into the lofty entrance of the Seagram Building is enough to suggest how much more august this building is than the many Park Avenue siblings which derive more or less from the teachings of Mies and the giants of his generation. There are two Skidmore, Owings & Merrill buildings of the late 1950s—the Union Carbide on 47th and 48th, and the Pepsi-Cola on 59th—which are distinctive contributions to Park Avenue's glistening mirror façade, but which are far more elaborate than Mies's uncompromisingly classic tower. The Union Carbide Building is distinguished by its unusual main floor, a flight above ground, which hovers enticingly above the pedestrian's eye level. The Pepsi-Cola building has been called a palazzetto by Ada Louis Huxtable because of its relatively smaller size and scale. But it is a palazzetto much admired by those who seek the floating, dematerialized qualities of the glass curtain wall. Its plate glass panels are 9 feet high and 13 feet wide, and held by only the lightest aluminium spandrels and slightly protruding mullions, imposing an impression of lightness. This simple glass box all but floats away in its fragility and weightlessness.

No progeny can be counted from the other major monument, the Guggenheim Museum by Frank Lloyd Wright, although its presence must certainly have stimulated younger architects to seek less orthodox modes of modernity. From its inception, in the early 1940s, the museum was a source of contention. Wright's extravagant vision of

▷

King of Kings (undated) by Constantin Brancusi. Wood, 118 3/8" high. Solomon R. Guggenheim Museum.

Reclining figure, *1963, by Henry Moore,*
set serenely in the terrace pool of Lincoln Center.

a single, continuing space as the proper form for a museum found opposition all along the way, particularly among those of New York City's appointed building overseers who could control the licensing of the plans and site. The continuous quarrelling, which lasted some sixteen years, did not stop, even when the opened museum proved to be a great attraction for New York's visitors. Jokes were rife, and museum personnel dolefully referred to the architect as 'more wrong than Wright'. The functional aspects of the museum were less than satisfactory, as nearly all art experts agreed, but no one could claim that the building itself was not a work of art; a unique and ingenious structure defying habitual notions of architecture.

Many of the principles illustrated in Wright's museum had remained unchanged throughout the octogenarian's lifetime. In his 1908 essay, 'In the Cause of Architecture', he recalled that as early as 1894 he had established that 'a building should appear to grow easily from its site, shaped to harmonize with its surroundings if Nature is manifest there, and if not try to make it as quiet, substantial and organic as She would have been were the opportunity hers.' In the same essay, he hinted at an innate antipathy for paintings: 'Pictures deface walls more often than they decorate them.'

When he designed the museum for an unfortunately cramped site on

Lincoln Center
(Above) Guichet, *stabile*
by Alexander Calder

◁
The Metropolitan
Opera House.

Fifth Avenue between 88th and 89th Streets, Wright quite understood that Nature was not manifest there, despite the leafy facing
spaces of Central Park. He attempted in his spiralling concrete structure to suggest that the museum grew from the site, and that it was
substantial and organic. Many visitors, standing at the entry and
peering upward do, in fact, experience a sense of awe, and some
apprehension of the meaning of this enormous single space, extending
like a chambered nautilus to its full 90 feet and beyond.

Once inside, the spectator can look upwards to the glass dome—the
only source of light envisioned by Wright—which does appear to
merge with the limitless spaces of nature. It is true that he might
find the contemplation of paintings difficult as he leans against
gravity on the steep ramps; he might sense the great well of space
behind him, even though a waist-high parapet protects him; he might
be disturbed by the vista across that gulf, of half-blocked paintings;
and he might sense some rebellion as the relentless curve forces him
always upward or downward. (Wright's original idea—that the paintings lean against the outcurving walls—was found completely unten-
able by the museum's first director, James Johnson Sweeney, who
helped to invent a new mode of exhibiting after Wright's death by
placing paintings on bars projected from the walls, and by installing

lights in the clerestories.) But, despite the obvious difficulties such a monument presents in terms of its designated function as an exhibition space, the building itself is a powerful source of architectural pleasure.

The insistent sense of meaning in the building itself can certainly diminish the individual meanings in the Guggenheim's extraordinary collection of modern masters. With its basic collection of works by Kandinsky, certainly the most important in the world, significant paintings by Chagall, Léger, Seurat, Cézanne, Picasso, Klee and scores of others, and with its fine collection of sculpture, the Guggenheim will shortly have to expand its exhibition facilities. Wright's plan was not adequate to the ever-increasing holdings. Sweeney's contribution during the years he was director was to build an exceptional sculpture collection, numbering no less than nine major works by Constantin Brancusi and many other capital pieces, and to fill in important gaps in the historical painting collection. Later, the accession of the Justin K. Thannhauser collection of some seventy-five works necessitated awkward changes and an unseemly addition to the clean lines of the ramp, denying yet again the functional appropriateness of Wright's vision of a museum.

The 1950s saw the first museum in New York devoted frankly to other than Western European cultures; this was the Museum of Primitive Art, housed in two of Nelson Rockefeller's town houses on East 54th Street. The museum under the directorship of Dr Robert Goldwater, whose specific interests are both modern and primitive art, is an excellent small-scale institution, exhibiting exceptional works from Africa, Oceania and the Americas.

New Regard for Urbanism

As one of the few twentieth-century prophets, Wright had long since won his battle. Those who, like the Museum of Modern Art, had seen him as a genius, but somehow beyond the pale in the early 1930s, began to look back and see that he was in many ways a spiritual companion to the more easily accepted Mies and Le Corbusier. Wright, too, they now understood, had had his urban visions. Had he not imagined a city, 'iridescent by day, luminous by night, imperishable! Buildings, shimmering fabrics, woven of rich glass; glass all clear or part opaque and part clear, patterned in colour or stamped to harmonize with the metal tracery that is to hold all together, the metal tracery to be, in itself, a thing of delicate beauty consistent with slender steel construction, expressing the nature of that construction in the mathematics of structure...'? (*Architectural Record,* April, 1928). In addition he had designed an apartment building for New York's lower East Side which in its landscaped site, and its glass exposures, would have come close to Le Corbusier's ideal, while yet remaining consistent with all the principles enunciated for decades by Wright himself.

Moreover, during the late 1950s Wright, with his reflexive love for the land and his implicit hatred for cities, nevertheless located some of the causes for urban despair and predicted what many young urbanists would maintain in the 1960s—that perpendicularity could

▷

The bandshell in the Lincoln Center for the Performing Arts.

no longer be regarded as a civilized and preserving factor in the
growth of cities. In *The Living City* published in 1958, Wright
noted that, 'In the present era's future (if it has one) the skyscraper
will be considered *ne plus ultra* of the *e pluribus unum* capitalistic
centralization. The New York skyscraper will be seen as the pranc-
ing of this great iron horse—the industrial revolution. The iron horse
rearing high hoofs in air for the plunge before the runaway—the runaway to oblivion by way of the atom bomb—or we go to the country!'
Although not all the urbanists who became vociferous in the 1960s
were as pessimistic about the survival of New York, many of them
recognized that what Wright called skyscraperism was a social disease that must be fought to extinction. It led to vigorous proposals
to 'rehabilitate' neighbourhoods, where four- to six-storey houses still
saw the light of day, and where, with proper planning, children and
adults could live according to the democratic standards of decency that
Wright proposed. There were well-organized campaigns against the
practices of city bureaucrats. City zoning laws and building codes
came in for new scrutiny, and while not many of the campaigns against

Indian feathers, *mobile*
by Alexander Calder
in the sculpture court of the
Whitney Museum
of American Art.

P. 180/181
Pocket playground at 29th Street
and Second Avenue, embellished
by a member of City Walls,
a cooperative group of artists
working to improve temporary
sites in the city.

high-rise monstrosities were successful, there was a definite public awareness of their dangers to the physical and psychological existence of the city.

As a new state of mind seemed apparent at the onset of the 1960s, and as various social forces had been mobilized to fight back, there were signs of rapid change in the city. Pressures were mounting to face the urban crisis, and young architects, urbanists, sociologists and artists jointly were increasingly concerned with their civic responsibilities. Although luxury housing and commercial office-building went on undeterred, many other projects were conceived, and some realized, which would make the quality of life in New York more tolerable. Even the architects most accustomed to building those huge repositories of office space began to talk about the social responsibility of the architect. It was during the 1960s that the university architecture departments reorganized in order to stress planning and urban rehabilitation.

In 1966, John V. Lindsay was elected mayor on the strength of his promises to make the city government serve the needs of the people. The

Summer Rental No. 2; *1960, Robert Rauschenberg.*
Whitney Museum of American Art.

shift in emphases can be noticed in his report for the following year. In contrast to those of the previous administration, Mayor Lindsay's report opens with a summary of the services his administration initiated, including neighbourhood government centres, pre-school childhood centres, vest-pocket parks, manpower training offices and the

model cities programme for which the City 'has been channelling virtually all available Federal housing funds into three core ghetto areas.' He announced that at long last the concern with the City's environment had led the City Planning Commission to add an urban design force of architects and planners. He also discussed at length

Philip Johnson's new wing of the Museum of Modern Art, an upward view.

the unprecedented activities of the Department of Parks, Recreation and Cultural Affairs which, under his administration, had taken on a significance it had never enjoyed before. Among such activities were free opera performances in the five boroughs; outdoor shows by theatre troupes and modern dance groups was the first organized attempt to bring living art to the people. In 1967 the Office of Cultural Affairs sponsored the largest, outdoor exhibition of avant-garde sculpture ever held in an American city. Called 'Sculpture in Environment', it led to subsequent programmes aimed at placing contemporary art in public sites all over the city.

This report reflects the growing pressures from the voters and responsible civic leaders to attend to the near-disaster proportions of urban problems. In addition to housing and employment crises, and problems of physical survival posed by pollution, the 1960s saw crises in many of its major cultural institutions as well. Universities were urged by citizens to open their doors to previously ignored minorities, and museums were urged to establish community annexes and projects outside the mere repository function they had for so long been fulfilling. The city was pressured by artists' organizations to preserve the loft districts that had so long served New York as the working headquarters of America's best known artists. Even Lincoln Center, which had been the source of extensive controversy from its early planning stages in the mid-1950s, was picketed by irate young citizens who found its 'cultural services' far beyond the means of most New Yorkers. The term 'elitist' came into extensive use as the 1960s drew to a close.

The private benefactors who had dreamed of a great centre in which all of New York's cultural resources in the performing arts would be brought together in a proclamation of New York's grandeur had little idea of the storms of criticism their plan would engender. They conceived of Lincoln Center as 'an idea embracing every aspect of the performing arts; the creative, educational, the organizational, the physical, the political, and the economic. It is an idea giving bold and concrete expression to confidence in man's survival, to the enduring values of art as a true measure of civilization.'

But man's survival and his relationship to the higher arts was precisely the issue which brought serious critics to the fore. In order to provide the cultural centre, the developers and the city had to raze heavily populated areas. This was a practice which already during the mid-1950s had caused grave alarm among humanistic planners. The idea of urban renewal seemed to the powers that ruled New York's planning commission until the early 1960s to consist in bulldozing whole neighbourhoods. Such 'planning' was criticized by one of America's most distinguished architectural historians, Vincent Scully, as a device 'to turn the old New Deal around in order to use the taxes of the poor to subsidize their own removal for the benefit of real estate men, bankers, suburbanites and center city retailers.'

In the case of Lincoln Center, the cultural centre was complemented by the building of Lincoln Towers, a massive high-rise cluster reserved for the middle and upper income citizens, displacing hordes of the poor. The critic Jane Jacobs in *The death and life of American cities* deplored the project, and attacked the planning of the cultural centre itself. When it was proposed to tear down Carnegie Hall, New York's venerable concert hall on 57th Street, she and others came forward to save it for the sake of the neighbourhood, and she used the metaphor of chessmen which are vital to the organic activity of a city. The threat to Carnegie Hall came, she said, from 'New York's decision to take all its most impressive, or potentially impressive, cultural chessmen out of play and segregate them in a planning island called the Lincoln Center for the Performing Arts ... Now this is a pitiful kind of planning, which would blindly destroy a city's existing pools of use and automatically foster new problems of stagnation, as a thoughtless by-product to pushing through new dreams.' From Miss Jacobs' point of view, the idea of a cultural centre itself is deadening to cities, since the animation of neighbourhoods is the city's life blood. Anyone who today challenges Miss Jacobs' judgment need only to wander through Lincoln Center on an off hour, to discover how unused, how desolate its open spaces are.

Moreover, the neighbouring areas are still blighted slums, from which people rarely venture. The painter Allen d'Arcangelo, who executed the murals on the surfaces of two linked tenements facing the Center, angrily pointed out that Lincoln Center is facing the other direction, and that nothing gracious or appealing was planned for its rear façades which, like city ramparts, close out the extra-mural poor. The City Walls group, to which d'Arcangelo belonged, was itself born of the anger of artists who saw unalleviated drabness and misery in blighted areas closing in upon themselves. Their wall-paintings—of limited tenure—were emergency efforts to compensate for the lack of initiative shown by the donors of such projects as Lincoln Center. Originally, in the mid-1950s, the project was announced for fifty-two acres, of which twenty-one would be reserved for housing. Within two years, another twenty acres were requisitioned. The Center for the Performing Arts was projected in 1956 as costing $175 million,

The Whitney Museum, Marcel Breuer's concrete, cantilevered home for a large collection of American art, completed in 1966.

with the idea of asking the Federal government for a slum clearance subsidy. In 1957, the city and the federal government contributed toward the acquisition of the sites, and handed over the project to private developers. An international committee was called in for consultation on the plans, including Alvar Aalto, Marcel Breuer, Sven Markelius, Philip Johnson and Henry Shapley, under the general leadership of Harrison and Abramovitz. Later, there were a great many discussions among the designated architects—Philip Johnson, Max Abramovitz, Wallace Harrison, Eero Saarinen, Pietro Belluschi and Gordon Bunshaft—concerning the nature of the grouping which would include the Metropolitan Opera House, Philharmonic Hall, New York State Theater for Ballet, the Vivian Beaumont Repertory Theater and Library of the Performing Arts, and the Julliard School of Music. At some point Philip Johnson proposed a harmonizing overall scheme, in the tradition of the Chicago World's Fair, but that was rejected, leading certain critics to satirize the whole as a series of separate performances brought together on a single stage

for reasons that no one ever made clear. Their sole concession to such harmony was the use of Roman travertine to face all three structures.

The final decision—to group the three major performance buildings around a traditional plaza, with something of Renaissance glamour imparted in a terrazzo floor and central fountain—left the three architects free to develop their pet theories of theatrical grandeur. The result seems to many a very tepid and temporary-looking demonstration of individualism. Most critics have found the Vivian Beaumont Theater, designed by Eero Saarinen, and the Library of the Performing Arts, designed by Skidmore, Owings & Merrill, the best buildings in the immediate complex, and the Julliard School, designed by Pietro Belluschi and his associates Eduardo Catalano and Helga Westermann, of exceptional merit. But even critics favourably inclined towards the individual buildings have had to admit that the lack of adequate transportation and parking facilities make this spectacular theatre compound a distressingly non-functional entity in the city.

The first of the buildings to open to the public was Max Abramovitz's Philharmonic Hall. A rectangular glass box with extended tapered columns of rather spindly cast, the hall was designed to seat 2,644 people. There are three terraced balconies within, well-designed so that few are seated beneath their overhang, and the seats are accoustically engineered. The acoustical baffles are intended to be decorative but are not pleasing in form. On the whole, the interior is pleasant, if unimaginative. The high lobby, which can be seen from the three promenades enclosing the hall, is somewhat narrow. Its height is mitigated by the two hanging sculptures of Richard Lippold, while at the entry level there is a bronze sculpture by Dimitri Hadzi to enliven the space.

Wallace Harrison's Metropolitan Opera House sits behind five very oddly scaled arches, neither powerful like those of the Romanesque period nor graceful in the Moorish style. These five arches in travertine only very slightly conceal the conventional glass screen through which, at night, can be seen the malapropos Chagall murals. Harrison clung to the conventional opera house plan, right down to the red and gold trappings. The winding staircases are from certain vantage points sufficiently eccentric to be exciting, although the glass chandeliers, the baubled interior of the hall, and numerous overdone details diminish the Opera's dignity.

Philip Johnson designed his New York State Theater, as if to reply to the vaulted arches with an emphatic nay. Like the Philharmonic, the State Theater has a tall porticoed façade in travertine but the grouping of the members is completely different; Johnson's exterior design is relatively severe with four groups of two columns, and a low plaza-level entrance through which visitors enter to begin their ascent of two grand stairways to the huge galleried promenade. This enormous space has character in itself, but Johnson's fussy details—tiers of filigreed balconies and lots of gold chain—mar the largesse of the space. In addition, a quixotic whim of Johnson's—to blow up beyond their minuscule scale two Elie Nadelman sculptures—is humour fallen into black humour. These sculptures could not be more ludicrously placed. Within the hall, with its five tiers of horseshoe balconies, the crystal central light and the myriads of spangles wherever one looks do much to make the theatre one of the most vulgar experiences of its kind. In the name of gaiety, Johnson provides a sad spectacle of lavish expense and mediocre results.

From the point of view of design and elegance, the Vivian Beaumont Repertory Theater by Saarinen, and the Library-Museum of the Performing Arts by Skidmore, Owings & Merrill, are far more successful in the immediate compound of the centre. The low-roofed, split-level structure with the massive roof housing the library, and properly scaled stairway leading from the plaza level are matched in good taste by the splendid theatre, certainly one of the most agreeable in New York. The only work of art which seems intimately related to the structuring of the Center is Henry Moore's sculpture in its formal pool which flanks the building. This outdoor space is most satisfyingly designed both from the outside stroller's point of view, and from that of the audience looking out from the theatre balcony.

Pietro Belluschi and his associates Eduardo Catalano and Helge Westermann designed the Julliard School to meet the special requirements of its curriculum. With four storeys below ground, and six above, they have given the building a graceful exterior, and an extremely

Cube *by Isamu Noguchi in front of the Marine Midland Grace Trust Co.*

lively interior with four performance halls, workshops, a library, and comfortable teaching studios. In the 960 seat Julliard Theater, there is a special ceiling which can be raised or lowered to permit acoustic adjustment, while Alice Tully Hall, an extremely agreeable auditorium seating some 1,000, is equipped for both chamber music performances and film showings.

There are numerous schemes in preparation to rectify some of the grosser errors of planning in the Lincoln Center area, but none has been formally adopted. Some suggestion of connecting the cultural centre with the low-income neighbourhood by causeways and promenades has been taken under consideration, but little can now be done to relate what has been called a cultural supermarket in a vital

The new artists' quarter, Soho, in downtown New York,

way to the citizenry. The back of Lincoln Center will always be cold and forbidding.

The one other cultural building added to New York during the 1960s occasioning both criticism and praise was Marcel Breuer's citadel on 74th Street for the Whitney Museum. The granite structure by Breuer and Hamilton Smith literally fortifies the life of American art with its moated entry and its massive projecting walls along both property lines of its crowded Madison Avenue site. The protruding windows, like oblique scanners on some science-fiction machine, are similar to the rare openings in embattled castles. To add to the fantasy character Breuer designed the building with three cantilevered steps, like an Aztec pyramid in reverse, the top one being a chunky overhang, its force lessened by the decorative window. The impression of reclusive power is enhanced by the device of the bridge leading

into the museum from which the visitor looks down into the sculpture court. The sculpture appears to be relegated to a dungeon from the sidewalk vista, but once down below, the visitor has more a feeling of austere storage space. This compromise with the idea of incorporating the street life and the idea of exhibiting sculpture was not as successful as the other exhibiting areas.

In the three main galleries, the innovations are spectacular. Breuer designed each floor as a huge loft with infinite possibilities for the installation. The floors are attractive split bluestone and the walls are white-painted canvas and bush-hammered concrete. Nothing competes with the exhibited objects. The ceilings are covered with a two-foot precast concrete grid that conceals an excellent lighting system and grooves for bracing temporary exhibition walls. The top exhibition gallery with its 17½-foot ceiling and 120-foot long area was prophetically conceived, is recent exhibitions of sculpture on a vast scale have proved. No other museum has the possibilities for quick and effective installation of outsized works that the Whitney now possesses.

The challenge to the concept of the centralized museum becomes more acute every day. Artists have doubted the significance of repositories in the centre of Manhattan which are rarely if ever penetrated by New York's millions of ghetto residents. Museum officials have been pressed to open auxiliary branches, or workshops, or children's centres rather than build still another storehouse for treasures. One of the notable by-products of new social agitation was Brooklyn Museum's successful children's branch, MUSE. Housed in a remodelled pool-room in a densely populated, seriously blighted area, the children's museum combines workshop facilities with exhibition spaces in a wholly satisfying scheme.

Art in the 1960s

With the exception of the Whitney, and Samuel Glazer's addition in 1963 to the original Jewish Museum, museum expansion slowed down in the 1960s, reflecting the emphases on other more pressing problems. The visual arts had been undergoing swift transitions ever since the mid-1950s. Many of the thrusts of the new generations seemed to be directed towards public-scale projects, reflecting the rise in civic responsibility in the 1960s. Much of the painting, for example, indicated the new generation's impatience with the arcane aspects of the more metaphysically oriented Abstract Expressionists. In the late 1950s, the work of Robert Rauschenberg, who claimed to bring his art into closer relationship with the life of the city itself, came into prominent focus. Rauschenberg's technique of using scraps of city waste, and fragments of New York newspaper photographs and headlines, seemed apposite to the new spirit. His contemporary, Jasper Johns, was equally celebrated for incorporating actual objects in his paintings, and for de-emphasizing the ethical or symbolic aspects of abstract painting Soon after, the literal realization of Rauschenberg's interest in bridging the gap between art and life, came to the fore in Pop art—a movement which utilized popular imagery from magazines to billboards to TV commercials and cartoons, its prominent practitioners being Roy Lichtenstein, Andy Warhol and James Rosenquist. At the same time, large enterprises got under way to merchandise what came to be called 'multiples'—moderately priced editions of objects and images. The urge to broaden the uses of art was implicit not only in the works of individual artists during the late 1950s and early 1960s, but also in the appearance of social protest art in the form of flats and peace murals, reviving the tradition of the 1930s.

Even more significant of the changing goals of many artists was the new interest in public-scale sculpture. From around 1960 to the present, sculpture took a predominant position in the art discourse of the metropolis. Veteran architectonic sculptors such as Tony Smith were suddenly exalted. Younger sculptor working in large-scale steel found encouragement from architects and city agencies. Mayor Lindsay's

▷

The United Nations complex,
designed by an international committee of architects, 1947-53.

Department of Cultural Affairs kept making temporary displays in the hope of stimulating permanent use of contemporary sculpture. Certain artists whose techniques were admirably suited to public-scale exhibition, such as Kenneth Snelson with his steel and wire held in tension, found new scope for their work. Though there were still very few opportunities for artists to be considered as part of the planning and designing team for new architectural projects, the practicability of their participation was growing.

Nevertheless, very few major sculptures for permanent installation were commissioned. An exception was made in the case of Isamu Noguchi, who for some forty years had been attempting to persuade New York to let him work in the embellishment of its spaces, particularly the children's recreational areas, to no avail. Finally, a major opportunity appeared when Skidmore, Owings & Merrill called him in for their mammoth Chase Manhattan Bank and Plaza project at Nassau, Pine and Liberty Streets. The tower of glass and aluminium rose 800 feet into the air, interrupting the skyline but in a distressing manner. At its foot was the first plaza in the downtown district, and in the plaza a sunken sculptured water garden.

The elements used by Noguchi consisted of a glass-walled circular well 16 feet below the open plaza and seven huge basalt rocks which

he himself had found in Japan. With these he created a unique sculpture that is at once a water garden and a work of art, with an undulating floor of patterned granite paving the 60-foot pool, and pipes in the rocks which permit slow trickles of water to burnish their surfaces. The success of this project led Skidmore, Owings & Merrill to call Noguchi in again for the 140 Broadway plaza in front of their sober Marine Midland Grace Trust Company Building. Here, Noguchi's cube, standing on a point, is a wholly suitable sculptural qualification of the spaces of plaza and building.

In painting, artists continued to prefer the large scale proposed by the first generation of abstract expressionists. The tradition established by Pollock, Rothko, Newman, Kline and other men of their generation was sustained, at least in terms of canvas size. Pollock, who said that he hoped eventually to do murals, often scaled his paintings to walls greater than the average apartment wall. The young who adopted the same ideals went even further toward the architectural solution, creating paintings in geometric or free-formed shaped canvases more like sculptural reliefs.

There were few actual paintings commissioned. Fritz Glarner's murals for the Time-Life Building and for the UN Library were among a handful. Rather it seemed that the lavish banks were furnished with

The new block-shaped skyline of Lower Manhattan.

195

New York at night.

paintings and sculptures as decor, and not as organic necessities. The majority of artists during the 1960s never even gave the mural possibilities a thought until spontaneous groups, such as City Walls, Inc. and Smokehouse, began to find outdoor sites for their work. Others who called themselves earth artists or conceptualists, produced works in city parks and even in the city streets, on temporary bases.

The movement into the streets brought many artists closer to the applied arts, erasing the stigma that had once attached to being a designer. Works of imagination were no longer categorized in terms of painting and sculpture, but found other designations according to their uses. Pop art and op art and minimal art found their way into commercial design, and commercial design found its way into art reciprocally. The spurt in lively shop designing remarked in the 1960s was one indication. A distinguished architect such as Ulrich Franzen could contribute his expertise to the design of apparel shops uptown and downtown. His Paraphernalia boutiques with their use of all the visual paraphernalia of the 1960s, from shiny black plastic to light shows, and their absence of the usual displays verge on fantasy, or high camp. Franzen was quoted as desiring the projected images, rather than the merchandise, to become the enticement. 'Everything was done to create an environment and the ambiance in which the people and the projections are the performance, in which the customers project themselves into a different context, into the ambiance of a discotheque.' The latest shop, at Lexington Avenue and 55th Street, certainly comes close to his ideal, and shows the impulse toward the popular arts as very strong even in commerce.

Another artfully designed shop, stressing unconventional values and imaginative display techniques, is Lucidity, with premises on upper Ma-

dison Avenue and also on Second Avenue at 51st street, designed by Alan Buchsbaum. Here new furnishings in plastic, and new forms resulting from the material's flexibility, are appropriately housed in a fresh style of retail shop design. Buchsbaum, and designers such as Barbara Stauffacher, reach out into the high visual arts for their sources, and use them to enliven the urban environment. Stauffacher's hoardings for buildings under construction, such as the Banco de Brasil on Fifth Avenue, by architect Paul Damaz, have offered fresh possibilities to the chaotically tearing-down-and-rebuilding atmosphere of New York. At the same time as the uptown shops were being brought into other visual contexts, uptown art galleries were more frequently exhibiting works of art which were based on technological possibilities. Light and electric circuitry became a new medium seen by many architects as possible accessories to buildings. Other forms of art which could not be easily acquired, such as photographic records of projects in great mountainous areas, or on the plains of the Midwest, also appeared, indicating the waning interest in objects as collectors' items. The average Madison Avenue gallery often found the scale of its walls and ceilings inappropriate for the new works made by younger artists who had luxuriated in Manhattan's manufacturing lofts as studios. During the late 1960s, scores of artists settled in the area below Houston Street where many huge lofts were available to those willing to clean them out and install amenities. The district became known as Soho, and was soon a lure for uptown sightseers and would-be collectors. It was also soon a lure to real estate profiteers. The

P. 198/199
The rectangular slab of the 1963 Pan Am Building offers an interesting contrast with the spire of the 1930 Chrysler Building.

fight to keep the artist's rights intact—both from city harassment and from landlords—continues, but meanwhile Soho replaces the old East 10th Street enclave of the 1950s as an artists' quarter.

Once the artists started the movement downtown, and once their works began to take on the dimensions permitted by huge lofts, galleries began to appear in Soho. They too were spectacular in size and design. One of the largest, the O.K.Harris Gallery on La Guardia Place, has enough exhibition space to have two very large one-man shows and a smaller one-man show at the same time, and to install, as was once done, a sculpture the size and shape of a private aeroplane. Art of warehouse proportions will undoubtedly call forth situations in which it can be used, although few of the exhibitors in Soho galleries have so far had any specific opportunities to work with architects.

Planning the Environment

Many of these artists profess to be practitioners of what they call 'environmental art'. Though there is no clear definition of what constitutes environmental art, the use of the term is significant. Throughout the 1960s the main currents of thought in many disciplines were eddying around the notion of total environment, and of dynamic interrelations among things and people. Nowhere was the discourse more pointed than in the fields of planning and architecture; art and philosophy; psychology and sociology. There were clear, bold theoretic speculations coming from various sciences and technology (all the systems-analysis discussion) and there was an opening cleared for experiment even in the ranks of the commercial builders. For instance, the widening discussion of 'field theory' was initiated by a team within the ranks of Skidmore, Owings & Merrill. Field theory, a method of analysis in behavioural science that describes actions or events as the result of dynamic interplay among sociocultural, biochemical and motivational forces, was adapted by SOM designers in their search for fresh and more human building designs. The results have been praised for the radical break that field theory has brought from the traditional simple rectangular grid. The whole feeling of environmental interdependency generated in such theory and discussion leads to diversification of form, and the solving of large-scale urban problems which heretofore had achieved rectangular solutions with alarming regularity. In line with this shift in thought is the tendency, among the youngest architects, to do battle with the rigours of the International Style. The Style, which became for so many years a vernacular in New York building, represents to them an autocratic decision on the part of Utopianists to make prototypal judgments. In the late 1960s the idea of 'non-judgmental' learning was broached, whereby a more practical attitude was intended toward the conditions that must be met by planners and architects. Rejecting the prototypal mode of thinking, which they found epitomized in Le Corbusier's Voisin Plan for the destruction and rebuilding of Paris, these younger architects seek specific solutions to specific urban problems of structuring neighbourhoods. At their most extreme, they advocate the acceptance even of the chaos and lack of planning. They have gone so far, as has their

◁
New York at night, showing the Hudson River.

leading spokesman, Robert Venturi, to see the 'beauty' of the gaudy gambling strip in Las Vegas, and by implication, the beauties of urban jungles such as the Times Square area in New York. Many of these younger architects rebel against the open-space ideal propounded by older architects, claiming that the nature of the city is counter to open plazas; that New Yorkers do not like to sit in open spaces, and that the grid plan works better with filled-out blocks. Implicitly, this is an attack upon the luxury builders whose prestige was announced largely by the amount of rentable space they would sacrifice. The younger architects envision salvaging open space for active city life, and keeping the close-knit integrity of the city block intact.

The philosophical resistance to the luxury builders, and their idea of urban embellishment, is epitomized by the attitudes of those who call themselves advocacy planners. The horrors of such projects as the Bronx's Co-Op City, where some 60,000 peoples are housed on only 300 acres, can be avoided, they claim. Some of the advocacy planners, such as Roger Katan, insist that the architect can function only if he is prepared to extend himself to activities which were previously considered beyond his realm of competence. Katan's attitude is a long way from the aristocratic distance of a Richardson, whose clients took his word for law, and were always rich. Katan's clients are the community as a whole; they are mostly the very poor in the ghettoes of Harlem, and they share with him the planner's task.

According to Katan, the only way to realize the human needs of urban citizenry is to work from every possible vantage point. He himself lives in East Harlem, has an open house system in which the neighbourhood clients are free to drop in, and spends a great deal of his time teaching the neighbours the principles of planning and design. By helping them to organize themselves and state their needs coherently, Katan is able to develop plans which make sense. He also recognizes the necessity of learning the intricacies of city bureaucracy, and how to deal with the political aspects of each citizen's existence. Over the years—he has lived in East Harlem for some seven years—Katan has slowly developed a number of alternative plans for rehabilitation and rebuilding in his neighbourhood. His models for the 'rejuvenation of an old public housing site and integration with the adjoining urban fabric' show visual imagination, but they also indicate his close understanding of the lives of the residents in East Harlem.

The housing Katan proposed for the sites incorporating the old housing projects would be built on a pre-fabricated shelf system with individuals buying or leasing lots in the sky. Katan defends the right of the community to look forward to economic amelioration and the possibility for each individual to make a better home without leaving his neighbourhood. 'The determination of his individual dwelling lies, as it has with the residential housing throughout human history, on his financial means, technical know-how, and personal whim. Only in this way can we open the way to the essential quality of organic diversity within the urban environment which has been the natural outcome of human settlement in the past. This diversity is an imponderable no architect can foresee, only the inhabitants and time can create. The architect provides constructions whose relationships suggest a certain way of life; the people make of these shells a city.'

An example of the fruits of Katan's public-spirited labours is a projected multi-service centre, a kind of shopping centre for social services, which was planned with local residents and the East Harlem Community

*The old Grand Central tower
weirdly overshadowed by the Pan-American building.*

Corporation. Katan offered the citizens a number of possibilities for housing such services as legal advice, day care, health, education, and took care of a host of other needs expressed by the residents of this teeming neighbourhood. They chose to design the building with an interior street three storeys high leading into a patio planted with tropical verdure (the neighbourhood is largely Puerto Rican and black). The youth workshops, in which Katan plans to install an active design and architecture programme, would be grouped around the patio, as would the library. Balconies would be festooned with vines. Katan also proposes a corner cafeteria, with indoor and outdoor facilities, which would be protected by the trellised vines he hopes to plant the entire length of the block. Emphasis would be on flexibility in the planning so that enlarging services as time goes by would not be blocked. A 24-foot module is accordingly used throughout the building.

Saarinen's CBS Building, 1965,
his only high-rise tower, presents
its sombre power on Sixth Avenue's
new skyscraper row (left and above).

The theory that no one knows another's needs until he is acquainted with the other, is increasingly preoccupying planners who are more and more often consulting citizen's groups before they design housing. A recent decision to allow the community to be consulted around Columbia University, where large-scale redevelopment plans are envisioned, and to incorporate community representatives on the planning team, was readily accepted by the architects, for instance, but looked upon with some displeasure by the trustees.

This is not to say that the battle between concerned citizens, such as Jane Jacobs, and the great financial forces of New York has yet been shifted in balance. Although Jane Jacobs and community groups in west Greenwich Village were able to stave off plans to destroy the Village and substitute mass commercial buildings with less residential space, they won only a small victory. Throughout the 1960s the building boom thrived, and plans to redefine Lower Manhattan were pushed through over residents' protest. Uptown, all along Sixth Avenue, the 1960s saw a tremendous transformation of a relatively run-down, low-rise neighbourhood into a chic commercial district of hotels and office buildings. But glorious monuments to economic power did rise there.

The most sophisticated testament to corporate power is Eero Saarinen's last work, the Columbia Broadcasting System Building at Sixth Avenue and 52nd Street completed in 1964. Stark and lowering, with its deep grey granite columns faceted and very closely spaced, the building's sheer 38-storey rise is emphasized in the columns that go from top to bottom, without even the usual lobby columns. This linear consistency is subtly altered by the angling of the granite columns which catches the light in various ways throughout the day. For all that, the building stands remote from the life below it, and the plaza spaces are mournful and uninviting. Far more inviting is Saarinen's Trans-World Airlines Terminal at Kennedy Airport. Here, Saarinen's pronounced gift for designing unexpected spaces, with many curvilinear elements and even a discreet symbolism, is fully exploited. The sculptural character of the interior halls and walkways brought considerable criticism when the building was unveiled in 1962, but it remains one of the most appealing and daring of the Kennedy ensemble which has too many modernistic clichés.

Saarinen's superior design for CBS is readily seen when compared to the dozen or so other office buildings on Sixth Avenue that have appeared since. Although Harrison & Abramovitz's rather commonplace design for the Time-Life Building is acceptable, some of the more hastily erected structures in the neighbourhood tell the often-repeated New York story of quick, commercial, and socially indifferent enterprise. Certainly William B. Tabler's gigantic New York Hilton Hotel completed in 1963 is grotesquely inconsistent with its surroundings, and poorly designed. Its public spaces are confused and labyrinthine; its so-called sculpture court totally meaningless; its details jejune. Such hotels, with their fake luxury and presumably deliberate vulgar taste, increasingly become the rule in New York. The elegance of the St Regis is nowhere to be found, even in the most expensive of the new hotels.

Like Sixth Avenue and Third Avenue, Lower Manhattan is rapidly changing its mores and appearance. At the very tip of Manhattan, once housing quaint old loft buildings, and some of the old romantically designed skyscrapers that used to define the skyline, much speculative building has occurred. The *Architectural Forum*, January-

Southern entrance to the Grand Central building.

February 1970, pointed out that between 1968 and 1971, about 12 million square feet of office space will have been completed in the two-block swatch along the East River between Battery Park and Fulton Street. Most of these structures are ungainly, and done in the usual curtain wall clichés that have characterized speculative building for the past decade. An exception is Carson, Lundin & Shaw's Hanover Trust operations centre. This brick-clad building, harmonizing with the few historical buildings in their fine brickwork, eschews the glass vernacular in favour of volumetric mass and surface texture. The brickwork plaza, the pyramidal mounds for the air ducts, and the deep arcade are all features distinguishing this building from its less attractive neighbourhood.

If the skyline at the Battery is hampered by these new buildings for commerce, it is treated even more cavalierly in the bleak design of the World Trade Center. Promoted by the city's own Port Authority, this great building designed by Minoru Yamasaki and Emery Roth & Sons goes back to the roaring '20s with its ambitions to reach for the skies not once, but twice. The twin towers are 110 storeys high, probably the highest buildings in the world, and tower threateningly over not only the waterfront, but City Hall Park as well. When completed the project will have ten million square feet of office space, and will house 50,000 workers, all this on a site of a mere sixteen acres. It is also equipped with a large plaza. Most of the criticism of this project comes from neighbouring communities such as artists in the loft districts, and from theorists who had thought that gigantism was a dead issue for New York. The architectural journals seemed to have limited themselves to admiring the techniques of the elevator system which will start not only from the main floor, but also from the 'sky lobbies' at other levels.

The desolation these mammoths spread will, it is hoped, be partly offset by the firm interference of the Urban Design Group which is recommending a series of linked open spaces to connect Chase Manhattan Plaza with the World Trade Center, and thereby impose some coherence in Lower Manhattan. The coherence that was hoped for when Conklin & Rossant, McHarg & Todd, and Wallace produced their Lower Manhattan Plan in 1966, seems a lost dream, now that developers have moved into the area.

This plan had envisioned numerous pedestrian thoroughfares, with automobile storage at the edges of carefully planned spaces, and a large, vitally nourished plaza that would be well-used by surrounding housing developments and commercial enterprises of various sizes. One of the planners, Rossant, takes a discouragingly dim view of the future of the Plan. 'It is probably not possible in our city in our lifetime for planning decisions to be realized. Masterplans are unfortunately used for bargaining issues, and everything is up for grabs— even by good guys.' Within the next decade there will have to be decisions, probably on a national level, to limit the profits in real estate, or the cities will perish.

But it is too late to intervene in many areas such as that around the Grand Central Terminal and lower Park Avenue. There, aesthetic disaster is spelled out in the 59-storey octagonal building surmounting the Grand Central Tower Building, blocking a respectable urban vista and desecrating a landmark of another era.

Not only have critics condemned the Pan Am building for the designers' indifference to problems of circulation, arrival and departure of workers and traffic in general, but they have recognized the commercial pressures which have made of its ground plan and its lobby interiors a wilderness of ugliness—this in spite of afterthoughts such as Josef Albers' mural, Richard Lippold's sculpture, and decor by Gyorgy Kepes.

This is compensated for—at least a little—by one of the more ambitious projects of the 1960s, the Ford Foundation Building, a superb example, most critics agree, of expensive institutional building. The Foundation has presented itself with a building by Kevin Roche and John Dinkeloo in which no expense has been spared, from the bronze facing on the curb of its loading entry to the smallest pushbuttons.

Roche has been quoted as saying that he wishes, in his design, to suggest a 'sense of the individual identifying with the aims and intentions of the group.' Since it is a group of some three hundred scholarly executives and their secretaries, charged with the heavy responsibilities of disbursing hundreds of millions of dollars each year, this building is a special case and has been treated as such.

Sited on 42nd Street and extending through to 43rd, the building occupies an almost square plot. Roche has successfully avoided the squatness of squareness by weighting his granite-clad columns on one side, and emphasizing in the glass and steel walls the ambiguities of his interior L-shaped space. The approach to the interior from 42nd

▷

The spire of St Paul's Chapel dwarfed by the World Trade Center's twin towers, under construction.

Street is gradual, leading from the confusion of the street into the unique glimmering green lobby where Roche's large interior garden forms a well from ground to skylighted ceiling. This garden, which is rather unimaginatively planted and serves more as a decorated public space than a place for repose, provides the main source of life to the very sober interior, with its tier of glazed offices rising nine storeys, and its two executive floors running on all four sides of the building. Secretaries and executives alike look out upon the dim green space from the carefully, expensively and practically appointed offices. The head of the Foundation himself sits in a glass sanctum and can be seen at work by all those entering the top floor cafeteria. All this reciprocity (I look at you, look at me, we all look at the garden and the interior garden looks out at the exterior garden) should suggest philosophical harmony, but to many it simply suggests magnificent organization of powerful economics, much as the glassed Manufacturers Trust does on Fifth Avenue and 43rd Street. The largesse and imaginative quality of Roche's vision distinguishes this building as one of the finest recent structures in New York. The excellence of detail, and such beautiful features as the lozenge-patterned skylight, recalling the best of the art nouveau architect, Hector Guimard, make for the true majesty a good architect can elicit in the urban environment.

For all the impediments, hazards and exasperating battles architects

The Bronx-Whitestone Bridge.

P. 212/213
*Night-view of downtown
Manhattan,
viewed from Brooklyn.*

have had to wage to improve the quality of life in New York, they did manage during the 1960s and early 1970s to build decent and even distinguished structures with increasing frequency. For instance, early in the 1960s the city became a conscientious client for the first time in many decades. Ideas were solicited for better ways to construct city schools not only from the architectural point of view, but from the point of view of humane education. The myriad problems encountered in city school building, ranging from red-tape and bureaucracy in various city offices to vandalism and other symptoms of serious social disorder affecting the schools, have made school building a province that tempts only the hardiest and most idealistic of architects.

Among them is Richard G. Stein whose Public School 55 in Richmond, Staten Island, remains one of the liveliest examples of sound school building. Stein was among the first architects to attempt an overall unity of school and playground, avoiding the desolate asphalt fenced squares usually called playgrounds in New York schools. Lawns, trees, a graded sloped with ramps and an amphitheatre move down the hillside to the play area. The school has four sculptures by Nivola, as well as graphic decor by Chermayeff and Geismar.

Shortly before he built the New York Cultural Center at Columbus Circle, which was roundly castigated for its fussy and exceedingly flimsy Venetian exterior, Edward Durrell Stone completed Public

A powerful institution in a commensurately powerful building, the Ford Foundation, and (right) its unique greenhouse court.

School 199 at 70th Street and West End Avenue. The school, in marked contrast to the dreadful massing of Lincoln Towers' 4,000 housing units, stands, dignified and free, against the confusing walls of dense housing behind it. Stone used a system of brick piers from ground to roof, simply articulated in pleasing rhythms, and lending an air of calm permanence to an otherwise chaotic neighbourhood.

In 1966, the young firm of Pedersen & Tilney completed Public School 306 at 970 Vermont Street in Brooklyn, described in the AIA Guide as a 'superb, cast-in-place concrete school. In an area of flat monotony and long eerie vistas down empty streets, the boldly raked stair towers and handsome massing of the long, low volumes of this building add richness and an air of mystery to the otherwise bland skyline.'

The incidence of distinguished ecclesiastical architecture is relatively low in New York City; during the 1960s, however, a few outstanding churches and synagogues were produced. The first of these—Church of the Resurrection at 325 East 101st Street—was completed by architect Victor A. Lundy in 1965. As Lundy remarked, 'the site for this small mission church in East Harlem is one of the worst slum streets in New York, an 80 by 100 foot lot hemmed in by dilapidated tenements...' Presumably, the tenements would be replaced by high-rise public housing, so Lundy planned the church as a total piece of sculpture to be viewed from above. As seen from the street, the church is a sober, masonry sculptured form with a prow-like projection into the sky, the proportions between two sections perfectly scaled. Within, Lundy has built a slow ramp ascent to the second-floor sanctuary

which is absolutely simple and awesome in construction and is lit by
a single skylight over the altar. Timbers have been used to stress
the movement toward the sanctuary's climax, moving in sweeps up
the ceiling toward the small single source of light.

The possibilities of sculpturally interesting form were realized in the
next significant church to be built in the 1960s, Belfatto & Pavarini's
Church of the Epiphany at the corner of 22nd Street and Second
Avenue. On a rather small site, in a visually undistinguished neighbourhood, the architects arranged their major forms in curving contoured vertical blocks, with variations in form occurring in the shapes
of the bell-tower and the crests of the adjacent sections. The whole
is smoothly wedded by the use of dark brown glazed brick lending an
air of sobriety and stern idealism to the entire neighbourhood. The
small plaza area has been tastefully laid out to separate the functions
of the church from the more mundane activities on Second Avenue.
Despite its small scale, the church succeeds in setting the commanding
tone for the surrounding area.

In another heavily commercial site, downtown Manhattan, architect
William Breger has added his sculptural note to ecclesiastic structures
in the Civic Center Synagogue on White Street between Church and
Broadway. This synagogue was designed for the special circumstances
provided by the financial district. Those who drop in for devotions
are not strictly speaking parishioners, but commuters to daily commercial jobs in the lower city. The site offered Breger was exceedingly
constricted, being only 50 feet wide. For this site he conceived of the

small terrace leading into the synagogue which would be the first step in a retreat from the noise and worldly bustle always present during the day in the Wall Street district. Above the entry is a gracefully curved, billowing form which is braced and framed by the two adjoining party walls of business buildings on either side. Inside, Breger designed three impressive curving shells to form the sanctuary which, since the congregation is not permanent, is the most important space. Meeting halls, offices and the other spaces usually provided in synagogues and churches, were not significant for this business district sanctuary. Breger's sense of sculptural form is highly developed, and this small-scale structure may be counted among the few imaginative attempts to deal with the city block with reasonable invention, and still not destroy the necessary scale and continuity of existing buildings.

The problem of scale found a few more reasonable solutions in the area of housing. By the mid-1960s, discussions of the problems of housing proliferated, not only for the poor who were rapidly being dispossessed to make way for new projects, but also for the so-called 'middle-income' families who could neither be housed in city projects for low-income groups, nor afford luxury apartments. It was pointed out that during the first decade or so of urban renewal under such Federal plans as Title I, 28,000 dwelling units had been built, but 126,000 had been demolished. Moreover, critics found that new building tended to fall into the same old ways, disregarding the environment as a whole and concentrating on getting the most out of the investment. If housing were for the poor, the economies practised by the builders resulted in dreary and unacceptably small units which multiplied themselves interminably. If it were for the rich, it generally showed the usual ostentation in lobby spaces and plaza areas, but little regard for the neighbourhood.

One of the first widely discussed projects which avoided most of the pitfalls was Kelly & Gruzen's Chatham Towers co-operative apartments, completed in 1965. The two striking towers in wood-grained concrete rise vigorously in an area that tradition had long established as depressed. Once known as the Five Points intersection, where New York City's destitute and depraved lurked in the early nineteenth century, and where, later in the century, the conventional grim tenements of the Lower East Side replaced the pothouses, Chatham Towers is a triumphant departure from tradition. Taking into consideration the generally disorganized character of Lower Manhattan, and the well organized colour of Chinatown, which the Towers face, the concrete towers with their well-scaled details, their differing planes of walkways, playgrounds and plazas serve as a focal point, an emphatic node. Aside from the excellent design and spacious layout of the apartments, the Towers offer visual pleasure in the strength of the sculptural details and the care in texturing the surfaces.

Shortly before Chatham Towers was completed, I.M. Pei's first unit of Kips Bay Plaza between 30th and 33rd Streets and First and Second Avenues was completed, and hailed as the first exposed concrete apartment house in New York. Pei's two 21-storey slabs are much more sternly entrenched in the International Style rigour than the two-tower project of Kelly & Gruzen. Pei set his towers facing one another across a vast and barren plaza. Dwellers in the apartments with floor-

◁
Battery Park landing stage for ferries to Staten Island.

to-ceiling windows are condemned to know their neighbours, but only at a distance. Their ground vistas are singularly cold and even the landscaping of the plaza is uninviting. Here, critics saw in Pei's scheme a realization of Le Corbusier's idea of the skyscraper dwelling within a park and many of them condemned it. Unquestionably the vast, inert space of the plaza and the cellular regularity of the towers has added a forbidding note to a neighbourhood which previously was teeming with life and the daily activities rated so important by social planners such as Jane Jacobs.

The extensive project called Riverbend by Davis, Brody & Associates, completed in 1968, has not lost this sense of activity and community thanks to a careful plan and a point of view which distinctly sought to relate the dwellers to the neighbourhood, the landscape and each other. Riverbend stands on what would have been considered by many builders an almost impossible site. It occupies a triangle along the Harlem River which is cut up by highway ramps and approaches and city sewers, and is cut off from the river by a six-lane highway. On this site, Davis and Brody built a middle-income (a truly middle-income) project which includes 624 apartments of which 200 are duplexes. The whole grouping consists of two apartment towers and five blocks of duplexes, connected with carefully planned ramps, terraces and playgrounds.

Unquestionably Riverbend affected building projects in New York. For one thing, ingenious economies occurred in the design of such details as the size of the brick (larger than normal to cut labour costs); the rough finish of the concrete, and the sharing of elevators—not, as is the usual case, in the interior spaces, which were conscientiously kept large. For another, the sidewalks in the sky—walkways the length of the duplex buildings through which tenants enter their own patios and thence their dwellings—offered a solution both to the problem of entry and exit on a site which is geared to the view of the river, and a suggestion for a means of relating the urban dweller to his community. The stress throughout the project on connecting—both physically and psychologically—served as a model for other architects who have come to understand the necessity for encouraging communication.

The same considerations guided Davis, Brody & Associates in their ambitious project of rejuvenation for Manhattan's midtown East Side. For East Midtown Plaza, they designed a series of ten-storey buildings, each with five layers of duplex apartments, flanked by two high-rise buildings, one of 22 storeys and one of 27 storeys. The area they had to plan for had long been deadened by the exclusive occupation of institutions, largely medical facilities which sprawl along the East River in considerable confusion. The life of the neighbourhood near East Midtown Plaza was considerably choked off by the absence of residents, small shops, restaurants and recreational facilities. The rather chilling presence of hospitals, the sole noises being the screams of ambulance sirens and the roar of riverside traffic, had to be offset by the warmth of small-scale housing and the incorporation of festive spaces.

▷

Church of the Epiphany (1967), a rare essay in modern church architecture with its curving, contoured, vertical forms tastefully grouped.

P. 220/221
Imaginative façade of the Civic Centre Synagogue in downtown New York.

To do this, the architects argued vigorously for permission to close 24th Street in order to make a through-block plaza which is flanked by the lower buildings. The intimacy of the space created here will eventually be enhanced with an outdoor café, and many vivid shops. The pleasing design of the buildings, the warmth of their brick faces and their generous apartment floor-plans immediately attracted tenants who are fast converting this once forbidding pocket into a vital neighbourhood.

Even in projects where the high-rise tower is still preserved, as in Paul Rudolph's Tracey Towers, the recent trend is toward diversity of design and more human living spaces. Rudolph's two towers, one 40 storeys and the other 42 storeys, stand in a landscaped area of the Bronx where there are educational parks and a reservoir, and the Jerome Subway Yards. Rudolph originally conceived of his project as high-rise towers in relation to some thirty-six townhouses. Now it appears that the townhouses idea has been abandoned and only the freely designed towers, with their rounded columns and sweeping ramps, will distinguish this part of the Bronx with their presence.

The most notable rehabilitation project in recent years is Westbeth, a unique housing scheme designed to meet the mounting crisis in the lives of painters, sculptors, writers, dancers and all other artists whose incomes are small and whose space needs are large. Financed by a private foundation in collaboration with the National Council on the Arts, the project began with the acquisition of a city block of factory facilities in the West Village, erected for Bell Telephone between 1898 and 1920. These buildings were conventional factory buildings, with high ceilings, thick walls and poured concrete floors, and were not very coherently related to one another.

Architect Richard Meier sought a unifying theme which he found in the enclosed courtyard formerly used as a loading dock for trucks. He removed the roof and fashioned a courtyard open to the sky which provided simultaneously a focal point for both residential units and commercial shops and galleries. He connected this narrow opening with three of the peripheral streets and opened it out to the small park on the site, giving the building complex a unity and intimacy.

In designing the interior spaces, Meier used great ingenuity by eliminating interior corridors in all but three floors of the ten-storey central portion of the building, designing the units on two levels. The space gained by removing corridors was for the use of the tenant who could now have the equivalent of a loft space from wall to wall and window to window. The units were left as nearly as possible bare of installations, enabling tenants with special requirements, such as painters, dancers or sculptors, to install themselves according to their tastes and needs. Storage space is provided in mobile units which double as room dividers.

New York has lagged behind for many years in providing studio space. Westbeth, which was not without problems for the architect constrained by certain rulings of the building authorities, has various planning flaws and functional problems. But it is nevertheless an impressive example of forceful designing on the architect's part, and enlightened planning on the part of the National Council on the Arts, the City of New York, and the Kaplan Fund.

It remains to be seen whether the incorporation of an art gallery, a theatre seating 800, and various community studio facilities will stimulate the lost sense of community in the art world. Dispersion, high rents and the lack of congenial meeting places have changed the

Westbeth, the renovation of an old industrial building to provide work space and housing for artists.

character of bohemia in New York City. The old Tenth Street Studio building where once the patrons attended soirées and met artists on their own ground was a more modestly scaled project, and reflected a cohesion which no longer exists in the art world.

The vast and significant changes in the nature of New York's artistic life is in some measure symbolized by another rehabilitation project, Automation House at 49 East 68th Street. Architects Lehrecke & Tonetti snatched a nineteenth-century mansion from extinction by converting its interior into a handsome and unique plant symbolizing, as its sponsors say, 'Man's wish to shape his future in a world of bewildering change.' The six-floor, 25 × 100 foot building is now the home of an unusual group of organizations including the American Foundation on Automation and Employment (in which labour unions have a huge stake), the Institute of Collective Bargaining and Group Relations, and strangest of all, Experiments in Art and Technology, for which much of the building is designed.

EAT, which arranges special exhibitions for the excellent gallery on the main floor of Automation House, is an artistic phenomenon born in the 1960s, and highly influential in the new realms of imaginative activity having to do with technology. It grew from the early collaboration of Dr Billy Kluver, a Bell Telephone laser expert, with various visual artists interested in harnessing technological discoveries for use in the arts. Kluver's early collaboration with Jean Tinguely led to further experiments with Robert Rauschenberg who then became a founder of EAT. Under the forceful leadership of these two adventurers, the organization grew into prominence very quickly, attracting to its ranks many sculptors and painters who wished to realize dreams that only scientists could help materialize. When it appeared that experiments in circuitry, laser beams and other sophisticated technological areas would be extremely costly, the leaders arranged liaisons with industry, bringing artists and scientists together under the aegis of large companies or labour unions. The next step was to bring them under one roof, and Automation House was born. This experiment is far from over. Nevertheless, the incorporation of motion, light, and extremely elaborate technical arrangements in the concept of the practising artist has led to significant changes in cultural attitudes. Where once a young artist was expected to shun industry and remain isolated in his studio, he is now encouraged to participate in the 'total environment' by taking part in many functions of the total society.

In line with EAT's ambition to civilize the sciences with the injection of artistic imagination is the design of Automation House. As its sponsors boast, it can be changed from a forum on collective bargaining into a museum in a matter of minutes. It is equipped with unprecedented electrical power facilities, with closed circuit communications, film facilities, and all kinds of visual equipment supported by 3,000 amperes of power—enough for an entire city block. The attractive ceiling grid is a flexible arrangement that supplies circuitry and power throughout the house. Such mixed-media happenings as Rauschenberg or Robert Whitman devise are easily presented in this first museum designed specifically for them.

Some civic groups are motivated by an enlightened attitude towards the past and are ready to convert the interior of a nineteenth-century museum into a twentieth-century marvel. One of the most interesting battles fought and won for preservation of the past to be used intelligently in the present concerns historic South Street Pier. This waterfront area, which was once an important docking area for nineteenth-century vessels, which housed the fish market, and numerous small businesses and old warehouses, was threatened by the encroachment of large commercial speculative building. A group of private citizens banded together to acquire the pier and the adjacent colourful neighbourhood in order to found a South Street Seaport Museum. Although they have run into considerable difficulty in the purchase of expensive land, and although the group has been forced to subsidize their project through selling air rights for skyscrapers, they have been singularly successful.

The pier, with its rugged timbers, has been refurbished and several nineteenth-century ships are berthed there. A small kiosk-like display of figureheads lends gaiety while the view of Lower Manhattan river traffic and bridges is superb. The past is honoured here, but so is the present. The board has authorized the use of the pier for various contemporary functions, such as the exhibition of sculpture made by the students of Cooper Union out of discarded flotsam found in the area. This outdoor sculpture project, led by the young sculptor Christopher Wilmarth, brought an air of vital festivity to the neighbourhood that it had not known for half a century. Such endeavours become more frequent now that New Yorkers have been alerted to the necessity of salvaging the past and enlivening the present. Whole areas of

▷

Chatham Towers, an experimental undertaking in housing and restoring a depressed area in the Chinese quarter.

Washington Square Village, one of the first large housing projects in Greenwich Village to make two block-long units shelter a plaza area

brownstones have won protection from the city, with the help of civic groups. Such attractive rehabilitation projects as the rows of rescued brownstones in Brooklyn's Park Slope area and Manhattan's West 80s and 90s are the direct result of citizens' intervention in their environmental destiny, a trend which is becoming healthily pronounced in the city of New York.

New York City has a large roster of colleges and universities, some of which are large property owners. Until the 1960s, the university as a patron of advanced architecture was almost unknown in New York. Most attention directed to universities in terms of building and property-holding was the product of community dissatisfaction. Students and community groups began to protest the notion of the university as slumlord; as real estate enterprise; as a walled fortress, indifferent to the needs of the community.

Under general pressure, both for expansion of facilities to meet the needs of a huge new population of students, and for concern in community development, several major institutions in New York embarked on ambitious architectural and housing projects. Certainly the most comprehensive was that proposed by New York University in the early 1960s.

Kips Bay Plaza, an integrated living area with free-standing apartment buildings reminiscent of Le Corbusier's work in Marseilles.

P. 228/229
Picasso's Portrait of Sylvette *in the plaza of I.M. Pei's university village on Washington Square campus.*

New York University is the largest private university in the United States. It has a student enrolment of some 40,000 dispersed in various locations held and developed by the University: at Washington Square, where the college of liberal arts is installed; at University Heights in the Bronx, which concentrates on science and engineering; at 78th Street where the Institute of Fine Arts trains art historians a few steps from the Metropolitan Museum; along the East River where the premises of the medical school are strung out; and in Wall Street where graduate studies in business administration appropriately take place. The importance of such a huge educational enterprise is grasped when the statistics concerning New York City's professionals are cited. More than half the dentists in New York City have been trained at NYU; one out of five doctors; one out of five lawyers, and thousands upon thousands of engineers and teachers.

In an effort to meet responsibility primarily to students, New York University decided to engage major architects for further planning and construction. The first to be commissioned was Marcel Breuer whose experiments with reinforced concrete on other campuses inspired the NYU committee. Breuer's first building was the Julius Silver Residence Hall for the University Heights campus. Given a difficult, hilly

*Aerial wiew of
Manhattan
looking uptown.*

site, Breuer resolved the problem of entry and exit with a series of ramps, at the same time providing a visual strength to the building. Not long after, he completed one of his finest structures: Begrisch Hall, a small science building relating beautifully to the Julius Silver residence. Begrisch Hall is a cantilevered building revealing Breuer's signature in the way he used the reinforced concrete for both practical and aesthetic effect. The wood grained concrete is cast in highly sculptural forms, making use of the highlights and shadows of sunlight both in the articulation of its interlocking parts and in the plaza on which it stands.

Breuer's other major work at University Heights is the new Technology II building, an H-shaped complex of an eight-storey laboratory and office wing, a three-storey classroom wing, and classrooms beneath a raised open plaza. In this, Breuer extends his experiment with

concrete, making load-bearing walls with 11-ton blocks of pre-cast concrete.

Downtown the construction programme for the 1960s and 1970s is no less ambitious. In 1964, the University named Philip Johnson architect for its Washington Square Center, asking him to draw up a master plan. His resulting proposals roused storms of controversy in the community, which was loath to see historic Washington Square tampered with, but the University marched intrepidly on with its plan. The first building in the Washington Square area was completed before Philip Johnson's entry as master planner. It is Warren Weaver Hall, a 14-storey building which is the largest centre for mathematical training and research in the western world. Certainly the most satisfying of NYU's enterprises, this building was designed by architects Warner, Burns, Toan and Lunde with notable restraint. An award

A piece of sculpture enlivens a previously drab neighbourhood near Bellevue Hospital.

citation from the City Club of New York praised it as a vigorous academic building: 'Its disciplined shapes are original; its materials modest but nobly used, indoors and out. In its reassuring simplicity, consistency, substance and quiet force, as well as its restraint from occupying all the footage of its site, it makes a good neighbour to both old and new buildings nearby.'

Of particular interest is the design of the building in which warm-toned brick columns punctuate the glassed bays, and are in turn punctuated by a band of cantilevered glassed bays around the perimeter of the 12th floor. This necklace of reliefs softens the verticality of the columns and is what most distinguishes the building.

Many critics would not be so generous about Philip Johnson's building. Johnson's sense of scale and place, in the opinion of many, falters badly in his notions for Washington Square. The major building is the Elmer Holmes Bobst Library on the southeast corner of Washington Square, designed to be the largest open-shelf library in the world, with space for two million books and 4,800 readers.

For this 12-storey building, Johnson and his associate Richard Foster chose to cloak the skeleton in a heavy red sandstone which, in a less massive building, might have joined its elder neighbours of nineteenth-century provenance with pleasant harmony. As it is, the incredible hue and the density of the heavy stone weighs down the square, dwarfs the trees in the park, and proclaims a horrifying might. As at Lincoln Center, the opportunity to equal the gracious proportions of Renaissance palaces is missed. Here, as in the three Lincoln Center theatres, the architects strive for verticality and therefore lose the sense of scale and design these buildings might have offered weary New Yorkers.

Certain of the University's obligations were discharged, it was felt, when three residential towers by I.M.Pei were completed, two for faculty housing and one for middle-income families. Pei's habitual functional clarity and severity is somewhat mitigated by the installation of an unsuccessful Picasso sculpture in sand-blasted concrete. In his enthusiasm for the large scale made possible in concrete—the sculpture is more than 36 feet high—Pei allowed Picasso to decide which of his small sculptures should be enlarged, and Picasso settled on a *Portrait of Sylvette*, hardly suitable for the site. (NYU's earliest sortie into commissioning modern artists resulted in the aluminium relief on Loeb Student Center by Reuben Nakian. More recently, NYU has sponsored a full-length wall painting by Tania at 683 Broadway, and a monumental sculpture by Gitou Knoop for University Heights.)

The areas along the East River occupied by medical institutions have long been out-of-bounds for ordinary residents. Moreover, the lack of planning and environmental emphasis led to a breakdown in most services and recreational facilities. The East River piers and promenades were used only sparsely by the public due to traffic congestion along the periphery, and the generally unappealing atmosphere generated by the agglomeration of unplanned institutional buildings.

With the new emphasis on master-planning that characterized the Lindsay administration, many young architectural firms indicated their interest in the urbanist aspects of whole neighbourhoods. Davis, Brody & Associates were already well advanced with East Midtown Plaza when their plans for Waterside were approved. In their excellent brochure, *Bellevue Environs,* the architects took into account the diversity of the existing neighbourhoods and the potential for recreational pleasure that the river holds. They proposed that NYU and private developers in the area should co-operate on an overall plan which would link activities, housing and medical facilities in a balanced and civilized way. Their own plans for Waterside are eminently imaginative.

Waterside would be built on a platform extending over piles sunk into the riverbed from 25th Street to 30th Street. It would have 1,450 apartments in four towers and townhouses. But, as they write, 'the river will be reclaimed for far more than 1,450 families. Terraces and plazas, shops, restaurants and a cinema are planned for the public at large. A boardwalk will run along the very edge of the river.'

Waterside is not yet finished, but many of the projects conceived in the mid-1960s are already realized, or in construction, indicating that the pressures from newly-aroused civic groups who in turn alerted the public to fresh environmental experiment, were effective.

Language is often a gauge of the deepest preoccupations of a society. When a word such as *environment* begins to take on new connotations, as it did in the early 1960s, it is obvious that many social forces have converged to invest the word with dynamic qualities. The frequency with which the term environment occurred in the public press and specialized journals from around 1962 to the present is a clear sign of awareness. From the initial awareness of environment rose the more complex awareness of ecological considerations, which served to bring a host of disciplines—from social psychology to biology and art—into the problems of designing a workable, and more important, livable city.

The evolution of awareness, of a fresh way of apprehending the living spaces, both physical and psychological, is implicit in much of twentieth-century history and perhaps most easily discerned in the development of the arts. Painting and sculpture in the twentieth-century have, at various moments, declared themselves the progeny of environmental thinkers. The popularity of the mural during the 1930s, the resurgence of interest in the mural in the 1960s, the increasing interest in public sculpture, are quickly perceived indicators. More subtle is the force of the idea of what came to be called 'environmental art'—a loose term which gathered unto itself painters, such as Rothko and Newman, who intended their works to transcend the traditional frame and envelop the spectator, and sculptors who tried to make of a many-membered structure an embracing environment rather than an object in space. From there, it is a short step to the works of electronic artists whose lights and sounds are geared literally to alter the environment of public spaces.

The Artist in the Public Domain

The opportunities for entering the public domain were all too rare for the artist in the years between the Depression and the 1960s. A few American artists had persistently attempted to introduce their skills and insights into the urban environment during those years only to be met with resistance on the part of officials and planners. A signal example is Isamu Noguchi, whose social instincts were apparent (but not encouraged) very early in his career.

Noguchi was already dreaming of ecological projects in the early 1930s. His mind had turned to problems of relating his sculpture to the earth, which he attempted in his first playground proposal, Play Mountain, in 1934 — rejected by the New York Parks commissioner. Noguchi's description of Play Mountain is as follows: 'This was an original concept to expand playable space in a given city lot by tilting the surface into vari-dimensional steps of a pyramid, or of a roof, whose interior could also be used. In the shape of a spiral; the ridge is a slide for sleds in winter. There is another steeper slide with water flowing into a shallow pool...'

The prototypal aspects of Noguchi's model are obvious. The following year, he proposed an earth sculpture for the Newark Airport which would be seen from the sky. This radical view of sculpture as both the environment (for it would have been an environment to those on its earth) and a visual experience (as it would have been from the airplane) is now quite a common idea which has even achieved the status of a genre of art—earthworks. In 1935 Noguchi's proposal was met with outright derision.

Again in 1941, Noguchi returned to his idea of sculpturing the earth in order to provide an environment for children with his contoured playground made up entirely of earth modulations with areas for hiding, sliding and games, and with flowing water in warm weather.

The Washington Arch, at the foot of Fifth Avenue,
designed by Stanford White (1892), leading to Washington Square.

Again Noguchi's visionary impulse was checked, this time the excuse being the outbreak of the Second World War. But the ideas he developed in 1941 remained important to him, and when, in 1960, he was approached by a citizens' committee to remake a portion of Riverside Park as a children's playground, he entered a partnership with architect Louis I. Kahn, in order to realize the idea of playgrounds as sculptural landscape. From 1960 to 1965, Noguchi and Kahn grappled with various forces, ranging from the traditional opposition of city authorities to opposition from neighbourhood groups on various grounds. Finally, once again, the project, with its play mountain, its giant slides built into the topography of the hilly site, its sand and pebble areas and maze, its theatre and its all weather nursery building, was annihilated. But not before the various models, plans, and philosophical statements had gained wide currency in the press. The fact is that Noguchi's vision had already entered the consciousness of young planners and designers, some of whom readily acknowledge his influence.

Among the lessons implicit in the heated controversy that accompanied Noguchi and Kahn's project was the knowledge that public projects could no longer be conceived and effected by experts without consulting the public. The mood of rebellion and the insistence on democratic participation that overtook New York ruled out such schemes, no matter how inspired. Subsequent proposals for new environments and recreational areas were made first to community representatives, whose assent would have made Noguchi's original scheme acceptable.

235

Successfully engaging in community consultation, the architect Richard Dattner accomplished the building of the first American playgrounds to be based on the humane and sociologically sound principles advocated by Noguchi in the early 1930s and showing his aesthetic insight. Dattner studied the habits of children, their ethnic and social determinants, and the works of eminent child psychologists, notably Piaget. He concluded that 'play is freedom' and that the quality of playing spaces could be a direct influence on social function. His criteria for play spaces reflect the general shift to environmental thinking. A playground should be like a small-scale replica of the world, with as many as possible of the sensory experiences to be found in the world included in it. His Adventure Playground on Central Park West was thoughtfully created to meet these ideals. There are certain features which directly reflect Noguchi's original ideas, such as the pyramid between the two main areas of the playground with stepped sides for sliding which also function as a storage room. The so-called volcano and concentric mounds recall Noguchi's prototypical plans for modulating surfaces of the play areas. What is impressive in the Dattner playgrounds (there is another at Central Park West and 81st Street) is the clear evidence of close attention to children's needs, important among which are visual stimulation and reaction to portions of the environment where aesthetic control is evident.

The quality of attention to both the physical and psychological needs of people using recreational spaces is not limited to designers of children's playgrounds. The creators of a superb vest-pocket park on 53rd Street between Madison and Fifth Avenue, the Samuel Paley Plaza by Zion and Breen, made an elegant resting place for walkers, office workers and Fifth Avenue shoppers which cools them in the summer via a wall-like cascade, and reposes them in cold weather with the agreeable network of delicate trees.

Both the needs of adults and children were sharply apparent to M. Paul Friedberg who can truthfully be called the 'Wunderkind' of recreational space design. In his work of the early 1960s, such as the landscaping of Chatham Towers, he began experimenting with various levels to break the towering monotony of vertical housing. By 1965, when he worked with architects Pomerance and Breines on low-income housing for the city, the Carver Houses at 99th Street and 101st from Madison to Park Avenue, he was already beginning to formulate a point of view that would go far beyond the mere landscaping of spaces between city slabs. The pedestrian mall, left over from misunderstood Le Corbusier tenets, had been traditionally a grassy area with hundreds of coercive restrictions. Friedberg transformed a grim plaza into a lively pattern of socializing designs, introducing smaller plazas, graded walkways, an elegant trellised walk, a small amphitheatre and wonderful climbing walls.

In 1966, Friedberg's plan to overhaul the spaces in the Jacob Riis Houses between 7th Street and 10th Street and Avenues A and B, was greeted with unqualified admiration. This housing project, embedded in a traditionally poor and overcrowded neighbourhood taxed with problems ranging from drug addiction to ethnic adversity, was originally equipped with the usual desolate grassy areas, with the usual injunctions against their use. There was no variety, either visually or in terms of activity, offered to residents and the spaces were almost never used by the children who preferred the arresting bustle of the city street. Friedberg, working again in collaboration

*I.M. Pei's soaring buildings forming
the university village on the Washington Square campus.*

with Pomerance and Breines, removed all lawn areas that required signs or fences, replacing them with textured paving. He introduced sculptured terracing and embankments for aesthetic variety, and changed the pattern of resting space in the multi-level scheme. The playground, which remains a model for vivacity and functional variety, is laid out in a group of sculptural block mounds. As Friedberg observes, 'relationships between the mounds are critical for they form the basis of "linked

M. Paul Friedberg play area in Jacob Riis Houses (above and right).

play", a concept offering exciting, decision-making possibilities as
the child goes from one experience to the next.'

In Riis, Friedberg demonstrated the soundness of his decision to use
materials that are mostly natural—wood, granite block, water and
sand. As in Carver, he made ample use of trellises to connect and
make intimate the pedestrian areas. In his view, it is the environment
—not just the facilities—to which the child responds. The obvious
need of children is not just a place to play—a circumscribed area with
three of four pieces of equipment, swing by sandbox, slide by teeter-
totter, side by side—but a total world to which he can respond. The
total world happily includes work by visual artists in most of Friedberg's projects such as the schoolyard of Public School 166, with its
relief by sculptor Mon Levinson; and various painted walls and sculptures in the vest-pocket parks of Manhattan and Brooklyn.

Friedberg's growing concern with larger issues than the play space
was demonstrated when he worked with I.M.Pei to restore the
dignity of a dreadful slum in the Bedford-Stuyvesant area in Brooklyn.
Known as the Superblock, it encompasses three square blocks in the
area between St Marks Avenue and Prospect Place, in which two
interior streets have been developed as landscaped recreational areas.
By widening the street eight feet and planting trees, by making a multi-
level plaza with a fountain, a pedestrian walkway, benches and play
area, the designers honoured the suggestions of the community which
had been consulted long before the work got under way. The resulting
community pride has protected the Superblock from the usual vandalism. One resident proudly remarked that not one of the attractive
globes on the street lamps had been broken.

This experience led Friedberg to reconsider the principles on which
he had begun his spectacular career as an urban designer. In 1970,
he wrote that planners, sandwiched between the needs and requirements of the *de facto* client (the community) and the *de jure* client

(government or industry), have not produced salient results because the community, 'that sector of the society with the greatest need for action-oriented planning assistance has least access to it.' He concludes—as many young architects have come to recognize—that the planner must enter the political arena on both an individual and collective level. 'The planner must become politically active, set himself up as liaison between government, industry and community, be totally involved in the process, develop concepts which establish bridges between physical, social and economic planning...'

Just such a programme is commencing operation in Friedberg's latest collaboration with Davis, Brody & Associates for a spectacular reclamation of the Harlem River valley. Once upon a time, the area was a cool, vernal retreat for New Yorkers who, until the late nineteenth century, came to picnic, swim and go boating. With the unprincipled development of industry and its subsequent decay, the Harlem River valley in the Morris Heights section (in the West Bronx between 176th and 180th Streets) became a base for hideous junkyards and sinister empty lots.

The new plans call for a linear park development along the river's edge, punctuated by community nodes which will provide housing, commercial and community facilities. The planners have carefully considered the rest of the community, and have designed attractive overpasses, bringing the river into a new relationship with the residents. The two-tower apartments in this case represent not the usual builder's notion of skyscraper sensationalism and quantitative planning, but rather a practical solution to the problem of existing housing. The towers, pleasantly designed but avoiding the monolithic quality of most slabs, command a view of the entire valley, but minimize the obstruction of view for the existing community.

To these various functions of the planner and designer postulated by Friedberg another extraordinary figure, Laurence Halprin, adds a host of others. He is interested in what he calls the creative processes in the human environment, and although he is an architect, planner and designer of long standing, has reached out into all the arts and sciences to develop his theories and to realize them in public spaces. He thinks of himself as 'an environmental designer and planner involved in the broad landscape where human beings and nature interface.' In his writings, there is a clear bias against the 'goal-oriented' empiricism which has been a traditional American vice. His emphasis is on process, and he tries to persuade his reader to think of values implicit in doing and making rather than in achieving an inflexible predetermined goal. References to the I Ching, and even to tarot cards, underline his rebellion against the logical and positivistic strain in planning. Community design, he insists, is not a science and can never be a science. (Since one of his long-term studies has been of what he calls 'people motion in space,' he could hardly submit to the barren abstractions that turn up again and again in urban design surveys and committee proposals.)

The function of 'scoring,' a system of planning which Halprin has evolved, is to scatter power, destroy secrecy, and involve everyone in the process of evolving their own communities. He says that the new ruling class are those who utilize land as a commodity for economic gain and are the real architect planners of our environment. (They are not so 'new' for New York City.) 'They are largely responsible for the disintegration of the physical environment of our ghettos, for the appalling ugliness of urban and suburban sprawl... The artist-planner and the people are all at the mercy of the entrepreneur within the present context of our society.' Like Noguchi, Halprin has offered a few highly imaginative proposals for the enhancement of city life in New York which have not as yet met with any encouragement. But his model for a fountain—more like a watergarden taking up a whole city block—would have certainly been a splendid monument, and undoubtedly a time will come when Halprin's insight will be understood in New York City.

Advocacy has crept into the attitudes of many painters and sculptors who have committed themselves to public service in one way or another. New York has been exceedingly impoverished in terms of respectable monumental sculpture. Even now, very few important sculptors working in New York itself ever receive major commissions. The late David Smith who worked there for years was never honoured with a public commission, although Washington owns one of his large outdoor pieces, New York has yet to acknowledge his stature. A rare exception is James Rosati, whose refined, mature, steel sculpture has recently been sought out by large builders, and whose work for the World Trade Center will soon be installed.

Given the poverty of the aesthetic environment, and the new concern with ecology, it is not surprising that artists concerned with ghetto problems have banded together to form active programmes for the public aesthetic welfare. In the case of Smokehouse Associates, a largely black group who have designed large portions of the area

▷

Wall painting by Tania in the New York University downtown area.

P. 242/243
A natural fresco created by young New Yorkers.

VE HAVE

UT OF OUR

"WALD

RICH OF 102

HANCY & Arlene

Tony
Barbara Eddie
+

CHR

Power
David NAR

TiNY

Juan

I SAY
David

A DREAM

AIN COMES W

102

LOVE Preston

ES   sps   TERRY

Tony

bubbu

KIE

The new skyline at the Battery.

between 120th Street and 123rd, bordered by Second Avenue and Lexington, as well as 135th Street and Lenox Avenue, the basic concerns go far beyond purely aesthetic intentions. Smokehouse originally included only painters and sculptors who began by cleaning up vacant lots and abused, decayed city park areas, for which they designed murals and sculptures. The members quickly learned that in order to change the environment fundamentally, it would require more than a well-designed wall painting or a piece of sculpture. Architects, writers, lawyers, poets, community planners and actors were added to the group in order to search out the true needs of the community and encourage community expression. No project was undertaken without the advice and consent of the people who were to move about in the spaces. In a programme which includes lectures, poetry readings and analytic documentation, Smokehouse shows how the ecological approach has influenced artistic workers in many areas. Another group, City Walls, Inc., has limited itself more strictly to the enhancement of neighbourhoods where little colour normally survives. Artists such as Allen d'Arcangelo, who initiated the programme and Nassos Daphnis, Jason Crum, Tania and others have painted walls on tenements, abandoned warehouses, playground barriers and towers. The summit of a huge office building on Madison Avenue at 26th Street, decorated with Daphnis's geometric painting, is an example of how applied colour composition can neutralize the deadening effects of commercial building, and lend ordinarily dull areas a visual excitement. On the whole, the new attitudes toward the cultural role of the artist

Map of New York, pp. 246-7.

*The Empire State Building looming impressively
in its midtown site, p. 248.*

and architect are still far from being enacted fully. New York City is
no exception to the universal challenge to ideas received and experienced by the entire world since the Second World War. Many
New Yorkers sense turmoil and rapid change, particularly in the 1970s,
as potentially positive effects of the close of the industrial era. Despite oversimplifications of the idea of a post-industrial society, completely divorced from the values of the early part of the century, there
can be no question that the assumptions motivating artists and architects have undergone dramatic change. The visual results of such
drastically altered assumptions as the old modernist idea that form
follows function (challenged by ecological considerations), or that
light and air will change the attitudes of slum-dwellers (challenged by
all younger planners), or that architecture if beautiful is self-justifying
(challenged by many socially concerned architects), or that the visual
artist is a solitary genius (challenged by technologically oriented creators
and by artists' collaborative efforts)—all are registered all over New
York City today. Cultural New York is no longer limited to its
skyscrapers, its institutional piles, its masterpieces within those piles,
or even its designated parks. It no longer reflects exclusively the iron
will of those commercially potent forefathers who imposed the grid
plan. New York today, more than ever a perplexing organism whose
chief attribute is swift change, reflects instead the burgeoning conviction that man, and particularly urban man, must have physically
and symbolically satisfying environments, and that the energies of the
populace, so often grossly misapplied in the past, must be redirected.

Inset

Gallery of Modern Art
Columbus Circle

Ninth Avenue
W 49th St
W 48th St
W 47th St
W 46th St

Seventh Avenue
Central Park South

Americana Hotel
Hilton Hotel
Equitable Life Building
C B S Building
J C Penney Building
Eighth Avenue
W 58th
Time & Life Building
Sperry Rand Building
W 57th

Allied Chemical Building
W 42nd St
W 53rd
Museum of Modern Art
R C A Building
International Building
W 56th St
W 55th St
W 54th St

Rockefeller Center
Lever Building

Broadway
Times Square
Plaza
St
E 52nd St
Patrick's

Avenue of the Americas
Pan Am Building
Seagram Building
E 50th St

Bryant Park
New York Public Library
Chrysler Building

Fifth Avenue
Grand Central Station
Lexington Avenue

Madison Avenue
Park Avenue
Third Avenue

Hudson

Dewitt Clinton Park
W 65th
W 72nd
26 25
W 59th
Columb
Cer
15 Lincoln Center

North River
Central

Eleventh Avenue
Tenth Avenue
W 46th
33
Ninth Avenue
34th
See Inset
6 20
W 23rd
32
Eighth Avenue
Seventh
12
Central Park South
E 65th
8

W 14th
Avenue of the Americas
E 53rd
E 46th
Fifth Avenue
Madison Avenue

Christopher St
Houston St
W 4th
Avenue of the Americas
Madison Sq
28
Park Avenue
Lexington Avenue
Third Avenue
Second Avenue
First Avenue

Express Highway
Greenwich
Hudson St
Union Sq
United Nations
Queensbo
Bridge

Vestrey St
Greenwich Village
Washington Sq
1
Gramercy Park
E 23rd St
Roosevelt Drive

Varick
West Broadway
31
E 14th St
E 20th St
Franklin

Chambers Street
Canal Street
Broadway
30
4
Avenue D
East
River

Fulton
17
Lafayette
Schiff Parkway
E 4th Street
Avenue B

5
9
Bowery
Clinton

7
Park Row
E Broadway

10
Allen

Battery Park
Broad
Nassau
Wall St
St
Street
South Street

Statue of Liberty
Brooklyn Bridge
Manhattan Bridge
Williamsburg Bridge

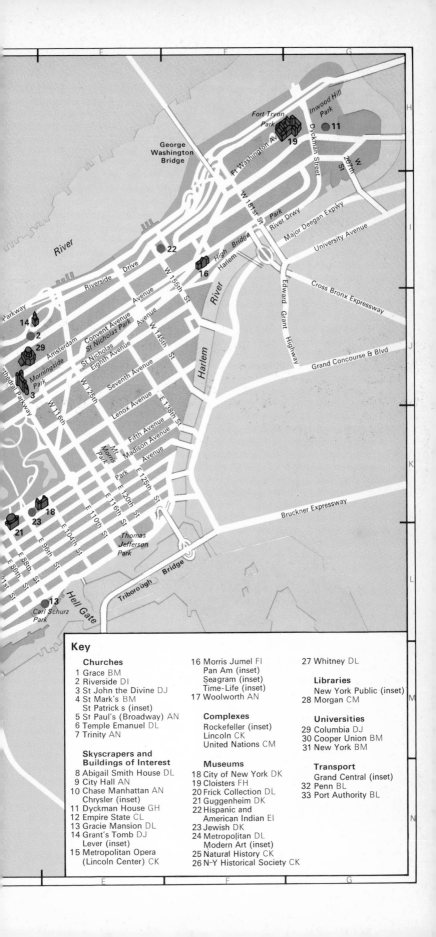

Bibliography

Andrews, Wayne *Architecture, Ambition and Americans* Harper, New York 1947

Baur, John I. H. *New Art in America* New York Graphic Society, Greenwich Conn., 1957; Hutchinson London 1957

Baur, John I. H. *Revolution and Tradition in American Art* Harvard University Press, Cambridge, Mass., 1951; Oxford University Press, London 1952

Blake, Peter *God's Own Junkyard* Holt, Reinhart, New York 1964

Burchard, John and Bush-Brown, Albert *The Architecture of America* Little, Brown, Boston 1961

Dattner, Richard *Design for Play* Van Nostrand, New York 1967

Duckworth, Sophia and Reed, Henry *Central Park* New York 1967

Giedion, Siegfried *Space Time and Architecture* Oxford University Press, London, 1949; Harvard University Press, 1950

Gowans, A. *Images of American Living* Lippincott, Philadelphia 1969

Halprin, L. *New York* American Heritage Press, New York 1968

Halprin, Lawrence *The RSVP Cycles* Braziller, New York 1969

Hamlin, Talbot *Greek Revival Architecture* Oxford University Press, New York 1944

Harris, Neil *The Artist in American Society* Braziller, New York 1966

Heyer, Peter *Architects on Architecture* Walker, New York 1966

Hitchcock, Henry-Russell and Johnson, Philip *The International Style* Norton, New York 1966

Huxtable, Ada Louise *Classic New York* Doubleday, New York 1964

Huxtable, A. *Four Walking Tours of New York* Doubleday, 1961

Jacobs, Jane *The Death and Life of American Cities* Random House, New York 1961

Kaufmann, Edgar Jr. (Editor) *The Rise of an American Architecture* Praeger New York 1970; Pall Mall Press, London 1970

Kimball, Fiske *American Architecture* 1928

Kowenhoven, John A. *The Columbia Historical Portrait of New York* Doubleday, New York 1953

Larkin, O. *Art and Life in America* Hol, Rinehart, New York 1949

Le Corbusier *When the Cathedrals were White,* Harcourt, Brace

Lerman, Leo *The Museum* Viking Press, New York 1969

Morrison, Hugh *Early American Architecture* Oxford University Press, New York and London 1952

Mumford, L. *The Brown Decades* Harcourt Brace, New York 1931

Mumford, Lewis *Sticks and Stones* Liverwright, New York 1924

Nevins, Allan (Editor) *The Diary of Philip Hone* 1922

Novak, Barbara *American Painting of the 19th Century* Praeger, 1969

Scully, Vincent Jr. *American Architecture and Urbanism* Praeger, New York 1969; Thames & Hudson London 1969

Scully, Vincent Jr. *Frank Lloyd Wright* Braziller, New York 1960

Stern, Robert A. M. *New Directions in American Architecture* Braziller, New York 1969; Studio Vista, London 1969

Still, B. *Mirror for Gotham* Oxford University Press, New York 1956

Sullivan, Louis H. *The Autobiography of an Idea* New York 1949

Trumbull, John *Autobiography* Wiley & Putnam, New York 1841

Weisman, W. *Architectural Review* Dec. 1950 Vol. CVIII no. 648

White, Norval and Willensky Elliot (Editors) *AIA Guide to New York* Macmillan, New York 1967

Museums and Galleries

Page references are given at the end of each entry. Numbers in italics refer to the captions.

American Academy of Arts and Letters

National Institute of Arts and Letters, W. 155th Street and Broadway (Audubon Terrace). Tuesday-Sunday 1-5.
The Academy (50 members) has a collection of manuscripts and first editions of past and present members; and owns works by the American Impressionist, Childe Hassam. Periodic exhibits of newly elected members' achievements. 32.

American Museum of Natural History

Central Park West between 77th and 81st Street. Monday-Saturday 10-5; Sundays and holidays 1-5. Admission by contribution.
Founded 1869, formerly at the Arsenal, the Museum of Natural History is now the largest of its kind in the world. The monumental Romanesque Revival 77th Street building (designed by J. C. Cady, 1867) and the building on Central Park West, with its classic Roman façade (designed by John Russell Pope, 1936) provide some 40 acres of floor space. Specimens from all fields of natural history, a library, and the *Hayden Planetarium*, where daily shows dealing with astronomy, space and the universe are given. Exhibits show natural processes and their products (The Hall of Gems and Minerals houses a famous collection of precious stones, including the De Long star ruby and the Star of India sapphire, given by J. P. Morgan), birds and animals in their natural habitats or demonstrating points of scientific interest (the Hall of Ocean Life; a diorama of birds of the world) and the life of primitive peoples and alien civilizations. Includes the Hall of Man in Africa (masks and sculpture); the Hall of Peoples of the Americas (gold work from Central America and Peru, pottery from Peru, and sculpture from Mexico); the Hall of Indians of the Northwest (masks and totem poles); Hall of the Peoples of the Pacific (tribal art Oceania). *76, 80.*

Asia House Gallery

112 E. 64th St between Park and Lexington Ave. Monday-Friday 10-5; Saturdays 11-5; Sundays 1-5. Admission free.
Designed by Philip Johnson; 1959. Attached to the Asia Society and the Japan Society. Three exhibitions yearly presented by the Asia Society, of Oriental art from various private and public collections. Library, research facilities. 160.

Brooklyn Museum

Eastern Parkway and Washington Ave., Brooklyn. Monday-Saturday 10-5; Sundays and holidays 1-5. Admission free.
Classical design by McKim, Mead & White; main building 1897; additions to 1924; flanking the entrance are two sculptures by Daniel Chester French, *Manhattan* and *Brooklyn*, 1916. Collections organized in 1884. *First floor*: large collection of primitive and tribal art, including work by peoples of Mexico, Central and South America (pottery, jewelry and stone sculpture) as well as a wide range of North American tribal art (wood-carvings of the Northwest Coast Indians, masks and totem poles; the Jarvis collection of art of the Plains Indians). From Africa there are masks and Benin bronzes; from New Guinea elaborate initiation masks. *Second floor*: Oriental and Indian collections, print collection of mainly 19th- and 20th-century works. *Third floor*: Egyptian collections, especially later periods, including Coptic; the Wilbour Library of Egyptology (by Howe & Lescaze; 1935); the Middle Eastern galleries, with twelve alabaster slabs from Nimrud, as well as smaller statuary and jewelry. *Fourth floor*: Decorative Arts of Europe and America, including twenty-five furnished American rooms, and the reconstructed Schenk House, a Dutch farmhouse built in Brooklyn in 1675. *Fifth floor*: American and European paintings galleries. The European collection includes representative works from Italian Primitive and Renaissance schools, the Dutch school, and French 19th- and 20th-century paintings. The American collection includes primitive paintings, such as Edward Hicks' *The Peaceable Kingdom*, landscape paintings of the Hudson River school, Thomas Eakins' *William Rush carving his Allegorical Figure of the Shuylkill River*, 1908, and 20th-century works from the Ashcan school through the Abstract Expressionists. Sculpture includes work by Gaston Lachaise, David Smith, and Seymour Lipton, and bronze works by the 19th-century French sculptor Antoine-Louis Barye. A garden behind the museum houses architectural elements and sculpture from New York buildings which have been destroyed, including portions of McKim, Mead & White's Pennsylvania Station and Louis Sullivan's Condict Building façade.

Brooklyn Children's Museum - *see* MUSE

China House Gallery

125 E. 65th St. Monday-Friday 10-5; Saturdays 11-5; Sundays 2-5 during exhibitions. Admission free.
The China Institute sponsors here in spring and autumn loan exhibitions of Chinese art objects.

The Cloisters

In Fort Tryon Park. Tuesday-Saturday 10-5; Sundays and holidays 1-5; closed Mondays. Admission by contribution. Recorded concerts of medieval music are broadcast in the Cuxa Cloister on Tuesday and Saturday afternoons at 3.30.

Housing the Metropolitan Museum's collection of medieval art, built to include elements from several European buildings, composed into a group by the architect Charles Collens, working with Henry Breck and James J. Rorimer of the Metropolitan. Portions of the cloisters from St Michel-de-Cuxa (12th century), St Guilhem-le-Desert (13th century), Bonnefont-en-Comminges and Trie (15th century, southern France), together with other medieval works, were assembled early in the 20th century by the American sculptor George Gray Barnard and shown to the public in a building on Fort Washington Avenue in 1914. John D. Rockefeller Jr. bought the collection for the Metropolitan in 1925, which he presented, together with the site of Fort Tryon Park, and some other medieval sculpture, to the city in 1930. The Cloisters opened in 1938, and has expanded in the intervening years, the latest addition being the Romanesque apse of a Spanish church from Fuentiduena, Segovia. The Cloisters' tower is modern, but is designed to resemble those of St Michel-de-Cuxa. Medieval tapestries are shown in three rooms, including the six Unicorn tapestries, woven in France, probably for Anne of Brittany, in the late 15th and early 16th centuries. The Nine Heroes tapestries, woven in France in the late 14th century are, with the tapestries at Angers, France, the only works of this early date known. The third tapestry group, from the late 15th century, is Flemish. The sculpture collection includes the 12th-century Romanesque Madonna in the Langon Chapel, the 13th-century Virgin from Strasbourg and the 14th-century Madonna and Child, both in the Early Gothic Hall, and the Catalan tombs of the 13th and 14th centuries, in the Gothic Chapel. Stained glass is housed in the respective chapels and in the Boppard room. Objects of art, sculpture and architectural details, frescoes and paintings, including the 15th-century *Annunciation Altarpiece* by Robert Campin, are found in the Treasury, Langon Chapel, Fuentiduena Chapel, Romanesque Hall, Early Gothic Hall and Spanish Room. *99, 112, 116, 119, 121.*

Cooper-Hewitt Museum for the Arts of Decoration

2 E. 91st Street. Monday-Saturday 10-5. Admission free.

In the Carnegie Mansion, a heavy neo-Georgian house designed by Babb, Cook & Willard; 1901. Collection, owned by Cooper Union, of textiles, drawings, wallpaper, birdcages, prints, metalwork, embroidery, and other material from the history of design and decoration, as well as a large collection of the works of Winslow Homer. Reference library.

Finch College Museum of Art

62 E. 78th Street. Tuesday-Sunday 1-5. Admission free.

Primarily a study museum for Finch art students, but open to the public. Paintings include Italian Baroque works, with canvases by Guercino and Guido Reni.

The Frick Collection

1 E. 70th Street at Fifth Avenue. Tuesday-Saturday 10-6. June, July and August open Wednesdays and Sundays 1-6, Thursday-Saturday 10-6, closed Mondays and Tuesdays. Admission free. Chamber music concerts are given on Sunday afternoons during the winter (tickets free, but must be applied for in writing). Brief organ concerts daily, 11.30 a.m.

Designed by Thomas Hastings; 1914. Remodelled as a museum by John Russell Pope, 1935. The collection of Henry Clay Frick (1849-1919) is shown on the first floor of his former residence, a mansion of more than forty rooms built in a formal Renaissance style. Dutch and Flemish works, French art of the 18th century, and Italian, British and Spanish art. In the East Gallery, works by Jacob Van Ruisdael, Giovanni Tiepolo, Jean Baptiste Greuze, Jean Chardin, J.A.McN. Whistler and Claude Lorrain. The Oval Room has portraits by Thomas Gainsborough and Anthony van Dyck, and a *Diana* by the French sculptor Jean-Antoine Houdon. In the long West Gallery there are pictures by Rembrandt, including *The Polish Rider* and a late self-portrait; works by Bronzino and El Greco, Van Dyck's portraits of Frans Snyders and his wife, and Diego Velazquez's *Philip IV of Spain.* Besides other Dutch paintings, by Van Ruisdael and Meindert Hobbema, there are in the West Gallery two paintings by J.M.W. Turner, Georges de La Tour's *Education of the Virgin*, two works by Paolo Veronese and Francisco Goya's *The Forge.* The Enamel Room, off the West Gallery, houses a collection of Limoges enamels of the 16th and 17th centuries, *The Temptation of Christ*, a panel by the 14th-century Sienese painter Duccio di Buoninsegna and Piero della Francesca's *St John the Evangelist. The Virgin and Child with St Catherine and Donors* by the Flemish painters Jan van Eyck and Petrus Christus is in the North Hall. The Living Hall houses great riches, with El Greco's *St Jerome as Cardinal*, Giovanni Bellini's *St Francis in Ecstasy*, Titian's portrait of *Pietro Aretino*, and two paintings by Hans Holbein, *Thomas More* and *Thomas Cromwell.* The Library contains a collection of Chinese porcelain and Italian and French bronzes of the 16th and 17th centuries. In the Dining-room are works by English painters of the 18th century: Thomas Gainsborough, George Romney, William Hogarth, Joshua Reynolds and John Hoppner. Several rooms house French art of the 18th century. The Fragonard room contains four panels by Jean Honoré Fragonard for Madame Du Barry, as well as other work by this artist. The Boucher Room is devoted to François Boucher's eight panels, *The Pursuits of Man*, painted for Madame de Pompadour. Boucher's *Four Seasons* are hung in a vestibule nearby. Two paintings by Jan Vermeer hang in the South Hall, also a work by Paolo Veneziano, and another work by Boucher. Reference library. 112, *119,* 120, 121.

Guggenheim Museum - *see* Solomon R. Guggenheim

Hispanic Society of America
155th Street and Broadway (Audubon Terrace). Tuesday-Saturday 10-4.30, Sundays 2-5. Admission free.
Founded by Archer M. Huntington in 1904, the society houses his collection of Spanish art and his library. There are several works by Goya, including *The Duchess of Alba* and paintings from the Medieval and Renaissance periods by El Greco (*Pietà, The Holy Family, St Jerome*), Luis Morales, Antonio Moro, José de Ribera, Francesco de Zurbarán, Diego Velazquez (*Count-Duke of Olivares, Portrait of a little girl*) and others. The sculpture exhibit contains a 13th-century *Mater Dolorosa.* Tombs and tomb effigies from the 16th and 17th centuries; Hispano-Moorish lustre ware and tiles, metalwork, textiles and coins, and statuary and mosaics from the Roman-Iberian period. A separate room houses modern paintings of Spain by Joaquin Sorolla y Bastida.

Jacques Marchais Center of Tibetan Art
340 Lighthouse Avenue, Staten Island. Tuesday-Friday 2-5; second and fourth Saturday and Sunday of each month 2-5; closed October 31-April 1. Charge for admission.
A research centre for Oriental art, particularly that of Tibet; originated by Mrs Harry Klauber (known professionally as Jacques Marchais), and housing her collection and library of books on Asian subjects. Stone figures of elephants and other animals adorn staircases in the terraced gardens, which also contain a lifesize Buddha and a lotus pool, a wishing well and an aviary. The museum building has the form of a Tibetan temple. Prayer wheels, incense burners and tankas (wall banners) and a three-tiered lamasery granite altar.

Jewish Museum
92nd Street and Fifth Avenue. Monday-Thursday 12-5, Fridays 11-3, Sundays 11-6. Closed Saturdays. Charge for admission.
Housed in the former residence of Felix M. Warburg, designed in French Renaissance style by C.P.H. Gilbert; 1908. New wing, the Albert List Building, designed by Samuel Glazer; 1963. The museum is sponsored by the Jewish Theological Seminary of America, and display a large collection of Jewish ceremonial art. From the historical collection: Torah arks, Torah wrappers, Menorahs (seven-branched candelabrae), parchment Torah scrolls, a Torah shrine of faience (Persia 16th century), a 16th-century Torah ark from Urbino, a gold Torah crown (Poland, 18th century). Modern ceremonial objects, bronze plaques with portraits of noted Jews; collection of Hebrew coins. Louise Nevelson's black construction *Homage to the Six Million* is also on display. 192.

Library-Museum of the Performing Arts
Lincoln Center. Monday-Friday 10-9, Saturdays 10-6. Admission free.
A division of the New York Public Library, which holds exhibits related to the performing arts: posters, scene designs, short films etc., and contemporary sculpture and painting. 187, 188.

Metropolitan Museum of Art
Fifth Avenue between 80th and 84th Streets. Temporary exhibits, programmes of lectures and concerts. Monday-Saturday 10-5, Tuesday nights until 10, Sundays and holidays 11-5.45. Admission by contribution.
Founded in 1870 by a group of New York citizens, most of them members of the Union League Club. The museum opened in its first permanent building in 1880. The core of its collections was a gift of Cypriot antiquities by General Louis Palma de Cesnola, the museum's first director, and a group of some 170 paintings, mostly Dutch and Flemish. The *West Wing* is a Ruskinian Gothic structure designed by Calvert Vaux and J. Wrey Mould. A connecting structure by Theodore Weston was added to the south in 1888. In the 1890s the central building, a grandiose conception in Roman style by Richard Morris Hunt, was begun and completed in 1902 by Hunt's son, Richard Howland Hunt. Major renovations were made for the museum's hundredth anniversary in 1970. The museum is on three levels, covering almost 20 acres of floor space. *Ground floor*: European Ceramics, Glass and Metalwork; the Junior Museum; Costume Institute (closed during process of reorganization); educational and photographic services, a slide library, a bookshop and a snack bar.
Main floor: the Great Hall, with an information desk, checking facilities, book and gift shops; restaurant (south wing); the period rooms of European Decorative Arts, Greek and Roman Art (south wing), Egyptian Art and Art of the Ancient Near East (north wing), Arms and Armour, Medieval halls and Treasury; the Grace Rainey Rogers Auditorium; the Library, entered by way of the 16th-century marble patio from the castle of Vélez Blanco, Almeria, Spain. *Second floor*: Greek and Roman collection, including Etruscan works (south wing); Ear Eastern Art and Islamic Art (north wing); Musical Instruments; the European Paintings Galleries; the American Paintings Galleries; the Drawing and Print collection.
The *American Wing* is a separate three-storeyed building, entered through the Equestrian Hall of Arms and Armour on the main floor, and containing American rooms, furnishings, artifacts and paintings from the Colonial period. *European paintings*: Dutch and Flemish

17th-century paintings include more than thirty paintings by Rembrandt, among them *Aristotle Contemplating the Bust of Homer, The Lady with a Pink* and *Bathsheba.* There are works by Frans Hals (*Merry Company*), Jan Vermeer (*Young Woman with a Water Jug; Lady with a Lute*), Pieter de Hooch, Gerard Terborch, Jan Steen, Jacob van Ruisdael and Meindert Hobbema (*Venus and Adonis*), Peter Paul Rubens, and portraits by Anthony van Dyck. Flemish paintings from the 15th century include Hubert van Eyck's panels *Crucifixion* and *Last Judgment,* a portrait of a Carthusian monk by Petrus Christus, paintings by Hans Memling and Rogier van der Weyden (*Francisco d'Este* and *Christ Appearing to His Mother.*

Flemish paintings of the 16th century by Gerard David, Joachim Patinir and Pieter Bruegel the Elder (*Harvesters*).

Spanish painting includes El Greco's *View of Toledo, Cardinal Guevara,* and *The Vision of St John;* Jose de Ribera's *The Holy Family,* Velazquez's *Christ and the Pilgrims at Emmaus* and the portrait of his assistant, *Juan de Pareja.* Works by Francisco Goya include *Don Manuel Osorio de Zuniga* and *Dona Narcisa Baranana de Goicoechea.*

Among the *Italian paintings* are works by the Sienese Sassetta; the Florentines Andrea del Castagno, Piero di Cosimo (*Hunting Scene* and *Return from the Hunt*), Andrea Mantegna (*The Adoration of the Shepherds*), Domenico Ghirlandaio (*Francesco Sassetti and his Son Teodoro*); the Venetians Carlo Crivelli, Vittore Carpaccio and Giovanni Bellini, and Titian (*Venus and the Lute Player*), Paulo Veronese, Tintoretto, Raphael (*Colonna Madonna*) and Michelangelo Caravaggio (*Musicians*). From later periods there are paintings by Giovanni Tiepolo, Antonio Canaletto and Francesco Guardi.

Among the *French paintings* are works by Claude Lorrain, Nicolas Poussin (*Blind Orion searching for the Rising Sun*), Georges de La Tour (*The Fortune Teller*), François Boucher and Jean Honoré Fragonard, Antoine Watteau (*Mezzetin*), and Jean Chardin (*Boy Blowing Bubbles*). French classicism is represented by Jacques Louis David (*The Death of Socrates*) and J.A.D. Ingres (several portraits and *Odalisque in Grisaille*). There are works by Eugène Delacroix, Théodore Géricault, Gustave Courbet, J.C. Camille Corot, Edouard Manet and Rosa Bonheur, and Impressionist and post-Impressionist works, including Pierre Auguste Renoir's *Madame Charpentier and her Children,* Claude Monet's *Rouen Cathedral,* Edgar Degas' *Rehearsal of the Ballet on the Stage,* several works by Paul Cézanne (*The Card Players, Mont Sainte-Victoire*), Georges Seurat (*La Parade de Cirque*), Vincent van Gogh, Paul Gauguin, Henri de Toulouse-Lautrec, Pierre Bonnard, Amadeo Modigliani and Pablo Picasso (*Gertrude Stein*).

English painting includes portraits by Thomas Gainsborough, Henry Raeburn, Sir Joshua Reynolds, Sir Thomas Lawrence and landscapes by John Constable (*Salisbury Cathedral*) and J.M.W. Turner (*Grand Canal, Venice*). German paintings include Albrecht Dürer's *Virgin and Child with St Anne,* Lucas Cranach's *The Judgment of Paris* and Hans Holbein's *Portrait of a member of the Wedigh family.*

Modern European sculpture includes works by Antonio Canova, Auguste Rodin, Antoine Bourdelle, Edgar Degas, Aristide Maillol and Henry Moore.

Among *American paintings* are J.S. Copley's *Samuel Verplanck* and *Midshipman Augustus Brine,* several by Benjamin West, portraits by Thomas Sully and Samuel F.B. Morse (*The Muse—Susan Walker Morse*). The Hudson River school contains works by Thomas Cole (*The Oxbow*), Asher B. Durand, Frederick E. Church and Albert P. Ryder (*Toilers of the Sea*); the expatriate J.A.McN. Whistler (*Portrait of Theodore Duret*), John Singer Sargent (*Madame X*), Winslow Homer and Thomas Eakins (*Max Schmidt in a Single Scull*). Representative paintings of The Eight are shown, Alfred Stieglitz's bequest of paintings by Arthur Dove, John Marin, Marsden Hartley, Georgia O'Keeffe and Charles Demuth, and other works include Edward Hopper's *From Williamsburg Bridge,* paintings by the American regionalists, notably Thomas Hart Benton (*Cotton Pickers*), Charles Burchfield, Stuart Davis, Andrew Wyeth, and by artists of the New York school, such as Josef Albers, Hans Hofmann, Arshile Gorky, Franz Kline, Jackson Pollock (*Autumn Rhythm*), Willem DeKooning, Adolph Gottlieb, Morris Louis, Mark Rothko, Barnett Newman, Frank Stella. *American sculpture* is represented by artists such as Frederick MacMonnies, Karl Bitter and Daniel Chester French, George Gray Barnard (*The Two Natures of Man*), William Zorach, John Flannagan, Alexander Calder and David Smith. *The Art of Antiquity*: Egyptian collection, including the Old Kingdom tomb of Peryneb, the Egyptian gold room, mummies and a variety of wooden and large and small-scale statuary. Works in heavy stone include, from the New Kingdom, the marble figure of Queen Hatshepsut (XVII Dynasty) as a sphinx. Art of the Ancient Near East includes Assyrian glazed brick lions from Babylon and the guardian figures from the palace of Ashurnasirpal II at Nimrud. Works from Sumer and pottery from Iran; gold and bronze artifacts from the Achaemenian Empire and late Sassanian period. Greece and Rome: Cycladic works, a *Kouros,* Etruscan artifacts and Cypriot sculpture, Roman sarcophagi and portrait busts, the painted bedroom of a villa near Boscoreale, head of the Emperor Constantine. Far Eastern Art: Chinese porcelain and bronzes. The *Sackler Gallery of Oriental Art* displays Chinese Buddhist sculpture, a mural from Shansi and examples of Japanese, Korean and Indian art. A long gallery is devoted to Islamic art.

Early Christian art is shown in the gallery on the north flank of the great staircase on the main floor, medieval art in the gallery on the south flank and in the medieval tapestry and medieval sculpture halls. The Treasury houses Burgundian sculpture groups, *The Entombment* and a *Pietà* (16the century), reliquaries and Limoges enamels.

The *French rooms* of decorative art are largely of the 17th and 18th centuries and include a Louis XVI grand salon from the Hôtel de Tessé in Paris, and the reconstruction of an 18th-century shop from the Ile St Louis. Works by Hyacinthe Rigaud, Boucher, Houdon, Clodion and others are displayed.

The *English rooms* include 17th-century wood-carving by Grinling Gibbons, and two late 18th-century rooms, decorated by Robert Adam, from Croome Court, Warwickshire and the dining-room from Lansdowne House, London.

The Italian group includes the inlaid wood mosaic of the 'studiolo' from the Ducal Palace at Gobbio (15th century), a Venetian bedroom of the early 18th century and a collection of small bronzes of the 16th and 17th centuries.

European ceramics: metalwork and glass, including the Rospigliosi Cup. Arms and Armour (Equestrian Court): examples of armour, including the parade helmet of Francis I, three complete sets of armour worn by Philip II of Spain and Oriental arms and armour. The *American Wing* houses three floors of American furnishings, decoration and craft. American rooms from the 17th to the 19th century show the growth and change of styles: the Verplanck drawing-room from 3 Wall Street, the Assembly Room from Gadsby's Tavern in Alexandria, Virginia, the entry of the Van Rensaller house at Albany and Pennsylvania Dutch and Shaker work. The museum will soon open a new gallery of musical instruments, displaying some of their four thousand instruments, including a violin by Stradivarius.

Works in the *Drawings and Prints* and *Photographic* collections are shown in small, thematic exhibitions on the *second floor. 28, 35, 89, 90, 92, 95, 98-9, 111, 112, 121, 166, 170, 227.*

Morgan Library - *see* Pierpont Morgan

MUSE (Broklyn Children's Museum)
1530 Bedford Avenue, Brooklyn. Tuesday-Friday 10 a.m.-10 p.m., Saturdays 10-5, Sundays 1-5. Admission free.
Housed in a remodelled pool room in a Brooklyn neighbourhood. Arts, crafts and photographs dealing mostly with African-American subjects. Provides a wide variety of educational and cultural activities for local children, including art classes, dance programmes, scientific experiments and natural history. 192.

Museum of American Folk Art
49 W. 53rd Street.
Begun in 1963 to foster an appreciation of native craftsmen and anonymous folk artists through its permanent collection and loan exhibitions. Weathervanes, cigar-store Indians, whirligigs, decoys, samplers, Shaker furniture and New Mexican santos. Limestone figures by Nashville-born Will Edmondson and the so-called Chief Tammany weathervane.

Museum of the American Indian (Heye Foundation)
Broadway and 155th Street (Audubon Terrace). Tuesday-Sunday 1-5. Admission free.
Established by George Heye and opened to the public 1922. Crafts, objects from daily life, religious and artistic artifacts from tribes in North and South America, arranged geographically, covering Indians of the Plains (baskets, representational and abstract art), Southeast (Seminole appliqué work), Basin-Plateau, New England, Canada, the Northwest Coast (monumental wood jambs, carved with animal and anthropomorphic shapes), Southwest (Kachina dolls), Mexico (poterry and silverwork), Central America, the West Indies, Columbia and Peru (gold work and pottery), Equador, Brazil and the Argentine.

Museum of the City of New York
Fifth Avenue between 103rd and 104th Streets. Tuesday-Saturday 10-5; Sundays and holidays 1-5. Admission free.
Housed in Gracie Mansion before moving to its present Georgian-style building in 1932. Paintings, prints, photographs and furnishings of New York City. A museum of fire-fighting is housed on the ground floor. The *first floor* has a room devoted to Dutch New York, as well as space for temporary exhibits. Portraits include works by John Trumbull (*Alexander Hamilton and his wife*), Gilbert Stuart, John Wesley Jarvis, J.S. Copley, Rembrandt Peale and others. The *second floor* has an exhibit of New York silver, Tiffany glass and a Marine Museum. A diorama depicts the history of the Stock Exchange. On the *third floor* is a diorama of an old New York street, as well as a collection of 19th-century toys, and several period rooms, including a drawing-room of the Federal period with furniture by Duncan Phyfe. Displayed on the *fifth floor* are rooms in Victorian taste, including portions of the house of John D. Rockefeller, which stood at 4 W. 54th Street, and a box from the old Metropolitan Opera House, which stood at 40th Street and Broadway until 1966. Walking tours of the city are conducted by the museum from April to October of each year. 9.

Museum of Contemporary Crafts
29 W. 53rd Street. Monday-Saturday 11-6; Sundays 1-6. Charge for admission.
Opened in 1956. Exhibitions of ceramics, textiles, metalwork, glassware etc. Shows, dealing with the craft possibilities of materials such as paper and

plastics. Presentation of exhibits often involves participation by spectators.

Museum of Modern Art
11 W. 53rd Street, between Fifth and Sixth Aves. Mondays 12-7; Tuesday-Saturday 11-6; Sundays 12-6; Thursdays till 9 p.m. Admission charge which includes ticket to film shows by application on day of showing.

Designed by Philip Goodwin and Edward Durrell Stone. Founded 1929 by a group of New Yorkers including Mrs Lillie P. Bliss and Mrs John D. Rockefeller, Jr. under the direction of Alfred H. Barr, Jr. From its beginning, the museum has encouraged contemporary art, and it has been instrumental in securing international recognition of the New York school of painting, and consequently the recognition of New York City as an international centre of artistic activity. The museum carries on a regular schedule of exhibitions which utilize the rooms on the first floor. The sculpture garden, designed 1951 by Philip Johnson, displays works by Auguste Rodin (*Balzac* and *John the Baptist*), Elie Nadelman, Henry Moore (a *Family Group*), David Smith, Alexander Calder and others.

The *second and third floors* house work from the permanent collection, arranged in chronological order, with painters of the same school grouped together. 19th century: works by Paul Cézanne (*The Bather* and several landscapes), Henri Rousseau (*The Dream*), Paul Gauguin and Vincent Van Gogh (*A Starry Night*) Georges Seurat, Pierre Bonnard and Edouard Vuillard. Paintings by André Derain, George Rouault, Henry Matisse and others show the work of the Fauves. Matisse and Picasso are represented by works from all periods of their production. The first Cubist picture *Les Demoiselles d'Avignon* (Picasso, 1907) is here, also *The Three Musicians* and *Girl before the Mirror*. George Braques, Juan Gris, Marc Chagall, Fernand Léger and Roger de la Fresnaye are also represented. The Futurist movement is represented by Umberto Boccioni (the sculpture *Unique Forms of Continuity in Space*) and Giacomo Balla. Expressionist painting by Emil Nolde, Ernest Kirchner and others. Works from representational movements of the 20s, works by Otto Dix, Pavel Teheltichew, Giorgio de Chirico, René Magritte, Joan Miró, Christian Berard, Marcel Duchamp and Max Ernst, Ben Shahn, Peter Blume, Max Beckmann, Wassily Kandinsky, Paul Klee, Piet Mondrian, and Mexican painters Siquerios and Orozco. American works displayed on the *second floor* include Edward Hopper's *House by the Railroad*, and Andrew Wyeth's *Christina's World*. An entire room is reserved for the display of Claude Monet's vast, three-part painting of *Water Lilies*. This floor also houses the Philip Goodwin Galleries of Architecture and Design and displays modern furnishings from Art Nouveau to the present; chairs by G.T. Reitveldt, Marcel Breuer, Mies

van der Rohe; appliances, china, etc., many from work of the Bauhaus.

Paintings on the *third floor* include Picasso's *Guernica* and developments in art since 1940. Abstract French works include paintings by Georges Mathieu, Pierre Soulages and others; 'art brut' works by Jean Dubuffet and paintings by the Englishman, Francis Bacon. The New York school includes canvases by Arshile Gorky, Bradley Tomlin, Franz Kline, William Baziotes, Mark Rothko, Mark Tobey, Willem de Kooning, Sam Francis, Ad Rinehart and others. Pop artists include Robert Rauschenberg and Jasper Johns. Also on the *third floor* is sculpture by Wilhelm Lembruck (*Kneeling Woman* and *Standing Youth*), Alberto Giacometti (*The Palace at 4 a.m.*), Julio Gonzales, Alexander Calder, Seymour Lipton, Richard Lippold, Constantin Brancusi (*Bird in Space, Fish*) and others. Here are also the Paul Sachs Galleries of Prints and the Edward Steichen Photography Center. The museum has an art reference library, print room, film library and theatre on the *ground floor*. There are jazz concerts and classes for art in all ages are sponsored. 134, *137-41,* 142, 143, 145, *148,* 149, 150, 166, 170, 176, 184.

Museum of Primitive Art
15 W. 554th Street. Wednesday-Friday 11-5; Saturdays 12-5. Charge for admission.

Founded in 1957 by Governor Nelson Rockefeller. Art of native cultures of Oceania, Africa and the Americas. Masks, featherwork, Benin bronzes, Melanesian wood carvings. The permanent collection has recently been given to the Metropolitan Museum of Art, but for the time being will continue to be housed at the Museum of Primitive Art. 176.

New York City Hall
Between Broadway and Park Row in City Hall Park. Governor's Room open Monday-Friday 10-3; closed weekends and holidays. Admission free.

In the Governor's Room, Board of Estimate and Council Chamber hang many notable portraits by American artists: John Trumbull (*Washington, Clinton, Hamilton* and *Jay*); John Wesley Jarvis (*Oliver Hazard Perry*); Thomas Sully (*Stephen Decatur*); George Catlin (*De Witt Clinton*); *Martin Van Buren* by Henry Inman and the famous *Marquis de Lafayette* by Samuel F.B. Morse. 25.

New York Cultural Center (originally the Gallery of Modern Art)
2 Columbus Circle. Tuesday-Sunday 11-8. Charge for admission.

Designed by Edward Durrell Stone; 1964. In association with Fairleigh Dickinson University, the Cultural Center holds exhibitions of contemporary art in many mediums. Photographic exhibitions are frequently held. The small theatre is used for film programmes and concerts. 214.

New York Historical Society
Central Park West and 77th Street.

Tuesday-Friday and Sundays 1-5; Saturdays 10-5; closed Mondays and in August. Admission free.

Organized by John Pintard early in the 19th century, the society has been housed in its present building since 1908. *Basement:* turn-of-the-century carriages. *First floor:* 'elephant folios' of John James Audubon (*Birds of America*) and some of the 460 original Audubon watercolours owned by the society, from which they were made. New York silver, portraits from the Belknap collection, glass paperweights and early advertising. *Second floor:* antique toys, a gallery of artifacts, prints and drawings illustrating the history of New York and several rooms of the 17th and 18th centuries, complete with furnishings. *Third floor:* American folk arts and crafts, and a number of primitive paintings. *Fourth floor:* much of the society's collection of American paintings, including colonial portraits, many fine paintings by the Peale family and a large gallery of the work of the Hudson River school: Thomas Cole's *The Course of Empire*, a Cole self-portrait and paintings by Durand, Thomas Moran and J.F. Kensett. Portraits of American leaders from the early days of the Republic through Lincoln are shown in a separate gallery. There is also a group of European paintings drawn from collections bequeathed to the society in the 19th century. Research library with files of the architectural office of McKim, Mead & White. *12, 30, 32.*

New York Public Library

Central Building, Fifth Avenue between 40th and 42nd Streets. Monday-Saturday 9 a.m.-10 p.m. Admission free.

Designed by Carrère & Hastings; 1911. Formed from the combination of the Astor, Lenox and Tilden libraries early in this century, the New York Public Library now includes over 7,500,000 volumes, second in size only to the Library of Congress; almost 5,000,000 volumes are kept at the Central Building. Specialized collections include the Berg collection of manuscripts (the manuscript of T.S. Eliot's *The Waste Land* is a recent acquisition) and the Phelps Stokes collection of pictures relating to the history of New York. Asher B. Durand's painting, *Kindred Spirits*, hangs opposite the main reading room. *Third floor:* manuscripts, portraits, including works by J.S. Copley, Sir Joshua Reynolds, Henry Raeburn, John Trumbull, Samuel F.B. Morse and Gilbert Stuart, and the Print Room. Regular exhibitions of prints, books and documents are held in the Fifth Avenue lobby and library. *10, 40, 62, 119.*

Nicholas Roerich Museum

319 W. 107th Street. Monday-Friday and Sundays 2-5; closed Saturdays, holidays and during July and August. Admission free.

Devoted to the work and collections of Nicholas Roerich (1874-1947), artist, scene-designer, explorer and writer,

founder of the Master Institute and originator of the Roerich pact, an agreement to respect cultural sites and institutions in time of war. Exhibits include paintings by Roerich of mountains, saints and madonnas and a variety of objects from India, Tibet and the Himalayas.

Pierpont Morgan Library

29-33 E. 36th Street, between Madison and Park Avenues. Winter, Monday-Saturday 9.30-5; closed Sundays and holidays. Summer, Monday-Friday 9.30-5 (in August only the reading room is open). Admission free.

Designed by Charles F. McKim; 1906. Addition designed by Benjamin Wister Morris; 1928. The main building is a marble palace in severe Italian Renaissance style, built for J. Pierpont Morgan (1837-1913). Collection includes illuminated and textual manuscripts of the 6th to 16th centuries; autograph manuscripts by Milton, Keats, Byron and other notable writers; a Gutenberg bible on vellum and the famous section of the *Book of Hours of Catherine of Cleves*. Master drawings from the 14th to 18th centuries are shown in changing exhibitions of manuscripts, correspondence and art. Morgan's study, arranged as he left it, contains a number of paintings and other art works: *Virgin and Saints adoring the Child*, by Perugino; *Portrait of a Moor*, by Tintoretto; portraits of Martin Luther and his wife by Lucas Cranach the Elder; portraits by Hans Memling and several other paintings. Several small Renaissance sculptures in marble; also the Stavelot Triptych, a portable altar in gold and enamel, from the 12th century. *80, 112.*

Riverside Museum

310 Riverside Drive and 103rd Street. Tuesday-Sunday 1-5; closed Mondays, holidays and during July and August.

Connected with the Master Institute, a school of art, drama and dance founded by Nicholas Roerich, this privately endowed museum, founded in 1938, has a permanent collection of Nepalese, Tibetan and Japanese art, and arranges exhibits of contemporary art, graphics, photography and multi-media works.

Solomon R. Guggenheim Museum

1071 Fifth Avenue betwen 88th and 89th Streets. Tuesday-Saturday 10-6; Thursdays until 9 p.m.; Sundays and holidays 12-6. Charge for admission.

Designed by Frank Lloyd Wright, 1959, it is a controversial structure with a hollow five-storey cylinder of concrete, with a continuous ramp on the inside winding from top to bottom, and a glass dome 95 feet high. The Guggenheim began in 1937 as a museum of non-objective art, under the patronage of Solomon R. Guggenheim, but soon broadened its scope to include work from the entire range of modern art. The permanent collection of over 4,000 works includes numerous works by Wassily Kandinsky, Fernand Lèger, Henri Rousseau, Modigliani, Picasso and

Braque, the Eiffel tower series by French cubist Robert Delaunay, and sculpture by Constantin Brancusi. The Guggenheim also owns works by artists of the New York school: Franz Kline, Mark Rothko, Barnett Newman, Adolph Gottlieb, Ellsworth Kelly, Adja Junkers, Jackson Pollock, David Smith, Robert Rauschenberg, William Baziotes, Jasper Johns, and works by Jean Dubuffet. A ceramic wall by Joan Miró is installed at the first level of the ramp in the central gallery; an Alexander Calder mobile usually hangs in the well of the museum. The Justin K. Thannheuser bequest to the museum, housed in a gallery separate from the ramp, contains Impressionist and Post-Impressionist work, including Auguste Renoir (*Woman with a Parrot*), Paul Cézanne (*Portrait of the Artist's Wife*) and paintings by Vincent van Gogh, Edouard Vuillard, Henri de Toulouse-Lautrec (*Moulin de la Galette*, 1900) and the young Picasso. The museum holds retrospective exhibitions and exhibitions of contemporary art, and sponsors the annual Guggenheim International Exhibition. 150, 160, *165*, *166*, *170*, 174-6.

Studio Museum in Harlem
2033 Fifth Avenue at 125th Street. Mondays and Wednesdays 10 a.m.-9 p.m.; Thursdays and Fridays 10-6; Saturdays and Sundays 1-6. Admission free.
A museum of contemporary Black art, with regular exhibitions of painting, sculpture and works in other media. Occasional historical exhibits.

Whitney Museum of American Art
945 Madison Avenue at 75th Street. Monday-Saturday 11-5; Sunday 12-6. Charge for admission.
Designed by Marcel Breuer and Hamilton Smith; 1966. Founded by Gertrude Vanderbilt Whitney in 1929 with her personal collection, and is primarily of American art since 1900. Annual exhibitions of American painting and sculpture, retrospective and special exhibitions. The Eight and the Ashcan school are well represented (John Sloan's *Backyards, Greenwich Village*; George Luks' *Mrs Gamley*). Works by pioneer American modernists, including Max Weber, Arthur Dove, Marsden Hartley, as well as by Georgia O'Keeffe, Charles Sheeler and Joseph Stella (*Brooklyn Bridge: Variation on an old theme*); watercolours by Charles Burchfield and Edward Hopper (*Early Sunday Morning*). The American regionalists are represented. Stuart Davis (*Owh! in San Pão*) is a link between the group around Robert Henri and the Abstract Expressionists, such as Arshile Gorky, Barnett Newman, William Baziotes, Mark Rothko, Jackson Pollock and others. Paintings by pop and protopop artists, including Robert Rauschenberg and Jasper Johns. The sculpture collection, displayed in a sunken stone-flagged court, includes work by Gaston Lachaise, William Zorach, Alexander Calder, David Smith, Louise Nevelson and others. 124, *134*, *168*, *179*, *182*, *186*, 190-2.

Historic Buildings and Churches

Abigail Adams Smith House, *421 E. 61st St at York Ave*; 1799. A stone house in simple Georgian style, with a two-storey balustraded porch facing the East River. Once the stables of a house planned but never built by Col. William Smith, son-in-law of John Adams, second president of the U.S. Used as a residence from 1833; now headquarters of the Colonial Dames of America (seen by their permission). 22.

Adventure Playgrounds - *see* **Central Park.**

American Academy of Dramatic Arts, formerly Colony Club. Designed by McKim, Mead & White; 1905. A Georgian building with unusual, end-out brickwork.

American Radiator Building, *40 W. 40th St.* Designed by Raymond Hood; 1924. A Gothicized office building with distinctive facing of black brick and gold terra-cotta, and grand lobby. 128.

The Arsenal - *see* **Central Park.**

Astor Place, *between E. 8th St and the Bowery.* Centre of a fashionable district at the middle of the 19th century. Homes of the Vanderbilts, Delanos and Astors were nearby. Cooper Union was erected on the east in 1859. The Astor Library and LaGrange Terrace on Lafayette St are buildings of note in the vicinity. Burnham's Wanamaker store, now an office building, is on the west side of Astor Place. On a traffic island in the center Bernard Rosenthal's movable cubic sculpture, *Alamo*, has recently been erected. 64.

Audubon Terrace, *155th St and Broadway.* Designed by Charles P. Huntington; 1908. A courtyard of classic design, with balustrades and ornamental sculpture flanked by museum buildings which stand on land formerly part of John James Audubon's farm.

Automation House, *49 E. 68th St.* Designed by Lehrecke & Tonetti; 1969. Reconditioned 19th-century town houses with facilities and space for artistic, industrial and educational projects involving advanced technology. 223.

Banco do Brasil - *see* **Fifth Ave.**

Bartow-Pell Mansion, *Shore Road, in Pelham Bay Park, Bronx. Open Tuesday, Friday and Sunday 1-5. Admission charge.* Originally built in 1675 for the Lords of the Manor of Pelham. Remodelled and enlarged in the Federal style, probably by Minard Lafever, 1836-45. Now the headquarters of the International Garden Club, it has remarkable furnishings, extensive gardens, and a view of Long Island Sound.

The Battery. Originally a row of guns at the extreme lower tip of Manhattan, later the fortifications erected there, of which Castle Clinton, originally the West Battery, built in 1807 by John McComb, Jr., remains today. The East Battery, now Castle Williams, is on Governor's Island. Adjacent to the Park, ferries leave for Staten Island (24 hour service), and for the Statue of Liberty (every hour on the hour during the day). *25, 207, 208, 217, 244.*

Bayard (Condict) Building, *65 Bleeker St at Crosby St.* The only building by Louis Sullivan (1898) in New York. It has the vertical elements and decoration based on natural forms which are characteristic of his designs. Portions of the façade have been removed and are at the Brooklyn Museum. *101, 103.*

Begrish Hall - *see* **New York University,** University Heights Campus.

Bobst Library - *see* **New York University,** Washington Square Campus.

The Bowery, *extending from Cooper Square south to Canal St.* Settled early in the 19th century, the area and the street itself were once noted for their theatres and teeming city life, but dwindled to become a refuge for derelicts, who lived in the shadow of the Third Ave El, which passed through here. It is still an area for the down-and-out, though it is also a commercial district and artists have begun to recondition the many loft buildings in the vicinity. Many of the smaller buildings date from the Federal Period. *28.*

Bowling Green, *foot of Broadway.* Formalized as New York's first park in 1732. The present fence dates from 1771. Figure of Abraham de Peyster, Mayor of New York 1691-95, by George Bissell (1896).

801 Broadway (formerly **McCreery Store**), *at 11th St.* Designed by John Kellum; 1868. A large construction of cast-iron. *57.*

900 Broadway, *at 20th St.* Designed by McKim, Mead & White; 1887. An early product of the firm, rounded to the corner, with a finely detailed brick wall rising above high arches.

Bronx-Whitestone Bridge, *East River between Bron and Queens.* Designed by O. H. Ammann (engineer) and Aymar Embury II (architect); 1939. A notably well-designed suspension bridge built during the city's period of large-scale public works. *145, 211.*

Brookdale Dental Center, *First Ave and 24th St.* Designed by Pomerance & Breines; 1970. Sculptural vertical shafts break the expanse of glass walls.

Brooklyn Botanic Garden, *Eastern Parkway, Brooklyn.* Noted particularly for its Japanese Garden (1915), flowering cherry trees, and meticulously accurate replica of the stone garden of the Royanji Temple, Kyoto (1963), this 50-acre tract also includes a rose garden, herb garden and fragrance garden for the blind.

Brooklyn Bridge, *City Hall Park and the East River, between Manhattan and Brooklyn.* Planned and engineered by John A. Roebling and built by Washington Roebling, 1867-83. A single span hung from cables, springing from two double-arched masonry towers of Gothic aspect. A raised board-walk over the traffic lanes permits a spectacular view of Manhattan, Brooklyn, and the harbour. *64, 73, 79, 80, 111, 112.*

Brooklyn Heights, *Brooklyn Bridge to Atlantic Ave, Fulton St to the Esplanade, Brooklyn.* This residential area, built for the most part between 1820 and 1890, has many superb houses, from Federal to late Victorian in style. From the Esplanade (1950-51), built above the Brooklyn-Queens expressway skirting the East River, there is a superb view of Lower Manhattan and the upper bay.

Bryant Park, *behind the New York Public Library, W.40th to W.42nd St between Fifth and Sixth Ave.* Named for William Cullen Bryant in 1884, it occupies the site on which New York's Crystal Palace was erected. Its present formal layout dates from the 1930s. *63.*

Cadman Plaza, *at the Brooklyn Bridge, between Fulton and Adams St.* A park created in the 1950s as a result of the demolition of several blocks of houses and the elevated tracks which passed over the Brooklyn Bridge. J.Q.A. Ward's *Henry Ward Beecher* (1891) stands in the southern part of the park. Beecher once preached at nearby Plymouth Church in Brooklyn Heights. *90.*

Carl Schurz Park, *East End Ave to the East River at 86th St.* Named for Carl Schurz, a German immigrant and a prominent public figure in 19th-century New York. The setting for Gracie Mansion, this small park is lifted high above F.D.R. Drive and provides a view of the East River boat traffic and the bridges to the borough of Queens. *146.*

Carnegie Hall, *W. 57th St and Seventh Ave.* Designed by William B. Tuthill; Dankmar Adler and Richard Morris Hunt, consultants; 1891. Formerly the home of the New York Philharmonic, and renowned for its acoustics, it was saved from demolition and reconditioned in the 1960s. The Renaissance-style building also contains a recital hall, a theatre, and a number of studios and apartments; a multipurpose structure like Adler & Sullivan's Auditorium Building in Chicago. 185.

Carver Houses Plaza, *99th to 101st St, Madison to Park Ave.* Designed by Pomerance & Breines, J. Paul Friedberg, landscape architect; 1965. Multilevel plaza, with walls and walkways, sections for individual and group use. 236.

Cast-Iron District, *from Worth St north to Houston St, the Bowery west to West Broadway.* Most cast-iron construction from the late 19th century is concentrated in this area. Built for light manufacturing, some are still in use, though many have been converted into artists' studios and apartments. Canal St, Broadway, Worth St and Greene St have notable examples. *See also* Soho.

Cathedral of St John the Divine (Protestant Episcopal), *112th St and Amsterdam Ave.* The choir and crossing of this huge edifice were built to the original Byzantine-Romanesque design of Heins & LaFarge; 1891-1911. Ralph Adams Cram's revised design of 1911 was French Gothic, and the nave and west front were constructed to his plan 1911-42. Plans for finishing it, however, have been abandoned.

Central Park, *between Central Park South (59th St) and 110th St, Fifth Ave to Central Park West, comprising 840 acres.* Built on land set aside by a commission of citizens, which originally included Andrew Jackson Downing and William Cullen Bryant, in 1857, and landscaped, between 1860 and 1880, to a plan called Greensward, by Frederick L. Olmsted and Calvert Vaux. As well as footpaths, bridle-paths and carriage drives, kept separate by bridges in some spots, the plan includes four transverse roads, laid below the park level so that vehicular traffic does not interfere with the park, an innovation remarkable for its time.

A description of the park might best follow a route from south to north, beginning with the entrance at Fifth Ave and 59th St. To the right of this lies the Zoo, one of whose focii is the Arsenal (1847) designed by Martin Thompson, now the office of the New York City Department of Parks and Recreation. There is also a children's zoo, north of the main Zoo. To the left as one enters at Central Park South is Conservatory Pond with its wildlife refuge. Skirting its edge on the north, one comes to Woolman Rink, scene of winter ice skating and summer concerts. Not far beyond to the West is the carrousel, and further west lies a complex of lawns which reaches to the Columbus Circle entrance. Near Central Park West at 67th St is Richard Dattner's Adventure Playground, with its fresh structures for creative play, and Tavern on the Green, a restaurant made from an old sheep-fold. Sheep kept here used to graze on Sheep Meadow, the vast lawn to the east, now the scene of sports, concerts and demonstrations. East of Sheep Meadow lies the main

architectural grouping of the park: The Mall and The Terrace. The Mall is a long wide walk lined with statuary and flanked on the east by a bandshell; it leads north to The Terrace, from whose balustrades one passes down stone stairs with decorative railings to the Bethesda Fountain, with its sculpted *Angel of the Waters* by Emma Stebbins, at the centre of a small plaza which fronts on the lake. Rowboats may be rented at the boathouse at the lake's eastern end. North of the lake lies a complex of hilly paths and lawns called the Ramble, at the far end of which rises Belvedere Castle, a mock-medieval construction which closes the vista from The Terrace, and in turn overhangs the New Lake. North and slightly west of the New Lake is the Delacorte Theater, open-air home of the park's free, public summer Shakespeare productions. Further west, near the 81st St entrance, is another Adventure Playground. Between the Belvedere and the Delacorte lies a garden said to be planted with all the species mentioned in Shakespeare's plays. North of the Delacorte lies the vast oval Great Lawn.

From 72nd St north at the park's east side one finds Conservatory Water, where children sail model boats and clamber over the statues, figures of *Hans Christian Andersen* (by Georg Lober) and *Alice in Wonderland* (José de Creeft). At 81st St behind the Metropolitan Museum is The Obelisk, 1600 BC, erected here in 1877, the gift of the Khedive of Egypt. Tal Streeter's zig-zag, red-painted *Endless Column,* at 79th St and Fifth Avenue, stands in humorous contrast to it. North of the Metropolitan lies the large Reservoir, which runs north to 100th St. There are a number of sports fields, and on the west the Great Hill, with a Blockhouse. From the Pool at 100th St. Further east are more hills, and the one formal element is Conservatory Garden, planted with flowering trees, which lies along Fifth Ave near 104th St. 64, *64,* 70, 73, 97, 175, 236.

Century Association, *7 W. 43rd St, between Fifth and Sixth Ave.* Designed by McKim, Mead & White; 1891. A delicate Italian Renaissance façade graces this long-established club for intellectuals and 'men of accomplishment'.

Charlton St, *between Varick St and Sixth Ave in Lower Manhattan.* The block contains a row of typical New York town houses from the 1820s. 25.

Chase Manhattan Plaza, *between Nassau, William, Liberty and Pine St,* in the centre of New York's financial district. Designed by Skidmore, Owings & Merrill; 1960. Site of SOM's Chase Manhattan Bank Building, 800 feet tall, with a glass and aluminum curtain wall, which inaugurated the contemporary rebuilding of Lower Manhattan. In the large plaza's sunken courtyard is Isamu Noguchi's water garden. 194, 208.

Chatham Towers (1965), *Chatham Green (1961), south of Worth St, east* *of the Civic Center.* Designed by Kelly & Gruzen. The Towers are of concrete, in an interesting combination of forms; the buildings have outlines similar to monumental sculpture. Chatham Green has an undulating façade, with galleries. 79, 217, 224, 236.

Chelsea, *from 14th St to 30th St, Seventh Ave to the Hudson River,* a residential and commercial district of Manhattan. Originally divided into lots and settled in the 1830s, it still possesses rows of elegant town houses built in the middle and late 19th century. The Chelsea Hotel on 23rd St (Hubert, Pirsson & Co; 1884), with interesting wrought-iron balconies, was one of the first New York apartment houses. Plaques outside commemorate writers who have stayed there. 83-4, 146.

Chinatown, the area of Chinese immigrant settlement in New York, extends roughly from Canal St to the Brooklyn Bridge on Manhattan's lower east side. Mott St is lined with Chinese restaurants and shops. The area contains examples of early 19th-century church architecture (Mariners' Temple, q.v.) and, at its southern border, the modern apartment complexes, Chatham Towers and Chatham Green (q.v.). 218.

Chrysler Building, *42nd St and Lexington Ave.* Designed by William Van Alen; 1930. Third tallest building in New York (1048 feet to the top of the spire), it is ornamented with large expanses of stainless steel in Art Deco designs, some similar to those which appeared on Chrysler automobiles of the 1930s. *123*, 128.

Church of the Ascension, (Protestant Episcopal) *10th St and Fifth Ave.* Designed by Richard Upjohn; 1841. A Gothic Revival structure. The interior was remodelled 1885-89 by McKim, Mead & White. John LaFarge painted the large altar mural of the Ascension at that time and designed several of the stained glass windows. The marble altar reliefs are by Augustus St-Gaudens.

Church of the Epiphany, (Roman Catholic) *Second Ave and 22nd St.* Designed by Belfatto & Pavarini; 1967. A modern church, whose form is made from a combination of plain walls with rounded corners and sharply-angled roofs, plus a tube-like spire, all covered in dark brick. The overall L-shape permits a plaza in front of the church. 215, 217, *218*.

Church of the Resurrection, (East Harlem Protestant Parish) *325 E.101st St between First and Second Ave.* Designed by Victor Lundy; 1965. A windowless red brick church with a stark, dramatic sanctuary. 214.

City Hall - *see* **New York City Hall.**

Civic Center Synagogue, *White St between Church St and Broadway.* Designed by William Breger; 1963. The ballooning concrete façade of this building begins above the plaza level. The entrance is recessed deep under the

curve, a garden seen behind it, and the mass of the building seems to float. Murals by Tania in interior. 215, *218*.

College of the City of New York, *133rd to 140th St, bounded by Convent, Amsterdam, and St Nicholas Ave.* One of several municipal colleges. The south campus, with red-brick buildings in Flemish style, was once the property of the Academy (and Convent) of the Sacred Heart. The buildings of the north campus, designed by George B. Post; 1904, are of Manhattan schist, stone excavated during the construction of the nearby Broadway subway.

Colonnade Row - *see* **LaGrange Terrace.**

Columbia Broadcasting System (CBS) Building, *51 W. 52nd St at Sixth Ave.* Designed by Eero Saarinen; 1965. This striking, sombre tower is a free-standing 38-storey structure with a concrete frame, sheathed in dark gray granite. *205*, 206.

Columbia University, *roughly 114th St to 120th St between Broadway and Amsterdam Ave.* North campus designed by McKim, Mead & White; Low Library designed by McKim; 1897. The original complex of buildings, on land terraced above the level of surrounding streets, is dominated by Low Library, in Roman style, with an Ionic portico and a low dome. Around it, connected by a paved paths and balustrades, stand Italianate buildings of brick with corner quoins of stone, and an elaborate domed chapel, with a domed hall to balance it. The south campus, built later by a variety of architects, holds roughly to the style of the north campus, but arrangement is less complex. 88, 206.

Columbus Circle, *Broadway at 59th St, southwest corner of Central Park.* In the centre of this major traffic circle at the top of a column stands the figure of *Columbus* (Gaetano Russo, 1892). Around its base fountains have recently been added. At the Park corner is the *Maine Memorial,* designed by H. Van Buren Magonigle (1913) with sculpture by Attilio Piccirille. Around the edge of the circle, the most notable buildings are the New York Coliseum, a commercial exhibition hall; the office tower of the Gulf and Western Building; and Edward Durrell Stone's New York Cultural Center; 1965. 211.

Coney Island, *Gravesend section of south Brooklyn. Open in winter 10-5 daily and from Memorial Day to Labor Day 10-6. Admission charge.* An area of wooden beach hotels and piers in the 19th century, Coney Island became a famed public beach and amusement area with a boardwalk. Many of the rides and amusement areas are gone, but some remain, housed in extravagant buildings built by local carpenters and covered with bright signs. Nathan's Famous, noted for its hot dogs, is on the boardwalk, as is the New York Aquarium (Harrison & Abramovitz, 1955). 112.

Conference House (Billopp House), *foot of Hylan Boulevard, Staten Island;* 1680. *Open daily 10-5; closed Mondays. Admission charge for adults; children free if accompanied.* A large fieldstone house built by a British naval captain. In September 1776, it was the site of a conference between Lord Howe and delegates of the Continental Congress, who attempted to resolve differences between England and the Colonies without going to war. 16.

Co-op City, *west of Hutchinson River Parkway, Bronx.* Designed by Herman Jessor; 1971. A group of 35 high-rise structures and 236 two-family houses, built as middle-income housing on a once marshy tract in the North Bronx, providing housing for 60,000 people on 300 acres. 202.

Cooper Union, *7th St to Astor Place, Fourth Ave to Bowery.* Designed by Frederick Peterson; 1859. A tall Italianate brownstone school building, the oldest extant steel-framed structure in the U.S. Steel beams came from the factories of Peter Cooper, American industrialist and philanthropist, who founded the art and engineering school to provide training for talented and industrious students. Steel framing provides freedom of planning for the building's interior unavailable before. In the Great Hall Lincoln gave a significant speech in 1860. Augustus St-Gaudens' *Peter Cooper* (1897) stands in Cooper Square, south of the building, on a base designed by Stanford White. *61, 64, 90, 93, 224.*

Customs House - *see* **U.S. Customs House.**

Daily News Building, *220 E. 42nd St and Second Ave.* Designed by Raymond Hood and John Mead Howells; 1930. Addition by Harrison & Abramovitz; 1958. A purely vertical striped design using white and brown brick, it was one of New York's first buildings; in severely modern style. *128, 135.*

The Dakota, *Central Park West and 72nd St.* Designed by Henry Hardenbergh; 1884. A massive block of yellow brick with the pinnacles, gables and balconies of a European chateau, it was one of New York's first luxury apartment houses, and has always been a favoured address for persons prominent in the arts. 83.

DeVinne Press Building, *399 Lafayette St at 4th St.* Designed by Babb, Cook & Willard 1885. Broad, regular arches in the severe brick façade, and scrupulous detailing, make this massive masonry bearing-wall commercial structure a fine example of the influence of H.H. Richardson's Romanesque Revival style in New York. 82.

Dyckman House, *Broadway and W. 204th St. Open daily 11-5. Closed Mondays. Admission free.* Thought to be the oldest house in Manhattan. Rebuilt *c.* 1783 by William Dyckman, it has the gambrel roof and fieldstone lower

walls characteristic of a Dutch country house; contains family artifacts. 12, *13.*

East Midtown Plaza, *23rd to 27th St, Second to First Ave.* Designed by Davis, Brody & Associates; 1970. A complex of high-rise and low-rise apartments, interspersed with plazas, shops and walks, designed to revitalize this predominantly institutional area. Together with Waterside, also designed by Davis, Brody, and planned for construction between 23rd and 30th St east River Drive. 218, 233.

Ellis Island, *in New York Harbor, southwest of Lower Manhattan.* Site of the United States Immigration Station. The late Victorian buildings which housed the station are now deserted, and the island is scheduled for new use.

Empire State Building, *350 Fifth Ave between 33rd and 34th St. Observatory open 9.30 a.m.-midnight daily. Admission charge.* Designed by Shreve, Lamb & Harmon; 1931. The tallest building in the world for a long time, it is now surpassed in height by the towers of the World Trade Center (q.v.). An office building clad in limestone and aluminium, with a large setback from the first few floors to the tower proper. The observation deck at the 86th floor level is one of the best places from which to view New York. *121, 128, 245.*

Evening Post Building (now **Garrison Building**), *Vesey St between Church St and Broadway.* Designed by Robert D. Kohn; 1906. An office building with art nouveau decoration at the top. *105, 106.*

Federal Building - *see* **U.S. Federal Building.**

Federal Hall National Memorial, *28 Wall St at Nassau St. Open Monday-Friday 9-4.30. Admission free.* Designed by Ithiel Town, Alexander Jackson Davis, and John Frazee; 1842. Built in the form of a marble Doric temple, its major interior space is a rotunda. The most notable monument of Greek Revival style in New York, it served originally as a Customs House, then as a Sub-Treasury building. Built on the site of Federal Hall on whose balcony George Washington took the oath of office in 1789 as first president of the U.S., hence its name. The stone on which Washington stood is on display in the rotunda of the present building and there are rooms portraying American history. J.Q.A. Ward's full-length portrait sculpture of *Washington* (1883) is placed on a podium above the steps on the Wall Street Side. *86, 90.*

Fifth Avenue, *from 34th St north to the Plaza.* The city's famous shopping street. Parts of it have recently been zoned in order to protect the area from further office building construction. Speciality shops and department stores (Saks Fifth Avenue, F.A.O. Schwartz, B. Altman, Lord & Taylor) are here, as are the major jewellers (Tiffany, Cartier, Harry Winston). The street is also the location of many foreign airline offices, each of which has attempted an individual façade. Notable banks are the Israeli Discount Bank, at 43rd St; the Manufacturers Hanover Trust bank (q.v.) at 43rd; the Banco do Brasil at 44th St. There are also bookstores (Brentano's, Scribners (q.v.), Rizzoli), churches (St Patrick's Cathedral (q.v.) and St Thomas's (q.v.). In the lobby of the Corning Glass building (Harrison & Abramovitz; 1959) at 56th St there is a mural by Josef Albers. 79, 110, *126*, 197, 201.

First National City Bank, *55 Wall St.* Originally the Merchants' Exchange. Designed by Isaiah Rogers; 1842. Remodelled 1907 by McKim, Mead & White. An imposing Greek Revival structure of granite with Ionic colonnade. 49.

Flatiron Building, *23rd St between Broadway and Fifth Ave.* Designed by Daniel H. Burnham; 1902. Originally the Fuller building, its popular name derives from its sharply triangular shape. Faced with rusticated limestone, in a Renaissance fashion, but with a steel-cage structure and regular fenestration, it strikes a balance between eclectic decoration and modern construction design. 104, *108*.

Flushing Meadow Park, *Queens.* The site of two world's fairs, in 1939 and 1964, it has recently been developed as the major park for Queens. It contains a lake, and is near Shea Stadium, built in 1964, one of New York's major sports areas with facilities for baseball and football. From the 1964 fair, two notable structures remain: the Museum of Science and Technology, by Harrison & Abramovitz, and the New York State Pavilion, an open, circular structure with a translucent roof supported by cables, designed by Philip Johnson.

Ford Foundation Building, *E. 42nd St between First and Second Ave.* Designed by Kevin Roche, John Dinkeloo Associates, 1967. An elegant 15-storey building sheathed in granite. Its offices are arranged in an L-shape, all looking out onto a glass-enclosed, 130-foot high, skylighted indoor courtyard, planted with trees and shrubs. 210-11, *214*.

Fort Tryon Park, *W. 192nd St to Dyckman St, Broadway to Riverside Drive.* Designed by Frederick Law Olmsted, Jr. A gift to the city from the Rockefeller family, it contains the remains of Fort Tryon, a Revolutionary War fortification. Noted for its flower gardens and its view of the Hudson, the park is also the site of The Cloisters (q.v.). 121.

Franklin Delano Roosevelt Drive (East River Drive), *125th St south to the Manhattan Bridge, along the East River.* Designed by Harvey Stevenson and Cameron Clark; 1938. A well-planned and scenically exciting highway along the edge of the East River. Uptown it is placed well below the level of the city streets, parks and buildings, which are often continued over the drive, providing access to river views for residents. In its lower reaches it becomes an express highway with park-like strips between it and the river. 146.

Fraunce's Tavern, *54 Pearl St at Broad St. Open weekdays 10-4; Saturdays 10-3; closed Sundays and holidays and Saturdays during July and August. Admission free.* A conjectural reconstruction (1912) of the once-famous tavern which stood on this site in Revolutionary and pre-Revolutionary times.

Friends' Meeting House - *see* Stuyvesant Square.

General Motors Building, *Fifth Ave between 58th and 59th St.* Designed by Edward Durrell Stone and Emery Roth & Sons; 1968. A slab-like 50-storey office building sheathed in marble. It fills the block between Fifth and Madison Ave, though there is a small, sunken plaza on the Fifth Ave side. This fronts directly on Grand Army Plaza, and has been criticized for diluting the effect of the Plaza's space. *126.*

General Post Office, *Eighth Ave between 31st and 33rd St.* Designed by McKim, Mead & White; 1913. The obvious main feature of this façade is the row of enormous Corinthian columns two blocks long.

George Washington Bridge, *178th St and the Hudson River.* Designed by O.H. Ammann (engineer) and Cass Gilbert (architect); 1931. A single-span (3,500 feet) suspension bridge of steel as much admired by modern architects as by engineers. 145, 146, *152.*

George Washington Bridge Bus Terminal, *at 178th St between Fort Washington and Wadsworth Ave.* Designed by Pier Luigi Nervi for the New York Port Authority. The major feature of this structure is the reinforced concrete roof. 145.

Governor's Island, *off the tip of Manhattan.* Historically involved with the city's military defence, the island's buildings of note are Castle Williams (1811), built, with Castle Clinton on Manhattan, to fortify New York in the War of 1812. Fort Jay and the Governor's House are 18th-century constructions. The Commanding General's Quarters (1840) and the Block House (1843) were designed by Martin Thompson.

Grace Church, *Broadway and 10th St.* Designed by James Renwick Jr; 1846. Gothic Revival structure with a fine spire. Built of unpolished marble, with an accompanying vicarage in the same style, the church was based on designs from the handbooks of the Pugins, British Gothic Revivalists. The parish was a fashionable one in mid-19th-century New York. 50, *51.*

Gracie Mansion, *E. 88th St at the East River, in Carl Schurz Park. Not open to the public.* Built in 1799 as a country house by Archibald Gracie, it has later Federal details such as a fanlight doorway. A two-storey frame structure with chinoiserie balustrades, it was once used as the Museum of the City of New York. Often remodelled and enlarged, it now serves as the residence of New York's mayors. 19, *23*.

Gramercy Park, *20th to 21st St on the axis of Lexington Ave and Irving Place.* Designed by Samuel Ruggles; 1831. A small private park, similar to those of London, usable only by residents of the adjoining houses, who have keys to the locked gates. It has always been one of the most fashionable addresses in Manhattan. Alexander Jackson Davis designed the commodious houses with wrought-iron balconies at 3 and 4 Gramercy Park West. On Gramercy Park South are Stanford White's remodelling (1888) of Edwin Booth's house for the Players' Club and Calvert Vaux's residences for Samuel J. Tilden (1874), now the National Arts Club, which has a Ruskinian Gothic façade decorated in part with portrait heads of notable writers. Just east of the park on 20th St is a brownstone Friends' Meeting House, and west at 21st St and Park Ave South is James Renwick's brownstone Gothic Calvary Church (1846). 41, *41, 54,* 80.

Grand Army Plaza, *Brooklyn, Flatbush Ave at the entrance to Prospect Park.* Designed by Olmsted & Vaux; 1866. A large oval, divided into several park-like sections, whose focal point is the enormous classical Soldiers' and Sailors' Memorial Arch, by John Duncan (1892), with sculpture by Frederick MacMonnies (*Quadriga,* 1898; groups on south pedestal, representing the *Army and the Navy,* 1901), Thomas Eakins (bas-relief of *Lincoln* on interior, 1895) and William O'Donovan (bas-relief of *Grant* on interior, 1895).

Grand Army Plaza, *Manhattan, Fifth Ave between 58th and 60th St.* Known simply as The Plaza, and planned by Olmsted & Vaux in the 1860s as part of the approach to Central park, this open urban space is in two parts. The portion between 59th and 60th St, which cuts into Central Park and around which are the Park's entrances, now has as its major ornament St-Gaudens' equestrian monument to *General Sherman* (1903). The south portion has Carrère & Hastings' Pulitzer fountain, a pyramidal composition of basins surmounted by the figure of *Abundance* by Karl Bitter (1916). The Plaza Hotel faces the Plaza on the west, and the Bergdorf Goodman store stands on the south, where the Vanderbilt chateau once was. East is the General Motors building (q.v.), with its own small plaza. 93, *126*.

Grand Central Terminal, *42nd St at Park Ave.* Designed by Charles Reed and Allen Stem, Whitney Warren and viaducts, 1920. The major interior space, the Concourse, has a vault 125 feet in span and 116 feet high, hung from the roof trusses. Train gates are on two levels, and on the ramps to the lower level the tile vaulting is left exposed. On the façade, facing south, is a huge sculptural group by Jules Coutan, surrounding a clock. The traffic ramps around the building are integral to it, with shops and entrances to the terminal beneath them. 100, *104, 203, 207, 208.*

Grant's Tomb, *Riverside Drive at 122nd St.* Designed by John Duncan; 1897. The domed classical mausoleum of the nation's 18th president, Ulysses S. Grant, and his wife, set in a pleasant expanse of trees and lawn.

Greenwich Village, *roughly Broadway west of the Hudson River, 14th St south to Houston St.* Settled early in the 19th century, it has a varied street pattern, established before the grid, set by the 1811 commissioners' plan, went into effect, which remains for tourists and residents alike one of the major charms of this area of the city. Though tenements and apartment houses have been built in the Village over the years, there are still a great number of houses of the Federal and Victorian periods here, and a good portion of the Village has been designated a Historic District. The most notable rows of houses are on Washington Square North (some possibly designed by Martin Thompson; 1831), and on 9th through 12th St in the blocks on either side of Fifth Ave. Smaller and more modest houses of the same type together with their assorted mews and art buildings, also abound west of Sixth Aveune, and have long attracted the crowd of artists and writers who settled there early in the 20th century. Rents have risen ,and most of the artists have moved east or south, but their houses and apartments have been taken by young professional people and by families who desire life on a more human scale than the rest of the city provides. A large colony of Italian-Americans remains in the southern part of the Village. West 8th St is the main thoroughfare of Greenwich Village. Many shops are here and along Sixth Ave. The tourist bars and coffee-houses lie along Macdougal St and Bleeker St. Washington Square is the major open space in the Village. Once a potter's field, then a parade ground, it is now a park, closed to vehicular traffic, and well-used, especially on Sundays. The Washington Arch, designed by Stanford White (1892), at the foot of Fifth Ave, is a landmark and its most notable structure. Judson Memorial Church and the buildings of New York University edge the square, and the noble Greek Revival rows flank the north side. Other open spaces include Sheridan Square and Christopher Park, and in the far west Village Abington Square. Village Square, at the intersection of 8th St, Sixth Ave and Greenwich Ave (the Jefferson Market Library is nearby), is only nominally a square, but it provides a centre for the extremely varied life of the Village. 28, 25, 28, *36,* 50, 124, 128, 147, 206, *235.*

Hall of Fame - *see* **New York University,** University Heights Campus

Hamilton Grange, *287 Convent Ave. Not open to the public.* Designed by John McComb, Jr. Once the country residence of Alexander Hamilton. A frame building in Federal style, with a broad porch.

Harlem, *roughly from 110th St to 155th St.* The largest area of Black settlement in New York, Harlem stretches west to Morningside Heights and Hamilton Heights, dominated by the campuses of Columbia University and the City College of New York, and east to the Harlem River. The core of Black Harlem is 125th St, with shops, theatres and hotels. East Harlem houses distinct social enclaves: Spanish Harlem and Italian Harlem. Opened to Black residence early in this century, the area has many districts of fine houses and well-planned public spaces, but has been subject to municipal neglect and made to bear the strain of over-population because of restricted opportunity for Blacks to live elsewhere in the city. Despite a great deal of public housing built in the area since World War II, and developments such as Riverbend (q.v.) there is still overcrowding and poverty, for which a colourful and energetic street life cannot readily compensate. 202-3, 206, 218, 239-40.

Harmonie Club, *4 E. 60th St between Madison and Fifth Ave.* Designed by McKim, Mead & White. The building of New York's most prestigious Jewish club.

Harvard Club, *27 W. 44th St.* Designed by McKim, Mead & White; 1894, 1902, 1915. A neo-Georgian façade, which belies the vast spaces of the public rooms within. The building extends through the block to 45th St. 88.

Haughwout Building, *488-492 Broadway at Broome St.* Designed John P. Gaynor; 1857. Built of cast-iron sections whose design is taken from Sansovino's Library in Venice, this 19th-century mercantile palace had the first working passenger elevator. *57, 62.*

Herald Square, *34th to 35th St, at the crossing of Sixth Ave and Broadway.* Today New York's main middle-class shopping district, with R.H. Macy, 'The World's Largest Store', and Gimbel's nearby, as well as the hub of the garment district, its factories, showrooms and suppliers, the square was the centre of New York's Tenderloin vice district in the 1870s and 1880s. The New York Herald building by McKim, Mead & White from which the square takes its name stood at 35th St between 1895 and 1921.

House (formerly Museum of Modern Art guesthouse), *242 E.52nd St.* Designed by Philip Johnson; 1950. Behind a simple front of brick and glass, the house is in two sections, divided by a central pool. *151.*

House, *56 W. 10th St, between Fifth and Sixth Ave.* 1832. A typical builder-architect house in the Federal style. *25, 35.*

Houses, *157-165 E. 78th St, between Lexington Ave and Third Ave.* Designed by Henri Armstrong; 1861.

Jacob Riis Houses - *see* **Riis.**

Jefferson Market Library (originally Jefferson Market Courthouse), *Sixth Ave and W.10th St.* Designed by Vaux and Withers; 1876. An elaborate Victorian Gothic building, with stained-glass windows, steeply pitched roofs, polychrome brickwork, and a fire lookout tower, it was originally part of a courthouse-jail complex which replaced a market and an earlier fire lookout tower on the site. Restored and remodelled as a library by Giorgio Cavaglieri; 1967. 80.

John F. Kennedy International Airport, *Van Wyck Expressway and Southern Parkway, Queens.* New York's international air terminal has spawned this huge complex of striking, sometimes overwrought, buildings, often called Terminal City. Circulation through it is achieved by a complex system of roads. A large number of the buildings have been designed by Skidmore, Owings & Merrill, including the International Arrivals Building (1957), 2,000 feet long, containing the main customs hall, with a balcony for viewing passengers' processing, a large, arched lobby with a mobile by Alexander Calder; the adjacent control tower; and the United-Delta Air Lines terminal, in steel and glass, a long curved building with spare, clearly articulated interior spaces. Other notable structures are the concrete and glass National Airlines building by I.M. Pei (1970) and the expressionistic concrete TWA terminal by Eero Saarinen (1962), with its wing-like shape and curving interior spaces. 159, 206.

Judson Memorial Church, *55 Washington Square South.* Designed by McKim, Mead & White; 1892. An eclectic design which nonetheless has a distinct style of its own. The tower is reminiscent of Tuscan campaniles, but houses apartments. There are interesting decorative stone courses on the buff-coloured brick façade, which is dominated by large arcaded windows. The stained glass for these was designed by John LaFarge. Inside, the marble reliefs on the south wall of the chancel were planned by Augustus St-Gaudens.

Juilliard School of Music - *see* **Lincoln Center for the Performing Arts.**

Kips Bay Plaza, *30th to 33rd St, First to Second Ave.* Designed by I.M. Pei and associates; 1960, 1965. Two free-standing 21-storey apartment buildings of exposed concrete, with a distinctive window grid, facing each other across a landscaped park. The concept is related to that of Le Corbusier's *Unité d'habitation* in Marseilles. A shopping centre and underground garage are integrated in the plan. 217, 226.

Kennedy Airport - *see* **John F. Kennedy.**

LaGrange Terrace, or **Colonnade Row,** *428-34 Lafayette St, between 4th St and Astor Place.* Designed by Alexander Jackson Davis; 1836. A row of town houses united by a continuous colonnade of Corinthian columns, built for wealthy New Yorkers in the then fashionable district. *36, 38.*

La Guardia Airport, *Grand Central Parkway at 99th St, Queens.* Central terminal and Control Tower designed by Harrison & Abramovitz; 1965. Originally laid out in 1939, as New York's second municipal airport, it now serves domestic flights exclusively. The façade of the terminal is built in a sweeping arc. The cylindrical control tower is of concrete, curving out at the top, with circular windows.

Lambs' Club, *128 W. 44th St between Broadway and Sixth Ave.* Designed by McKim, Mead & White; 1904. An actors' club in Federal style, with a stage-like window.

Lefferts Homestead, *Flatbush Ave near Empire Boulevard, Prospect Park, Brooklyn. Open Monday, Wednesday and Friday 1-5. Admission free.* 1777-83. A Dutch colonial homestead with Revolutionary relics and 18th-century furnishings. *18.*

Lescaze Residence, *211 E. 48th St.* Designed by William Lescaze; 1934. An early residence in the modern style, utilizing glass brick windows on the façade. *143.*

Lever House, *390 Park Ave between 53rd and 54th St.* Designed by Skidmore, Owings & Merrill (Gordon Bunshaft, chief designer); 1952. A landmark of the International style in New York, it was revolutionary in using only a small portion of the available building space. The 18-storey vertical slab of offices, clad in a tinted-glass and stainless steel curtain wall, is raised above the north end of a horizontal slab which is itself set one floor above the street. Under this one passes through a metal-sheathed colonnade to the small open courtyard which the horizontal slab encloses. *156, 159.*

Lincoln Center for the Performing Arts, *62nd to 66th St, Columbus to Amsterdam Ave.* Designed by a board of architects chaired by Wallace K. Harrison, the centre was built 1962-68 on land formerly occupied by tenement housing. It provides permanent auditoriums for the city's major performing arts organizations and schools of the performing arts. The facing of all the buildings in the complex is travertine. The three major auditoriums are grouped around a plaza with a fountain, open on the Columbus Ave side. On the north side of the plaza is Philharmonic Hall, home of the New York Philharmonic, designed by Max Abramovitz (1962), enclosed in glass, with traver-

tined columns which form a sort of peristyle around it. These are extended as a colonade at the plaza side. Visible in the lobby are the brass space sculptures *Orpheus* and *Apollo* by Richard Lippold. There is other sculpture throughout the buiding, including Seymour Lipton's *Archangel* and Dmitri Hadzi's *The Hunt.* On the south side of the plaza is The New York State Theater (1964), used by the New York City Ballet and the New York City Opera, designed by Philip Johnson and Richard Foster, with a colonnade on the plaza side. The principal interior space aside from the auditorium is a grand foyer running the length of the front and separated from the plaza by gold-beaded curtaining, and wall of glass. At either end stand large marble sculptures of women, blown up from smaller works by Elie Nadelman. Around the foyer run balconies fronted with gold-coloured railings. The high ceiling is covered in gold-leaf. Other art in the building includes works by Lee Bontecu and Jasper Johns. On the west side of the plaza, in the principal position, is the largest auditorium in the group, the Metropolitan Opera House, designed by Wallace K. Harrison (1966), with a high-arched portico. Behind this is a screen of glass through which the curving balconies, making up the grand staircase, rise the height of the façade. A sculpture by Wilhem Lehmbruck is placed at the first level. The lobby is further ornamented by Austrian crystal chandeliers. At either end, facing the plaza, hang large murals by Marc Chagall. The plaza opens on the northwest to a smaller plaza, where trees flank the south side of a large formal pool, in which a sculpture by Henry Moore is placed. West of the pool is the Vivian Beaumont Theater, designed by Eero Saarinen (1965). Between the theatre and the side wall of the opera house is the entrance to the Library-Museum of the Performing Arts, designed by Gordon Bunshaft (1965), with a stabile, *Guichet* by Alexander Calder, fronting it. The Library-Museum is structurally a part of the Beaumont Theater, using space in its huge overhanging attic. A sculpture by David Smith stands in the glass-enclosed, recessed Beaumont lobby. North of the Beaumont's plaza rises the building of the Juilliard School of Music, designed by Pietro Belluschi, with Eduardo Catalano, Westermann and Miller (1968). Aside from class rooms and facilities for the Juilliard school, this building, severe and blocklike, but with warm wood decoration on the interior, contains Alice Tully Hall, used primarily for concerts. South of the opera house and west of the State Theater there is also a small park with a band shell, as well as the buildings of Fordham University's Manhattan campus. *172, 175, 176,* 184-90, 233.

Lincoln Towers, *West End Avenue between 66th and 70th Street.* A large, high-rise apartment development for middle and upper-middle income families, built in the 1960s.

Litchfield Mansion (Ridgewood; Grace Hill Mansion), *Prospect Park West between 4th and 5th St, Brooklyn.* Designed by Alexander Jackson Davis; 1857. The best and most elaborate surviving example of Davis's work in the Italianate style. Now used as a public office. *45.*

Little Italy, *Canal to Houston St, Lafayette St to Bowery.* Retains much of its population of Italian descent, with many restaurants and shops selling Italian specialities, and a great deal of street life in the warm months. Though some of the original immigrant families have moved away, they return for religious and family festivals. Old St Patrick's Cathedral, originally designed by Mangin (1815), but reconstructed after a fire, is in the area, between Mott, Prince and Mulberry St.

Lotos Club, *5 E. 66th St.* Designed by Richard Howland Hunt; 1900. Built as a residence, with an elaborate 19th-century French façade.

Low Memorial Library - *see* **Columbia University.**

Lower East Side, *roughly Bowery to the East River, 14th St south to the Williamsburg bridge.* From the 1880s to the First World War, this tenement area was the first American home of millions of Eastern European Jews. Railroad flats, with light only at each end of their 90-foot length, were built by speculators under the old law construction codes to house the immigrants. The Jews maintained much of the religious and social life of their homelands in the new surroundings, and the area was long rich in street life, with pushcarts and small traders. Some of this quality remains today, but many of the teeming tenements have been replaced by high-rise projects, some erected by Labour unions for their members. The Henry Street settlement, between Montgomery and Gran St, has preserved a group of Greek Revival townhouses, and other buildings of the Federal period can be found in the area.

Lucidity, *Second Ave at 51st. St.* Designed by Alan Buchsbaum; 1970. An imaginative shop selling plastics, which have also been used in the shop's design. *197.*

Madison Square, *23rd to 26th St, Fifth Ave to Madison Ave.* All that remains of the plan for a park, called The Parade, which would have extended from 23rd to 34th St, Third to Seventh Ave, Madison Square was laid out as a park in 1847. Notable sculpture in the park includes Augustus St-Gaudens' *Farragut* memorial, on a base by Stanford White (1880); J.Q.A. Ward's *Roscoe Conkling* (1893). McKim, Mead & White's original Madison Square Garden once stood at 26th St and Madison Ave, where the gilt-topped New York Life building by Cass Gilbert (1928,

now stands. Nasson Daphnis' wall painting can just be seen from the park. *90, 92, 101, 244.*

Madison Square Garden Center, *31st to 33rd St, Seventh to Eighth Ave.* Designed by Charles Luckman; 1967. This complex of modern buildings includes a circular sports arena, a slab-like office building, shops, and the underground railroad stations of the Penn Central and Long Island railroads. It replaces the monumental Pennsylvania Station of McKim, Mead & White, which stood on the site from 1912 to 1964. *100, 244.*

Manhattan House, *200 E. 66th St between Second and Third Ave.* Designed by Skidmore, Owings & Merrill with Mayer & Whittlesey. A full block of apartments, with balconies, faced with light grey glazed brick and with window frames of white-painted steel. *166, 168.*

Manufacturers Hanover Trust branch bank, (formerly Manufacturer's Trust Company). *510 Fifth Ave at 43rd St.* Designed by Skidmore, Owings & Merrill; 1954. A steel-framed wall of transparent glass reveals the interior of the bank to the passerby, including the huge vault at street level. On the second floor is a long welded metal screen, by Harry Bertoia. *169, 211.*

Manufacturers Hanover Trust Operations Center, *4 New York Plaza, near the Battery.* Designed by Carson, Lundin & Shaw; 1969. One of a group of gigantic new office structures at the tip of Manhattan, its relative warmth and appeal are partly due to its skilful massing of volumes and its facing of brick rather than glass. *158.*

Marine Midland Grace Trust Company, *140 Broadway.* Designed by Skidmore, Owings & Merrill; 1967. An elegant matt-black steel office building of steel and dark-tinted glass. It has its own plaza, on the Broadway side of which stands Isamu Noguchi's red-orange cubic construction. *189, 195-6.*

Mariners' Temple, *12 Oliver St at Henry St;* 1844. Often attributed to Minard Lefever. A late example of the Greek Revival church in New York, with beautiful interior detail.

McGraw-Hill Building, *330 W. 42nd St, between Eighth and Ninth Ave.* Designed by Raymond Hood, with Godley & Fouilhoux; 1931. Considered one of New York's first truly modern buildings, it is sparely designed, with continuous horizontal bands of blue-green terra cotta brick and a distinctive silhouette, the product of its setback pattern. *124, 130.*

Mercedes-Benz Showroom, *430 Park Ave at 56th St.* Designed by Frank Lloyd Wright; 1955. The curved ramp used here is characteristic of several Wright works, including his only other building in New York, the Guggenheim Museum. *169.*

Metropolitan Club, *1 E. 60th St at*

Fifth Ave. Designed by McKim, Mead & White; 1893. A large white stone palace, with a carriage entrance and courtyard, houses this club founded by J.P. Morgan.

Metropolitan Opera House - *see* **Lincoln Center for the Performing Arts.**

Morningside Park, *Cathedral Parkway and Manhattan Ave to Morningside Ave and W. 123rd St.* Designed by Frederick Law Olmsted. A rocky cliff rises at the west side of this strip of park to Morningside Heights and the Cathedral of St John the Divine. Harlem lies to the east, on the plain. At 114th St and Manhattan Ave, Bartholdi's sculpture, *Lafayette and Washington.*

Morris-Jumel Mansion, *Edgecombe Ave at 161st St; 1765, 1810. Open 11-5 daily; closed Mondays. Admission free.* Now a colonnaded Federal house with a pediment and wooden quoins, the house was originally built by Roger Morris as a country home. It played a part in the Revolution, serving as General Washington's headquarters until it fell into the hands of the British. After the Revolution it became a roadside tavern until bought and reconditioned in 1810 by Stephen Jumel, a wealthy West Indian plantation owner. It has an octagonal drawing-room, which is furnished in a combination of Georgian and French Empire taste. *19, 22.*

Mt Morris Park, *120th to 124th St, Mt Morris Park west to Madison Ave.* A small park in the Harlem district, containing the sole remaining Bogardus-built fire-watch tower.

Murray Hill, *33rd to 42nd St east of Fifth Ave.* This area was the seat of Robert Murray's country house in the 18th century. It is now a precinct of mid and late 19th-century town houses and modern apartment buildings. Interesting buildings in the area include the Morgan Library (*see* List of museums) and Sniffen Court, at 150 E. 36th St, a group of brick carriage houses on a mews, built between 1850 and 1860, tastefully refurbished as residences.

National Arts Club, - *see* **Gramercy Park.**

New School for Social Research, *66 W. 12th St between Fifth and Sixth Ave.* Designed by Joseph Urban; 1930. Additions and sculpture court by William J. Conklin of Mayer, Whittlesey & Glass; 1958. The main building has a spare 'modernist' façade, with horizontal bands of dark brick. The sculpture court contains work by Isamu Noguchi. Inside are murals by Thomas Hart Benton and José Orozco. *143.*

New York City Hall, *in City Hall Park between Broadway and Park Row.* Designed by Joseph F. Mangin and John McComb, Jr; completed 1812. An elegant combination of French Renaissance and Georgian architecture, it houses the centre of New York's municipal government. Two long pavilions flank

a central core from which a slender domed cupola arises. The exterior has notably graceful ornament and detail. Inside, a well-proportioned double staircase with wrought-iron railings rises from the main to the second floor. Interiors were restored by Grosvenor Atterbury early this century. The Governor's Room and other chambers contain paintings by American artists (*see* Museums and Galleries). *22-3, 25, 28.*

New York Hilton, *Sixth Ave between 53rd and 54th St.* Designed by William Tabler; 1963. From a large box-like podium containing the public rooms, a slim vertical slab of guest rooms rises, each with a blue-tinted bay window, making zig-zag patterns of the north and south walls. *206.*

New York Shakespeare Festival Theater, *425 Lafayette St between 4th St and Astor Place; 1849-1881.* Originally the Astor library, it was built in three stages. The central portion was designed by Griffith Thomas. Thomas Thomas designed the north portion, Thomas Stent the south portion. The whole is an Italianate structure of red brick. It has been remodelled into several theatres by Giorgio Cavaglieri (1967-70), but many of the interior spaces of the original have been conserved in the process, most notably the central reading hall. *63.*

New York State Theater - *see* **Lincoln Center for the Performing Arts.**

New York Stock Exchange, *8 Broad St between Wall St and Exchange Place.* Designed by George B. Post; 1903. The Greek Temple façade, with fluted Corinthian columns surmounted by a pediment with sculpture by J.Q.A. Ward, is backed by a glass wall which lights the vast hall of the interior, where the main work of bargaining goes on. Guided tours are available and visitors may watch the activity from the galleries. *86.*

New York Studio School, *8 W. 8th St.* Renovated 19th-century town houses, once the home of the Whitney Museum of American Art, are now used as an art school. *124.*

New York University-B e l l e v u e Medical Center, *30th to 34th St, First Ave to East River Drive.* Designed by Skidmore, Owings & Merrill; 1950. A complex of teaching hospitals, cleanly designed to a master plan by the architects and built over a number of years. *227, 237.*

New York University, *University Heights Campus, W. 180th St at University Ave, Bronx.* There are two groups of notable buildings here, the earlier by McKim, Mead & White, the later by Marcel Breuer and associates. At the crest of a ridge overlooking the Harlem River and Manhattan, the Hall of Fame (1896-1900), a semi-circular colonnade around whose perimeter are busts of notable Americans, frames Gould L i b r a r y (1900), a domed

Palladian structure with an extended portico, Baker Hall of Philosophy to the north (1912) and the Hall of Languages to the south (1894). Breuer's works are the two Technology buildings; (1964, 1969) and Begrish Lecture Hall boldly cantilevered structures, and the Julius Silver Residence, served by ramps which enter at the fourth floor because of the building's difficult hillside site. A sculpture by Guitou Knoop is placed on campus. 227, 230, 233.

New York University, *Washington Square Campus, north, east, and south of Washington Square.* Alexander Jackson Davis' Gothic Revival university building was torn down at the turn of the century to make room for the undistinguished high-rise classical structures which now face Washington Square on the east. Recently the university has begun to build new structures, most of them integrated in a campus plan designed by Philip Johnson and John Burgee. Built before the plan are the Loeb Student Center on Washington Square South (Harrison & Abramovitz; 1959), with a metal sculpture by Reuben Nakian on its façade, and Warren Weaver Hall (Warner, Burns, Toan & Lunde; 1966), a brick and glass tower with protruding bays at its top. The Elmer Holmes Bobst Library (Philip Johnson and Richard Foster; 1971) is a severe, imposing twelve-storey block of red-tinted cast stone and sets the scale and aspect of other buildings in the planned complex, such as Tisch Hall (1971) and the Meyer physics building (1971; actually a remodelling), also by Philip Johnson. *32, 50, 79, 227, 228, 231-3, 237.*

New York Yacht Club, *37 W. 44th St, between Fifth and Sixth Ave.* Designed by Warren & Wetmore; 1899. Windows like the sterns of ships are the extravagant feature of this façade.

Old Merchant's House (Seabury Treadwell House), *29 E. 4th St, between Bowery and Lafayette St; 1832. Open daily 1-5; closed Mondays. Phone in advance. Admission charge.* Attributed to Minard Lafever. A typical town house of the Federal period, with Greek Revival detailing. Original furnishings.

Paley Plaza, *E. 53rd St between Fifth and Madison Ave.* Designed by Zion & Breen, landscape architects; 1967. A 'vest-pocket' park contributed by William S. Paley to the city in memory of his father. The small space is given individuality by a cascade of water which forms its rear wall. 236.

Pan Am Building, *200 Park Ave at 45th St.* Designed by Emery Roth & Sons, Pietro Belluschi, and Walter Gropius; 1963. A sixty-storey slab, topped by a now-idle heliport, with 4,200,000 square feet of office space (more than the Empire State), clad in a cast concrete curtain wall. It has been criticized for changing the urban scale of Park Ave and for adding an enormous amount of pedestrian traffic to the Grand

Central complex without providing for proper circulation or amenities. The lobby connects with Grand Central Terminal's concourse, and contains a mural by Josef Albers, decor by Gyorgy Kepes, and a wire construction by Richard Lippold. *203, 208.*

Paraphernalia, *795 Madison Ave between 67th and 68th St; Lexington Ave and 55th St; Greenwich Ave at 10th St.* Designed by Ulrich Franzen; 1966-70. Boutiques with exciting decor. 196.

Park Avenue, *46th to 57th Street.* Once an area of luxury apartment houses and hotels north of Grand Central Terminal, this area has been transformed since the Second World War by the construction of tall office buildings. Some were built under the old building regulations, requiring setbacks. Under the new regulations buildings like the Union Carbide (q.v.) and the Seagram (q.v.) have risen. The only remaining notable hotel is the Waldorf-Astoria. North of 57th St, only the Pepsi-Cola building (q.v.) at 59th St stands out among the apartment buildings on the upper avenue, but it keeps to the prevailing height of the structures of the 20s and 30s. 169, 170, 208.

Park Ave Synagogue, *Milton Steinberg House, 50 E. 87th St.* Designed by Kelly & Gruzen, stained glass by Adolph Gottlieb; 1955. The façade of stained glass fronts an activities building. 169.

680 Park Ave (former **Pyne House**) *at 68th St.* Designed by McKim, Mead & White; 1911. An elaborate Georgian town house of brick and stone, setting the tone for its neighbours, designed at a later date on the same block.

Park Slope, *east of Fourth Ave and opposite Prospect Park, Brooklyn.* A dignified residential district, built late in the 19th century, whose houses in rows have richly diverse façades, many in brownstone. 226.

Pennsylvania Station - *see* **Madison Square Garden Center.**

Pepsi-Cola Building, *500 Park Ave at 59th St.* A compact office building in the International style. Built in scale with its surroundings, with a clear glass curtain wall. 170.

Philharmonic Hall - *see* **Lincoln Center for the Performing Arts.**

Pieter Claessen Wyckoff House, *5902 Clarendon Road at Ralph and Ditmas Ave, Flatlands section of Brooklyn; c. 1640.* A Dutch farmhouse, perhaps the oldest extant building in New York state. 12.

Players' Club - *see* **Gramercy Park.**

Plaza Hotel, *opposite Grand Army Plaza (The Plaza) on the west between 58th St and Central Park South.* Designed by Henry J. Hardenbergh; 1907. A severe façade of white glazed brick ends in variety of minarets and gables reminiscent of European chateaux. The hotel's elaborate entrances, marble lobbies and public spaces are notable. *106.*

Prospect Park, *south of Grand Army Plaza, Brooklyn.* Built to the plans of Olmsted & Vaux, in the romantic picturesque English style; 1867-72, with later classical additions, many by McKim, Mead & White. The two main entrances to the park are from Grand Army Plaza (q.v.), through columns and temples designed by Stanford White (1894), or from Park Circle, where there is another McKim, Mead & White entrance in classical style, with equestrian sculpture by Frederick MacMonnies (1897). The Lefferts Homestead, Litchfield Mansion, and a zoo are within the Park's precincts, and a drive runs around the park, but most of its features are best seen by taking the many paths which lead to the important areas: the Long Meadow, the Vale of Cashmere, the Nethermead, the Swan Lake, and the Music Grove. Some structures of interest are the Croquet Shelter (McKim, Mead & White; 1906), Nethermead Arches (Calvert Vaux ; 1870), the Oriental Pavilion (Calvert Vaux; 1874). *70, 73, 79.*

Public School 55, *Koch Boulevard and Woods of Arden Road, Staten Island.* Designed by Richard G. Stein; 1965. Playground; 1967. Surfaces of exposed masonry, sculpture by Nivola, graphics by Chermayeff & Geismar, and a multi-level playground with amphitheatre distinguish this recent school. 214.

Public School 166, *132 W. 89th St, between Amsterdam and Columbus Ave.* Playground designed by J. Paul Friedberg; 1969. Relief by Mon Levinson. 238.

Public School 199, *70th St and West End Ave, Manhattan.* Designed by Edward Durrell Stone; 1963. A relatively simple design, whose brick piers are used rhythmically, lending an air of calm to an area of aggressive slab-like apartments. 214.

Public School 306, *970 Vermont St at Cozine Ave, Brooklyn.* Designed by Pederson and Tilney; 1966. A concrete school, cast in place, whose towers and massing stand out in an otherwise flat area. 214.

Racquet and Tennis Club, *370 Park Ave, between 52nd and 53rd St.* Designed by McKim, Mead & White; 1918. The sober neo-Florentine façade, with regular fenestration, trimmed in rusticated granite, now serves as a perfect foil to the Seagram Building and its plaza opposite. *82, 170.*

Riis Plaza, *in Jacob Riis Houses, 6th to 10th St, Ave D to East River Drive.* Designed by Pomerance & Breines, with J. Paul Friedberg, landscape architect; 1966. Neither a park nor a city street, but with qualities of both. An elaborate play area, with structures encouraging participation by children as well as an amphitheatre for use by all ages, and a variety of places in which to sit, move around, through, etc. 236, 238, *238.*

Riverbend, *E. 138th St and Harlem River Drive.* Designed by Davis, Brody & Associates; 1968. The use of large red bricks and concrete, an interesting grouping of buildings and sharing of services, and walkways in the air between buildings, as well as apartments planned with generous spaces (many are duplexes) make this middle-income project an important development in urban housing. 218.

Riverside Church, *Riverside Drive and W. 122nd St.* Designed by Charles Collens; 1930. An enormous Gothic church of limestone, endowed by John D. Rockefeller, Jr. Richly decorated, with a massive and elaborate tower (which contains offices and classrooms).

Riverside Park, *Riverside Drive to the Hudson River, 72nd to 124th St.* Designed by Frederick Law Olmsted; completed 1911. Later modifications. The park of the upper west side, a strip of well-planted hilly land with walks, lawns, playgrounds and sports facilities. The Henry Hudson Parkway runs through the park, which is built covering the tunnel of the New York Central's freight line. Notable are the Soldiers' and Sailors' Memorial (to the Civil War dead) by Stoughton & Stoughton (1902), a classical structure derived from the Hellenistic Choragic Monument of Lysicrates, and, at the Park's northern end, Grant's Tomb (q.v.). 235.

Rockefeller Apartments, *17 W. 54th St to 55th St, between Fifth and Sixth Ave.* Designed by Harrison and Fouilhoux; 1936. Pleasant curved bay windouws enliven the façades. These are two buildings, one fronting on 55th St, which share a central garden. 142.

Rockefeller Center, *Fifth to Sixth Ave, 48th to 51st St. RCA building observatory open 9 a.m.-midnight April 1-October 1; 9 a.m.-7 p.m. the rest of the year. Admission charge.* Designed by Reinhard & Hofmeister; Corbett, Harrison & MacMurray; Hood & Fouilhoux; 1931-40. Thirteen buildings sheathed identically in limestone, which focus on a terraced, landscaped plaza with a skating rink, Rockefeller Center (much of the land was donated by John D. Rockefeller, Jr.) has served as a model for other high-density urban commercial developments. The Channel Gardens, with fountains and plantings, descend west from Fifth Ave between low buildings. Behind the skating rink at their end rises Paul Manship's gilded *Prometheus,* and behind that the tallest structure in the complex, the 70-storey RCA building. At right angles to each other, connected by a complex of underground passageways and on the surface by a carefully planned system of vehicular and pedestrian circulation, lie the other buildings of the group. Sculpture by Manzù adorns the Italian Building at Fifth and 50th St, and in front of International Building is Lee Lawric's *Atlas.* 128, 130-34, *130, 158.*

Roosevelt House, *28 E. 20th St*

between Broadway, and Park Ave South; 1848. *Open 9-4:30 daily. Admission charge.* The birthplace of Theodore Roosevelt, a large brownstone maintained in the style of the mid-19th century, complete with furnishings .

Sailors' Snug Harbor, *Richard Terrace between Tysen and Kissell Ave.* Designed by Martin Thompson; 1833. Dormitories for retired seamen in dignified Greek Revival style, laid on a 100 acre plot. Founded in 1801 by R.R. Randall, the Harbor is supported by income from what was onec his 21-acre estate in Greenwich Village, near Washington Square.

St Bartholomew's Church (Protestant Episcopal), *Park Ave between 50th and 51st St.* Designed by Bertram Grosvenor Goodhue; 1919. Community house; 1927. Portals from an earlier church, designed by McKim, Mead & White; 1902. The doors of this Romanesque-Byzantine edifice are elaborately sculpted; the church itself has severe, 'modernist' wall surfaces and a dome covered in mosaic. The vaulted interior is richly decorated but sober. *124.*

St Mark's-in-the-Bouwerie (Protestant Episcopal), *Second Ave and 10th St*; 1799. Greek Revival steeple designed by Town and Thompson; 1835. Cast-iron portico; 1858. Essentially a Georgian country church, built on land which was originally a part of Peter Stuyvesant's estate, it is the second oldest church in Manhattan, after St Paul's Chapel. *16, 18.*

St Patrick's Cathedral (Roman Catholic), *50th to 51st St, Fifth to Madison Ave.* Designed by James Renwick, Jr; 1758-79. A Gothic Revival structure in granite, said to be modelled after Cologne Cathedral. Twin towers, 330 feet high, rise from the Fifth Avenue façade. *45, 50.*

St Paul's Chapel of Trinity Parish (Protestant Episcopal), *Broadway between Fulton and Vesey St.* Designed by Thomas McBean; 1766. Steeple; 1796. The only extant pre-Revolutionary church in Manhattan, it is built of Manhattan schist, the underlying rock of the island, in high Georgian style, with a steeple modelled after that of St Martins-in-the-Fields, London, by James Gibbs. The portico on the Broadway side is at the opposite end of the church to the steeple. *13, 15, 16.*

St Regis Hotel, *2 E. 55th St at Fifth Ave.* Designed by Trowbridge & Livingston; 1904. An elaborate hotel in Beaux Arts style, which has retained its elegance and popularity to the present. *206.*

St Saba (Serbian Eastern Orthodox), formerly Trinity Chapel, *15 W. 25th St between Fifth and Sixth Ave.* Designed by Richard Upjohn; 1855. A later church in the Gothic Revival style by the architect for Trinity Church, of· which this once was the uptown chapel.

St Thomas Church (Protestant Epis-

copal), *Fifth Ave and 53rd St.* Designed by Cram and Goodhue; 1914. A 20th-century French Gothic design, with large plain surfaces and skilful massing of forms, an elaborate tower and façade, and a richly decorated interior; the carved reredos is notable.

Scribner Building, *597 Fifth Avenue between 48th and 49th St.* Designed by Ernest Flagg; 1913. The two-storey bookstore is seen through a handsome steel and glass façade.

Seabury Treadwell House - *see* **Old Merchant's House.**

Seagram Building, *375 Park Ave between 52nd and 53rd St.* Designed by Mies van der Rohe and Philip Johnson; 1958. Set back from Park Ave, approached across a plaza edged by pools with fountains and flanked by trees, this 38-storey office tower is the epitome of refinement in the use of elements of the International Style. The entrance is recessed behind the façade, so that a colonnade is formed about the building's base; the curtain wall is of brown-tinted glass in a structure of bronze; at the rear of the lobby, in the entrance to the Four Seasons Restaurant, designed by Philip Johnson, hangs Picasso's backdrop for 'Le Tricorne' (1929). Inside the restaurant, a brass construction by Richard Lippold hangs over the bar. *82, 160, 160, 169-70.*

Silver Residence Hall - *see* **New York University,** University Heights Campus.

Shakespeare Festival Theater - *see* **New York.**

Singer Building, *561 Broadway,* with façades on Broadway and Prince St. Designed by Ernest Flagg; 1907. An early use of steel and glass though within a masonry frame; this building prefigures later use of the curtain wall in commercial structures. Flagg's later, more elaborate, Singer building of 1908 has been demolished. *104.*

Sniffen Court - *see* **Murray Hill.**

Soho, *below Houston St, west of the Bowery to Sixth Ave.* The newest New York artists' quarter, it grew up in the 1960s as artists sought living and working space in the area's warehouses and lofts. Somewhat later, many galleries moved their quarters downtown from Madison Ave. Of these, perhaps the best-known is O. K. Harris, on LaGuardia Place. *190, 197.*

South Street Pier, *on the East River in Lower Manhattan. Museum open 10-6 daily; Sundays 12-6. Admission to museum and pier free.* With the South Street Seaport Museum on Fulton Street nearby, this is an attempt to give New Yorkers some sense of what the port was like in earlier days. Berthed at the reconditioned pier are ships of many kinds from the 19th century. *224, 226.*

Statue of Liberty, *on Liberty Island (formerly Bedloe's Island) at the entrance to New York Harbour. Ferry* *service from the Battery every hour on the hour during the day.* The monumental figure of *Liberty enlightening the World*, by Frédéric Auguste Bartholdi, was fabricated in France and mounted here in 1886 on a base designed by Richard Morris Hunt, over an armature designed by the French engineer Gustave Eiffel. A gift to the U.S. from France, the figure with uplifted torch has always been symbolic of the new world's opportunity, especially to immigrants. An elevator and stairs inside take visitors to the figure's crown, for a spectacular view of Manhattan and the harbour. *9.*

Stuyvesant Town, *E. 14th to E. 20th St, First Ave to Ave C.* Designed by Irwin Clavan and Gilmore Clarke; 1947. A group of brutally functional high-rise apartments in red brick, developed by the Metropolitan Life Insurance Company for middle-income families. Though the development has trees, lawns, playgrounds and a road system; the units are set quite closely together. *155.*

Stuyvesant-Fish House, *21 Stuyvesant St, between Third and Second Ave; 1804.* A simple, but unusually wide, Federal façade fronts this house, which was the home of Nicholas Stuyvesant and the birthplace of Hamilton Fish. *25, 30.*

Stuyvesant Square, *Rutherford to Perlman Place, 15th to 17th St.* Given to the city by Rutherford Stuyvesant in 1837. Split in half by Second Avenue, this pleasant park is bordered on the east by the buildings of Beth Israel hospital and on the west by churches and town houses of the 19th century and apartment buildings. On Rutherford between 16th and 17th St, the brownstone Romanesque St George's Church (Protestant Episcopal) stands, together with its chapel and, on E 16th St, its massive Gothic parish house (by Leopold Eidlitz; 1887).

Superblock, *St Mark's Avenue, Brooklyn.* 1971 I. M. Pei and J. Paul Friedburg. An attempt to make a more livable area out of a combination of city blocks.

TWA Terminal - *see* **John F. Kennedy International Airport.**

Technology buildings - *see* **New York University,** University Heights Campus.

Time-Life Building, *Sixth Ave at 50th St.* Designed by Harrison & Abramovitz; 1960. A glass-walled office slab, fronted on Sixth Ave by a small plaza with fountains. The murals in the lobby are by Fritz Glarner, and there is a street level exhibition hall. *195, 206.*

Times Square, *Broadway and 42nd St north along Broadway to 47th and 48th St.* The old triangular Times Tower, designed by Cyrus Eidlitz (1904), has been remodelled in white marble as the Allied Chemical Tower, but the band of lights around it still delivers news flashes. A district once overwhelmed with neon lights, trick advertising displays, giant billboards and movie theatres, the scene of New Year's Eve celebrations and a multifarious street life, Times Square has recently become an area of office building construction as well. The theatre district is nearby, however, and to keep it here plans have been made to build new theatres into the office structures. *202, 240.*

711 Third Ave, *at 44th St.* Designed by William Lescaze; 1956. A steppedback office tower with a lower element in light brick and a blue brick top. The lobby elevators are wrapped in a mosaic mural by Hans Hoffman. *169.*

919 Third Ave, *at 55th St.* Designed by Skidmore, Owings & Merrill; 1970. A matt-black, dark glass office building with its own plaza. The red brick P.J. Clarke's tavern, which has been retained, sets it off.

Tisch Hall - *see* **New York University,** Washington Square Campus.

Tracey Towers, *Bronx.* Designed by Paul Rudolph; 1971. Two freely-designed high-rise apartment towers, sited and planned to bring a more human feeling to high-rise housing. *222.*

Trinity Church, *Broadway & Wall St. (Protestant Episcopal).* Designed by Richard Upjohn; 1846. A major monument of the Gothic Revival in New York, impressively detailed, with a fine steeple ornamented with sculpture. It is set in its churchyard at the head of Wall St. *48, 50, 52, 100, 208.*

Union Carbide Building, *270 Park Ave between 47th and 48th St.* Designed by Skidmore, Owings & Merrill. A 53-storey tower with a lobby exhibition space lifted high above the street. The building's curtain wall is of grey glass and steel, and there is a 13-storey wing at the rear, connected to the main building by a narrow bridge. *170.*

Union Square, *14th to 17th St, Park Ave South to Union Square West.* Laid out as a private park, called Union Place, in the 19th century, it was the centre of a fashionable residential district *c.* 1840. From the late 19th century onward, the park became the focal point for gatherings of radicals, and political rallies are held there to the present day. Today it is flanked by office buildings and 'bargain' department stores such as S. Klein. Sculpture in the park includes *Washington* (1856) by H.K. Brown, his *Lincoln* (1866) and Bartholdi's *Lafayette* (1876). *48, 79, 146-7, 147, 148.*

United Nations, *First Avenue between 42nd and 48th St.* Designed by an international committee of architects, chaired by Wallace K. Harrison; 1947-53. Built on land donated by John D. Rockefeller, Jr. The overall conception of the buildings is that of Le Corbusier, though much of the detailing is by Harrison. The slab-like Secretariat dominates the composition. North of it rises the curved roof, with a dome, of the General Assembly building. Along the river front is the Conference building, and on the southern corner of the plot a library named for Dag Hammarskjöld has been built (Harrison & Abramovitz; 1963). A sculpture by Barbara Hepworth is placed in the forecourt of the Secretariat; the hall of the General Assembly has decorations by Léger. The conference building interiors are by the Swedish architect Sven Markelius; the library contains murals by Fritz Glarner, and there are stained glass windows by Chagall. *154, 155, 155-60, 160, 192, 199.*

U.S. Customs House, *Bowling Green.* Designed by Cass Gilbert; 1907. A monumental grey granite building, in elaborate eclectic style, with engaged Corinthian columns. The main façade facing Bowling Green, is ornamented with four large limestone sculptures representing the continents, executed by Daniel Chester French.

University Club, *1 W. 54th St at Fifth Ave.* Designed by McKim, Mead & White; 1899. An elaborate, rusticated stone Italian Renaissance palace of three storeys, all of a great height to accommodate the salons and amenities of this private club. *84.*

University Village, *between Mercer St and West Broadway, Bleeker to Houston St.* Designed by I.M. Pei (1966). Three elegant 30-storey apartment towers of exposed concrete, grouped around a courtyard in which a large sand-blasted version of Picasso's *Portrait of Sylvette* is set. *228, 233, 237.*

U.S. Federal Building, *641 Washington St, between Barrow and Christopher St.* Designed by Willoughby J. Edbrooke; 1899. A 10-storey example of Richardsonian Romanesque in red brick, also showing influence of the Chicago school of architecture.

Van Cortlandt Manor, *Broadway at 246th St, in Van Cortlandt Park, Bronx; 1748. Open daily 10-5; Sundays 2-5; closed Mondays and during February. Admission charge; free on Friday and Saturday.* A fieldstone country house, with a rich Georgian interior and 17th- and 18th-century furnishings. *25.*

Verrazano-Narrows Bridge, *between Brooklyn and Staten Island.* Designed by O.H. Ammann; 1964. A suspension bridge with a 4,260 foot span and a maximum clearance of 228 feet above the water, it bridges The Narrows at the entrance to New York Bay.

Villard Houses, *Madison Ave between 50th and 51st St.* Designed by McKim, Mead & White; 1886. Built for Henry Villard, a railroad magnate, in Italian Renaissance style, these are sober yet rich city mansions, with meticulous detailing and elaborate ironwork, fronting on a formal courtyard, with the fourth side open to Madison Ave. Now offices for the Roman Catholic Archdiocese of New York. *84, 86.*

Voorlezer (lay reader) house, *Arthur Kill Road opposite Center St, Richmondtown, Staten Island;* 1969. *Open daily 2-5; Sundays 2-6. Admission free.* Built as a school and a residence for the lay reader, who served as teacher of the church school. The oldest known elementary school in America, it houses a replica of a colonial classroom. *18.*

Wall St, *east of Broadway to the East River.* With Trinity church at the Broadway end, this is the spine of the financial district, and its name is often applied generically to the entire area. The street's name is exact. In 1653 the Dutch built a wall here to guard against English invading from the northern part of the island. *34, 48, 100, 217, 227.*

Warren Weaver Hall - *see* **New York University,** Washington Square Campus.

Washington Square Village, *W. 3rd St to Bleeker St, Mercer St to West Broadway.* Designed by S. J. Kessler; 1958. Two multi-coloured brick apartment slabs, facing each other across a landscaped lawn. *35, 224.*

Waterside, *23rd to 30th Streets*, built on piles in the East River. An innovative apartment development, currently building, which will include boating facilities, arcades, shops and a waterfront promenade.

Welfare Island, *in the East River, between 50th St and 86th St.* There are several hospitals here, some functioning, some abandoned.

Westbeth, *463 West St.* Designed by Richard Meier; 1970. The former Bell Telephone Laboratories have here been remodelled to house artists with modest incomes but needing space for work, to which the lofts of these buildings were well adapted. *222, 223.*

Wise Stephen Towers, *Amsterdam to Columbus Ave, 90th to 91st St.* Designed by Knapp & Johnson; 1964. Play area by Richard G. Stein, with sculpture and murals by Constantino Nivola.

Woolworth Building, *233 Broadway between Park Place and Barclay St.* Designed by Cass Gilbert; 1913. Almost 800 feet tall, with a façade designed to emphasize its verticality. The style of decoration adopted is Gothic, and the building has an elaborate, pinnacled, pyramidal crown. *97, 104, 111.*

World Trade Center, *bounded by West, Washington, Barclay, Vesey, Church and Liberty Streets, and West Broadway.* Designed by Minoru Yamasaki and Emery Roth & Sons; to be completed 1975. Two 110-storey buildings, both higher than the Empire State, and several low structures of ten storeys or so, enclose a plaza larger than the plaza of St Marks in Venice. *97, 207, 208, 240.*

Yorkville, *east of Park Ave to the East River, 79th St to the 90s.* 86th is the major shopping street of this traditionally German area.

Painters, Sculptors and Architects

The publishers wish to thank the owners of works reproduced and S.P.A.D.E.M.

Aalto, Alvar (b. Kuortane, Finland, 1898). In New York, served on committee for Lincoln Center for the Performing Arts; responsible for design of conference rooms at the Institute of International Education. *186.*

Abramovitz, Max (b. Chicago, Illinois, 1908), architect, partner in Harrison & Abramovitz (q.v.), designer of Philharmonic Hall, Lincoln Center. *135, 186.*

Adler, Dankmar (b. Eisnach, Germany, 1844, d. 1900), architect. With Louis Sullivan, designed the Auditorium, Chicago; in New York, consultant on Carnegie Hall.

Albers, Josef (b. Westphalia, Germany, 1888), painter, noted for series of geometrical colour paintings *Homage to the Square.* Mural in lobby of Pan Am Building, reliefs in lobby of Corning Glass Building, 5th Ave & 56th St; work in MMA, MOMA, WMAA, Gu, BM. *126, 208.*

Ammann, Othmar H. (b. Geneva, Switzerland, 1879, d. 1965), engineer, responsible for many New York bridges, including George Washington Bridge (Cass Gilbert, architect), Bronx-Whitestone Bridge (Aymar Embury II, architect), Verrazano-Narrows Bridge. *145-6, 152, 211.*

Atterbury, Grosvenor (b. Detroit, Michigan, 1869, d. 1956), architect and restorer. Designed American wing of MMA. Responsible for restoration of City Hall interiors. *25.*

Audubon, John James (b. Haiti, 1785, d. 1851), artist and naturalist. Drawings for *Birds of America* at NYHS. Land formerly his farm in upper Manhattan used for Audubon Terrace.

Avery, Milton (b. Altmar, New York, 1893, d. 1964), painter, particularly admired by the Abstract Expressionists; noted for his handling of colour in works which hover between simplified representational mode and abstraction. Work in MOMA, WMMA.

Babb, Cook & Willard (George W. b. New York, N.Y., 1843, d. 1916), architects. Their Carnegie Mansion (now Cooper-Hewitt Museum), 2 E.91st St, typical Fifth Ave eclectic work of turn of the century; their DeVinne Press Building a full-bodied example of Richardsonian Romanesque. *82.*

Badger, Joseph W., portrait and miniature painter active in New York 1832-7. Exhibited at National Academy.

Baker, George A. (b. New York, N.Y., 1821, d. 1880), portrait and miniature painter. *97.*

Barnard, George Gray (b. Bellafonte, Pennsylvania, 1683, d. 1938), sculptor and collector. His *Struggle of the Two Natures in Man* is at MMA. His collection of medieval architecture and artifacts formed the nucleus of the collection now at The Cloisters. *121.*

Bartholdi, Frédéric Auguste (b. Colmar, France, 1834, d. 1904), French sculptor of the *Statue of Liberty*, also *Lafayette* in Union Square and *Washington and Lafayette,* 114th St & Manhattan Ave. *9.*

Baziotes, William (b. Pittsburgh, Pennsylvania, 1912, d. 1963), painter of the Abstract Expressionist school, noted for work including biomorphic forms, in muted colour. Work in MMA, MOMA, WMAA, Gu. *150, 152.*

Beckmann, Max (b. Leipzig, Germany, 1884, d. 1950), expressionist painter. Work in MOMA, Gu, BM.

Belfatto & Pavarini (Joseph Belfatto b. New York, N.Y. 1925; George Pavarini b. New York City 1926), architects, designers of churches, including Church of the Epiphany, 2nd Ave & 22nd St. *215, 218.*

Bellows, George (b Columbus, Ohio, 1882, d. 1925), painter associated with the Ashcan School, noted for naturalistic portraits, city scenes, paintings of sport. Work in MOMA, WMMA, BM.

Belluschi, Pietro (b. Ancona, Italy, 1899), architect. Spare modern style seen in his Juilliard School of Music, Lincoln Center (with Catalano and Westermann & Miller), much less distinct in Pan Am Building, designed with Walter Gropius (q.v.) and Emery Roth & Sons (q.v.). *186-8.*

Benjamin, Asher (b. Greenfield, Massachusetts, 1771, d. 1845), builder-architect, whose ideas were widely followed in the early 19th century. No work in New York. *36.*

Benton, Thomas Hart (b. Neosho, Missouri, 1889), painter of the American regionalist school, known for energetically expressive murals and paintings of American life. Murals at New

School; work in MMA, MOMA, WMAA, BM.

Bertoia, Harry (b. San Lorenzo, Italy, 1915), sculptor. Metal screen in Manufacturers Hanover Trust Bank, 5th Ave & 43rd St. Work in MOMA. 169.

Bierstadt, Albert (b. Germany, 1830 d. 1902), landscape painter, second generation of the Hudson River School. His *The Rocky Mountains* is at MMA; work at BM.

Bingham, George Caleb (b. Augusta County, Virginia, 1811, d. 1879), painter of the American frontier. Work in MMA.

Bissell, George (b. New Preston, Connecticut 1839, d. 1920), sculptor of the figure of *Abraham De Peyster* at Bowling Green.

Bitter, Karl (b. Vienna, Austria, 1847, d. 1915), sculptor of *Abundance* on Pulitzer Fountain at the Plaza, figures on doors of Trinity Church.

Blume, Peter (b. Russia, 1906), painter, noted for dreamlike scenes to which his virtuoso painting technique gives exaggerated realism. Work in MMA, MOMA, WMAA.

Bogardus, James (1800-74), inventor and manufacturer, developed a system of prefabricated building with cast-iron and foresaw combination of cast-iron construction with non-bearing curtain walls. In New York, Edgar Laing Stores, now dismantled (his first cast-iron structure); 85, 87, 89 Leonard St; cast-iron watchtower in Mount Morris Park. *58*, 60, 62-3, 100.

Bonheur, Rosa (b. France 1822, d. 1899), painter, especially of animals. *The Horse Fair* is at MMA. 88.

Bontecu, Lee (b. Providence, Rhode Island, 1931), artist, noted for her constructions of cloth over metal armatures. Work in New York State Theater, Lincoln Center; MOMA, WMAA.

Brancusi, Constantin, (b. Rumania 1876, d. 1957), sculptor. Work at MOMA, Gu.

Breger, William (b. New York, N.Y., 1925), architect, designer of Civic Center Synagogue. 215, *218*.

Breton, André (b. Tinchebray, Orne, France, 1896, d. 1966), surrealist poet and art theorist. Active in New York in 1940s; influential with first generation of Abstract Expressionists. 150, 152.

Breuer, Marcel (b. Pécs, Hungary, 1902), architect trained at the Bauhaus, designer of numerous recent buildings in New York characterized by use of cantilevered elements and severe surfaces in concrete and granite: Begrish Hall, Technology buildings, Silver Residence Hall (all at New York University, Bronx); Whitney Museum of American Art (with Hamilton Smith). 186, *186,* 190-1, 192, 227, 230.

Brooks, James (b. St Louis, Missouri, 1906), painter of the Abstract Expres-

sionist school. Work in MOMA, WMAA. 154.

Brown, Henry Kirke (b. Leyden, Massachusetts 1814, d. 1886), sculptor. His equestrian *Washington* and his *Lincoln* are in Union Square Park.

Brown, Lawford & Forbes (Geoffrey Lawford, b. Leicestershire, England, 1903; Edwin Forbes, b. Scranton, Pennsylvania, 1899), architects; designers of Thomas J. Watson Library at MMA, and Study and Storage Gallery at BM.

Bruegel, Pieter (b. Brueghel? Holland *c.* 1525-30, d. 1569), painter., famous for satirical scenes of country life. Work at MMA.

Buchsbaum, Alan (b. Savannah, Georgia, 1935), architect, shop designer, including Lucidity, 2nd Ave at 51st St. 197.

Bunshaft, Gordon (b. Buffalo, New York, 1909), architect, partner in Skidmore, Owing & Merrill (q.v.). *156*, 159, 169, 186.

Burchfield, Charles (b. Ashtabula, Ohio, 1893, d. 1967), painter and watercolourist, known for his scenes of American town and landscape in which menace and movement of dream are evoked in an expressionistic style. Work in MMA, MOMA, WMAA.

Burgee, John (b. Chicago, Illinois, 1933), architect, designer with Philip Johnson, of the new campus of New York University at Washington Square, and of a city for Welfare Island.

Burgis, William, designer and engraver of views, active in 1916-31. Work in NYHS.

Burnham, Daniel H. (b. Henderson, New York, 1846, d. 1912), architect, though a pioneer, with his partner John Wellborn Root (b. Lumpkin, Georgia, 1850, d. 1891), of the Chicago school of architecture. Became proponent of The City Beautiful, which relied on grand classical buildings of the sort produced for World's Columbian Exposition of 1893 under his direction. In New York, designed Flatiron Building and 'new' Wanamaker store, Broadway & 9th St, now an office building. 98, 101, 104,

Cady, J.C. (b. Providence, Rhode Island, 1839, d. 1919), architect, responsible for Romanesque Revival design of 77th St Building, American Museum of Natural History. 76.

Calder, Alexander (b. Philadelphia, Pennsylvania, 1898), sculptor, creator of the *mobile. Guichet,* stabile, at entrance to Library-Museum of the Performing Arts, Lincoln Center; mobile in lobby of International Arrivals Building, Kennedy Airport; mobile at Chase Manhattan branch bank, Park Ave & 55th St; work in MMA, MOMA, WMAA, Gu. *175, 179.*

Campin, Robert (b. Tournai, Belgium 1378-79, d. 1444), Flemish painter. His *Annunciation Altarpiece* is at The Cloisters. *112,* 121.

Carrere & Hastings (John M. Carrere, b. Rio de Janeiro, Brazil, 1858, d. 1911; Thomas Hastings, b. New York, N.Y., 1860, d. 1929), architects, responsible for private houses and public buildings in late 19th, early 20th century New York, in variations of the eclectic Beaux Arts style, notably the Frick Collection (originally H.C. Frick's residence), New York Public Library, Pulitzer Fountain at The Plaza, approaches to Manhattan Bridge. *62, 99,* 119.

Carson, Lundin & Shaw (Earl H. Lundin b. Detroit, Michigan 1902; Arvin Shaw III, b. Los Angeles 1906; Robert L. Thorson, b. Iowa, 1930), architects, noted for office structures, especially 666 Fifth Ave and Manufacturers Hanover Operations Center; Esso Building at Rockefeller Center. 207-8.

Carstenson, George, engineer, designer of New York's Crystal Palace with Charles Geldemeister. 63.

Cassatt, Mary (b. Pennsylvania 1855, d. 1926), Impressionist painter. Work at MMA, BM.

Catalano, Eduardo (b. Buenos Aires, Argentina 1917), architect, designer, with Belluschi, and Westerman & Miller, of the Juilliard School of Music at Lincoln Center. 187, 188.

Catlin, George (b. Wilkes-Barre, Pennsylvania, 1796, d. 1872), painter, especially noted for his paintings of Indians. Work at MMA, City Hall.

Cavaglieri, Giorgio (b. Venice, Italy, 1911), architect, responsible for functional remodelling of two historic structures, New York Shakespeare Festival Theater (Astor Library) and Jefferson Market Library (Jefferson Market Courthouse). 64.

Cézanne, Paul (b. Aix-en-Provence, 1839, d. 1906), French Post Impressionist painter, forerunner of cubism. Work in MMA, MOMA, BM, Gu. 111, 134, *135, 137,* 176.

Chagall, Marc (b. Vitebsk, Russia, 1887), painter. Murals at Metropolitan Opera House, Lincoln Center; windows at United Nations; work in MMA, MOMA, Gu, BM. 150, 176, 188.

Chamberlain, John (b. Rochester, Indiana, 1927), sculptor, noted for large-scale metal sculpture, often made from junked automobile bodies. Work in MOMA, WMAA.

Chermayeff & Geismar (Ivan Chermayeff b. London, England, 1932 Thomas H. Geismar b. New Jersey 1931), designers Graphic. MOMA typography is theirs, as are graphics and typography at P.S. 55, Staten Island. 211.

Church, Frederick E. (b. Hartford, Connecticut, 1826, d. 1900), painter of the later Hudson River School, noted for his panoramic landscapes. Work in MMA, BM. 76, 88.

Clark, Cameron, (b. Holyoke, Massachusetts 1887, d. 1957), engineer, co-designer with Harvey Stevenson of FDR Drive. 146.

Clarke, Gilmore, (b. New York City 1892), engineer and landscape architect, designer, with Irwin Clavan, of Stuyvesant Town.

Clavan, Irwin (b. Newport News, Virginia, 1900), architect, designer, with Gilmore Clarke, of Stuyvesant Town.

Cole, Thomas (b. Bolton-le-Moor, Lancashire, England, 1801, d. 1848), painter of the Hudson River School, noted for his landscapes, allegorical and narrative paintings. *Course of Empire* at NYHS. Work in MMA, BM. *28,* 30, *39-40, 52, 58.*

Collens, Charles (1873-1956), architect, designer of Riverside Church and of The Cloisters. *112, 116,* 119, 121.

Conklin & Rossant, McHarg, Wallace & Todd (William J. Conklin b. Hebron, Nebraska, 1923; James S. Rossant b. New York, N.Y., 1928; Ian McHarg b. Clydebank, Scotland; David Wallace b. 1917; Thomas G. Todd b. Stonington, Connecticut, 1928), designers and planners, authors of the controversial Lower Manhattan Plan. Separately Conklin working with Mayer, Whittlesey & Glass (q.v.), is responsible for the design of the addition to the new school. 208.

Copley, John Singleton (b. Boston, Massachusetts, 1738, d. 1815), portrait painter, active in New York 1771-74, after which he worked in England. Work in MMA, BM, NYPL. 16.

Corbett, Harvey Wiley (b. San Francisco, 1872, d. 1954), architect, member of committee for design of Rockefeller Center. 133.

Cornell, Joseph (b. Nyack, New York, 1903), painter and assemblagist, known for his constructions in which Romantic imagery is used to surrealist effect. Work in MOMA, WMAA.

Coutan, Jules (b. France 1848, d. 1939), sculptor of the group surrounding the clock on the south façade of Grand Central Terminal.

Cram & Goodhue (Ralph A. Cram, b. Hampton Falls, New Hampshire, 1863, d. 1942; Bertram G. Goodhue, b. Pomfret, Connecticut, 1869, d. 1929), architects. Cram, latter-day Gothic and Tudor revivalist, reworked plans of Cathedral of St John the Divine from Romanesque-Byzantine to Gothic; designed the nave and west front. With Goodhue, responsible for Gothic St Thomas Church, 5th Ave. Goodhue alone designed Byzantinesque St Bartholomew's, Park Ave. *124.*

Crum, Jason (b. LaHarpe, Illinois 1935), painter, member of City Walls. 244.

Damaz, Paul (b. Oporto, Portugal, 1912), architect, designer of the new façade for Banco do Brasil, Fifth Ave at 45th St. 197.

Daphnis, Nassos (b. Krokeai, Greece 1914), painter. Large wall painting at 26th St, seen from Madison Square Park. Work in MOMA, WMAA. 244.

D'Arcangelo, Allan (b. Buffalo, New York, 1930), painter noted for his geometric landscapes, sometimes using pop imagery, and his abstractions; active in wall painting. Painting on buildings near Lincoln Center; work in MOMA, WMAA. *185, 244.*

Dattner Richard (b. Poland, 1937), architect, noted for his Adventure Playground in Central Park. *236.*

Davies, Arthur B. (b. Utica, New York, 1862, d. 1928), painter of romantic and allegorical landscapes, member of The Eight, organizer of Armory Show. Work in MMA, MOMA. *110.*

Davis, Alexander Jackson (b. New York, N.Y., 1803, d. 1892), architect, partner with Ithiel Town, 1829-44, versatile and popular architect through most of 19th century. Designed Colonnade Row (LaGrange Terrace) and, with Town, Federal Hall National Memorial (Sub-Treasury, originally Customs House), both in Greek Revival style. 3 and 4 Gramercy Park W., his. *35, 36, 38, 45, 49, 50, 54, 58, 86.*

Davis, Brody & Associates (Lewis Davis b. Orange, New Jersey, 1925; Samuel Brody b. Toledo, Ohio, 1926), architects responsible for some of best-designed urban housing complexes in contemporary New York: Riverbend, Waterside, East Midtown Plaza. *218, 222, 233-4, 239.*

Davis, Stuart (b. Philadelphia, Pennsylvania, 1894, d. 1964), painter, pioneer modernist in his use of cubist techniques with everyday American subject matter, in a style that makes brilliant rhythmic use of colour and line. Work in MMA, MOMA, WMAA. *110, 111, 143.*

De Creeft, Jose (b. Guedalara, Spain, 1884), sculptor of *Alice in Wonderland* at Conservatory Water, Central Park.

Degas, Edgar (b. Paris, France 1834, d. 1917), French painter. Work at MMA, MOMA, BM, Gu. *111, 135.*

Demuth, Charles (b. Lancaster, Pennsylvania, 1883, d. 1935), painter of the Precisionist Group, known for his geometrical paintings of American artifacts and his delicate watercolours. Work in MMA, MOMA, WMAA, BM.

Diaper, Frederick (b. England, 1810, d. 1905), architect whose houses in New York, in Italianate style, hastened break-up of the Greek Revival. *73.*

Dickinson, Edwin (b. Senaca Falls, New York, 1891), painter of mystic landscapes and still life. Work in MMA, WMAA.

Dove, Arthur B. (b. Canandaigua, New York, 1880, d. 1946), painter and collagist, one of first American abstractionists. His paintings usually attempt to render growth and movement in nature through form and colour. Work in MMA, MOMA, WMAA, BM. *110.*

Downing, Andrew Jackson (1815-52), landscape architect; practised the Romantic, English variety of landscape planning, one of first to seek a park for New York. *55, 57, 58, 64-70.*

Duchamp, Marcel (b. Blainville, France, 1887, d. 1968). French dadaist painter, his *Nude descending a Staircase* was a *cause célèbre* of Armory Show, 1913. Little production after 1920 but work influential in New York where he settled in '40s. Work in MOMA. *111, 128.*

Duncan, John (1855-1929), architect. Designer of Grant's Tomb and the Soldiers' and Sailors' Memorial Arch at Grand Army Plaza, Brooklyn.

Durand, Asher B. (b. Maplewood, New Jersey, 1796, d. 1886), landscape painter of the Hudson River School. *Kindred Spirits* at NYPL: work in MMA. *28, 30, 38, 40, 52, 55, 76-7.*

Eakins, Thomas (b. Philadelphia, Pennsylvania, 1844, d. 1916), painter, perhaps most important of American 19th century; richly painted realistic work marked by both scientific precision and psychological depth. Bas-relief of Lincoln on Soldiers' and Sailors' Memorial Arch, Grand Army Plaza, Brooklyn; work in MMA, BM. *73.*

Edbrooke, Willoughby J. (b. England, 1843, d. 1896), architect, designer of the U.S. Federal Building, Washington St, in a style derived from the Chicago school.

Eidlitz, Cyrus L.W. (b. New York, N.Y., 1853, d. 1921), architect, son of Leopold Eidlitz, designer of Times Tower, one of first New York skyscrapers, now altered.

Eidlitz, Leopold (b. Prague, Bohemia, 1823, d. 1906), architect of Gothic Revival structures in New York, now destroyed, with exception of Parish House, St George's Church, E.16th St. With H.H. Richardson and F.L. Olmsted, planned New York State Capitol at Albany. *73.*

Eiffel, Gustave (b. Dijon, France 1832, d. 1923), engineer. Designer of the Eiffel Tower, in New York he designed the armature supporting the *Statue of Liberty.*

El Greco (Domenico Theotocópuli, b. Crete 1541, d. 1614), painter. Work in MMA, BM, Frick, Hispanic Society. *90, 119.*

Embury, Aymar, II (b. New York City 1880, d. 1966), architect. Worked with O.H. Ammann on Bronx-Whitestone Bridge. *211.*

Ernst, Max (b. Brühl, Germany, 1891), surrealist painter. Work in MOMA, Gu. *150.*

Feininger, Lyonel (b. New York, N.Y., 1871, d. 1956), painter known for his geometrical paintings of ships and architecture, in Germany until 1936, then New York. Work in MOMA, WMAA, Gu.

Flagg, Ernest (b. Brooklyn, New York, 1857, d. 1947), architect, designer of notable apartment and office structures in New York. Of his three Singer buildings, one (at 561 Broadway) remains. His structures often innovative in plan and in use of materials (steel, glass, concrete), despite grounding in Beaux Arts style. Scribner Store, 5th Ave & 49th St; Cherokee Apartments, E.77th St & Cherokee Place. 99.

Flagg, George (b. New Haven, Connecticut, 1816, d. 1877), genre and portrait painter. 39, 104.

Flannagan, John (b. Fargo, North Dakota, 1895-1942), sculptor, noted for his animal forms carved in stone. Work in MMA, MOMA, WMAA.

Foster, Richard (b. Pittsburgh, Pennsylvania 1919), architect, co-designer, with Philip Johnson, of New York State Theater, Lincoln Center, Bobst Library, and New York University's Washington Square campus. 232.

Fouilhoux, Jacques André (b. Paris, France, 1879, d. 1945), architect, co-designer, with Raymond Hood and Frederick Godby of McGraw-Hill Building, with Wallace K. Harrison of Rockefeller Apartments; also involved in the planning of Rockefeller Center. *124,* 130, 133, 143.

Fragonard, Jean Honoré (b. Grasse, France, 1732, d. 1806), French painter. Work in MMA, Frick. 121.

Francis, Sam (b. San Mateo, California, 1923), painter of the Abstract Expressionist school, known for his paintings in which freely-worked areas of strong colour stand forth on otherwise empty canvas. Work in MOMA, WMAA, Gu. *144.*

Frankenthaler, Helen (b. New York, N.Y., 1928), painter, known for her lyrical paintings in which colour is stained into raw canvas in loose and flowing fashion. Work in MOMA, WMAA, BM.

Franzen, Ulrich (b. the Rhineland, Germany, 1921), architect, designer of Paraphernalia boutique, Madison Ave & 67th St; Lexington Ave & 55th St; also in Greenwich Village, Greenwich Ave on 10th St. 196.

Frazee, John (b. Rahway, New Jersey 1790, d. 1852), sculptor and designer. Most likely responsible for Greek Revival interiors of Federal Hall National Memorial. *86.*

French, Daniel Chester (b. Exeter, New Hampshire, 1850, d. 1931), sculptor, known for monumental *Lincoln* in Lincoln Memorial, Washington. In New York, four figures at entrance to Customs House, Bowling Green; *Brooklyn* and *Manhattan* flanking entrance to Brooklyn Museum; *Alma Mater,* Columbia University.

Friedberg, M. Paul (b. New York, N.Y., 1931), landscape architect, developer of innovative play areas of Carver Houses ,and Jacob Riis Houses, P.S. 166, 236-7, 238, *238,* 239.

Gauguin, Paul (b. Paris, France 1848, d. 1903), French Post-Impressionist

painter. Work in MMA, MOMA, BM, Gu. 111, 134, 135.

Gaynor, John P., engineer, designer of cast-iron Houghwout Building, first commercial building with proper passenger elevator. *57, 63.*

Geldemeister, Charles, engineer, designer, with George Carstenson, of New York's Crystal Palace. 63.

Gibbs, James (b. Aberdeen, Scotland 1682, d. 1754), English architect of the Georgian period. His St Martin-in-the-Fields, London, the model for St Paul's Chapel, by Thomas McBean. 13.

Gilbert, Cass (b. Zanesville, Ohio, 1859, d. 1934), architect, designer of Customs House, Bowling Green; later adapted his style to skyscraper, in Gothic design for Woolworth Building; also designed New York Life Building, Madison Ave & 26th St; Auditorium and Gallery of American Institute of Arts & Letters, Audubon Terrace; architect of George Washington Bridge. *97, 104, 152.*

Gilbert, C.P.H. (d. 1952), architect, designer of the French Renaissance-style Felix Warburg House, now the Jewish Museum.

Glackens, William (b. Philadelphia, Pennsylvania, 1870, d. 1938), painter of the Ashcan School, member of The Eight, known for warmly-painted scenes of lower-class and middle-class life. Work in MMA, WMAA, BM. 108.

Glarner, Fritz (b. Zürich, Switzerland, 1899), painter of geometrical abstractions. Murals in Time-Life Building and Hammarskjöld Library, United Nations. Work in MMA, MOMA, WMAA. 195.

Glazer, Samuel (b. Latvia, 1902), architect, designer of addition to Jewish Museum. 192.

Gleizes, Albert (b. France 1881, d. 1953), French cubist painter. Work in MOMA, Gu. 150.

Godley, Frederick A. (b. Jersey City, New Jersey, 1886, d. 1961), architect, designer with Hood and Fouilhoux, of McGraw-Hill Building; member of committee planning Rockefeller Center. *124,* 130, 133.

Goodwin, Philip L. (b. New York, N.Y., 1885, d. 1958), architect, co-designer of Museum of Modern Art; collection of modern design there named for him. 143.

Gorky, Arshile (b. Hayetz Dzore, Armenia, 1905, d. 1948), painter, one of the foremost of the Abstract Expressionist school. From style derived from Picasso's cubism, but dependent on a personal mythology, Gorky worked toward style in which, using rich yet delicate palette, he wove together abstract biomorphic forms and line. Work in MMA, MOMA, WMAA, JM, BM. 146, 147, 150.

Gottlieb, Adolph (b. New York, N.Y., 1903), painter of Abstract Expressionist school, noted for his formalized compositions in which stark f o r m s are positioned in field of deep colour, with mythic or totem content. Glass wall at Park Ave Synagogue; work in MMA, MOMA, WMAA, Gu. 152, 169.

Graham, John (b. Kiev, Russia, 1881, d. 1961), painter, known for cubist works, and for eccentric and esoteric paintings of women. Work in WMAA.

Graves, Morris (b. Fox Valley, Oregon, 1910), painter influenced by Oriental art and thought, noted for his intense, mystic paintings, often of birds. Work in MMA, MOMA, WMAA.

Greenough, Horatio (b. Boston, Massachusetts 1805, d. 1852), sculptor and art critic. Work in MMA. 58.

Gris, Juan (b. Madrid, Spain, 1887, d. 1921), Spanish cubist painter. Work in MOMA, Gu. 150.

Gropius, Walter (b. Berlin, Germany, 1883, d. 1969), architect, founder of the Bauhaus, articulate spokesman for architecture and design in which form follows function and craftsmanship is high. In America since the '30s, became Chairman of Harvard Graduate School of Design and influential practitioner of the International Style. Worked on design of Pan Am Building, with Pietro Belluschi and Emery Roth & Sons. 136, 203.

Guimard, Hector (b. Paris, France, 1867, d. 1942), French architect and designer. Work in MOMA design collection. 210.

Guston, Philip (b. Montreal, Canada, 1913), painter of the Abstract Expressionist school, noted for his heavily-painted lyric abstractions, often using pastel colours; more recently for burlesque figurative paintings. Work in MMA, MOMA, WMAA, Gu. 154.

Hadzi, Dmitri (b. New York, N.Y., 1921), sculptor. Abstract bronze sculpture, *The Hunt*, in Philharmonic Hall, Lincoln Center; work in MOMA, WMAA. 188.

Halprin, Lawrence (b. New York, N.Y., 1916), architect and planner, author of schemes for reclamation of Harlem River Valley, and for a New York City Fountain. 239-40.

Hals, Frans (b. Antwerp, Belgium 1581/5-d. 1666), Dutch painter. Work in MMA, Frick. 88.

Hardenbergh, Henry J. (b. Brunswick, New Jersey, 1847, d. 1918), architect. Designed several major New York hotels, including the Plaza, and the early luxury apartment house, the Dakota, in eclectic style, with decorative devices imitative of European chateaux. Consolidated Edison's headquarters, building his design. 82, *106.*

Hare, David (b. New York, N.Y., 1917), sculptor active in the Abstract Expressionist school. Metal sculpture in MOMA, WMAA.

Harrison & Abramovitz (Wallace K. Harrison, b. Worcester, Massachusetts, 1895; Max Abramovitz, b. Chicago Illinois, 1908), architects. Responsible for variety of structures in contemporary New York, including major office structures (Socony Mobil Building, 3rd Ave & 42nd St; Time-Life Building; Corning Glass Building, 5th Ave & 56th St), academic and public buildings (Loeb Student Center, New York University; Columbia University Law School; Hammarskjöld Library, United Nations; Central terminal and central tower. La Guardia Airport. *135,* 158, 160, 186, 188, *192,* 206.

Harrison, Wallace K. (b. Worcester, Massachusetts, 1895), architect, partner in Harrison & Abramovitz (q.v.), member of group which planned Rockefeller Center, Chairman of the international committee for the design of United Nations headquarters, Director of Board of Architects of Lincoln Center for the Performing Arts and designer of the Metropolitan Opera House there. Designer (with J.A. Fouilhoux) of Rockefeller Apartments. 133, *135,* 142, 182.

Hartley, Marsden (b. Lewiston, Maine, 1877, d. 1943), painter, noted for his early abstractions, and for later paintings of Maine and New Mexico, in primitivist expressionistic style. Work in MMA, MOMA, WMAA. 110, *168.*

Heins & LaFarge (George Heins, b. Philadelphia, Pennsylvania, 1860, d. 1907; Christopher G. LaFarge, b. Newport, Rhode Island, 1862, d. 1938), architects, responsible for original, Romanesque-Byzantine design of Cathedral of St John the Divine; also many buildings at Bronx Zoo. La Farge, son of painter John LaFarge.

Held, Al (b. New York, N.Y., 1928), painter, hard-edge abstractionist. Work in WMAA.

Henri, Robert (b. Cincinnati, Ohio, 1865, d. 1929), painter, leader of the Ashcan School, member of The Eight, known for his energetically painted, naturalistic portraits. As teacher to a generation of American artists, influenced painters as diverse as Edward Hopper and Stuart Davis. Work in MMA, WMMA. 108, 110.

Hepworth, Barbara (b. Wakefield, England, 1903), British sculptor, noted for her works of metal, polished stone, wood. *Single Form* in courtyard of United Nations Secretariat. Work in MOMA, *154,* 159-160.

Hicks, Edward (b. Langhorne, Pennsylvania, 1780, d. 1849), primitive painter. His *The Peaceable Kingdom* at BM.

Hofmann, Hans (b. Neissenberg, Germany, 1880, d. 1966), painter and teacher, of the Abstract Expressionist school; noted for his masterly use of colour. Mosaic mural at 711 3rd Ave. Work in MMA, MOMA, WMAA, Gu. 154, 168.

Hofmeister, Henry (b. New York, N.Y., 1890, d. 1942), architect, member of Rockefeller Center design team. 133.

Holbein, Hans (b. Augsburg, Germany, 1497, d. 1543), painter. Work in MMA, Frick. 119.

Holland, John Joseph (b. England, 1776, d. 1820), townscape and theatrical scene painter, sometimes called George Holland. His watercolour of Broad Street is at NYPL.

Homer, Winslow (b. Boston, Massachusetts, 1836, d. 1910), painter and illustrator, known especially for seascapes and genre paintings. Work in MMA, WMAA, C-HM. 79.

Hood, Raymond (b. Pawtucket, Rhode Island, 1881, d. 1934), architect, designer (with J.M. Howells) of the Gothicized Chicago Tribune Tower. In New York, his American Standard Building (American Radiator Building) is also Gothicized, but later McGraw-Hill Building (with J. A. Fouilhoux) and Daily News Building (with Howells) were among first in city to embody principles of the International Style. Hood member of group which planned Rockefeller Center. *124, 128, 130, 133, 135, 136.*

Hopper, Edward (b. New York, N.Y., 1882, d. 1967), realist painter, student of Henri, noted for his paintings of American life, strangely lighted, often with effect of mystery or loneliness. Work in MMA, MOMA, WMAA. 135.

Howe & Lescaze (George Howe, b. Worcester, Massachusetts, 1886, d. 1955; William Lescaze, b. Geneva, Switzerland, 1896), architects, noted for their pioneering work in the International Style, PSPS Building in Philadelphia. Lescaze alone has designed office structures in New York (711 3rd Ave, U.S. Plywood Building, 3rd Ave & 48th St), and designed for himself one of first modern town houses in the city (211 E. 48th St.).)136, 143, 169.

Howells, John Mead (b. Cambridge, Massachusetts, 1868, d. 1959), architect, with Raymond Hood designed New York Daily News Building, as well as Chiacgo Tribune Tower. *135.*

Hubert, Pirsson & Co. (Philip G. Hubert, b. Paris, France, 1830, d. 1911; James W. Pirsson, b. New York, N.Y. 1833, d. 1888), architects, noted for their apartment buildings, one of which is now the Chelsea Hotel. 84.

Hunt, Richard Howland (b. Paris, France, 1862, d. 1931), architect, son of Richard Morris Hunt; completed his father's work on 5th Ave building of Metropolitan Museum; relatively modest Lotos Club his design.

Hunt, Richard Morris (b. Brattleboro, Vermont, 1828, d. 1895), architect; major contributor to New York architecture of late 19th century, influential designer of elaborate 'country cottages' for the rich (The Breakers, Newport). An eclectic, trained at École des Beaux Arts, Hunt designed 5th Ave building of the Metropolitan Museum (in Roman style), the doors of Trinity Church (in Italian Renaissance style), and the base of the *Statue of Liberty*. 73, 82, 86, *89,* 90, 98, 99.

Huntington, Charles P. (b. Logan-

sport, Indiana, 1874, d. 1919), architect, designed Audubon Terrace and most of buildings there, in classical style.

Huntington, Daniel (b. New York City 1816, d. 1906), portrait, historical and landscape painter.

Inman, Henry (b. Utica, New York, 1801, d. 1846), portrait painter. Work in MMA, City Hall. 31.

Jarvis, John Wesley (b. England, 1780, d. 1840), portrait painter. Work in MMA, City Hall. 30.

Jenney, William LeBaron (b. Fairhaven, Massachussets 1832, d. 1907), engineer-architect. Responsible for first important building of Chicago school of architecture, Home Insurance Building in Chicago. No work in New York. 101.

Jessor, Herman, architect, designer of Co-Op City in the Bronx.

Johns, Jasper (b. Augusta, Georgia, 1930), painter, especially noted for his paintings of flags and targets; uses iconography and often artifacts from popular culture in his work, but technique that of the best Abstract Expressionism. Painting in New York State Theater, Lincoln Center; work at MOMA, WMAA.

Johnson, Eastman (b. Lowell, Maine, 1824, d. 1906), genre and portrait painter popular with middle class in New York, 19th century. Work at MMA. 76.

Johnson, Philip (b. Cleveland, Ohio, 1906), architect. Collaborator with Henry-Russell Hitchcock on exhibition and book, *The International Style* early in the 30s; as an architect after Second World War worked in style of Mies van der Rohe (former Museum of Modern Art Guesthouse, Asia Society, Museum of Modern Art Sculpture Garden) and collaborated with Mies on Seagram Building. Taste for the extravagant, seen in design for Four Seasons Restaurant, Seagram Building, has since found its way into his architectural style. Latest additions to Museum of Modern Art his. Chosen to design immigration monument for Ellis Island. 137, 139, 145, 148, 151, 155, 160, 169, 170, *184,* 187, 188, 231, 232.

Kahn, Louis (b. Ösel Island, Estonia, 1901), architect, major architectural theoretician and teacher; especially noted for his expressive Richards Medical Research Building in Philadelphia. In New York, worked with Isamu Noguchi on design for Riverside Park, to include a variety of play areas, and plans for Welfare Island. 235.

Kandinsky, Wassily (b. Russia 1866, d. 1944), abstract painter. Work in MOMA, Gu. 111, 150, 152, *166,* 176.

Katan, Roger (b. Algiers 1931), French-born architect and planner, designer of Multi-service Center for East Harlem. 202, 203, 206.

Kellum, John (b. New York, N.Y., 1807, d. 1871), builder; handling of cast iron seen in 801 Broadway building. 57.

Kelly & Gruzen (Hugh Kelly b. Jersey City, New Jersey, 1888, d. 1966; b.

Riga, Latvia, 1903), Sumner Gruzen now Gruzen & Partners, architects; designers of notable modern apartment complexes in New York, Chatham Towers (in reinforced concrete) and Chatham Green; also Park Avenue Synagogue. 169, 217, 218, *224.*

Kelly, Ellsworth (b. Newburgh, New York, 1923), painter of the hard-edge school, noted for his large colour paintings, which utilize only a few geometric forms, and for his drawing of natural forms. Work in MMA, MOMA, WMAA, Gu.

Kensett, John F. (b. Cheshire, Connecticut, 1818, d. 1872), painter of the Hudson River School; landscapes and seascapes noted for handling of light and smoothly-finished detail. Work in MMA, NYHS. 76-77, 97.

Kepes, Gyorgy (b. Selyp, Hungary, 1906), painter and designer, noted for his decor for public buildings and spaces, often utilizing advanced technology. Decor of lobby, Pan Am Building. 208.

Kessler, S.J. (b. New York, N.Y., 1913), architect; designer of Washington Square Village. *224.*

Kiesler, Frederick (b. Vienna, Austria, 1896, d. 1965), designer and architect; designed interior and furnishings for New York stores, restaurants and galleries (since destroyed, including Peggy Guggenheim's Art of this Century gallery); expounded visionary notion of the nature and function of architecture in modern society. Work in MOMA. 147, 150.

Klee, Paul (b. Bern, Switzerland 1879, d. 1940), Swiss painter and musician. Work in MOMA, Gu. 150, 176.

Kline, Franz (b. Wilkes-Barre, Pennsylvania, 1910, d. 1962), one of the foremost painters of the Abstract Expressionist school; in his dynamic large paintings, mostly in black and red, great slashing strokes delineate picture's space and form. Work in MMA, MOMA, WMAA, Gu. 195.

Knoop, Guitou (b. Moscow, Russia, 1911), sculptor. Her monumental sculpture at New York University, Bronx. 154, 233.

Kohn, Robert D. (b. New York City 1870, d. 1953), architect, designer of Evening Post Building. 105, *106.*

de Kooning, Willem (b. Rotterdam, Holland, 1904), painter, one of the foremost of the Abstract Expressionist school; noted for his abstractions, done with broad brushwork, and his paintings of women, in which figures disappear into the energetic rythm of the painting surface. Work in MMA, MOMA, WMAA, Gu, BM. 152, 154.

Lachaise, Gaston (b. Paris, France, 1882, d. 1935), sculptor, noted for his expressively handled, rhythmic, massive sculptures of women. Work in MMA, MOMA, WMAA, BM.

LaFarge, John (b. New York, N.Y., 1835, d. 1910), painter, known especially for his church decoration; decorated Richardson's Trinity Church in Boston. In New York, chancel painting of the *Ascension* in Church of the Ascension, 5th Ave, for which he also designed some of the windows; stained glass in Judson Memorial Church.

Lafever, Minard (b. Morristown, New Jersey, 1797, d. 1854), builder-architect and author of architectural style books, *The Modern Builder's Guide. The Beauties of Modern Architecture, The Young Builder's General Instructor,* which elaborated decoration, mostly of Greek Revival style. His work in New York often identified by reference to material in the books, and so not certainly his. Old Merchant's House (Seabury - Treadwell House); St James' Church; Mariners' Temple; Bartow-Pell Mansion; portions of Church of the Holy Apostoles, 9th Ave & 28th. Certainly his are several Gothic Revival churches in Brooklyn. 36.

Lawrie, Lee (b. Rixford, Germany, 1887, d. 1963), sculptor; of *Atlas* at International Bulding, Rockefeller Center.

Lassaw, Ibram (b. Alexandria, Egypt, 1913), sculptor, noted for his works in metal and wire. Work in MOMA, WMAA. 148.

Latrobe, Benjamin Henry (b. Fulneck, near Leeds, England, 1764, d. 1820), British-trained architect, inaugurator of architectural profession in America, as opposed to builder-architect tradition; leading spirit of Greek Revival, architect of the Capitol, Washington, 1803-17. No work in New York. 34.

Le Corbusier, pseudonym of Charles-Edouard Jeanneret (b. La Chaud-de-Fonds, Switzerland, 1887, d. 1965), architect, known for writings on architecture and the modern city, as well as his buildings often raised on massive concrete stilts. Only work in New York as member of international committee responsible for design of United Nations complex, in general form thought to represent his conception. 128, 130, 133, 134, 136, 139, 145, 155, 159, 167, 176, 178, 202, 218, 226, 236.

Léger, Fernand (b. Normandy, France, 1881, d. 1955), painter, noted for machine forms. Murals at United Nations General Assembly Building; work in MOMA, Gu. 159, 176.

Lehmbruck, Wilhelm (b. Germany 1881, d. 1919), German sculptor. Work at Metropolitan Opera House, Lincoln Center; in MOMA.

Lehrecke & Tonetti (Thomas C. Lehrecke b. Dresden, Germany 1928), architects; designers Automation House. 223.

Leibl, Wilhelm (b. Cologne, Germany, 1844, d. 1900), German painter of the realist school, influenced by Courbet. 88.

L'Enfant, Pierre Charles (b. Paris, France, 1754, d. 1825), architect and engineer; planned Washington, D.C. In New York, designed Federal Hall, where Washington took oath of office as President, on site of present Federal Hall National Memorial. 19.

Leutze, Emmanuel (b. Württemburg, Germany 1816, d. 1868), historical and portrait painter. Work at MMA.

Levine, Jack (b. Boston, Massachusetts, 1915), painter, known for depiction of grotesque ceremonies of American Life, painted in elaborate style utilizing blur. and distortion. Work in MMA, MOMA, WMAA.

Levinson, Mon (b. New York 1926), sculptor. Relief at P.S. 166. Work in WMAA. 238.

Lewitt, Sol (b. Hartford, Connecticut, 1928), conceptual artist, noted for his cubic sculptures. Work in MOMA, WMAA.

Lichtenstein, Roy (b. New York, 1923), painter, noted for his large-scale, blown-up, pop art painting in the style of cartoon illustrations. Work in MOMA, WMAA, Gu.

Lienau, Dietlef (b. Holstein, Germany, 1818, d. 1887), architect with lucrative practice in New York, beginning in 1848, which marked change in building style of New York houses, from Greek Revival to more generally eclectic style. His Schiff House at 5th Ave & 10th St (destroyed) was thought to be first in city with Mansard roof. 73.

Lippold, Richard (b. Milwaukee, Wisconsin, 1915), artist noted for his wire and metal constructions. Works in Four Seasons Restaurant, Philharmonic Hall, lobby of Pan Am Building; work in MMA, MOMA, WMAA. 169, 188, 208.

Lipchitz, Jacques (b. Lithuania, 1891), sculptor, noted for his early cubist work and later monumental abstract sculpture. Work in MOMA.

Lipton, Seymour (b. New York, N.Y., 1903), sculptor, noted for his work in metal suggesting primordial forms. Sculpture, *Archangel* at Philharmonic Hall, Lincoln Center; work in MMA, MOMA, WMAA.

Lober, Georg (b. Chicago, Illinois, 1893, d. 1961), sculptor of *Hans Christian Andersen*, at Conservatory Water, Central Park.

Louis, Morris (b. Baltimore, Maryland, 1912, d. 1962), painter of the Abstract Expressionist school, noted for striped canvases stained with intense colour. Work in MMA, MOMA, WMAA, Gu.

Luckman, Charles (b. Kansas City, Missouri, 1909), architect, designer of the newest Madison Square Garden, with its accompanying Pennsylvania Station.

Luks, George (b. Williamsport, Pennsylvania, 1867, d. 1933), painter of the Ashcan School, member of The Eight, originally a newspaper illustrator; known for his scenes of common life, painted in a broad, bold style imitative of Hans. Work in MMA, WMAA. 110.

Lundy, Victor (b. New York, N.Y., 1923), architect, designer of the Church of the Resurrection, E. 101st St, and of

interior, I. Miller store, 5th Ave & 57th St. 214.

MacMonnies, Frederick (b. Brooklyn, N. Y., 1863, d. 1937), sculptor of figures above fountains at New York Public Library, and much of the sculpture on Soldiers and Sailors' Memorial Arch, Grand Army Plaza, Brooklyn.

Magonigle, H. Van Buren (b. Beizen Heights, New York, 1867, d. 1935), architect, designer of Maine Memorial, Columbus Circle.

Maillol, Aristide (b. France, 1861, d. 1944), sculptor, of female heroic nudes. Work in MMA, MOMA, BM. 135.

Mangin, Joseph François, French architect designer, with John McComb, Jr., of New York City Hall and the Georgian Gothic old St Patrick's Cathedral, Mott St (reconstructed, but walls of Mangin's building remain). 22, 25.

Manship, Paul (b. St Paul, Minnesota, 1885, d. 1966), sculptor of the stylized, gilded *Prometheus* which dominates skating rink at Rockefeller Center. Work at MMA. 134.

Manzù, Giacomo (b. Bergamo, Italy, 1908), sculptor. Work at Italian Building, Rockefeller Center; MOMA.

Marca-Relli, Conrad (b. Boston, Massachusetts, 1913), painter of the Abstract Expressionist school, noted for collages. Work in MMA, MOMA, WMAA, Gu.

Marin, John (b. Rutherford, New Jersey, 1870, d. 1953), painter and watercolourist, known for landscapes, seascapes, and city scenes, in style derived from Cézanne and the cubists, but expressionistic as well; often considered forerunner of Abstract Expressionism because of interest in picture surface and texture. Work in MMA, MOMA, WMAA. 110, 111, *111.*

Markelius, Sven (b. Stockholm, Sweden, 1800), Swedish architect, designer of interiors and decoration of Conference Building, United Nations. Member of planning committee for Lincoln Center. 159, 186.

Masson, André (b. Balagny, France, 1896), French surrealist painter, active in U.S. 1941-46. Works in MOMA, Gu. 150.

Matisse, Henri (b. LeCateau, France, 1869, d. 1954), French painter. Works in MMA, MOMA, Gu. 110, 111, 134.

Matta (Echuarren), Roberto (b. Santiago, Chile, 1912), surrealist painter, worked in New York during Second World War, influenced Abstract Expressionists. Work in MOMA. 154.

Maurer, Alfred (b. New York, N.Y., 1868, d. 1932), painter, noted for his cubist and expressionist work among the first American examples. Work in MMA, MOMA, WMAA. 110.

Mayer & Whittlesey (and Mayer, Whittlesey & Glass) (Albert Mayer b. New York, N.Y., 1897; Julian Whittlesey, b. Greenwich, Connecticut, 1905; Milton M. Glass b. New York City 1906), architects, designers with Skidmore, Owing & Merrill of Manhattan House. M. Milton Glass, with William J. Conklin in charge, designed addition to New School for Social Research. 166.

McBean, Thomas, Scottish architect of St Paul's Chapel, which greatly resembles St Martin-in-the-Fields church in London by British architect, James Gibbs, of whom McBean was a follower. 13, *15*, 16.

McComb, John, Jr. (b. New York, N.Y., 1763, d. 1853), architect and builder, designer, with Joseph F. Mangin, of New York City Hall; Castle Clinton on the Battery; 7 State St (Watson House) attributed to him. Most of his work talented American builder's adaptation of English Georgian design. 22, *25*, 49.

McKim, Mead & White (Charles Follen McKim, b. Isabella Furnace, Chester City, Pennsylvania, 1847, d. 1909; William Rutherford Mead, b. Brattleboro, Vermont, 1846, d. 1928; Stanford White b. New York, N.Y., 1855, d. 1906), architects responsible for many of the principal buildings erected in New York in last quarter of 19th, first quarter of 20th century. Work wide-ranging in type and style; included large-scale public buildings based on Roman models (Pennsylvania Station, now destroyed; General Post Office; Low Library, Columbia University; Hall of Fame, New York University, Bronx), clubs and private mansions in style of Renaissance palaces or Georgian houses (University Club, Metropolitan Club, Villard Houses, Racquet & Tennis Club, Century Association, Morgan Library, Harvard Club, Colony Club—now American Academy of Dramatic Arts, houses at 680-686 Park Ave at 68th St), the Renaissance-inspired Judsen Memorial Church, portals to St Bartholomew's Church. Firm's eclecticism derived from Beaux Arts training and inspiration of European buildings from all great architectural periods, reinforced by participation in World's Columbian Exhibition, Chicago, 1893, inaugurating Imperial age of American architecture. Stanford White's talents put to use separately in variety of odd monuments in city: Washington Arch, Washington Square; bases of Farragut memorial, Madison Square Park, and Cooper Memorial, Cooper Square; redecoration of Church of the Ascension, 5th Ave; remodelling of Players' Club, Gramercy Park S. Other buildings by McKim, Mead & White: Croquet Shelter in Prospect Park, Brooklyn; Harmonic Club, Lambs' Club, Brooklyn Museum, wings of Metropolitan Museum. *80, 82,* 86, *84,* 86, 92, 98, 99, 100, 112, *124, 235.*

Meier, Richard (b. Newark, New Jersey, 1934), architect; his rehabilitation of Westbeth a notable example of building conversion. 222, *223.*

Meissonier, Ernest (b. Lyons, France, 1815, d. 1891), French painter. Emulat-

ed Dutch little masters, but noted for his historical and battle paintings as well. 88.

Mies van der Rohe, Ludwig (b. Aachen, Germany, 1886, d. 1969), architect, known for elegance of proportion, precision and refinement in use of metal and the curtain wall. Buildings prime examples of the International Style. In New York, sole work Seagram Building, designed with Philip Johnson. 136, *160,* 169, 170, 176.

Milles, Carl (b. Lagga, Sweden 1875, d. 1955), sculptor, especially of fountains. Work in MMA.

Miró, Joan (b. Barcelona, Spain, 1893), painter. Work in MOMA, Gu. *141,* 150.

Mondrian, Piet (b. Amersfoort, Holland, 1872, d. 1944), Dutch painter, leader of *de stijl,* noted for his geometric paintings; spent last four years of his life in New York. Work in MOMA, Gu. *139,* 148.

Moore, Henry (b. Castleford, England, 1898), English sculptor, known for his use of simple massive forms. Sculpture at Lincoln Center, in reflecting pool between Beaumont Theater and Philarmonic Hall; work in MMA, MOMA, Gu. 172, 189.

Moran, Thomas (b. England, 1837, d. 1926), painter, member of later Hudson River School. Work in MMA, BM, NYSH.

Morris, Benjamin Wister (b. Portland, Oregon, 1870, d. 1944), architect; designer of addition to Morgan Library. One of consultants (Joseph Urban the other) on the first design of Rockefeller Center. 131, 133.

Morse, Samuel F.B. (b. Charlestown, Massachusetts, 1791, d. 1872), portrait painter, inventor of the telegraph. His *Allegorical Landscape with New York University* at NYHS; work at MMA, HYPL. 30, 32, *32,* 35, 50.

Motherwell, Robert (b. Aberdeen, Washington, 1915), one of the foremost painters and theorists of the Abstract Expressionist school, known for work in which picture plane divided into areas of strong colour, with frequent use of motifs of decorative character and treatment. 150, 154.

Mould, J. Wrey (b. England, 1825, d. 1884), architect, designer, with Calvert Vaux, of first building for MMA. 98.

Mount, William S. (b. Setauket, Long Island, New York, 1807, d. 1868), genre painter, mostly of scenes from country life on Long Island. Work in MMA, NYPL. 39, 40.

Nadelman, Elie (b. Warsaw, Poland, 1882, d. 1946), sculptor. His witty figures of men and women characterized by flowing curves and smooth surfaces. Large white marble versions of two small Nadelmans placed at either end of grand foyer, New York State Theater, Lincoln Center. Work in MMA, MOMA, WMAA. 188.

Nakian, Reuben (b. College Point, New York, 1899), sculptor, mature work related to Abstract Expressionist painting, intended to embody spirit of classical myths. Sculpture on Loeb Student Center, New York University, Washington Square; work in MOMA, WMAA, New School. 233.

Nervi, Pier Luigi (b. Sondrio, Lombardy, Italy, 1891), Italian engineer and architect, noted for use of pre-stressed concrete; designed George Washington Bridge Bus Station.

Neutra, Richard (b. Vienna, Austria 1892, d. 1970), architect, featured in Hitchcock and Johnson's International Style exhibit at MOMA. No work in New York. 136.

Nevelson, Louise (b. Kiev, Russia, 1900), artist, known for her constructions, usually painted a single colour, in which great variety of forms built into boxes of wood or metal, which in turn form 'walls' or 'environments'. Work at Juilliard School, Lincoln Center; in MOMA, WMAA, JM, RM, BM.

Newman, Barnett (b. New York, N.Y., 1905, d. 1970), one of the foremost painters of the Abstract Expressionist school; known for works in which large areas of colour edged with or divided by vertical bands of different hue. Sometimes called 'non-relational' paintings; dispose of convention to express primitive painter's 'abstract thought-complex'. Work at MMA, MOMA, WMAA, Gu. 152, 195, 234.

Niemeyer, Oscar (b. Rio de Janeiro 1907), architect and planner. In New York, consultant UN building.

Nivola, Constantino (b. Sardinia, 1911), architectural sculptor and painter, known for his murals, play sculptures, architectural decoration. Play Area, W. 90th St between Columbus Ave & Amsterdam Ave; Play Area, P.S. 55, Staten Island; P.S. 46, Brooklyn. 211.

Noguchi, Isamu (b. Los Angeles, California, 1904), architectural sculptor. known for his use of simple, organic forms and polished surfaces; long a proponent of public sculpture, author of scheme for redesigning Riverside Park, with Louis Kahn. Water garden at Chase Manhattan Plaza; up-ended red cube, 140 Broadway; sculpture, interior court of New School; waterfall and ceiling in arcade, 666 5th Ave. Work at MMA, MOMA, WMAA, Gu. 189, 194-5, 196, 234-5, 235, 240.

Noland, Kenneth (b. Asheville, North Carolina, 1924), painter, noted for large paintings of stripes and chevrons. Work in MOMA, WMAA, Gu.

O'Donovan, William (b. Preston City, Virginia 1844, d. 1920), painter and sculptor. Bas-relief of Grant on interior face of Soldiers' and Sailors' Memorial Arch, Grand Army Plaza, Brooklyn.

O'Keeffe, Georgia (b. Sun Prairie, Wisconsin, 1887), painter associated with Stieglitz, noted for her subtle palette of earth colours, simplified forms derived from nature, visionary quality of her compositions. Work in MMA, MOMA, WMAA, BM.

Oldenburg, Claes (b. Stockholm, Sweden, 1929), pop painter, sculptor, deviser of happenings; noted for 'soft' sculpture. Work in MOMA, WMAA.

Olmsted, Frederick Law (b. New York, N.Y., 1822, d. 1903), landscape architect and conservationist; designer, with Calvert Vaux, of Central Park and Prospect Park, Brooklyn; alone, designed Morningside Park and Riverside Park. *64,* 70-1, 79, 98.

Olmsted, Frederick Law, Jr. (b. New York City 1870), d. 1957), landscape architect; designer of Fort Tryon Park.

Orozco, José Clemente (b. Zapotlan, Mexico, 1883, d. 1949), Mexican painter and muralist. Murals at New School; work in MOMA, NYCC. 143, 148.

Oud, J.J.P. (b. Holland, 1890, d. 1963), architect; several of his buildings—especially for housing developments—were featured in Hitchcock and Johnson's International Style exhibit at MOMA. No work in New York, 136.

Pascin, Jules (b. Bulgaria, 1885, d. 1930), painter, noted for his freely-handled paintings of nudes. Work in MOMA, WMAA. 128.

Peale, Rembrandt (b. Bucks County, Pennsylvania, 1778, d. 1860), portrait painter. Work in MMA, NYHS, MCNY, NYPL. 32.

Pederson & Tilney (William Pederson, b. Stamford, Connecticut, 1908; Bradford Tilney, b. Lynton, England, 1908), architects, noted for their schools, especially IHS 43, Brooklyn. 214.

Pei, I.M. (b. Canton, China, 1917), architect, designer of Kips Bay Plaza Apartments and University Village Apartments, which make use of exposed concrete grids, characteristic of his work. In his Domestic Arrivals Building at Kennedy Airport, exposed concrete again major building material. 217, *226, 228, 233, 237,* 238.

Peterson, Frederick, architect, designer of Cooper Union Building. *61.*

Picabia, Francis (b. Paris, France, 1878, d. 1953), French cubist and dadaist painter, visited New York at about time of Armory Show; with Duchamp, influenced development of American painting '20s. Work in MOMA, Gu. 128.

Piccarilli, Attilio (b. Massa, Italy 1866, d. 1945), sculptor of figures on Maine Memorial, Columbus Circle, and Firemen's Monument in Riverside Park.

Picasso, Pablo (b. Malaga, Spain, 1881), painter and sculptor. Backdrop for *Le Tricorne* at entrance to Four Seasons Restaurant, Seagram Building; monumental enlargement of cubistic *Portrait of Sylvette* in forecourt of University Village Apartments. Best and most complete collection of work at MOMA; work in MMA, Gu, Bm. 110, 111, *138,* 145, 150, 152, 170, 176, 233.

Pollock, Jackson (b. Cody, Wyoming, 1912, d. 1956), painter, one of the foremost of the Abstract Expressionist school, mature style characterized by rhythmic linear working of paint, dripped and swirled into mural-size compositions, creating effect of energetic movement and play of forces. Work in MMA, MOMA, WMAA, Gu, BM. *141, 148, 150, 152, 195.*

Pope, John Russell (b. New York, N.Y., 1874, d. 1937), architect, noted for elaborate classical public buildings; designed Theodore Roosevelt Memorial Building of American Museum of Natural History, renovation of the Frick Mansion for use as a museum. *76.*

Post, George B. (b. New York, N.Y., 1837, d. 1913), architect, one of first New York skyscraper builders; designer of Union Trust Building and of Vanderbilt House, 5th Ave & 57th St (both now destroyed), New York Stock Exchange, North Campus of City College. *86, 98, 104.*

Potter, E.C. (b. New London, Connecticut 1857, d. 1923), sculptor of the lions which flank the stairs of the New York Public Library.

Pousette-Dart, Richard (b. St Paul, Minnesota, 1916), painter of the Abstract Expressionist school. Work in MOMA, WMAA.

Prendergast, Maurice (b. St Johns, Newfoundland, 1859, d. 1924), painter, member of The Eight; known for his sun-dappled Post-Impressionist painting, which has affinities with the work of Vuillard. Work in MMA, MOMA, WMAA.

Rauschenberg, Robert (b. Port Arthur, Texas, 1925), painter. While using characteristic brushwork of Abstract Expressionism, incorporated detritus of daily life into his painting, giving it problematic relation to art that was to be thoroughly explored by pop art. Works in MOMA, WMAA, Gu. *182, 192, 223.*

Ray, Man (b. Philadelphia, Pennsylvania, 1890), surrealist painter and photographer. Work in MOMA. *128.*

Redon, Odilon (b. France, 1840, d. 1910), French symbolist painter. Work in MMA, MOMA. *135.*

Reed & Stem (Charles Reed, b. 1911; Allen Stem b. Van Wert, Ohio, 1859, d. 1931), architects, designers, with Warren & Wetmore, of Grand Central Terminal. *104, 203, 207.*

Reinhard, L. Andrew (1892-1964), architect, member of board of architects for Rockefeller Center. *133.*

Reinhardt, Ad (b. Buffalo, New York, 1913, d. 1967), painter, known for his geometrically organized abstract painting in which subtle colour modulation from area to area is characteristic. Work in MOMA, WMAA. *149.*

Rembrandt Van Rijn (b. Leyden, Holland 1606, d. 1669), the greatest Dutch painter. More than thirty works at MMA; three works at Frick. *119.*

Renoir, Pierre Auguste (b. Limoges, France, 1841, d. 1919), French Impressionist painter; work in MMA. *95, 111, 112, 135.*

Renwick, James, Jr. (b. New York, N.Y., 1818, d. 1895), engineer and architect, designed Grace Church on Broadway, following handbooks of the Pugins, English Gothic Revival architects. Most important later work St Patrick's Cathedral; others, Calvary Church 21st St & Park Ave S. *45, 50, 51.*

Richardson, Henry Hobson (b. St James Parish near New Orleans, Louisiana, 1838, d. 1886), architect, chief exponent of Romanesque Revival. His use of masonry influenced architects of the Chicago school. No building in New York, but such buildings as De Vinne Press Building, U.S. Federal Building, Washington St, and 77th St building, American Museum of Natural History, characteristic of his style. *80, 86, 202.*

Rietveld, Gerrit Thomas (b. Utrecht, Holland 1888, d. 1964), architect. Work in MOMA design collection. No buildings in city.

Rivera, Diego (b. Guanajuato, Mexico, 1886, d. 1957), painter and muralist; while working in New York in 30s, stimulated artists of first generation of Abstract Expressionists. Work in MOMA. *148.*

Rivera, José de (b. New Orleans, Louisiana, 1904), sculptor, noted for his flowing, clean-lined, design. Work in MOMA, WMAA.

Rivers, Larry (b. New York, N.Y., 1923), painter known for his pop imagery and free, often sketchy, rendition of complicated and surrealist themes. Work in MMA, MOMA, WMAA, BM.

Robertson, Archibald (b. Moneymusk, Scotland, 1765, d. 1835), draughtsman of many early views of New York.

Roche, Dinkeloo & Associates (Kevin Roche, b. Dublin, Ireland, 1922; John Dinkeloo, b. Holland, Michigan, 1918), architects, designers of elegant Ford Foundation Building, new plaza and entrance to Metropolitan Museum and renovation of its Great Hall. *208, 210, 214.*

Roebling, John (b. Mühlhausen, Germany, 1806, d. 1869), engineer, designer of Brooklyn Bridge; died before construction was far advanced; work completed by son, Washington Roebling (b. Saxonburg, Pennsylvania, 1837, d. 1926). *64, 73, 79, 80.*

Rogers, Isaiah (b. Marshfield, Massachusetts, 1800, d. 1869), architect. Worked in Greek Revival style, mostly on hotels. In New York, designed Astor House, Astor Place Opera House (both destroyed), Third Merchants' (Mercantile) Exchange on Wall St, still existing, though altered. *36, 49.*

Rohe, Mies van der - *see* **Mies**

Rosati, James (b. Washington, Pennsylvania, 1912), sculptor. His monumental steel sculpture designed in plaza of World Trade Center. Work in WMAA. 240.

Rosenquist, James (b .Grand Forks, North Dakota, 1933), painter, originally of billboards; juxtaposes images from advertising in odd combination, sometimes at billboard scale, in a flat painting style. Work in MOMA, WMAA.

Rosenthal, Bernard (b. Highland Park, Illinois, 1914), sculptor. His *Alamo* is placed near Cooper Union, in Astor Place, sculpture in plaza E. 59th St between Park and Lexington Aves, work in WMAA.

Roszak, Theodore (b. Poznan, Poland, 1907), sculptor of abstract, expressive metal works, often suggesting mythic figures. Work in MOMA, WMAA.

Roth, Emery, & Sons, architectural firm. (Emery Roth b. Czechoslovakia, 1877, d. 1948; Jilian Roth b. New York; Richard Roth b. New York, N.Y. 1904). In contemporary New York, they have designed or co-designed many office structures, notably Pan Am Building, World Trade Center. *203,* 207, *208.*

Rothko, Mark (b. Dwinsk, Russia, 1903, d. 1970), painter, one of the foremost of the Abstract Expressionist school, known for his large paintings in which rectangles of deeply glowing colour are juxtaposed, with calming, meditative effect, on a subtly-related ground of colour. Work in MMA, MOMA, WMAA, Gu. *143,* 152, 170, 195, 234.

Rudolph, Paul (b. Elkton, Kentucky, 1918), architect, known for his buildings of dramatic, sculptural shape, often faced with concrete; designer of Tracey Towers, Bronx. 222.

Ryder, Albert Pinkham (b. New Bedford, Massachusetts, 1847, d. 1917), painter, lived most of his life as a recluse; known for his dark, highly-worked paintings, especially of the sea at night, which embody seemingly mystical vision. Work in MMA, MOMA, EMI. 88.

Saarinen, Eero (b. Kirkkonummi, Finland, 1910, d. 1961), Finnish-born architect, responsible for three elegant and dramatic contemporary buildings in New York: CBS Building, faced with black granite; massive, low-roofed Vivian Beaumont Theater, Lincoln Center; TWA Terminal at Kennedy Airport, expressionistically designed in concrete. 186, 187, *205,* 206.

Saint-Gaudens, Augustus (b. Dublin, Ireland, 1840, d. 1907), sculptor, known especially for his portrait work. Equestrian monument of *Sherman* at The Plaza; Farragut in Madison Square Park; Peter Cooper at Cooper Square; Chancel marbles, Judson Memorial Church; Altar marbles, Church of the Ascension, 5th Ave: work in MMA. *61,* 88, 92-3, *101.*

Sargent, John Singer (b. Florence, Italy, 1856, d. 1925), painter, noted for his brilliantly-executed society portraits and his water colours. Work in MMA. *95.*

Segal, George (b. New York, N.Y., 1924), sculptor, of the pop art group, noted for his environmental tableaux with white plaster figures. Work in MOMA, WMAA.

Seurat, Georges (b. Paris, France 1859, d. 1891), French painter. Work at MMA, MOMA, Gu. 134, 150, 176.

Shahn, Ben (b. Kaunas, Russia, 1898, d. 1969), painter, often concerned with social and political themes; work executed in a graphic style, figures often close to caricature. Murals in Bronx Post Office, at Grady H.S., Brooklyn; work in MMA, MOMA, WMAA, JM.

Sheeler, Charles (b. Philadelphia, Pennsylvania, 1883, d. 1965), painter and photographer of the precisionist group, known for his paintings of industrial America.

Shepley, Henry (b. Brookline, Massachusetts, 1887, d. 1963), architect, with practice mostly in Boston. Member of committee for Lincoln Center for the Performing Arts in New York. No building in city. 186.

Shinn, Everett (b. Woodtown, New Jersey, 1876, d. 1953), painter of the Ashcan School, member of The Eight; painted theatre and society in the manner of Degas. Work in MMA, WMAA, BM. 110.

Shreve, Lamb & Harmon (Richmond H. Shreve, b. Cornwallis, Nova Scotia, Canada, 1877, d. 1946; William Lamb, b. Brooklyn, New York 1883; Arthur Harmon, b. Chicago, Illinois, 1918, d. 1958), architects, chiefly notable for design of the Empire State Building. *121,* 128, *245.*

Siqueiros, David Alfaro (b. Mexico City, Mexico, 1898), painter and muralist, worked in New York in 30s, with influence on early Abstract Expressionists. Work in MOMA. 48.

Skidmore, Owings & Merrill (Louis Skidmore, b. Lawrenceberg, Indiana, 1897; Nathaniel Owings, b. Indianapolis, Indiana, 1903; John Merrill, b. St Paul, Minnesota, 1896), architects, responsible for many important structures in contemporary New York, most in the International Style. Lever House (Gordon Bunshaft, b. Buffalo, New York, 1909, chief designer); Manufacturers Hanover Trust bank, 5th Ave & 43rd St; Pepsi-Cola Building; Union Carbide Building; Chase Manhattan Bank Building; Chase Manattan branch bank, Park Ave & 55th St; Equitable Building; 140 Broadway; 919 Third Ave Manhattan house apartments; Library-Museum of the Performing Arts, Lincoln Center (by Gordon Bunshaft). At Kennedy Airport: International Arrivals Buildings and others. Two recent SOM buildings have exposed concrete frames: American Bible Society Building; American Red

Cross Building. *156, 158,* 159, 166, 169, 170, 188, *189,* 194, 201.

Sloan, John (b. Lock Haven, Pennsylvania, 1871, d. 1951), painter of the Ashcan School, member of The Eight; known for his warmly-rendered naturalistic paintings of New York scenes. Work in MMA, WMAA, BM.

Smith, David (b. Decatur, Illinois, 1906, d. 1965), sculptor; utilized geometric, plant-like, and machine forms in welded metal sculpture whose effects range from a sense of drawing in space to the monumental and architectonic sculpture in lobby, Vivien Beaumont Theater, Lincoln Center, Work in MMA, MOMA, WMAA, Gu, BM. 146, 240.

Smith, Hamilton (b. Bronxville, New York, 1925), architect, co-designer, with Marcel Breuer, of Whitney Museum of American Art. 190.

Smith, Tony (b. Paterson, New Jersey, 1912), architect and sculptor; noted for his monumental black sculpture, of single, extended geometrical forms. Work in MOMA. 192.

Snelson, Kenneth (b. Pendleton, Oregon, 1927), sculptor, noted for work of tubular steel and wire under tension. Work in MOMA, WMAA. 194.

Stamos, Theodore (b. New York, N.Y., 1922), painter of the Abstract Expressionist school. Work in MMA, MOMA, WMAA. 154.

Stankiewicz, Richard (b. Philadelphia, Pennsylvania, 1922), sculptor, noted for junk sculpture. Work in MOMA, WMAA.

Stebbins, Emma (b. New York City 1815, d. 1882), sculptor of the *Angel of the Waters,* on the Bethesda Fountain in Central Park.

Steichen, Edward (b. Luxembourg, 1879), photographer; promoter, with Alfred Stieglitz, of modern painting and photography; curator of the first museum collection of photography, at the Museum of Modern Art, which bears his name. Work in MMA, MOMA.

Stein, Richard G. (b. Chicago, Illinois, 1916), architect, noted for his schools. Designer of P.S. 55, Staten Island, with Play Area, and Play Area of Stephen Wise Towers (with Constantino Nivola). 211.

Stella, Frank (b. Malden, Massachusetts, 1936), painter, known for his 'stripe' paintings. Work in MMA, MOMA, WMAA.

Stella, Joseph (b. Muro-Locano, Italy, 1882, d. 1946) futurist painter, known especially for his paintings of Brooklyn Bridge. Work in MMA, MOMA, WMAA. 80, 111, 112.

Stent, Thomas, architect, designer of section, New York Shakespeare Festival Theater (Astor Library).

Stevenson, Harvey (b. Croton-on-Hudson, New York, 1894), architect, designer of FDR Drive, with Cameron Clark. 146.

Stieglitz, Alfred (b. Hoboken, New Jersey, 1864, d. 1946), photographer and art entrepreneur. Introduced the work of major modernist painters and sculptors, European and American, in his gallery. Work as a photographer ranges from views of New York life in 1890s to near-abstract photographs of clouds, called 'equivalents'. Work in MMA, MOMA, WMAA. 110, 134.

Still, Clyfford (b. Grendin, North Dakota, 1904), painter of the Abstract Expressionist school; known for his large-scale paintings of heavily-worked, often flame-shaped areas of colour. Work in MOMA, WMAA. 152.

Stone, Edward Durrell (b. Fayetteville, Arkansas, 1902) architect, noted for his use of stone grills; co-designer of original building, Museum of Modern Art; New York Cultural Center; General Motors Building; Hallmark Gallery, and his own town house on E. 64th St. *126,* 143, 211.

Stoughton & Stoughton (Charles W. Stoughton, b. New York, N.Y., 1871, d. 1945; Arthur Stoughton b. Mt. Vernon New York 1867, d. 1955), architects of the Soldiers' and Sailors Memorial, Riverside Drive at 89th St.

Streeter, Tal (b. Oklahoma City, Oklahoma, 1934), sculptor. His *Endless Column* is in Central Park at 79th St. Work at N.Y.U.

Stuart, Gilbert (b. North Kingston, Rhode Island, 1755, d. 1828), portrait painter, especially noted for his portraits of George Washington. Studied under Benjamin West. Work in MMA, NYPL, City Hall.

Sturgis, Russell (b. Baltimore, Maryland 1832, d. 1903), architect and architectural historian. Worked mostly in Gothic Revival style. 86.

Sullivan, Louis H. (b. Boston, Massachusetts, 1866, d. 1924), architect of the Chicago school; known for his advanced treatment of vertical elements of steel-frame design and distinctive use of ornament derived from natural forms. In New York, sole work Bayard Building (Condict Building); portions of ornament from façade in BM. 99, 100, 101, *103,* 134, 136.

Sully, Thomas (b. Lancashire, England, 1783, d. 1872), portrait painter. Works in MMA, MCNY, NYPL, NYHS, City Hall.

Tabler, William B. (b. Momence, Illinois, 1914), architect, chiefly of hotels; designer of New York Hilton. 206.

Tanio (Schreiber), (b. Warsaw, Poland, 1924), painter, associated with wall painting. Work in New York Civic Center Synagogue; at N.Y.U.

Thomas, Griffith (b. Isle of Wight. England, 1820, d. 1878), architect, son of Thomas Thomas; designer central section, New York Shakespeare Festival Theater (Astor Library); also many cast-iron buildings.

Thomas, Thomas, English-born architect, designer of south section, New York Shakespeare Festival Theater (Astor Library).

Thompson, Martin (b. New York, N.Y., 1789, d. 1877), builder-architect, sometime partner with Ithiel Town; worked in Greek Revival style. Designer of Bank of the United States (later U.S. Assay Office), whose façade is now in MMA; Arsenal in Central Park; most likely town houses on Washington Square and steeple of St Mark's-in-the-Bouwerie. *18, 34, 35.*

Tiffany, Louis Comfort (b. New York, N.Y., 1848, d. 1933), painter and stained-glass designer, originator of Tiffany Glass. Work in MMA, MOMA, MCNY.

Tinguely, Jean (b. Freiburg, Switzerland, 1925), sculptor. Work, MOMA. 223.

Tobey, Mark (b. Centerville, Wisconsin, 1890), painter, known for his use of 'white writing', related to oriental techniques. Work in MMA, MOMA, WMAA, BM.

Tomlin, Bradley Walker (b. Syracuse, New York, 1899, d. 1953), painter of the Abstract Expressionist school, known for his use of calligraphy. Work in MMA, MOMA, WMAA. 154.

Town, Ithiel (b. Thompson, Connecticut, 1784, d. 1844), architect, inventor of the Town Truss for bridges; active in New York from 1826, first in partnership with Martin Thompson, then, from 1829, with Alexander Jackson Davis; an important influence on architecture of city in period of Greek Revival. With Davis, designed Federal Hall National Memorial (Sub-treasury, originally Customs House); with Thompson, steeple of St Mark's-in-the-Bouwerie. No other work remains. 16, *18, 35, 36, 86.*

Trowbridge & Livingston (S. B. Parkmen Trowbridge, b. New York, N. Y., 1862, d. 1925), architects, designers of the St Regis Hotel.

Trumbull, John (b. Lebanon, Connecticut, 1756, d. 1843), historical and portrait painter. Work at NYPL, MCNY, NYHS, City Hall. 18, 29.

Tuthill, William B. (b. New York, N. Y., 1855, d. 1929), architect of Carnegie Hall, studied with Richard Morris Hunt.

Tworkov, Jack (b. Biala, Poland, 1900), painter of the Abstract Expressionist school; brushwork often agitated and slashing, colour rich. Work in MMA, MOMA, WMAA. 154.

Upjohn, Richard (b. Shaftesbury, Dorset, England, 1802, d. 1878), architect, influential exponent of Gothic Revival; designer of Trinity Church and Trinity Chapel, W. 35th St (now St Saba). *48, 50, 52, 73.*

Urban, Joseph (b. Vienna, Austria, 1872, d. 1933), architect, designer of New School, involved in planning of Rockefeller Center. 131, 143.

Van Alen, William (b. Brooklyn 1883, d. 1954) architect, designer of Chrysler Building. *123,* 128.

Van Brunt, Henry (b. Boston, Massachusetts, 1830, d. 1903), architect, active in Boston and Kansas City. One the first supporters of the use of iron as an architectural material. 62, 98.

Vanderlyn, John (b. Kingston, New York, 1775, d. 1852), painter. Work in MMA, City Hall.

Van Gogh, Vincent (b. Grott-Zundert, Holland, 1853, d. 1890), Post-Impressionist painter. Work in MMA, MOMA, Gu. 111, 134, *135, 138.*

Vaux, Calvert (b. London, England, 1824, d. 1895), architect; with Frederick Law Olmsted, planned Central Park and Prospect Park, Brooklyn. Working in Victorian Gothic style, designed National Arts Club (Samuel Tilden Residence), Jefferson Market Library (Jefferson Market Courthouse, with Frederick O. Withers), original building of Metropolitan Museum (with J. Wrey Mould). *64,* 70-1, 73, 98.

Velazquez, Diego (b. Seville, Spain, 1599, d. 1660), painter. Work at MMA, Frick, Hispanic Society. 119, *119.*

Vicente, Esteban (b. Segovia, Spain, 1906), painter of the Abstract Expressionist school. Work in WMAA. 154.

Walter, Thomas U. (b. Philadelphia, Pennsylvania, 1804, d. 1887), architect of U. S. Capital 1851-65, and organizer of American architectural associations. No work in New York. 36.

Ward, John Quincy Adams (b. Urbana, Ohio, 1830, d. 1910), portrait sculptor, popular in late 19th century. Washington at Federal Hall National Memorial; Horace Greely at City Hall Park; Roscoe Conkling in Madison Square Park; Henry Ward Beecher, Cadman Plaza, Brooklyn; sculpture on pediment of New York Stock Exchange. *86,* 88, 93, 97.

Warhol, Andy (b. Pittsburgh, Pennsylvania, 1930), pop artist and filmmaker, known for his paintings, objects, stage designs, etc., which show American development of sources in dada and surrealism. Work in MOMA, WMAA.

Warner, Burns, Toan & Lunde (Danforth Toan b. New York City 1918; Frithjof M. Lunde b. Scandinavia 1921), architects, designers of Warren Weaver ton Square. 231.

Warren & Wetmore (Whitney Warren, b. New York, N. Y. 1864, d. 1943; Charles D. Wetmore, b. Elmira, New York 1867, d. 1941), architects, designed many residences and office structures in late 19th century, early 20th, in New York. Most notable Grand Central Terminal (with Reed & Stem), New York General (Central) Building, Consolidated Edison Tower, New York Yacht Club. *104, 203, 207.*

Weber, Max (b. Byelostok, Russia, 1881, d. 1961), painter, pioneer of

287

cubism in America. Work in MMA, MOMA, WMAA, BM. 110.

West Benjamin (b. Springfield, Pennsylvania, 1738, d. 1820), historical painter resident in England from 1763; first American painter professionally trained. Work in MMA. 16.

Westermann & Miller (Helge Westermann, b. Esbjerg, Denmark, 1914; Richard Miller, b. Wisconsin, 1925), architects, designers, with Belluschi and Catalano of the Juilliard School of Music, Lincoln Center. 187.

Weston, Theodore (b. 1832, d. 1919), architect, designer of southwest wing, Metropolitan Museum. 98.

Whistler, James A. McNeill (b. Lowell, Massachusetts, 1834, d. 1903), expatriate painter of portraits and landscapes. Work in MMA.

Whitman, Robert (b. New York, N.-Y., 1935), mixed-media artist; devises and organizes happenings, often involving advanced technology. 224.

Whittredge, Worthington (b. Springfield, Ohio, 1820, d. 1910), landscape painter. Work in MMA. 97.

Wilmarth, Christopher (b. Sonoma, California, 1943), sculptor. Many of his works are in glass. 224.

Wright, Frank Lloyd (b. Richland Center, Wisconsin, 1869, d. 1959), architect, considered unique architectural genius; particularly noted for his 'organic' approach to design and use of materials in building, and accommodation of buildings to their natural sites.

His Guggenheim Museum remains a controversial structure; curving ramp there prefigured in only other work in New York, Mercedes-Benz showroom on Park Ave. 134, 136, 139, *165,* 169-70, 174-6, 178, 179.

Wyeth, Andrew (b. Chadds Ford, Pennsylvania, 1917), painter, known for his precisely realistic painting of country scenes and people. Work in MMA, MOMA.

Yamasaki, Minoru (b. Seattle, Washington, 1912), architect, known for his romantic treatment of elements of the International Style; responsible for design of World Trade Center (with Emery Roth & Sons). 207, *208.*

Youngerman, Jack (b. Louisville, Kentucky, 1926), painter, known for his large paintings of graceful shapes in style of post-painterly abstraction. Work in MOMA, WMAA.

Yunkers, Adja (b. Riga, Latvia, 1900), painter of the Abstract Expressionist school, noted for his gestural abstractions, and utilizing few colours and controlled, simplified forms. Work in MMA, MOMA, WMAA, Gu, BM.

Zion & Breen (Robert L. Zion b. New York City 1921; Harold Breer b. New York City 1923), landscape architects, responsible for design of Paley Plaza. 236.

Zorach, William (b. Eurburick-Kovno, Russia, 1887, d. 1966), sculptor, known for his stone figures of women, which draw on archaic styles; work in MMA, MOMA, WMAA.

Americans [...]
infiltrate[...]
troops[...]
tio[...]

silenced, the infantry m[...]
of the [pill]box and cal[...]
to come out. This was[...]
one [pill]box, only 13[...]
grenade was thrown[...]
and seven more eme[...]
If any German s[...]
that they could n[...]
wounded, the ad[...]
explosion. 'Afte[...]
they somehow[...]
attackers shou[...]
use a flameth[...]
hiding. Men[...]
'ointment b[...]
only two i[...]
Finally, the[...]
with blow[...]
prevent[...]
pillboxe[...]
sector[...]
On on[...]
and v[...]
capt[...]
pat[...]
tak[...]

c[...]
con[...]
and i[...]
cans a[...]
the steel[...]
containing[...]
they still re[...]
with a fragm[...]
ventilation shaft[...]
And a white phos[...]
the same air-shaft is[...]
reviser [of attitudes]'. [...]
'Kamerad?' and 'Wir s[...]
won't shoot!'). 'If all this [...]
blast the rear of the pillbo[...]
dozer to fill in the hole [and b[...]
Soldiers were advised neve[...]
pillbox; they should make the defe[...]
out. 'When the doors and ports h[...]
blown in,' the 41st Armored Infantry[...]
ment with the 2nd Armored Division[...]
ported, 'and enemy automatic weapon [...]

ved *to* the blind side
…ed fo*r* the occupants
…obeye*d* promptly. At
…prisoners came out. A
…through a *b*lasted port
…rged.'
…oldier called ba*c*k to say
…t move because *th*ey were
…ice recommended another
…a second charge o*f* TNT,
…nanage to walk out.' B*u*t the
…ld still throw in grenad*e*s or
…rower in case anyone was left
…had to be careful to watch for
…x mines' which were very small,
…ches across and an inch deep.
…y needed to seal up the steel doors
…torches or a thermite grenade to
…Germans from reoccupying the
…s. One unit had six pillboxes in its
…which had to be retaken three times.
…e occasion, a whole platoon, exhausted
…vet from the incessant rain, piled into a
…ared pillbox and fell asleep. A German
…ol returned and the whole platoon was
…en prisoner without a shot being fired.

…n the centre of First Army, VII Corps ad-
…vanced on the city of Aachen, the ancient
capital of Charlemagne and *lieu sacré* of the
Holy Roman Empire. The young commander
of the corps, Major General J. Lawton Col-

lins, was known to his troops as 'Lightning Joe' for his dynamism. With Aachen situated in a slight salient of German territory, the Siegfried Line ran round the west and southern side, with another line of fortifications behind the city. Collins wanted to avoid a house-to-house battle of attrition, so he decided to surround the city in the hope that the Germans might decide to pull out. But this reasoning failed to take into account Hitler's 'fortress' mentality and his obsessive refusal to give up towns, especially a place as historically significant as Aachen. Göring later said in a 1945 interrogation: 'The Führer wanted to defend Aachen to the last stone. He wanted to use it as an example for every other German city, and defend it, if necessary, until it was levelled to the ground.'

The sudden approach of American forces on 11 September triggered a panic. Nazi Party officials, Luftwaffe flak detachments, local functionaries, the police and troops fled east towards Cologne. According to the chief of staff of the German Seventh Army: 'The sight of the Luftwaffe and SS troops retreating, with the commanders leading the retreat, was very bad for morale. They simply got into their vehicles and took off. There was a riot in Aachen about it.'

Hitler ordered that the civilian population should be evacuated, forcibly if necessary. He suspected that they preferred an American occupation which would end the bombing. All those who did not leave would be considered traitors. But things did not turn out as he had expected. On 12 September, the 12th Volksgrenadier-Division was rushed to the sector, but the 116th Panzer-Division, which had retreated from Normandy, reached the city first. Its commander, Generalleutnant Gerhard Graf von Schwerin, promptly cancelled the Gauleiter's evacuation order. Schwerin was considered by colleagues to be too clever, and too contemptuous of the Nazis, for his own good. He had been sacked in Normandy for telling a corps commander what he thought of him, but then reinstated because he was such an effective leader. This perhaps encouraged him to think that he could get away with anything.

Schwerin first re-established order, with his panzergrenadiers instructed to shoot looters. He then sent an appeal to the American commander explaining that he had stopped the 'absurd' evacuation, and requested that the population be treated mercifully. Collins, however, carried on with his plan of encirclement. The 1st Infantry Division advanced from the south-east, with the 3rd Armored Division guarding its right flank. But the state of tank engines after the long advance from Normandy, and the shortage of every calibre of ammunition, greatly limited its striking power. The 1st Division was even short of rations. 'We were reduced to eating emergency D Rations — rock-hard chocolate bars full of artificial nutrients,' wrote Lieutenant Gardner Botsford. 'Three chocolate bars a day can make you very tired of chocolate bars.'

When it became clear to the Nazi authorities that Aachen was not immediately threatened, officials rushed back to restart the evacuation of civilians while a counter-attack was prepared from the north-east to prevent encirclement. News of Schwerin's letter leaked out, and the rash young general had to hide from arrest on charges of defeatism and even treason. Hitler, surprisingly, forgave him later. The forcible evacuation was carried out brutally. Most civilians wanted to stay. Wild rumours had spread of typhus in Cologne as a result of Allied bacteriological bombs. Many also believed that the Allies had bombs containing leprosy and plague bacilli.

'You should have seen how they treated their own German people in the evacuation areas,' Unteroffizier Huttary stated. 'They drove away cattle without giving any receipt for them. Then they made the owner himself go. The SA [Nazi Brownshirts] drove the cattle away in herds.' An engineer soldier called Bayer added: 'And when the houses were empty they looted them. They put up notices or announced that unrationed bread would be available at such and such a place from 2 to 4 o'clock. Then the women took up their places at the shop and when a queue had formed, trucks drove up and they were loaded into them. They picked up children on the street and threw them into the vehicles. Then they just took them out of the immediate danger zone, put them down on the road and left them to their fate.' Fear of a possible rising by foreign forced labourers prompted the SS to consider mass executions, but in the chaos nothing was done.

During the second half of September an intense debate had arisen, both in Washington and at SHAEF headquarters, over the wording the Supreme Commander should use when addressing the German people. If too conciliatory then the Germans would see it as a sign of weakness and be encouraged. If it sounded too harsh then it might persuade them to fight to the bitter end. On 28 September, SHAEF finally published Eisenhower's proclamation: 'The Allied Forces serving under my command have now entered Germany. We come as conquerors, but not as oppressors.' It went on to emphasize that they would 'obliterate Nazism and German militarism'.

The Nazi authorities soon countered with their own bizarre attempts at propaganda, even dropping leaflets by bomber over their own lines to strengthen the determination of

The Battle for Aachen
October 1944

Siegfried Line defences
German front 7 October
German front 20 October

N

NETHERLANDS

GERMANY

2

29   30

116Pz

3Pzg

Eschweiler

12VG

Aachen

Cathedral

Stolberg

1

3

0   1   2   3 km

their troops. One claimed that 'American officers [are] using riding whips on German women' and promised that 'Every German will fight in secret or openly to the last man.' The 'secret' fight was the first hint of Nazi plans for a resistance movement, the Werwolf, which would continue the fight and target Germans who collaborated with the Allies. But the leaflets did not succeed in raising morale. According to a German NCO, 'the troops were indignant, fearing that the Allies would capture one of these leaflets, and that their imminent captivity would be made most unpleasant'.

Early in October, the US Ninth Army took over the left flank of Bradley's 12th Army Group next to the British Second Army. This gave Hodges's First Army a greater density, especially round Aachen, where the 1st Infantry Division coming from the south-east worked its way towards the 30th Infantry Division advancing from the north to cut off the city entirely. By now the state of American vehicles had improved and supplies of ammunition had resumed.

The 12th Volksgrenadier-Division, recently arrived from the eastern front, faced the 1st Infantry Division near Stolberg. One of its officers wrote to a friend to say that their 'former proud regiment had been smashed completely at Mogilev'. Only six officers out of the whole regiment had survived and three of those were in hospital. The regiment had been completely rebuilt with new personnel and equipment and was now in action. It had suffered badly when thrown into a counter-attack as soon as it detrained at the railhead. 'The Americans laid down artillery barrages of such intensity that many an old combat soldier from the East was dazed.' The writer himself was wounded with a hole in his foot 'the size of a fist' and was now lying in hospital.

On 11 October IX Tactical Air Command bombed and strafed Aachen for two days, and on 14 October the battle for the city began. Despite attempts by the Nazi authorities to evacuate its 160,000 civilians, some 40,000 remained. Women and old men were horrified to see German troops turning their houses into bunkers with reinforced concrete. The defending force of nearly 18,000 men was a very mixed collection under the command of Oberst Gerhard Wilck, with regular troops, Waffen-SS, Kriegsmarine sailors serving as infantry and low-quality fortress battalions. Before Aachen had been completely encircled on 16 October, the Germans rushed in a battalion of SS, the artillery of the 246th Infanterie-Division, the 219th Assault Gun Brigade and some combat engineers. Men from the fortress battalions were the most likely to surrender at the first opportunity, but Major Heimann of the 246th Infanterie-Division observed: 'I had the most excellent troops, half of whom were naval personnel intended for the U-Boat arm.' He also had 150 men from the SS *Leibstandarte Adolf Hitler,* but they wanted to pull out on their own. Heimann had to give them a severe warning that the Führer's order to hold the town to the last applied to them just as much as to everyone else.

The American attack began with two battalions from the 1st Division coming from the north and north-east, 'a job that should have been done by two regiments', as one of their officers complained later. The essential point was to make sure that adjacent companies remained in close contact to prevent the enemy slipping between them to attack from the flank or rear. 'To make sure that no individuals or small groups were overrun, we searched every room and closet of every building. In addition every sewer was blown in. This not only gave our fighting troops assurance that they would not be sniped at from the rear, but it enabled command and supply personnel to function more efficiently behind the lines.'

The 1st Division operated with tanks and tank destroyers well forward, each guarded by a squad of infantry against Germans with Panzerfaust rocket-propelled grenades. The M-4 Shermans mounted an extra .50 machine gun on the right front of the turret. This proved very useful in Aachen street fighting for suppressing fire from upper windows. Knowing that German soldiers moved from basement to basement, tank crews would first shoot into the cellar if possible with high-explosive shells from their main armament, then fire at the ground floor and work their way up the house. Others would deal with any Germans still sheltering in cellars by throwing in fragmentation and white phosphorus grenades. Flamethrowers often 'resulted in a quick enemy surrender'.

Bazookas or explosive charges were used to smash through walls from house to house, an activity which became known as 'mouse-holing'. It was safer to blast through a wall, which would shock anyone in the room beyond, than enter through the door. As soon as an opening into the next-door house had been made, one of the team would throw a hand grenade into the adjoining room, and they would rush in following the explosion. Soldiers carried armour-piercing rounds to shoot up through the ceiling or down through the floor. They then dashed to the top of the house and worked their way down, forcing the Germans into the cellar. When a whole block had been cleared, guards were posted to prevent Germans from sneaking back in. The Germans also used their Panzerfausts in a similar fashion. 'When attacked in this way,' a report admitted, 'American strong-point crews surrendered in most cases immediately, [once] deprived of sight due to dust clouds caused by explosions.'

The Americans soon found that mortar and longer-range artillery fire was uncertain and often dangerous to their own men in urban combat, so they insisted on direct fire wherever possible. In any case, fuses on American mortar rounds were so sensitive that they exploded as soon as they touched a roof, and did little damage to the inside of a building. But their artillery fire was so intense that Oberst Wilck, the commander of the German forces in the town, had to move his command post to an air-raid shelter. 'The few assault guns which we had just received were put out of action straight away,' Wilck recounted afterwards. 'You can't hold a town with just carbines!' The Germans in fact had more than carbines, and managed to use their heavy 120mm mortars very effectively.

Allied aircraft were closely managed by a ground controller, but it was impossible to identify specific points in the ruins, so 'no close-in bombing missions were undertaken'. In any case, the presence of friendly aircraft overhead certainly seemed to bolster the morale of the troops on the ground and kept German heads down. There were firm orders in place not to damage the cathedral, which was spared from ground fire. Even so, the destruction was so great that VII Corps could report that 'the flattened condition of the buildings' at least allowed 'actual physical contact [to] be maintained among adjacent units'.

'The operation was not unduly hurried,' VII Corps reported. 'It was realized that street fighting is a slow, tedious business which requires much physical exertion and time if buildings are searched thoroughly.' House clearing, the GIs had been told, meant firing constantly at every window until they were inside the house, then with one man ready with a grenade in his hand and two others covering him with rifles, or ideally Thompson sub-machine guns, they would go from room to room. But they soon found that they needed to mark houses occupied by their own troops. 'Numerous times we have had casualties by grenades thrown into buildings or shooting into them by our own troops after we had occupied the building.'

As the Red Army had discovered, heavy artillery at close range was the most cost-effective, as well as destructive, means of advance. The Americans in Aachen used 155mm self-propelled 'Long Toms' at ranges as close as 150 metres. Oberst Wilck admitted after his surrender that 'the direct fire of the 155mm self-propelled gun was very devastating and demoralizing. In one instance a shell completely pierced three houses before exploding in and wrecking the fourth house.'

'Civilians must be promptly and vigorously expelled from any area occupied by our troops,' one American officer in Aachen emphasized. 'Failure to do so costs lives.' Holding pens were constructed and guarded by MPs, but Collins's corps did not have enough trained interpreters or members of the Counter Intelligence Corps to filter out Nazi supporters, or interview the hundreds of foreign forced labourers. At one point during the battle, three small boys found a rifle. They fired at an American squad. A sergeant spotted them, ran over to grab the rifle off them and cuffed the boy who held it. This story somehow spread and was taken up as an example of heroism by German propaganda, which claimed with shameless exaggeration that 'they held up all the enemy troops there'. But as the diarist Victor Klemperer pointed out, the example was surely self-defeating. The Nazis now claimed to be using partisans, whom they had always condemned as 'terrorists'. It also underlined the weakness of German forces when, according to Nazi newspapers, 'Eisenhower is attacking with seven armies, with two million men (men not children!),' Klemperer emphasized.

On 16 October, the 30th and 1st Divisions finally met up north-east of Aachen, having suffered heavy casualties. Two days later, Himmler declared that 'Every German homestead will be defended to the last.' But on 21 October Oberst Wilck surrendered with the remainder of his exhausted and hungry men. He was not a devotee of Hitler and knew that the killing went on because Hitler was living in his own fantasy world. 'Even the Führer's adjutant told me how the Führer is surrounded by lies,' he remarked in captivity. Knowing that it would please Hitler, Himmler would come in with a beaming face to say: '*Heil mein Führer,* I wish to report the establishment of a new division.'

One of Wilck's men later complained that the worst part of being taken prisoner was being marched through Aachen. 'The civilian population behaved worse than the French,' he said. 'They shouted abuse at us and the Americans had to intervene. We can't help it if their houses have been smashed to smithereens.' German women had soon emerged from cellars under the rubble to search for food. They could be seen butchering a fallen horse in the street hit by shellfire, and wheeling back turnips in little wooden baby carriages.

Goebbels tried to lessen the impact of the defeat. German propaganda assured the German people that 'the time gained at Aachen, Arnhem and Antwerp has made Fortress Germany impregnable. The Luftwaffe is being rejuvenated and Germany now has more artillery and tanks to throw into battle.'

■ ■ ■ ■

The most frustrating delay for the Allies was their inability to use the port of Antwerp. This gave the Germans the breathing space they needed to rebuild and redeploy their armies for Hitler's new plan. But other factors also played a part. Encouraged by victory fever and the idea that the European war would be over by Christmas, American commanders in the Pacific had seized the chance to boost their own strengths. SHAEF suddenly woke up to the fact that the 'Germany first' policy, originally agreed in 1941, had slipped out of the window, resulting in alarming shortages of ammunition and men.

The Nazis, with Germany now threatened from the east, the southeast and the west, suffered their own internal tensions. On 15 October, Admiral Nikolaus Horthy, after secret negotiations with the Soviet Union, declared over the radio that Hungary was changing sides. The Germans knew of his betrayal. A commando led by SS-Obersturmbannführer Otto Skorzeny, the enormous Austrian who had snatched Mussolini from the Gran Sasso, kidnapped Horthy's son as a hostage in a street ambush just before the broadcast.[*] Horthy himself was

_____

[*] German army officers joked that Skorzeny had received the Knight's Cross of the Iron Cross for

brought back to Germany and the government was handed over to the fascist and fiercely anti-semitic Arrow Cross.

In East Prussia, as the Red Army advanced on to German territory for the first time, the power struggle behind the scenes intensified. General der Flieger Kreipe, the chief of staff of the Luftwaffe, was now persona non grata in the Wolfsschanze. Keitel and even Hitler's Luftwaffe adjutant Oberst von Below turned their backs on him as a 'defeatist'. Göring decided to extend his deer hunt near by at Rominten, Kreipe noted in his diary, because 'he has to watch Himmler and Bormann a little closer. Himmler has now requested some squadrons for his SS.' This appears to have been Himmler's first attempt to increase his military empire beyond the ground forces of the Waffen-SS. Part of the power game around the Führer depended on the two gate-keepers: Bormann, who controlled access over anyone outside the Wehrmacht and SS, and Keitel. 'Before the Generals or anyone get to Adolf to make a report,' a captured general remarked to his companions, 'they are given detailed instructions by Keitel what they are to say, how they are to say it, and

having freed Mussolini, but 'he would have been given the [even higher distinction of the] Oak Leaves if he had taken him back'.

97

only then are they allowed into Adolf's presence.'

On an inspection of flak batteries nearer the front, Kreipe wrote on 18 October of the Red Army incursion: 'Fears in East Prussia, the first refugee treks to be seen, horrible.' Göring had to leave Rominten in a hurry, and Keitel tried to persuade Hitler to leave the Wolfsschanze, but he refused. A few days later, Kreipe visited the Panzer Corps *Hermann Göring* at Gumbinnen. 'Gumbinnen is on fire,' he noted. 'Columns of refugees. In Nemmersdorf, shot women and children have been nailed to barn doors.' Nemmersdorf was the site of an atrocity, which was almost certainly exaggerated in Nazi propaganda, and Kreipe had probably not visited the scene.

Also on 18 October, just as the battle for Aachen was coming to an end, Eisenhower, Bradley and Montgomery met in Brussels. Since the British and the Canadians were so involved clearing the Scheldt estuary, Eisenhower decided that the US First Army should focus on obtaining a bridgehead across the Rhine south of Cologne, while the recently arrived Ninth Army protected its left flank. As might be imagined Montgomery was not pleased that the First Army was to be given priority, but he had been silenced for the moment after his climbdown. For the Americans, on the other hand, this strategy led to the plan to advance through the Hürtgen Forest. Neither the commanders nor the troops had any idea of the horrors that awaited them there.

4
Into the Winter of War

The brief Soviet rampage on to East Prussian territory in October prompted Goebbels to play up stories of rape, looting and destruction by the Red Army. He tried to invoke the idea of *Volksgemeinschaft,* or national solidarity, in the face of mortal danger. Yet on the western front Wehrmacht generals were shocked by reports of German soldiers looting German homes.

'The soldiers' behaviour today is unbelievable,' said a doctor with the 3rd Fallschirmjäger-Division. 'I was stationed in Düren and the soldiers there robbed their own people. They tore everything out of the cupboards.... They were like wild animals.' Apparently this behaviour had started when the division was in Italy. And other formations which had looted during the retreat through France and Belgium did not change their habits when back on German soil. Their tattered uniforms had not been replaced, some 60 per cent of them were estimated to be infested with lice, and they were permanently hungry. Just behind the front line, there were reports of soldiers blinding horses so that they could be slaughtered and eaten.

This did not mean that they were reluctant to fight on, for the knowledge that the Red Army had reached the borders of the Reich had concentrated their minds. Significantly, a captured German army doctor called Dammann considered that 'German propaganda urging the men to save their Fatherland has helped to keep down the number of cases of combat exhaustion.'

Looting by German soldiers was not the only reason for relations between civilians and troops to deteriorate sharply in western Germany. Women wanted the fighting to end as quickly as possible. For them, East Prussia was very far away. 'You've no idea what morale is like at home,' an Obergefreiter told fellow prisoners. 'In the villages the women cursed and yelled: "Get out! We don't want to be shot to bits!" ' A member of the 16th Fallschirmjäger-Regiment agreed. 'They called us "prolongers of the war", and that wasn't just in one place either, but in fifty towns and villages in the West.' An Unteroffizier Mükller said that in Heidelberg 'The mood there is shit, yet the hatred is not directed at the enemy, but against the German regime.' People were saying: 'If only the Allies would hurry up and come to end the war.' While most within the armed forces were still eager to believe in Hitler's promises of secret weapons, cynicism was much greater in civilian circles, except of course for the Party faithful and the desperate. In some places the unreliable V-1 flying bomb was already referred to as 'Versager-1', or 'No. 1 Dud'.

Goebbels seized every opportunity to make civilians in the west of Germany fear an Allied victory. The announcement in September of the plan by Henry Morgenthau, Roosevelt's secretary of the treasury, to turn Germany 'into a country primarily agricultural and pastoral in character' was disastrous. It enabled Goebbels to claim that 'every American soldier will bring Morgenthau along with him in his duffle bag' and Germany would be broken up. This idea clearly influenced Wehrmacht forces in the west. An officer taken prisoner was asked by his American interrogator whether he regretted the destruction of the Rhineland. 'Well, it probably won't be ours after the war,' he replied. 'Why not destroy it?'

The Nazi newspaper the *Völkischer Beobachter* warned: 'The German people must realize that we are engaged in a life and death struggle which imposes on every German the duty to do his utmost for the victorious conclusion of the war and the frustration of the plans of destruction planned by these cannibals.' The fact that Morgenthau was Jewish also played straight into the hands of the propaganda ministry and its conspiracy theories of a Jewish plot against Germany. The ministry tried to increase the effect with some dubious quotations from the British press, including 'Henningway' cited in the *Daily Mail* as saying: 'The power of Germany will have to be destroyed so thoroughly that Germany will never rise again to fight another battle. This goal can only be achieved by castration.'

After the presidential election in the United States, Goebbels said that President Roosevelt had been re-elected as 'generally expected', with the support of American Communists at Stalin's urging. Yet German propaganda also played a double game, encouraging the belief that the alliance of the Reich's enemies would soon fall apart. According to the US Counter Intelligence Corps, the Germans circulated leaflets showing 'Tommy and his Yankee pal regarding with disgust the spectacle of Russians taking over and policing Brussels, Berlin, etc.; the Teuton being apparently unable to get out of his head that when it comes to an abject fear of Bolshevism we're All Krauts Together'. Other leaflets tried to make the point that 'while Americans are being slaughtered by the thousand, Monty's troops are indulging in a "Dutch Holiday Slumber" '.

'German civilians don't know what to expect,' the Counter Intelligence Corps reported. 'They are torn between belief in the "terror" stories of German authorities and those which cross the lines, by rumor and Allied radio, about the fairness of our treatment of civilians in captured areas.' The Allies were of course helped by accounts which circulated within Germany of Nazi Party corruption at home and of the shameless looting in France by senior officials of the military administration. Gauleiters were amassing great wealth, and their children were allowed cars and petrol when even the heads of companies were rationed to forty litres a week.

The Counter Intelligence Corps admitted that it had crossed into German territory 'armed with a few directives, no precedents, uncertainty as to its potentialities, and [with an] uneasy expectation of partisan warfare'. Its priority was to seize Nazi Party records quickly, but its operatives found themselves overwhelmed by the numbers of 'suspicious civilians' arrested by American soldiers for screening along with the prisoners of war. German soldiers and civilians found it very easy to escape from American compounds. The other problem which the CIC faced was the number of Belgian and French Resistance members crossing into Germany to loot, or on 'intelligence missions of their own'.

In Aachen the Counter Intelligence Corps estimated that up to 30 per cent of the population had defied Nazi orders to evacuate the city. 'Don't kick them around,' was the CIC advice on treating Germans under American occupation, 'but don't let them fool you. The Germans are accustomed to taking orders, not complying with requests.' Many were indeed willing to denounce Nazis and to provide information, but it was often hard for Allied intelligence units to know exactly what to believe. Word had spread of the unrest in bomb-shattered Cologne, where police were engaged in running battles with the so-called 'Edelweiss Pirates': bands of dissident youth, plus an estimated 2,000 German deserters and absconded foreign workers sheltering in the ruins.

Allied bombing had not only flattened cities. Travel by train had become very difficult, if not impossible. German officers and soldiers who had finally obtained home leave found that almost all of their precious days were spent sitting in trains or waiting in stations. 'A Leutnant of ours went to Munich on leave [from Rheine near the Dutch border],' a Luftwaffe Unteroffizier Bock recounted. 'He was away ten days, but he only had one day at home.'

Hardly any soldier chose to go to Berlin on leave unless he had family or a sweetheart there. Everyone in the capital was exhausted from sleepless nights, as RAF Bomber Command fought its own 'Battle of Berlin', hammering the city night after night. 'What is cowardice?' ran a typical example of the city's gallows humour. 'When someone in Berlin volunteers for the Eastern Front.'

Visitors were often amazed how its inhabitants from all classes had adapted to the conditions. 'I am so accustomed now to living among these ruins,' wrote Missie Vassiltchikov in her diary, 'with the constant smell of gas in the air, mixed with the odour of rubble and rusty metal, and sometimes even the stench of putrefying flesh.' Apartments were particularly cold during that winter of fuel shortages. There was little glass available to repair windows and people opened their windows wide when the sirens sounded in the hope of saving any remaining panes from bomb blast.

During air raids, the packed cellars and concrete air-raid shelters shuddered and shook. The low-wattage bulbs flickered, dimmed still further, went out and then came back. Children screamed, many adults buried their heads between their knees. After the all-clear had finally sounded, many admitted to a curious exhilaration when they found themselves still alive. But some people stayed in the cellars even after the others had trooped off. It was warmer and less threatening there.

'Skin diseases', a doctor reported, 'have become very common both in the Army and at home, owing to the poor quality of the soap available, overcrowding in air-raid shelters and in those houses which are still standing, shortage of clothing, poor hygiene etc.' Workers in industrial areas were increasingly succumbing to diphtheria, and venereal diseases had spread, partly as a result of German troops returning from France, Belgium, the Balkans and Poland.

According to a court-martial judge, there were estimated to be 18,000 Wehrmacht deserters in Berlin. Many were hiding in huts on allotments. They no doubt subscribed to the German army joke: 'War is just like the picture-house: there's a lot going on up in the front, but the best seats are right at the back.' Ordinary Germans were at last ready to shelter deserters, usually sons or nephews but sometimes even strangers, at terrible risk to themselves. By the end of the year, the Wehrmacht had executed some 10,000 men, a figure which was to increase significantly in the final months of the war.

The families of deserters were also liable to severe penalties. 'During the night of 29–30 October', the commander of the 361st Volksgrenadier-Division announced in an order of the day, 'Soldat Wladislaus Schlachter of the 4th Company, 952nd

Grenadier-Regiment, deserted to the enemy. The court martial assembled on the same day passed the death sentence on Schlachter. Thus he was expelled forever from the community of our people and may never return to his home. Most ruthless reprisals will be enacted against the members of his family, measures which are a necessity in this struggle for the survival of the German people.' Threats were also made against the families of prisoners of war who told their American captors too much.

The more prosperous classes increasingly feared the tens of thousands of foreign workers in and around the city. Some were volunteers, but most had been brought to Germany as forced labourers. The authorities were losing control of them. Barracks were often burned down, leaving the foreigners homeless. German shopkeepers would claim that gangs of them had broken in to their establishments and stolen supplies, when in fact they themselves had sold the missing items on the black market. Alongside food, cigarettes were the most sought-after commodity. In Berlin, according to one captured officer, a single English cigarette sold for five Reichsmarks, while a Camel went for twice as much. Real coffee was out of almost everyone's reach at 600 Reichsmarks a kilo. According to one officer, most of the black market in coffee was organized by the SS in Holland.

Coffee, because of its rarity, was the conspicuous consumption of choice for the Nazi hierarchy. A horrifying and bizarre conversation between two captured Kriegsmarine admirals was secretly recorded in their camp in England in 1945. Konteradmiral Engel told Vizeadmiral Utke about fellow admirals entertained by Arthur Greiser, the notorious Gauleiter of the Wartheland, who was later hanged by the Poles.

'Greiser boasted: "Do you know that the coffee you're drinking now, cost me 32,000 Jewish women?" '

'Where did they go?' Vizeadmiral Utke asked.

' "Into the incinerators probably," Greiser said to us at the time. "Let's hope we all get as easy a death as they had." That was the first thing he said. All the admirals sat around laughing themselves sick and thinking of the human suffering behind the coffee they were drinking.'

Following the Roman tradition of bread and circuses, the Nazi administration organized an ice show in the bomb-damaged Sportpalast to distract people from the shortage of rations. The Deutsches Frauenwerk welfare organization produced bakery booklets and brochures on how to save food. One was entitled 'Main meal without meat', which no doubt prompted another Berlin joke that the next one would be how to produce a main meal without food. A satirical song, sung to the tune of the Nazi anthem, the 'Horst Wessel Lied', went:

The prices rise
The shops are firmly shuttered
Starvation marches
With the German race
Yet those who starve
Are just the little comrades.
While those above
Can merely sympathize.

Leave was much easier for the Allied armies on the western front. The British and Canadians went to Brussels and the Americans to Paris. Senior officers could always find a good excuse to visit SHAEF at Versailles or Com Z in the city itself. From mid-September, almost 10,000 American soldiers were arriving in Paris every day on seventy-two-hour passes. The priorities of what the poet-paratrooper Louis Simpson called 'the overheated soul of the dogface fresh from his dugout' were predictable. Paris became known as 'the silver foxhole', and the term 'zig-zag' covered both drink and sex. Pigalle became known as 'Pig Alley' where prostitutes, both professional and amateur, charged anything up to 300 francs or five dollars.*

* A private from a quartermaster company picked

General Lee, the authoritarian commander of Com Z, was appalled by the informal and at times insulting behaviour of GIs on leave in Paris. He tried to instil some smartness by sending out officers from his headquarters to take the name of any soldier who failed to salute. The Avenue de Kléber soon became known as the 'Avenue de Salute' among front-line soldiers who resented the officers and MPs trying to make them behave.

GIs offset the expense of prostitutes and drink by buying cartons of Chesterfield, Lucky Strike and Camel cigarettes for fifty cents through the US Army's PX organization, then selling them for anything from fifteen to twenty dollars. French authorities complained in vain that US troops were exploiting their exemption from both import duties and exchange controls. American soldiers were able to make a killing at the expense of the French government by converting their pay in francs back into dollars at

---

up, 'according to his VD contact form, nine different women in the vicinity of the same corner, took them to six different hotels, and actually managed seven sexual exposures', all within eight hours. The VD rate in the European Theater of Operations doubled during the year, with more than two-thirds of venereal infections acquired in France originating in Paris.

the official rate, then selling the dollars on the black market at a huge profit. Soldiers lured women with the offer of cigarettes, tinned ham, nylon stockings and other items posted from the States.

University graduates and anyone with a feel for European culture sympathized with the French and yearned, not just for carnal reasons, to see Paris, the intellectual capital of the world. But those with little knowledge of foreign countries tended to despise the French as losers who could not speak a proper language. They expected French girls and women alike to be ready to service the desires of their liberators. One of the very few phrases that many of them bothered to learn was 'Voulezvous coucher avec moi?' The American embassy described US troops in Paris as 'ardent and often very enterprising' in the pursuit of women. In fact the lack of subtlety soon became counter-productive. Summoned in a café by a whistle and a prof-fered pack of Lucky Strike, one young woman earned the cheers of French onlookers by taking a cigarette from the GI, dropping it to the ground and grinding it under her foot. Young French males, unable to compete with American largesse, became increasingly bitter at what they saw as the presumption of their liberators. Mutual suspicion and resentment grew on both sides. 'The French, cynical before defeat; sullen after rescue,' wrote Louis

Simpson. 'What do the sons of bitches want?'

If the black market in Berlin was flourishing, in Paris it became rampant when American deserters teamed up with local criminal gangs. The profits from stolen US Army gasoline were so large that even drug dealers were drawn to this new market. Up to half the jerrycans in continental Europe went missing. Increased criminal penalties, making the fuel more traceable by adding coloured dye, and numerous other attempts by the American authorities failed to dent a trade which made the supply situation at the front even worse. Paris soon became known as 'Chicago-sur-Seine'.

The most notorious racket that autumn was perpetrated by the railway battalion. These troops would stop the train on a bend so that the MPs guarding against theft at the end of the train could not see, then unload meat, coffee, cigarettes and canned goods to their confederates. A twenty-pound drum of coffee could go for $300 and a case of 10-in-1 rations for $100. Blankets and uniforms were also stolen from hospital trains. Some 180 officers and enlisted men were eventually charged and sentenced to terms of imprisonment ranging from three to fifty years. Altogether some 66 million packs of cigarettes disappeared in a single month.

French dislike for the 'new occupation' increased with the signs of American military privileges. White-helmeted American MPs directing traffic on the Place de la Concorde gave priority to US vehicles approaching the American embassy. Roosevelt had delayed recognition of the provisional government because he suspected that de Gaulle wanted to be a military dictator, but after much pressure from the State Department and Eisenhower, the President gave in. On Monday 23 October Jefferson Caffery, the US ambassador, Duff Cooper, the British ambassador, and Aleksandr Bogomolov, the Soviet representative, finally presented their letters of credence. De Gaulle invited Cooper and his wife to dinner that night, but he was still in such a bad mood that the British ambassador in his diary described the evening as an 'extremely frigid and dreary party, worse even than his entertainments usually are'.

Caffery was far more sympathetic towards the French than most of the senior officers at SHAEF, and as a result a number of them held him in contempt. He was an awkward man, both formal and ill at ease, and clearly did not enjoy diplomatic life. The Francophobe senior officers were determined to subordinate him to their own hierarchy and not allow any diplomatic independence. Caffery and Georges Bidault, the inexperienced French foreign minister, commiserated with each other over their difficulties. Bidault was constantly apologizing to Caffery and

Cooper for de Gaulle's needless provocations. He even said to Caffery later that 'there is absolutely no one else in sight and that it must be admitted that de Gaulle loves France, even if he doesn't like Frenchmen'. Cooper's main problem was his old friend Winston Churchill. The Prime Minister wanted to visit SHAEF, without saying a word to de Gaulle beforehand, an act which would have been seen as an insult. Eventually, Churchill was persuaded to formalize his visit, and he walked down the Champs-Elysées with General de Gaulle, acclaimed by vast crowds. Their furious contretemps on the eve of D-Day was tactfully forgotten.

De Gaulle's displays of bad temper were due in part to the grave economic and political difficulties his government faced. Food and fuel supplies were uncertain, causing frequent protests. SHAEF estimated that 1,550,000 buildings had been destroyed during the war. Factories and mines were still not working properly, and the country's ports and transport system remained half paralysed after all the destruction from Allied bombing and German looting. De Gaulle also needed to deal with an embittered Resistance movement, which resented both its own loss of influence and the re-establishment of state power by the Gaullists returned from London. The French Communist Party and its supporters were the most vocal in their protests. Their hopes of carrying liberation into revolution had been thwarted, but they did not know that Stalin was totally opposed to the idea. He feared that the United States might cut off Lend-Lease support if there were disturbances in France behind Allied lines.

De Gaulle played his trump card towards the end of October. He would allow the French Communist Party leader Maurice Thorez to return to Paris from Moscow, but in return the two Communist ministers in his government would have to support his decree to abolish the 'patriotic militias' and force them to surrender their weapons. With uniforms and weapons provided by SHAEF, de Gaulle began to incorporate the patriotic militias into the regular French forces, sending the majority to General Jean-Marie de Lattre de Tassigny's First French Army advancing towards Strasbourg at the southernmost part of the Allied line.

One person who had no intention of surrendering his weapons was Ernest Hemingway, who had played at partisans around Rambouillet just before the liberation of Paris. At the beginning of October, Hemingway had to leave his roving court on the German frontier where the 22nd Infantry Regiment of the 4th Division had been breaching the Siegfried Line. After committing perjury to a court of inquiry into his illegal military activities at Rambouillet, he was acquitted and allowed to remain in France as an accredited war correspondent.

Although he took time and trouble in Paris to encourage the writing of Sergeant J. D. Salinger of the 4th Division, who had already started *Catcher in the Rye,* Hemingway remained an inveterate war tourist: he was after all the man who had coined the term 'whore de combat' during the Spanish Civil War. He returned to the Ritz in Paris to drink and sleep with Mary Welsh, the next Mrs Hemingway. Some time later, when drinking with Colonel 'Buck' Lanham, the commander of the 22nd Infantry Regiment, he seized a photograph of Mary's husband, threw it into the lavatory and fired a German machine pistol at it, with disastrous effects on the Ritz plumbing.

He also flirted paternally with Marlene Dietrich, who was in France entertaining American troops. One of Dietrich's 'ardent admirers' was General Patton, who gave her a set of pearl-handled pistols. Another was Jim Gavin of the 82nd Airborne, the extraordinarily young and good-looking paratrooper major general who became her lover. Gavin also later became the lover of Martha Gellhorn, the third Mrs Hemingway, who now could not stand the sight of 'Papa' any more. Paris was indeed a turbulent feast for the last year of the war.

Brussels was the leave centre for the First Canadian and the Second British Army. British officers used to say wistfully that, for someone who loves Paris, to go to Brussels was like having tea with the sister of the girl you love. The Belgian capital may not have been as riotous as Pigalle, but for their soldiers it offered the beer and women they so eagerly sought. And it too became a haven for deserters and black marketeers.

The political situation in Brussels was perhaps even more complicated than the one in Paris. Major General G. W. E. J. Erskine, the head of the SHAEF mission in Belgium, had tried to help the Belgian government of Hubert Pierlot re-establish order after its return from exile in London. The largely left-wing Resistance movements, rather like their counterparts in France, were hardly enthusiastic at being told what to do by conservative politicians who had spent the war years in the safety of London while they had suffered such dangers. Totalling some 30,000 members at the beginning of September, their numbers grew to 70,000. Those who had fought closely with British and American forces did not welcome the idea of being brigaded into the Belgian army and gendarmerie to act in a subordinate role.

General Eisenhower issued an order of the day on 29 September praising the work of the Resistance but also supporting the request of the Belgian government for them to hand over their arms and equipment and volunteer for military service in special battalions as auxiliaries. At a time of acute coal and food shortages when Belgium was short of manpower, this was greeted with a mixture of scorn and irritation. On 21 October, General Erskine pointed out to the Supreme Commander that the fractious members of the Resistance who refused to give up their weapons outnumbered the police and gendarmerie by more than ten to one. A breakdown in governmental control was a distinct possibility. Eisenhower then prompted the Belgian government to declare that the unauthorized possession of weapons in a combat zone was not permissible.

On 9 November Eisenhower made an official visit to the Belgian capital, where he addressed parliament. A few days later the Belgian ministry of national defence announced that all Resistance forces would be demobilized on 18 November. Two Communist ministers and a representative of the Resistance resigned from Pierlot's cabinet in protest. But General Erskine managed to convince them at a meeting later that SHAEF fully supported the government on this measure, and nobody should want to see clashes between the Resistance and Allied forces. Resistance groups backed down and agreed to hand over all weapons to the 'inter-Allied authorities'.

On 25 November, however, British troops and armoured vehicles were moved in to support police and gendarmerie facing a large demonstration in the government district of Brussels. Rather as was happening in Greece, this made it look as if the British had decided to maintain an unpopular government in power. Erskine was forced to justify his actions publicly, on the grounds that order had to be maintained behind the lines of a combat zone. However, until elections could be held, the military authorities had no option but to support governments which had survived in exile and were totally out of touch with all those who had suffered through a long occupation.

While American veterans of the fighting in Normandy had their seventy-two-hour passes back to Paris, a constant stream of replacements for those killed or wounded in action were sent forward from Cherbourg to holding camps. Most were teenagers freshly arrived from the United States, but there were many older men reassigned to infantry rifle platoons which had suffered about 80 per cent of the casualties, a far higher proportion than predicted.

Just about the only improvement that winter to the depressingly unimaginative system was to change the name 'replacements' to 'reinforcements' in an attempt to take away the idea that newcomers were just filling dead men's boots. This did little good. A regimental officer with the 28th Infantry Division said: 'We're still a first-class outfit, but not nearly as good as when we came across the beach [in Normandy]. We have a great deal more prodding to do now. The replacements, both officers and men, are green. They don't know how to take care of themselves. They become casualties very fast sometimes. They don't know their leaders and their buddies well, and it is hard to get them worked in as members of the team.' In one company twenty men reported sick, mostly with colds and trench foot, otherwise known as 'immersion foot'. All were new arrivals who had not been taught even the most basic rules of hygiene in the field, of which the most important was to change your socks. Their company commander admitted that he had lost twenty-six men to hospital in ten days because of trench foot. J. D. Salinger in the 4th Division was indeed fortunate to receive each week a pair of woollen socks knitted by his mother.

The Communications Zone personnel in charge showed little interest in the fate of their charges. For them, it was simply a question of processing the required numbers. Replacement depots were known as 'repple depples', and they resembled a gangmaster's collection point for casual labour. 'Each morning,' wrote a newcomer called Arthur Couch, 'some 1,000 men would stand outside a headquarters unit where someone would read out a list of some 100 or more soldiers' names who would go off in trucks to their division or regiment. The rest of us would go back to our tents until another name calling.' Young replacements had often been made even more apprehensive by wounded veterans returning from hospital to combat, who took pleasure in recounting weird and gruesome tales of fighting at the front.

Men often arrived with none of the training qualifications which their forms stated. Many could not swim. After losing a large number of men crossing the Moselle, a company commander in Patton's Third Army described the attack on Fort Driant with replacements for his casualties. 'We couldn't get the new untrained and inexperienced troops to move. We had to drag them up to the fort. The old men were tired and the new afraid and as green as grass. The three days we spent in the breach of the fort consisted in keeping the men in the lines. All the leaders were lost exposing themselves at the wrong time in order to get this accomplished. The new men seemed to lose all sense of reasoning. They left their rifles, flamethrowers, satchel charges and what not laying right where it was. I was disgusted and so damned mad I couldn't see straight. If it had not been for pre-planned defensive artillery fire [the Germans] would have shoved us clean out of the fort with the caliber of troops we had. Why? — The men wouldn't fight. Why wouldn't they fight? — They had not been trained nor disciplined to war.'

In all too many cases, replacements joined their platoon at night, not knowing where they were or even which unit they were with. They were often shunned by the survivors of the platoon they were joining who had lost close buddies. And because replacements were seen as clumsy and doomed, the veterans kept their distance. This became almost a self-fulfilling prophecy as badly led platoons would use the new arrivals for the most dangerous tasks rather than risk an experienced soldier. Many never survived the first forty-eight hours.

Replacements were sometimes treated little better than expendable slaves, and the whole system bred a cynicism which was deeply troubling. Martha Gellhorn, in her novel *Point of No Return*, repeats a clearly common piece of black humour: 'Sergeant Postalozzi says they ought to shoot the replacements at the repple depple and save trouble. He says it just wastes time carrying all them bodies back.'*

Only if a replacement was still alive after forty-eight hours at the front, did he stand a hope of surviving a little longer. One of Bradley's staff officers mused on the fate of a newly arrived 'doughboy'. 'His chances seem at their highest after he has been in the line — oh, perhaps a week. Then you know, sitting in a high headquarters, like an actuary behind an insurance desk, that the odds on his survival drop slowly but steadily and with mathematical certainty always down, down, down. The odds drop for every day he remains under fire until, if he's there long enough, he is the lone number on a roulette wheel which hasn't come up in a whole evening of play. And he knows it too.'

'I was lucky to be with old soldiers who wanted to help a new replacement to survive,' Arthur Couch wrote of his good fortune to be sent to the 1st Infantry Division. He was taught to fire a burst with the Browning Automatic Rifle, then immediately roll sideways to a new position because the Germans would direct all their fire back at any automatic weapon. Couch learned quickly, but he

* Hemingway repeated a very similar joke himself in *Across the River and into the Trees,* but after the bitterness of their marriage breakdown, neither would of course admit that they had heard it from the other.

124

must have been in a minority. 'The quality of replacements has declined appreciably in recent weeks,' his division reported on 26 October. 'We receive too many men not physically fit for infantry combat. We have received some men forty-years-old who cannot take exposure to cold, mud, rain etc. Replacements are not sufficiently prepared mentally for combat. They have not been impressed with the realities of war — as evidenced by one replacement inquiring if they were using live ammunition on the front.'

Front-line divisions were furious with the lack of training before their arrival. 'Replacements have 13 weeks basic training,' a sergeant in III Corps commented. 'They don't know [the] first thing about a machinegun, don't know how to reduce stoppage or get the gun in action quickly. They are good men but have not been trained. Up in the fight is no place to train them.' Another sergeant said that, in training back in the States, the raw recruits had been told that 'enemy weapons could be silenced and overcome by our weapons'. They arrived thinking the only danger was from small-arms fire. They had not imagined mines, mortars, artillery and tanks. In an attack, they bunched together, offering an easy target. When a rifle fired or a machine gun opened up, they would throw themselves flat on the ground, exposing themselves to mortar bursts, when the safest course was to rush forward.

The principle of 'marching fire', keeping up a steady volume at likely targets as they advanced, was something that few replacements seemed able to comprehend. 'The worst fault I have found', reported a company commander, 'has been the failure of men to fire weapons. I have seen them fired on and not fire back. They just took cover. When questioned, they said to fire would draw fire on themselves.' Paradoxically, when German soldiers tried to surrender, replacements were nearly always the first to try to shoot them down, which made them go to ground and fight on. Newcomers also needed to learn about German tricks which might throw them. 'Jerry puts mortar fire just behind our own artillery fire to make our troops believe that their own fire is falling short.' Experienced troops were well used to this, but replacements often panicked.

Divisions also despaired at the lack of preparation for officer and NCO replacements. They argued that officers needed to serve at the front before being given responsibility for men's lives. NCOs who arrived without any combat experience should be reduced in rank automatically before they arrive, and then be promoted again once they had proved they could do the job. 'We actually had a master sergeant sent to us,' one division reported. 'All he had done since being in the Army was paint a mural in the Pentagon. He is a good man but we have no job for him in grade.'

'My first contact with the enemy found me rather in a dazed frame of mind,' a young officer replacement admitted. 'I could not quite grasp the significance of what it was all about . . . It took me about four days to get where I did not think every shell that came over was for me.' He doubtless turned out to be a good platoon leader. But many, through no fault of their own, were utterly unsuited to the task. Some lieutenants were sent to tank battalions having never seen the inside of a tank. An infantry division was horrified to receive 'one group of officer replacements [who] had no experience as platoon leaders. They had been assistant special service officers, mess officers, etc.'

Commanders, in an attempt to galvanize their replacements, tried to stir up a hatred of the enemy. 'Before entering combat I have my leaders talk up German inhumanities,' stated a battalion commander with the 95th Division involved in the reduction of fortresses at Metz. 'Now that we have been in combat, we have lots of practical experience to draw on in this regard and it takes little urging to get the men ready to tear the Boche limb from limb. We avoid putting it on thick but merely try to point out that the German is a breed of vicious animal which will give us no quarter and must be exterminated.'

5
THE HÜRTGEN FOREST

Hemingway's friend and hero Colonel Buck Lanham of the 4th Division had soon found himself back in a world far removed from the comforts of the Ritz. At the end of October, General Eisenhower issued his orders for the autumn campaign. While the Canadian First Army finished securing the Scheldt estuary to open the port of Antwerp, the other six Allied armies under his command would advance to the Rhine with the industrial regions of the Ruhr and the Saar as their next objectives.

First Army's breaching of the Siegfried Line round Aachen put it no more than thirty kilometres from the Rhine, a tantalizingly small distance on the map. Some fifteen kilometres to the east lay the Roer river, which would have to be crossed first. The left wing of First Army, supported by the Ninth Army just to its north, would prepare to cross as soon as Collins's VII Corps and Gerow's V Corps secured the Hürtgen Forest and adjoining sectors.

Lieutenant General Courtney H. Hodges chose the old health resort of Spa for his headquarters. At the end of the First World War, Spa had been the base for Generalfeldmarschall Paul von Hindenburg and Kaiser Wilhelm II. There, in November 1918, the leadership of the Second Reich faced the sudden disintegration of their power as mutinies broke out back in Germany: the 'stab in the back' which Hitler was now obsessed with preventing twenty-six years later. Hodges took over the Grand Hôtel Britannique, while his operations staff set up their collapsible tables and situation maps under the chandeliers in the casino. The town's parks were packed with Jeeps and other military vehicles which had churned the grass into a mass of mud. The combat historian Forrest Pogue noted that, although less than thirty kilometres from the front line, nobody bothered to carry a weapon or wear field uniform.

First Army headquarters was not a happy place. It reeked of resentment and frustration at the slow progress during that stalemated autumn. Hodges, a strictly formal, colourless man with a clipped moustache, always held himself erect and seldom smiled. He had a southern drawl, was reluctant to take quick decisions and showed a lack of imagination for manoeuvre: he believed in simply going head-on at the enemy. More like a business-man in head office than a soldier, he hardly ever visited the front forward of a divisional command post. His decision to attack straight through the Hürtgen Forest as part of the plan to close with the Rhine led to the most gruesome part of the whole north-west Europe campaign.

South-east of Aachen, the Hürtgen Forest was a semi-mountainous expanse of deep pinewoods, with a few patches of oak and beech and some pasture on the ridges. Before the noise of war dominated its eerie peace, the only sounds were those of the wind in the trees and the mew of buzzards circling above. The forest, riven diagonally by ravines, had all too many vertiginous slopes. They were too steep for tanks and exhausting for heavily laden infantry, slipping and sliding amid the mud, rock and roots. The pine forest was so dense and so dark that it soon seemed cursed, as if in a sinister fairy-tale of witches and ogres. Men felt that they were intruders, and conversed in whispers as if the forest might be listening.

Tracks and firebreaks gave little sense of direction in this area of just under 150 square kilometres. There was little sign of human habitation except for a handful of villages, with woodcutters' houses and farms built in the local grey-brown stone at ground level, and timber-framed above. Piles of firewood were neatly stacked under shelters outside each dwelling.

After the initial forays into the edge of the forest by the 3rd Armored and the 1st Infantry Divisions in the second week of September, Hodges and his staff should have realized what they were asking their troops to take on. The subsequent experience of the 9th Infantry Division during the second half of September and October should have been a further warning. Progress had been good at first, advancing south-east towards the key town of Schmidt. Surprise was achieved because, in the words of the German divisional commander facing them, 'In general it was believed to be out of the question that in this extensive wooded area which was difficult to survey and had only a few roads, the Americans would try to fight their way to the Roer.' Once the German infantry were supported by their corps artillery, the forest fighting turned into a terrible battle of attrition.

The Germans brought in snipers to work from hides fixed high in the trees (closer to the ground there was little field of vision). They had been trained at Munsterlager in a *Scharfschutzen-Ausbildungskompanie,* or sniper-training company, where every day they had been subjected to half an hour of hate propaganda. 'This consisted of a kind of frenzied oration of the NCO instructors and usually took the following form:

'NCO: "Every shot must kill a Jewish Bolshevik."

'Chorus: "Every shot."

'NCO: "Kill the British Swine."

'Chorus: "Every shot must kill." '

The American 9th Infantry Division was attacking the sector held by the 275th Infanterie-Division led by Generalleutnant Hans Schmidt. Schmidt's regiments' command posts were log-huts in the forest. The division was only 6,500 strong with just six self-propelled assault guns. It had some soldiers with an idea of forest fighting, but others, such as the 20th Luftwaffe Festbataillon, had no infantry experience. One of its companies consisted of the Luftwaffe Interpreter School, which in Schmidt's view was 'absolutely unfit for employment at the front'. The following month 'almost the entire company went over to the enemy'. His troops were armed with a mixture of rifles, taken from foreign countries occupied earlier in the war.

Fighting in the Hürtgen Forest, Schmidt acknowledged, made 'the greatest demands on [the soldiers'] physical and psychological endurance'. They survived only because the Americans could not profit from their overwhelming superiority in tanks and airpower, and artillery observation was very difficult. But German supplies and rear-echelon personnel suffered badly from fighter-bomber attacks. The difficulties of bringing hot food forward meant that German troops received nothing but 'cold rations at irregular intervals.' Men in soaking uniforms had to remain in their foxholes for days in temperatures close to freezing.

On 8 October, the division was joined by Arbeitsbataillon 1412, consisting of old men. 'It was like a drop of water on a hot stove,' Schmidt commented. Virtually the whole battalion was annihilated in the course of a single day. An officer cadet battalion from the Luftwaffe was also torn to pieces. And on 9 October, when the division had already suffered 550 casualties 'without counting the great number of sick', a police battalion from Düren was thrown into the battle east of Wittscheide. The men, aged between forty-five and sixty, were still in their green police uniforms and had received no training since the First World War. 'The commitment of the old paterfamilias was painful,' Schmidt admitted. Casualties were so heavy that staff officers and training NCOs from the Feldersatzbataillon, their reserve and replacement unit, had to be sent forward to take command. Even badly needed signallers were sent in as infantrymen.

Only the very heavy rain on 10 October gave the 275th Division the chance to re-establish its line. Schmidt was impressed by the American 9th Infantry Division and even wondered whether it had received special training in forest warfare. That afternoon when his corps and army commanders paid a visit, they were so shaken by the condition of the division that they promised reinforcements.

Reinforcements did arrive, but to launch a counter-attack rather than strengthen the line. They consisted of a well-armed training regiment 2,000 strong, half of whom were officer candidates, commanded by Oberst Helmuth Wegelein. Hopes were high. The attack was launched at 07.00 hours on 12 October with heavy artillery support. But, to the despair of German officers, the advance became bogged down under very effective American fire. It appears that the battalion commanders of this elite training regiment became confused and the whole attack collapsed in chaos. A second attempt in the afternoon also failed. Training Regiment Wegelein lost 500 men in twelve hours, and Wegelein himself was killed the next day. On 14 October, the Germans were forced to pull back to reorganize, but as General Schmidt guessed with relief, the American 9th Division was also totally exhausted.

The 9th Division's painful and costly advance came to a halt on 16 October after it had suffered some 4,500 battle and non-battle casualties: one for every yard it had advanced. American army doctors, operating on both badly wounded GIs and German soldiers, had begun to notice a striking contrast. Surgeons observed that 'the German soldier shows an aptitude for recovery from the most drastic wounds far above that of the American soldier'. This difference was apparently due to 'the simple surgical fact that American soldiers, being so much better fed than the Germans, generally have a thick layer of fat on them which makes surgery not only more difficult and extensive, but also delays healing. The German soldier on the other hand, being sparsely fed and leaner, is therefore more operable.'

To the dismay of divisional commanders, First Army headquarters was unmoved by the casualties of the 9th Division's offensive and still took no account of the terrain. Once again Hodges insisted on attacking through the most difficult parts and the thickest forest, where American advantages in tank, air and artillery support could never play a part. He never considered advancing on the key town of Schmidt from the Monschau corridor to the south, a shorter and generally easier approach. The trouble was that neither his corps commanders nor his headquarters staff dared to argue with him. Hodges had a reputation for sacking senior officers.

The First Army plan for the Hürtgen For-

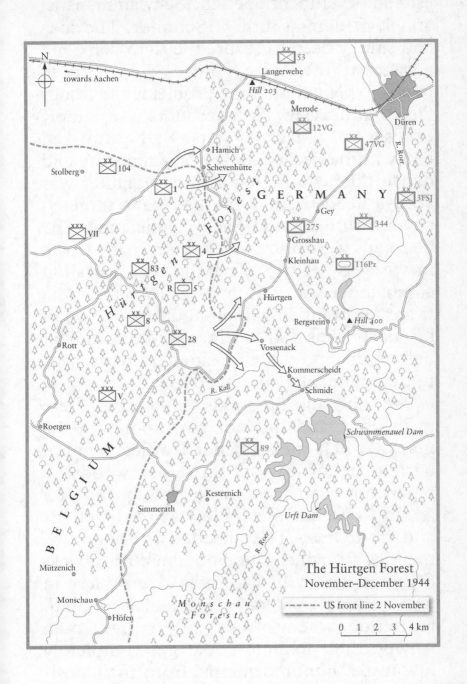

N

towards Aachen

⊠⊠ 53
Langerwehe
▲ Hill 203
Merode
⊠⊠ 12VG
⊠⊠ 47VG
Düren
R. Roer

Hamich
Schevenhütte
⊠⊠ 104
Stolberg
⊠⊠ 1
GERMANY
⊠⊠ 3FSJ
Gey
⊠⊠⊠ VII
⊠⊠ 275
⊠⊠ 344
Grosshau
⊠⊠ 4
Kleinhau
⊠⊠ 116Pz
⊠⊠ 83
R ⊠ 5
Hürtgen
⊠⊠ 8
Bergstein
▲ Hill 400
Rott
⊠⊠ 28
Vossenack
⊠⊠⊠ V
Kommerscheidt
R. Kall
Schmidt
Roetgen
⊠⊠ 89
Schwammenauel Dam

BELGIUM
Kesternich
Urft Dam
Simmerath
Mützenich
R. Roer
Monschau
The Hürtgen Forest
Höfen
November–December 1944
Monschau
Forest
------ US front line 2 November

0   1   2   3   4 km

est had never mentioned the Schwammenauel and Urft dams south of Schmidt. The idea had simply been to secure the right flank and advance to the Rhine. Hodges did not listen to any explanation of the problems the troops faced. In his view, such accounts were simply excuses for a lack of guts. Radios worked badly in the deep valleys, heavy moisture and dense pinewoods. A back-up signaller was always needed since the Germans targeted anyone with a radio pack on his back. The Germans were also swift to punish any lapses in wireless security. The slip of a battalion commander who said in clear over the radio 'I am returning in half an hour' led to two of his party being killed in a sudden mortar bombardment on their customary route back to the regimental command post.

The trails and firebreaks in the forest were misleading and did not correspond to the maps, which inexperienced officers found hard to read anyway. 'In dense woods,' a report observed, 'it is not too infrequent for a group to be completely lost as to directions and front line.' They needed the sound of their own artillery to find their way back. Sometimes they had to radio the artillery to fire a single shell on a particular point to reorientate themselves. And at night men leaving their foxhole could get completely lost just a hundred metres from their position, and would have to wait until dawn to discover where they were.

Most unnerving of all were the screams of those who had stepped on an anti-personnel mine and lost a foot. 'One man kicked a bloody shoe from his path,' a company commander later wrote, 'then shuddered to see that the shoe still had a foot in it.' American soldiers soon found that the Germans prided themselves on their skills in this field. Roadblocks were booby-trapped, so the trunks dropped across trails as a barrier had to be towed away from a distance with long ropes. New arrivals had to learn about 'Schu, Riegel, Teller and anti-tank mines'. The Riegel mine was very hard to remove as it was 'wired up to explode upon handling'. Germans laid mines in shellholes where green troops instinctively threw themselves when they came under fire. And well aware that American tactical doctrine urged troops to approach a hill whenever possible via 'draws', or gullies, the Germans made sure that they were mined and covered by machine-gun fire.

Both sides mined and counter-mined in a deadly game. 'When mines are discovered,' a report stated, 'this same unit places its own mines around the enemy mines to trap inspecting parties. The Germans, in turn, are liable to booby-trap ours, and so on.' A member of the 297th Engineer Combat Battalion noticed a mine poking through the surface of the ground. Fortunately for him, he was suspicious and did not go straight to it. A mine detector showed that the Germans had buried a circle of other mines all around it and he would have had a leg blown off. 'The Germans are burying mines as many as three deep in the soft muddy roads in this sector,' Colonel Buck Lanham's regiment reported soon after reaching the Hürtgen Forest. The engineers would locate and remove the top one, not realizing that there were more. Once spotted, they resorted to blowing them with dynamite and then repairing the hole in the road with a bulldozer.

Another danger was from trip-wires among the pine trees. Officers complained that soldiers spent so much time staring at the ground just in front of them in an attempt to spot wires and mines that they never looked up and around when on patrol. The Americans also improvised trip flares in front of their forward positions, with wires stretched out in several directions between the trees. These consisted of a half-pound block of TNT taped to a 60mm mortar illuminating shell, with a firing device. They soon discovered that they had to be sited at least fifty yards in front of the machine-gun pits covering the approach, otherwise the gunner would be blinded by the light. But in the Hürtgen Forest nothing was simple. As another officer observed: 'The effective range of rifle fire in woods and forests seldom exceeds fifty yards.'

Both sides suffered badly from the chilling autumn rains. Even when it was not pouring down, the trees dripped ceaselessly. Rusty ammunition caused stoppages. Uniforms and boots rotted. Trench foot could lead rapidly to debilitation, and even the need to amputate. American officers were slow at first to recognize the gravity of the problem. Regiments, weakened by the loss of so many men, made efforts to issue a fresh pair of socks to each man with his rations. Men were told to keep their spare socks dry by putting them inside their helmet, and to use the buddy system, rubbing each other's feet briskly, and sleeping with their feet up to help the circulation.

The constant chill felt by men soaked to the skin for days on end in water-filled foxholes made battalion officers aware of the need to allow men to get warm at least once a day. Bell tents with heaters inside were set up behind the lines, with hot coffee and hot food on offer. Another heated tent was used for drying uniforms. But all too often the constant attacks and the Germans' aggressive patrolling prevented those in the forward foxholes from getting away. Trench-foot rates soared as the men were simply doomed to shiver under pelting rain and chew on cold rations. As a heater and cooker, some resorted to using a C-Ration can filled with earth and soaked in gasoline, which they dug into a hole a foot deep. They would then warm up their food or liquid in a larger No. 10 can which had been perforated round the top.

Resilient constitutions, both mental and physical, were needed in such conditions, especially when the snow began to fall in November at higher altitudes. 'Men over thirty are too old to stand up under combat conditions,' a VII Corps officer observed, 'while men under twenty are not sufficiently matured, mentally and physically.' Unfortunately, the vast majority of replacements were either under twenty or over thirty.

Even providing overhead cover for the two-men foxholes was a dangerous matter. The German artillery fired tree bursts, deliberately exploding their shells in the tops of the tall pines to rain splinters and metal shrapnel down on anyone sheltering below. So part of the foxhole had to be covered with logs under a thick layer of earth, camouflaged in turn with moss or branches. But cutting logs to size with an axe was dangerous. The sound carried a long way and the Germans, knowing that men were above ground, would fire a rapid mortar barrage. Handsaws had to be used instead.

The Germans, as had been their practice in Normandy and on the eastern front, manned their foremost line very lightly, relying on automatic weapons. They then used better-quality troops to launch their counter-attacks, backing them with tanks. And when the Americans attacked, they did not shrink from calling down artillery fire on their own positions. The Americans soon discovered that they could do the same, because with the shells coming in from behind, the spray of deadly splinters and shell fragments went forward against the attackers rather than down on their own men, sheltering in their foxholes. 'It took guts, but it worked,' a colonel commented.

On 1 November, Hodges accompanied by Gerow, the V Corps commander, visited the headquarters of the 28th Division at Rott. He told 'Dutch' Cota, who had so proudly watched his men march through Paris, that they would be attacking the next morning as the first stage before VII Corps began to advance on their left. The plan, Hodges assured him, was 'excellent'. In fact the plan was just about as inept as it could be. Not only was the 28th to advance across the steepest ridges and valleys, but Hodges ordered Cota to split his division in different directions, effectively making his attacking force far weaker than the defenders. Not even a whole regiment was to advance on the town of Schmidt. Cota tried tactfully to point out the flaws but his objections were ignored.

Obstinacy and a failure to listen were even greater at the top of the Third Reich. The very next morning, General der Flieger

Kreipe, having been forced to resign as chief of staff of the Luftwaffe, made his farewell to Reichsmarschall Göring on his special train at the Wolfsschanze. The conversation came round to the outcome of the war. 'Certainly there will be a Nibelungen battle,' Göring said, 'but we will stand at the Vistula, at the Oder or at the Weser River.' Kreipe doubted that a civilian population could be expected to engage in such suicidal warfare. He begged the Reichsmarschall 'to prevail upon the Führer to see to it that politics will take a hand in the matter. Göring was silent for a while,' he wrote in his diary, 'and finally told me that he was unable to do this since this would rob the Führer of his self-confidence.'

At 09.00 on 2 November, just as Kreipe met Göring, the 28th Infantry Division advanced eastwards out of a small salient into the mist-covered forest. The 110th Infantry Regiment on the right suffered badly from machine guns in pillboxes of the Siegfried Line which had not been dealt with earlier. The 109th Infantry on the left were equally unfortunate, running straight into an unmarked minefield covered by heavy fire. The German 275th Infanterie-Division defending the sector was by then experienced in forest fighting, but had been ground down so badly that its commander, Generalleutnant Schmidt, clamoured for its relief. Some of his soldiers, on surrendering to the Americans, claimed that mines had been laid behind as well as in front to prevent desertion. Several of their comrades had been executed for making the attempt.

In the centre, the American 112th Infantry Regiment attacked down towards the village of Vossenack, running along to the end of a saddleback ridge above the 200-metre-deep ravine of the Kall river. Artillery concentrations of white phosphorus shells set most of the houses on fire. Sherman tanks fired at the church steeple, on the assumption that it contained at least a German artillery observer or snipers. Expecting a counter-attack after they had occupied the smoking village, the company commander told his men to dig in and have their rifles ready. To his surprise 'one big, old country boy remarked, "The last time I fired this thing, it cost me 18 bucks in a summary court. I was liquored up on Calvados." '

On 3 November at dawn, the 112th Infantry began to advance down the very steep slope to the River Kall below and then climb up the equally steep escarpment on the south-east side which led to the village of Kommerscheidt. One battalion, displaying considerable endurance, leap-frogged on ahead towards the town of Schmidt, which it seized to the astonishment of the utterly unprepared German troops there. Sergeant

John M. Kozlosky stopped a horse-drawn ammunition wagon. 'When the driver found that Kozlosky could speak Polish, he jumped from the wagon and kissed Kozlosky on both cheeks.' He was one of the many Poles forced into the Wehrmacht. Below Schmidt lay the great, meandering Schwammenauel reservoir and its dam, just two and a half kilometres from where the soldiers of the 112th stood. Cota could not resist basking in the congratulations he received on this triumph, even if it seemed too good to be true.

Only a few days before, officers at First Army headquarters had suddenly realized that if the Germans opened the dams when American forces downstream were trying to cross the River Roer, a wall of water could sweep away pontoon bridges and cut off any troops in bridgeheads on the east bank. Hodges started to take this in only when news of the capture of Schmidt arrived, but it was too late to do anything. And to make a bad situation worse, Hodges had just encouraged Collins to delay the VII Corps attack until a fourth division arrived to reinforce his advance. As a result the 28th Division was left totally exposed.

Cota's division could hardly have been a worse choice for such a hopeless task. Earlier losses meant that most of its troops were replacements and it had a very high rate of self-inflicted wounds and desertion. As a warning, Private Eddie Slovik, a repeat deserter from the division, was selected as the only soldier in the United States Army in Europe to be executed for the offence.

The Germans had been taken by surprise because they could not understand the reason for the strong American attacks in the Hürtgen Forest, 'after the effectiveness of the German resistance' against the 9th Division the previous month. But, in one of those coincidences of war, Generalfeldmarschall Model, the commander-in-chief of Army Group B, was holding a map conference at that very moment in Schloss Schlenderhan, near Quadrath, west of Cologne. He and his staff were looking at the possibility of an American attack along the boundary between the Fifth Panzer Army and the Seventh Army. So as soon as Model received word of the American occupation of Schmidt, he wasted no time. He sent Generalleutnant Straube, the commander of the LXXIV Corps in charge of the sector, straight back to his headquarters. Then, with General Erich Brandenberger of the Seventh Army and General der Panzertruppe Hasso von Manteuffel of the Fifth Panzer Army, he worked out their best response with the other officers present.

The 116th Panzer-Division was ordered to move with all speed to attack the northern flank of the American advance along with the

89th Infanterie-Division. The 116th Panzer was now commanded by Generalmajor Siegfried von Waldenburg, following the storm created by his predecessor, Generalleutnant Graf von Schwerin, who had cancelled the evacuation of Aachen. Waldenburg also left the map exercise rapidly with his operations officer, Major Prinz zu Holstein, to rejoin their division. Model, who had been ordered by Führer headquarters not to commit the 116th Panzer, felt obliged to ignore this instruction purely 'to prevent American troops from spilling out of the woods on to the open ground'.

That night, men of the 3rd Battalion of the 112th Infantry Regiment holding Schmidt were exhausted after their efforts. Rather than dig foxholes, they went to sleep in houses. Their officers never imagined that the Germans would react immediately, so they did not send out patrols or position outposts. As a result the battalion was totally surprised when German infantry and tanks appeared at dawn, following a sudden artillery bombardment. Short of bazooka rounds and shocked by the unexpected attack from three directions, most of the battalion panicked. In the confusion, some 200 men ran straight into more Germans coming from the southeast, and only sixty-seven of them were left alive afterwards. Officers lost control of their men. The rest of the battalion, abandoning their wounded, rushed back towards Kommerscheidt to join up with the 1st Battalion.

In his command post at Rott, some thirteen kilometres to the west of Schmidt, Cota at first had little idea of the disaster overtaking his division. On 8 November, he was inundated by a chain of commanders. General Hodges arrived to find 'General Eisenhower, General Bradley and General Gerow talking the situation over with General Cota. Pleasantries were passed until the official party left,' Hodges's aide recorded, 'then General Hodges drew General Cota aside for a short sharp conference on the lack of progress made by 28th Division . . . General Hodges, needless to say, is extremely disappointed over the 28th Division's showing.' Hodges also blamed Gerow, the corps commander, even though the supposedly 'excellent' plan, sending a single division alone into the Hürtgen and then splitting it up, had been the work of his own First Army headquarters. He forced Cota to send an order to the 112th Infantry to retake Schmidt, which revealed his total ignorance of what was happening on the ground.

Sherman tanks sent forward to take on the Panther and Mark IV panzers could not negotiate the steep winding tracks, the mines and the mud. Low cloud and rain meant that the fighter-bombers could not take off. And all the time, the two American battalions cut off in Kommerscheidt were subjected to concentrated shelling from tanks and all the artillery battalions which Model had ordered in from neighbouring corps. On 7 November, the 2nd Battalion in Vossenack broke and ran. Cota sent in the 146th Engineers, fighting as infantry, and they managed to hold on to the western part of Vossenack against panzer-grenadiers and tanks. The situation was so grave that part of the 4th Infantry Division had to reinforce the 28th Division.

On the night of 8 November, American artillery laid a heavy bombardment around Kommerscheidt to allow the survivors of the two battalions to sneak out through the Kall ravine. The 28th Infantry Division had been forced back almost to where it had started, having suffered 5,684 battle and non-battle casualties. For Cota, who had watched his division so proudly in Paris, it must have been the most bitter day of his life. The 112th Infantry alone had lost more than 2,000 men and was now no more than 300 strong. As one of Bradley's staff officers observed: 'When the strength of an outfit in the line drops below a certain point, something very bad happens to it and its effectiveness falls away sharply. What happens to it is that there are not enough experienced men left in it to make the replacements — "the reinforcements" — savvy.'

German propaganda wasted no time in

boasting of the successful counter-attack, as well as the recapture of Goldap in East Prussia and the failure of the Red Army to take Budapest. 'The surrounded American task force was destroyed. The villages of Vossenack and Kommerscheidt have been cleared of the small groups, which defended themselves desperately, but then gave up their senseless resistance.'

General Hodges refused to consider another plan. Even now, knowing the importance of the dams, he did not plan to swing round to the south. He ordered the 1st, the 8th and the 104th Infantry Divisions as well as the 5th Armored Division and the rest of the 4th Division into the Hürtgen Forest. This would constitute the right flank of the joint Ninth and First Army offensive. On 12 November, the British Second Army began its offensive east from its Nijmegen salient. Despite the rain, mud and mines, over the next ten days it cleared the west bank of the Maas up to Venlo and Roermond, both close to the Dutch–German border. Also that day, the 1st Division left its rest area west of Aachen in trucks for the northern sector of the forest.

The third offensive into the Hürtgen Forest began, after several delays, on 16 November. By then sleet had started to turn to snow on the higher ground. The 1st Division in the north was to advance from the Stolberg corridor on the town of Düren, which along with Eschweiler and Jülich was almost totally flattened under the weight of 9,700 tons of bombs dropped by the Allied air forces. Düren was also shelled nightly by American artillery.

Soon after the leading elements of the 1st Division had entered the pinewoods, they and their supporting tanks came under heavy artillery and small-arms fire from the 12th Volksgrenadier-Division. 'There was a stream of wounded soldiers coming out of the woods,' wrote the novice machine-gunner Arthur Couch. 'One man I noticed was holding onto his stomach in an effort to hold in a large wound that was allowing his intestines to spill out. Quickly a front line medic came up and helped the man lie down and he put on a large bandage around his stomach and then injected him with morphine. An old sergeant told me to lie low behind large rocks and then move towards the last German artillery shell blast. He said that was the safest thing to do since the German gunners always turned the crank on their gun a few notches to hit another position. I did run into the last shell burst and the next shell landed 30 yards away. This was life-saving advice.'

Once again, as a 1st Infantry Division officer observed, the Germans tried to pin the American attackers down with small-arms fire 'then blast hell out of us with artillery and mortars'. Newcomers had been told to stand close behind a large tree, as it offered some protection from tree bursts. The one thing to avoid was lying flat on the ground as that increased your chances of being hit by shards of steel or wood splinters. The Americans tried to use heavy 4.2-inch mortars in support, but their crews soon found a wide dispersion in the fall of their rounds because of the effect of the cold, wet weather on the propellant. And when the ground was saturated, the base plate would be hammered further into the mud with each round.

'The German artillery', wrote Couch, 'was pre-aimed on the forest roads and also had been set to explode when hitting a tree top so the shell fragments sprayed down on us. This caused many dangerous wounds or deaths. I was seeing many wounded or dying men . . . at first I used to kneel down and talk to them but I soon found that too much to bear. I think seeing such wounds was starting to break through my defensive shield.' His greatest admiration was for the medics who ran to help the wounded 'even under heavy artillery or machine guns while we would stay in more protected places'.

In the forest, most German soldiers lost their fear of tanks. They could stalk them with the Panzerfaust. Or at a slightly longer range, they used the Panzerschreck, known as an 'Ofenrohre' or 'stovepipe', which was a larger version of the American bazooka. The German soldier or *Landser* also used the Panzerfaust as close-range artillery in the forest. Not surprisingly, as the chief of staff of the Seventh Army pointed out, the Germans found it 'easier to defend in the woods than in the open', because American tanks had such difficulties operating there. Engineers would remove most of the mines along the narrow, muddy tracks, but almost always one would be missed and the first tank through would be immobilized and block the route.

The 1st Infantry faced bitter resistance, and heavy artillery fire. 'Just before dawn,' continued Couch, 'a large bombardment began mainly hitting the trees above us. Being night and really dangerous, the new troops became very anxious and started moving around in panic. I tried to hold onto one or two of them, saying stay in your foxholes or you may get killed . . . This was the first time I had seen battlefield panic and could understand how some men get very traumatized and shell-shocked . . . Other later cases were sent to the rear for treatment. It is too dangerous for the rest of us to have such disturbances in our midst while we need to move forwards.'

The 4th Division, with Colonel Buck Lanham's 22nd Infantry Regiment in the centre, set out eastwards up the great ridge which ran down to Schmidt. The plan was to begin with Grosshau almost at the top, while the

8th Division on its right attacked the village of Hürtgen, and then Kleinhau. But the casualty rate for every metre of ground gained was appalling. American commanders had no idea that the reason for the desperate German defence was to prevent a break-through just north of the start-line for the forthcoming Ardennes offensive.

Even the tiny villages, often no more than a hamlet in size, had their own church solidly built in the same grey and brown stone. Schmidt's 275th Infanterie-Division had sent a number of men off for intensive sniper-training courses. American officers had to wear their field glasses inside their shirt to avoid being targeted, and yet, as Colonel Luckett of the 4th Division pointed out, visibility seldom stretched beyond seventy-five yards, making it very difficult for snipers on the ground. The Germans also made use of a flak battery of 88mm guns south-west of Mariaweiler, which fired at Allied bombers on their way to German cities. At the same time, a forward observation post could warn them if their guns needed to be switched to an anti-tank role.

Schmidt's officers could rely on local forest-ers for much of their intelligence in the area, which gave them a great advantage. The Americans, they noticed, bothered to carry out reconnaissance only when about to at-tack a particular sector, which thus revealed their objective for the next day. German officers and NCOs were adept at exploiting American mistakes. Junior American commanders were often tempted to pull back at night after taking ground, but the Germans would move in and it would become impossible to dislodge them next day. And an attack was not the only time GIs bunched together. Whenever a prisoner was captured, 'twelve to twenty men will pile around, and that is going to cause a lot of casualties'.

The Germans kept their tanks well dug in and camouflaged, and used them mostly as a psychological weapon. 'In the daytime,' an American officer reported, 'they are comparatively quiet, but at dawn, dusk and at intervals during the night they become active. They continually move around and shoot, just enough to keep our troops in an almost frantic state of mind.' American officers resolved to keep their tank destroyers well forward to reassure their men. Infantry tended to panic and retreat once their supporting tanks moved back to replenish with fuel and ammunition, so whenever possible a reserve platoon of tanks needed to be ready to take their place. It was not easy because armoured vehicles were so vulnerable in the dark woods. Each platoon of light tanks needed a squad of infantry, and a mine-removal squad from the engineers. Tank crews seem to have been even more frightened than the infantry in the forest. 'One time we didn't get out of the tanks for four days,' recorded one soldier. 'Heavy artillery, 88s, mortars, screaming meemies [from the German Nebelwerfer rocket launcher] pounding in all around us. You got out of your tank to take a leak and you were a dead duck. We used our damn helmets and dumped them out of the turret.'

As Colonel Lanham's 22nd Infantry Regiment slogged its way up the thickly wooded hill towards the hamlet of Kleinhau, it found that the Germans had cut the lower branches from the trees to the front to provide better fields of fire for their MG-42 machine guns. A sudden charge forced the first outposts to flee, but further on the Americans were stopped by a 'booby-trapped stretch of tangle-foot barbed wire twenty-five yards deep'. As they surveyed the obstacle, a sudden salvo of mortar fire hit them. This was just the start of their Calvary. All three of Lanham's battalion commanders were killed. In one of the most horrific incidents, three German soldiers stripped a badly wounded American of his possessions, then placed an explosive charge under him which would explode if he was moved. He was not found for seventy hours, but had just enough strength left to warn his rescuers.

The 4th Infantry Division gradually adapted to forest fighting. Each company was divided into two assault groups and two support groups. The assault groups carried only personal weapons and grenades. The support groups behind, keeping just within sight, had the mortars and machine guns. The scouts and the assault group in front needed to maintain 'direction by compass' because it was so easy to lose all sense of direction in the woods. As they advanced, the support group would reel out signal wire for communications, but also, rather like Hansel and Gretel, to guide runners, ammunition carriers and litter bearers.

American divisions in the forest soon found that tracks, firebreaks and logging trails should be used not as boundaries but as centre lines. Units should advance astride them, although never up them because they were so heavily booby-trapped and targeted by the Germans in their artillery fire-plans. The Germans had zeroed in their mortars on every track, as part of the 1st Infantry Division had found to its cost; so to save lives the division attacked through the forest itself. It also sited command posts well away from trails, even though this too cost time.

In mid-November the weather turned very cold. Many exhausted men had thrown away their heavy wool overcoats when they became impregnated with rain and mud. 'A heavy snow two feet or more fell on the whole forest,' wrote Couch with the 1st Infantry

Division. 'One day we were walking through a forward area where another company had made an earlier attack. I saw a line of about six soldiers standing leaning forward with pointed rifles in the deep snow — seemingly in an attack. But I then noticed they didn't move at all. I said to a comrade: they must be dead and are frozen stiff as they were hit. I had taken the precaution of stuffing my left breast pocket with German coins to block a bullet or shrapnel to my heart — but I knew it was silly.'

Further south, General Patton continued to pressure his commanders to attack. On Saturday 11 November, the 12th Army Group diarist joked that it was both 'Armistice Day and Georgie Patton's birthday: the two are incompatible'. Exactly a week later, Patton's Third Army finally encircled Metz, and four days later resistance within the fortress city ceased. Patton's obsession with capturing Metz had led to heavy losses among his own troops. His arrogance and impatience, after the lightning victories of the summer, had contributed greatly to the heavy casualties. The constant rain, which had swollen the Moselle over its flood plain, made the crossing south of Metz a sodden nightmare. Patton told Bradley how one of his engineer companies had taken two days of frustration and hard work to connect a pontoon bridge across the fast-flowing river. One of the first vehicles across, a tank destroyer, snagged on a cable which then snapped. The bridge broke loose and swung downstream. 'The whole damn company sat down in the mud', Patton related, 'and bawled like babies.'

In the south, a US Seventh Army attack on the Saverne Gap in mid-November enabled the French 2nd Armoured Division to break through and into Strasbourg itself, thundering right up to the Kehl bridge over the Rhine. And on the 6th Army Group's right flank, General de Lattre's First Army liberated Belfort, Altkirch and Mulhouse to advance south of Colmar, where it would be halted by German resistance within what became known as the 'Colmar pocket'.

The defence of Strasbourg was an inglorious episode in the history of the German army. The SS had looted Strasbourg before withdrawing. According to one general defending Strasbourg, soldiers ordered to 'fight to the last round' tended to throw most of their ammunition away before the battle, so that they could claim they had run out and then surrender. Generalmajor Vaterrodt, the Wehrmacht commander, was scornful about the behaviour of senior officers and Nazi Party officials. 'I am surprised that Himmler did not have anyone hanged in Strasbourg,' he told fellow officers after he had been captured. 'Everyone ran away, Kreisleiter, Ortsgruppenleiter, the municipal authorities, the mayor and the deputy mayor, they all took to their heels, government officials — all fled . . . When things began getting a bit lively in the early morning they crossed the Rhine.' The Landgerichtspräsident or chief judge of Strasbourg was seen fleeing with a rucksack towards the Rhine. Vaterrodt had more sympathy in his case. 'He was right. He had had to sign so many death warrants, summary sentences, that it was really terrible.' The judge was an Alsatian born in Strasbourg, so he would have been the first to be tried or lynched.

Many German officers turned up with their French girlfriends, claiming 'I've lost my unit.' 'They were all deserters!' Vaterrodt exploded. The most spectacular was Generalleutnant Schreiber, who arrived in Vaterrodt's office and said: 'My staff is down there.' Vaterrodt looked out of the window. 'There were about ten wonderful brand-new cars down there, with girls in them, staff auxiliaries, and over-fed officials, with a terrific amount of luggage which of course consisted mainly of food and other fine things.' Schreiber announced that he intended to cross the Rhine. 'Then at least I shall be safe for the moment.'

The liberation of Strasbourg by General Leclerc's 2nd Armoured Division produced great joy in France, and for Leclerc it was the culmination of his promise at Koufra, in North Africa, that the *tricolore* would fly again from the cathedral. For them the liberation of Strasbourg and Alsace, taken by the Germans in 1871 and 1940, represented the final objective in France. Leclerc was admired and liked by senior American officers. The same could not be said of the mercurial and flamboyant General de Lattre de Tassigny, who believed it was his duty to keep complaining about the failure to supply enough uniforms and weaponry to his forces in the First French Army on the extreme southern flank. To be fair to him, he faced immense problems, integrating some 137,000 untrained and unruly members of the French Resistance into his army. De Gaulle wanted to start withdrawing colonial forces to make the First Army appear more ethnically French, and the North African and Senegalese colonial troops had suffered terribly in the cold of the Vosges mountains. In heavy snow, Lattre's First Army had finally broken through the Belfort Gap to the Rhine just above the Swiss frontier.

On 24 November, Eisenhower and Bradley arrived to visit Lieutenant General Jacob L. Devers, who commanded the 6th Army Group with Lieutenant General Alexander M. Patch's Seventh Army and Lattre's First French Army. Devers was an ambitious young general who put many backs up, including Eisenhower's. He had not had a chance to discuss his plans with SHAEF, largely because Eisenhower took little interest in his southern flank. Devers was convinced he could cross the Rhine easily at Rastatt, south-west of Karlsruhe, despite some counterattacks on his left flank. He had clearly expected that Eisenhower would be thrilled at the possibility of seizing a bridgehead across the Rhine. But as Devers outlined the operation he handled his arguments badly, and became deeply upset when the Supreme Commander rejected his plan out of hand. The fault lay mainly with Eisenhower, who had his eyes on the Ruhr and Berlin and had never really considered what his strategy should be in the south. He simply wanted to follow his overall idea of clearing the west bank of the Rhine all the way from the North Sea to Switzerland. Eisenhower's decision showed an unfortunate lack of imagination. A bridgehead across the Rhine at Rastatt would have offered a useful opportunity, and if carried out quickly, it might well have disrupted Hitler's planning for the Ardennes offensive.

As the fighting in the Hürtgen Forest ground on, both sides relied more and more on artillery. Schmidt's division alone had a total of 131 guns in direct support, although its artillery regiments were equipped with a mixture of German, Russian, Italian and French guns, which made ammunition resupply difficult. The American concentration of firepower was even greater.

The result was a chaotic nightmare of trees smashed, shredded, gashed and sliced by shellfire and mortars, bodies mangled by mines, abandoned helmets and rusty weapons, the burned-out carcasses of vehicles, ammunition containers, ration packs, gasmasks and sodden mud-encrusted overcoats abandoned because of their weight. 'Especially distressing was the personal clothing of the soldiers,' General Straube, the German corps commander, admitted. In the wet and intense cold his men suffered from hypothermia, trench foot, frostbite and illness. Yet mortar rounds caused the largest proportion of battle casualties on both sides.

Many German officers believed that the fighting in the Hürtgen Forest was worse than fighting in the First World War, or even on the eastern front. One described it as 'an open wound'. Generalmajor Rudolf Freiherr von Gersdorff called it a 'death-mill'. Hemingway, having attached himself again to Lanham's 22nd Infantry, witnessed the scenes of snow, mud and smashed pines. He said that the Hürtgen was 'Passchendaele with tree bursts'.

Hemingway, again armed with a Thompson

sub-machine gun despite the recent inquiry into his martial activities, was also carrying two canteens, one filled with schnapps and the other with cognac. He certainly demonstrated his own fearlessness under fire on several occasions, and even took part in one battle. Journalism was not high on his priorities. He referred to himself mockingly as 'Old Ernie Hemorrhoid, the poor Poor Man's Pyle', in a mild jibe against Ernie Pyle, the most famous American war correspondent. But he studied the men around him and their conduct under fire because he had plans for writing the great American novel about the war. As his biographer observed, 'Ernest gloried in the role of senior counsellor and friend to both officers and men.' He was fascinated by the nature of courage and derided psychiatrists' views about a man's breaking point.

J. D. Salinger, little more than a mile away with the 12th Infantry Regiment, continued to write short stories furiously throughout this hellish battle, whenever, as he told his readers, he could find 'an unoccupied foxhole'. This activity seems at least to have postponed Salinger's own psychological collapse until the end of the war.

Combat exhaustion, that military euphemism for neuro-psychiatric breakdown, spread rapidly. 'After five days up there you talk to the trees,' ran one of the few jokes.

'On the sixth you start getting answers back.' With perhaps cynical exaggeration one of Bradley's staff officers, who visited the sector, wrote: 'The young battalion commanders who came out of the Hürtgen Forest were as near gibbering idiots as men can get without being locked up for it.' One of them apparently said to him: 'Well, it's not too bad until the doughs get so tired that when they are coming out of the line and there is a dead dough from their own outfit lying on his back, in their way, they are just too goddam tired to move their feet and they step on the stiff's face, because what the hell . . .'

Stress made the men yearn for nicotine and alcohol. Most officers were generous in sharing their own privileged supplies of whisky and gin, but rumours of cigarette rations being stolen by quartermasters in the rear to sell on the black market could almost provoke a riot. 'The men accept poor or short rations without grumbling,' remarked an officer with the 4th Division; 'in fact, [they] would rather go short on rations to get more cigarettes.'

Physical casualties also soared. 'You drive by the surgical tents in the morning, going up, and there are two or three stiffs there on the ground; you come back in the afternoon and there are thirty or forty . . . They are short-handed in the Graves Registration squad.' In the first three days of the offensive, the 22nd Infantry in the 4th Division suffered 391 battle casualties, including 28 officers and 110 NCOs. Sometimes new company and platoon leaders survived for such a short time that their men never even knew their names.

German losses were also severe. Model, determined to 'keep control of the dominant terrain', threw one hastily organized battalion or regiment after another into the battle. More elderly policemen and under-trained Luftwaffe ground crew were marched forward to die. Many were killed by American artillery before they even reached the front line. Whenever the sky cleared, American fighter-bombers attacked German artillery batteries using white phosphorus bombs. Although freezing in his threadbare uniform and badly under-nourished due to meagre and infrequent rations, the German *Landser* fought on because there appeared to be no alternative.

Constant German counter-attacks against the 1st, 4th and 8th Infantry Divisions delayed the American advance through the smashed woodland, but painfully and slowly it continued: whatever the cost, and despite the freezing rain, and the mud and the mines which prevented tanks from coming up to support them. American troops became embittered. 'Our men appear to have developed fully a requisite psychological attitude towards battle,' a sergeant wrote in his diary.

'They are killers. They hate Germans and think nothing of killing them.'

For 23 November, Thanksgiving Day, Eisenhower had ordered that every soldier under his command should receive a full turkey dinner. Battalion cooks tried to comply in the Hürtgen Forest, if only with turkey sandwiches, but as men climbed out of their foxholes to line up, they were hit by German artillery fire. A major who witnessed that day of heavy casualties confessed that he had never been able to eat another Thanksgiving dinner again. He 'would get up and go to the backyard and cry like a baby'.

Nobody felt there was much to celebrate. It needed another six days of very heavy casualties to take Kleinhau and Grosshau. The 8th Division finally captured the village of Hürtgen in a mad charge followed by close-quarter fighting in the houses, with grenades, rifles and Tommy guns.

The 83rd Division began to replace the 4th Infantry Division. These troops too were shaken by the damage caused by 'tree bursts that sent shell fragments screaming from the treetops in every direction'. To prepare for their assault on the village of Gey, the massed artillery organized a 'time on target', with every gun synchronized to fire at the same moment at the same target. They nevertheless faced 'gruelling house-to-house combat' when they entered the village. It was not until the end of the first week in December that the Americans were out of the forest, and looking down on the open countryside of the Roer valley. But they had still failed to capture the town of Schmidt and the dams. RAF Bomber Command, after repeated requests, finally made three attempts to destroy the dams, with five cancellations due to bad weather. Little damage was done and Bomber Command refused to try again. Finally, Hodges decided to try attacking towards them from the south-west with the 2nd Infantry Division, but the great German offensive soon halted that attempt. The dams would not be secured until February 1945.

The cost to both sides in battle casualties, nervous breakdown, frostbite, trench foot and pneumonia had been horrendous. In October, some 37 per cent of US troops had to be treated for common respiratory diseases, the worst level in the whole war. Fighting in the Hürtgen Forest produced 8,000 cases of psychological collapse on the American side. The Wehrmacht did not acknowledge this to be a legitimate reason to be spared front-line duty, so it had no figures. 'There were few cases of combat exhaustion,' the chief German medical officer said later. 'However since these men were not relieved, I could not say what percent this would be of total casualties.' 'In some cases,' wrote Brandenberger's chief of staff at Seventh Army, 'soldiers were found dead in their foxholes from sheer exhaustion.'

In the Hürtgen Forest campaign, the United States Army suffered 33,000 casualties out of the 120,000 men deployed. The 4th Infantry Division alone sustained 'more than 5,000 battle casualties and over 2,500 non-battle losses'. To help the division to recover, General Hodges ordered it to move to the 'quiet' VIII Corps sector across the Ardennes. Over the next twelve days, the 4th Division's three regiments took over the positions of the 83rd Infantry Division and came under the command of Troy Middleton's VIII Corps, with its headquarters in Bastogne. The 4th Division had to man a fifty-six-kilometre front, yet it was only at half strength when the German Ardennes offensive struck a few days later.

6
THE GERMANS PREPARE

On 20 November, Hitler boarded his special train in the camouflaged siding in the Wolfsschanze. The Führer's *Sonderzug* included a flak wagon at both ends with four quadruple guns, two armoured coaches and six passenger coaches in between. All were painted dark grey.

Hitler must have known in his heart that he would never return to East Prussia, but in a characteristic act of denial he ordered the building work on defences to continue. His staff and his secretary Traudl Junge also climbed aboard the train 'with the rather melancholy feeling of saying a final farewell'. Hitler, who spoke only in a loud whisper, was nervous because next day in Berlin a specialist was going to remove a polyp from his vocal chords. Hitler admitted to Traudl Junge that he might lose his voice. 'He knew very well', she wrote, 'that his voice was an important instrument of his power; his words intoxicated the people and carried them away.

How was he to hold crowds spellbound if he couldn't address them any more?' His entourage had been begging him for weeks to speak to the nation. 'My Führer, you must address the German people again. They've lost heart. They have doubts about you. There are rumours that you're not alive any more.'

Hitler wanted to reach Berlin after dark. He said that this was to keep his presence there a secret, but his entourage knew that he did not want to see the effects of Allied bombing. When they disembarked at the Grunewald station and drove off to the Reichschancellery, 'the column of cars tried to drive down streets that were still intact', wrote Junge. 'Once again, Hitler had no chance to see Berlin's wounds as they really were. The dipped headlights of the cars merely touched on mounds of rubble to right and left of the road.'

Hitler's most important reason for coming to Berlin was to supervise the planning for the Ardennes offensive, the vision which had come to him when bedridden in the second week of September at the Wolfsschanze. Hitler had been sick with an attack of jaundice, and was therefore unable to attend the situation conferences. 'Hitler had all day in which to think,' Generaloberst Jodl later recalled. 'I saw him alone as he lay in bed — he usually disliked anyone seeing him in bed except his aides — and he spoke of the idea.

I made a rough sketch on a map, showing the direction of attack, its dimensions, and the forces required for it.'

Hitler was determined never to negotiate, a fact of which Göring was well aware when he rejected General der Flieger Kreipe's entreaty to persuade the Führer to seek a political solution. Hitler continued to convince himself that the 'unnatural' alliance between the capitalist countries of the west and the Soviet Union was bound to collapse. And he calculated that, instead of being ground down in defensive battles on both eastern and western fronts, a final great offensive stood a far better chance of success. 'By remaining on the defensive, we could not hope to escape the evil fate hanging over us,' Jodl explained later. 'It was an act of desperation, but we had to risk everything.'

On the eastern front, a concentrated attack with thirty-two divisions would be absorbed and smothered by the immense forces of the Red Army. A sudden victory on the Italian front would change nothing. But Hitler believed that in the west, by driving north to Antwerp, two panzer armies could split the western Allies, forcing the Canadians out of the war and perhaps even the British in 'another Dunkirk'. It would also put paid to their threat to the war industries of the Ruhr.

Hitler had selected the Ardennes as the sector for the breakthrough because it was so thinly held by American troops. He was certainly conscious of the success of the 1940 attack on that sector, and wanted to repeat it. The great advantage was the thickly forested Eifel region on the German side of the frontier, which offered concealment for troops and tanks from Allied airpower. Everything would depend on surprise and on the Allied leadership failing to react quickly enough. Eisenhower, he assumed, would have to consult with his political masters and other Allied commanders, and that could take several days.

Until Hitler's unexpected announcement at the Wolfsschanze on 16 September, only Jodl knew of the Führer's plan. From then on, everyone informed had to sign a piece of paper accepting that they would be executed if they mentioned it to anyone not specifically authorized. Jodl used his small staff for working out details of the plan according to Hitler's wishes. Keitel, although theoretically in charge of the OKW, was not involved in the planning, only in the allocation of fuel and ammunition for the operation. And Rundstedt, despite his position as commander-in-chief west, received no information at all. This was why he was so irritated later when the Americans kept referring to the 'Rundstedt offensive' as if it had been his plan.

On 22 October, Rundstedt's chief of staff

General der Kavallerie Siegfried Westphal and Model's chief of staff General der Infanterie Hans Krebs answered a summons to the Wolfsschanze. Fearing a tirade from Hitler over the fall of Aachen and suspecting that their request for more divisions would be angrily rejected, they were surprised when made to sign a pledge of secrecy on pain of death before entering the conference room. Jodl's deputy presented a secret study entitled 'Wacht am Rhein' — 'Watch on the Rhine', a codeword designed to give an entirely defensive impression. There was at that stage no hint of the Ardennes offensive, just the transfer of troops to the western front in the general area of Aachen, supposedly to counter-attack an imminent American onslaught.

After lunch, the two chiefs of staff were included in Hitler's daily situation conference. A number of officers were asked to leave after the general briefing, and about fifteen men remained in the room. Hitler began to speak. The western front, he said, had been asking for reinforcements, and considering the fact that during the First World War there had been 130 German divisions, this was understandable. He had not been able to reinforce it because he could not afford more troops just for defence. But now things were different because he had evolved a plan for a surprise attack towards

Antwerp. It would take place south of Liège, and would be supported by 2,000 aircraft, an exaggerated figure which no officer present believed for a moment.

He wanted to launch the attack in November, the period of fogs, although he realized that it would take most of the month to prepare. The main breakthrough would be made by the Sixth Panzer Army just south of the Hürtgen Forest. Manteuffel's Fifth Panzer Army would support its left flank, while the Seventh Army would in turn guard against counter-attacks from Patton's Third Army to the south. Westphal had many questions to put to Jodl afterwards, but found himself 'whisked away'. He had been tempted to say that the forces allocated were clearly insufficient even to reach the River Meuse, but he knew that if he had raised these objections, the 'Wehrmachtführungsstab [operations staff] probably would have accused me of defeatism'.

Westphal briefed Rundstedt on returning to Schloss Ziegenberg, the headquarters of the commander-in-chief west near Frankfurt-am-Main. It was next to the carefully camouflaged Adlerhorst, Hitler's western field headquarters, which Albert Speer had built for him before the campaign of 1940. Westphal also reported his impression that even Jodl probably did not believe that they would ever get to Antwerp.

Although Rundstedt cannot have been pleased at the lack of prior consultation, he was determined not to allow such an over-ambitious operation to proceed without modification. Model, the commander-in-chief of Army Group B, had similar feelings when briefed by his own chief of staff. One can only speculate as to his reaction on hearing that he was strictly forbidden from using any of the divisions earmarked for the great offensive. They had to be withdrawn from the front to be re-equipped, reinforced and retrained. The American attack into the Hürtgen Forest forced him to break that order less than two weeks later when he had to send forward the 116th Panzer-Division to help retake Schmidt. A number of other divisions nominated for the offensive also had to be brought in to prevent a collapse in the Hürtgen Forest. And further south the 17th SS Panzergrenadier-Division *Götz von Berlichingen,* which was needed to hold the advance of Patton's Third Army, never could be extracted to join the Ardennes offensive as planned. These 'German divisions were gradually worn down and could no longer be reconditioned prior to the Ardennes offensive', acknowledged the chief of staff of the Seventh Army.

'The old Prussian' and the short, aggressive Model could hardly have been more different in appearance, tastes and political outlook, but they at least agreed that Hitler's 'grand slam', or 'large solution', was one of his map fantasies. Rundstedt maintained that the only realistic option on the Ardennes–Aachen front was a double envelopment, with the two panzer armies wheeling inside the great bend of the Meuse to cut off Hodges's First Army and part of Lieutenant General William H. Simpson's Ninth Army, while the Fifteenth Army further north near Roermond swung out to meet them near Liège. This alternative became known as the 'small solution' or 'little slam'. Model was sceptical about the Fifteenth Army's role. He wanted to use any spare forces as a follow-up to the main attack, broadening the breakthrough as they advanced, creating 'a snowplow effect'.

On 27 October, at a conference at Model's headquarters near Krefeld, the plans were discussed with the army commanders: SS-Oberstgruppenführer Sepp Dietrich of Sixth Panzer Army, Manteuffel of the Fifth Panzer Army and Brandenberger of the Seventh Army. Model, accepting that he would not be able to get his version of the 'small solution' approved by the OKW without his chief's support, acceded to Rundstedt's plan. But even Jodl's gradual attempts to win the Führer round to a 'small solution' made no headway. Hitler stubbornly ignored warnings that much greater forces would be needed, not just to reach Antwerp, but to secure the corridor against Allied counter-attacks.

Jodl warned Rundstedt that the Führer was immovable, so the commander-in-chief west put his views in writing. He clearly could not face another frenzied meeting with Hitler, outraged at the idea that any of his generals could disagree with him. Even Model's later tactic of suggesting the 'small solution', to be followed upon success by a drive north to Antwerp, was firmly rejected. Hitler thought that the American forces in front of Aachen were too powerful, so the only way to weaken them was by outflanking them across the Meuse and then cutting off their supply base.

Generaloberst Heinz Guderian again protested at the concentration of all available German forces in the west. He knew that the Red Army was preparing to strike its next blow on the eastern front as soon as the ground froze hard enough for its tank armies to charge forward from the Vistula. 'In our current situation,' Jodl explained to him on 1 November, 'we cannot shrink from staking everything on one card.' Guderian's son was to take part in the Ardennes offensive as Ia, or chief operations officer, of the 116th Panzer-Division.

The field commanders knew that fuel was going to be the chief problem, despite all assurances that they would receive what was needed. On 23 November, at a major conference in Berlin, they raised the question. Dietrich complained that there was no sign of the supplies he had been promised. General Walter Buhle of the OKW tried to prove that they had been delivered by showing pieces of paper, but most of the fuel supplies were still stuck east of the Rhine as a result of Allied bombing. Manteuffel, knowing the effects of the difficult terrain and the mud on fuel consumption, had requested fuel for 500 kilometres, but his army received enough only for 150 kilometres. Keitel had accumulated 17.4 million litres of fuel, but Jodl later admitted that Keitel wanted to hold some back 'on principle, otherwise the commanders would have been too extravagant with it.'

Any hope of keeping to Hitler's original plan of attacking in November disappeared. Even the beginning of December looked increasingly uncertain. The transport of fuel, ammunition and the divisions themselves was delayed, partly due to Allied bombing of the transport network and partly due to the earlier difficulties of withdrawing formations to prepare. Hardly a single panzer division found the time and fuel to train many of the novice tank drivers. German forces on the western front had been receiving priority for the replacement of panzers, assault guns and artillery. Waffen-SS divisions received the bulk of the new equipment and had the pick of reinforcements, but even then they tended to be mainly youngsters transferred from the

Luftwaffe and Kriegsmarine. The shameless preference for SS formations, which had Hitler's backing, was justified on the grounds that the Sixth Panzer Army had the major breakthrough role, but Jodl conceded later that the panzer divisions in Manteuffel's Fifth Panzer Army were more effective. 'There was a certain political interference in the conduct of the war,' he said.

On 2 December, Model came to Berlin with Manteuffel and Sepp Dietrich, who had been Hitler's loyal escort commander from the Nazis' street-fighting days. Both men also supported the 'small solution'. Hitler insisted that the Antwerp plan remain as he had stated. All preparations were to be made on that basis. Rundstedt did not attend the conference. He sent instead his chief of staff Westphal, who said virtually nothing. Hitler later 'expressed his astonishment at this conduct' to Jodl. But Rundstedt was clearly signalling what he thought of the whole project over which he had no control. The final orders were annotated by the Führer 'Not to be altered'. Rundstedt and Model were told expressly that their task was simply to pass on orders from the OKW 'to their subordinate commands'.

Model appears to have been fatalistic. He took the view that this was a 'last gamble' and he had no choice but to carry it out. Manteuffel later said that it was at this conference on 2 December that he privately decided that his 'final objective would be the Meuse' and not Brussels, as Hitler insisted for his army. He knew that 'the Allied ability to react would be the cardinal factor'.

Manteuffel was a tough little cavalryman who had served in the Zieten Hussars in the First World War. During the revolutionary upheavals which followed the Armistice he became adjutant to the Freikorps von Oven, which took part in suppressing the Spartacists in Berlin and the Räterepublik in Munich. In the Second World War he rapidly proved himself to be an outstanding leader on the eastern front, first with the 7th Panzer-Division and then with the Panzergrenadier-Division *Grossdeutschland*. 'Surprise, when it succeeds,' he explained, 'is a decisive part of the success of the panzer formation. Slackness, softness, etcetera amongst all ranks must be sternly put down.'

Hitler's obsession with secrecy never slackened. No troops were to be briefed until the evening before the attack. Even regimental commanders would know nothing until the day before. No registering of artillery could take place in advance. Despite pleas from the army commanders, the OKW, on Hitler's instruction, refused permission to brief anyone other than corps commanders, their chief artillery officers and one staff officer.

Commanders of corps artillery had to reconnoitre all the gun positions themselves. Not
surprisingly, many officers were soon able to
work out that a major offensive was in preparation, since the artillery dispositions alone
indicated that the deployments were not for
defensive purposes.

Troops, as they moved on night marches
into their concentration areas in the Eifel,
were to be billeted in villages by day, with all
vehicles concealed in barns. There were to be
no fires and no movement in daylight in case
of American reconnaissance flights. Charcoal
was provided for cooking as it made little
smoke. German officers were amazed that
Allied air reconnaissance failed to spot villages and woods 'full to bursting point'. They
half expected a massive air attack at any moment.

Maps were to be distributed only at the very
last moment, for security reasons. Total radio
silence was to be observed, but that also
meant signals nets could not be established
until the opening bombardment. For the
move to their attack positions, all roads were
restricted to one-way traffic. No routes were
to be marked in case this was spotted by
enemy agents. Recovery vehicles were to be
ready to cope with breakdowns. Storch
aircraft would fly constantly overhead at night
to check on progress and to spot any lights
showing, but also to disguise the noise of

engines. The civilian population was to be tightly controlled and all telephone lines in the Eifel must be cut. Gestapo officers were sent forward to check on all security measures. Volksgrenadier divisions received the order to take away their men's paybooks and identity documents so that they would be shot as spies if they deserted.

A fake headquarters north of Aachen transmitting instructions gave the impression that the Sixth Panzer Army was in position there, ready to counter-attack an expected American offensive across the River Roer. And a fake Twenty-Fifth Army was created in the same way as the Allies had invented a 1st US Army Group in eastern England before D-Day. Manteuffel himself 'started a rumour in a restaurant early in December, to the effect that we were preparing to attack in the Saar area in January. I mentioned this in a loud voice to some of my commanders while we were having dinner one night.'

Goebbels, meanwhile, kept repeating the mantra of the Nazi leadership that 'the political crisis in the enemy camp grows daily'. But many of their most loyal followers were not convinced by this message of hope; they simply felt that there was no choice but to fight on to the bitter end. A secret recording of a captured Waffen-SS Standartenführer revealed the diehard view of the moment. 'We have all been brought up from the cradle to consider Leonidas's fight at Thermopylae as the highest form of sacrifice for one's people,' he told a fellow officer. 'Everything else follows on from that and if the whole German nation has become a nation of soldiers, then it is compelled to perish; because by thinking as a human being and saying — "It is all up with our people now, there's no point in it, it's nonsense" — do you really believe that you will avoid the sacrifice of an appreciable number of lives? Do you think you will alter the peace terms? Surely not. On the other hand it is well known that a nation which has not fought out such a fateful struggle right to the last has never risen again as a nation.'

The vision of Germany as a phoenix arising from the ashes had a wide currency among true believers. 'The only thing is to continue the fight until the last,' said Generalleutnant Heim, 'even if everything is destroyed. Fighting until the last moment gives a people the moral strength to rise again. A people that throws in the sponge is finished for all time. That is proved by history.'

Tensions between the Waffen-SS and the German army were growing because of Hitler's insistence on saving SS formations in a retreat while ordinary divisions were left to fight on as a rearguard. And the SS never forgot a perceived injury. An officer in the 17th SS Panzergrenadier-Division claimed that, in the escape from the Falaise pocket at the end of the battle for Normandy, General der Panzertruppe Freiherr von Lüttwitz of the 2nd Panzer-Division had refused to lend a vehicle to evacuate the wounded commander of the SS Division *Leibstandarte,* who had been shot in the thigh. 'What a filthy trick!' he said. He then asserted that Lüttwitz himself had been saved by the commander of an SS panzergrenadier battalion.

'There were many comments', acknowledged General Warlimont, 'to the effect that the SS no longer considered itself a member of the Wehrmacht but had its own organisation.' Sepp Dietrich wanted his Sixth Panzer Army to be designated an SS panzer army, but this was denied because he had non-SS formations in his command. Dietrich even refused to have General der Artillerie Kruse as his chief artillery officer because he was not a member of the Waffen-SS. Manteuffel, like many others, had little respect for Dietrich's generalship. He thought that the Sixth Panzer Army 'was not commanded as one formation, and its component parts did not fight with the same sense of duty as the Army divisions'. Dietrich was regarded as a bad joke by senior army officers. When asked the objectives of his Sixth Panzer Army in the first and second days of the offensive, he is said to have replied: 'Objectives, objectives! If I had to give everybody objectives, wherever should I be? You general staff officers!'

Oberstleutnant von der Heydte was even more scathing, after meeting him to discuss his parachute drop in front of the Sixth Panzer Army. He said that Dietrich liked to pose as 'a people's general', but he was 'a conceited, reckless military leader with the knowledge and ability of a good sergeant. He has no moral scruples.' Heydte, although a German nationalist, detested the Nazis. As a cousin of Oberst Claus Graf von Stauffenberg, he had been exasperated by a questionnaire following 20 July which asked whether he was related to aristocracy of non-German blood or to the former ruling house of Germany, or whether he had been educated abroad or in a Jesuit institute. When Heydte asked about his overall plan, Dietrich could say only that it was to push through to Antwerp 'and then give the English a good beating'.

Heydte, the head of the Fallschirmjäger Army Combat School, had first been warned of his mission by Generaloberst Kurt Student on the evening of 8 December at Student's headquarters in Holland. 'The Führer has ordered a parachute attack in the framework of a powerful offensive,' Student told him. 'You, my dear Heydte, are ordered to carry out this task.' He was to assemble a force of some 1,200 men to drop behind enemy lines to seize key road junctions. He rejected Heydte's suggestion of using his 6th Fallschirmjäger-Regiment, since that might be spotted by the enemy and secrecy was vital.

Kampfgruppe Heydte was to drop on the first night south of Eupen. Its mission was to block American reinforcements coming south from the Aachen sector. Over the next two days, Heydte received his men and sent them off to Sennelager for a short and intensive training course. Hitler's refusal to attempt airborne operations after the heavy losses on Crete in 1941 meant that many had never received proper training, and even some of the veterans had not been up in an aircraft since that invasion.

Heydte then went to Limburg to see General Pelz to discuss aircraft requirements. He was not impressed. 'There was nothing but French girls in the mess of the XII Flieger Korps commanded by Pelz at Limburg,' he noted.* Pelz complained of their disastrous

* It is striking how many accounts at this time refer to young French women who had accompanied their lovers on the retreat to Germany because they knew that the Resistance would seek revenge for their *collaboration horizontale*. It is, however, very hard to get an idea of their subsequent fate. Many of them must have lost their 'protector' in the savage fighting over the last six months of the war. And

188

situation and said: 'Germany's last reserves of fuel are being thrown into this Ardennes enterprise.' Heydte discovered that 112 Junkers 52 transports had been allocated for the mission; but half of the pilots had never dropped paratroopers, nor flown over enemy territory, nor been trained to fly in formation. 'Only two pilots were old Stalingrad flyers,' he noted, referring to those veterans who had flown in and out of the Stalingrad encirclement during the doomed attempt to resupply Paulus's Sixth Army in December 1942.

On 11 December, taking the most experienced pilot with him, Heydte went on to see General der Flieger Beppo Schmidt, the most disastrous intelligence officer the Wehrmacht ever produced. Schmidt had constantly predicted all through the Battle of Britain that RAF Fighter Command was at its last gasp, yet Göring had protected and promoted his toady ever since. Schmidt, 'who was heavily under the influence of alcohol', declared that 'Success or failure in the German attack on Antwerp will decide the outcome of the war.' Schmidt told Heydte that he was to split his force in two, with one group to drop west

---

German women, convinced that French women had done nothing since 1940 except try to seduce their menfolk, would not have taken them in.

of Malmédy and the other near Eupen. Heydte said this was ridiculous. They would be too small to be effective since many men would not make the dropping zone. And when Heydte warned that the lack of training of both pilots and paratroopers was so serious that the operation would fail, Schmidt cursed his two visitors and dismissed them for questioning the abilities of Luftwaffe personnel.

After a long drive through the night, Heydte went on to see Generalfeldmarschall Model in a hunting lodge south of Münstereifel. Model was blunt. He said the operation was not his idea and asked whether it stood a one in ten chance of success. Heydte had to agree that it was possible. Model apparently replied that 'the entire offensive had not more than a ten percent chance of success', but 'it was the last remaining chance of concluding the war favourably'. Model then sent him to see Sepp Dietrich, whose headquarters were half an hour's drive further to the south.

While Heydte waited most of the morning to see Dietrich, an orderly-room clerk told him the secret plan for sabotage operations by a Kampfgruppe led by Otto Skorzeny, an astounding breach of security for which he could have been shot. Finally, Heydte was shown into Dietrich's office. Heydte thought he looked like 'an old non-commissioned officer permanently addicted to alcohol'. Dietrich opened the conversation by demanding: 'What can you paratroopers do, anyhow?' Heydte replied that, if told the mission, he could judge whether or not it was possible. Failing to obtain a clear reply, Heydte then asked what was known of enemy strength in the area. 'All that was known', Heydte recorded, 'was that the front line was held by American units; and that behind them there were only "a couple of bank managers and Jewboys" ', in Dietrich's words. 'As for tactical and operational reserves, nobody could tell me anything.'

Heydte later entertained fellow officers in captivity with his version of how the conversation went, imitating Dietrich's thick Swabian accent. When he tried to explain some of the problems the operation faced, Dietrich clearly considered this defeatism. The offensive would crush the Americans.

'We'll annihilate them,' he shouted.

'But what about the enemy, Herr Oberstgruppenführer?'

'Good Lord, I don't know. You'll find out soon enough.'

'Who will you send in first?'

'I can't tell you yet — whoever is the first to turn up.'

Heydte's account continued: 'When I added that you can only jump when the wind is favourable, he said: "Well, I'm not responsible for the Luftwaffe's shortcomings! It's just another example of their uselessness." '

The only useful aspect to this bizarre encounter was that Dietrich agreed he should not split his force in two. Heydte discovered more from Dietrich's chief of staff, SS-Brigadeführer Krämer — 'a highly overstrung and overworked man', which was hardly surprising since he had to do everything for Dietrich. Krämer told him that the panzer spearhead of the 12th SS Division *Hitler Jugend* would be with them 'within twenty-four hours'. Heydte demanded an artillery forward observation officer to drop with them and he was provided with SS-Obersturmführer Etterich. Heydte then heard that the drop was to take place on the morning of 16 December between 04.30 and 05.00 hours, just before the opening bombardment. Motor transport would be laid on to take his force to the airfields at Paderborn and Lippspringe.

The other special operation which the OKW planned was a commando venture, using picked troops in captured American vehicles and uniforms to penetrate Allied lines and cause mayhem in the rear. Hitler had summoned SS-Obersturmbannführer Otto Skorzeny to East Prussia on 21 October for a personal briefing long before Rundstedt or Model knew anything of the offensive. 'Skorzeny,' Hitler said, 'this next assignment will be the most important of your life.' Skorzeny, two metres tall and with a large scar on his left cheek, towered over the bent and sickly Führer. Heydte described the huge Austrian as a 'typical evil Nazi' who used 'typical SS methods. So he formed a special body of people of the same type as himself.' General der Panzertruppe von Thoma also regarded Skorzeny as an Austrian criminal, and described him as 'a real dirty dog . . . shooting is much too good for him'.

Skorzeny was given unlimited powers to prepare his mission. His officers obtained whatever they wanted simply by saying 'order from the Reichsführer'. Officers and NCOs from the army, Waffen-SS, Kriegsmarine and Luftwaffe who spoke English were ordered to report to the camp at Schloss Friedenthal outside Oranienburg for 'interpreter duties'. Around half of them came from the navy. There they were interrogated in English by SS officers. They were told that they would be part of a special unit designated the 150th Panzer-Brigade and were sworn to secrecy. They had to sign a paper which stated: 'Everything I know about the commitment of 150th Panzer-Brigade is secret. Secrecy will be maintained even after the war. Breach of the order is punishable by death.' Their commander, the wonderfully named Oberstleutnant Musculus, had blond hair and facial scars from student duels. He promised them that the activities of the 150th Panzer-Brigade would have a 'decisive effect on the course of the war'.

A young naval officer, Leutnant zur See Müntz, was sent along with all the others to the heavily guarded camp of Grafenwöhr. He was then given the task of collecting 2,400 American uniforms, including those of ten generals and seventy officers, from prisoner-of-war camps by 21 November. Müntz first went to Berlin to the department of prisoners of war. The officer in charge, Oberst Meurer, was taken aback by the Führer order they presented signed by Hitler himself. He mentioned that such activities were illegal under international law, but provided them with written instructions to all camp commanders. Müntz set off with a truck and various helpers to collect the uniforms as well as identity papers, paybooks and so forth, but they had great difficulty obtaining what they needed from the prisoner-of-war camps. At Fürstenberg-ander-Oder, the camp commandant refused the order to strip field jackets from eighty American soldiers. Müntz was recalled to Grafenwöhr in case the Red Cross heard of the row and word of it then reach the Allies. His mission partly failed because of the grave shortage of US Army winter clothing, as GIs had already found to their cost in the Hürtgen Forest, Lorraine and Alsace.

At Grafenwöhr, all ranks had to salute in the American style, they were fed on

K-Rations and were kitted out in the few uniforms which Müntz and his group had managed to obtain. Every order was given in English. They were made to watch American movies and newsreels to learn the idiom, such as 'chow-line', and to improve their accent. They also spent two hours a day on language and American customs, including how to eat 'with the fork after laying down the knife'. They were even shown how to tap their cigarette against the pack in an American way. All the usual commando skills were also taught, such as close-quarter combat training, demolition and the use of enemy weapons.

When given more details of the forthcoming Operation *Greif,* as it was called, those who expressed doubts about going into action in American uniforms were threatened by SS-Obersturmbannführer Hadick. He 'emphasized that the Führer's orders would be obeyed without question, and that anyone who chose to disagree would be sentenced to death'. Morale was also rather shaken when they were issued with ampoules of cyanide 'concealed in a cheap cigarette-lighter'.

Men from SS units almost worshipped Skorzeny as a super-hero after his exploits in Italy and Budapest, while he treated them with 'conspicuous friendship'. One of them wrote later: 'he was our pirate captain'. Many rumours ran around the camp about what their true mission was likely to be. Some thought that they were to be part of an airborne operation to reoccupy France. Skorzeny himself later claimed that he had encouraged the story that certain groups would be tasked with heading to Paris, to kidnap General Eisenhower.

Kampfgruppe Skorzeny was split into a commando unit, Einheit Steilau, and the 150th Panzer-Brigade. For the commandos, Skorzeny picked 150 men out of 600 English-speakers. Mounted mostly in Jeeps and wearing American uniforms, they included demolition groups to blow up ammunition and fuel dumps and even bridges; reconnaissance groups to scout routes to the Meuse and observe enemy strength; and other teams to disrupt American communications by cutting wires and issuing false orders. Four men were mounted in each Jeep, which was a mistake since the Americans themselves seldom packed as many on board, and each team had a 'speaker', the one with the best grasp of American idiom. The German soldiers in American uniforms waiting to advance in their Jeeps were clearly nervous. In an attempt to reassure them, an officer from brigade headquarters told them that 'according to the German radio, US soldiers in German uniforms had been captured behind the German lines, and that . . . a lenient view would be taken, and the US soldiers treated as prisoners of war'.

The 150th Panzer-Brigade was much stronger with nearly 2,000 men, including support units. There was a paratroop battalion, two tank companies with a mixture of M-4 Shermans and badly disguised Panthers, panzergrenadier companies, heavy mortars and anti-tank guns in the event of their securing one of the Meuse bridges at Andenne, Huy or Amay. The plan was to get ahead of the panzer spearheads once they reached the Hohes Venn plateau on a line with Spa, by taking side roads and tracks. They would hide up by day, then race forward in the dark to seize the three bridges.

Skorzeny also had plans to blow up the five bridges over the upper Rhine at Basle, in case the Allies entered Switzerland to outflank German defences in the south. In fact on 5 December SHAEF studied the possibility of outflanking German forces in the south by going through Switzerland, but Eisenhower turned this idea down. (Stalin, who clearly hated the Swiss, had urged the Allies at the Teheran conference a year before to attack southern Germany through Switzerland.)

As X-Day for the Ardennes offensive approached, the defensive cover-name was changed from *Wacht am Rhein* to *Herbstnebel,* or 'Autumn Mist'. The delays in the delivery of fuel and ammunition became worse and the attack had to be pushed back to dawn on 16 December. Altogether some 1,050 trains were needed to bring the divisions to their concentration areas. Each panzer division needed seventy trains alone.

So far, nobody below the level of corps command had been informed. But SS-Obersturmbannführer Joachim Peiper of the 1st SS Panzer-Division *Leibstandarte Adolf Hitler* guessed what was afoot on 11 December when Krämer, the Sixth Panzer Army's chief of staff, wanted to discuss a hypothetical offensive in the Eifel region. He asked Peiper how long it would take a panzer regiment to move eighty kilometres at night. To be sure of his answer, Peiper himself took out a Panther for a test run over that distance in darkness. He realized that moving a whole division was a much more complicated matter, but what he and his superiors had underestimated was the state of the roads and the saturated ground in the Ardennes.

Hitler reached his western headquarters at the Adlerhorst that day in a long motorcade of huge black Mercedes. His main concern was maintaining secrecy. He had become nervous when Allied bombers flattened the town of Düren, the main communications centre just behind the start-line for the operation. His mood swings were highly erratic, from total dejection to groundless optimism. According to his Luftwaffe adjutant Oberst von Below, he 'was already seeing in his mind's eye the German spearhead rolling into Antwerp'. The next morning, Sepp Dietrich was summoned to his bunker concealed under fake farm buildings.

'Is your army ready?' Hitler asked straight out.

'Not for an offensive,' Dietrich claimed to have replied.

'You are never satisfied,' the Führer answered.

Late that afternoon, buses brought divisional commanders to the Adlerhorst to be addressed by Hitler. Each officer was searched by SS guards and had to surrender his pistol and briefcase. At 18.00 hours, Hitler limped on to the stage. Generals who had not seen him for some time were shocked by his physical deterioration, with pallid face, drooping shoulders and one arm which shook. Flanked by Keitel and Jodl, he sat behind a table.

He began with a long self-justification of why Germany was in the state it was at that stage of the war. A 'preventative war' had been necessary to unify the German peoples and because 'life without *Lebensraum* is unthinkable'. Never for a moment did he consider how other nations might react. Any objection was part of a conspiracy against Germany. 'Wars are finally decided by the recognition on one side or the other that the war can't be won any more. Thus, the most important task is to bring the enemy to this realization. The fastest way to do this is to destroy his strength by occupying territory. If we ourselves are forced on to the defensive, our task is to teach the enemy by ruthless strikes that he hasn't yet won, and that the war will continue without interruption.'

Hitler reminded the assembled generals that some of them had feared taking the offensive against France in 1940. He claimed that the Americans had 'lost about 240,000 men in just three weeks' and 'the enemy might have more tanks, but with our newest types, ours are better'. Germany was facing a fight that had been inevitable, which had to come sooner or later. The attack had to be carried through with the greatest brutality. No 'human inhibitions' must be allowed. 'A wave of fright and terror must precede the troops.' The purpose was to convince the enemy that Germany would never surrender. 'Never! Never!'

Afterwards the generals went to a party to toast Rundstedt's sixty-ninth birthday at his headquarters in the nearby Schloss Ziegenberg, a gloomy building rebuilt in neo-Gothic style. Nobody felt much like celebrating. According to Dietrich, they did not dare discuss the offensive because of the death penalty threatened against anyone who mentioned it.

On 13 December, Dietrich visited the

headquarters of Army Group B. Model said to him that this was 'the worst prepared German offensive of this war'. Rundstedt noted that out of the thirty-two divisions promised, four divisions were withdrawn just before the attack, including the 11th Panzer-Division and the 17th SS Panzergrenadier-Division. Only twenty-two were assigned to take part in the opening of the offensive. The rest were held back as an OKW reserve. While most generals were deeply sceptical of the operation's chances of success, younger officers and NCOs, especially those in the Waffen-SS, were desperate for it to succeed.

Peiper's regiment received its march order from east of Düren to its assembly area behind the front. It set off after dark following the plain yellow arrows which marked the route. No divisional insignia or numbers were shown. The night and the following morning were foggy, which allowed the men to slip into their assembly areas without being spotted by air reconnaissance. Other divisions also removed their divisional insignia from vehicles just before the advance.

Joachim, or 'Jochen', Peiper was twenty-nine years old and good looking with his brown hair slicked back. In the Waffen-SS he was seen as the beau idéal of a panzer leader, a convinced Nazi and utterly ruthless. In the Soviet Union he was well known for torching villages and killing all the inhabitants. On 14 December, shortly before noon, he reported to the headquarters of the 1st SS Panzer-Division *Leibstandarte Adolf Hitler* where Brigadeführer Wilhelm Mohnke issued its orders for X-Day on 16 December. The division had been reinforced with an anti-aircraft regiment with 88mm guns, a battalion of heavy howitzers and an extra engineer battalion for repairing bridges. Each Kampfgruppe was to be accompanied by one of the Skorzeny units, with captured Shermans, trucks and Jeeps, but the division had no control over them. On his return Peiper briefed his battalion commanders in a forester's hut.

Only on the evening of 15 December were officers allowed to brief their troops. Hauptmann Bär, a company commander in the 26th Volksgrenadier-Division, told his men: 'In twelve or fourteen days we will be in Antwerp — or we have lost the war.' He then went on to say: 'Whatever equipment you may be lacking, we will take from American prisoners.' Yet, in SS formations especially, the mood was one of fierce exultation at the prospect of revenge. NCOs appear to have been among the most embittered. Paris was about to be recaptured, they told each other. Many regretted that the French capital should have been spared from destruction while Berlin was bombed to ruins. In the 10th SS Panzer-Division *Frundsberg,* the briefing on the offensive produced 'an extraordinary optimism' because the Führer had 'ordered the great blow in the West'. They believed that the shock of an unexpected attack would represent a massive blow to Allied morale. And according to an officer in the highly experienced 2nd Panzer-Division, 'the fighting spirit was better than in the early days of the war'. Dietrich's Sixth Panzer Army alone had more than 120,000 men, with nearly 500 tanks and assault guns and a thousand artillery pieces. Manteuffel's Fifth Panzer Army had another 400 tanks and assault guns. The Allied command had no idea of what was about to hit them on their weakest sector.

7

Intelligence Failure

Hitler's prediction of tensions in the Allied camp did come about, but certainly not to the degree he had hoped. Both Field Marshal Sir Alan Brooke, the chief of the imperial general staff, and Montgomery had again become concerned with the slowness of the Allied advance, which they ascribed to Eisenhower's incapacity as a military leader. Both wanted a single ground force commander, ideally in the shape of Bernard Law Montgomery. Yet Brooke thought Montgomery harped on about it too much. He was awake to the political reality that everything had changed. The war in north-west Europe had become an American show, as Britain struggled to maintain its armies around the world. So if there were to be a single ground commander, in Brooke's view, it would have to be Bradley and not Montgomery. But the diminutive field marshal had clearly learned nothing and forgotten nothing, except his promise to Eisenhower that he would hear no more on the subject of command from him.

On 28 November, Eisenhower came to 21st Army Group headquarters at Zonhoven in Belgium. Montgomery always pretended to be far too busy to visit his Supreme Commander even when little was happening on his front. Eisenhower should not have put up with his behaviour. He sat in Monty's map trailer while Montgomery strode up and down, lecturing him for three hours on what had gone wrong, and why a single ground commander was needed. Montgomery felt that the natural dividing line was the Ardennes, and that he should command all the Allied forces north of that sector, which would have given him most of the First US Army and all of Lieutenant General William H. Simpson's Ninth Army. Unfortunately, Eisenhower's silence — he was speechless from exhaustion and boredom — gave Montgomery the idea that it indicated tacit consent with his argument that the Allies had suffered a strategic reverse by failing to reach the Rhine and by the fruitless bloodbath in the Hürtgen Forest. Afterwards, to the astonishment of his own military aide, the field marshal sent a signal to Brooke in London indicating that Eisenhower had agreed with everything he said. And in a cable to Eisenhower on 30 November, Montgomery outlined what he thought had been agreed.

The next day Eisenhower visited Bradley at

his headquarters in the Hôtel Alfa in the city of Luxembourg. Bradley was a pitiful sight in bed, suffering from flu and hives. Although Eisenhower was furious with Montgomery over his allegation of a strategic reverse, the letter which he dictated in reply was not pointed enough to penetrate Montgomery's armoured complacency. A meeting on 7 December was agreed in Maastricht.

On Wednesday 6 December, Eisenhower returned to Bradley's headquarters, bringing his deputy Air Chief Marshal Tedder to discuss tactics before meeting Montgomery. Major Chester B. Hansen, Bradley's aide, feared that his general was 'pathetically alone'. 'It is his knowledge of the critical times facing him that has caused the nervousness now evident in him for the first time. He is not irritable but he is more brusque than usual, he looks tired and the slight physical irritations have combined to wear him down physically as well as mentally.' Eisenhower listened to him, 'with his face heavily wrinkled as he frowned, his neck stuck deeply into the fur collar of the flying jacket he wears'.

Bradley was also exasperated with the Allies' lack of progress. 'If we were fighting a reasonable people they would have surrendered a long time ago,' he said. 'But these people are not reasonable.' Hansen then added in his diary: 'The German has proved unexpectedly resistant, however, and he dies only with great difficulty . . . He has been told by Goebbels that this is a fight to the finish, that the weak shall be exterminated in the labor camps of Siberia. It is little wonder, therefore, that we find them fighting our advance savagely, causing us to kill them in great numbers.' Goebbels, in an attempt to stop German soldiers surrendering in the west, had indeed put out a story that the Americans had agreed to hand over all their prisoners of war to the Soviets for reconstruction work. He came up with the slogan 'Sieg oder Sibirien!' — 'Victory or Siberia!'

The next day at Maastricht, with Montgomery, Hodges and Simpson, Eisenhower discussed the next stage. He spoke of 'sledgehammer blows that will carry them across the Roer and up to the banks of the Rhine'. Eisenhower then expressed his concerns about crossing the Rhine. He was afraid of mines or ice floes destroying pontoon bridges, thus cutting off any troops in the bridgehead. Field Marshal Brooke had been horrified when Eisenhower told him in mid-November that the Allies probably would not be across the Rhine until May 1945. This remark, coming at the end of Brooke's tour of the front, strongly influenced his view that Eisenhower was not up to the task of Supreme Commander.

Montgomery once again put forward his arguments for a heavy attack across the Rhine north of the Ruhr industrial region while all the other American armies were virtually halted. Eisenhower, no doubt gritting his teeth, once again repeated his position that a thrust towards Frankfurt was also important and he had no intention of stopping Patton. 'Field Marshal Montgomery', the notes of the meeting recorded, 'could not agree that a thrust from Frankfurt offered any prospect of success. In his view, if it were undertaken, neither it nor the thrust north of the Ruhr would be strong enough . . . Field Marshal Montgomery said that the difference of view about the Frankfurt–Cassel thrust was fundamental.' To avoid a clash, Eisenhower tried to convince him that the difference was not very great. Montgomery's 21st Army Group would have the major role with Simpson's Ninth Army under his command.

Bradley had to hide his anger when Montgomery went on to argue that 'all operations north of the Ardennes should be under one command; all south of the Ardennes under another'. This would mean leaving Bradley with just the Third Army. Eisenhower retorted that future operations dictated that the Ruhr in front of them should be the dividing line. Bradley made his feelings clear to Eisenhower soon afterwards. If his 12th Army Group were to be placed under Montgomery, then he would regard himself as relieved of his duties for having failed in his task as a commander.

Most of the action at that time was taking place on the Third Army front. Patton's forces were crossing the River Saar in several places, and a few days later the last fortress in the Metz area was taken. 'I think only Attila [the Hun] and the Third Army have ever taken Metz by assault,' Patton wrote with satisfaction in his diary. He was also preparing a major offensive to begin on 19 December. Yet it is wrong to suggest that Montgomery was acting through jealousy of Patton, as some have suggested. He was far too self-absorbed to be envious. He also appeared quite incapable of judging the reactions of others to what he said. In fact, one might almost wonder whether Montgomery suffered from what today would be called high-functioning Asperger syndrome.

Patton was becoming infuriated with the one element he could not control, the relentless rain. On 8 December, he rang the Third Army chaplain, James O'Neill. 'This is General Patton. Do you have a good prayer for weather?' The chaplain asked if he could call back. He could not find anything in the prayer books, so he wrote out his own. 'Almighty and most merciful Father, we humbly beseech Thee, of Thy great goodness, to restrain these immoderate rains with which we have had to contend. Grant us fair weather for Battle. Graciously hearken to us as soldiers who call upon Thee that, armed with Thy power, we may advance from victory to victory, and crush the oppression and wickedness of our enemies, and establish Thy justice among men and nations. Amen.' Patton read and firmly approved. 'Have 250,000 copies printed and see to it that every man in the Third Army gets one.' He then told O'Neill that they must get everyone praying. 'We must ask God to stop these rains. These rains are the margin that holds defeat or victory.' When O'Neill encountered Patton again, the general was in bullish form. 'Well, Padre,' said Patton, 'our prayers worked. I knew they would.' And he cracked him across the helmet with his riding crop to emphasize the point.

In the south, the neglected US Seventh Army in Alsace redeployed towards the northern flank of its salient to support Patton's offensive in Lorraine with its own attack up towards the area of Bitche. This meant that the neighbouring French First Army under General de Lattre de Tassigny felt exposed. Lattre considered his forces undermanned, partly because so many French units were still besieging German garrisons on the Atlantic coast. This, he maintained, was the reason for his army's inability to crush the Colmar pocket despite the addition of a US infantry division, a failure which prompted many disobliging remarks from American officers. To make matters worse, the bitter cold of the Vosges mountains had badly affected the morale of his troops.

One of the great debates about the Ardennes offensive has focused on the Allied inability to foresee the attack. There were indeed many fragmented pieces of information which taken together should have indicated German intentions, but as in almost all intelligence failures, senior officers discarded anything which did not match their own assumptions.

Right from the start, Hitler's orders for total secrecy cannot have been followed. Word of the forthcoming offensive even circulated among senior German officers in British prisoner-of-war camps. In the second week of November, General der Panzertruppe Eberbach was secretly recorded saying that a Generalmajor Eberding, captured just a few days before, had spoken of a forthcoming offensive in the west with forty-six divisions.*

* The secret recording of conversations among selected German prisoners of war was carried out by the Combined Services Detailed Interrogation Centre (CSDIC). Interpreters, most of whom were German Jewish refugees, listened to conversations picked up by concealed microphones and recorded on wax discs. Transcripts of relevant material were

Eberbach believed this was true, and that it was a last try. Even a Leutnant von der Goltz, captured on South Beveland during the clearing of the Scheldt, had heard that 'the big offensive, for which they were preparing 46 divisions, was to start in November'. These secretly recorded conversations were reported by MI 19a on 28 November to the War Office in London and sent on to SHAEF, but this rather vital information does not appear to have been taken seriously. No doubt it was simply dismissed as a desperately optimistic rumour circulating among captured officers, especially since the figure of forty-six divisions seemed so impossibly high.

During the first week of November, a German deserter recounted in a debriefing that panzer divisions redeployed to Westphalia were part of the Sixth Panzer Army. This also highlighted the fact that SHAEF intelligence had not heard of the Fifth Panzer Army for several weeks. Both SHAEF and Bradley's 12th Army Group assumed that the Germans were preparing a strong counter-attack against an American crossing of the Roer. A German spoiling attack before Christmas was also considered to be quite likely, but hardly

---

distributed afterwards to the War Office, Admiralty, the Secret Intelligence Service, ministries and also SHAEF from 1944.

anybody expected it to come from the Eifel and through the Ardennes, even though the Germans had used this route in 1870, 1914 and 1940.

The Allies could not believe that the Germans in their weakened state would dare to undertake an ambitious strategic offensive, when they needed to husband their strength before the Red Army launched its own winter onslaught. Such a gamble was definitely not the style of the commander-in-chief west, Generalfeldmarschall Gerd von Rundstedt. This was true, but the Allied command had gravely underestimated Hitler's manic grasp on the levers of military power. Senior officers have always been encouraged to put themselves in their opponents' boots, but it can often be a mistake to judge your enemy by yourself. In any case, SHAEF believed that the Germans lacked the fuel, the ammunition and the strength to mount a dangerous thrust. And the Allies' air superiority was such that a German offensive into the open would surely play into their hands. In London, the Joint Intelligence Committee had also concluded that 'Germany's crippling shortage of oil continues to be the greatest single weakness in her capacity to resist.'

Wehrmacht troop movements into the Eifel around Bitburg were observed, but other divisions seemed to move on so it was assumed the area was just a staging post, or a sector for preparing new formations. Unfortunately, the Ardennes sector was deemed a low priority for air reconnaissance, and as a result of bad weather very few missions were flown in the region. Just six days before the great attack in the Ardennes, Troy H. Middleton's VIII Corps headquarters in Bastogne concluded: 'the enemy's present practice of bringing new divisions to this sector to receive front line experience and then relieving them out for commitment elsewhere indicates his desire to have this sector of the front remain quiet and inactive'. In fact the Germans were playing a clever form of 'Find the Lady', shuffling their formations to confuse Allied intelligence.

Patton's Third Army headquarters noted the withdrawal of panzer formations, and his chief intelligence officer, Brigadier General Oscar W. Koch, feared that VIII Corps in the Ardennes was very vulnerable. The conclusion of many, including General Bradley, was that the Germans might well be planning a spoiling attack to disrupt Patton's major offensive due to begin on 19 December. A number of other intelligence officers became wise after the event and tried to claim that they had predicted the great offensive, but nobody had listened. Several within SHAEF and Bradley's 12th Army Group did indeed predict an attack, and a couple were very close to getting the date right, but none of them specifically identified the Ardennes as the threatened sector in time.

Eisenhower's senior intelligence officer Major General Kenneth Strong included an offensive in the Ardennes as one of several options. This had made a marked impression on Eisenhower's chief of staff Bedell Smith in the first week of December. Bedell Smith told Strong to go to Luxembourg and warn Bradley, which he did. In their conversation, Bradley said that he was 'aware of the danger', but that he had earmarked certain divisions to move into the Ardennes area should the enemy attack there.

The most controversial Cassandra was Colonel B. A. Dickson, the G-2 (or senior intelligence officer) at US First Army. A colourful character, Dickson was not always trusted by his peers because he had an unfortunate knack of identifying German divisions in the west when their position had been confirmed on the eastern front. In his report of 10 December, he commented on the high morale of German prisoners, which indicated a renewed confidence. Yet even though he noted a panzer concentration in the Eifel, he predicted that the attack would come further north in the Aachen area on 17 December. Several prisoners of war had spoken of an attack to recapture Aachen 'as a Christmas present for the Führer'. Then, on 14 December, Dickson received the debriefing of a German-speaking woman who had reported troop concentrations and bridging equipment behind enemy lines in the Eifel. Dickson was now convinced that the attack was definitely coming in the Ardennes between Monschau and Echternach. Brigadier General Sibert at Bradley's 12th Army Group, irritated by Dickson who loathed him in return, rejected his report as no more than a hunch. Dickson was told on 15 December to take some leave in Paris.

Hitler's order for total radio silence among the attack formations had been followed, thus depriving Bletchley Park analysts of a clear picture through Ultra material. Regrettably, SHAEF relied far too much on Ultra intelligence, and tended to think that it was the fount of all knowledge. On 26 October, however, it had alighted upon 'Hitler's orders for setting up a special force for special undertaking in west. Knowledge of English and American idiom essential for volunteers.' And on 10 December, it worked out that radio silence had been imposed on all SS formations, which should have rung an alarm bell at SHAEF.

Unlike the German army the Luftwaffe had once again been incredibly lax, but SHAEF does not appear to have reacted to Bletchley transcripts. Already on 4 September, the Japanese ambassador in Berlin had reported after interviews with Ribbentrop and Hitler that the Germans were planning an offensive in the west in November 'as soon as replenishing of air force was concluded'. The subsequent inquiry into the intelligence failure stated, 'The GAF [Luftwaffe] evidence shows that ever since the last week in October, preparations have been in train to bring the bulk of the Luftwaffe on to airfields in the West.'

On 31 October, 'J[agd]G[eschwader] 26 quoted Goering order that re-equipment of all fighter aircraft as fighter bombers must be possible within 24 hours.' This was significant because it could certainly indicate preparations for an attack in support of ground troops. And on 14 November, Bletchley noted: 'Fighter units in West not to use Geschwader badges or unit markings'. On 1 December, they read that courses for National Socialist Leadership Officers had been cancelled owing to 'impending special operation'. The Nazi over-use of the word 'special' was probably the reason why this was not seized on. And on 3 December, a report was called for by Luftflotte Reich 'on measures taken for technical supply of units that had arrived for operations in the west'. The next day fighter commanders were summoned to a conference at the headquarters of Jagdkorps II. Soon after, the whole of SG 4, a specialized ground-attack Geschwader, was transferred to the west from the eastern front. That should have raised some eyebrows.

The head of the Secret Intelligence Service considered it 'a little startling to find that the Germans had a better knowledge of the US order of battle from their signals intelligence than we had of the German order of battle from Source [Ultra]'. The reason was clear in his view. 'Ever since D-Day, US signals have been of great assistance to the enemy. It has been emphasized that, out of thirty odd US divisions in the west, the Germans have constantly known the locations, and often the intentions, of all but two or three. They knew that the southern wing of US First Army, on a front of about eighty miles, was mostly held either by new or by tired divisions.'

The understandably tired 4th and 28th Infantry Divisions were licking their wounds after the horrors of the Hürtgen Forest. They had been sent to rest in the southern Ardennes, a steeply sloped area known as the 'Luxembourg Switzerland', and described as a 'quiet paradise for weary troops'. It seemed to be the least likely sector for an attack. The men were billeted in houses, to make a change from the extreme discomforts of foxholes in the Hürtgen Forest.

In the rear areas, soldiers and mechanics settled down with local families, and the shops were stocked with US Army produce. 'The steady traffic and the slush soon gave nearly every village the same drab, mud-splashed touch. In most of the drinking and eating places the atmosphere was that of some far western town of the movies where the men gathered at night to spice their lives with liquor. These soldiers, for the most part, had made their deal with the army. They didn't care for the life, but they proposed to make the best of it.'

The Germans, despite all orders forbidding reconnaissance, had a very clear picture of certain sectors of the front, especially those which were lightly held, such as the 4th Infantry Division frontage in the south. German civilians could move back and forth, slipping between outposts along the River Sauer. The Germans were thus able to identify observation posts and gun positions. Counter-battery fire was an essential part of their plan to protect their pontoon bridges over the Sauer in the first vital hours of the attack. Some of the more experienced agents even mingled with off-duty American soldiers in villages behind the lines. After a few beers, many soldiers were happy to chat with Luxembourgers and Belgians who spoke a little English.

Locals ready to converse were rather fewer than before. The joy of liberation in September and initial American generosity had turned sour later in the autumn as collaborators were denounced and suspicions increased between Walloon and German-speaking communities. Resistance groups made increasingly unjustifiable demands for food and supplies from farmers. But, for the eastern cantons closest to the fighting along the Siegfried Line, the greatest dismay was caused by the decision of the American civil affairs administration to evacuate the majority of civilians between 5 and 9 October. Only a small picked number would be allowed to remain in each village to look after livestock. In one way, this would prove to be a mercy because even more farming families would have been killed otherwise.

Over the previous 150 years, the border areas of Eupen and St Vith had moved back and forth between France, Prussia, Belgium and Germany, depending on the fortunes of war. In the Belgian elections of April 1939, more than 45 per cent of those in the mainly German-speaking 'eastern cantons' voted for the Heimattreue Front which wanted the area reincorporated into the Reich. But by 1944 the privilege of belonging to the Reich had turned bitter. The German-speakers of the eastern cantons had found themselves treated as second-class citizens, jokingly known as *Rucksackdeutsche* who had been gathered up and carried along after the Ardennes invasion of 1940. And so many of their young men had been killed or crippled on the eastern front that now most German-speakers longed for liberation by the Reich's enemies. Yet there were enough left still loyal to the Third Reich to constitute a considerable pool of potential informers and spies for German intelligence, known as *Frontläufer*.

Parties from the divisions in the Ardennes were allowed back to the VIII Corps rest camp at Arlon or to Bastogne, where Marlene Dietrich went to perform for the GIs, crooning huskily in her long sequinned gown which was so close-fitting that she wore no underwear. She nearly always sang 'Lili Marlene'. Its lilting refrain had gripped the hearts of Allied troops, despite its German provenance. 'The bloody Heinies!' wrote one American soldier. 'When they weren't killing you they were making you cry.'

Dietrich loved the response of the soldiers, but she was much less enamoured of the staff officers she had to deal with. 'La Dietrich was bitching,' Hansen wrote in his diary. 'Her trip among the corps of the First Army had been a rigorous one. She didn't like the First Army. She didn't like the competition between corps, armies and divisions. Most of all she disliked the colonels and generals of Eagle Main [12th Army Group rear headquarters] at Verdun where she lived on salmon because her meal times did not correspond to the chow periods and no one took an interest in her.' She also claimed that she caught lice, but that did not stop her from accepting General Bradley's invitation to cocktails, dinner 'and a bad movie' at the Hôtel Alfa in Luxembourg. General Patton, whom she claimed to have slept with, was clearly much more her sort of general. 'Patton believes earnestly in a warrior's Valhalla,' Hansen also observed that day.

On the evening of Sunday 10 December, there was a heavy fall of snow. The next morning, Bradley, now partially recovered, went to Spa to see Hodges and Simpson. It would be their last meeting for some time. He returned in the afternoon after a long drive past Bastogne. Snow covered the whole area and the roads were thick with slush as a result of the blizzard the previous night. A pair of shotguns which he had ordered were waiting for him. General Hodges seemed to have had the same idea. Three days later, he spent 'a good part of the afternoon' with Monsieur Francotte, a renowned gunmaker in Liège, ordering a shotgun to be made to his specifications.

Bradley's headquarters remained quietly optimistic about the immediate future. That week staff officers concluded: 'It is now certain that attrition is steadily sapping the strength of German forces on the western front and that the crust of defence is thinner, more brittle and more vulnerable than it appears on our G-2 maps or to the troops in the line.' Bradley's chief worry was the replacement situation. His 12th Army Group was short of 17,581 men, and he planned to see Eisenhower about it in Versailles.

At a press conference on 15 December to praise the IX Tactical Air Command, Bradley estimated that the Germans had no more than six to seven hundred tanks along the whole front. 'We think he is spread pretty thin all along,' he said. Hansen noted that as far as air support was concerned, 'Little doing today . . . Weather prevents their being operational even a quarter of the time.' The bad visibility to prevent flying, which Hitler had so earnestly desired, was repeated day after day. It does not, however, appear to have hampered artillery-spotting aircraft on unofficial business in the Ardennes. Bradley received complaints that 'GI's in their zest for barbecued pork were hunting [wild] boar in low-flying cubs with Thompson submachine guns.'

Also on 15 December, the G-3 operations officer at the daily SHAEF briefing said that there was nothing to report from the Ardennes sector. Field Marshal Montgomery asked General Eisenhower if he minded his going back to the United Kingdom the next week for Christmas. His chief of staff, General Freddie de Guingand, had just left that morning. With regrettable timing on the very eve of the German onslaught, Montgomery stated that the shortages of 'German manpower, equipment and resources precluded any offensive action on their part'. On the other hand, VIII Corps in the Ardennes reported troop movements to its front, with the arrival of fresh formations.

In the north of the VIII Corps sector, the newly arrived 106th Infantry Division had just taken over the positions of the 2nd Infantry Division on a hogsback ridge of the Schnee Eifel. 'My men were amazed at the appearance of the men from the incoming unit,' wrote a company commander in the 2nd Division. 'They were equipped with the maze of equipment that only replacements fresh from the States would have dared to call their own. And horror of horrors, they were wearing neckties! Shades of General Patton!'* During the handover a regimental commander from the 2nd Division told Colonel Cavender of the 423rd Infantry: 'It has been very quiet up here and your men will learn the easy way.' The experienced troops pulling out took all their stoves with them. The green newcomers had none to dry out socks, so many cases of trench foot soon developed in the damp snow.

Over the following days the 106th Division heard tanks and other vehicles moving to

* General Patton was renowned for making his military police charge any soldier without a necktie for being improperly dressed.

their front, but their lack of experience made them unsure of what it meant. Even the experienced 4th Division to their south assumed that the engine noises came from one Volksgrenadier division being replaced by another. In fact there were seven panzer and thirteen infantry divisions in the first wave alone, coiled ready for the attack in the dark pinewoods ahead.

In Waffen-SS units especially, the excitement and impatience were clearly intense. A member of the 12th SS Panzer-Division *Hitler Jugend* wrote to his sister on the eve of battle. 'Dear Ruth, My daily letter will be very short today — short and sweet. I write during one of the great hours before an attack — full of unrest, full of expectation for what the next days will bring. Everyone who has been here the last two days and nights (especially nights), who has witnessed hour after hour the assembly of our crack divisions, who has heard the constant rattling of Panzers, knows that something is up and we are looking forward to a clear order to reduce the tension. We are still in the dark as to "where" and "how" but that cannot be helped! It is enough to know that we attack, and will throw the enemy from our homeland. That is a holy task!' On the back of the sealed envelope he added a hurried postscript: 'Ruth! Ruth! Ruth! WE MARCH!!!' That must have been scribbled as they moved out, for the letter fell into American hands during the battle.

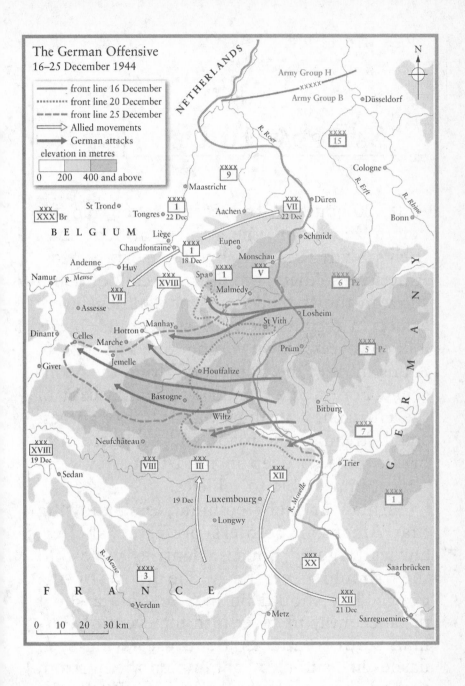

The German Offensive
16–25 December 1944

front line 16 December
front line 20 December
front line 25 December
Allied movements
German attacks

elevation in metres
0   200   400 and above

NETHERLANDS

Army Group H
XXXXX
Army Group B

Düsseldorf

XXXX
15

Cologne

R. Roer

R. Erft

R. Rhine

BELGIUM

St Trond

XXX
XXX Br

Maastricht

XXXX
9

Tongres   XXXX
1
22 Dec

Aachen

XXX
VII
22 Dec

Düren

Bonn

Schmidt

Liège

Chaudfontaine

XXXX
1
18 Dec

Eupen

Monschau

Andenne   Huy

Namur   R. Meuse

XXX
XVIII

XXX
VII

Spa   XXXX
1

XXX
V

Malmédy

XXXX
6   Pz

G

Assesse

Losheim

Manhay

St Vith

Hotton

Celles

Dinant

Marche

Jemelle

Houffalize

Prüm

XXXX
5   Pz

E

Givet

Bastogne

Wiltz

Bitburg

XXXX
7

R
M

Neufchâteau

XXX
XVIII
19 Dec

XXX
VIII

XXX
III

XXX
XII

Trier

A

Sedan

19 Dec   Luxembourg

Longwy

R. Moselle

XXXX
1

N

R. Meuse

XXXX
3

F   R   A   N   C   E

Verdun

Metz

XXX
XX

XXX
XII
21 Dec

Saarbrücken

Sarreguemines

Y

0   10   20   30 km

N

8
SATURDAY 16 DECEMBER

At 05.20 hours on 16 December, ten minutes before 'zero hour', the artillery of Sepp Dietrich's Sixth Panzer Army opened fire. Most American soldiers, avoiding the chill of damp snow in the sixteen hours of darkness, were asleep in farmhouses, foresters' huts, barns and cowbyres. Dawn was not due until 08.30. Along most of the front, south from the Monschau Forest, the terrain was reminiscent of the Hürtgen, with thick woods, rocky gorges, small streams, few roads and saturated firebreak trails so deep in mud that they were almost impassable to vehicles.

German artillery commanders, knowing that American soldiers preferred shelter, always targeted houses. Sentries were told they should never be in the house by the door. They should be in a foxhole a short distance away to cover it in the event of German surprise attacks. Sentries, having seen flashes like summer lightning on the horizon, rushed in to wake those inside. But it was

228

only when the shells began to explode all around that there was a panic-stricken scramble by the men to extricate themselves from their sleeping bags, and grab equipment, helmets and weapons.

There had been odd bombardments before, but this was much more intense. Some of the civilians allowed to stay in the forward area to look after their livestock were terrified to see shells setting hay-barns alight, with the fire quickly spreading to the farmhouse. Unable to control the blaze, they fled with their families towards the rear. Some were killed in the bombardment. In the tiny village of Manderfeld, five died, including three small children.

To the south, on the Fifth Panzer Army frontage, artillery batteries remained silent. Manteuffel had disregarded Hitler's insistence on a long opening bombardment. He considered such a barrage to be 'a World War I concept and completely out of place in the Ardennes, in view of the thinly held lines . . . Such a plan would merely be an alarm clock to the American forces and would alert them to the daylight attack to follow.' A few days earlier, Manteuffel had sneaked forward in disguise to reconnoitre the deep valley of the River Our, and the River Sauer at the southernmost end. The Sauer was 'a significant obstacle due to its steep banks and limited crossing sites'.

He then questioned his soldiers and officers on the habits of the Americans opposite them. Since the 'Amis' retired after dark to their houses and barns, and only returned to their positions an hour before dawn, he decided to cross the river and infiltrate their lines without waking them up. Only when the attack had really started did his army use searchlights, bouncing their beams off low cloud to create artificial moonlight. This helped his infantry spearheads find their way forward in the dark woods. His engineer battalions meanwhile had started bridging the River Our, so that his three panzer divisions, the 116th, the 2nd and the Panzer Lehr, could surge forward.

Hitler had laid down in his prescriptive way that infantry divisions would make the breakthrough so that the precious panzer divisions would start fully intact for the Meuse bridges. The first reports to reach the Adlerhorst were most encouraging. Jodl reported to Hitler 'that surprise had been achieved completely'. Surprise had indeed been achieved, but what the Germans really needed was momentum to turn surprise into a paralysing shock. Some American troops lost their heads and began to save themselves. In many cases, frightened civilians begged to be allowed to accompany them. A few of the German-speakers still loyal to the Reich, on the other hand, watched the chaotic scenes with undisguised satisfaction. 'If in places there was panic,' an officer in the 99th Division reported, 'in other places there was supreme valor.' These feats of extraordinary courage would slow down the German onslaught with critical results.

Four kilometres north of Manderfeld, the hamlet of Lanzerath stood opposite the Losheim Gap, the line of advance of the 1st SS Panzer-Division led by the Kampfgruppe Peiper. Almost on the top of a ridge, it had a magnificent view out towards Germany. On a knoll, overlooking the houses and the road, an outpost of eighteen soldiers from the intelligence and reconnaissance platoon of the 394th Regiment of the 99th Division manned foxholes on hillside pasture. To their right rear a thick pinewood offered a means of escape, but also a route for an attacking force to outflank them. The importance of this position lay in the fact that a couple of hundred metres to the left was the road junction leading north-west to Honsfeld, and then to the valley of the River Amblève.

Even though the inexperienced 99th Division was part of V Corps, this platoon commanded by Lieutenant Lyle J. Bouck Jr was just over the boundary into the VIII Corps sector, which at its northern end was weakly held by the 14th Cavalry Group. Some tank destroyers attached to the 14th Cavalry were down below them among the houses. When the eastern horizon came alive with the

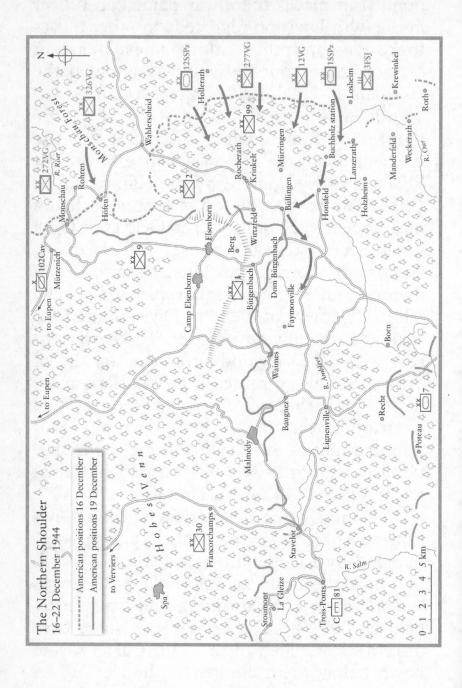

The Northern Shoulder
16–22 December 1944

American positions 16 December
American positions 19 December

N

Monschau forest
Hohes Venn

to Eupen
to Eupen
to Eupen
to Verviers

102Cav
Mützenich
Monschau
Rohren
Höfen
Wahlerscheid
Rocherath
Krinkelt
Mürringen
Büllingen
Dom Bütgenbach
Faymonville
Bütgenbach
Berg
Wirtzfeld
Elsenborn
Camp Elsenborn
Warnes
Baugnez
Malmédy
Ligneuville
Recht
Poteau
Born
Holzheim
Lanzerath
Buchholz station
Losheim
Honsfeld
Manderfeld
Weckerath
Roth
Krewinkel
R. Our
R. Amblève
R. Salm
Stavelot
Trois-Ponts
La Gleize
Stroumont
Spa
Francorchamps

326VG
272VG
125SPz
277VG
12VG
1SSPz
3FSJ
99
2
9
1
30
7
C 81

R. Roer

0 1 2 3 4 5 km

flashes from the muzzles of hundreds of guns, the reconnaissance platoon had ducked down into its foxholes. Lanzerath was an obvious target for German artillery. The soldiers were grateful for the overhead cover on their well-constructed trenches, which had been prepared by the 2nd Division. After the bombardment lifted, they saw the tank destroyers down in the village pull out past them and then turn left down the Honsfeld road. 'They might at least wave goodbye,' one soldier remarked.

Bouck radioed his regimental headquarters to report on the bombardment, and he was told to send a small patrol into Lanzerath to check and observe. Now in the grey, dawn light, he took three men down to have a look. They entered a house to hear a man talking German. Lanzerath, only just within the Belgian border, was very much part of the Germanophone eastern cantons. Bouck's men were convinced the man was talking to the enemy and he had to stop them from killing him. As the light improved a little on that heavily overcast morning, they saw large numbers of figures in the distance approaching in a column. They would be coming up the road past the platoon's position. Bouck ran back to radio a request for artillery fire on the road below Lanzerath, but he was met by disbelief at regimental headquarters.

Through his field glasses, Bouck watched

what turned out to be a twin column of German paratroopers in their distinctive helmets and smocks marching, with a file on either side of the road. Their weapons were slung, not at the ready, and they had no scouts out ahead or on the flanks. They could have been on a route march. This was the 9th Regiment of the 3rd Fallschirmjäger-Division, whose task was to break open the front for the Kampfgruppe Peiper. The platoon waited tensely, their machine guns and other automatic weapons cocked ready for the perfect ambush. Bouck wanted the main body to be within their field of fire before his men opened up. He then sighted a small group who were clearly officers. He signalled to his men to prepare to open fire. But at the very last moment a little fair-haired girl of about thirteen rushed out of a house and pointed up the hill at the recon platoon's position. Bouck hesitated, not wanting to kill the girl, but the German officer screamed an order, and his men threw themselves into the ditches on either side of the road.

The ambush may have aborted, but the opportunities for killing the under-trained teenagers had not disappeared, due to the obduracy of their commander. He sent them into one frontal attack after another. The recon platoon machine-gunners simply scythed them down as they struggled to climb a snow-fence across the field just below the American

234

positions. The range was so short that they could see their faces clearly. Bouck radioed a second time, urgently requesting artillery support. He was told that the guns were on other fire missions. He asked what he should do. 'Hold at all costs!' came the reply. Several of his men had been hit, but they were able to fight on.

Sickened by piles of dead and the wounded building up in the fields below, Bouck could scarcely believe that the German regimental commander could continue this futile sacrifice instead of trying to outflank them. A white flag appeared, and Bouck ordered a ceasefire while German medical orderlies collected their wounded. The battle began again and continued until after dark, by which time Bouck and his men were almost out of ammunition. Only after nightfall did the German commander attempt to outflank the defenders. They rushed and overran the position. Bouck and almost all his men were taken prisoner. His platoon had held off a whole regiment for a day, killing and wounding over 400 paratroopers, at a cost of just one man dead and several wounded. But it was the delay inflicted which counted most.

Peiper knew that it had been a mistake to let the infantry go first, and he was furious. Already his Kampfgruppe had been held up because the bridge over the railway line north-west of Losheim, which had been blown by the Germans during their withdrawal three months earlier, had not been repaired. It was not ready until 19.30 hours that evening. The 12th Volksgrenadier-Division's horse-drawn artillery also went ahead of Peiper's column, adding to the delay. The roads were clogged but Peiper ordered his vehicles 'to push through rapidly and to run down anything in the road ruthlessly'. In his impatience to get ahead, he told his tank commanders to drive on through an American minefield: five panzers were disabled as a result.

His divisional headquarters ordered him to divert to Lanzerath to meet up with that part of the 3rd Fallschirmjäger-Division which had been repulsed. Peiper was to take over the regiment and attack. According to one inhabitant of Lanzerath, Peiper's men were highly agitated as they entered the village, 'shouting that they were going to drive the Americans all the way back to the Channel', and they kept saying that their troops were already on the Meuse at Liège.

Peiper showed his contempt for the parachute regiment officers, who insisted the American positions were very strong although they had not been near them. He was also exasperated with the Kampfgruppe Skorzeny combat team attached to his force, with four Shermans, trucks and Jeeps. 'They might just as well have stayed at home,' he said later, 'because they were never near the head of the column where they had planned to be.' Peiper ordered his men and the paratroopers forward towards Buchholz and Honsfeld.

The small force from the 99th Division, surrounded at Buchholz station, fought off attacks from the 3rd Fallschirmjäger. A young forward observation officer was sent to direct artillery support. 'We pulled our jeep off the road and backed it into a barn,' he recorded later. 'It was a quiet, cold night . . . We could clearly hear the SS panzer troops shouting back and forth, the racing of tank engines, the squeal of bogie wheels.' On their SCR-536 radio, they also heard German signallers taunting them in English. 'Come in, come in, come in. Danger, danger, danger. We are launching a strong attack. Come in, come in, anyone on this channel?' The defenders of Buchholz station were doomed when Peiper's flak panzers arrived. They mounted quadruple 20mm guns that could obliterate any defenders unprotected by concrete, or by several inches of armour-plate.

On Peiper's right flank, the 12th SS Panzer-Division *Hitler Jugend* was struggling as it advanced slowly on the twin villages of Rocherath and Krinkelt. This division, which had been ground down by the British and Canadians in Normandy, had never fully recovered. 'There were fellows among them whose discipline was not quite up to standard,' an officer in another SS formation commented. 'These were boy-scout types and the sort of swine who think nothing of cutting a man's throat.' The division also seemed to lack technical skills. The *Hitler Jugend* suffered a high rate of mechanical breakdowns with its Panther Mark V panzers.

At the northernmost end of the 99th Infantry lines, the 3rd Battalion of the 395th Infantry held the village of Höfen just south of Monschau. The small Höfen salient in the Monschau Forest was an obvious target for attack. Generalfeldmarschall Model wanted to break through either side of Monschau to block the roads to Eupen and Aachen, and stop any American reinforcements coming from the north. He forbade any bombardment on Monschau itself. At Höfen, however, the American battalion found artificial moonlight playing in its favour. As the 326th Volksgrenadier-Division advanced through the mist, the glow silhouetted the approaching German infantry. 'At 06.00 the Germans came,' an officer reported. 'Out of the haze, they appeared before the battalion position. They seemed to be in swarms moving forward in their characteristic slow walk. The artificial moonlight outlined the approaching Germans perfectly against the backdrop of snow, and every weapon the battalion possessed opened fire . . . The German losses were terrific and

at 06.55, they began to withdraw.' The battalion's ten 81mm mortars were also used,
and when communications were restored
with the 196th Field Artillery, they added
their fire.

Less than two hours later, another, stronger
attack began, reinforced by tanks and armoured cars. 'On the K Company front, the
German infantry moved forward of the tanks
and shouting like wild men, they charged the
company position.' The assault was fought off
only after the mortars and artillery — the
155mm 'Long Toms' — targeted the sector.
At 09.30 came yet another attack. A large
number of Germans managed to seize four
houses. The battalion commander ordered
his two 57mm anti-tank guns to start smashing the walls with armour-piercing rounds.
Rifle and automatic fire was concentrated on
all the windows to prevent the Germans
shooting at the anti-tank gun crews. 'From
the screams within the house one could readily ascertain that the anti-tank guns were
creating havoc.' A reserve platoon crept up
and began throwing white phosphorus grenades through the windows. The survivors
soon surrendered. Some seventy-five dead
were apparently found inside.

The 2nd Battalion of the 393rd Infantry had
been attached to the 2nd Division, which had
just started a new V Corps advance north

towards the Roer dams near Schmidt. When they heard heavy firing to the south they thought that the rest of the division was now joining in the same attack. They still had no idea of the German offensive.

An aid man called Jordan, helped by a couple of riflemen, began bandaging the wounded in the comparative shelter of a sunken road. 'We administered plasma to a boy whose right arm was attached by shreds,' a soldier recounted, 'tried to soothe him and held cigarettes for him to smoke. He was already in shock, his body shaking badly. Shells exploding hundreds of feet away made him flinch. "Get me out of here! For God's sake get me out of here. That one was close — that one was too damn close. Get me out of here," he kept saying.' Jordan, the aid man, received a bullet through the head. 'We heard later that day that our boys shot a German medic in retaliation, somewhat mitigated by the fact that he was carrying a Luger.' Not knowing what was going on, and angry at having to give up ground they had just taken in the advance towards the dams, they were ordered to halt and turn round. Orders were to withdraw south-west towards Krinkelt to face the 12th SS Panzer-Division.

While most of the 99th Division fought valiantly in the desperate battles, 'a few men broke under the strain', an officer acknowledged, 'wetting themselves repeatedly, or vomiting, or showing other severe physical symptoms'. And 'the number of allegedly accidental rifle shots through hands or feet, usually while cleaning the weapon, rose sharply'. Some men were so desperate that they were prepared to maim themselves even more seriously. A harrowing example in the 99th Infantry Division was a soldier who was said to have 'lain down beside a large tree, reached around it, and exploded a grenade in his hand'.

The newly arrived and even less experienced 106th Infantry Division to the south, in the Schnee Eifel, would be shattered by the German offensive over the next three days. It was rapidly outflanked when the 14th Cavalry Group in the Losheim Gap, covering the area between the 99th Division and the 106th, retreated without warning. This also left the right flank of the 99th vulnerable. As its 395th Infantry Regiment pulled back in desperate haste, soldiers bitterly remembered the slogan 'The American Army never retreats!' Having received no rations, they forced open some drums of dried oatmeal. So desperate were they that they tried to stuff handfuls of it into their mouths and fill their pockets. An officer recorded that one soldier even offered another $75 for a thirteen-cent can of Campbell's soup.

The cavalry group had faced an almost

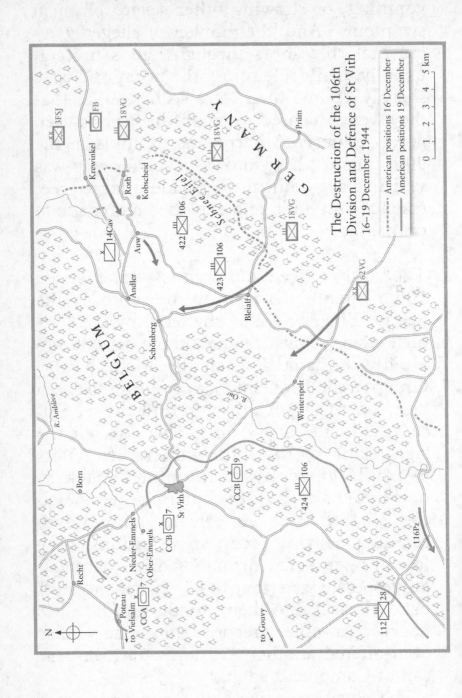

The Destruction of the 106th
Division and Defence of St Vith
16–19 December 1944

American positions 16 December
American positions 19 December

0 1 2 3 4 5 km

GERMANY

BELGIUM

N

Born

R. Amblève

Recht

Poteau

to Vielsalm

Nieder-Emmels

Ober-Emmels

St Vith

CCA 7

CCB 7

CCB 9

424 106

112 28

116Pz

to Gouvy

Winterspelt

R. Our

Schönberg

Andler

Auw

Bleialf

Roth

Kobscheid

Krewinkel

14Cav

3FSJ

FB

18VG

18VG

18VG

62VG

422 106

423 106

Schnee Eifel

Prüm

impossible task. Strung out in isolated positions across a front of nearly nine kilometres, its platoons could only attempt to defend fixed positions in villages and hamlets. There was no continuous line and the cavalry was not manned, trained nor equipped for a stationary defence. All it had were machine guns dismounted from reconnaissance vehicles, a few anti-tank guns and a battalion of 105mm howitzers in support. The very recent arrival of the 106th meant that no coordinated plan of defence had been established.

In the days before the offensive, German patrols had discovered that there was a gap nearly two kilometres wide between the villages of Roth and Weckerath in the 14th Cavalry sector. So, before dawn, the bulk of the 18th Volksgrenadier-Division, supported by a brigade of assault guns, advanced straight for this hole in the American line, which lay just within the northern boundary of the Fifth Panzer Army. Manteuffel's initial objective was the town of St Vith, fifteen kilometres to the rear of the American front line on the road from Roth.

In the murky grey daylight, the men of the 14th Cavalry at Roth and Weckerath found that the Germans were already behind them, having slipped through partly concealed by the low cloud and drizzle. Communications collapsed as shell bursts cut field telephone cables and German intercept groups played records at full volume on the wavelengths which the Americans used. The surrounded cavalry troopers in Roth fought on for much of the day, but surrendered in the afternoon.

The 106th Division did not collapse immediately. With more than thirty kilometres of front to defend, including a broad salient just forward of the Siegfried Westwall, it faced major disadvantages, especially when its left flank was burst open on the 14th Cavalry sector around Roth. With eight battalions of corps artillery in support, it inflicted heavy casualties on the volksgrenadiers, used as cannon fodder to break open the front for the panzer divisions. But the 106th Division did little to counter-attack the flank of the German breakthrough on its left, and this would lead to disaster the next day.

As Model's artillery chief observed, the difficult terrain of wooded country slowed the advance of the German infantry and made it very hard for his artillery to identify its targets. Also Volksgrenadier divisions did not know how to make proper use of artillery support. They were not helped by the strict orders on radio silence, which had prevented signals nets from being established until the opening bombardment.

Communications were even worse on the American side. Middleton's VIII Corps headquarters in Bastogne had no clear idea of the scope of the offensive. And at First Army in Spa, General Hodges assumed that the Germans were mounting 'just a local diversion' to take the pressure off the V Corps advance towards the Roer river dams. And yet although V-1 'buzz-bombs', as the Americans called them, were now passing overhead every few minutes to bombard Liège, Hodges still did not recognize the signs.* Despite General Gerow's urging, he refused to halt the 2nd Division's advance north. In Luxembourg at 12th Army Group headquarters during the 09.15 briefing, the G-3 officer reported no change on the Ardennes sector. By then General Bradley was on his way to Versailles to discuss manpower shortages with General Eisenhower.

A diary kept by Lieutenant Matt Konop with the 2nd Division's headquarters gives an idea of how Americans, even those close to the front, could take so long to comprehend the scale and scope of the German offensive. Konop's entry for 16 December began: '05.15: Asleep in Little Red House with six other officers — hear loud explo-

---

* The worst disaster resulting from the V-1 bombardment took place in Antwerp that evening when one struck a cinema, killing nearly 300 British and Canadian soldiers and wounding another 200 as well as many civilians.

sions — must be a dream — still think it's a dream — must be our own artillery — can't be, that stuff seems to be coming in louder.' Konop got up in the dark and padded to the door in his long johns. He opened it. An explosion outside sent him scurrying back to wake everyone else. They all rushed down into the cellar in their underclothes, finding their way with flashlights. Eventually, when the shelling eased, they returned upstairs. Konop called the operations section to ask if there was anything unusual to report. 'No, nothing unusual,' came the answer, 'but [we] had quite a shelling over here. Nothing unusual reported from the lines.' Konop crawled back to his mattress, but could not get back to sleep.

It was still dark at 07.15 when he reached the command post at Wirtzfeld. The progress of the 2nd Division's advance appeared satisfactory on the situation map. Its 9th Infantry Regiment had just captured the village of Wahlerscheid. An hour later Konop looked round Wirtzfeld. There were no casualties from the shelling, except that a direct hit on a heap of manure resulted 'in the pile being suddenly transported over the entire kitchen, mess-hall and officers' mess of the Engineer Battalion'. Later in the morning, he agreed with the division's Catholic chaplain that after the morning's bombardment they should be careful about holding mass in the church next day because it was an obvious target.

At 17.30 hours, Konop saw a report that German tanks had broken through the 106th Division. This was described as a 'local enemy action'. Having nothing else to do, he returned to his room to read. He then spent the evening chatting with a couple of war correspondents who had arrived to doss down. Before going to 'hit the hay', he showed the two journalists the door to the cellar in case there was another bombardment the next morning.

Cota's 28th Division, adjoining the 106th to the south-west, was initially taken by surprise because of the bad visibility, but the Germans' use of artificial moonlight proved a 'blunder'. 'They turned searchlights into the woods and then on clouds above our positions, silhouetting their [own] assault troops. They made easy targets for our machine-gunners.'

Fortunately, before the offensive began the division had trained infantry officers and NCOs to act as forward observers for the artillery. One company of the division's 109th Infantry Regiment, which was dug in, brought down 155mm howitzer fire just fifty metres in front of its own position during a mass attack. It claimed a body count of 150

Germans afterwards for no American casualties.

The compulsion to exaggerate achievements and the size of enemy forces was widespread. 'Ten Germans will be reported as a company,' a battalion commander in the division complained, 'two Mark IV tanks as a mass attack by Mark VIs. It is almost impossible for commanders to make correct decisions quickly unless reports received are what the reporter saw or heard and not what he imagined.'

The 112th Infantry Regiment of Cota's 28th Division found that 'on the morning of the initial assault, there were strong indications that the German infantry had imbibed rather freely of alcoholic beverage . . . They were laughing and shouting and telling our troops not to open fire, as it disclosed our positions. We obliged until the head of the column was 25 yards to our front. Heavy casualties were inflicted. Examination of the canteens on several of the bodies gave every indication that the canteen had only a short time before contained cognac.'

Waldenburg's 116th Panzer-Division attacked on the boundary between the 106th and 28th Divisions. But, instead of finding a gap, the Germans were taken in the flank by the extreme right-hand battalion of the 106th and a platoon of tank destroyers. In the forest west of Berg, Waldenburg reported, the assault company of his 60th Panzergrenadier-Regiment was not merely stopped but 'nearly destroyed' when the Americans 'fought very bravely and fiercely'. The Germans rushed forward artillery to cover the river crossings, but the woods and hills made observation very difficult and the steep slopes offered few places to site their batteries.

Waldenburg's 156th Panzergrenadier-Regiment to the south, on the other hand, advanced rapidly to Oberhausen. Then he found that the dragons' teeth of the Siegfried Line defences made it impossible for the panzer regiment to follow its prescribed route. He had to obtain permission from his corps headquarters to allow it to follow the success of the 156th Panzergrenadiers who had seized crossing points over the River Our. The heavy rains and snow in the Ardennes had made the ground so soft that panzer units were restricted to surfaced roads. Tank tracks churned the mud of lesser routes to a depth of one metre, making them impassable for wheeled vehicles, and even other panzers. The bad weather which Hitler had wanted to shield his forces from Allied airpower came at a high price, and so did the wild, forested terrain, with which he had concealed his purpose.

Further south, the 26th Volksgrenadier-Division had the task of opening the front for Manteuffel's most experienced formations,

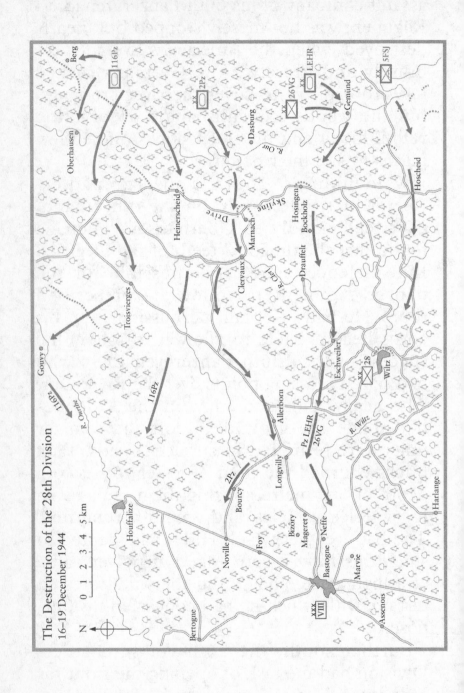

The Destruction of the 28th Division
16–19 December 1944

N

0 1 2 3 4 5 km

116Pz

R. Ourthe

Gouvy

Troisvierges

116Pz

Oberhausen

Berg

116Pz

2Pz

Dasburg

R. Our

26VG

LEHR

Gemünd

5FSJ

Hoscheid

Heinerscheid

Skyline Drive

Marnach

Hosingen
Bockholz

Clervaux

R. Clerf

Drauffelt

Eschweiler

28

Wiltz

R. Wiltz

Pz LEHR

26VG

Allerborn

Longvilly

2Pz

Bourcy

Noville

Foy

Bizory
Magret

Neffe

Bastogne

Marvie

Harlange

Houffalize

Bertogne

Ascenois

VIII

the 2nd Panzer-Division and the Panzer Lehr Division. They hoped to reach Bastogne, which lay less than thirty kilometres to the west as the crow flies, during that night or early the next morning. But Generalmajor Heinz Kokott, the commander of the 26th Volksgrenadiers, had an unpleasant surprise. The 28th Division fought on even after its line along the high ground and road known as 'Skyline Drive' had been broken. What had not been expected, he wrote later, 'was the fact that the remnants of the beaten units did not give up the battle. They stayed put and continued to block the road.' This forced the German command to accept that 'the infantry would actually have to fight its way forward', and not just open a way for the panzer divisions to rush through to the Meuse. 'At the end of the first day of the offensive, none of the objectives set by the [Fifth Panzer] Army were reached.' The 'stubborn defense of Hosingen' lasted until late in the morning of the second day.

Even though the 26th Volksgrenadiers eventually forced a crossing, repairs to the bridge over the Our near Gemünd were not ready until dusk at 16.00 hours. Traffic jams with the vehicles of both the 26th Volksgrenadier and the Panzer Lehr built up, because the Americans had blocked the road to Hosingen with enormous craters and 'abatis' barriers of felled trees. German pioneer battalions had to work through the night to make the road passable. The 26th Volksgrenadier lost 230 men and eight officers, including two battalion commanders, on the first day.

On the American 28th Division's right flank, the German Seventh Army pushed forward the 5th Fallschirmjäger-Division to shield Manteuffel's flank as his Fifth Panzer Army headed west for the Meuse. But the 5th Fallschirmjäger was a last-minute replacement to the German order of battle and struggled badly. Although 16,000 strong, its officers and soldiers had received little infantry training. One battalion, commanded by the flying instructor Major Frank in the 13th Fallschirmjäger-Regiment, had twelve officers with no field experience. Frank, in a conversation secretly taped after his capture, told another officer that his NCOs were 'willing but inept', while his 700 soldiers were mostly just sixteen or seventeen years old, but 'the lads were wonderful'.

'Right on the very first day of the offensive we stormed Führen [held by Company E of the 109th Infantry]. It was a fortified village. We got to within 25 metres of the bunker, were stopped there and my best Kompaniechefs were killed. I stuck fast there for two and a half hours, five of my runners had been killed. One couldn't direct things from there, the runners who returned were all shot up. Then, for two and a half hours, always on my stomach, I worked my way back by inches. What a show for young boys, making their way over flat ground and without any support from heavy weapons! I decided to wait for a forward observation officer. The Regimental commander said: "Get going. Take that village — there are only a few soldiers holding it."

' "That's madness," I said to the Regimentskommandeur.

' "No, no, it's an order. Get going, we must capture the village before nightfall."

'I said: "We will too. The hour we lose waiting for the forward observation officer I will make up two or three times over afterwards . . . At least give me the assault guns to come in from the north and destroy their bunker."

' "No, no, no."

'We took the village without any support and scarcely were we in it when our heavy guns began firing into it. I brought out 181 prisoners altogether. I rounded up the last sixty and a salvo of mortar shells fell on them from one of our mortar brigades right into the midst of the prisoners and their guards. Twenty two hours later our own artillery was still firing into the village. Our communications were a complete failure.'

The divisional commander Generalmajor Ludwig Heilmann clearly had no feeling for his troops. Heydte described him as 'a very ambitious, reckless soldier with no moral scruples', and said that he should not be commanding a division. His soldiers called him 'der Schlächter von Cassino', the butcher of Cassino, because of the terrible losses suffered by his men during that battle. And on the first day of the Ardennes offensive, his units were battered by American mortar fire as they floundered across the River Our, which was fast flowing and had a muddy bottom.

Just to the south the American 9th Armored Division held a narrow three-kilometre sector, but was pushed back by the 212th Volksgrenadier-Division. To its right, outposts of the 4th Infantry Division west and south of Echternach failed to see German troops crossing the Sauer before dawn. Their outposts on bluffs or ridges high above the river valley may have had a fine view in clear weather, but at night and on misty days they were blind. As a result most of the men in these forward positions were surrounded and captured very rapidly because German advance patrols had slipped through behind them. A company commander, while finally reporting details of the attack by field telephone to his battalion commander, was startled to hear another person on the line. A voice with a heavy German accent announced: 'We are here!' One squad in Lauterborn was caught entirely by surprise and taken prisoner. But the over-confident Germans marched them down the road past a mill, which happened to be occupied by Americans from another company who opened fire. The prisoners threw themselves in the ditch where they hid for several hours, and then rejoined their unit later.

Once again, field telephone lines back from observation posts were cut by shellfire and radios often failed to work due to the hilly terrain and damp atmospheric conditions. Signals traffic was in any case chaotic, with careless or panic-stricken operators jamming everyone else. Major General Raymond O. Barton, the commander of the 4th Infantry Division, only heard at 11.00 hours that his 12th Infantry Regiment either side of Echternach was under strong attack. Barton wasted no time in committing his reserve battalion and sending in a company from the 70th Tank Battalion. As darkness fell later that afternoon, the 12th Infantry still held five key towns and villages along the ridge route of 'Skyline Drive'. These were the all-important crossroads which blocked the German advance. 'It was the towns and road junctions that proved decisive in the battle,' concluded one analysis.

The 4th Infantry had also dropped tall pines across the roads to make abatis barriers, which were mined and booby-trapped.

The division's achievement was all the more remarkable when considering its shortages in manpower and weaponry after its recent battles in the Hürtgen Forest. Ever since the fighting in Normandy, the 4th Infantry Division had seized as many Panzerfausts as it could to use them back against the Germans. Although their effective range was only about forty metres, the infantrymen found them much more powerful in penetrating the Panther tank than their own bazooka. Forty-three of their fifty-four tanks were still undergoing repair in workshops to the rear. This did not prove as disastrous as it might have done. Manteuffel had wanted to provide Brandenberger's Seventh Army with a panzer division to break open the southern shoulder, but none could be spared.

General Bradley's journey that day on the icy roads from Luxembourg to Versailles took longer than expected. Eisenhower was in an expansive mood when he arrived, for he had just heard that he was to receive his fifth star. Bradley congratulated him. 'God,' Eisenhower answered, 'I just want to see the first time I sign my name as General of the Army.'

Major Hansen, who had accompanied Bradley, returned to the Ritz where Hemingway was drinking with a large number of visitors. 'The room, with two brass beds,' wrote Hansen, 'was littered in books which over-

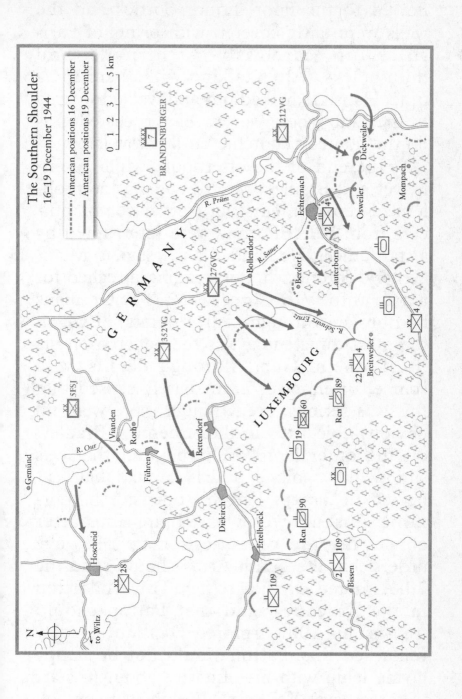

The Southern Shoulder
16–19 December 1944

········· American positions 16 December
━━━━━━ American positions 19 December

0 1 2 3 4 5 km

GERMANY

LUXEMBOURG

BRANDENBURGER

212VG

276VG

352VG

5FSJ

R. Prüm

R. Sauer

R. Schwarz Ernz

R. Our

Echternach

Bollendorf

Berdorf

Dickweiler

Osweiler

Mompach

Lauterborn

Breitweiler

Vianden

Roth

Führen

Bettendorf

Diekirch

Ettelbrück

Bissen

Hoscheid

Gemünd

to Wiltz

N

12

4

4

4

22 4

89 Rcn

60

19

9

90 Rcn

109

109

28

1

2

N

flowed to the floor, liquor bottles and the walls were fairly covered with prints of Paris stuck up carelessly with nails and thumbtacks.' After talking with them for a time, Hansen 'ducked out and walked wearily to the Lido where we saw bare breasted girls do the hootchy kootchie until it was late'.

At the end of the afternoon, while Eisenhower and Bradley were discussing the problem of replacements with other senior officers from SHAEF, they were interrupted by a staff officer. He handed a message to Major General Strong who, on reading it, called for a map of the VIII Corps sector. The Germans had broken through at five points, of which the most threatening was the penetration via the Losheim Gap. Although details were sparse, Eisenhower immediately sensed that this was serious, even though there were no obvious objectives in the Ardennes. Bradley, on the other hand, believed that this was simply the spoiling attack he had half expected to disrupt Patton's offensive in Lorraine. Eisenhower wasted no time after consulting the operations map. He gave orders that the Ninth Army should send the 7th Armored Division to help Troy Middleton in the Ardennes, and that Patton should transfer his 10th Armored Division. Bradley remarked that Patton would not be happy giving it up with his offensive about to start in three days. 'Tell him', Eisenhower snarled, 'that Ike is running this war.'

Bradley had to ring Patton straight away. As he had predicted, Patton complained bitterly, and said that the German attack was just an attempt to disrupt his own operation. With Eisenhower's eyes upon him, Bradley had to give him a direct order. The men of the 10th Armored Division were horrified to hear that they were to be transferred from Patton's Third Army to First Army reserve. 'That broke our hearts because, you know, First Army — hell we were in Third Army.' Patton, however, had an instinct just after the telephone call that it 'looks like the real thing'. 'It reminds me very much of March 25, 1918 [Ludendorff's offensive]', he wrote to a friend, 'and I think will have the same results.'

Bradley then rang his headquarters in Luxembourg and told them to contact Ninth Army. He did not expect any trouble there. Lieutenant General William H. Simpson was a tall but quietly spoken Texan known as 'the doughboy general', whom everybody liked. He had an engaging long face on a bald head with prominent ears and a square chin. Simpson was examining the air-support plan for crossing the Roer when at 16.20 hours, according to his headquarters diary, he received a call from Major General Allen, the chief of staff at 12th Army Group. 'Hodges [is] having a bit of trouble on his south flank,' Allen said. 'There is a little flare-up south of you.' Simpson immediately agreed to release the 7th Armored Division to First Army. Exactly two hours later, Simpson rang to check that the advance party of the 7th Armored Division was on its way.

Eisenhower and Bradley, having despatched the two divisions, drank a bottle of champagne to celebrate the fifth star. The Supreme Commander had just received a supply of oysters which he loved, but Bradley was allergic to them and ate scrambled eggs instead. Afterwards they played five rubbers of bridge, since Bradley was not returning to Luxembourg until the following morning.

While the two American generals were in Versailles, Oberstleutnant von der Heydte in Paderborn was woken from a deep sleep by a telephone call. He was exhausted because everything had gone wrong the night before and he had not been to bed. His Kampfgruppe had been due to take off in the early hours of that morning, but most of the trucks to bring his men to the airfield had not received fuel in time, so the operation had been postponed; then it looked as if it would be cancelled. General Peltz, the Luftwaffe general on the telephone, now told him that the jump was back on because the initial attack had not progressed as rapidly as hoped.

When Heydte reached the airfield, he heard

that the meteorological report from Luftflotte West estimated a wind speed of twenty kilometres per hour over the drop zone. This was the highest speed permissible for a night drop on a wooded area, and Heydte was being deliberately misinformed so that he would not cancel the operation. Just after all the paratroopers had climbed aboard the elderly Junkers 52 transport planes, a 'very conscientious meteorologist' rushed up to Heydte's plane as it was about to taxi, and said: 'I feel I must do my duty; the reports from our sources are that the wind is 58 kph.'

The whole operation turned into a fiasco. Because most of the pilots were 'new and nervous' and unused to navigating at night, some 200 of Heydte's men were dropped around Bonn. Few of the jumpmasters had ever performed their task before, and only ten aircraft managed to drop their sticks of paratroopers on the drop zone south of Eupen, which had been marked by two magnesium flares. The wind was so strong that some paratroopers were blown on to the propellers of the following aircraft. Survivors of the landing joined up in the dark by whistling to each other. By dawn Heydte knew that his mission was 'an utter failure'. He had assembled only 150 men, a 'pitifully small muster', he called it, and very few weapon containers were found. Only eight Panzerfausts out of 500 were recovered and just one

81mm mortar.

'German People, be confident!' stated Adolf Hitler's message to the nation. 'Whatever may face us, we will overcome it. There is victory at the end of the road. Under any situation, in battle where the fanaticism of a nation is a factor, there can only be victory!' Generalfeldmarschall Model declared in an order of the day to the troops of Army Group B: 'We will win, because we believe in Adolf Hitler and the Greater German Reich!' But that night some 4,000 German civilians died in an Allied bombing raid on Magdeburg, which had been planned before the offensive.

Belgian civilians at least had the choice of fleeing the onslaught, but some stayed with their farms and animals, resigned to another German occupation. They did not know, however, that the SS Sicherheitsdienst security service was following hard on the heels of Waffen-SS formations. As far as these SD units were concerned, the inhabitants of the eastern cantons were German citizens and they wanted to know who had disobeyed the orders in September to move east of the Siegfried Line with their families and livestock. Locals avoiding service in the Wehrmacht and those who had collaborated with the Americans during the autumn were liable to arrest, and even execution in a few cases. But their main targets were those young

Belgians in Resistance groups which had harried the retreating German forces in September.

General Hodges, finally aware of the danger, ordered the 1st Division then resting behind the lines to prepare to move. 'We heard a siren-like sound', wrote Arthur Couch, 'and an announcement that all American troops were to return to their units and prepare to move out — there had been a large German attack in the Ardennes area. We gathered our combat gear and climbed onto trucks taking us to the new front line. We were told that a German tank attack had broken through an inexperienced new division straight from America. They were in a chaotic retreat.' At 22.00 hours, another order from First Army headquarters instructed the 2nd Division to halt its attack north and prepare to move back towards the eastern flank of the Elsenborn ridge to block the advance of the 12th SS Panzer-Division.

After all the delays on the first day, that night Peiper forced his men forward to Honsfeld. His Kampfgruppe had been allotted 'the decisive role in the offensive', and he had no intention of failing. 'I was not to bother about my flanks, but was to drive rapidly to the Meuse river, making full use of the element of surprise.' His column of tanks, half-tracks and other vehicles stretched almost twenty-five kilometres in length, and because the roads were so narrow he could not change the order of march. He therefore decided to have a strong fighting element right at the front, with panzergrenadiers mounted in half-tracks, followed by a company of Panthers and Mark IV tanks. The heavy battalion of Tiger tanks would follow on behind.

Before the offensive began, Peiper really had believed that if the German infantry managed to break through at dawn on 16 December as planned, then he could reach the Meuse in just over twenty-four hours. Now he knew that his test-drive of a Panther over eighty kilometres before the offensive had been utterly misleading. The farm roads allotted to him were muddy tracks. The fact that the Führer himself had chosen Peiper's route for him was hardly a consolation in the circumstances. As Manteuffel had predicted, the panzers' fuel consumption in this terrain was more than twice what Keitel and the OKW had estimated. Having been warned at the divisional briefing that two trainloads of fuel had failed to arrive and that the spear-heads were to make use of captured supplies, Peiper consulted his map. The divisional Ic intelligence officer had marked the position of American fuel dumps at Büllingen and Stavelot. However, the main US Army gaso-line dump at Francorchamps between Malmédy and Spa, which held more than 2 million gallons, was not shown.

9
SUNDAY 17 DECEMBER

For Lieutenant Matt Konop with the 2nd Infantry Division headquarters, the first sign of anything 'unusual' came on the second morning when the telephone by his mattress rang shortly before seven. The operations officer told him that a report had come in of paratroopers landing south of Eupen, and that some thirty German tanks had broken through to their east. Konop turned on the light and reached for a map to try to work out if anything important was going on. A few minutes later the telephone rang again.

'Say, Konop, I want you to alert everybody.' Konop could not identify the voice. 'Get every gun, man and whatever you can get to prepare a last ditch defense of the C[ommand] P[ost]! Enemy tanks have broken through and are on the road to Büllingen now.'

'Yes, sir,' Konop replied. 'By the way, who is this?'

'This is General Robertson,' replied his

divisional commander, a man known for his calm, good sense. Konop felt obliged to remind him that the only soldiers available were 'those men who drive the trucks and former battle exhaustion cases'. Robertson told him to get together every individual he could find. So Konop formed cooks, clerks, drivers and any man who could still hold a weapon into an improvised defence platoon and rushed them down the road from Wirtzfeld. He could already hear machine-gun fire in the distance while he placed bazooka teams and their two 57mm anti-tank guns to cover any side tracks which a panzer commander might select. He put a cook sergeant and his own Jeep driver to man a .50 machine gun and set up observation posts with radios. A military police officer arrived with twenty men, and even though his 'snowdrops' were armed only with pistols, they too went into the line.

General Hodges had at last been forced to face reality. At 07.30 hours on 17 December, twenty-four hours after the German offensive began, he finally allowed General Gerow, the commander of V Corps, to halt the 2nd Division in its attack north from Wahlerscheid. Gerow wanted to pull it back towards the twin villages of Rocherath–Krinkelt, which were now threatened. The 99th Division had been forced to retreat by the 277th Volksgrenadier-Division and the 12th SS

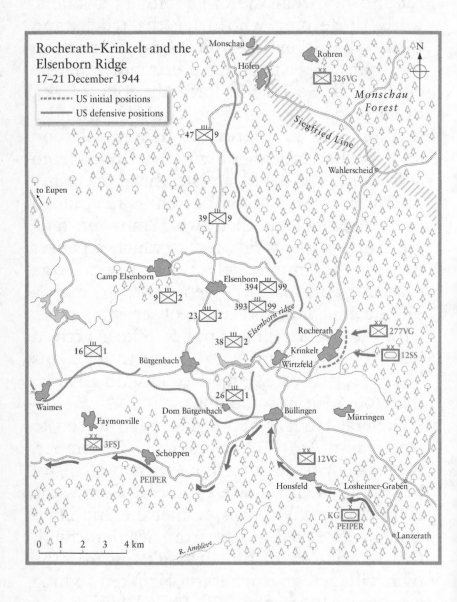

Rocherath–Krinkelt and the
Elsenborn Ridge
17–21 December 1944

········· US initial positions
———— US defensive positions

Monschau

Rohren

326VG

Höfen

Monschau
Forest

Siegfried Line

47⊠9

Wahlerscheid

to Eupen

39⊠9

Camp Elsenborn

Elsenborn

394⊠99

9⊠2

393⊠99

23⊠2

Elsenborn ridge

Rocherath

277VG

38⊠2

Krinkelt

12SS

16⊠1

Bütgenbach

Wirtzfeld

26⊠1

Dom Bütgenbach

Büllingen

Mürringen

Waimes

Faymonville

3FSJ

Schoppen

12VG

PEIPER

Honsfeld

Losheimer-Graben

KG
PEIPER

Lanzerath

0 1 2 3   4 km

R. Amblève

N

Panzer-Division *Hitler Jugend*. He and General Robertson agreed that they must protect the road north from Rocherath–Krinkelt to Wahlerscheid so that he could extricate his two regiments.

Gerow did not subscribe to the pointless slogan that the American army never retreats. He had immediately sensed that holding the northern shoulder of the breakthrough was what mattered, and the key to that would be the Elsenborn ridge, which began just west of Rocherath–Krinkelt. They had to hold the twin villages long enough to establish firm positions along the ridge, where he was already bringing in artillery regiments.

Robertson ordered forward his only reserve, a battalion of the 23rd Infantry Regiment, from Elsenborn in trucks. These troops dismounted east of Rocherath, and looked with foreboding at the thick pinewoods. All they knew was that a unit of the 99th Division, which 'had had the hell knocked out of them', was withdrawing in front of the 12th SS *Hitler Jugend*. Behind them, bursts of firing could be heard as anti-aircraft half-tracks blazed away at the V-1 buzz-bombs flying overhead. 'The snow around the road junction had been churned into a yellowish mixture of snow and dirt from recent heavy shelling,' wrote Charles MacDonald, a company commander.

He took his men forward to the edge of the

woods. Even in the open, visibility extended no more than a hundred metres in the damp mist. They could hear small-arms fire ahead of them, mainly the ripping noise of rapid-fire German automatic weapons, rather than the slower, more deliberate cadence of their American counterparts. Then, a salvo of 'screaming meemies' came over. As soon as MacDonald's men heard artillery shells they picked a thick pine tree to stand behind, hoping to avoid any splinters from an overhead burst. With little enthusiasm except the instinct of self-preservation, MacDonald's company returned to digging foxholes. It was hard work with the small shovels because of the tree roots under the wet snow.

The threat that morning to the 2nd Division's headquarters in Wirtzfeld, which Lieutenant Konop prepared to defend, did not come from the *Hitler Jugend* Division to the east: it came from Peiper's Kampfgruppe to the south. Peiper, horrified by the state of the tracks he was expected to follow, had decided to ignore his orders and the route prescribed by Hitler. His corps commander later agreed. 'Owing to the wretched condition of the roads,' he wrote, 'the wheeled vehicles had be towed in places for considerable distances.'

Before dawn on 17 December, the Peiper Kampfgruppe launched an attack on Hons-feld. Its leading vehicles simply followed in the wake of a retreating American column. Even though the small American force was taken by surprise, the Kampfgruppe lost two Mark V Panthers, but captured a large number of trucks and half-tracks. Peiper's SS panzergrenadiers executed nineteen American prisoners in a field, and two villagers who were made to face a wall were shot in the back of the head. For the panzergrenadiers, it could have been the eastern front again where they had slaughtered prisoners and civilians without a second thought. They proceeded to loot the houses and the chapel. Peiper detailed a small group to stay behind to guard his line of communications. Two days later, five of these panzergrenadiers forced Erna Collas, a beautiful sixteen-year-old girl, to show them the way to a farm. She was never seen again until her body was found in a foxhole five months later. She had been riddled with bullets, almost certainly after she had been raped.

Peiper decided to leave most of the trucks in Honsfeld because of the mud, and ordered the commander of the 9th Fallschirmjäger-Regiment to stay there to mop up and secure the area. Then, instead of driving due west to the valley of the Amblève as he had been instructed, Peiper pushed north to Büllingen where the American 2nd Division's fuel dump was marked on his map. The Kampfgruppe took the village unopposed soon after

08.30 hours that Sunday morning, and destroyed twelve American light aircraft parked on a landing strip. A civilian emerged wearing a swastika armband to greet them. He gave the Nazi salute as each vehicle passed, then showed the SS soldiers where the Americans stored their fuel. The panzergrenadiers put their prisoners to work refuelling vehicles and loading jerrycans on to the half-tracks. One wounded soldier was finished off with a *Kopfschuss,* a pistol shot through the head at close range, but according to civilian witnesses the other prisoners were more fortunate than their comrades in Honsfeld. The American official history, on the other hand, states that fifty were shot at Büllingen.

Just west of Büllingen, Company B of the 254th Engineer Battalion was overrun by German tanks. The panzers did not just 'iron' the foxholes by charging over them, they halted to twist back and forth on their axis to collapse the trench walls and bury the occupants in mud and snow. Fortunately, help was on the way. The 26th Infantry Regiment of the 1st Division, after travelling in trucks through the early hours, reached Camp Elsenborn on the ridge at 09.00 hours. One of its battalions was immediately sent south to Bütgenbach.

On the way down, it skirmished with an advance patrol of paratroopers from the 3rd

Fallschirmjäger's reconnaissance battalion. After urging the civilians in Bütgenbach to shelter in their cellars, the Americans pushed on towards the next hamlet of Dom Bütgenbach, two kilometres west of Büllingen, where they heard that SS troops had taken the village. On some high ground by the road, they found a scratch force made up of around fifty clerks and supply personnel from the 99th Infantry Division who had been taken in hand by a captain from a tank-destroyer battalion. The battalion of the 26th Infantry wrongly assumed that the enemy force in Büllingen was from the 12th *Hitler Jugend* Division. These infantrymen could not understand why it did not continue to attack north. But the reason for the lull was that Peiper's spearhead had already set off south-west, to regain the route to the Amblève valley.

Despite the delays in the initial breakthrough, German morale was high. 'I think the war in the west is again turning,' wrote a Gefreiter in the 3rd Panzergrenadier-Division, waiting that day to advance. 'The main thing is that the war will soon be decided and I will be coming home again to my dear wife and we can again build a new home. The radio is now playing bells from the homeland.'

General Bradley, returning that morning from Paris to Luxembourg in his own olive-drab Cadillac, found an escort of machine-gun-mounted Jeeps waiting for him in Verdun because of reports of German paratroopers. Hansen asked about the possibility of moving 12th Army Group headquarters, because German divisions were now less than thirty kilometres to their north. 'I will never move backwards with a headquarters,' Bradley replied. 'There is too much prestige at stake.' This defiance would serve him ill over the next few days.

Both men sensed that a German reoccupation of the Grand Duchy might be brutal after the warm welcome its people had accorded to the Americans less than three months before. When entering the city of Luxembourg, Bradley saw the Stars and Stripes hanging from a house. 'I hope he doesn't have to take it down,' he murmured. The city of Luxembourg had so far been spared the full horrors of war. It was dubbed 'the last air-raid shelter in Europe', because it had not been bombed by either the RAF or the USAAF.

The Cadillac drew up outside the 12th Army Group's forward headquarters known as 'Eagle Tac', four blocks from the general's residence in the Hôtel Alfa. Bradley hurried up the stairs. He came to a halt in front of the situation map and stared at it in fascinated horror. 'Pardon my French,' he said, 'I think the situation justifies it — but where in hell has this son of a bitch gotten all his strength?'

Bradley and his staff were shaken by the way German intelligence had identified the weakest part of their whole front. And since the Americans' policy was one of attack, their lines had not been built in depth with reserve formations. Yet Bradley still wanted to believe that a major redeployment could be avoided. First Army at Spa that day wondered 'whether 12th Army Group fully appreciates the seriousness of the situation'. Third Army also appears to have been surprised at the slow reaction. 'The Army Group commander called General Patton on the phone,' the chief of staff recorded, 'and told him that he might have to call on him for two more divisions. The decision was not to be made for forty-eight hours.'

At Ninth Army headquarters, nobody seemed to have any idea of the size of the attack. Staff officers could indulge only in confused speculation. A Luftwaffe attack on their front prompted suggestions that this was 'a diversion for a larger counter-offensive in First Army zone'. Ninth Army staff officers told war correspondents desperate for information that 'everything depends on what troops are at von Rundstedt's disposal'.

Back at SHAEF, the danger became clearer thanks to some captured German instructions. Eisenhower ordered that all reserve formations should be brought in. He told Bedell Smith, Strong and Major General John Whiteley, the British head of the operational planning staff, to organize the details. In the chief of staff's office, the three men stood around a large map spread out on the floor. Strong pointed with a German ceremonial sword to Bastogne. The town was the hub of the central Ardennes, and most of the main roads leading to the Meuse passed through it. It was the obvious place to block the German advance to the Meuse, and everyone present agreed.

SHAEF's immediate reserve consisted of the 82nd and 101st Airborne Divisions, resting in Reims after their operations in Holland. The question was whether they could reach Bastogne before Manteuffel's panzer spearheads arrived from the east. Strong considered it possible, and the orders for them to move were issued immediately.

It was ironic that Bradley's headquarters in Luxembourg should have feared an ambush by Heydte's paratroopers, for they had dropped more than a hundred kilometres to the north as the crow flies. And Heydte, accepting that there was little he could do with such a weak force, decided to hide most of his men in the forest. He sent out standing patrols to watch the main roads from Eupen to Malmédy and from Verviers. They were to ambush single Jeeps and messengers. Once the sounds of battle came closer, then perhaps his men could assist by seizing a key point just before Dietrich's tanks arrived. His standing patrols soon collected a range of prisoners and a haul of intelligence on the American order of battle, but since their radios had been lost in the parachute drop Heydte had no way of passing the information back. He had asked Sepp Dietrich for carrier pigeons, but the Oberstgruppenführer had simply laughed at the idea.

On the evening of 17 December, Heydte's force doubled in size to around 300 men when more stragglers and a large group which had dropped too far to the north joined them. That night he released all his prisoners and sent them off with some of their own wounded. Then he moved camp. Heydte and his men had no idea of the course of events, except for the rumble of artillery from the Elsenborn ridge more than a dozen kilometres to their south.

While the 99th Division was being battered east of Rocherath–Krinkelt, the 106th Division to its south was in an even worse state, attacked by the 18th and 62nd Volksgrenadier-Divisions. Major General Alan W. Jones, the 106th's hapless commander, felt powerless as he sat in a school in St Vith, which he had taken over as his command post. Two of his regiments, the 422nd and the 423rd, were almost surrounded in the Schnee Eifel, while his third regiment, the 424th, was holding the line down to the south with a combat command of the 9th Armored Division. His son was with the headquarters of one of the beleaguered regiments, which increased his anxiety.[*]

The day before, Jones had failed to comprehend the gravity of the German thrust through the 14th Cavalry's position on his north flank, and he had not reacted when its commander Colonel Mark Devine warned that he was having to pull back. Devine added that he would try to counter-attack with the 32nd Cavalry Squadron, but their attack was repulsed in the afternoon, and most of his force withdrew to the northwest unable to close the widening breach. Only a single cavalry troop remained in the valley of the River Our, attempting to block the road to St Vith. Jones sent his last reserve battalion to Schönberg in the valley, but it became lost in the dark and turned in the wrong direction. And on the right of the 106th Division's sector, the 62nd Volksgrenadier-Division had forced Jones's right-hand regiment, the 424th, back towards the village of Winter-

[*] See map, The Destruction of the 106th Division, p. 236 above.

spelt and the River Our.

General Jones, overtaken by events, had tended to rely on the promise of help from outside rather than on his own actions. He expected Combat Command B of the 7th Armored Division to be with him in St Vith by 07.00 hours on Sunday 17 December. He was counting on it to launch a counter-attack to free his two regiments. When Brigadier General Bruce C. Clarke, a 'great bear of a man', arrived at his command post at 10.30 hours, Jones asked him to mount an attack immediately. Clarke had to tell him that he was on his own. His tanks had been held up by chaotic traffic, caused by units falling back in panic. Jones now bitterly regretted having committed the 9th Armored Division combat command to his right flank the evening before. The two men could only sit and wait.

To Clarke's astonishment, he heard Jones tell his corps commander in Bastogne on the telephone that the situation was under control. Jones's mood veered between irrational optimism and despair. Clarke was even more concerned because there was little radio contact with the two regiments out on the Schnee Eifel, apart from their demands for resupply by airdrop.* Colonel Devine of the

* 'One futile effort' was made the next day, but due to bad co-ordination with Transport Carrier Command no drop took place.

14th Cavalry Group then appeared in the command post, claiming that German tanks were just behind him. Jones and Clarke saw that Devine had lost his nerve, so Jones told him to report to General Middleton in Bastogne. Yet Devine had not imagined the German tanks. Another SS Kampfgruppe was breaking through ten kilometres to the north.*

At 14.30 hours, they heard small-arms fire. Jones and Clarke went up to the third floor of the school and sighted German troops emerging from the woods in the distance. Jones told Clarke that he should now take over the defence of St Vith. Clarke accepted, but wondered what troops he had, apart from the two engineer service companies and headquarters personnel already out on the road east to Schönberg. Half an hour later this force, miraculously joined by a platoon of tank destroyers, was attacked. The tank

* Staff officers described Devine as 'excited, nervous, over-talkative, agitated, could barely control his actions, and gave undue attention to trivial personal injuries. At no time did he present the appearance of a competent commander.' He was treated with sedatives in hospital and released on 19 December, but was then found directing traffic in La Roche-en-Ardenne while trying to order a battalion of tanks to turn round. He was again sedated and evacuated.

destroyers managed to scare the panzers back into the woods beyond the road. But the main reason for the slowness of the German advance on 17 December came from the state of the roads and the traffic jams, which blocked artillery and other panzer units coming forward.

Volksartillerie units had not moved forward because their draught horses could not cope with hauling heavy guns through the deep mud churned up by panzer tracks. Even some of the self-propelled artillery of the 1st SS Panzer-Division had to be left behind because of the shortage of fuel. Both Model and Manteuffel were seething with impatience. Model, on finding several artillery battalions still in their original positions, ordered General der Panzertruppe Horst Stumpff to court-martial their commanders. 'When I told him it was because of the fuel shortages and road conditions that they hadn't moved, he rescinded the order.' At one stage, out of sheer frustration, Manteuffel began to direct traffic at a crossroads. 'I expected the right-hand corps to capture St Vith on the first day,' he acknowledged later. Like Bastogne, St Vith's network of paved roads was vital for a rapid advance to the Meuse.

While the Germans held back east of St Vith and made little more than skirmishing thrusts, Clarke sent his operations officer out on the road west to Vielsalm to await his combat command. The scenes along the road shocked officers in the 7th Armored Division. 'It was a case of "every dog for himself"; it was a retreat, a rout,' one officer wrote. 'It wasn't orderly; it wasn't military; it wasn't a pretty sight — we were seeing American soldiers running away.' At one stage the combat command took two and a half hours to move five kilometres, and then they had to bulldoze vehicles off the road.

In Malmédy, their artillery encountered civilians fleeing in a variety of vehicles, with 'panic stricken soldiers running through the square towards the west . . . A field hospital north of Malmédy was being evacuated and ambulances were darting up and down. A truck loaded with nurses went through the square at top speed. The nurses' hair was flying.' Just over a kilometre from St Vith, part of Clarke's combat command came around a bend and spotted three panzers and an infantry company coming towards them. They quickly set an ambush, 'head-on at the bend of the road at point-blank range'. The three panzers were knocked out, and the infantry scattered, losing some fifty men.

Clarke himself went to the Vielsalm road and was horrified to see a field artillery battalion retreating, having abandoned its guns. He asked his operations officer why he had let them block the road. He replied that the lieutenant colonel in command had threatened to shoot him if he interfered. Clarke found him and said that he would shoot him if he did not get his trucks off the road. The lieutenant colonel, intimidated by Clarke's superior rank and build, finally did as he was told.

Another artillery officer proved very different. Lieutenant Colonel Maximilian Clay appeared with a battalion of self-propelled 105mm guns, saying he wanted to help. His 275th Armored Field Artillery Battalion had been supporting the 14th Cavalry Group, which was now far away to the north. Clarke welcomed him warmly and told him where to go. Finally, at 16.00 hours, Clarke's own reconnaissance squadron arrived, followed by the rest of his combat command. Clarke sent them straight through the town to strengthen the thin defence line on the eastern side. Not long afterwards, Clarke's divisional commander Brigadier General Robert W. Hasbrouck joined Jones and Clarke to discuss the situation. He too had been disturbed by 'the continuous stream of frenzied soldiers hurrying to the "safety" of the rear'. To Jones's despair, Hasbrouck ruled out a counter-attack to rescue the two stranded regiments. Holding on to St Vith was far more important. Jones observed bitterly that no general in the American army had lost a division so quickly. Late that afternoon, the two prongs of the 18th Volksgrenadier-

Division closed on Schönberg and cut off the two regiments completely.

The defence of St Vith would take the form of a large horseshoe. The town stood on a small hill, which was surrrounded a couple of kilometres further out by a circular ring of higher hills covered in woods, which the infantry, the reconnaissance squadron and the scratch units would defend with support from the tanks. 'The build-up of a defensive cordon around the town', wrote Hasbrouck, 'was a piecemeal procedure with units being placed in the line as they arrived in Saint Vith.' At that stage they did not know that the Kampfgruppe Hansen, based on the 1st SS Panzergrenadier-Regiment, had slipped through to their north and attacked Combat Command A of the 7th Armored near Recht. This was the panzer unit which had so unsettled Colonel Devine. The battle between the Americans and the SS lasted all night. The luckier villagers managed to escape to a nearby slate quarry, while their houses were blasted from both sides. These unfortunate 'border Belgians' were regarded with suspicion by American soldiers because they spoke German and had framed photographs of sons in Wehrmacht uniform. And Germans distrusted them because they had defied the September order to move into Germany beyond the Siegfried Line. Around a hundred men from St Vith had been killed serving in the German forces during the war. Others had deserted and were now determined not to be caught by the Feldgendarmerie or the SD, following closely behind the lead formations.

Peiper's long column had turned west, picking up speed. By midday it was close to the crossroads at Baugnez, five kilometres southeast of Malmédy. Peiper despatched a small force of panzergrenadiers and tanks to Baugnez to reconnoitre. His troops had just missed bumping into Combat Command R of the 7th Armored Division, on its way south to support the defence of St Vith.

Oblivious to the threat ahead the next unit of the 7th Armored Division, part of the 285th Field Artillery Observation Battalion, followed on through Malmédy. As the men were driven in open trucks through the town, locals who knew of the sudden German advance from refugees tried to warn them by pointing ahead shouting, 'Boches! Boches!', but the soldiers did not understand and just waved back. Their vehicles motored on towards the crossroads at Baugnez, and there the convoy ran straight into the SS half-tracks and panzers.

The German tanks opened fire. Trucks were set ablaze as men tumbled off to seek shelter or run for the forest. Panzergrenadiers rounded up some 130 prisoners and herded them into a field by the road. The SS took rings, cigarettes, watches and gloves from their prisoners. When one of their officers opened fire, they began to shoot their prisoners with automatic weapons and the tanks joined in with their machine guns. Some American soldiers made it to the trees, others feigned death, although many were still shot through the head with pistols. Although the mass killing took place at Baugnez, it was to become infamous as the Malmédy massacre. Altogether, eighty-four Americans died, as well as several civilians who tried to shelter some escapees.

Peiper, who had continued on the road to Ligneuville, was not present when the killings took place. But if one takes into account the murder of prisoners in Honsfeld, to say nothing of his record of extreme brutality on the eastern front, one cannot imagine that he would have objected. He claimed later that the firing started only when the prisoners ran for the trees. The few soldiers who escaped the massacre made it back to American lines by the late afternoon.

A patrol from an engineer combat battalion in Malmédy reached Baugnez that same afternoon after the departure of the SS, and saw the bodies. A military policeman on traffic duty at the crossroads, who had witnessed the whole incident, was brought to First Army headquarters at Spa. He described to

Hodges and his assembled officers how the prisoners had been 'herded together into a side field and an SS officer fired two shots from his pistol and immediately there came the crackle of machinegun fire and whole groups were mown down in cold blood'. Staff officers at Spa were shaken and furious. 'Immediate publicity is being given to the story,' General Hodges's chief of staff noted. Word spread like wildfire to all command posts, to SHAEF and to the 12th Army Group in Luxembourg, where Hansen recorded that the news 'took the breath away from the room for an instant — as though the room had suddenly become a vacuum'. Major General Elwood R. Quesada of IX Tactical Air Command made sure that his pilots were fully briefed the next morning. Revenge was clearly going to be the order of the day.*

Peiper's spearhead pushed on to Ligneuville where it met heavy resistance for the first time in the form of American tanks. A short, fierce battle left a Panther and two half-

---

* When news of the massacre reached England, German army generals held prisoner there were shaken. 'What utter madness to shoot down defenceless men!' said one. 'All it means is that the Americans will take reprisals on our boys.' Another added: 'Of course the SS and the paratroopers are simply crazy, they just won't listen to reason.'

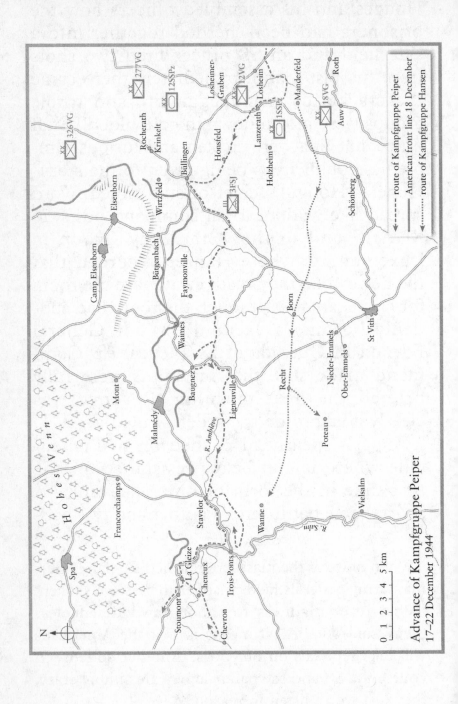

N

327VG

125SPz

Losheimer-
Graben

12VG

Losheim

Manderfeld

18VG

Roth

326VG

Rocherath

Krinkelt

Büllingen

Lanzerath

Losheim

1SSPz

Auw

Honsfeld

Holzheim

Elsenborn

Wirtzfeld

Schönberg

3FSJ

Bütgenbach

Camp Elsenborn

Faymonville

Born

St Vith

Waimes

Nieder-Emmels

Baugnez

Ligneuville

Recht

Ober-Emmels

Mont

R. Amblève

Malmédy

Wanne

Poteau

Francorchamps

Vielsalm

H o h e s   V e n n

Stavelot

R. Salm

Spa

La Gleize

Cheneux

Trois-Ponts

Stoumont

Chevron

route of Kampfgruppe Peiper

American front line 18 December

route of Kampfgruppe Hansen

Advance of Kampfgruppe Peiper
17–22 December 1944

0 1 2 3 4 5 km

tracks burning, while the Americans lost two Shermans and an M-10 tank destroyer. Peiper's men shot another eight American prisoners. Ahead in the town of Stavelot on the River Amblève, civilians were appalled to see their American liberators fleeing in vehicles. Many began to pack bags with their valuables and some food. They feared more German vengeance after the Resistance actions in September. Twenty-two men and women had been killed then in nearby Werbomont by German troops and Russian auxiliaries. The rush to escape beyond the River Meuse and the chaos which that would cause on the roads prompted the American authorities to forbid any civilian movement. Fortunately for the Americans and the fleeing Belgians, Peiper halted his column at dusk just short of Stavelot.

Since the main road was on the side of a very steep hill there was no room for Peiper's tanks to manoeuvre, and the sharp curve in the road just before entering the town meant that the defenders could focus all their anti-tank fire on one point. Peiper pulled back his Kampfgruppe and bombarded the village with mortar and artillery fire instead. Meanwhile he sent off some of his tanks to find a way to bypass Stavelot to the south, by crossing the River Salm at Trois-Ponts. But as other vehicles followed they were hit in the flank by a circuitous American counterattack from Stavelot. This was beaten off, but Peiper ordered another assault on the town, this time using his panzergrenadiers on foot. But after suffering nearly thirty casualties, he decided to wait for the rest of his panzergrenadier battalion to catch up. As night fell, the Kampfgruppe could see in the distance the lights of American military vehicles escaping to the west, so they opened fire with their tanks at maximum range on the road.

While the Peiper Kampfgruppe forged west down the valley of the Amblève, more battalions from the US 1st Division arrived to strengthen the southern approach to the Elsenborn ridge. The 2nd Battalion of the 26th Infantry prepared positions facing Büllingen during the afternoon. It was ready with four M-10 tank destroyers in support, to take on the advancing Germans who had been held back by American artillery fire from the ridge behind them.

The vital battle to defend the ridge was already taking place on its eastern flank around Rocherath–Krinkelt. General Robertson of the 2nd Division, having thrown his 23rd Infantry Regiment into a line east of the twin villages as the 99th Division was beaten back, began bringing the 38th Infantry back down the road from Wahlerscheid. A barrage by American artillery at midday kept the Germans' heads down as they pulled back from their forward positions. In such a confused situation, friendly fire was a real danger. That morning, a P-47 Thunderbolt pilot jettisoned his bombs to engage a Messerschmitt over the 3rd Battalion and caused twelve casualties.

With reinforced platoons flanking the eastern side of the Wahlerscheid–Rocherath road, General Robertson himself went out to meet the battalions with trucks to take them to the new positions near Rocherath.

At least the far left of the line, some fourteen kilometres north of Elsenborn, appeared solid. The 326th Volksgrenadier-Division had attempted one attack after another on either side of Monschau, but American artillery had broken each one. The new top-secret proximity, or Pozit, fuse was used on shells for the first time in action, without authority from higher command, but with great success as they exploded over the attackers in accurate air bursts.

An armoured infantry battalion from the 5th Armored Division would reach Mützenich to strengthen the line not long after dark. And to their rear the 18th Regiment from the 1st Infantry Division was starting its sweep of the forests south of Eupen, to deal with Heydte's isolated paratroopers. General Gerow was puzzled as to why the Sixth Panzer Army had not attacked in much greater strength on the northern flank, rather than concentrate its forces just south of the Elsenborn ridge. This was of course at Hitler's insistence, but Manteuffel still felt that Dietrich had made a great mistake in restricting himself to such a narrow frontage, with so little room for manoeuvre.

East of Rocherath–Krinkelt, as the light began to fade and the sound of firing came closer, the soldiers of Robertson's 2nd Division dug harder and harder to make their foxholes deep enough under the snow before the tanks of the SS *Hitler Jugend* Division hit them. Their sweat would turn very cold as soon as they stopped. There were chaotic scenes as the 1st Battalion of the 9th Infantry Regiment moved into its positions under fire from the wooded high ground to its east. Many of the men from the shattered 99th Division were so determined to escape that they would not listen to orders to halt and join the defensive line. 'Against this demoralizing picture, the Battalion moved in with orders to hold,' its commander, Lieutenant Colonel McKinley, reported. 'Streams of men and vehicles were pouring down the forest roads through the junction in wild confusion and disorder. Control in the 99th Division had been irretrievably lost and the stragglers echoed each other with remarks that their units had been surrounded and annihilated.

One of our own battalions from the 23rd Infantry had also been engulfed in what actually was a flight to the rear.'

McKinley's men laid 'daisy-chains' or 'necklaces' of six anti-tank mines each across any track or approach likely to be used by German tanks. The first attack came as darkness fell. Artillery fire along the length of the approach road proved effective, to judge by the 'screaming among the enemy'. During a lull, men slipped forward to lay anti-tank mines borrowed from the tank-destroyer battalion, and two-man bazooka teams improved their positions covering the road, knowing full well that they were in the target zone of their own artillery.

The American infantry's 57mm anti-tank gun stood little chance of knocking out a German Panther tank except from the side or rear, at close range. And tank-destroyer units with towed guns were at a severe disadvantage in the mud and snow, when limbering up to pull back. 'In heavy and close combat,' one analysis stated, 'the towing vehicle was often destroyed while the gun, dug in, remained intact.'

Lieutenant Colonel Barsanti of the 38th Infantry warned his platoon commanders that because of all the men from the 99th Division pulling back through their positions, they were not to open fire until they had positively identified the enemy. In the darkness it was impossible to be sure until they came close. As a result, two German tanks got through his K Company using their spotlights to blind the men looking out from their foxholes. But the two tanks were knocked out, one by artillery, the other by a bazooka team. Panzergrenadiers came close behind. 'One enemy soldier came so close to the position that he grabbed the barrel of a light machinegun and the gunner was forced to finish him off with a .45 pistol.'

Members of one company, forced to pull back from its forward position in a wood, 'plunged through the thickly interlaced branches of little firs. Bullets followed us,' their commander wrote, 'lashing the firs on all sides, and I wondered if maybe I had been hit. I felt no pain, but I could not see how any human being could endure those hails of bullets and not be wounded.' He wrote later of their escape back to Rocherath: 'I felt like we were helpless little bugs scurrying blindly about now that some man monster had lifted the log under which we had been hiding.'

The SS panzergrenadiers attacked using automatic weapons and throwing potato-masher grenades. One SS man seized a prisoner, and forced him to walk and answer challenges. Both he and his luckless human shield were shot down. Yet some stragglers who arrived from the 99th Division in the middle of this night battle were identified in time and not killed by their own side. A medic from the 99th also arrived, but he was a prisoner sent by the Germans. Apparently, some 150 Americans were surrounded by 200 Germans in the area shelled by the field artillery battalions on the Elsenborn ridge. 'The Germans had sent him to the US positions to try to get them to surrender on threat of annihilation of the prisoner GIs.'

During a lull in the battle, to the astonishment of the defenders, a large convoy of trucks full of troops from the 99th Division appeared. Their officers asked for directions to Camp Elsenborn. It was a miracle that they had come through the German units without being identified as American.

In the holding battle forward of Rocherath–Krinkelt, bazooka teams were sent to deal with the panzers. Whenever they achieved a hit, forcing the Germans inside to bale out, 'the crews were picked off by American riflemen', as Lieutenant Colonel McKinley observed. At 22.00 hours, two sergeants from his battalion grabbed a can of gasoline and crept up in the dark on a panzer, which although immobilized was causing heavy casualties with its machine gun and main armament. They poured the fuel over the tank and set it alight. Fifteen minutes later, a lieutenant stalked a Mark VI Tiger with a bazooka and knocked it out. But the attacks continued throughout the night in waves, and the main assault would not come until shortly before dawn the next morning.

In the south, Manteuffel's Fifth Panzer Army was having greater success against Cota's 28th Infantry Division due east of Bastogne. The 28th, which had been badly weakened in the Hürtgen Forest, was still short of men and weapons. But even though battered by the 116th Panzer-Division, the 2nd Panzer-Division and the Panzer Lehr, Cota's men managed to inflict considerable casualties and slow them down by holding crossroads and villages for as long as possible. The German corps commander considered the 28th to be 'a mediocre division with no reputation as a great fighting unit'. But although the 28th had certainly lost most of its experienced men in the Hürtgen Forest, some of its companies performed a heroic and vital role.

When fighting to defend a small town east of Wiltz, soldiers from Cota's 109th Infantry Regiment sighted tanks. They thought they were Mark VI Tigers, but they might have been Mark IVs which looked similar although much smaller. They had no anti-tank gun. 'A group of men nearby had a couple of bazookas and ammunition,' an officer recorded later, 'but said that they did not know how to use them. I took one and bumped right into a Tiger as I came round a corner. The tank was head on but I let it have one anyway, hitting it right in front. The tank stopped but was not damaged and fired its 88 at the house I had ducked behind. I then got up in the second story of an adjoining house where I was to the flank and above the tank. I fired two more shots at it; the first striking the rear deck at an angle. It exploded but the tank did not appear to notice it. My third shot hit the turret just above where it joins the hull of the tank. It didn't penetrate but a lot of sparks flew and it must have jarred the crew as the tank immediately backed up and withdrew to a position about 800 yards away from which they shelled us.' The bazooka was not as powerful as its shoulder-launched counterpart, the German Panzerfaust. From the front, all that could be achieved was a broken track. But if hunting groups managed to get round the back of a Tiger or a Panther with a bazooka, then they stood a chance. It was generally agreed that the anti-tank rifle grenade was a dangerous waste of time.

On the 28th Division's northern flank, the ancient town of Clervaux above the River Clerf came under threat. The attack of the 116th Panzer-Division to the north was pushing back the 112th Infantry of the 28th Division up into the 106th Division's sector, where it became the far-right flank in the defence of St Vith. Clervaux, where Colonel Fuller commanding the 110th Infantry had set up his command post in a hotel, was partly shielded by the resolute defence of Marnach by one of his companies. But the 2nd Panzer-Division forced on past this obstacle. At 05.00 on 17 December, a field artillery battery five kilometres north-east of Clervaux was overrun by panzergrenadiers.

Before dawn German patrols reached Clervaux, which had already been infiltrated by an artillery observation team equipped with a radio. Then infantry slipped in unobserved and concealed themselves in the pharmacy just below the mainly fifteenth-century castle, with round towers surmounted by spires like witches' hats. The castle still stands on a rocky spur projecting into the middle of the town, which curves round it in a horseshoe. By 09.30, Panther tanks and self-propelled assault guns were in action from the high ground overlooking Clervaux. General Cota sent a platoon of Shermans and some infantry to help Fuller, who had no more than his regimental headquarters personnel and sixty men retrieved from the divisional rest centre. As darkness fell that afternoon, Fuller reported to Cota in Wiltz that the town was surrounded and a panzer was 'sitting in his front door firing in'. At an aid station someone called out, 'If you're a Jewish GI, throw your dog tags away because there are SS troops here.' At least one soldier tossed his, marked with an 'H' for 'Hebrew', into a pot-bellied stove.

The headquarters personnel with soldiers from the rest centre pulled back to the castle, where they continued to hold out on the following day. Among the civilians sheltering in the castle was the sixteen-year-old Jean Servé, who described how in one room a GI was playing the piano while an American sniper, with a cigarette hanging from his lips, was calmly shooting Germans, one after another. Servé watched as one of his victims rolled down the hill behind the Hôtel du Parc. As the battle continued, the wounded were placed in the cellars along with the civilians. But soon the defenders ran out of ammunition, and with the castle on fire they had no choice but to surrender.

Next to the 28th Division on the southern flank was General Barton's 4th Infantry Division. It too had been badly weakened in the Hürtgen Forest, but at least its attackers were less formidable than Manteuffel's panzer divisions. Barton's 12th Infantry Regiment held the towns of Dickweiler, Echternach, Osweiler, Lauterborn and Berdorf against the 212th Volksgrenadier-Division. His plan had been to deny the Germans use of the road network west of the Sauer by occupying villages and hamlets at key intersections with a company apiece. The main thrust hit the 2nd Battalion of the 22nd Infantry Regiment, but it held its ground. Almost all these defended points were surrounded. But by the evening of 17 December the situation had been stabilized with the arrival of task forces from the 10th Armored Division, and they were soon relieved.

The 'Tigers of the Tenth' moved north through Luxembourg on 17 December. The news that they were to lead the fight back against the offensive was greeted with elation, for they had feared they were destined to be a rearguard. Late that afternoon, Combat Command A under Brigadier General Edwin W. Piburn 'rolled headlong into a very surprised German force' near the Schwarz Erntz gorge. The battle continued for three days, but the German advance was halted. The southern shoulder was secure.

At First Army headquarters in Spa, however, the mood on the evening of 17 December was sombre, with the Peiper Kampfgruppe forging west and the 28th Division unable to hold back Manteuffel's panzer divisions. 'The G-2 estimate tonight', the war diary recorded, 'says that the enemy is capable of attempting to exploit his initial gains by driving through our rear areas and seizing bridgeheads over the Meuse river.'

The greatest threat was to Bastogne. The Panzer Lehr Division was heading due west straight for its southern side, while the 2nd Panzer-Division was aiming to circumvent it to the north. The 26th Volksgrenadier-

Division was to take the town. They all received orders from General der Panzertruppe Heinrich Freiherr von Lüttwitz, who commanded the XLVII Panzer Corps. The 5th Fallschirmjäger-Division to the south was held up at Wiltz by Cota's 28th Division. There was no mention of Bastogne in its orders from the Seventh Army. It was just told 'to advance as rapidly as possible, to secure a large enough area for General von Manteuffel's Fifth Panzer Army to maneuver in'. But that afternoon Lüttwitz suddenly became aware of Bastogne's importance to the Americans. His headquarters intercepted a radio message saying that an airborne division would be coming to Bastogne in convoys of trucks. This presumably came from the US military police radio net, which broadcast in clear and gave the Germans some of their best intelligence. Lüttwitz was confident that his panzer divisions would get there first.

After their extended combat role in Holland in waterlogged foxholes, both the 82nd and the 101st Airborne Divisions were recuperating at the French camp of Mourmelon-le-Grand near Reims. Their rest period had consisted of playing football, compulsive gambling, drinking cheap champagne and indulging in bar-room brawls between the two divisions. The decision taken that morning in Versailles to pass XVIII Airborne Corps from SHAEF reserve to the First Army at first led to a good deal of confusion. A number of senior officers were absent. Major General Matthew B. Ridgway, the corps commander, happened to be in England. Major General Maxwell D. Taylor, the commander of the 101st, was back in the United States. His deputy, Brigadier General Gerald J. Higgins, was also in England, lecturing on Operation Market Garden. So Brigadier General Anthony C. McAuliffe, the 101st Division's artillery commander, had to take their men into battle.

McAuliffe, on receiving the order at 20.30 hours to prepare to move, immediately summoned unit commanders and staff for a meeting. 'All I know of the situation', he told them, 'is that there has been a breakthrough and we have got to get up there.' Many of their men were on leave in Paris, determined to enjoy themselves in an unrestrained airborne way, especially those who, following their wartime tradition, had pinned their 'Dear John' letters from unfaithful sweethearts on the unit noticeboard. Orders went out to the military police in Paris to round up all the airborne personnel, while an officer commandeered a train to bring them back. Many of those snatched back from leave were the worse for wear from their excesses. And 'most of them, to hear them tell it,' remarked Louis Simpson, 'were suffering from *coitus interruptus*'. There had been a good deal of jealousy from those who had lost all their back pay gambling and could not afford to go.

The 101st was well below strength and had not yet been re-equipped. Some 3,500 men had been lost during the fighting in Holland, and the division received comparatively few replacements during its time at Mourmelon. So after receipt of the movement order, prisoners on disciplinary sentences, mostly for fighting or striking an NCO, were released from the stockade and ordered to report immediately to their companies. Officers went to the military hospital and called for those almost cured to discharge themselves. On the other hand, some commanders advised their officers to leave behind any men whose nerves were still badly shaken. There had been several suicides from combat fatigue in the previous ten days, including the divisional chief of staff who had put his .45 automatic in his mouth and pulled the trigger.

The 82nd had had more time to integrate replacements and re-equip after the losses in Holland, while the 101st was short of everything, especially winter clothing. During that night, everyone tried to beg, borrow or steal whatever they were missing. Quartermasters simply opened their stores. Com Z, meanwhile, rose to the challenge of assembling enough ten-ton trucks to move two divisions.

Their exhausted drivers, who had been with the Red Ball Express, were not exactly enthusiastic at the prospect of delivering airborne troops to the front line in the Ardennes, but they more than did their duty.

Even though SHAEF tried to suppress news of the German advance, word spread rapidly. The rumour was that the Germans were heading for Paris. French collaborators in prison began to celebrate and taunt their guards. This was unwise. Many of their jailers came from the Resistance and they swore that they would shoot every one of them before the Germans arrived.

Partly due to the lack of clear information, anxiety in Paris had reached a feverish level. General Alphonse Juin accompanied by other senior French officers came to SHAEF at Versailles to discuss the breakthrough. They were met by General Bedell Smith. 'As we walked through the halls,' Bedell Smith wrote later, 'I saw the officers casting puzzled glances into offices where normal routine seemed to be going on. Then a French general behind me said to our Intelligence Chief, General Strong: "What! You are not packing?" '

Ernest Hemingway heard of the German attack at the Ritz in the Place Vendôme, where he was installed with his paramour, Mary Welsh. She had returned from a dinner with the air force commander Lieutenant

General 'Tooey' Spaatz, during which aides had rushed in and out bearing urgent messages. The Ritz lobby was in chaos, with officers running backwards and forwards. Although still not recovered from the bronchitis he had picked up in the Hürtgen Forest, Hemingway was determined to rejoin the 4th Infantry Division. He started to pack and assemble his illegal armoury. 'There's been a complete breakthrough,' he told his brother Leicester, who was passing through Paris. 'This thing could cost us the works. Their armor is pouring in. They're taking no prisoners . . . Load those clips. Wipe every cartridge clean.'

10
MONDAY 18 DECEMBER

The main attack against the last battalion of the 2nd Infantry Division in front of Rocherath–Krinkelt came at 06.45 hours, more than an hour before dawn. The Germans followed their usual practice of making the maximum amount of noise in night attacks, with 'yells, catcalls and many other forms of noises including banging on mess gear'. The battle continued for four hours, with the American field artillery taking on fire mission after fire mission in support of the forward infantry foxholes. In a number of cases, companies were calling for fire on their own positions as they were overrun. Lieutenant Colonel McKinley's 1st Battalion of the 9th Infantry Regiment had covered other units as they pulled back to the twin villages.

Again at first light twelve panzers, each escorted by a platoon of panzergrenadiers, advanced out of the mist until halted by artillery fire. The 2nd Division found that it would have been far more useful to have a dozen bazooka teams than three 'cumbersome' 57mm anti-tank guns in the anti-tank platoon. 'The 57mm anti-tank guns proved very unsatisfactory, only one effective hit being scored on the turret of one enemy tank,' an after-action report stated. Another officer described it as 'practically a useless weapon'. Lieutenant Colonel McKinley thought the 57mm had 'no place in an infantry battalion', because it was so hard to manoeuvre in mud, and it was impossible to put into position if the enemy was already in contact. He wanted tank destroyers as an integral part of the unit so that they did not disappear whenever they felt like it. But that day at Rocherath–Krinkelt, tank destroyers, as well as Shermans, bazookas and the artillery accounted for a number of Panther and Mark IV tanks.

The Americans always tried to prevent the Germans from recovering and repairing disabled panzers, or from using them as temporary firing positions just in front of their lines. So whenever the SS panzergrenadiers were forced back 'tanks knocked out of action, but not destroyed, were set afire with gasoline-oil mixes poured on them, and with thermite grenades set in gunbarrels which burned through the barrels'.

But then another attack overran the front line. Panzers fired down into the foxholes, and twisted back and forth on top to bury the men in them. Only twelve soldiers from one platoon of around thirty men emerged alive. The left-hand platoon of one company had no anti-tank ammunition left, so some six or seven men started to run towards the rear in despair. McKinley stopped them and sent them back to their platoon. Aid men, struggling heroically to evacuate the wounded through the snow, improvised sleds by nailing raised crosspieces to a pair of skis to carry a litter.

In due course the battalion received orders to pull back, but the fighting was so close that McKinley felt that he would not be able to extricate any of his men. At the critical moment, however, four Shermans from the 741st Tank Battalion appeared. They were able to cover the withdrawal, even scoring hits on three German tanks. 'When the Battalion assembled in Rocherath,' McKinley recorded, 'it was found that of the total strength of 600 men that had started the fight, 197 were left, including attachments.' Yet only nine men from the whole of the 2nd Division abandoned the battle and headed for the rear. They were picked up by military police as 'stragglers'. Most men found that they did not get the 'shakes' at the height of a battle: it hit them afterwards when the firing had died away.

The sacrificial stand of the 1st Battalion of the 9th Infantry Regiment helped save the rest of the 2nd Division, and thwart the breakthrough of the 12th SS Panzer-Division. But even McKinley acknowledged afterwards that 'it was artillery that did the job', saving his unit from complete destruction. All the time remnants of the 99th Division, which had faced the initial onslaught, continued to slip through to American lines. They were directed back to Camp Elsenborn where they were fed and ammunitioned, then placed in a new line behind Rocherath–Krinkelt. One battalion commander, accused by his own officers of 'cowardice and incompetence', was relieved.

Around 10.00, a group of seven American trucks approached. A tank destroyer fired a round over the leading truck at a range of 500 metres, compelling it to halt. A patrol went forward to make sure that the trucks were genuine, and not captured vehicles. But as they came close, men in the trucks opened fire. It had been a 'Trojan Horse trick' to penetrate American lines in the confusion. Around 140 German soldiers leaped from the trucks and tried to escape back towards the woods. The battalion's mortars and heavy machine guns opened up, and the battalion commander estimated that three-quarters of them were killed, but a number may have feigned death and crept away later. Several of the wounded were taken prisoner, and proved to be members of the 12th SS Division *Hitler*

Jugend. One of the more badly hit refused a transfusion of American blood at the aid station.

The battle for the twin villages continued, with civilians trapped and deafened from explosions in their cellars. As the fog lifted at about 08.30 hours and daylight strengthened a little, the woods beyond the snowfields became visible. More Panther and Mark IV tanks advanced accompanied by groups of panzergrenadiers and some broke into Rocherath–Krinkelt. The mortar officer in the 38th Infantry Regiment formed four bazooka teams, for stalking tanks around the village. Some men wore goggles because of the flash when firing, but only noticed the burns on their face later. The worst fate was to find a dud round stuck in the bazooka and see the enemy tank traverse its gun towards you. Guile was needed. 'A tank was observed approaching on a road,' V Corps reported. 'A sergeant stationed a bazooka in concealment on each side of the road, and then drove a herd of cows out in front of the tank. The tank slowed to a halt, was knocked out by bazooka fire, and the crew killed by small arms fire as they baled out.'

German tanks began blasting houses at point-blank range, even sticking their gun through a window. 'The bayonet was little used,' another American officer observed later, 'even in close-in fighting in Rocherath where rifle butts or bare fists seemingly took preference.' Two Shermans parked by the battalion command post in Rocherath and crewed by a mixture of 'gunners, drivers, assistant drivers, cooks and mechanics' fought back. Lieutenant Colonel Robert N. Skaggs suddenly saw a Mark VI Tiger tank approaching some American soldiers guarding German prisoners of war. Skaggs alerted the two tanks and they both opened fire. They missed. The Tiger halted and traversed its turret to fire back at both of them, but both of its shots also missed. Allowed a second chance, the scratch crews of the two Shermans made sure that they did not miss again, and the Tiger burst into flames. As soon as a German tank was hit, American infantry brought their rifles up to their shoulders ready to shoot down any of the crew trying to escape from the turret or hull. If they were on fire and screaming, then they were simply putting the poor bastard out of his misery. Captain MacDonald of the 2nd Division 'saw a soldier silhouetted against the tracers, throw a can of gasoline at a tank. The tank burst into flames.'

In another incident in the twin villages, the crew of a Sherman of the 741st Tank Battalion 'observed a Mark VI [Tiger] approaching frontally. The tank commander knew the difficulty of penetrating the frontal armor, and desired to utilize the faster turret action of the Sherman. The tank was quickly turned round and routed round a small group of buildings to enable the Sherman to bring fire to bear on the side or rear of the Mark VI. The German simultaneously sensing the maneuver followed, and the two tanks were chasing each other round in a circle endeavoring to get into position to fire. The team mate of the Sherman observed the action, [and] as the Mark VI in its course around the buildings exposed its rear, brought fire to bear on it and knocked it out.' The two commanders jumped out to shake hands jubilantly, climbed back into their tanks and then went back to work.

Rifle grenades again proved useless, and only one tank was disabled in this way. A sergeant saw a 'man from another outfit' fire six or seven rounds of anti-tank grenades at a panzer, and although they were hitting the target they had no effect. In other cases too, the grenades 'just glanced off'.

One Mark VI Tiger in Krinkelt in front of the church began firing at the battalion command post. Lieutenant Colonel Barsanti sent out five bazooka teams to stalk the tank. They achieved two hits, but the Tiger was barely damaged. Even so, its commander decided that it was too exposed in the village and made a run for it towards Wirtzfeld. But as the tank charged off, it rounded a corner at full speed and flattened a Jeep. The two occupants had managed to throw themselves into a ditch just in time. This slowed the Tiger just enough for the crew of a 57mm anti-tank gun to get off a round which wrecked the turret traverse mechanism. As it continued on its way, a Sherman fired and missed, but a tank destroyer further down the road brought it to a halt with two rounds. Riflemen then picked off the black-uniformed crew as they tried to escape. 'None of them got away.'

The 2nd Division later claimed that in the extended battle around Rocherath–Krinkelt seventy-three panzers had been knocked out by Shermans, bazookas, tank destroyers and artillery, while two Mark VI Tigers had been knocked out by bazookas. These, of course, were rare victories during that onslaught. American losses in men and tanks were very heavy. On the other hand, the determination to fight back and make the enemy pay dearly for every step of his advance proved probably the most important contribution to the eventual outcome of the Ardennes offensive. The Sixth Panzer Army had underestimated both the power of American artillery and the commanding position of the Elsenborn ridge. The SS divisions were sharply disabused of their arrogant assumptions about the low quality of American infantry units.

The fighting went on all day and into the night, with more and more buildings ablaze. The artillery observer from the 99th Division who had been sent forward to Buchholz on the first evening gazed at the conflagration in Rocherath–Krinkelt and kept thinking of a line from an Alan Seeger poem: 'But I've a rendezvous with death at midnight in some flaming town.'

While the fighting in Rocherath–Krinkelt reached its climax, part of the 1st Infantry Division five kilometres to the south-west was consolidating its positions and patrolling to establish the direction and strength of the German advance. Sepp Dietrich, frustrated by the fierce American defence of the twin villages, ordered the 277th Volksgrenadier-Division to continue the attack there. The 12th SS Panzer meanwhile was to move to the south-west, and advance from Büllingen and push further west towards Waimes. The small town of Waimes contained the 47th Evacuation Hospital and part of the 99th Division's medical battalion. General Gerow ordered a mixed force from the 1st Division with tank destroyers, light tanks and engineers to extricate the medics and the wounded in time.

The *Hitler Jugend* was to find that the southern flank of the Elsenborn ridge was as strongly held as the eastern flank. The 1st Division alone was backed by six battalions of artillery and a battery of 8-inch guns. The Americans were also fortunate that the ground was so soft in many places that it made off-road movement for the German tanks almost impossible. When American anti-tank guns and tank destroyers knocked out the leading panzer on a road, the others were blocked. Anti-aircraft half-tracks with quadruple .50 machine guns known as 'meatchoppers' then proved very effective in forcing back the SS panzergrenadiers.

Neither General Gerow nor General Hodges had any idea that Hitler had forbidden the Sixth Panzer Army to head north towards Liège. The Führer, wanting to avoid the concentration of American forces around Aachen, had dictated that the SS panzer divisions strike due west towards the Meuse and not vary their route. But Peiper's direction of advance had already convinced the American command that they had to extend the northern shoulder westward. General Ridgway's XVIII Airborne Corps was to establish a defensive line from Stavelot, deploying both the experienced 30th Infantry Division and the 82nd Airborne, which was already heading for Werbomont.

Following the Malmédy massacre of the day before, the American command issued an urgent warning to all troops: 'It is dangerous at any time to surrender to German tank crews, and especially so to tanks unaccompanied by infantry; or to surrender to any units making a rapid advance. These units have few means for handling prisoners, and a solution used is merely to kill the prisoners.' The lesson was: 'Those that fought it out received fewer losses. Those that surrendered did not have a chance.'

Peiper launched his attack on Stavelot at dawn, having let his exhausted men catch up on sleep during the night. Major Paul J. Solis had arrived in the early hours with a company of the 526th Armored Infantry Battalion, a platoon of anti-tank guns and a platoon of towed tank destroyers. He was still positioning his men and guns when they were surprised by two Panther tanks and a company of panzergrenadiers, charging around the hillside on the road to the bridge over the Amblève. The first Panther was hit and caught fire, but it had built up such momentum that it smashed into the anti-tank barrier erected across the road. The second Panther pushed on and occupied the bridge in Stavelot, to be followed rapidly by the panzergrenadiers.

The Americans did not have time to blow up the bridge. Solis's force was driven back into the town. Peiper's men alleged, without any justification, that Belgian civilians fired on them and they proceeded to shoot twenty-three of them, including women. After heavy fighting throughout the morning, Solis's small force had to withdraw a little way up the road to Francorchamps and Spa. The main American fuel dump at Francorchamps had not been marked on Peiper's map, and he decided to carry on west along the valley of the Amblève. In any case, General Lee's Communications Zone troops had succeeded in evacuating the bulk of the fuel supplies potentially within Peiper's grasp. Between 17 and 19 December, American supply troops removed more than 3 million gallons of fuel from the Spa–Stavelot area. The biggest Allied loss was 400,000 gallons, destroyed on 17 December by a V-1 strike on Liège.

That afternoon a misleading report reached Hodges's headquarters that Spa itself was threatened. General Joe Collins, who was sitting next to the First Army commander, heard its chief intelligence officer whisper to Hodges: 'General, if you don't get out of town pretty quickly, you are going to be captured.'

'The situation is rapidly deteriorating,' the headquarters diary noted. 'About three o'clock this afternoon there were reports that tanks were coming up from Stavelot headed towards Spa. Only a small roadblock and half-tracks stood between them and our headquarters.' Hodges rang Simpson, the Ninth Army commander, at 16.05. 'He says that the situation is pretty bad,' Simpson recorded. 'He is ready to pull out his establishment. He is threatened, he says.' Spa was evacuated, and the whole of First Army staff

317

moved to its rear headquarters at Chaudfontaine near Liège, which they reached at midnight. They learned later that, as soon as they left Spa, 'American flags, pictures of the President and all other Allied insignia were taken down and that the mayor released 20 suspected collaborationists out of jail.'

Earlier that evening two officers from the 7th Armored Division, who had just returned from leave, found that their formation had left Maastricht. Setting out to find them, they first went to Spa and in Hodges's abandoned headquarters they gazed in astonishment at the situation maps which had not been removed in the rush to evacuate. They took them down and carried on to St Vith, where they handed them over to Brigadier General Bruce Clarke. Clarke studied the maps in dismay. They revealed, as nothing else could, the First Army's failure to understand what was going on. 'Hell, when this fight's over,' Clarke said, 'there's going to be enough grief court-martialling generals. I'm not in the mood for making any more trouble.' He promptly destroyed them.

Peiper, in an attempt to find an alternative route, had sent off a reconnaissance force of two companies south of the Amblève to Trois-Ponts, a village on the confluence of the Amblève and the Salm. It appears that they became hopelessly lost in the dark. From Trois-Ponts the road lay straight to Werbomont. Peiper, having forced the Americans out of Stavelot, left behind a small detachment on the assumption that troops from the 3rd Fallschirmjäger-Division would arrive, and then set off for Trois-Ponts himself.

The 51st Engineer Battalion, which had been based at Marche-en-Famenne operating sawmills, had received orders the evening before to make for Trois-Ponts to blow the three bridges there. Company C arrived while Peiper's force was attacking Stavelot and set to work placing demolition charges on the bridge over the Amblève and the two bridges over the Salm. They also erected roadblocks across the road along which the Peiper Kampfgruppe would come. A 57mm anti-tank gun and its crew were pressed into service, as was a company of the 526th Armored Infantry Battalion on its way to St Vith to join up with the rest of the 7th Armored Division.

At 11.15 hours, the defenders of Trois-Ponts heard the grinding rumble of tanks approaching. Peiper's vanguard included nineteen Panthers. The crew of the 57mm anti-tank gun were ready and its first round hit the track of the leading Panther, bringing it to a halt. The other tanks opened fire and destroyed the gun, killing most of its crew. At the sound of firing the engineers blew up the bridges. Peiper's route to Werbomont was blocked. The defenders in houses on the west bank opened fire on panzergrenadiers trying to cross the river. Using various ruses, including a truck towing chains to make the noise of tanks and infantrymen firing bazookas to imitate artillery, the defenders convinced Peiper that their force was much stronger than it was.

Furious at this setback, Peiper decided to return to Stavelot and take the road along the north bank of the Amblève instead. His column thundered along the road towards La Gleize. The steep, forested slopes on the north side of the valley allowed no room for manoeuvre. Peiper still felt that, if only he had enough fuel, 'it would have been a simple matter to drive through to the River Meuse early that day'.

Finding no resistance in La Gleize, Peiper sent off a reconnaissance group who discovered a bridge intact over the Amblève at Cheneux. They were seen by an American spotter aircraft flying under the cloud. Fighter-bombers from IX Tactical Air Command were alerted and soon dived into the attack, despite the bad visibility. The Kampfgruppe lost three tanks and five half-tracks. Peiper's column was saved from further punishment by the early fall of darkness at 16.30 hours, but the Americans now knew exactly where they were. The 1st SS Panzer Corps, which had been out of radio contact with Peiper, also found out by intercepting the Americans' insecure transmissions.

Peiper pushed on under the cover of darkness but when the lead vehicle reached a bridge over the Lienne, a small tributary of the Amblève, it was blown up in their faces by a detachment from the 291st Engineer Combat Battalion. Peiper, who suffered from heart problems, must have nearly had a stroke at this further setback. He sent a tank company to find another bridge to the north, but just as they thought they had found one unguarded, they were attacked in a well-executed ambush. It was in any case a fruitless diversion because the bridge was not strong enough for their seventy-two-ton Königstiger tanks. Thwarted and with no more bridges left to try, the column turned round with great difficulty on the narrow road and returned to La Gleize to rejoin the Amblève valley to Stoumont three kilometres further on. Peiper halted the column to rest for the night before attacking Stoumont at dawn. This at least gave civilians in the village the chance to get away.

Peiper had no idea that American forces were closing in. A regiment of the 30th Infantry Division already lay ahead, blocking the valley road another two and a half kilometres further on, and the 82nd Airborne was starting to deploy from Werbomont. The trap was also closing behind him. A battalion from another regiment in the 30th Infantry

Division, strengthened with tanks and tank destroyers, relieved Major Solis's men north of Stavelot, and that evening fought its way into the northern part of the town.

While the 82nd Airborne had rushed on ahead to Werbomont, the 101st started to mount up back at Mourmelon-le-Grand. A long line of 380 ten-ton open trucks were waiting to take up to fifty men apiece. Roll calls by company took place. Men bundled up 'in their winter clothing looked like an assembly of bears'. Many, however, lacked greatcoats and even their paratrooper jumpboots. One lieutenant colonel, who had just arrived back from a wedding in London, would march into Bastogne still in his ceremonial Class A uniform. The division band, which had been ordered to stay behind, formed up in angry mood. Its members asked the chaplain whether he could speak to the commander of the 501st Parachute Infantry Regiment, to persuade him to allow them to go. He said that the colonel was too busy, but tacitly agreed that they could always climb aboard with the others. He knew that every man would be needed.

The first trucks left at 12.15 with airborne engineers, the reconnaissance platoon and part of divisional headquarters. The orders were to head for Werbomont. Brigadier General McAuliffe left almost immediately, and two hours later the first part of the main column set off. Altogether 805 officers and 11,035 enlisted men were going into battle. Nobody knew exactly where they were headed, and many thought it strange that they were not going to parachute into battle, but were being transported in like ordinary 'straight-leg' infantry. Packed into the open trucks, they shivered in the cold. The column did not stop, and as there was no room to move to the back to relieve themselves over the tailgate, they passed around an empty jerrycan instead. When darkness fell later in the afternoon, the drivers switched on their headlights. The need for speed was deemed to be greater than the risk of encountering a German night-fighter.

When McAuliffe reached Neufchâteau, thirty kilometres south-west of Bastogne, an MP flagged down his command car. He was given a message from Middleton's VIII Corps headquarters to say that the 101st Airborne had been attached to his command, and that the whole division should head straight for Bastogne. The advance party, unaware of the change of plan, had already gone on to Werbomont, forty kilometres further north as the crow flies. McAuliffe and his staff officers drove on to Bastogne and, just before dark, found General Troy Middleton's corps headquarters in a former German barracks on the north-west edge of the town. The scenes of panic-stricken drivers and soldiers fleeing on foot heading west were not an encouraging sight.

McAuliffe found Middleton briefing Colonel William L. Roberts of Combat Command B of the 10th Armored Division, one of the two formations which Eisenhower had ordered to the Ardennes that first evening. Roberts had a better idea of how desperate the situation was than McAuliffe. That morning General Norman Cota had sent him an urgent request to come to the aid of his battered 28th Division near Wiltz, where the 5th Fallschirmjäger-Division was attacking. But Roberts had received firm orders to go straight to Bastogne, so was forced to refuse. The Panzer Lehr Division and the 26th Volksgrenadier had already broken through just to the north, heading for the town.

'How many teams can you make up?' Middleton asked Roberts.

'Three,' he replied.

Middleton ordered him to send one team to the south-east of Wardin, and another to Longvilly to block the advance of the Panzer Lehr. The third was to go north to Noville to stop the 2nd Panzer-Division. Although Roberts did not like the idea of splitting his force into such small groups, he did not contest Middleton's decision. 'Move with the utmost speed,' Middleton told him. 'Hold these positions at all costs.'

■ ■ ■ ■

In the race for Bastogne, hold-ups on the roads caused tempers to flare in the XLVII Panzer Corps. But the main setback to the timetable had been caused by the courage of individual companies from the 28th Infantry Division. Their defence of road junctions along the north–south ridge road known as 'Skyline Drive', at villages such as Heiner-scheid, Marnach and Hosingen, had made a critical difference. 'The long resistance of Hosingen', Generalmajor Heinz Kokott acknowledged, 'resulted in the delay of the whole advance of 26th Volksgrenadier-Division and thereby of Panzer Lehr by one and a half days.' Company K's defence of Hosingen until the morning of 18 December, as the commander of Panzer Lehr also recognized, had slowed his division so much that it 'arrived too late in the Bastogne area'. This proved decisive for the battle of Bastogne, when every hour counted.

General Cota in Wiltz knew that his division was doomed. He ordered unsorted Christmas mail to be destroyed to keep it from the Germans, so letters, cards and packages were piled up in a courtyard, doused with gasoline and set on fire. During the afternoon, the remnants of the 3rd Battalion of the 110th Infantry fell back towards Wiltz.

The hungry and exhausted men formed up to defend the howitzers of a field artillery battalion south-east of Wiltz, while Cota prepared to pull his divisional command post back to Sibret, south-west of Bastogne.

That morning, in mist and drizzle, the spearhead of the Panzer Lehr had finally crossed the bridge over the River Clerf near Drauffelt while the 2nd Panzer-Division crossed at Clervaux, having been delayed by the defence of the town and its castle. Congestion was then caused by tanks breaking down — the Panthers were still the most susceptible to mechanical failure — while the horse-drawn artillery of an infantry division struggling on the same muddy track as armoured formations produced furious scenes.

The commander of Panzer Lehr, Generalleutnant Fritz Bayerlein, a short and aggressive veteran of North Africa and Normandy, blamed his corps commander for having allowed this chaos. Congestion was so bad that the marching infantry of the 26th Volksgrenadier reached Nieder Wampach at about the same time as the panzer troops in their tanks and half-tracks. When vehicles bogged down in the mud, infantrymen took their heavy machine guns and mortars off the vehicles and carried them on their shoulders.

As darkness was falling on 18 December, and the Panzer Lehr advanced on Bastogne, Bayerlein witnessed a tank battle going on

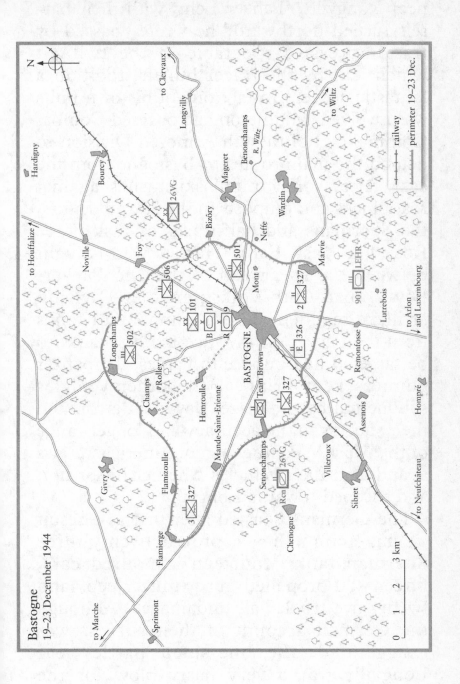

Bastogne
19–23 December 1944

N

to Marche
Sprimont

to Houffalize
Hardigny
Bourcy
Noville
Foy
Longchamps
Champs
Rolley
Givry
Flamierge
Flamizoulle
Hemroulle
Mande-Saint-Etienne
3 327
502
506
101
B 10
R 9
BASTOGNE
Team Brown
1 327
Senonchamps
Chenogne
Rcn 26VG
Villeroux
Sibret
Assenois
Hompré
to Neufchâteau
326
E
2 327
Mont
Neffe
Marvie
Lutrebois
Remonfosse
901 LEHR
to Arlon
and Luxembourg
Bizôry
501
Magaret
Benonchamps
R. Wiltz
Wardin
26VG
to Clervaux
Longvilly
to Wiltz

railway
perimeter 19–23 Dec.

0   1   2   3 km

near Longvilly. 'Panzer Lehr, with their barrels turned northward,' he wrote, 'passed by this impressive spectacle in the twilight which, cut by the tracer bullets, took on a fantastic aspect.' In fact one of his own units was involved. Middleton had ordered Combat Command R of the 9th Armored Division to defend the main routes to Bastogne from the east. After some initial skirmishes against roadblocks and outposts in the late afternoon, the Shermans and half-tracks of Task Force Rose and Task Force Harper were caught between the spearhead of the 2nd Panzer-Division, a 26th Volksgrenadier-Division artillery regiment, and a company of tanks from the Panzer Lehr. Once the first tanks to be targeted had burst into flames, the panzer gunners kept firing at the other vehicles silhouetted by the blaze. Bayerlein attributed their success to the accuracy and longer range of the Mark V Panther's gun. American crews abandoned their vehicles whether hit or not, and escaped towards Longvilly.

The Germans boasted later that as a result of this action they captured twenty-three Sherman tanks, fourteen armoured cars, fifteen self-propelled guns, thirty Jeeps and twenty-five trucks, all undamaged. Although the German account of their success was exaggerated, the one-sided battle near Longvilly was a very nasty blow for the Americans.

■ ■ ■

The only welcome development that evening in Bastogne was the arrival of the 705th Tank Destroyer Battalion, which had managed to fight its way through from the north. Colonel Roberts of the 10th Armored Division had already briefed his three team leaders and sent them on their way. Each had a mixture of Sherman tanks, armoured cars and half-tracks carrying the infantry. Team O'Hara set off to Wardin where it took up position on some high ground just to the south of the village. There was no sign of the Germans, but small groups of exhausted men from the 28th Division, bearded and filthy from three days of fighting, came through heading for Bastogne.

Major William R. Desobry of the 20th Armored Infantry Battalion was ordered north to Noville. An MP led the way in a Jeep to put him on the right road as they had no maps. On reaching the edge of Bastogne, the MP said: 'Noville is two towns up, straight down the road.' Desobry sent the reconnaissance platoon on ahead, through Foy and on to Noville. Both villages were deserted.

Desobry set up a defence on the north and eastern side of Noville with outposts of infantry squads and pairs of Sherman tanks guarding the roads coming in, then got some sleep soon after midnight. He knew that there was a big battle to come. 'We could hear gunfire out to the east and to the north and we could see flashes. We could see searchlights and so on. During the night a number of small units came back into our lines and a lot of stragglers. They essentially told us horror stories about how their units had been over-run by large German units with lots of tanks, Germans in American uniforms, Germans in civilian clothes and all sorts of weird tales.'

Roberts had given Desobry the authority to grab any stragglers and take them under command, but he found that their 'physical condition and mental condition was such' that it was easier to send them on to the rear. The only groups that seemed to be worth taking on were an infantry platoon from the 9th Armored Division and a platoon of engineers, but even the engineers were sent on their way the next morning. Reinforcements were coming in the shape of paratroopers, but Desobry sensed that the Germans would attack before they arrived.

Lieutenant Colonel Henry T. Cherry's team, with the 3rd Tank Battalion, a company of infantry, some engineers and a platoon of the 90th Cavalry Squadron, advanced from Bastogne towards Longvilly and the sound of firing. They halted short of the village, whose narrow street was jammed with rear-echelon vehicles from Combat Command R. Colonel

Cherry went forward on foot to find out what was happening, but none of the officers in their temporary command post seemed to have any idea of the situation. As at Wardin, stragglers from the 28th were retreating to Bastogne.

Cherry positioned his tanks and infantry a kilometre west of Longvilly and returned to report to Colonel Roberts in Bastogne. He set off back to his men shortly before midnight, and heard over the radio that the remnants of Combat Command R of the 9th Armored Division had pulled out completely. On reaching Neffe, Cherry was warned by a wounded soldier that the road ahead had been cut at Mageret by a reconnaissance group from the Panzer Lehr. Cherry called one of his officers on the radio to tell him to send a small force back to clear them out. But when the half-track with two squads of infantry reached Mageret, they found the German force consisted of three tanks and a company of infantry.

When Colonel Cherry heard what they had discovered, he knew that Longvilly could not be defended, despite Colonel Roberts's admonition to hold it 'at all costs'. He ordered his team to pull back to Neffe, fighting their way through if necessary. Cherry, having spotted an ancient chateau with thick walls, decided to set up his command post there. Like Desobry, he sensed that the real battle would start in the morning.

Even though his panzer divisions had at last broken through in the south, General der Panzertruppe von Manteuffel was furious at the delays in capturing St Vith. Part of the trouble came from the fact that the only roads west led through the town, and the boundary with the Sixth Panzer Army lay just six kilometres to the north. And since, in Manteuffel's view, Dietrich's army was already attacking on far too narrow a front, some of his forces had moved on to Fifth Panzer Army routes, increasing the traffic chaos.

Shortly after dawn, the Germans attacked Hasbrouck's defence line in front of St Vith. Panzers fired tree bursts, bringing down pine branches which made the Americans duck deep in their foxholes. Volksgrenadiers attacked, firing automatic weapons. The 18th Volksgrenadier-Division was considerably more experienced than the 62nd advancing towards the south of St Vith. A second attack late in the morning was supported by a massive Ferdinand self-propelled gun, but a Sherman knocked it out twenty-five metres from the American positions with an armour-piercing round which bounced and penetrated its belly.

A Greyhound armoured car concealed in some trees slipped in behind a Tiger tank on the Schönberg road so as to fire its puny 37mm gun at point-blank range. The Tiger commander, on spotting it, tried to traverse his turret round to engage, but the crew of the Greyhound managed to get within twenty-five metres and fire off three rounds into the thinly protected rear of the Tiger. 'There was a muffled explosion, followed by flames which billowed out of the turret and engine ports.'

The third attack came in the afternoon, with a battalion of infantry supported by four tanks and eight self-propelled assault guns. The assault was only broken up by the enfilade fire of Shermans. The temperature dropped sharply that day, with some snow flurries.

Manteuffel, seeing little progress, decided to commit his reserve in the form of the *Führer Begleit* Brigade commanded by Oberst Otto Remer. That afternoon, Remer received the order to advance to St Vith, but his column of vehicles was soon brought to a halt by the appalling conditions of the roads. One of Remer's officers recorded that the '*Führer Begleit* Brigade was involved in a vast traffic jam with two other infantry formations, all claiming the same road'. Remer ordered his men to keep 'pushing forward and not to worry about minor considerations'. When told to advance further round to the north, Remer at first 'declined to move in that direction', but eventually took up position in a wood south of Born. As the Führer's favourite, he could clearly get away with behaviour which would have landed any other officer in front of a court martial. Remer's high-handed attitude during the offensive became something of a black joke among fellow commanders.

All major American headquarters lacked information on the true state of affairs. Hodges's First Army staff now at Chaudfontaine appeared to be paralysed in the face of disaster, while at Simpson's Ninth Army headquarters in Maastricht officers appeared very optimistic. 'There's not the slightest feeling of nervousness in American quarters with regard to an attack,' the Australian war correspondent Godfrey Blunden wrote. 'On the contrary there is satisfaction that the enemy has chosen to join battle [in the open] instead of lying down behind a barrier of mud and water.' Reports of air battles above the clouds at altitudes of up to 20,000 feet, between P-47 Thunderbolts and Focke-Wulf 190s and Me 109s caused great excitement.

General Bradley still had no idea that General Hodges had abandoned his headquarters at Spa. At 22.30 hours, Bradley rang Patton to summon him to Luxembourg for a conference as soon as possible. Patton and three key staff officers left within ten minutes.

As soon as Patton arrived, Bradley again said to him: 'I feel you won't like what we are going to do, but I fear that it's necessary.' Bradley was surprised at how nonchalant Patton was about postponing his offensive in the Saar. 'What the hell,' he said. 'We'll still be killing Krauts.'

On the map Bradley showed the depth of German penetration, which was also much greater than Patton had imagined. Bradley asked him what he could do. Patton answered that he would halt the 4th Armored Division and concentrate it near Longwy, prior to moving north. He could have the 80th Infantry Division on the road to Luxembourg by the next morning, with the 26th Infantry Division following within twenty-four hours. Patton rang his chief of staff and told him to issue the necessary orders and assemble transport for the 80th Division. He confessed that driving back in the dark with no knowledge of how far the Germans had advanced rattled him. 'A very dangerous operation, which I hate,' he wrote in his diary.

When Patton called Luxembourg on his return, Bradley said: 'the situation up there is much worse than it was when I talked to you'. He asked Patton to get the 4th Armored moving immediately. 'You and a staff officer meet me for a conference with General Eisenhower at Verdun at approximately 1100.'

335

11
Skorzeny and Heydte

Eight of Obersturmbannführer Skorzeny's nine Jeep teams had slipped through American lines on the night of 16 December. They consisted of the best English-speakers, but even they were not good enough. Some carried vials of sulphuric acid to throw in the faces of guards if stopped. Some groups cut wires and carried out minor sabotage, such as changing road signs. One even managed to misdirect an entire infantry regiment. But the greatest success of the operation, combined with Heydte's disastrous parachute drop near Eupen, was to provoke an American over-reaction bordering on paranoia.

A Jeep with four men was stopped at a bridge on the edge of Liège by military police. The four soldiers wore US Army uniforms, and spoke English with an American accent, but when asked for a work ticket they produced several blanks. The MPs ordered them out, found German weapons and explosives, and swastika brassards under their uniform. The Jeep, it turned out, had been captured from the British at Arnhem.

Their officer, Leutnant Günther Schultz, was handed over to Mobile Field Interrogation Unit No. 1. Schultz appeared to co-operate fully. He admitted that he had been part of Skorzeny's Einheit Steilau and told the team from the Counter Intelligence Corps that, according to his commander Major Schrötter, 'the secret orders of the *Fernaufklärer* [long-range reconnaissance teams] were to penetrate to Paris and capture General Eisenhower and other high ranking officers'. All of this came from the rumour at the Grafenwöhr camp which Skorzeny had encouraged, but it is still not clear whether Schultz himself believed it, or whether he hoped to cause chaos, or perhaps in a wild attempt to impress his interrogators to save his skin.

Schultz told them of an 'Eisenhower Aktion' carried out by a 'special group' commanded by an 'Oberleutnant Schmidhuber', directly under Skorzeny's orders. Approximately eighty people were involved in the plot to kidnap or assassinate General Eisenhower. They would rendezvous at the Café de l'Epée or the Café de la Paix in Paris, he was not sure which. He also claimed that Brandenburger commandos, who had crossed the Soviet frontier just before the invasion in June 1941, were involved. Another report claimed that they 'may have a captured German officer as a ruse, pretending to take him to higher headquarters for questioning'. Despite the improbable image of eighty German soldiers meeting in a Parisian café, the Counter Intelligence Corps believed Schultz's account. The next morning, Eisenhower's security was stepped up to such a degree that he almost found himself a prisoner.

General Bradley made sure that when he went out he was sandwiched between another machine-gun-mounted Jeep in front and a Hellcat tank destroyer behind. He had been told by the Counter Intelligence Corps, alarmed by the assassination rumours, that he should not use a car, especially getting in and out on the street outside the main entrance of the Hôtel Alfa in Luxembourg. In future, he was to use the kitchen entrance round the back, and his room was changed to one further back in the hotel. All plates with a general's stars had been removed from vehicles and even those on his helmet had to be covered over.

The idea of German commando troops charging around in their rear areas turned the Americans into victims of their own nightmare fantasies. Roadblocks were set up on every route, greatly slowing traffic because the guards had to interrogate the occupants to check that they were not German. Instructions were rushed out: 'Question the driver because, if German, he will be the one who speaks and understands the least English . . . Some of these G.I. clad Germans are posing as high-ranking officers. One is supposed to be dressed as a Brigadier General . . . Above all don't let them take off their American uniform. Instead get them to the nearest PW cage, where they will be questioned and eventually put before a firing squad.'

American roadblock guards and MPs came up with their own questions to make sure that a vehicle's occupants were genuine. They included a baseball quiz, the name of the President's dog, the name of the current husband of Betty Grable and 'What is Sinatra's first name?' Brigadier General Bruce Clarke gave a wrong answer about the Chicago Cubs. 'Only a kraut would make a mistake like that,' the MP declared. Having been told that he should look out 'for a kraut posing as a one-star general', he was convinced he had discovered his man, and Clarke found himself under arrest for half an hour. Even General Bradley was stopped and held for a short time, despite having given the right answer to the capital of Illinois. The MP thought differently.

British personnel in the American Ninth Army rear area aroused considerable suspicion during the panic. The actor David Niven, a Phantom reconnaissance officer in Rifle Brigade uniform, was challenged by one

American sentry with the question: 'Who won the World Series in 1940?'

'I haven't the faintest idea,' Niven claimed to have replied with characteristic insouciance. 'But I do know that I made a picture with Ginger Rogers in 1938.'

'O.K. beat it, Dave,' came the reply, 'but watch your step for Crissake.'

At a more senior level Major General Allan Adair, the commander of the Guards Armoured Division, accompanied by his ADC, was stopped at a checkpoint manned by African-American soldiers. Adair's much loved but famously incompetent ADC Captain Aylmer Tryon could not find their identity documents. After much fruitless searching for them, the large NCO finally said, to Adair's delight, 'General, if I were you, I'd get myself a new aide.'

Another way of checking was to make the soldier or officer in question lower their trousers to check that they were wearing regulation underwear. A German Jew, who had escaped to England soon after Hitler came to power, asked his commanding officer in the Royal Army Service Corps for permission to visit Brussels. Born Gerhardt Unger, he had, like many other soldiers of German Jewish origin, anglicized his name in case of capture by the Nazis. On the evening of 16 December, Gerald Unwin, or Gee, as he was known, began drinking with some

American soldiers from the First Army in a bar. They told him of their German Jewish intelligence officer, a Lieutenant Gunther Wertheim. Gunther was his cousin and had escaped from Germany to America. So, on the spur of the moment, he decided to accompany his new friends back to their unit when they left early the next morning.

As they came closer to the Ardennes front, they became aware of heavy firing in the distance and scenes of panic. At a roadblock near Eupen, Gee was arrested. He had no movement order or authorization to be in the area, and although he wore British uniform, he spoke with an unmistakable German accent. Hauled off to an improvised cell-block in a local school, Gee was fortunate not to have been shot out of hand in the atmosphere of rumour and fear then caused by Heydte's paratroopers. He was saved for the moment by the fact that his underwear was standard British army issue, but he was locked up nevertheless in the school until summoned for interrogation the next day. As he was marched into the room, the intelligence officer gasped in astonishment: 'Gerd?' he said. 'Gunther!' Gee exclaimed in relief, on seeing his cousin.

One of Skorzeny's teams was captured on the evening of 18 December at Aywaille, less than twenty kilometres from the Meuse. The three men were found with German papers, and large sums in American dollars and British pounds. They were tried and sentenced to death five days later. Altogether sixteen members of Einheit Steilau were captured and sentenced to 'be shot to death with musketry'. One group asked for a reprieve on the grounds that they were following orders, and faced certain death if they had refused to do so. 'We were sentenced to death,' their appeal stated, 'and are now dying for some criminals who have not only us, but also — and that is worse — our families on their conscience. Therefore we beg mercy of the commanding general; we have not been unjustly sentenced, but we are de facto innocent.' Their appeal was refused and the sentences confirmed by General Bradley.

One of the group taken at Aywaille repeated the story about the plan to seize or kill General Eisenhower, thus confirming the worst fears of the Counter Intelligence Corps. There were also reports of a group of Frenchmen, former members of the Vichy Milice and the SS *Charlemagne* Division, who had been given the task of penetrating Allied lines to sabotage fuel dumps and railway cars. They were said to be wearing American coats, and pretending to be forced labourers who had escaped from a factory.

Another three members of Einheit Steilau, due to be executed at Eupen on 23 December, made a last request just before their execution. They wanted to hear some Christmas carols sung by German nurses interned near by. While the firing squad stood ready, 'the women sang in clear strong voices'. The guards looked at the condemned men, and apparently 'hung their heads struck by the peculiar sentimentality of it all'. The officer in command of the squad was 'half afraid that they'd shoot at the wall instead of the man when the command was given'.

On 23 December, when British troops from the 29th Armoured Brigade guarded the bridge over the Meuse at Dinant, 'visibility was almost nil' due to fog, the commanding officer of the 3rd Royal Tank Regiment wrote. 'An apparently American Jeep drove through one of the road blocks approaching the bridge on the east side of the river. This road block, as were all the others, was mined by the 8th Rifle Brigade who had established a movable barrier and arranged for mines to be pulled across the road should any vehicle break through the barrier without stopping. As we were by now in contact with the Americans, this Jeep was not fired on, but as it refused to stop the mines were drawn across the road and it was blown up.' It was found to contain three Germans. Two were killed and one taken prisoner.

This was probably the same incident (recorded with a certain artistic licence by Bradley's aide Chester Hansen) in which four

Germans in a Jeep lost their nerve on a guarded bridge and tried to smash their way through. The sentry pulled a string of mines across the road, and the Jeep blew up. Three of the Germans were killed instantly, the fourth wounded. The guards walked up, shot the fourth one dead, then tipped the Jeep and all the bodies into the river, 'swept up the bridge' and resumed their post.

Skorzeny's 150th Panzer-Brigade proved a complete anticlimax. Their tanks, most of which were German Mark IVs and Panthers unconvincingly camouflaged to look like Shermans, were painted in olive-drab paint with the white Allied star, in some cases with the surrounding circle omitted. Skorzeny himself knew that they would not have fooled the Americans except perhaps at night. He soon gave up all idea of thrusting through to the Meuse bridges after being bogged down in mud and thwarted by the immense traffic jams which built up behind the 1st SS Panzer-Division. On the evening of 17 December he asked Sepp Dietrich to commit his force instead as an ordinary panzer brigade. Dietrich gave his consent and told Skorzeny to take his force to Ligneuville. Dietrich had another reason for agreeing so readily. The commanding general of I SS Panzer Corps asked for Skorzeny's forces to be withdrawn, as they were 'hindering the operation of the corps by driving between vehicles and doing exactly as they pleased'.

On 21 December, the 150th Panzer-Brigade attacked north to Malmédy in a freezing fog. They forced back a regiment of the 30th Infantry Division until the American artillery ranged in, using the new and highly secret Pozit fused shells, which exploded on proximity to their target. More than a hundred men were killed and 350 wounded in the day's fighting, including Skorzeny, who was badly wounded in the face by shrapnel and nearly lost an eye. The 150th Panzer-Brigade was withdrawn entirely from the offensive and Operation *Greif* was over. But in its only action it managed, purely by chance, to sow confusion, just as Einheit Steilau had done. First Army became convinced by the attack on Malmédy that the Sixth Panzer Army was preparing a drive north.

The original contributor to Allied confusion, Oberstleutnant von der Heydte, was increasingly depressed in his Kampfgruppe's forest hideout south of Eupen. He was bitter about the 'amateurish, almost frivolous manner displayed at the higher levels of command, where the order for such operations originated'. Dietrich had assured him that he and his men would be relieved within a day. But there was no indication of a breakthrough round Monschau, and the American artillery on the Elsenborn ridge to the south still thundered away. Without radios, there was no hope of discovering the progress of the battle.

Heydte's 300 paratroopers had little food left, having jumped with emergency rations: two rolls of pressed bacon, two portions of sausage, two packets of 'Soya Fleischbrot', dextro-energen tablets, some of the German army hard bread called *Dauerbrot,* marzipan and Pervitin, a benzedrine substitute which had by then been banned. Under the cover of darkness, a group of his men had crept up to an American artillery battery during the night of 17 December and managed to steal some boxes of rations. But these did not last long when divided between 300 men.

Heydte's outposts near the road never attempted to attack a convoy, but picked off single vehicles. The Americans found a single strand of wire stretched across at neck height for anyone sitting in a Jeep. This was attributed to Heydte's men, and it prompted the decision to fit an angled iron attachment on the front of Jeeps to cut any wires strung across roads or trails. There were very few incidents of this sort, but it was considered necessary to reassure drivers, especially when they advanced further into Germany because of the rumours of Werwolf resistance groups made up of Hitler Youth fanatics.

On 17 December Sergeant Inber of the

387th Anti-Aircraft Artillery, driving south from Eupen, overtook a slow column of trucks with ease. But 400 metres ahead of it he was 'ambushed, captured and whisked off the road before the leading vehicle of the convoy reached the point'. Inber was led off to Heydte's main lair, about a kilometre into the woods, where the paratroopers treated him well. Heydte told Inber that he would release him if he could guide two of his injured men to an American aid station. The other American wounded whom they had captured were placed by the road where an ambulance could pick them up.

Isolated paratroopers and air crew from the scattered drop soon fell into American hands. A survivor from a Junkers 52, brought down behind the Ninth Army, told his interrogators that they had 'taken off believing they were on a practice flight, but learned while in the air that they were on a special mission'.

After moving their hiding place, Heydte's force clashed on 19 December with some of the troops from the 18th Infantry Regiment of the 1st Division who were combing the forest. There were a dozen casualties on both sides. Some of the soldiers searching for the German paratroopers did not report the parachutes they found; they simply cut them up to make silk scarves.

Heydte, who was sickening and suffered from trench foot, gave up any idea of an advance on Eupen and decided to move east instead toward Monschau. His men were visibly weakened by malnutrition. They struggled through forest and marshes, and were soaked in the freezing waters of the Helle river which they had to wade. On 20 December, after another, heavier skirmish, Heydte told his men to make their way back to German lines in small groups. Altogether thirty-six were captured, but the rest reached safety. The thirty-seven fatal casualties in the Kampfgruppe were entirely from anti-aircraft fire on the first night.

On 22 December Heydte, by then feeling very ill and utterly exhausted, went into Monschau on his own and broke into a house. When discovered by a civilian, he was relieved when the man told him that he would have to report him to the American military authorities. After a spell in hospital, Heydte was transferred to a prison camp in England. It was comfortable, but he and other officers held there never realized that their conversations were being recorded.

12
TUESDAY 19 DECEMBER

On 19 December at dawn, Peiper's Kampf-gruppe attacked Stoumont with a battalion of panzergrenadiers, a company of paratroopers, and tanks in support on the road. The first assault failed. Stoumont seemed solidly held, and the 119th Infantry of the 30th Division launched a counter-attack on their right flank. But a little later in the thick morning mist the trick of Panther tanks charging at maximum speed worked once more. The anti-tank gunners did not stand a chance in the bad visibility. Only ghostly bazooka teams stalking panzers in the fog managed to achieve a couple of kills from the rear. A 90mm anti-aircraft gun sent to Stoumont in desperation managed to knock out a Tiger from the 501st Heavy Panzer Battalion.

Peiper's Kampfgruppe cleared Stoumont nevertheless, crushing the infantry company defending it. Two platoons of Shermans arrived too late, and had to pull back. Peiper's force pushed on four kilometres to the west to Stoumont station. American officers assembled a scratch force just in time. It included the reserve battalion from the 119th, fifteen incomplete Shermans extracted from a nearby ordnance depot by the newly arrived 740th Tank Battalion, a battery of howitzers and another 90mm anti-aircraft gun. With short cliffs on the north side of the road, rising to steep, wooded hillsides above, and a sharp drop on the south side down to the railway track along the river, this position could not be outflanked. Even though First Army headquarters feared that Peiper's force would turn north towards Liège, Stoumont station would be the furthest point of his advance. The rest of the 30th Infantry Division and General Jim Gavin's 82nd Airborne were concentrating in the area just in time: the 30th to counter-attack the German spearhead and the 82nd to advance from Werbomont to support the defenders of St Vith.

Around 260 Belgian civilians, in an attempt to escape the fighting in Stoumont itself, went down into the cellars of the Saint-Edouard sanatorium, which from the steep hillside overlooked the Amblève valley. But the Germans took over the building as a strongpoint. Priests held masses to calm the frightened women and children when the Americans counter-attacked next day and fought their way in.

The civilians thought they were saved, and greeted the GIs with joy, but the Germans came back in the night. 'Sister Superior led the crowd in reciting twelve rosaries for those fallen in battle.' The Americans again launched an attack, with Sherman tanks firing at point-blank range into the sanatorium. The roof collapsed, walls were blasted down, and parts of the basement ceiling came down in a cloud of dust and smoke. The priest gave general absolution, but by a miracle none of the women and children was hurt.

On the morning of 19 December, Peiper heard that the Americans had retaken Stavelot to his rear, thus cutting his Kampfgruppe off from any hope of resupply when it was almost out of fuel. He sent his reconnaissance battalion back to retake the small town. Peiper sensed failure. He still bitterly regretted that his Kampfgruppe had been forced to wait for the infantry to open the way on the first day of the offensive. It should have been a surprise attack without artillery preparation, he believed, but with armoured combat teams as well as infantry. In the subsequent advance west, the long snaking column had proved a big mistake. They should have had many smaller groups, each one probing for intact bridges and a way through.

His Waffen-SS troopers continued to kill prisoners at almost every opportunity. In La

Gleize on the route back, a member of the 741st Tank Battalion, cut off by the German attack the day before, remained hidden in the church. 'From his place of concealment,' a report stated, 'this soldier observed the [German] tanks and infantry halt an American armored car. The occupants surrendered and were told to get out. They were promptly fired upon by machine weapons as they stood there with hands up. The Germans then took the vehicle and moved away.' And Rottenführer Straub of the reconnaissance battalion later recounted another incident to fellow prisoners from the 26th Volksgrenadier-Division. 'Our battalion advanced to Stavelot and on to La Gleize. From there we went back to Stavelot. Our Sturmführer just shot [prisoners] outright . . . There were twelve of them the first time. He just shot them because they were in the way.'

SS panzergrenadiers convinced themselves of the most extraordinary stories to justify their actions. An eighteen-year-old soldier from the 1st SS Panzer-Division told a fellow prisoner of war that the reputation of one of their senior NCOs for shooting unarmed men was so well known that they had to deal with Americans who pretended to surrender but were secretly bent on revenge. 'Some of them came along', he said, 'waving a white flag and we knew very well that they were out for our Oberscharführer, because he'd killed so many of them, so we took our machine pistols and shot them before they could do a thing. That's the way we work.'

After dark on the evening of 19 December, American soldiers from the 105th Engineer Battalion managed to infiltrate Stavelot and destroyed the main bridge across the Amblève, despite enemy tank and machine-gun fire. Peiper was furious: part of his force was now cut off north of the river and there was little sign of bridging equipment coming up from his division.

The 3rd Fallschirmjäger-Division, which Peiper's Kampfgruppe had expected to catch up with them, was just one of Sepp Dietrich's formations battering away without success at the southern edge of the Elsenborn ridge. The I SS Panzer Corps headquarters had sent the paratroopers to take Faymonville and then Waimes, from where the American field hospital had been evacuated. But the bulk of the 3rd Fallschirmjäger never advanced further than Faymonville.

The lack of progress by the Sixth Panzer Army had started a cascade of criticism from Hitler and the OKW, via Rundstedt and Model down to a frustrated and angry Dietrich. In a fresh attempt, Dietrich ordered the 12th SS Panzer-Division to move round from Rocherath–Krinkelt to attack the American 1st Infantry Division positions from Büllingen. The Germans urgently needed to open the road west to Malmédy. Panzergrenadiers of the SS *Hitler Jugend,* battalions of the 12th Volksgrenadier and tanks assembled in the early hours in Büllingen ready to crush the American 26th Infantry Regiment. The battle for Dom Bütgenbach was to be as intense as that for Rocherath–Krinkelt to the north-east.

To continue the attacks around Rocherath–Krinkelt and Wirtzfeld, Dietrich sent in his reserve, the 3rd Panzergrenadier-Division, to support the 12th and 277th Volksgrenadiers. The hard pounding intensified, as the massed American artillery regiments on the Elsenborn ridge smashed every village in range now held by the Germans. Their first priority on the morning of 19 December was to break up the renewed attacks against Rocherath–Krinkelt, a task at which the 155mm Long Toms excelled. But the casualty rate among young artillery officers acting as forward observers was very high.

In the shattered twin villages, the remaining units of the 2nd Division and the Sherman and tank-destroyer platoons continued to fight off the volksgrenadiers and panzergrenadiers. They also prepared their withdrawal to new positions on the side of the Elsenborn ridge. During the afternoon, they started to destroy vehicles, guns and equipment which would have to be left behind. Radiators and oil reservoirs were emptied and the engines revved until they seized. Artillerymen rolled thermite grenades into their gun barrels. And at 17.30 hours, just over an hour after dark had fallen, the first units began their withdrawal. Along the rutted road, engineers had taped TNT blocks to the trees on either side, ready to blow them down to block the way.

Exhausted after the three-day battle of Rocherath–Krinkelt which had blunted the Sixth Panzer Army, the men slipped and slid in the muddy slush, cursing and sweating. They were so tired that on firmer patches they fell asleep as they continued to trudge forward. Late that night, a small patrol sneaked back to the edge of the twin villages. They returned to report that there were around a thousand Germans there with about a hundred American prisoners.

A dozen kilometres to the south, the two unfortunate regiments of the 106th Division, trapped in the Schnee Eifel east of St Vith, tried to fight their way back to American lines. The inexperienced officers and soldiers were utterly demoralized. They were short of ammunition, out of radio contact mainly due to German jamming, and the scale of the disaster appeared overwhelming. Many tried to raise each other's spirits with assurances that a relief force must be on its way.

Kurt Vonnegut, who was with the 423rd Infantry Regiment, described his comrades as a mixture of college kids and those who had enlisted to avoid jail. Many were 'poor physical specimens' who 'should never have been in the army'. Few had received infantry training. Vonnegut was a battalion scout who knew about weapons only because his 'father was a gun-nut, so [he] knew how all this crap worked'.

Some tried to get away in vehicles, but when the Germans opened fire with anti-tank guns, they abandoned them and immobilized the rest. Their commanders, who were 'flying blind', sent off scouts to find out what was happening, but they could not even find the artillery battalion which was supposed to be supporting them. The Germans had brought up loudspeakers to play music by Benny Goodman, Artie Shaw and other American bandleaders, interrupted with promises of 'showers, warm beds, and hotcakes for breakfast if you surrender'. This provoked an obscene chorus in response. One soldier in a ditch, weeping violently, shouted: 'Go blow it out your ass, you German son of a bitch!'

The two regimental commanders decided to give up when their units were bombarded by German artillery from all sides. At 16.00 hours an officer went forward waving a snow cape. Officers and men were marched off with their hands on their heads, stumbling and tripping. Their guards later told them to put the contents of their pockets into their helmet liners so that they could pick out what they wanted. A large number found themselves herded into a farmyard surrounded by a stone wall. At dusk a voice called out: 'Do not flee. If you flee, you will be machine weaponed.' They could only cling together for warmth in the long, cold night.

Vonnegut called it 'the largest surrender of Americans under arms in American military history'. (In fact the surrender at Bataan in 1942 was much greater, but the capitulation of some 8,000 men in the 106th was certainly the biggest in Europe.) Vonnegut and a dozen others tried to find their way back to American lines through the snow-bound forest, but the Germans of the 18th Volksgrenadier-Division who were mopping up trapped them in the bed of a creek. Loudspeakers broadcast an order to surrender. To hurry them, the Germans fired tree bursts over their heads. Deciding that they had no alternative, the cornered Americans stripped their weapons and threw the working parts away. They emerged with their hands up, and thus began their imprisonment which, in Vonnegut's case, led to Dresden and the firestorm of February 1945, described in *Slaughterhouse Five*.

Officers at VIII Corps headquarters in Bastogne were horrified when they heard of the surrender. The deputy chief of staff 'inferred that the two surrounded regiments might have put up a stronger fight. He characterized a force of that size as "two wildcats in a bush" which might have done some clawing of the enemy instead of surrendering as they eventually did.'

The Germans could not believe how many men they had surrounded. One of their officers wrote in his diary: 'Endless columns of prisoners pass; at first, about a hundred, later, another thousand. Our vehicle gets stuck on the road. I get out and walk. Model himself directs traffic. (He's a little undistinguished looking man with a monocle.) The roads are littered with destroyed American vehicles, cars and tanks. Another column of prisoners pass. I count over a thousand men. In Andler there is a column of 1,500 men with about 50 officers and a lieutenant colonel who had asked to surrender.'

To Model's frustration, German traffic east of St Vith was hardly advancing. The 7th Armored Division's artillery kept up a steady bombardment on the approach roads. After the previous day's failure to take St Vith, the Germans tried probing and outflanking movements mainly against the 31st Tank Battalion. The 38th Armored Infantry Battalion was 'licking its wounds' after the mauling it had received, and platoons needed to be amalgamated because of their losses. But even so the Germans seemed to have come off worst.[*]

In the trees in front of them, the 38th Armored Infantry reported, 'the only Jerries we found were dead ones — most of them killed apparently as they tried to dig themselves in behind some tree or fallen log. Those who were not equipped with shovels had attempted to scoop shallow holes with their helmets, bayonets and even with their fingernails.' A firebreak, which had been covered by a heavy-machine-gun section on the right flank, was found to have 'nineteen paratroopers stretched out at almost parade-ground intervals, five yards apart, each one with at least five to eight slugs in his chest or throat'. According to Major Boyer, the 'paratroopers' were later found to have been wearing *Grossdeutschland* uniform and insignia 'under their jump jackets'. During another attack that afternoon, the 90mm guns of a tank-destroyer platoon managed to knock out a Mark V Panther tank and one of the two assault guns supporting the infantry.

The main threat to Brigadier General Hasbrouck's defence line lay in the north where the 18th Volksgrenadiers and the *Führer Be-*

---

[*] See map, The Destruction of the 106th Division, p. 236 above.

gleit Brigade were pushing round. But although the *Führer Begleit* saw itself as an elite formation, it also had its psychological casualties. Apparently one member of its staff, Rittmeister von Möllendorf, was 'hysterical and a nervous wreck. He cries whenever Hitler's name is mentioned.'

An even greater threat to Hasbrouck's rear came when the 9th SS Panzer-Division *Hohenstaufen* followed the same route a little further north, via Recht and Poteau, which the Kampfgruppe Hansen had taken earlier. In the fighting near Poteau, an SS runner received a stomach wound when an American shell exploded. As his comrades put him on a stretcher, with some of his intestines protruding, one of them made a move to take his steel helmet off, but he begged him to leave it on. At company headquarters an Unterscharführer tried to remove the helmet, but the man screamed his protest. By the time they reached the dressing station, he was barely conscious. A medic 'lifted the man's head up, undid the chin strap and took the helmet off. The top of the skull with the brain came off with it. The man must have realised that he had taken another piece of shrapnel right under the rim of his helmet. It had sheared through his skull. He lived until his helmet was removed.'

Hasbrouck knew that if the Germans diverted south and took Vielsalm and Salmchâteau some ten kilometres to the west of St Vith, then his forces would be cut off. But both the 9th SS Panzer and the 116th Panzer-Division twenty kilometres to the south-west were heading towards the Meuse either side of the St Vith breakwater. He knew he simply had to hold on there to block the 18th and 62nd Volksgrenadier-Divisions which, having now dealt with the two beleaguered American regiments in the Schnee Eifel, could concentrate all their strength against St Vith.

Verdun, in the words of one of Bradley's staff officers, was 'an ugly professional garrison town', with a population considered hostile by the Americans. 12th Army Group's rear headquarters was based 'within great loops of barbed wire, up and down which sentries walked'.

Eisenhower arrived with Air Chief Marshal Tedder in the Supreme Commander's armour-plated Cadillac. Patton appeared in his 'fabulous Jeep with plexiglass doors and thirty caliber machinegun mounted on a post'. Together with the two American army group commanders, Bradley and Devers, they trooped upstairs in the grey stone barracks followed by a bevy of staff officers. A single pot-bellied stove was the only source of heat in the long room, so few outer clothes were removed.

Resolved to set the right tone, Eisenhower

opened proceedings. 'The present situation is to be regarded as one of opportunity for us and not of disaster,' he said. 'There will be only cheerful faces at this conference table.'

'Hell, let's have the guts to let the sons of bitches go all the way to Paris,' Patton called down the table. 'Then we'll really cut 'em off and chew 'em up.' This prompted nervous laughs. Patton's instinct to attack the enemy salient at the base found few supporters. Eisenhower was unamused. 'George, that's fine,' he said. 'But the enemy must never be allowed to cross the Meuse.'

Thanks to fresh Ultra intercepts, SHAEF by now had a much clearer picture of German ambitions in Operation *Herbstnebel*. Eisenhower was determined to rise to the challenge as a field commander, and not preside over the battle as a distant figurehead. This feeling may well have been strengthened by the suspicion that he had not imposed himself strongly enough over the past months.

Standing by the large map of the Ardennes hanging on the wall, staff officers briefed the assembled array of generals on the situation. Eisenhower then listed the divisions being brought over to France. Commanders could give ground if necessary, but there was to be no withdrawal behind the Meuse. General Devers's 6th Army Group in Alsace was to extend north to take over part of Patton's Third Army front. This was to free up Patton's divisions for a counter-attack from the south.

'When can you start?' Eisenhower asked, turning to Patton.

'As soon as you're through with me.'

Eisenhower wanted him to be more specific. Patton could not resist a display of bravado. 'On the morning of December 21st, with three divisions', he replied.* 'The 4th Armored, the 26th and the 80th.' Patton did not say that a combat command of the 4th Armored and a corps headquarters were already on the move, and the rest were starting to leave that morning. The idea that the bulk of an army could be turned around through ninety degrees to attack in a different direction within three days produced stunned disbelief around the table.

'Don't be fatuous, George,' Eisenhower said. 'If you try to go that early, you won't have all three divisions ready and you'll go piecemeal. You will start on the twenty-second and I want your initial blow to be a strong one!' Eisenhower was right to be concerned that an over-hasty attack would

* In most accounts of the meeting, Patton apparently said the morning of 21 December, but in his own diary Patton puts 22 December. It is impossible to tell whether this was what he believed he said at the time, or whether he changed it because he recognized that Eisenhower was right.

reduce the desired effect. But there can be little doubt that Third Army's energy and staff work produced one of the most rapid redeployments known in the history of warfare.

All through the meeting, Patton's superior General Bradley said very little. Already suffering from stress and hives, he was also a martyr to his sinuses. Bradley felt very much on the defensive since it had been his decision to leave the Ardennes weakly defended. He felt completely sidelined, for Eisenhower was taking all the decisions and giving orders to Patton over his head. Bradley had also isolated himself by refusing to move his headquarters from the city of Luxembourg on the grounds that this would frighten its inhabitants, but pride certainly played a large part in that decision. In any event, the result was that he remained cut off from Hodges's First Army headquarters near Liège by the German advance. Neither he nor any of his staff officers had visited an American headquarters since the offensive began. To make his mood even worse, Bradley clearly felt snubbed after the meeting when he invited Eisenhower to lunch. The Supreme Commander declined the offer, saying he would have a sandwich in the car on his way back to Versailles.

As Eisenhower was about to get into the staff car, he turned again to Patton. 'Every time I get a new star I get attacked,' he joked, referring also to his previous promotion just before Rommel's surprise offensive at Kasserine in Tunisia.

'And every time you get attacked, I pull you out,' Patton retorted, clearly feeling on top of the world. He then went to a telephone and called his own headquarters in Nancy to confirm the movement order for his divisions using a prearranged codeword. Patton returned, smoking a cigar, to talk to Bradley, who, according to his aide Chester Hansen, was 'fighting mad'.

'I don't want to commit any of your stuff [i.e. formations] unless I have to,' Bradley said to Patton. 'I want to save it for a damn good blow when we hit back and we're going to hit this bastard hard.' This suggests that Bradley still resented Eisenhower's decision that Patton should launch a rapid counterattack. But when Bradley and his retinue drove back towards Luxembourg, they passed a convoy of Patton's III Corps already on the road. Third Army staff had not wasted a moment.

Eisenhower had been right to dismiss Patton's instinct to cut off the German offensive at its base. Although American forces in the Ardennes had doubled to nearly 190,000 men, they were still far too few for such an ambitious operation. The Third Army was to secure the southern shoulder and the city of

Luxembourg, but its main priority was to advance north to Bastogne where the 101st Airborne and part of the 10th Armored Division were soon to be surrounded.

The situation in the whole area was chaotic. Colonel Herman of the 7th Tank Destroyer Group took over the defence of Libramont, south-west of Bastogne. Nobody there knew what was happening, so he stopped all stragglers and even an artillery column passing through the town. 'Where are you going?' he demanded.

'We're retreating, sir,' came the reply.

'The hell you are,' said Herman. 'This is where you turn around and fight.' By midnight on 19 December, Herman had collected a force of some 2,000 men, to which he added another leaderless artillery battalion the next morning.

Resistance still continued in Wiltz even though the road west to Bastogne had been cut by German patrols, thus blocking efforts to resupply the remnants of the 28th Division in the town with rations and ammunition. At 14.30 the 5th Fallschirmjäger-Division, blowing whistles and supported by forty tanks and self-propelled assault guns, attacked the town from several sides. By nightfall, the defenders had been pushed back to the centre of the town, amid burning buildings. General Cota sent a message to their commander: 'Give them hell!' That night survivors were ordered to break into small groups and head for Bastogne. A convoy of thirty vehicles tried to leave but ran into heavy fire and was abandoned. Having blown the bridges, the last engineer unit did not leave Wiltz until 11.00 the next day.

The trucks and trailers heading for Bastogne packed with paratroopers were directed to Mande-Saint-Etienne, half a dozen kilometres to the west, so as not to clog the town. Roads leading out of Bastogne were blocked by panic-stricken army drivers trying to escape. Even their officers had to be threatened with pistols to force them to move their vehicles aside to allow the 101st Airborne through. Paratroopers frozen from the long journey jumped down stiffly. Everybody realized the need for speed, with two panzer and one infantry division closing on Bastogne. Those who had to shoulder mortar tubes and their base-plates staggered along under the load like 'a hod-carrying Egyptian slave', in the words of Louis Simpson with the 327th Glider Infantry.

Unaware of the vital part played by the shattered 28th Division, the paratroopers of the 101st Airborne were disgusted by the bearded and filthy stragglers fleeing west through the town. They grabbed ammunition, grenades, entrenching tools and even weapons from them or from abandoned vehicles to make up for their own shortages.

Belgian civilians, on the other hand, emerged from their houses with hot soup and coffee for the soldiers, and walked along beside them as they gulped it down.

The first regiment to arrive, Colonel Julian Ewell's 501st Parachute Infantry Regiment, marched east towards Longvilly in the pre-dawn darkness to support Team Cherry of the 10th Armored. The men could hear firing ahead through the damp, chill fog. Soon they encountered traumatized survivors from the destruction of Combat Command R the evening before, who told them: 'We have been wiped out.'

Colonel Cherry had reached the chateau just south of Neffe during the night of 18–19 December, but any hope of making it his command post was dashed at dawn. The reconnaissance platoon of the 3rd Tank Battalion and part of the 158th Engineer Combat Battalion holding the crossroads in Neffe were attacked by an advance detachment of the Panzer Lehr. A bazooka team knocked out one Mark IV tank, but the weight of machine-gun fire and shellfire coming at the reconnaissance platoon was so great that they had to pull back along the road which ran up a valley to Bastogne.

Two men managed to warn Cherry in the chateau of what had happened. Another four tanks including a Mark VI Tiger, as well as an armoured car and another hundred panzergrenadiers, were sighted coming from the east. Cherry and his handful of headquarters personnel prepared to defend the chateau, a square solid building with a single tower. They dismounted the machine guns from their vehicles and set them up in the windows. For Cherry, it was terrible moment. His main force between Mageret and Longvilly had been cut off, and was blocked in a traffic jam with the remnants of the 9th Armored Division's Combat Command R. Cherry could only watch as the Germans prepared their trap.

At around 13.00 hours the noise of battle became audible. The 77th Grenadier-Regiment of the 26th Volksgrenadier-Division launched an immediate attack on the jammed column. Artillery and assault guns joined in as well as a company of tanks from the Panzer Lehr. 'The surprise was complete,' the rather professorial Generalmajor Kokott noted. The Americans were surrounded, and chaos ensued as vehicles collided with each other as they tried in vain to escape. The battle was over in an hour and a half. Only a few vehicles managed to escape towards the north. Several officers and a hundred men were captured.

As they approached Neffe, Colonel Ewell's 1st Battalion of the 501st Parachute Infantry could hear shooting clearly through the fog and drizzle. Ewell spread his men out on both sides of the road with the order to dig in. As they were preparing foxholes, tanks could be heard. Desperate cries for bazooka teams followed.

The 2nd Battalion, meanwhile, was moving to defend Bizôry, two kilometres to the north of Neffe. It too would be caught in a bitter battle, and was soon renamed 'Misery'. Morale among the German forces had been greatly boosted by the two highly successful engagements against American armoured columns, but they were about to receive a sharp disappointment. Later that afternoon the 26th Volksgrenadier reconnaissance battalion and the 78th Grenadier-Regiment found themselves involved in heavy fighting around both Mageret and Bizôry. The attack on Bizôry produced 'painful losses'. Part of the Panzer Lehr Division was also heavily engaged at Neffe. The Americans had won the race to Bastogne, with their reinforcements.

Colonel Ewell established a defensive line along high ground less than three kilometres west of Bastogne's market square. 'The enemy had made good use of the time!' the commander of the 26th Volksgrenadiers acknowledged ruefully. And the Panzer Lehr was so desperate for fuel that it was reduced to draining the tanks of captured or knocked-out vehicles.

This 'day of surprises' made it clear to Bayerlein that the higher command idea of taking Bastogne off the march was now impossible. But the commander of the XLVII Panzer Corps, General der Panzertruppe Freiherr von Lüttwitz, blamed him for the failure to take Bastogne. Bayerlein retorted by blaming the 26th Volksgrenadier-Division, and Lüttwitz himself, who had slowed him down by committing the Panzer Lehr to battle east of the River Clerf contrary to the original plan. Bayerlein also said that Lüttwitz's leadership was 'not sufficiently coherent and energetic'. He had failed to concentrate the three divisions into a full-scale attack, and had allowed them to become 'scattered'.

That night the exhausted German troops dug in as the rain came on. 'Ammunition and rations were brought up,' recorded the commander of the 26th Volksgrenadiers. 'Now and then there was a nervous burst of machinegun fire or the thunder of mortar fire which lasted a couple of minutes and after a few salvos died down again.'

Eight kilometres north of Bastogne, the twenty-six-year-old Major William Desobry commanding the 20th Armored Infantry Battalion had spent an anxious night in Noville. The tall and athletic Desobry with his 400 men awaited the onslaught of what he would later discover to be the bulk of the 2nd

Panzer-Division. At around 04.00 hours, Desobry's men noticed that no more stragglers were coming through. Soon afterwards, they heard the first shots. The outpost along the road to Bourcy, having opened fire, pulled back into the town as ordered. Its sergeant, who had been shot in the mouth, reported with difficulty that Germans had appeared in half-tracks.

Desobry could hear the distinctive noise of German armoured vehicles to the north. Although he knew that 'sounds at night are much louder and seem much nearer', this was clearly quite a force with tanks from the clanking noise of their tracks. 'Oh brother!' Desobry said to himself. 'There is really something out there.'

Heavy firing with automatic weapons and tank gunnery could be heard to the northeast. This came from the destruction of the third team from the 9th Armored Division's ill-fated Combat Command R. They had unfortunately withdrawn right into the path of the 2nd Panzer-Division. As at Longvilly the night before, German Panthers picked their targets with ease once the first vehicles were ablaze. Lieutenant Colonel Booth, the American commander, had a leg crushed under one of his own half-tracks as he tried to redeploy his trapped column. Survivors abandoned their armoured vehicles, and escaped across country towards Bastogne.

Some 200 men were lost as well as all the Shermans and half-tracks.

The sergeant commanding Desobry's outpost on the northern route to Houffalize, however, felt that as he had seen some American tanks pulling back through their position earlier, they should check before opening fire. He gave his challenge in the darkness, and although he received an answer in English, he realized his mistake. A German tank opened fire, knocking out one of the Shermans. The remaining vehicles rapidly pulled back into Noville. Desobry immediately called in the third group to the northwest. Dawn brought little clarity to the situation because of a heavy ground fog, but soon the sound of German tanks could be heard coming down the northern road from Houffalize. The American defenders prepared their 57mm anti-tank gun and bazooka teams in a cemetery on the edge of Noville. As soon as the enemy vehicles emerged from the fog, they opened up with everything that they had against the Panther tanks and panzergrenadiers.

Two of the Panthers were disabled and provided a good roadblock. But just to make sure that German tank-recovery teams did not manage to sneak up, Desobry sent out a small group with explosives to blow their tracks and wreck their main armament. The ground everywhere was so waterlogged that the Germans would find it difficult to send their panzers round the knocked-out Panthers blocking the road. Desobry's small force was then strengthened by the arrival of five M-18 Hellcat tank destroyers from Bastogne. He kept them back as his reserve.

Later in the morning the fog began to lift, and to their horror the Americans saw that the ridge to the north and north-east was covered in German panzers and half-tracks. The battle began in earnest. Many of the panzers got to within a hundred metres of the perimeter, and one even broke into the town before it was shot to a standstill. After an intense two-hour firefight, the Germans pulled back behind the ridge. Then the Germans tried probing attacks from different directions. They were not too difficult to fight off, but German mortar and artillery fire started to cause casualties.

Desobry ignored an order from Bastogne to send a patrol to Houffalize, because it would have had 'to go through the whole daggone German army to get there'. With Noville half surrounded by ridges, he suggested to his combat command headquarters back in Bastogne that it would be better if his force withdrew to defend the ridge between Noville and Foy. Colonel Roberts told him that it was his decision, but a battalion of the 101st Airborne was marching up the road from Bastogne to join him. Desobry sent a

Jeep for the battalion's commander, Lieutenant Colonel James LaPrade, just before midday. LaPrade agreed entirely with Desobry's assessment that they had to take the ridgeline ahead if they were to hold Noville.

As with other battalions of the 101st Airborne, LaPrade's unit was short of weapons and ammunition. So the 10th Armored Division's service company loaded their trucks, drove up the road and threw the paratroopers what they needed: bandoliers of rifle ammunition, machine-gun belts, grenades, mortar and bazooka rounds and even spare weapons. As the parachute battalion reached Noville, Desobry called on the supporting artillery battalion to fire at the ridgeline. The paratroopers fanned out and went straight into the attack towards the ridge, with Desobry's Shermans firing in support. 'They spread out across the fields,' he wrote, 'and those guys when they attacked, did it on the dead run. They would run for 50 metres, hit the ground, get up and run.' But it turned out that the Germans had planned another attack at the same time, so the two sides 'were engaged in a head-on clash'. One company made it to the ridgeline, only to be counter-attacked by tanks and panzergrenadiers from beyond. All the companies were taking such heavy losses that LaPrade and Desobry agreed to pull everyone back into the village. The number of badly wounded men overwhelmed the tiny aid station set up in the village.

That night, Desobry and LaPrade conferred in their command post in Noville's school on what they could do to hold on to the village. General McAuliffe in Bastogne had asked General Middleton, who had been ordered to take his VIII Corps headquarters back to Neufchâteau, if he could pull back the force in Noville, but Middleton had refused. While Desobry and LaPrade were studying the map upstairs, the 10th Armored's maintenance officer, who was responsible for recovering damaged vehicles, drove up and parked right outside. This was contrary to all standard practice as it gave away the whereabouts of a command post. The Germans concentrated all their fire on the building. LaPrade and a dozen others were killed. Desobry, coated in dust, had a head wound, with one eye half out of the socket.

Desobry was evacuated in a Jeep. On the way back to Bastogne, they were stopped in Foy by a German patrol from the 26th Volksgrenadier-Division. The volksgrenadiers, seeing he was in a bad way, generously allowed the Jeep to continue. Desobry, despite his pain, was shaken to find that the Germans had cut the road behind his force at Noville. Just to the south of Foy, Easy Company of the 506th was digging in when they heard engines through the fog. A soldier said to Lieutenant Jack Foley, 'You know those sound like motorized vehicles.' 'Vehicles?' another soldier cried. 'Hell, they're tanks!' The fear was heightened because they could not see 'what was out there'. 'All you could do was hear.'

Desobry, in spite of his stroke of luck at being let through, was again to suffer the misfortunes of war. One of the most serious mistakes made in the defence of Bastogne was to leave the 326th Airborne Medical Company at a crossroads near Sprimont, a dozen kilometres north-west of the town. They had set up their tents and were already treating the first casualties to arrive as refugees continued to stream by. The company was so exposed that a surgeon went into Bastogne to ask General McAuliffe for permission to move into the town. 'Go on back, Captain,' McAuliffe said. 'You'll be all right.'

That night, as they were operating on badly burned men and other victims, a Kampfgruppe from the 2nd Panzer-Division attacked. Machine-gun fire ripped through the tents killing and wounding many of the men lying on stretchers. With no troops to defend them, the senior American officer had no option but to surrender immediately. The Germans gave them forty-five minutes to load all the wounded, equipment and supplies on to their trucks.

Their German captors escorted them towards Houffalize. Desobry recovered consciousness on a halt in the journey and, on hearing German voices, thought that they must have taken many prisoners. He was cruelly disabused by his American driver. Desobry tried to persuade him to make a dash for it, but the driver was not prepared to take the risk. The bitter truth sank in. He was a prisoner of war.*

For the Germans of the 2nd Panzer-Division, it was a great coup to have captured so much equipment and medical supplies, especially morphine. For the 101st Airborne, it was a disaster. Their wounded were now condemned to suffer in fetid cellars and the garage of a barracks in Bastogne, where the short-staffed medics lacked morphine and other drugs. The conditions were primitive, with no latrine and a single electric light bulb in the main garage ward. The wounded were 'laid in rows on sawdust covered with blankets'. Those deemed unlikely to survive lay nearest the wall. 'As they died they were

---

* Desobry encountered a number of paradoxes during his imprisonment, such as listening in a German hospital train near Münster to a recording of Bing Crosby singing 'White Christmas', while British bombers smashed the city. He was then held in a panzergrenadier training establishment in Hohne next to Belsen concentration camp, along with British paratroopers captured at Arnhem.

carried out to another building' used as a morgue.

Montgomery, at his tactical headquarters outside Zonhoven in Belgium, was deeply disturbed by the lack of information on the battles raging to his south. On the morning of 19 December he sent two of his young liaison officers, whom he used as old-fashioned 'gallopers', to report back on the state of the battle. They were accompanied by Lieutenant Colonel Tom Bigland, who was his link with Bradley. Driving through freezing fog in a Jeep, they headed for General Hodges's advance headquarters in Spa.

'We arrive at First Army HQ, located in an hotel,' Captain Carol Mather noted at the time, 'and find it abandoned. A hurried evacuation has evidently taken place. The tables in the dining room are laid for Christmas festivities. The offices are deserted.' The place felt like the *Marie Celeste*. 'The truth begins to dawn. The German attack is more serious than we had thought, for the evacuation of the headquarters shows every sign of a panic move.' They collected some of the classified papers left lying around to prove that they had been there in case anyone disbelieved them later.

Montgomery did not wait for instructions from SHAEF. His staff officers began to issue detailed orders to the SAS and Phantom reconnaissance teams. Lieutenant General Brian Horrocks's XXX Corps received a warning order to move to defend the Meuse. Brigadier Roscoe Harvey, the commander of 29th Armoured Brigade, was summoned back from shooting woodcock. He expostulated that his brigade had not 'got any bloody tanks — they've all been handed in'. This was true. They were waiting to receive the new Comet, the first British tank produced in five years of war that would be a match for the Tiger and Panther. Harvey was told to take back his old Shermans, those that were still 'runners', and move with all speed to Dinant to block the very crossing points on the Meuse which Major General Erwin Rommel had seized in 1940.

Montgomery's gallopers meanwhile drove through 'oddly deserted countryside' to Hodges's rear headquarters at Chaudfontaine south-east of Liège, where they found him. 'He is considerably shaken,' Mather reported, 'and can give no coherent account of what has happened. Nor is he in touch with General Bradley's 12th Army Group. Communications seem to have completely broken down.' While Bigland set off on a circuitous route to Bradley's headquarters in Luxembourg, the two captains drove back to Zonhoven as quickly as the icy roads permitted.

Montgomery was 'clearly alarmed' when the two young officers recounted what they had seen. He told Mather to drive straight back to First Army headquarters. 'Tell Hodges he must block the Meuse bridges!' Mather asked how he was to transmit such orders when Hodges was not under 21st Army Group.

'Just tell him,' Montgomery said. 'The Liège crossings in particular must be defended at *all* costs. He *must* block the bridges by any means. Call up L[ine] of C[ommunications] troops. Use any obstacles he can find, including farm carts! He must hold the bridges all day tomorrow, and make sure that officers supervise each operation. You can tell him so from me!' Mather was also to inform Hodges that Phantom teams and SAS in Jeeps would be sent straight to the bridges. The British XXX Corps would move with all speed to the north bank of the Meuse to block routes to Antwerp. Montgomery insisted that he must see Hodges the next morning. 'If possible bring him back here tonight!' Eisenhower, equally adamant about the Meuse crossings, had already given orders to General Lee's Com Z headquarters. It was to move any available engineer units to mine the bridges and send in scratch battalions of rear-area troops. The French also offered seven battalions, but they were poorly armed and trained.

Montgomery was already convinced, with a good deal of justification, that Bradley in

Luxembourg could not direct First Army, which was cut off on the northern side of the German salient, or 'Bulge' as it was soon to be known. He told Major General Whiteley, the senior British operations officer at SHAEF, to tell Eisenhower that he should be put in command of all Allied forces north of the German salient. Whiteley, who was no admirer of the field marshal and his demands for increased powers, felt that this time he had a point. He discussed the situation with Major General Strong, Eisenhower's intelligence chief and a fellow Briton, and the two of them went that night to see Bedell Smith, the SHAEF chief of staff.

Bedell Smith, woken from his sleep, exploded at what he saw as a British plot. He called them 'Limey bastards' and told them that they should both consider themselves relieved of their duties. Then, after some reflection, he changed his mind. Bedell Smith was unimpressed by Hodges's First Army headquarters and its relationship with Bradley's 12th Army Group, but his real concern was that Bradley was out of touch. He rang Eisenhower to discuss giving Montgomery command of the northern front and suggested that this would also push the 21st Army Group into committing British forces to the battle.

Eisenhower agreed to the proposal, partly because Bradley had taken no steps to reinforce the line of the Meuse as he had ordered. He began to consult the map to decide where the boundary line should be drawn. He decided it would go from Givet on the Meuse, and run north of Bastogne to Prüm behind German lines. Montgomery would command all Allied forces to the north, thus leaving Bradley with just Patton's Third Army and Middleton's VIII Corps, which would be attached to it.

Bedell Smith rang Bradley in Luxembourg to warn him that Eisenhower thought of giving Montgomery command over the Ninth and First Armies. According to Bedell Smith, Bradley admitted that he had been out of touch with Hodges and the First Army for two or three days. 'Certainly if Monty's were an American command,' Bradley acknowledged revealingly, 'I would agree with you entirely. It would be the logical thing to do.'

Next morning, Eisenhower rang Bradley to confirm his decision. Bradley had by now worked himself into a frenzy of outrage. 'By God, Ike, I cannot be responsible to the American people if you do this. I resign.'

'Brad, I — not you — am responsible to the American people,' Eisenhower replied. 'Your resignation therefore means absolutely nothing.' He then dealt with further complaints, and terminated the conversation by saying: 'Well Brad, those are my orders.'

A senior RAF officer present at 12th Army

Group headquarters described how, after the call, an 'absolutely livid' Bradley 'walked up and down and cursed Monty'. Bedell Smith later found it ironic that 'Montgomery for a long time thought Bradley was very fond of him; he didn't know he couldn't stand him.' The dislike in fact went much deeper. Bradley saw Montgomery 'as the personal inspiration of all his troubles', an American staff officer remarked. 'He had long since acquired a distaste for the little man with the beret and the bark.' In his increasingly paranoid mood, a humiliated Bradley saw Eisenhower's decision 'as a slam to me'.

13
WEDNESDAY 20 DECEMBER

Captain Carol Mather left Montgomery's headquarters again at midnight, uneasy at his 'extremely delicate' mission to General Hodges. The journey, slowed by ice and roadblock guards checking for Skorzeny groups, took some two hours. From time to time V-1 missiles flew overhead through the night sky towards Liège. On arrival at First Army headquarters at Chaudfontaine, an MP took him straight to the bedroom of Hodges's authoritarian chief of staff, Major General Bill Kean. Many thought that Kean was the real army commander. Kean was in his pyjamas with a blanket round his shoulders telephoning.

Mather presented the handwritten letter from Montgomery. During a pause, Kean put his hand over the receiver and asked after Montgomery's chief of staff Major General Freddie de Guingand. They then went next door to wake Hodges. Mather described how the First Army commander sat up in bed also with a blanket round his shoulders to read Montgomery's letter. He felt that Hodges was 'completely out of touch' with events. He passed every question to Kean. 'On the important question of the Meuse crossings,' Mather recorded, 'General Hodges had nothing to say. He implied that it was of no great consequence and had been or would be looked after'.

Mather, suffering from loss of sleep, was back with Montgomery well before dawn. The field marshal sat up in bed sipping a cup of tea as he listened to Mather's report. He intended to meet Hodges later that day, but first he wanted an accurate picture of the German breakthrough. Five liaison officers, including two Americans attached to his headquarters, set off in Jeeps immediately. They wore the newly issued tank suits in pale-brown canvas to ward off the cold, but these increased the suspicions of nervous American soldiers manning roadblocks.

On that morning of 20 December, Montgomery took a call from Eisenhower. According to General Miles Dempsey, the commander of the Second British Army, who was with Montgomery when Eisenhower rang, the extraordinarily brief conversation went as follows:

'Monty, we are in a bit of a spot.'

'So I gathered,' the field marshal replied.

'How about taking over in the north?'

'Right.'

Montgomery drove to Chaudfontaine intending to sort out the situation. Mather's report had convinced him that Hodges was in a state of near collapse. In the memorable description of one of his own staff officers, the field marshal arrived at First Army headquarters 'like Christ come to clean the temple', even if Our Lord would not have appeared in a dark-green Rolls-Royce with pennants flying and motorcycle outriders.

Mather, although the most loyal of aides, felt that Montgomery put American backs up unnecessarily on his arrival by ignoring the American generals and summoning his liaison officers who had arrived with their reports of the fighting. 'What's the form?' he demanded, and they crowded round the bonnet of a Jeep with their maps. General Hodges and General Simpson, the commander of the Ninth Army, could only look on in embarrassment. 'It was a slight uncalled for on that day,' Mather wrote.

Montgomery had now taken command of all Allied armies north of that line from Givet on the Meuse to Prüm. He was also deeply concerned about Hodges. On his return, he telephoned Bedell Smith to say that as a British officer he was unwilling to relieve an American general, but that Eisenhower should consider it.[*] Bedell Smith asked for a twenty-four-hour delay. Montgomery sent a message the next day that things could stay as they were, even though Hodges was hardly the man he would have picked. This was a view shared by Bedell Smith, who considered Hodges 'the weakest commander we had'.

Bradley later claimed that Montgomery and SHAEF had grossly exaggerated the danger for their own ends, to deprive him of the First Army. But the situation appeared desperate. Hodges was close to breaking down, and Kean had taken over. Even Kean said the following day that they would not know until Friday 'whether we can hold or will have to withdraw to a defense line such as the Meuse'.

Bradley clearly regretted having chosen the city of Luxembourg for his Eagle Tac headquarters and now felt trapped. It was not just a question of prestige, as he had said to Hansen. If he pulled out, the Luxembourgers would believe they were being abandoned to German vengeance. And even though Brad-

---

[*] There are several accounts of Hodges's collapse at this time. One comes in his aide's diary three days later. 'The General is now well located in a private home. With a chance for rest, and with good food again provided, he is obviously feeling fitter and better able to cope with the constant pressure of this work and strain.'

ley tried to downplay the threat of the enemy offensive, his own staff officers took it very seriously. 'We sandwiched the thermite grenades in amongst the most secret of our papers,' one them wrote, 'to be ready to destroy them if we saw any grey uniforms across the hills.' But unbeknown to all of them, Generaloberst Jodl had persuaded Hitler not to include the city of Luxembourg as an objective in Operation *Herbstnebel.*

The capital of Luxembourg had in any case been ably defended by the 4th Infantry Division, holding the southern shoulder of the breakthrough. Its commander Major General Barton declared stoutly, if not very originally, during the battle: 'The best way to handle these Heinies is to fight 'em.' Barton had refused to allow his artillery battalions to move back. Their task was to maintain fire on the bridges over the Sauer, and he made sure that they were well defended by infantry. This prevented the Germans from bringing forward their heavy weapons, especially anti-tank guns. They were therefore unable to fight back effectively against the 10th Armored Division, which was arriving to support the 4th Division.

Like General Cota of the 28th Division, Barton used reinforced companies to hold key villages and thus block crossroads. Along with the 9th Armored Division on his immediate left, Colonel Luckett's task force was pushed back up the Schwarz Erntz gorge, but held fast at the village of Müllerthal to thwart the Germans as they attempted to break into the rear areas of the division.

In Berdorf, halfway down the east side of the gorge, a small mixed force of 250 men from the 10th Armored and two companies of the 4th Infantry had held on for three days. A heavy attack left them with little ammunition and many wounded in need of evacuation. Three assaults, supported by Nebelwerfer rockets and artillery, were beaten off. But just as the small force feared that they would not be able to hold back another attack, a group of two Shermans and three half-tracks broke through to the town with ammunition and supplies, and then left with the severely wounded. Later, the tank commander in Berdorf, Captain Steve Lang of the 11th Tank Battalion, received orders to withdraw. Each tank carried fifteen infantrymen, 'four inside and eleven clinging for life on the outside'. An artillery barrage was laid on to cover the noise of the tanks moving, and the small force managed to escape before the Germans discovered what was happening.

German attacks along that sector of the front began to weaken on 20 December, and the arrival of more units from General Patton's III Corps meant that the 212th and 276th Volksgrenadier-Divisions made no further advance to the south. Only thick fog prevented the Americans from counter-attacking. The stalwart defence of the southern shoulder meant that the Germans lacked room for manoeuvre, and that the Third Army could concentrate its forces against the encirclement of Bastogne.

Hemingway, eager not to miss the big battle even though he was suffering from influenza, managed to reach Colonel Buck Lanham's command post near Rodenbourg. The house had belonged to a priest suspected of being a German sympathizer. Hemingway took great delight in drinking a stock of communion wine and then refilling the bottles with his own urine. He claimed to have relabelled them 'Schloss Hemingstein 1944' and later drank from one by mistake.

The Germans had already found that their salient was too narrow and that Bastogne controlled the road network. Both Bayerlein of the Panzer Lehr and Kokott of the 26th Volksgrenadier-Division argued that since a swift attempt to take Bastogne had failed, then its defenders must be crushed by the whole corps. But General von Lüttwitz, the commander of XLVII Panzer Corps, was under strict instructions to send his two panzer divisions past Bastogne and straight on to the Meuse.

The German drive to the Meuse was also not helped when the 116th Panzer-Division was ordered to change direction to the northwest. This 'caused a considerable waste of time', wrote its commander Generalmajor Siegfried von Waldenburg, and led to chaos on the overcrowded roads. This decision, he maintained, 'became fatal for the Division'.

The mixed force of paratroopers and 10th Armored in Noville, north of Bastogne, were attacked again and again in rushes by panzers and panzergrenadiers emerging out of the fog. They knew that the road behind them had been cut by another German unit, but not that the battalion of the 506th Parachute Infantry Regiment had been pushed back south of Foy. This would make their escape far more difficult. In the middle of the morning, the fog lifted, and the tanks of the 2nd Panzer-Division opened fire from the high ground. When radio contact was finally reestablished with the beleaguered force in Noville, General McAuliffe told them to prepare to break out. He had decided that despite his orders from General Middleton not to pull them back, he must either rescue or lose them. He told Colonel Sink to launch a renewed assault on Foy to open the road, with his paratroopers of the 506th. German tanks were firing tree bursts in the woods just south of Foy to keep the paratroopers' heads down. Easy Company of the 506th had no anti-tank weapons, but fortunately the Germans never put in a proper armoured attack against them.

By a stroke of luck the fog rolled in again, just as the defenders of Noville were about to withdraw. The infantry left on foot, the wounded and the body of Lieutenant Colonel LaPrade were loaded on half-tracks, the Shermans carried as many men as possible, and the Hellcat tank destroyers acted as rearguard. Demolitions set in the church made the tower collapse across the road as planned. But, as they reached Foy, the armoured visor on the lead half-track came down, obscuring the driver's vision. He brought it to an abrupt halt, and all the following half-tracks rammed into one another: this gave three German panzers, out to the flank, stationary targets to fire at. The leading vehicles caught fire. A soldier further back in the column noted that 'the fog up front turned bright orange'. Crews baled out, and the same soldier watched from the ditch as German fire poured into the column. 'Dead were lying all around on the road and in the ditches. Some were hanging out of their vehicles; killed before they could get out and seek cover. Our trucks and half-tracks were either burning or had been torn to shreds.'

Chaos was finally averted when a Sherman, with paratroopers manning the gun, managed to knock out one of the tanks, and the other two pulled back rapidly. The force with which Desobry and LaPrade had held Noville had lost 212 men and eleven out of fifteen Shermans in less than two days.

General Troy Middleton's determination to maintain an extended perimeter had proved costly, but the sudden withdrawal from Noville seemed to encourage Lüttwitz in the belief that the capture of Bastogne would be straightforward. Generalmajor Kokott claimed that when Lüttwitz visited the headquarters of the 26th Volksgrenadier-Division at Wardin that morning, he said: 'The 2nd Panzer-Division has taken Noville. The enemy is in flight-like retreat to the south. 2nd Panzer-Division is in steady pursuit. The fall of Foy — if it has not already taken place — is to be expected at any moment. After taking Foy, the 2nd Panzer-Division will, according to its orders, turn west and drive into open country.' Lüttwitz, a large, smoothly shaved panzer general with a well-fed face and a monocle, also convinced himself that the Panzer Lehr Division had taken Marvie on the south-eastern edge of Bastogne. Lüttwitz strenuously asserted later that he had urged Fifth Panzer Army to capture Bastogne first, and Bayerlein believed his version.[*]

* Bayerlein claims that on 19 December, after the first attack failed, he had convinced Lüttwitz that the whole corps should be concentrated against Bastogne, because they could not afford to leave such a

Kokott argued that the decision to send on the 2nd Panzer was the major mistake in the failure to take Bastogne. He blamed a lack of clear thinking at Fifth Panzer Army and XLVII Corps level. 'Is Bastogne to be captured? Or is Bastogne to be merely encircled and the Maas River reached?' Only with 2nd Panzer attacking from the north and west, and Panzer Lehr and the bulk of the 26th attacking from the south-west, could they sort out this 'Eiterbeule' or pus-filled boil. But in fact even Manteuffel himself had little say in the matter. Führer headquarters would brook no alteration to the plan.

Orders for the next day were categoric. The 2nd Panzer and Panzer Lehr were to push on westwards with the bulk of their force, leaving the 26th Volksgrenadier plus a panzergrenadier regiment from Panzer Lehr to encircle and capture Bastogne all on their own. 'The Division dutifully expressed its doubts,' wrote Kokott, but Lüttwitz dismissed them, apparently on the grounds that American forces in Bastogne could not be very strong, with 'parts of an Airborne division'

---

centre of road communications untaken in their rear. Lüttwitz is said to have referred the proposal upwards, but it was firmly rejected. Bayerlein heard from him that they 'considered Bastogne child's play'.

and 'the remnants of those enemy divisions which had been badly battered at the Our River and which had taken refuge in Bastogne'. Corps headquarters apparently also believed that 'on the basis of prisoner of war interviews, the fighting quality of the forces inside Bastogne was not very high'.

The 26th Volksgrenadier, having expressed its need for artillery support in the attack ordered on Bastogne, was at least given time to deploy its 39th Regiment which had been guarding the southern flank, while most of the 5th Fallschirmjäger-Division was delayed in the Wiltz valley. Kokott was bemused by Lüttwitz's optimism. His two regiments confronting the Americans in the Foy–Bizôry sector had not detected any weakness. The rest of his division was then sent round to the south of Bastogne towards Lutrebois and Assenois, to attack the town from the south. But through gaps in the mist he spotted American vehicles rushing south from Neffe to Marvie. To the north, 'the deep rumble of artillery could be heard — in the wooded areas west of Wardin, in addition to the crashing impact of the mortars, the fire of rapid German and slower American machineguns was audible'. Roads and forest tracks had been blocked by craters, so the soldiers had to take their heavy weapons off the vehicles and manhandle them.

At about 13.00 hours, American artillery

observers sighted the concentration of vehicles round the divisional headquarters of the 26th Volksgrenadiers in Wardin. Battalion salvoes crashed into the village 'with devastating effects on this assembly of men and machines', Kokott reported. That afternoon he heard that his reconnaissance battalion, when crossing the southern road to Arlon, had come into contact with the enemy. Matters were not helped by the chaos on roads and tracks south of Bastogne, with vehicles from the Panzer Lehr, the 26th Volksgrenadier and now an advance unit of the 5th Fallschirmjäger all trying to push on to the west but getting hopelessly entangled. Youngsters of the 5th Fallschirmjäger had to pull their own few vehicles when they broke down.

One of Kokott's Volksgrenadier battalions managed to break in from the north-east along a railway track, which was guarded by little more than a strong patrol because it was on the boundary between the 506th and the 501st Parachute Infantry Regiments. The patrol's resistance slowed the Volksgrenadier advance. Both Colonel Sink south of Foy and Colonel Ewell reacted quickly, sending a company each to block the penetration. Soon they found that the enemy force was larger than they had realized, and more units had to be hurried in, including, to their own disbelief, those who had escaped that day from Noville. The battle carried on well into the next day.

Another attack on the Neffe sector that evening by the Panzer Lehr was hit by a rapid response of concentrated artillery fire. McAuliffe could now count on eleven artillery battalions, several from the 101st, but also others from divisions which had withdrawn via Bastogne, including two battalions of African-American gunners. This gave him a total of around 130 pieces, but ammunition shortages would soon become a problem. Hellcats from the 705th Tank Destroyer Battalion firing tracer from their machine guns, as well as every automatic weapon in Ewell's 1st Battalion, caught the two battalions of panzergrenadiers in the open, exposed in the dark by the deathly glow of illuminating flares. They had been slowed down in this night attack by barbed-wire cattle fences. The carnage was sickening. Daylight next morning revealed a hideous sight of corpses caught on the wire like scarecrows battered by a freak storm.

General Middleton in his VIII Corps headquarters at Neufchâteau, some thirty kilometres south-west of Bastogne, was impatient for Patton's counter-attack from the south to begin. The 4th Armored Division Combat Command B had reached Vaux-les-Rosières halfway between the two towns. To the irritation of the commander of III Corps, Middleton's headquarters ordered it to send a combat team north immediately, rather than wait for the major attack which Patton had promised. Patton too was furious, and ordered the combat team to be recalled. Whether or not such a small force could have secured the road is open to question, but some historians believe that it would have made the advance from the south much less expensive in lives and tanks. In any case, the town of Bastogne was cut off from the south that evening, shortly after General McAuliffe had driven back from a meeting with Middleton. The town was not entirely surrounded, but most people assumed it was.

For the paratroopers of the 101st, encirclement by the enemy was seen as part of the job. Louis Simpson, the poet and company runner, was sent back on an errand to battalion headquarters. On the way he came across a Sherman tank, with a sergeant from the 10th Armoured Division 'seated negligently in the turret, as if on the saddle of a horse'. Fifty metres down the road, a panzer burned. He asked the sergeant what had happened. 'They tried to get through,' the sergeant replied in a bored voice and turned away. Simpson pondered the fact that this was behind his own company's line. They would have been cut off if the 'appallingly casual' sergeant had not fired first. 'I saw Tolstoy's sergeant at Borodino, with his pipe stuck in his mouth, directing the fire of his battery. On men like this the hinge of battle swung. They did not see themselves in a dramatic role. They would do great tasks, and be abused for not doing them right, and accept this as normal.'

At battalion headquarters he heard that they were now surrounded within the Bastogne perimeter. When he returned to his foxhole in the snow, his neighbour called across: 'Welcome home! So what's new?'

'We're surrounded.'

'So what's new?'

First Army and Montgomery's headquarters lacked a clear idea of the situation round St Vith. Montgomery's instinct was to pull back Hasbrouck's forces there before they were crushed, but the US Army had a proud dislike of abandoning ground. First Army wanted to send the 82nd Airborne forward to reinforce the defenders. At midday on 20 December, while they were discussing the problem, a letter reached Major General Bill Kean from Hasbrouck in St Vith outlining their embattled state. His horseshoe line extended from Poteau to the north-west of St Vith, down and round to Gouvy station to the south-west. His southern flank and rear were now totally exposed following the advance of the 116th Panzer-Division towards Houffalize.

Montgomery was convinced that the defence of St Vith had served its purpose well. The threat now lay further to the west, with three panzer divisions heading for the Meuse. He agreed, however, that the 82nd Airborne should continue its advance to the River Salm, but only to help extricate Hasbrouck's forces through the gap between Vielsalm and Salmchâteau.

In the afternoon the division's 504th Parachute Infantry Regiment advanced towards Cheneux, which was held by the light flak battalion of the SS *Leibstandarte* and a battalion of its panzergrenadiers. Colonel Reuben H. Tucker, the regimental commander, sent two companies into the attack through the mist. Coming under heavy machine-gun and 20mm-flak fire, they went to ground, suffering many casualties. When darkness fell, they pulled back to the woods behind. On hearing of this, Tucker ordered them to attack again. They managed to get closer in the dark, but barbed-wire fences across the fields held them up. Exposed to an even greater concentration of fire, men torn on the fences were shot down on all sides. The attack was about to stall when Staff Sergeant George Walsh yelled, 'Let's get those sons of bitches!' Only a handful of men made it to the roadblock on the edge of the village. One managed to throw a grenade into a flak half-track and a second cut the throat of a gunner on another. But the two companies suffered 232 casualties, including twenty-three killed. Their action was heroic, but Tucker's gung-ho decision was shockingly wasteful. The next day, Tucker sent another battalion around the flank, which is what he should have done the first time. With comparatively few losses, the 3rd Battalion took the village, along with fourteen flak wagons, another six half-tracks and a battery of self-propelled guns.

On 20 December the fighting round St Vith approached a climax as Model and Manteuffel became desperate to seize the town in an all-out assault. The Germans used their Nebelwerfer rocket launchers, targeting American mortar pits, whose crews were causing savage losses to the ranks of the Volksgrenadier battalions. Under heavy shellfire, many soldiers, bunched into a foetal position in the bottom of their foxholes, would keep repeating the 23rd Psalm, as a mantra to calm themselves 'in the valley of the shadow of death'.

Visibility was 'still very bad', Hasbrouck reported. 'Twenty-one enemy attacks were launched from north, east and south. Tanks were coming in from all directions accompanied by infantry.' The five American field artillery battalions fired almost 7,000 rounds on that day alone. 'The only way ammunition supply had been kept up was by hunting for and finding abandoned dumps toward the front . . . The 434th Field Artillery Battalion was reported to have fired even some old propaganda shells [used for leaflets] just to keep projectiles whistling around German ears.'

One attack was led by SS panzergrenadiers from the *Leibstandarte Adolf Hitler,* using a captured American half-track at the front of the column in the hope of confusing the defenders. But Shermans and bazooka teams managed to deal with them. 'We stressed to every man', wrote Major Boyer of the 38th Armored Infantry Battalion, 'that "no ammunition could be wasted — that for every round fired, a corpse must hit the ground," and that fire should be held until Germans were within 25 yards,' when fighting in the woods around the town. This order was also to discourage men from revealing their positions by firing too early.

Oberst Otto Remer's *Führer Begleit* Brigade finally did what it had been told, and began a probing attack on St Vith down the road from Büllingen. But Remer considered American resistance to be 'too heavy' and moved his brigade north and into thick woods below Born. He decided that he would take the main road west towards Vielsalm, but was then rather affronted when told to move back to the south. He claimed that he did not have enough fuel for his tanks, but the objective he had been given — the twin villages of Nieder-Emmels and Ober-Emmels — were little more than five kilometres away.

That evening after firing had died away, Hasbrouck's men could hear the sound of tanks. They knew that the Germans were almost certainly preparing an even greater onslaught for dawn the next morning.

With his Kampfgruppe under attack from all directions, Peiper brought back his outlying group from west of Stoumont. They then abandoned the town and pulled back to counter-attack the 117th Infantry from the 30th Division. Peiper had been bitter about the lack of support from his own division. He claimed later that he had been told that unless he reported on the state of his fuel supplies, he would not receive any more. Radio contact had been non-existent until the night before when an officer from the *Leibstandarte* had managed to get through, with a new and more powerful radio. Peiper learned that the division had sent forward the 2nd SS Panzergrenadier-Regiment to open a route. These troops had bridging equipment and before dawn they waded 'neck-deep' into the fast-flowing and freezing River Amblève supported by machinegun and tank fire. But, by the light of illuminating flares fired overhead, American soldiers crouching at windows in houses which overlooked the river began to

pick off the SS pioneers and panzergrenadiers. 'Them bastards was hopped up,' one of
them said later. Three times the Americans
were driven out of their positions in the
houses by the river, 'forced out by direct fire
from tanks, and three times the infantry came
back and drove out the SS men'.

Peiper's panzergrenadiers had continued
their casual killing of civilians. They had
murdered two women and a man 'in a nearby
street for no apparent reason', and later they
put nine men against the walls of houses and
killed them too. An SS trooper in an armoured vehicle 'emptied his machine gun
into a house', killing a fourteen-year-old boy.
The killing spree continued, but some bodies
were not found until several days later.
Belgian civilians were killed on the road
towards Trois-Ponts: five were found shot in
the head, while a woman was killed lying in
bed. On the evening of 19 December, twenty
townsfolk, mainly women and children, were
forced out of a basement at gunpoint and
shot by a hedge. Altogether more than 130
civilians, mostly women and children, were
murdered in and around Stavelot. The young
men had fled beyond the Meuse to avoid
retribution for Resistance attacks in September, or to escape being marched off for forced
labour in Germany. Waffen-SS claims that
their killings were reprisals for partisans
shooting at them had no basis in truth.

At 11.15 hours Peiper's troops again tried to establish a bridgehead over the river, with panzergrenadiers swimming and wading across. Rapid rifle and machine-gun fire killed many of them in the water and bodies were washed downstream. Only a few made it to the northern bank and they too were soon dealt with. A simultaneous attack was mounted from the west, forcing back the 1st Battalion of the 117th Infantry a hundred metres or so, where they held on until the firing petered out at dusk around 16.00 hours.

Peiper's difficulties had increased from another direction. Combat Command B of the 3rd Armored Division reached the Amblève valley that morning, coming from Spa via woodland tracks. One task force, commanded by Lieutenant Colonel William B. Lovelady, emerged from the trees on to the road between La Gleize and Trois-Ponts, and there surprised and destroyed a column of German trucks carrying fuel escorted by assault guns and infantry.

The desperate position of the Kampfgruppe Peiper was not due solely to the courageous resistance shown by the 30th Infantry Division, tank battalions and engineer units. The powerful defence of the Elsenborn ridge to the east had prevented the rest of the 1st SS Panzer-Division and the 12th SS *Hitler Jugend* from reinforcing Peiper's advance. II SS Panzer Corps, with the 9th SS Panzer-

Division *Hohenstaufen,* had started to advance parallel with I SS Panzer Corps. The 2nd SS Panzer-Division *Das Reich* was supposedly following, but the single-track roads were so jammed with traffic that it had sought a route further south.

The Sixth Panzer Army blamed these failures on the fact that the only road was 'for the most part impassable because of the mire'. In many places, the mud was axle-deep, but in fact it was the American 1st Division's resolute defence of Bütgenbach which prevented the I SS Panzer Corps from using the much better road to the north. As a result, the 12th SS Panzer and the 12th Volksgrenadier-Division were kept battering away at the southern flank of the Elsenborn ridge, while the 3rd Panzergrenadier-Division and the 277th Volksgrenadiers attacked the eastern end above the twin villages of Rocherath–Krinkelt and Wirtzfeld. The 2nd Infantry Division continued to find that 'under almost continuous, heavy enemy artillery fire, wire lines went out nearly as soon as they were laid or repaired and communication was primarily by radio'.

Camp Elsenborn was a typical army post with officer apartments near the main gate, surrounded by single-storey barracks, garages and armouries. It stood in the middle of hilly, barren, windswept firing ranges. The barracks teemed with exhausted, dirty and bearded stragglers who were fed, rested briefly and then sent back into the line. Doctors and medics provided first aid to the wounded before evacuating them further back, now that the 47th Field Hospital in Waimes had been relocated just in time. Men discovered buddies they thought had been killed, and asked after others who were missing. Stories circulated of SS troopers killing wounded and executing prisoners and, coming on top of the news of the massacre at Baugnez, the determination to resist at all costs increased. Refugees packed the village of Elsenborn, and American troops became deeply suspicious of them, seeing them as potential German sympathizers. But until they were evacuated on Christmas Day, their fate under German artillery fire was little better than if they had stayed in their farms and houses below.

On the eastern side of the Elsenborn ridge, the 2nd Infantry Division and the remnants of the 99th found digging in on the shale hillside very hard, so they filled wooden ammunition boxes with dirt, and covered their foxholes with doors ripped out of the barracks. Short of stretchers, they scrounged several from Camp Elsenborn, although they were still sticky with blood and smelled bad when warm. On the exposed hillside, they shivered in uniforms damp from the mud and wet snow, so they made makeshift heaters for their foxholes, either using some gasoline-soaked earth in a tin, or burning bits of wood in a jerrycan with a large hole cut out at the bottom as a fire-door. These inventions concealed the flames from observation, but the foxhole-dweller's unshaven face soon became impregnated with a black, oily grime. Many tried to create a warm fug in their foxhole by covering it and their stove with a waterproof cape, causing a few to asphyxiate themselves in the process. Almost everyone suffered from thudding headaches, brought on by the barrages fired over their heads by the field artillery just behind. The fact that the rounds were coming from their own guns did not stop men who had been under heavy enemy fire over the last few days from flinching at the noise.

They again faced the 3rd Panzergrenadiers, which consisted of little more than a large Kampfgruppe in its total strength, and the 277th Volksgrenadiers, worn down by the earlier battles. These two formations attacked north of Rocherath–Krinkelt past a cross-roads the Germans named 'Sherman Ecke', or Sherman Corner, because of some knocked-out Sherman tanks with drooping barrels. But, as they mounted the little valley of the Schwalm, they were crushed by the weight of American artillery fire. 'The concentrated enemy artillery fire from the Elsenborn area was so strong', wrote the commander of the panzergrenadiers, 'that all roads leading to the front and all assembly areas were covered, and all our attacks brought to a standstill.'

The Elsenborn ridge provided the Americans with perfect fire positions for their sixteen field artillery battalions with 155mm Long Toms and 105mm howitzers, and seven battalions of corps artillery, including 4.5-inch and 8-inch guns. The longer-range artillery batteries were able to hammer villages and crossroads up to sixteen kilometres into the German rear. The unfortunate Belgian civilians trapped there could only sob and say their prayers in cellars, as their houses shook from the bombardment. 'Farmers learned to take care of cattle during the briefest of morning lulls that were soon known as the Americans' *Kaffeepause.*' It was impossible to bury the dead while the battle raged. Most were laid out in the local church wrapped in blankets. When the temperature dropped suddenly two days before Christmas, nobody could dig graves in the frozen ground.

During the night of 20–21 December, the Germans launched their largest attack on the southern flank against the 26th Infantry Regiment of the 1st Infantry Division around Dom Bütgenbach. Supported by more than thirty tanks and assault guns, two battalions of SS *Hitler Jugend* were sent into battle. A Belgian farmer had watched as twenty exhausted German youngsters, from fifteen to

410

seventeen years old, were dragged weeping from his cellar in Büllingen by NCOs to force them into battle.

A total of twelve American artillery battalions and a battalion of 4.2-inch mortars placed 'a ring of steel' around the 1st Division's defensive positions. Yet a group of the *Hitler Jugend* panzers broke through on the 26th Infantry's right flank and began to 'iron' the foxholes of the forward defence line, running over them and firing into them. Arthur S. Couch was operating a 60mm mortar near battalion headquarters. 'Soon I noticed that tank shells were coming right over my head, along with tracer machine gun bullets. It was a foggy night so at first I couldn't see the German tanks, but as dawn started I could see a number of German tanks maneuvering around about 200 yards in front of my position. I soon ran out of mortar shells so I asked by radio for some more from battalion headquarters in a manor house about 400 yards to my left. To my welcome surprise, two men from battalion came running with large numbers of new shells in a cart. The German tanks seemed to know we had a mortar position but they couldn't see it in the foggy conditions. Another phone call said one of my mortar shells had landed in a German tank and blown it up. After a few more minutes I could see that a German tank was going along our front line and firing directly

411

into the foxholes. I kept firing because I was very concerned that German infantry troops would soon be able to advance the 200 yards towards my position if I didn't stop them. I got word on my phone that German tanks were in the battalion headquarters.'

Several of these panzers were knocked out by anti-tank guns and Shermans, but only the arrival of a platoon of tank destroyers with the high-velocity 90mm gun managed to smash the attack. The losses inflicted on the *Hitler Jugend* were devastating. A Graves Registration unit counted 782 German dead. The 26th Infantry suffered 250 casualties.

More assaults on the ridge were mounted, but it became clear to both Rundstedt and Model that Hitler's beloved Sixth Panzer Army had utterly failed in its task, both around Monschau in the north, which was now reinforced with the 9th Infantry Division, and above all in front of Elsenborn. Its commander Sepp Dietrich was both angry and resentful, feeling that he was not to blame for the Führer's disappointment.

When the Ardennes offensive started, several British officers at 21st Army Group were teased by Belgian friends, who said that their Resistance groups were making preparations to hide them. When they replied that that would not be necessary as everything was well in hand, they received the answer: 'That is precisely what you said in 1940, and you left us next day.' Montgomery had no intention of allowing anything of the sort to happen again.

At 17.30 hours on 19 December, the day before Eisenhower gave him command in the north, Montgomery had ordered Lieutenant General Brian Horrocks's XXX Corps to secure the Meuse crossings. The 61st Reconnaissance Regiment in Bruges 'bombed-up, tanked up, loaded up and drove into the night'. Reinforced with an anti-tank troop, one squadron also headed to the bridge at Dinant. As well as watching for 'Germans masquerading as Yanks', they were to guard against enemy frogmen. Any flotsam in the river was blasted with Bren-gun fire. The 3rd Royal Tank Regiment, also at Dinant, worked with American MPs checking traffic and 'a small but steady trickle of American stragglers', as the bridges were prepared for demolition.

SAS and Phantom reconnaissance teams were already in position. On de Gaulle's orders, they were followed by the seven badly armed French battalions under Général de Division André Dody, and also by some scratch units from General Lee's Com Z supply troops. General Bedell Smith was greatly relieved by the commitment of XXX Corps. He said later that 'I felt that we were all right if [the Germans] went north because if they angled towards Liège–Namur we had Horrocks's Corps of four veteran divisions. We knew Horrocks and knew he had good men.'

Because of their severe losses in tanks, the Americans also asked the British 21st Army Group for replacements. Altogether it would send about 350 Shermans, with the Guards Armoured Division bringing the first batch of eighty down itself with their radios removed, as the Americans used different sets.

While the line of the Meuse was secured, SHAEF's insistence on controlling news of the Ardennes offensive drew heavy criticism. This was partly an ineffectual attempt to conceal the fact that it had been caught out by the surprise attack. *Time* magazine soon declared that SHAEF and 12th Army Group 'clamped down a censorship thicker than the pea-soup fog that shrouded the great German counterattack'. And even when news was finally released, 'communiqués were as much as 48 hours behind the event', and deliberately vague. Some senior officers at SHAEF simply regarded journalists as an unnecessary evil. Bedell Smith told Third Army headquarters on the telephone: 'Personally I would like to shoot the lot of them.'

Not only correspondents complained. Senior British officers at SHAEF felt that this policy was having 'disastrous results on Belgian and French morale if not all western allies . . . It is undermining the credibility of our own news; it is encouraging people to listen to German broadcasts in order to find out the truth; and it is giving rise to a flood of rumours . . . The present SHAEF policy is merely leading the public to believe that serious disasters are being concealed.'

In Paris, many became convinced that the German attack was heading straight for the French capital. Wild rumours began to circulate. The Communists even tried to claim that the Americans had been so angry about the Franco-Soviet treaty signed in Moscow earlier that month by General de Gaulle that they were letting the Germans through simply to give the French a fright.

At the Adlerhorst Hitler was still elated, even though the advance was far behind schedule. News of the great counter-attack was released in Germany. 'The wholly unexpected winter offensive in the Ardennes', wrote a staff officer with Army Group Upper Rhine, 'is the most wonderful Christmas present for our people. So we can still do it! . . . We had thought that this sixth Christmas of the war would hardly be festive and happy.' Unfortunately for the Nazis, the desperation to believe in something positive raised expectations far too high. Many persuaded themselves that France would be reconquered and the war brought to an end.

Some women were encouraged in this delusion by letters from their menfolk taking part in the battle. 'You cannot imagine what glorious hours and days we are experiencing now,' a Leutnant wrote to his wife. 'It looks as if the Americans cannot withstand our important push. Today we overtook a fleeing column and finished it . . . It was a glorious bloodbath, vengeance for our destroyed Homeland. Our soldiers still have the same old zip. Always advancing and smashing everything. The snow must turn red with American blood. Victory was never as close as it is now. The decision will soon be reached. We will throw them into the ocean, the arrogant big-mouthed apes from the New World. They will not get into our Germany. We will protect our wives and children from all enemy domination. If we are to preserve all tender and beautiful aspects of our lives, we cannot be too brutal in the deciding moments of this struggle.'

Goebbels noted that, following the announcement of the offensive, the entire Christmas ration of schnapps was consumed in Berlin. But sceptical Berliners, on the other hand, were less impressed. With characteristic gallows humour, they joked about the approach of a very unfestive Christmas: 'Be practical, give a coffin.' Their thoughts focused more on the threat from the east, and many privately prayed that the Americans would break through and reach the capital before the Red Army.

News of the offensive produced very different reactions among the German generals held prisoner in Britain. A secretly recorded conversation showed that Generalleutnant Ferdinand Heim, captured at Boulogne, Generaloberst Ramcke, the veteran paratrooper who had led the defence of Brest, and Standartenführer Kurt Meyer, the former commander of the 12th SS Panzer-Division *Hitler Jugend,* were all excited. Heim called it 'The Battle of the Long Nights'. 'Just rumble forward at night,' he cried out, 'just keep rumbling on!'

'Panzermeyer' agreed. 'The old principle of tank warfare: "forward, forward, forward!" . . . This is where the superiority of German leadership and especially of German junior commanders comes into play.' As a panzer leader, he was however concerned that the replacement tank gunners did not have enough experience. He was also in two minds whether the offensive might be over-ambitious and thus counterproductive, but Ramcke was having none of that. 'This offensive is terrific!' he insisted. 'The German people cannot be got down. You'll see that we shall chase the Allies right across France and hurl them into the Bay of Biscay!'

Others, on the other hand, were scathing. General der Panzertruppe Heinrich Eberbach said of Hitler: 'That man will never stop having illusions. When he is standing under the gallows he will still be under the illusion that he's not going to be hanged.' And Generalleutnant Otto Elfeldt, who had been captured in the Falaise Gap, reminded his listeners: 'It's Wednesday today, and if they have advanced only 40 kilometres in five days, I can only say that that is no offensive. A slow-moving offensive is no good at all because it allows the enemy to bring up reserves far too quickly.'

1. US Infantry advancing through a hole blasted in the Siegfried Line, or Westwall, in October 1944.

2. Fallschirmjäger mortar crew in the Hürtgen Forest. Mortars accounted for the highest number of casualties on both sides.

3. 1st Infantry Division in the Hürtgen Forest.

4. Medics with wounded soldier.

5. French troops in the Vosges. The North African soldiers in the First French Army attacking the Colmar Gap south-west of Strasbourg suffered terribly from the cold.

6. 7 December 1944, Maastricht meeting with (*l* to *r*) Bradley, Tedder, Eisenhower, Montgomery and Simpson.

7. German prisoners captured in early December in the Hürtgen Forest near Düren.

8. Generalfeldmarschall Walter Model, commander-in-chief Army Group B.

9. Field Marshal Montgomery appears to be lecturing an increasingly exasperated Eisenhower once again.

10. General der Panzertruppe Hasso-Eccard Freiherr von Manteuffel of the Fifth Panzer Army.

11. Oberstgruppenführer-SS Sepp Dietrich of the Sixth Panzer Army wearing his Knight's Cross with oak leaves.

12. Oberst then Generalmajor Heinz Kokott, the rather more enlightened commander of the 26th Volksgrenadier-Division at Bastogne.

13. Oberstleutnant Friedrich Freiherr von der Heydte, the law professor turned paratroop commander.

14. The briefing of panzer commanders in a snow flurry just before the Ardennes offensive on 16 December 1944.

15. Two SS panzergrenadiers enjoying captured American cigarettes.

16. 16 December. A Königstiger tank of the Sixth Panzer Army carrying soldiers of the 3rd Fallschirmjäger-Division on the first day of the advance.

17. German infantry in a Volksgrenadier division advance loaded down with machine-gun belts and panzerfaust anti-tank grenade launchers.

18. The first killing of American prisoners by SS panzergrenadiers from the Kampfgruppe Peiper in Honsfeld who then proceeded to loot the bodies. The boots have been removed from the victim on the left.

19. SS panzergrenadiers from the Kampfgruppe Hansen pass a burning convoy of American vehicles near Poteau.

20. American prisoners taken by the 1st SS Panzer-Division *Leibstandarte Adolf Hitler*.

21. 17 December. Part of the 26th Infantry Regiment (1st Infantry Division) arrives just in time to defend Bütgenbach at the base of the Elsenborn ridge.

22. Members of the same regiment manoeuvring an anti-tank gun in the mud as the Germans approach.

23. Belgian refugees leaving Langlir (south-west of Vielsalm) as the Fifth Panzer Army advances. Most wanted to cross the Meuse to escape the fighting and German reprisals for Resistance activities earlier in the year.

24. As the Germans advanced on the town of St Vith following the encirclement of the 106th Infantry Division, the people of Schönberg fled the fighting to shelter in caves.

25. American medics turned skis into improvised toboggans to drag the wounded on stretchers back to a point where they could be loaded on to Jeeps.

26. With a comrade already dead in the foreground, American troops dig in hastily on the forward edge of a wood to avoid the effect of tree bursts.

27. As the Germans advance on Bastogne and the first members of the 101st Airborne arrive to defend it, townsfolk start to flee in farm carts.

28. A platoon of M-36 tank destroyers emerge from the mist near Werbomont in support of the 82nd Airborne Division also rushed in by huge convoys of trucks.

29. German Volksgrenadiers taken prisoner in the fighting round the twin villages of Rocherath–Krinkelt.

30. Brigadier General Robert W. Hasbrouck, who commanded the 7th Armored Division and the defence of St Vith, receiving the silver star from Lieutenant General Courtney Hodges of the First Army.

31. In the wake of the scare caused by Otto Skorzeny's disguised commandos behind American lines, US military police check the identities of Belgian refugees near Marche-en-Famenne.

32. Dinant. Belgian refugees rush to cross the Meuse to safety to avoid German reprisals and the fighting.

33. A bazooka team from Cota's 28th Infantry Division withdraw after three days of fighting in Wiltz. This helped delay the Germans and allow the 101st Airborne just enough time to establish a defensive perimeter around Bastogne.

34. A young SS trooper taken prisoner near Malmédy, fortunate not to have been shot out of hand after the massacre nearby at Baugnez.

35. Civilians murdered by Kampfgruppe Peiper at Stavelot.

36. Vapour trails over Bastogne. On 23 December, the skies suddenly cleared to Allied relief and German anxiety. This allowed the Allied air forces to deploy the overwhelming strength of their air forces.

37. The change in the weather at last allowed the US Air Force to send in its C-47 Dakota transport aircraft to drop supplies into the Bastogne perimeter.

38. Unable to evacuate their wounded from Bastogne, the American command had to leave their casualties in cellars in the town, where they lay on straw awaiting the arrival of surgical teams dropped in by glider.

39. Paratroopers of the 101st Airborne sing carols on Christmas Eve just a few hours before the all-out German attack on the perimeter.

40. The end of the German thrust to the Meuse. Remnants of the Kampfgruppe Böhm from the 2nd Panzer-Division in a farmyard in Foy-Notre-Dame.

41. General Patton (*right*) reaches Bastogne on 30 December and decorates both Brigadier General Anthony McAuliffe (*left*) and Lieutenant Colonel Steve Chappuis (*centre*), the commander of the 502nd Parachute Infantry, with the Distinguished Service Cross.

42. American reinforcements advancing in steeply wooded Ardennes terrain.

43. A patrol from the British XXX Corps in the Ardennes wearing snowsuits made out of villagers' bedsheets.

44. The Allied counter-offensive in January 1945. Soldiers from the 26th Infantry Regiment of the 1st Division finally advance from Bütgenbach, which they had defended since 17 December.

45. La Roche-en-Ardenne was so badly destroyed that when swallows returned to rebuild their nests in the spring, they became disorientated.

46. Investigators start the work of identifying the American soldiers massacred at Baugnez near Malmédy.

47. After the massacre of American soldiers near Malmédy, their comrades, with the encouragement of senior commanders, shot most Waffen-SS soldiers who surrendered. Yet many had been forced into SS uniform against their will, or were pathetically young, like this boy.

48. Joachim Peiper on trial for war crimes including the massacre near Malmédy. Although the death sentence was commuted, members of the French Resistance killed him later.

14
THURSDAY 21 DECEMBER

By the morning of 21 December, the Kampf-gruppe Peiper was in a desperate situation, 'pocketed without adequate supplies', as its leader put it. He received a message from 1st SS Panzer-Division that it intended to advance through Trois-Ponts to relieve him. But Peiper's reduced strength could not even hold Stoumont and Cheneux, and the relief force failed to get through. The enraged troops looted the Château de Detilleux south of the Amblève and destroyed whatever they did not take. Others in Wanne murdered five men and a woman, claiming that villagers must have been signalling to the American artillery. Another group of nine SS soldiers later seized food from a house in Refat and raped three women there after they had eaten.

In Stavelot on the morning of 21 December, another 100 German soldiers tried to swim the river to obtain a foothold on the north bank. Eighty of them were shot in the water by soldiers of the 117th Infantry who boasted of their 'duck shooting'; and the rest turned back. Peiper's position became even more critical when American combat engineers managed to block the road from Stoumont to La Gleize by blasting trees across it and mining the route. He had no alternative but to withdraw most of his remaining troops into La Gleize, where the 30th Division's artillery began to bombard the village.

The battle against the Kampfgruppe had become savage. 'After we saw those dead civilians in Stavelot, the men changed,' one of the soldiers recorded. 'They wanted to pulverize everything there was across the river. That wasn't impersonal anger; that was hatred.' Few SS soldiers were taken alive. Officers in the Waffen-SS apparently turned news of the Malmédy massacre to their own advantage, hoping to frighten their men into fighting to the bitter end. They told them that if captured, they would be tortured and then killed.

'The prisoner bag is thus far small,' an officer at First Army headquarters noted. 'Our troops know of the atrocities committed by the enemy and know that now it is a matter of life or death, we or they.' A number of senior officers made it clear that they approved of revenge killing. When General Bradley heard soon afterwards that prisoners from the 12th SS Panzer-Division *Hitler Jugend* had spoken of their heavy casualties, he raised his eyebrows sceptically. 'Prisoners from the 12th SS?'

'Oh, yes sir,' the officer replied. 'We needed a few samples. That's all we've taken, sir.'

Bradley smiled. 'Well, that's good,' he said.

Bradley was encouraged by the sight of Patton's troops rolling north to attack Manteuffel's southern flank. He and members of his staff stood outside the Hôtel Alfa in Luxembourg on 21 December to watch the columns of 5th Infantry Division vehicles, 'caked in mud', passing through the city all day. 'The GIs looked cold,' Hansen wrote in his diary, 'bundled in brown against the winter wind that tore through their open vehicles, sitting stone-facedly on the piles of baggage in their trucks as they rode through town, staring back vacantly at the civilians who looked earnestly to them.'

Montgomery, all too conscious of the Germans' determination to cross the Meuse with their panzer divisions, recognized that First Army had to extend its line westward, well beyond the 30th Division's block on the Peiper Kampfgruppe. Major General Matthew B. Ridgway, a tall and formidable paratrooper who never appeared without grenades hooked on both shoulder straps of his webbing harness, had arrived to take command of the XVIII Airborne Corps west of the River Salm. Beyond, stretching towards the Meuse, Montgomery insisted on having the young Major General J. Lawton Collins in command of VII Corps. Montgomery regarded him as one of the very best American corps commanders, and Hodges also rated him highly. The First Army chronicler noted that 'General Collins is full of his usual fighting Irish vigour.' Collins was to have the 3rd Armored Division, the 84th Infantry Division and the 2nd Armored Division, Patton's old outfit known as 'Hell on Wheels'.

Ridgway, supported by Kean, the chief of staff First Army, and now Collins, argued that they should drive on St Vith while the defenders continued to hold out. 'Monty would come down about every other day to my command post,' Collins recorded. 'He would call Ridgway over to meet me at the same time, and would discuss the situation with us . . . I had gotten to know Monty well enough, and somehow or another we hit it off well. I could talk to him and disagree with him and he didn't get mad.' Montgomery opposed the idea of a corps attack towards St Vith partly on the grounds that a single road was insufficient to support a whole corps. 'Joe, you can't support a corps over a single road,' he said, no doubt remembering the route to Arnhem.

'Well, Monty, maybe you can't, but we can,' Collins retorted.

But both Hasbrouck, the commander of the

7th Armored Division, and Bruce Clarke of Combat Command B strongly disagreed with the plan to relieve St Vith. They felt afterwards that Montgomery had been right when he wanted to withdraw its defenders. They also thought that Ridgway was unnecessarily gung-ho and, as a paratrooper, did not understand the use of armoured formations.

Having heard the noise of tanks during the night of 20–21 December, the defenders of St Vith had expected an attack at dawn, but it did not come until towards the end of the morning. German volksgrenadiers began knocking out American machine-gun positions with grenades and the 'dread Panzerfaust'. They were so close that the American machine-gunners used 'swinging traverse', spraying fire in all directions. Hasbrouck's artillery battalions, although short of shells, responded to calls for fire missions within two to four minutes, 'bringing down fire within fifty yards of our own men'.

At 15.15 hours the battle died down, but Major Boyer suspected that it 'would prove to be only the lull before the storm'. They had no reserves left. Half an hour later, the German Nebelwerfer batteries suddenly opened fire again. Trees were lacerated. 'Huge gashes were cut in the logs over our holes, and all around us we could hear the crash and ripping of tree tops and even of trees as the merciless hail of steel swept and lashed through the forest. Again and again we heard the anguished scream of some man somewhere who had been hit, and yet all we could do was cower in our foxholes with our backs against the forward walls, hoping that we would not receive a direct hit. It seemed as if our very nerves were being torn out by the roots as the screaming steel crashed around us.'

The Germans attacked through the woods under the cover of the barrage. Boyer shouted out 'Heads up!' as the bombardment lifted. His infantrymen opened fire as the Germans tried to rush across the logging road. An American with a bazooka managed to knock out a self-propelled assault gun. And 'a Panther was destroyed when one soldier with a bazooka climbed out of his hole, ran forward and pressing his tube against the fender line, pulled the trigger. As he fired, he slumped to the ground dead.'

Two Panthers began methodically knocking out the foxholes one after another with direct fire. One of Boyer's officers called over the radio 'with tears in his voice' asking where the tank destroyers were to deal with the Panthers. 'Goddamn it, they've two heavy tanks here on the crest, and they're blasting my men out of their holes one at a time.' But no Shermans or tank destroyers were in their sector. Soon after nightfall, Boyer reported that he thought they could hold through the night, but just after seven the German on-slaught began again, with Nebelwerfers and panzers eliminating foxholes one by one.

The German attacks came from three directions astride the main roads into the town from the north, east and south-east. The defenders were soon overwhelmed. Every machine gun in Boyer's battalion had been manned by several crews. 'As soon as one team was destroyed, it was replaced by other men.' By 22.00 'German tanks had blasted their way through the center of the line and were entering Saint-Vith.' This cut off the 38th Armored Infantry on the south-east side of the town after five days of battle with no sleep, little food and many suffering from frostbite. Boyer's battalion of 670 men was reduced to 185 men still on their feet. All the rest were dead or severely wounded. Snow began to fall heavily.

Brigadier General Clarke of Combat Command B issued the order: 'Reform. Save what vehicles you can; attack to the west through Saint-Vith. We are forming a new line west of the town.' Finding the order impossible to carry out, Boyer told his men to break out in groups of four or five, taking only personal weapons. He sent a runner to the mortar platoon with the instruction to destroy vehicles, but salvage their mortars and bi-pods. A medic volunteered to be left behind with the wounded. The exhausted men trudged through the falling snow into the forest. A point man led them by compass, and each soldier was told to hold on to the equipment of the one in front of him.

St Vith's streets were littered with rubble and broken glass, the slaughterhouse was on fire, and terrorized cattle rampaged in the streets. During the heavy shelling the day before, many civilians in the town had packed some belongings and sought refuge in the St Josef Kloster, which had solid vaulted cellars. As the bombardment intensified, Father Goffart decided to join the refugees below. 'He took a chalice and wafers with him and built a small altar in one of the subterranean storage rooms.' By the time of the all-out German attack that day, the place was so packed that nobody else could fit in. Many of them were wounded American soldiers who had dragged themselves there and forced the civilians to make room.

Soldiers retreating through the town included the intelligence and reconnaissance platoon of the 423rd Infantry, from the ill-fated 106th Division. 'Nothing much could be seen in the darkness but outlines in the snow,' one of them wrote, 'except when the blinding lights of the flares and muzzle blasts made it seem brighter than day.' The last three Shermans left in St Vith, with the intelligence and reconnaissance platoon alongside, 'proceeded cautiously down another street, the Rodterstrasse, that led to the northwest. At the edge of the town, some climbed aboard the tanks, lying as flat as they could, clinging to anything they could get hold of while the rest of the group flanked the tanks on foot. The tanks took off in the midst of a murderous crossfire coming from either side of the road — a crossfire marked by machine-guns firing red tracers, scaring the living hell out us. Luckily, the Germans were firing too high and the tracers criss-crossed safely a few feet above our heads. At the top of a small hill about a mile to the west of town, we pulled off the road. The tanks took up position at the edge of a small patch of woods. The I&R moved down the forward slope of the hill a few yards, spread out and dug in as best we could.' The temperature had dropped significantly in the snowstorm.

The cold and famished Germans of the 18th and 62nd Volksgrenadier-Divisions charged into the town, desperate to seek shelter and loot what food they could find from houses and abandoned American stores. Hasbrouck's forces had pulled back to a new line west of St Vith, and now it was the turn of American field artillery battalions to bombard the doomed town.

To the north-west, Generalmajor Siegfried von Waldenburg's 116th Panzer-Division had orders to push on east of the River Ourthe to

Hotton. The day before, Waldenburg's panzer group had attacked Samrée and Dochamps, while the 560th Volksgrenadier on their right had a harder fight. The Panthers managed to disable about a dozen American tanks in the battle, but they were so short of fuel that 156th Panzergrenadier-Regiment, the artillery and the reconnaissance battalion had to be halted. Relief came after capturing Samrée, where they discovered a fuel dump of 25,000 gallons, which Waldenburg described as 'a God-sent gift'. American prisoners told them that it had been sabotaged with sugar, but he claimed that it 'suited the German engines very well'.

'Nothing was to be seen of the long awaited II SS Panzer Corps,' he complained, but in fact the 2nd SS Panzer-Division *Das Reich* was not that far behind. Having been blocked near St Vith by the continuing traffic chaos on the roads, it had swung round to the south and was about to attack north against the line of the 82nd Airborne, but then had to wait for fuel supplies. The *Das Reich* burned with impatience at this hold-up. 'It was known that the army's 2nd Panzer-Division was pushing towards the west without meeting heavy enemy resistance and already was close to Dinant. No air activity — the route to the Meuse lies open — but the whole division is stuck for 24 hours unable to move because of a lack of fuel!' Montgomery was almost certainly right to extend the northern shoulder westward to face the threat, and reject the idea of an advance on St Vith as Ridgway and First Army wanted.

The 116th Panzer attacked Hotton later in the day with the 156th Panzergrenadier-Regiment supported by tanks, but they were repulsed by a battalion of the 325th Glider Infantry from the 82nd Airborne, a platoon of tank destroyers and some tanks from Major General Maurice Rose's 3rd Armored Division which had arrived in the early hours. The commander of the 116th Panzer-Division acknowledged that the Americans fought well. His Kampfgruppe lost several tanks and his men were exhausted. 'The troops began slowly to realize that the decisive plan must have failed, or that no victory could be won. Morale and efficiency suffered.'

The 2nd Panzer-Division, meanwhile, had only reached Champlon some eighteen kilometres to the south of Hotton as the crow flies. It had been held up at a crossroads south-east of Tenneville by just one company of the 327th Glider Infantry, and Lüttwitz later wanted to charge the divisional commander Oberst Meinrad von Lauchert with cowardice. As well as the battle at Noville, the division had also been delayed by the late arrival of fuel supplies. Some of its units had only just passed north of Bastogne.

Once the fighting was over, civilians in Bourcy and Noville emerged from their cellars to the sight of destruction all around, and the smell of damp smoke, carbonized masonry, burned iron and the seared flesh of farm animals killed in the bombardments. But even the comparative relief that the shelling had stopped was short lived. They found themselves rounded up by one of the SS security service groups from the Sicherheitsdienst. Brutal interrogations began, in an attempt to identify members of the Belgian Resistance and those who had welcomed the Americans in September. The SD officials had newspaper photographs with them of the event. One man in Bourcy, after a savage beating, was taken outside and killed with hammers. They had found a home-made American flag in his cellar. The group moved on to Noville where they murdered seven men, including the priest, Father Delvaux, and the village schoolmaster.

Patton had achieved miracles by regrouping his Third Army so rapidly, but he was hardly enthusiastic about having to concentrate on the relief of Bastogne. He would have much preferred to head for St Vith to cut off the Germans. He was also reluctant to wait until he had a larger force, as Eisenhower had ordered. 'Ike and [Major General] Bull [the G-3 at SHAEF] are getting jittery about my attacking too soon and too weak,' he wrote in his diary that day. 'I have all I can get. If I wait, I will lose surprise.' Never one to suffer from humility, Patton also wrote to his wife that day: 'We should get well into the guts of the enemy and cut his supply lines. Destiny sent for me in a hurry when things got tight. Perhaps God saved me for this effort.' But Patton's hubris was to embarrass him over the next few days when the breakthrough to Bastogne proved so much harder than he had imagined.

The reconnaissance battalion commanded by Major Rolf Kunkel and the 39th Fusilier Regiment from Kokott's 26th Volksgrenadier-Division were already seizing villages along the southern perimeter of Bastogne. They were followed by the lead Kampfgruppe of the Panzer Lehr. General Cota of the 28th Division, who had established his headquarters in Sibret, nearly seven kilometres southwest of Bastogne, attempted to organize its defence with a scratch force of stragglers. But they broke under the force of the attack, and Cota had to pull out rapidly. Kokott, visiting the sector, witnessed stragglers from the 28th Division and thought that they came from the Bastogne garrison. A Belgian he spoke to at Sibret assured him that the defenders of Bastogne were falling apart. He became much more hopeful, thinking that perhaps Lüttwitz's optimism was justified after all.

Kunkel's Kampfgruppe pushed north, causing considerable alarm in McAuliffe's headquarters because the VIII Corps artillery based round Senonchamps was vulnerable. Soldiers panicked in one field artillery battalion and fled; but a rapidly improvised force, backed by anti-aircraft half-tracks with quadruple .50 machine guns, arrived just in time. The 'meat-choppers' did their gruesome work, and Kunkel's attack collapsed.

The famished German troops took over farmhouses and villages, glad of shelter now that the temperature was dropping sharply. They slaughtered pigs and cows, seized food from families and exulted when they discovered abandoned stocks of American equipment and rations. They treated villagers with as much suspicion as many American soldiers treated the Belgians within the encirclement.

Further to the south the 5th Fallschirmjäger-Division had reached the road from Bastogne to Arlon, ready to block Patton's advance. The other German divisions had little confidence in their ability to halt a major counter-attack.

The fight to crush the German incursion along the railway track to Bastogne between Bizôry and Foy continued in the fog. Platoons of paratroopers advanced cautiously through pinewoods planted densely in neat rows with no underbrush. 'It was like a tremendous hall with a green roof supported by many brown columns,' wrote Major Robert Harwick, who commanded the 1st Battalion of the 506th which had escaped from Noville the day before. They paused at every firebreak and logging trail to observe, before crossing. Orders were given in whispers or by hand signals. From time to time shells from German guns exploded in the tree tops.

The German positions were well concealed, so the paratroopers had no idea where the shots were coming from when they were fired on. Once the enemy foxholes were spotted, the men in an extended skirmish line began to advance in short sprints, while others covered them in classic 'fire and maneuver'. Attacked from two directions, a number of the volksgrenadiers panicked. Some fled straight into the arms of Harwick's men and surrendered. 'Two prisoners came back,' Harwick wrote. 'They were terribly scared and kept ducking their heads as the bullets buzzed and whined. Finally, a close burst and they dove for a foxhole. The guard took no chances and threw a grenade in after them. He walked up to the hole and fired four shots from his carbine and returned to the fighting in front . . . The fight was not long, but it was hard — it was bitter, as all close fighting is. A wounded man lay near to where I had moved. I crawled over. He needed help badly. Beside him was an aid man, still holding a bandage in his hand but with a bullet through his head.'

His men brought in more prisoners once the battle was truly finished. 'One, terrified, kept falling on his knees, gibbering in German, his eyes continually here and there. He kept repeating in English, "Don't shoot me!" He finally fell sobbing on the ground and screamed as we lifted him. The rest had an attitude between this man and the coldly aloof lieutenant, who was so aloof, that somehow, somewhere, he got a good stiff punch in the nose.' The prisoners were forced to carry the American wounded back to the nearest aid station.

Bastogne itself was relatively well provided with food and large supplies of flour, but there was a distinct shortage of rations for the front line. The K-Rations brought for the first three days were soon used up, so soldiers survived mainly on hotcakes and pancakes.

McAuliffe's main concern was the shortage of artillery shells, especially the 105mm for the short-barrelled howitzers of the 101st Airborne field artillery. Fuel stocks were also a major worry. The tank destroyers and Shermans consumed a vast amount and they were essential in the defence. But, ever since the loss of the field hospital, the mounting number of wounded and the shortage of doctors haunted everyone. The low cloud cover meant that airdrops were out of the question. Like Patton and Bradley in Luxembourg, in fact like every commander and American soldier in the Ardennes, medical staff prayed for flying weather.

The German artillery began to concentrate that day on the town of Bastogne itself. The accuracy of their fire led to unjustified suspicions among the military police that there were fifth columnists among the refugees and civilians directing German fire. The town was an easy target, and those in the cellars of the Institut de Notre-Dame could feel the ground trembling. One shell hit a small ammunition dump, causing a huge explosion. McAuliffe had to move his headquarters down into cellars. He had been joined by Colonel Roberts, who, having conducted the operations of his 10th Armored Division combat command independently, was now under McAuliffe. The two men worked well together, and McAuliffe's expertise as an artilleryman was very useful in a defence which depended so much on that arm.

Since the 26th Volksgrenadier-Division was to be left with just a Kampfgruppe of the Panzer Lehr to take Bastogne, Lüttwitz the corps commander ordered General Bayerlein to send in a negotiator to demand the town's surrender to avoid total annihilation. Lüttwitz was under strict instructions from Führer headquarters not to divert any more troops for the capture of Bastogne, so this demand for surrender, which was to be delivered next day, was simply a bluff.

The defensive perimeter around Bastogne was porous to say the least, as the infiltration along the railway line had proved. Darkness in the long nights and bad visibility by day made it easy for German groups to slip through and cut a road behind forward positions, in an attempt to provoke a retreat. Whenever this happened, reserve platoons were sent off to deal with them, so there was a lot of 'rat-hunting' in damp woods as patrols searched for survivors. The low-lying fog also led to returning patrols being fired on by their own side, and to soldiers on both sides wandering into enemy-held territory by mistake. Captain Richard Winters, the executive officer with the 2nd Battalion of the 506th near Foy, even saw a German soldier with his trousers down, relieving himself behind their command post. 'After he was finished, I hollered to him in my best German, "Kommen sie hier!" (Come here), which he did. All the poor fellow had in his pockets were a few pictures, trinkets and the butt end of a loaf of black bread, which was very hard.'

The only reserve held back in Bastogne for emergencies was a scratch battalion of some 600 men known as 'Team SNAFU' (Situation Normal All Fucked Up). Stragglers from the 28th Infantry Division and survivors from the destruction of the 9th Armored Division combat command east of Bastogne, as well as soldiers suffering from borderline combat fatigue, were all drafted into it. One advantage of the encirclement meant that the defenders, using interior lines, could reinforce threatened sectors rapidly along the roads out of Bastogne. In the meantime, Team SNAFU was used to man roadblocks close to the town and to provide individual replacements for casualties in front-line units.

That night, it began to snow again, and a hard frost was about to set in. It brought mixed blessings, both for Hasbrouck's force holding on west of St Vith and for the 101st Airborne at Bastogne.

15
FRIDAY 22 DECEMBER

West of St Vith, the falling snow could have allowed Hasbrouck's depleted forces to disengage, but no permission to withdraw had arrived. General Ridgway still wanted them to hold out between St Vith and the River Salm.

In the early hours of the morning, Remer's *Führer Begleit* Brigade launched an attack on the small town of Rodt some four kilometres west of St Vith. Rodt was defended by American service troops — drivers, cooks and signallers — and by late in the morning Remer's well-armed force had cleared the place.

Some of Hasbrouck's men still remained out of contact north-east of St Vith, unaware of the general retreat. At 04.00 a company of armoured infantry received a radio message passed on by the 275th Field Artillery. 'Your orders are: Go west. Go west. Go west.' The company commander ordered his platoons to return from outposts one at a time in single file, with 'each man firmly gripping the belt or pack-straps of the man in front of him'. Visibility was almost non-existent in the heavy snow. They used a compass to aim west. On the way, trudging through the snow, the men became separated from each other, with most killed or captured. Those who escaped through the woods, small canyons and steep hills finally reached the line of light tanks and armoured cars which formed the rearguard of the 7th Armored Division.

The exhausted intelligence and reconnaissance platoon from the 106th Division, which had escaped St Vith with the three Shermans, was woken before dawn by their engines starting up. The tank crews had received an order to pull back, but they had not thought of warning the platoon which had been guarding them. 'We crawled wearily out of our makeshift foxholes and gathered together in the edge of the woods. Some of the guys had to be supported as they tried to stand, and to a man, walking was painful. Our legs had stiffened up over night and our near frozen feet had become more swollen as we crouched in our defensive positions.'

The tanks attracted German fire as they reached the road to Vielsalm, which revealed that the enemy had advanced beyond them. 'So, again in the cold wind and snow, we started cautiously southwest through the patch of woods.' They could hear the heavy fighting in Rodt as the *Führer Begleit* attacked. So 'taking advantage of scrub growth and the ever present fog, we made our way further southwest over country lanes until we came to the small village of Neundorf. Approaching the village over a small bridge, we came to a cluster of farmhouses at the edge of the village.'

'As we crossed this bridge,' another member of the platoon continued, 'we were met by a large number of Belgians — men, women and children. I explained who we were and what had happened in Saint-Vith. I shall never forget, as long as I live, the actions of these people. There they were, in front of the advancing German armies and in the midst of the fleeing American army. And what did they do? They very quickly divided us into small groups and took us into their homes. The group I was with, was taken to the home of a wonderful Belgian lady. I don't know how in the world she did it but it seemed, in minutes, she had a long table loaded with food. There was a huge pot of stewed meat, two large pitchers of milk, boiled potatoes, and loaves of hot bread. You can imagine what happened. We just gorged ourselves. There was a fire going in the fireplace, and it wasn't long before Irish [PFC John P. Sheehan] was asleep in an old rocking chair in front of the fire. We no sooner had finished eating than we heard the sound of German machine guns a short ways behind us. As we scrambled to leave, we took all the money we had been able to salvage, out of our pockets, and put it in the middle of the table. We could do no less for these wonderful people.'

The advance of the *Führer Begleit* had split Hasbrouck's force in two, so he had to pull back further to avoid encirclement. Hasbrouck was furious with Ridgway and his XVIII Airborne Corps headquarters, who wanted him to form a 'goose-egg'-shaped defence east of the River Salm. Hasbrouck was deeply concerned about his southern flank, because during the night he heard that his task force on the right had captured a German officer from the 2nd SS Panzer-Division *Das Reich*. If the *Das Reich* was heading for Gouvy, as the prisoner said, the very weak force there did not stand a chance. Later in the morning of 22 December a fresh German force around Recht, just north of Poteau, was identified as part of the 9th SS Panzer-Division *Hohenstaufen.* If it was heading for the River Salm, as appeared to be the case, then it threatened to cut off the line of retreat of Combat Command A of the 7th Armored Division. Its commander Colonel Rosebaum reacted quickly. He withdrew his tanks fighting the *Führer Begleit* and concentrated his force round Poteau to block the SS *Hohenstaufen.*

That morning one of Montgomery's British liaison officers appeared at Hasbrouck's command post in Commanster, twelve kilometres southwest of St Vith. He asked Hasbrouck what he thought should be done. Hasbrouck replied that if higher command believed it essential to maintain an all-round defence, then he would hold on as long as possible, but he considered that withdrawal was preferable because the woods and lack of roads made it an almost impossible terrain to hold. This was reported back to Montgomery.

Hasbrouck then sent a detailed assessment of his position to Ridgway. German artillery would soon be able to shell his men from all sides, and his supply route via Vielsalm was in danger with the advance of the SS *Das Reich.* He argued that his remaining forces would be of more use strengthening the 82nd Airborne to resist the *Das Reich.* Losses in infantry especially had been so great that he doubted whether they would be able to withstand another all-out attack. He added a postscript. 'I am throwing in my last chips to halt [the Germans] . . . In my opinion if we don't get out of here and up north of the 82nd before night, we will not have a 7th Armored Division left.'

Ridgway still rejected the recommendation to withdraw, but Montgomery overruled him in the middle of the afternoon during a visit to First Army headquarters. He sent a signal to Hasbrouck: 'You have accomplished your mission — a mission well done. It is time to withdraw.' It was indeed well done. Hasbrouck's very mixed force had managed to delay the Fifth Panzer Army's advance by nearly a whole week.

Fortunately for the Americans, the German stampede into St Vith had caused a massive jam. Many of the vehicles were American Jeeps and trucks captured in the Schnee Eifel, and their new owners refused to let them go. The Feldgendarmerie lost control, and a furious Generalfeldmarschall Model was forced to dismount and walk into the ruins of the town his troops had taken so long to seize. The chaos around the key road junction meant that the German commanders would take some time to redeploy their forces. This breathing space gave Brigadier General Clarke the chance to pull back his Combat Command B to a new line. Then an even greater miracle occurred. Hasbrouck's artillery had been down to their last rounds when a convoy of ninety trucks unexpectedly arrived that morning via circuitous back routes, with 5,000 shells for the 105mm howitzers.

The intelligence and reconnaissance platoon joined up with the 424th Infantry, the only regiment of the 106th Division to escape, having formed the right wing of Hasbrouck's force. For the first time they heard of the massacre near Malmédy. 'The line troops vowed that no prisoners would be taken in their sector,' wrote one of them.

'Two of the platoon, on liaison to one of the companies, were visiting the front line fox-holes of one of the rifle platoons. Across a fifty yard gap in the woods, a white flag appeared, whereby a sergeant stood up and motioned the Germans to advance. About twenty men emerged out of the woods. After they had advanced closer to the line, the sergeant gave the command to open fire. No prisoners were taken.'

Only German troops who had circumvented St Vith were in a position to advance. That evening panzers and infantry attacked along the railway line to Crombach. The fight for Crombach was furious. One company fired 600 rounds in twenty minutes from its 81mm mortars and 'broke the base plates which were welded to the floor of the halftrack'. German panzer crews used their trick of firing bright flares to blind American gunners and thus got off their rounds first with devastating effect.

As Hasbrouck had predicted, nearly the whole division was now coming under heavy shellfire. Orders for the withdrawal were issued, and the artillery began moving out at midnight. It began to freeze hard. To the joyful disbelief of Brigadier General Clarke, the ground finally became solid enough not only for cross-country movement, but also along the deeply mired woodland tracks. This was essential if they were to extricate all the different components towards the three-kilometre gap between Vielsalm and Salm-château, and the two bridges over the river. But German attacks during the night prevented the two combat commands from pulling out during darkness. The careful plan for the withdrawal was thrown out of synchronization, but despite many rearguard skirmishes the bulk of the retreating forces managed to cross the River Salm on 23 December.

A survivor from one infantry company, who managed to escape with the 17th Tank Battalion, recounted how after several running firefights they finally reached the lines of the 82nd Airborne. A paratrooper digging a foxhole put down his shovel and said: 'What the hell are you guys running from? We been here two days and ain't seen a German yet.' The exhausted infantryman retorted: 'Stay right where you are, buddy. In a little while you won't even have to look for 'em.'

On the southern slope of the Elsenborn ridge, the 12th SS Panzer-Division *Hitler Jugend* again tried to break through with tanks at Bütgenbach. The American defenders herded civilians into the convent's cellars and provided them with food. In houses outside and on the edge of the town, women and children cowered in cellars as the house above them was fought over, captured and recaptured by both sides. Bazooka teams stalked panzers which had broken into the town. American fighter-bombers then attacked the village. One explosion threw a cow on to a farm roof. By the time the fighting had finished, the bodies of twenty-one civilians had been wrapped in blankets, ready for burial when the opportunity arose. Most were elderly and disabled residents from the nursing home.

This was the last major attempt to break the American defence of the Elsenborn ridge. The 12th SS *Hitler Jugend* Division was ordered to pull out and reorganize before being diverted to join the Fifth Panzer Army further south. Gerow's V Corps had defeated the attempt of the Sixth Panzer Army to break through.

In the early hours of 22 December, German Junkers 52 transport planes dropped fuel, rations and ammunition to Peiper's Kampfgruppe, but only about a tenth of the supplies could be recovered from the restricted drop zone. The Luftwaffe refused Sixth Panzer Army's requests for further missions. Attempts by the 1st SS Panzer-Division to break through to support and resupply Peiper were thwarted at Trois-Ponts by a regiment of the 82nd Airborne defending the line of the River Salm just below its confluence with the Amblève. General Ridgway knew that he needed to eliminate the Peiper Kampfgruppe in its pocket at La Gleize and Stoumont as soon as possible so that he could redeploy the 30th Division and the 3rd Armored Division. The threat was growing further west with the advance of the 116th Panzer-Division to Hotton, and the 2nd Panzer-Division on its left.

Ridgway had hoped for a clear sky that day, after the hard frost of the night before, but he soon heard that no aircraft would be flying in their support. At least Stoumont was finally cleared by the infantry from the 30th Division supported by Sherman tanks. The Germans pulled out, leaving wounded from all three battalions of the 2nd SS Panzer-grenadier-Regiment. But west of Stavelot a panzergrenadier company slipped in to block the road and captured an American aid station. This was retaken by combat engineers and tanks next day.

Peiper acknowledged that his situation was 'very grave'. There was house-to-house fighting in La Gleize, where some buildings were burning from American artillery firing phosphorus shells. Peiper claimed that the church in La Gleize, 'conspicuously marked with a red cross', had been targeted by US tanks and artillery. His men, most of them still teenagers, were exhausted and half starved. Most of them wore articles of American uniform taken from the dead and prisoners because their own were falling to pieces.

Since all attempts to break through by the relief force from his division had failed, Peiper decided that evening that his Kampfgruppe would have to fight its way out.

While Peiper's morale was sinking, Generalmajor Kokott on the south side of Bastogne began to feel much more optimistic. His 26th Volksgrenadier command post had just heard reports of the rapid advance of the panzer divisions towards the Meuse. He also began to think that perhaps Lüttwitz's corps headquarters must have good intelligence on the state of the American defenders of Bastogne, otherwise it would not have ordered just 'a single infantry division' to surround and capture the town. Lüttwitz, visited the night before by General der Panzertruppe Brandenberger, was assured that the 5th Fallschirmjäger-Division could hold the southern flank against Patton's drive north from Arlon.

In bitterly cold weather, with more flurries of snow and the ground frozen hard, Kokott began a concentric attack. His 39th Regiment advanced on Mande-Saint-Etienne in the west, while his reconnaissance battalion, Kampfgruppe Kunkel, fought around Senonchamps and Villeroux, south-west of Bastogne. 'In the course of the [day],' Kokott recorded, 'news arrived from Korps [headquarters] to the effect that the commander in charge of the Bastogne forces had declined a surrender with remarkable brevity.'

When soldiers of the 327th Glider Infantry had seen four Germans coming towards them, waving a white flag, they assumed that they wanted to surrender. A German officer speaking English announced that according to the Geneva and Hague conventions they had the right to deliver an ultimatum. They produced their own blindfolds and were led to the company command post. Their letter was then sent to divisional headquarters. Brigadier General McAuliffe, who had been up all night, was catching up on sleep in the cellar. The acting chief of staff shook him awake, and told him that the Germans had sent emissaries asking the Bastogne defenders to capitulate or face annihilation by artillery fire. McAuliffe, still half asleep, muttered 'Nuts!' Not knowing what to recommend as a reply, one member of the 101st staff suggested that McAuliffe should use the same reply as he had given to the chief of staff. So back went the message to the unidentified 'German commander', who was in fact Lüttwitz, with the single word. Manteuffel was furious with Lüttwitz when he heard about the ultimatum. He regarded it as a stupid bluff, because the Germans simply did not have the artillery ammunition to carry out the threat. McAuliffe, on the other hand, could not be sure that it was a bluff.

The change in the weather meant that uniforms stood out conspicuously against the snow. In Bastogne and surrounding villages, American officers asked the local mayor if they could obtain sheets to be used as camouflage. In Hemroulle, the burgomaster went straight to the church and began to toll the bell. Villagers came running and he told them to bring their sheets as the American soldiers needed them. Some 200 were provided. The paratroopers began cutting them up to make helmet covers, or strips to wrap round rifle and machine-gun barrels. Those who made poncho-style capes for going out on patrol soon found, however, that they became damp and froze. This made them crackle and rustle as they moved. Other soldiers scoured Bastogne and its surrounding villages for cans of whitewash to camouflage their vehicles and tanks.

In their foxholes round the Bastogne perimeter, the ill-equipped paratroopers of the 101st suffered badly in the freezing temperatures, especially with their feet in sodden boots. Some soldiers discovered a store in Bastogne with a couple of thousand burlap sacks. These and others were distributed rapidly for the soldiers to wrap around their feet, yet non-battle casualties from trench foot and frostbite were soon to rise alarmingly.

Despite the wretched conditions, the paratroopers surprised the Germans by the vigour of their counter-attacks on that day. The Germans had begun by attacking the Mande-Saint-Etienne sector at dawn. During the fighting there, a family of refugees sought shelter along with others in the last house in the village. The two brothers who owned the farm milked the cows and brought in pails of it for their guests to drink in the attached stable. Suddenly, the door was kicked open and two German soldiers with 'Schmeisser' MP-40 sub-machine guns entered. The refugees cowered against the wall, because the two men appeared drunk. While one of them trained his weapon on the civilians, the other walked over to the pails of milk, undid his trousers and urinated in them one by one. They both thought that this was funny.

The 26th Volksgrenadier-Division lost just on 400 men in its attacks that day, and it had to bring in replacements from the divisional supply battalion and the artillery regiment as infantrymen to make up numbers. Because of the counter-attacks, Generalmajor Kokott even thought that the defenders were about to attempt a breakout from the encirclement. His men had heard from civilian refugees leaving Bastogne that there was great tension in the town and that vehicles were being loaded up. German shells during the night had hit the 101st Division's command post and killed several officers in their sleeping bags.

An airdrop planned for that day had to be cancelled because of the bad visibility. The 101st was running very short of artillery ammunition and the number of barely treated wounded was mounting fast. Yet morale was high, particularly when news of the rejected demand to surrender rapidly made the rounds. Some senior officers at SHAEF, particularly Major General Strong, the British chief of intelligence, feared that the 101st Airborne would not be able to defend Bastogne. 'I was never worried about the operation,' Bedell Smith said later. 'Strong was, however. He asked me three times in one day if I thought we would hold at Bastogne. I thought [we could]. He said, "How do you know?" I said: "Because the commanders there think they can hold." We had at Bastogne our best division. When the commander said [they were] OK, I believed he would [hold].'

Major General 'Lightning Joe' Collins wasted little time in organizing his VII Corps to resist the advance of the German panzer divisions heading for the Meuse. For the moment he had only the 84th Infantry Division, but the 2nd Armored Division was on its way, and so was the 75th Infantry Division. He travelled in an armoured car to reach the town of

Marche-en-Famenne. 'The fog was sitting right on the tree tops,' he recorded later. There he found Brigadier General Alex Bolling, the commander of the 84th Infantry Division, who had pushed out reconnaissance forces to identify the enemy's line of approach. He was reassured to find Bolling 'very calm', but their conversation convinced him that Bradley was wrong to believe that his entire corps should be held back for a counter-attack. VII Corps was about to be 'engaged in a fight for its life'. Collins decided to set up his corps headquarters in a small chateau at Méan, fifteen kilometres due north of Marche.

The advance Kampfgruppe of the 2nd Panzer-Division had started early on 22 December heading for Marche. It met no resistance until it clashed with a detachment of Bolling's 335th Infantry Regiment at a crossroads two kilometres south of Marche, in rolling country of fields and woods. While a force of panzergrenadiers continued the battle, the lead elements of the 2nd Panzer turned west towards Dinant. Alarm was caused by an unconfirmed report from the British 23rd Hussars, forward of the Meuse crossing at Givet, that panzers had been sighted at Vonêche, a dozen kilometres to the south-east.

The lead elements of the 2nd Panzer were by then only twenty-five kilometres from the

Meuse bridge at Dinant, but constant attacks by Bolling's division forced the 2nd Panzer to detach troops for flank protection. An attack from Marche by American infantry in the morning failed, but another, stronger attempt supported by tanks in the afternoon retook the high ground south-west of the town. A major reverse was prevented by the 2nd Panzer's anti-aircraft battalion taking on the Shermans in the open, but it suffered heavy losses in the process. That night the panzergrenadiers managed to retake part of the heights and open the road to the west.

American service troops and other detachments in the area soon woke up to the danger. One group, who had billeted themselves in the ancient Château d'Hargimont between Marche and Rochefort, slept in their uniforms and boots with grenades to hand in case they were surprised in the night by the German advance. On hearing gunfire, they pulled out rapidly and headed back towards Dinant. So too did most of the young Belgian men, either on bicycles or on foot. They had a well-justified fear of reprisals for the attacks by the Resistance in September, and they also knew that if they stayed, they risked being marched off to Germany for forced labour.

Taking refuge in cellars as artillery shells began to fall, Belgians had no idea of the state of the battle. They could, however, identify the different sounds made in the street by

American boots with rubber soles and the hobnailed jackboots of the Germans. They backed away when Germans entered, not just from a fear of violence, but also because they knew the enemy soldiers were covered in lice. German troops during that advance were intent on searching for Americans in hiding or for members of the Resistance. Any young Belgian who had been unwise enough to pick up a couple of live rounds was liable to be shot as a 'terrorist' if searched. And when the Germans decided to make themselves at home, they stacked their rifles and Panzer-fausts in a corner, which the civilians could not help eyeing nervously. The locals spoke Walloon among themselves, knowing that the soldiers could not understand, unless one of them happened to be a conscript from the eastern cantons.

In cellars, lit by storm-lamps or candles, the Ardennais sometimes sang folk-songs when there was a long lull. But when the shelling started again in earnest, people began reciting the rosary, their lips moving fast. Conditions during long periods of bombardment rapidly deteriorated, encouraging dysentery. Buckets could be taken up and emptied on the dung-heap only when there was a lull in the firing. Farmers and their sons would also rush out to milk cows in the byre and feed the pigs. They brought back pails of milk for those sheltering downstairs to improve the diet of potatoes. If there was time, they would rapidly butcher livestock killed by shellfire. The fortunate would have brought an Ardennes ham, which they shared out. Many stuffed pails and bottles with snow and waited for it to melt as drinking water, because going to the pump was too dangerous. Those who fled to the woods when their homes were shelled could do no more than pack together for warmth. Their only water came from sucking icicles.

All over the Ardennes, the old and infirm were looked after in a community spirit; in fact examples of selfishness seem to have been rare. People whose houses had stone cellars would shelter neighbours who only had floorboards over theirs. And the owner of a local chateau with deep cellars would invite the villagers to take shelter there, but such a prominent building was always likely to attract the interest of artillery observers, whether Allied or German.

Generalmajor von Waldenburg, the commander of the 116th Panzer-Division, was in a bad mood that morning. At 04.00 hours, he had received an order from his corps commander to stop his attack on Hotton from east of the River Ourthe, which was valiantly defended by an American engineer battalion and service troops. Manteuffel wrongly believed that the defence was too strong and would hold up Waldenburg's division. He ordered the 560th Volksgrenadier-Division to take over at Hotton, while the 116th Panzer was to go back through Samrée and La Roche-en-Ardenne, then proceed north-west again on the other side of the Ourthe to break through between Hotton and Marche. Waldenburg was convinced that if they had been sent that way earlier, they could have advanced well beyond Marche by then. This diversion certainly allowed General Collins more time to organize his defence line further to the west.

In Luxembourg, General Bradley's staff noticed that he now seldom left his bedroom or office. But that morning Hansen entered Bradley's office to find him on his knees bent over a map on the floor, peering through his bifocals at the road net being used by the Germans, and marking routes with brown crayon. It was the day on which General Patton's attack from the south towards Bastogne began with III Corps, including the 4th Armored Division and the 26th and 80th Infantry Divisions on its right. XII Corps, starting behind the 4th Infantry Division on the southern shoulder, would also advance north with the 5th Division and part of the 10th Armored.

After the heavy snowfall of the night before, Hansen described the view from the hotel as 'a veritable postcard scene with tiny snow covered houses'. The fog had eased and the temperature had dropped, but low cloud cover still prevented the deployment of Allied airpower in all its strength. As the population of Luxembourg was still anxious, the 12th Army Group civil affairs officer decided to take Prince Jean, the son of the Grand Duchess Charlotte, round the city in a car, to reassure the people that he had remained with them. Bradley's staff were angry that Radio Luxembourg, with the most powerful transmitter in Europe, had gone off air when its staff pulled out in a panic, taking most of their technical equipment with them.

Fears over Skorzeny's commandos had still not been put to rest. Counter Intelligence Corps men were 'acutely worried over the safety of our generals', Hansen noted in his diary that day. 'German agents in American uniforms are supposedly identified by their pink or blue scarves, by two [finger] taps on their helmets and by the open top button on their coats and jackets. When Charlie Werten-baker [of *Time* magazine] came this evening, we pointed to his maroon scarf, warned him of a shade of pink and he promptly removed it.'

Eisenhower, also suffocating under security precautions at Versailles, issued an order of the day to all formations. 'The enemy is mak-ing his supreme effort to break out of the desperate plight into which you forced him by your brilliant victories of the summer and fall. He is fighting savagely to take back all that you have won and is using every treacherous trick to deceive and kill you. He is gambling everything, but already in this battle, your unparalleled gallantry has done much to foil his plans. In the face of your proven bravery and fortitude, he will completely fail.'

The day before, in an attempt to defend Bradley from any suggestion that he had been caught off-guard in the Ardennes, Eisenhower recommended his promotion to full general. He wrote to General Marshall to say that the 12th Army Group commander had 'kept his head magnificently and . . . proceeded methodically and energetically to meet the situation. In no quarter is there any tendency to place any blame on Bradley.'

Bradley, egged on by his staff according to Bedell Smith, convinced himself that Montgomery had panicked. If nothing else, this completely distorted view demonstrated that his Eagle Tac headquarters in Luxembourg was totally out of touch with the reality on the ground. 'We learned that the entire British Army was in retreat,' wrote one of his staff officers. 'Leaving only a skeleton force in the line, and with remarkable agility for a man who was often so cautious, Montgomery moved the bulk of the British Second and the Canadian First Armies back from Holland to a defensive semicircle round Antwerp, prepared for the last ditch battle he apparently thought he would have to fight there.' Bradley's staff clearly had no idea that Horrocks's XXX Corps was on the Meuse, with the 29th Armoured Brigade already on the east bank, ready to link up with the right wing of Collins's VII Corps.

16
SATURDAY 23 DECEMBER

All over the Ardennes, American commanders on the morning of 23 December gazed in
wonder at the cloudless blue sky and blinding winter sun. The temperature had dropped
even further, because a 'Russian High' of
crystal-clear weather had arrived from the
east. Air controllers joyfully reported 'visibility unlimited' and scrambled P-47 Thunderbolt fighter-bombers to go tank hunting.
An ebullient General Patton exclaimed to his
deputy chief of staff: 'God damn! That
O'Neill sure did some potent praying. Get
him up here, I want to pin a medal on him.'
Chaplain O'Neill was rushed from Nancy to
Luxembourg so that Patton could decorate
him with the Bronze Star next day.

Bradley's staff, like many of the inhabitants
of Luxembourg, went out into the street to
squint up against the brightness at the condensation trails of Allied heavy bombers flying over to attack Trier and its marshalling
yards. Morale soared in foxholes as men

461

stared at the bombers and fighter-bombers once more streaming overhead, glinting like shoals of silver fish.

Allied air support produced another bonus. German artillery batteries did not want to reveal their gun positions by firing while there were fighter-bombers around. 'As soon as the enemy air force appeared the effect of the artillery was reduced to fifty or sixty percent,' Model's artillery commander reported.

Later in the morning, however, 12th Army Group headquarters was shaken to hear that part of the 2nd Panzer-Division was advancing on Jemelle, just east of Rochefort. This was the site of the army group's radio repeater station, and it was guarded by no more than a platoon of infantry and some tank destroyers. Bradley immediately called First Army headquarters to see if reinforcements could be sent, but 'as he was speaking the line went dead'. The soldiers guarding the repeater station had just removed all the tubes. They were withdrawing as the Germans approached, but they did not destroy the equipment in the hope that the place could be recaptured soon.

At least air-reconnaissance missions could now clarify the movements of the panzer divisions heading north-west for the Meuse. Yet First Army headquarters was still convinced that the Germans wanted to break through towards Liège. Staff officers did not know that Hitler had insisted on a drive westward.

General Rose, with his command post in the embattled town of Hotton, had been forced to split his 3rd Armored Division in all directions. One combat command was still tied down crushing the Kampfgruppe Peiper around La Gleize, while another was on its way to join him from Eupen. The rest of the division was split into three task forces. Two of them were ready to block the advance of the 2nd SS Panzer-Division *Das Reich* as it advanced up the road from Houffalize towards Manhay on the road to Liège, but Task Force Hogan was surrounded at Marcouray ten kilometres to the south-east of Hotton and out of fuel. An attempt to drop supplies was made that day, but the parachute bundles fell more than six kilometres away, and on the following day they fell nearly ten kilometres away.

On the Houffalize–Liège highway, Baraque-de-Fraiture consisted of three farmhouses by a crossroads close to a village called Fraiture. It lay on the boundary between the 82nd Airborne and the 3rd Armored Division and had been overlooked. But Major Arthur C. Parker III, a survivor of the 106th Division's débâcle in the Schnee Eifel, recognized the importance of its position. He had started to prepare a defence with his own gunners and a mixture of sub-units retreating that way.

They included four anti-aircraft half-tracks with quadruple .50 machine guns — the notorious 'meat-choppers'.

The small force at 'Parker's crossroads', as Baraque-de-Fraiture was soon known, had been attacked before dawn on 21 December by a large fighting patrol from the 560th Volksgrenadier-Division. The 'meat-choppers' had cut them to pieces. Among the wounded, an officer from the SS *Das Reich* was identified. Task Force Kane defending Manhay to the north sent a reconnaissance platoon. And General Gavin, once aware of the danger, sent a battalion of the 82nd to Fraiture to protect Parker's left flank, and a company of the 325th Glider Infantry also arrived.

Little happened on 22 December because the *Das Reich* had been waiting for fuel supplies to arrive and for Remer's *Führer Begleit* to catch up. But at dawn on 23 December the 4th SS Panzergrenadier-Regiment attacked both the crossroads and the paratroopers at Fraiture, whom it surprised eating breakfast. The real attack on Parker's crossroads came late in the afternoon, with the whole of the 4th SS Panzergrenadiers and two companies of tanks. The fall of snow had revealed the defenders' positions, rather than camouflaging them, and their Shermans had no room for manoeuvre. Panzer gunners knocked out the armoured vehicles and shot up one foxhole after another. General Gavin

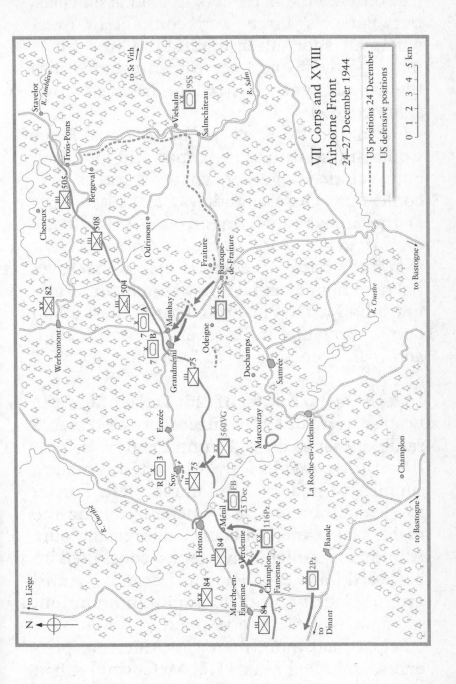

N
↑ to Liège

to St Vith

to Bastogne

to Bastogne

to Dinant

N
0 1 2 3 4 5 km

VII Corps and XVIII
Airborne Front
24–27 December 1944

········· US positions 24 December
———— US defensive positions

Stavelot
R. Amblève
Trois-Ponts
Cheneux
Bergeval
Odrimont
Vielsalm
Salmchâteau
R. Salm
Werbomont
Manhay
Fraiture
Baraque-
de-Fraiture
Odeigne
Dochamps
Samrée
Grandménil
Erezée
Soy
Marcouray
La Roche-en-Ardenne
Champlon
Hotton
Ménil
Verdenne
Champlon-
Famenne
Bande
Marche-en-
Famenne
R. Ourthe
R. Ourthe

505
508
504
82
7 A
7 B
255
75
560VG
3 R
75
84
84
84
116Pz
2Pz
955
FB
25 Dec

had ordered the defenders to hold at all costs, but Parker's force was completely overwhelmed soon after nightfall. Three Shermans got away, and some men escaped into the woods when a herd of frenzied cows stampeded.

Gavin and Rose, afraid that the *Das Reich* would smash through Manhay and into their rear, scraped together whatever forces they could find. General Ridgway lost his temper at this unexpected threat, and ordered the exhausted survivors of the 7th Armored Division, who had just escaped across the River Salm, to hold Manhay. He was in an unforgiving mood after Hasbrouck and Clarke had opposed his plan to fight on west of St Vith, and then been supported by Montgomery.

In the early hours of 23 December, the headquarters of I SS Panzer Corps received a radio message from Kampfgruppe Peiper. 'Position considerably worsened. Meagre supplies of infantry ammunition left. Forced to yield Stoumont and Cheneux during the night. This is the last chance of breaking out.' American artillery and tanks continued to bombard La Gleize. The much feared Kampfgruppe, lacking both fuel and ammunition, was now powerless to respond.

Peiper held more than 150 American prisoners, including Major Hal McCown. He had already attempted to interrogate McCown and to proclaim his own belief in Nazism and its reasons for fighting the war. McCown had been moved to a small cellar that morning with four other American officers. During the afternoon, an American 105mm shell hit the wall, blasting a large hole in it and throwing the German guard halfway across the room. Another shell landed just outside, sending fragments and stones flying through the cellar. An American lieutenant was killed and three Germans were wounded.

Later, McCown was taken to see Peiper again, who told him that he was going to break out on foot but did not know what to do with his American prisoners. Peiper had just received permission to make his way back to German lines. He proposed a deal. He would leave all the prisoners and his own wounded behind, and take just McCown with him as a hostage. McCown would then be set free if the American commander released the German wounded. McCown replied that he obviously could not make any agreement about prisoners of war. All he could do was sign a paper saying that he had heard Peiper's suggestion. That night Peiper's men began to prepare their surviving vehicles for demolition. They would have to wade across the River Amblève in the dark to slip into the trees on the southern side.

The Ninth Army commander General Bill Simpson was proud of his 30th Division's ruthless fightback against the Peiper Kampf-gruppe. 'American troops are now refusing to take any more SS prisoners,' his aide wrote, 'and it may well spread to include all German soldiers. While we cannot order such a thing, the C[ommanding] G[eneral] himself personally hopes that every GI will hear these stories and make that a battle rule, as the 30th Division did.' Simpson was pleased to hear that Germans now called the division 'Roosevelt's Butchers'. He had also received a report on prisoners taken in the Malmédy sector that their commanders had 'promised them that in this new fight they would not have to fight the 30th Div. They fear it that much.'

On the Elsenborn ridge, American artillery continued to pound the villages and towns below with white phosphorus and high explosive, even after the main attacks had petered out. The small town of Faymonville on the southern side, occupied by a detachment of the 3rd Fallschirmjäger, had been targeted day after day. The local priest begged a German officer to arrange a ceasefire so that non-combatants could be evacuated. On the morning of 23 December, the Germans instead simply ordered the 600 civilians trapped in Faymonville to leave for Schoppen, a village further behind the German lines. An officer told them that anyone who tried to walk towards American positions would be shot. The priest urged them to think again, but the Germans replied that they would start shooting his parishioners, five at a time, if they refused to leave.

At 11.00 hours, the terrified townspeople set off into the open. Unfortunately, the pilot of an American spotter plane saw the column trudging with difficulty through the deep snow, and identified it as an enemy concentration. American artillery on the Elsenborn ridge opened fire. As shells began exploding all around, the old men, women and children panicked, running in all directions. The priest ran back to Faymonville to ask the Germans to radio the Americans to cease their firing but they refused to do anything. Eight or so were killed or died later and many others were injured, before they reached the relative safety of Schoppen.

The German besiegers of Bastogne somehow still believed that the Americans were hoping to escape the encirclement. On 23 December, they tried to strengthen their presence on the west side of the town, continuing the attack round Senonchamps and Mande-Saint-Etienne to tighten the ring and to cut off any further 'attempts to break out'. Hitler, refusing to believe 'Manteuffel's report that he could not take Bastogne with the forces he had', sent an officer to check on 23 December. He, however, supported Manteuffel's assessment.

The defenders were certainly very short of food, but they still appear to have been better fed than Kokott's volksgrenadiers, whose supply situation was so bad that 'up to ten men had to share half a loaf'. And while American paratroopers suffered in the extreme cold from their lack of winter uniforms, they at least had villages round the perimeter in which they could warm up. Their volksgrenadier opponents were even worse off, which was why they stripped American bodies of boots and items of clothing for themselves. And in the continuing tension caused by the Skorzeny commandos, this led to the shooting of some of those who wore American kit when they surrendered. Apart from weapons, the only piece of German equipment which American soldiers hankered after was the German army's brilliantly simple knife–fork–spoon combination. The Germans had also proved more foresighted by issuing snow camouflage suits, while the Americans had to improvise.

'The first enemy fighter-bombers', Generalmajor Kokott recorded, 'appeared towards 0900 hours, swooped down on communication roads and villages and set vehicles and farmyards on fire.' Unfortunately for the paratroopers on the south-western perimeter, little air support appeared. The drastic drop in temperature during the night froze the turret-traverse mechanism on many of their supporting tanks and tank destroyers. Even anti-tank guns could not be moved as they had been frozen into the ground. Cross-country movement for infantry was also difficult, with a hard crust on the top of half a metre of snow.

The main German attacks that day to break the ring were mounted against the Flamierge sector in the north-west at noon, and another later against Marvie on the south-east side by the 901st Panzergrenadier-Regiment from the Panzer Lehr Division. Towards the end of the morning, however, an unexpected threat appeared from the south. The Fifth Panzer Army had not imagined that General Patton would have been able to move any of his forces north so quickly.

'Towards noon,' Kokott wrote, 'at first singly, but then in droves, men of the 5th Fallschirmjäger appeared near the divisional command post at Hompré. They were coming from the front lines and moving east. Barely an officer was in sight. When questioned, the men yelled: "The enemy has broken through! They've advanced north with tanks and have captured Chaumont!" ' Chaumont was no more than three kilometres to the south of Kokott's headquarters.

The stragglers were soon followed by vehicles and the horse-drawn carts of the

Fallschirmjäger division. In no time at all, American fighter-bombers had sighted the congestion in Hompré and wheeled in to attack. Any German with a weapon began 'firing wildly' at the attacking planes. 'Houses caught fire, vehicles were burning, wounded men were lying in the streets, horses that had been hit were kicking about.'

This chaos coincided with a massive supply drop all around Bastogne. German soldiers, on seeing the quantity of white and coloured parachutes to their north, assumed in alarm that this was the start of a major airborne operation. They took up the cry: 'Enemy paratroopers are landing to our rear!' Even Kokott was shaken by an eventuality that he had never considered. But a sort of order was gradually established, with volksgrenadiers halting the young soldiers of the 5th Fallschirmjäger who were fleeing. An anti-aircraft battery near Hompré received the order 'about face'. The gunners were to switch from aerial targets to prepare their guns for ground operations.

Kokott then improvised combat groups, taking command of four tanks which happened to be near by, an artillery detachment and some engineers, and reorganized some of the fleeing paratroopers who had recovered from 'their initial shock'. He ordered them to move south to take up position blocking the roads. The situation soon appeared to be restored. The American armoured force in Chaumont had only been a reconnaissance probe by forward elements from Patton's Third Army and, lacking sufficient strength, it pulled back.

The first warning the Germans received of the American airdrop to resupply the 101st Airborne and its attached units came soon after midday. The 26th Volksgrenadier-Division received the signal: '*Achtung!* Strong enemy formation flying in from west!' The Germans sighted large aircraft flying at low level accompanied by fighters and fighter-bombers. They expected a massive carpet-bombing attack, and opened rapid fire with their 37mm anti-aircraft guns.

They do not seem to have noticed the first pair of C-47 transports which dropped two sticks of pathfinders at 09.55 that morning. On landing, the pathfinders had reported to McAuliffe's command post in Bastogne to establish the best sites for the drop zones. Their mission had been deemed essential by IX Troop Carrier Command, because of fears that Bastogne might have already been over-run. The pathfinders then set up their homing beacons just outside the town and waited until the drone of approaching aircraft engines gradually built to a roar.

'The first thing you saw coming towards Bastogne', recorded a radio operator in the first wave of C-47 transports, 'was a large flat plain completely covered with snow, the whiteness broken only by trees and some roads and, off in the distance, the town itself. Next, your eye caught the pattern of tank tracks across the snow. We came down lower and lower, finally to about 500 feet off the ground, our drop height.' As the parachutes blossomed open, soldiers emerged from their foxholes and armoured vehicles, 'cheering them wildly as if at a Super Bowl or World Series game', as one put it. Air crew suddenly saw the empty, snowbound landscape come alive as soldiers rushed out to drag the 'parapacks' to safety. 'Watching those bundles of supplies and ammunition drop was a sight to behold,' another soldier recounted. 'As we retrieved the bundles, first we cut up the bags to wrap around our feet, then took the supplies to their proper area.' The silk parachutes were grabbed as sleeping bags.

Altogether the 241 planes from IX Troop Carrier Command, coming in wave after wave, dropped 334 tons of ammunition, fuel, rations and medical supplies, including blood, 'but the bottles broke on landing or were destroyed when a German shell blew up the room where they were stored'. Nine aircraft missed the drop zone or had to turn back. Seven were brought down by anti-aircraft fire. Some air crew were captured, some escaped into the forest and were picked up over the following days, and a handful made it to American lines. 'Not a single German aircraft could be seen in the skies!' Kokott complained. Luftwaffe fighters did attempt to attack the supply drop, but they were vastly outnumbered by the escorts and were chased away, with several shot down.

As soon as the transport planes departed, the eighty-two Thunderbolts in their escort turned their attention to ground targets. They followed tank tracks to where the Germans had attempted to conceal their panzers, and attacked artillery gunlines. Despite the best efforts of the air controllers, the Thunderbolts made several attacks on American positions. In one case a P-47 began to strafe and bomb an American artillery battery. A machine-gunner fired back, and soon several aircraft joined in the attack. Only when an officer ran out waving an identification panel did the pilots understand their mistake and fly off.

The attack of the 901st Panzergrenadiers against Marvie went ahead after dusk following the departure of the fighter-bombers. Artillery fire intensified, then Nebelwerfer batteries fired their multi-barrelled rocket launchers, with their terrifying scream. The German infantry advanced behind groups of four or five panzers. The 327th Glider Infantry and the 326th Airborne Engineer Battalion fired illuminating flares into the sky. Their light revealed Panther tanks, already painted white, and the panzergrenadiers in their snowsuits. The defenders immediately opened fire with rifles and machine guns. Bazooka teams managed to disable a few of the tanks, usually by hitting the tracks or a sprocket, which brought them to a halt but did not stop them from using their main armament or machine guns.

A breakthrough along the road to Bastogne was only just halted after McAuliffe threw in his last reserves and ordered the artillery to keep firing, even though their stocks of shells were perilously low. In fact the defenders fought back so effectively that they inflicted grievous losses. Kokott eventually abandoned the action. He then received an order from Manteuffel's headquarters that he was to mount a major attack on Bastogne on Christmas Day. The 15th Panzergrenadier-Division would arrive in time, and come under his command. Kokott might have been sceptical of his chances, but the defenders were just as hard pushed, especially on the western side.

The Americans could not cover the perimeter frontage in any strength, and they sorely lacked reserves in the event of a breakthrough. With the front-line foxholes so spread out in places, paratroopers resorted to their own form of booby-traps. Fragmentation grenades or 60mm mortar shells were attached to trees with trip wires extending in different directions. Fixed charges of explosive taped to trunks could be detonated by pullwires running back to individual emplacements.

Just south of Foy, part of the 506th Parachute Infantry continued to hold the edge of the woods. Their observation post was in a house, outside which a dead German lay frozen stiff with one arm extended. 'From then on,' a sergeant remembered, 'it was a ritual to shake hands with him every time we came or left the house. We figured that if we could shake his hand, we were a helluva lot better off than he was.' Even with the sacks and bags from the airdrop, frostbite and trench foot affected nearly all soldiers. And Louis Simpson with the 327th Glider Infantry observed, 'in this cold the life in the wounded is likely to go out like a match'.

Facing the attack around Flamierge, Simpson wrote: 'I peer down the slope, trying to see and still keep my head down. Bullets are whining over. To my right, rifles are going off. They must see more than I do. The snow seems to have come alive and to be moving, detaching itself from the trees at the foot of the slope. The movement increases. And now it is a line of men, most of them covered in white — white cloaks and hoods. Here and there men stand out in the gray-green German overcoats. They walk, run and flop down on the snow. They rise and come towards us again.'

■ ■ ■ ■

Bastogne had naturally been a priority for American air support, and so were the hard-pressed 82nd Airborne and the 30th Division on the northern flank. But the top priority that day, with half of all Allied fighter-bomber units allocated, had been to stop the German panzer divisions from reaching the Meuse.

From the moment the weather improved and the Allied air forces were out in strength, incidents of friendly fire, both from the air and from the ground, increased dramatically. Anti-aircraft gunners and almost anyone with a machine gun seemed almost physically incapable of stopping themselves from shooting at any aircraft. 'Rules for Firing' and instructions on 'Air-Ground Recognition' were forgotten. Soldiers had to be reminded that they were not to fire back at Allied aircraft who might be shooting them up by mistake. All they could do was to keep throwing out yellow or orange smoke grenades to make them stop, or firing an Amber Star parachute flare. The self-control of the 30th Infantry Division was the most sorely taxed. These soldiers had suffered attacks by their own aircraft in Normandy, and now in the Ardennes they were to suffer even more.

Bolling's 84th Infantry Division and parts of the 3rd Armored Division continued, with great difficulty, to hold a line south of the Hotton–Marche road against both the 116th Panzer-Division and the 2nd SS *Das Reich*. Combat Command A of the 3rd Armored was pushed further round to the west, as a screen for the assembly of Collins's VII Corps. The 2nd Armored Division, Patton's former command known as 'Hell on Wheels', was arriving by forced march in great secrecy for a counter-attack planned for 24 December. The advance of the 2nd Panzer-Division was faster than expected. But Collins had been greatly relieved to hear from Montgomery, 'chipper and confident as usual', that the bridges over the Meuse at Namur, Dinant and Givet were now securely defended by the British 29th Armoured Brigade. It was that night that the 8th Rifle Brigade killed two Skorzeny commandos in a Jeep. The main problem at the bridges was the flood of refugees fleeing across the Meuse to escape. 'The German push has unsettled the whole population,' wrote an officer with civil affairs, 'and they seem to fear the worst. Already the refugees are moving along the roads and we are out to stop them causing trouble to traffic.' Blocked at the bridges, Belgians resorted to boats to cross the Meuse.

Montgomery also assured Collins that the brigade would advance to link up with Collins's right flank on the next day, 23 December, but A Squadron of the 3rd Royal Tank

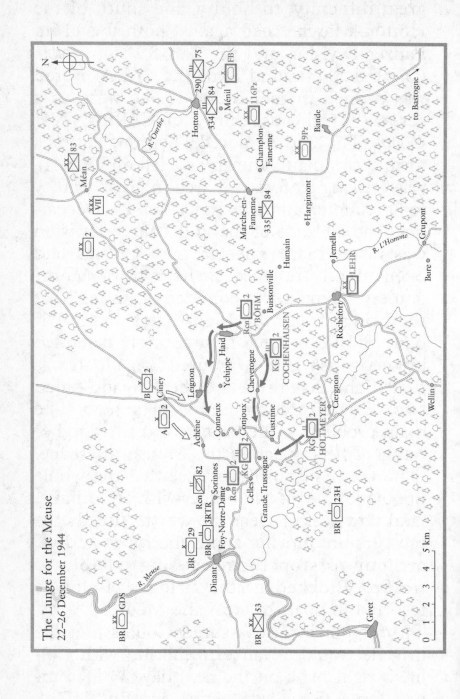

The Lunge for the Meuse
22–26 December 1944

N

R. Ourthe

Hotton

290 [III] 75
FB

334 [III] 84 Ménil

116Pz Champlon-Famenne

9Pz Bande

Mean [XX] 83

VII [XXX]

Marche-en-Famenne

335 [III] 84

Hargimont

[XX] 2

Humain

Jemelle R. L'Homme

Bure Grupont

LEHR [XX]

Buissonville

Rcn [II] 2 BÖHM

Rochefort

Ciney B [X] 2

Leignon

Haid

Ychippe

Chevetogne

KG [III] 2 COCHENHAUSEN

Ciergnon

Wellin

A [X] 2

Achêne

Conneux

Conjoux

Custinne

KG [III] 2 HOLTMEYER

Sorinnes

Rcn [II] 82

KG [II] 2

Celles

3RTR [II]

Grande Trussogne

BR [X] 29

BR [X]

Foy-Notre-Dame

Dinant

BR [IIII] 23H

R. Meuse

BR [XX] GDS

BR [XX] 53

Givet

0 1 2 3 4 5 km

to Bastogne

Regiment commanded by Major Watts was already at Sorinnes, six kilometres east of Dinant. Watts had no idea where either the Americans or the Germans were, so he spread his eighteen tanks out to cover every route into Dinant, using them more like an armoured reconnaissance regiment. For the three armoured regiments in the brigade, the great frustration was to be going into battle with their 'battle-weary Shermans', rather than their new Comet tanks.

The British also started to receive valuable help from locals. The Baron Jacques de Villenfagne, who lived in the chateau at Sorinnes, just three kilometres north of Foy-Notre-Dame (not to be confused with the Foy near Bastogne), was a captain in the Chasseurs Ardennais and leader of the Resistance in the area. He acted as a scout for Watts's squadron on his motorcycle, and reported on the advance of the 2nd Panzer-Division in their direction.

The approaching battle made one thing very clear to farming folk. They needed to prepare food for what could be a long siege, sheltering in their cellars. At Sanzinnes, just south of Celles, Camille Daubois, hearing of the advance of German forces, decided it was time to slaughter his prize pig, a beast of 300 kilos. Because it was so large, he felt he could not do it himself, and called the butcher, who was about to take refuge beyond the Meuse.

He only agreed to help with the slaughter, but when he arrived and saw the animal, he exclaimed: 'That's not a pig, that beast's a cow!' Not prepared to use the knife he insisted on an axe, with which he severed the head. They strung it up to drain the blood and the butcher dashed off. But when men from a Kampfgruppe of the 2nd Panzer arrived later, the pig's carcass disappeared, no doubt to their field kitchen known as a *Gulaschkanone*.

Oberst Meinrad von Lauchert, the commander of the 2nd Panzer-Division, split his force just north of Buissonville to search out the quickest route to the Meuse. The armoured reconnaissance battalion, under Major von Böhm, moved on ahead towards Haid and Leignon because it had been refuelled first. Two panzers in the lead sighted an American armoured car and opened fire. The armoured car was hit, but the crew escaped. Its commander Lieutenant Everett C. Jones got word to Major General Ernest Harmon, the commander of the 2nd Armored Division. The pugnacious Harmon, who was itching to go into the attack, ordered his Combat Command A under Brigadier General John H. Collier to advance immediately.

That evening the main panzer column, commanded by Major Ernst von Cochenhausen, reached the village of Chevetogne, a dozen kilometres north-west of Rochefort. The inhabitants of the village had so far had little more to fear than the V-1s flying overhead towards Antwerp, one of which had exploded in the woods near by. Apart from that, the war seemed to have passed them by. They had seen no American troops since the liberation of the area in September, and never imagined that the Germans would return.

Woken soon after midnight by the vibrations caused by tanks rumbling up the main street, the villagers crept to the windows of their houses to see if this force was American or German, but the vehicles were moving without lights and it was too dark to distinguish. The column came to a halt a little way up the hill, and then, to their alarm, they heard orders barked unmistakably in German. News of the massacres of civilians further east by the Kampfgruppe Peiper had spread rapidly. The black panzer uniforms with the death's-head badge prompted many to believe that these troops were also SS. But the 2nd Panzer-Division was different, and its behaviour towards civilians was on the whole correct. On entering a farm kitchen in Chapois, one of its officers warned the surprised housewife that she had better hide her hams. His soldiers were famished and they would not hesitate to take them.

In the early hours of 24 December, Kampfgruppe Cochenhausen reached Celles, a small and ancient town in a dip just a few kilometres south of Foy-Notre-Dame. Major von Cochenhausen attempted to push through the small town to head straight for Dinant, but the lead Panther tank hit a mine laid the day before by American engineers. According to local folklore, two German officers stormed into the little restaurant on the corner called Le Pavillon Ardennais. The *patronne,* Madame Marthe Monrique, who had just been woken by the blast, met them downstairs in her dressing gown. They demanded to know how many kilometres they still had to cover to reach Dinant. With great presence of mind, she apparently replied that there were only a dozen kilometres. 'But the road is mined, you know! The Americans have buried hundreds of mines.' Cursing, the Germans decided to pull back into nearby woods in case Allied aircraft caught them in the open at dawn.

Cochenhausen established his command post in the woods at a local grotto known as the Trou Mairia. His force included the 304th Panzergrenadier-Regiment, a battalion of the 3rd Panzer-Regiment, a panzer artillery regiment and most of the division's anti-aircraft battalion. Signs pointing to the divisional field hospital or *Feldlazarett* bore the trident symbol of the 2nd Panzer-Division. To prevent information getting back to the Allies, panzergrenadiers were put to work sawing down telephone poles and cutting wires. Another detachment of the 2nd Panzer-Division was just to the east at Conjoux. The villagers there were reminded how in September the local German commander had sworn, just before pulling out, that they would be back.

After Leignon, Böhm's Kampfgruppe had turned west in the night towards Dinant. Just before Foy-Notre-Dame, near the farm of Mahenne, a British Firefly Sherman of the 3rd Royal Tank Regiment lay in wait. The Firefly had the longer and far more powerful 17-pounder or 76.2mm high-velocity gun. Sergeant Probert, the commander, hearing the unmistakable noise of tracked vehicles approaching, woke his crew. The first round missed the leading vehicle but hit a munitions truck, causing an explosion which must have shaken the whole German column. After rapidly reloading, Probert's crew got off another round which destroyed a Mark IV panzer. Then, following the Royal Armoured Corps slogan of 'shoot and scoot', they reversed out rapidly before the Panthers in the column targeted their position. They reported back to Major Watts at Sorinnes. Major von Böhm, unsure after the ambush how strong the Allies were in the area, and because his vehicles were almost out of fuel, decided to halt at the small village of Foy-

Notre-Dame. His crews concealed their vehicles in farmyards, and packed into the houses to warm up and find food.

During that night of 23–24 December, the thermometer dropped to minus 17 Centigrade, and the moon shone on the frozen, snowbound landscape. The Baron de Villenfagne, with his friend Lieutenant Philippe le Hardy de Beaulieu, both dressed in white, managed to identify several of the main German positions. They came across a group of amphibious vehicles concealed under trees at Sanzinnes, which was subsequently shelled by American artillery. The two men returned to the Château de Sorinnes at 04.00 hours and woke Major Watts. Lieutenant Colonel Alan Brown, the commanding officer of the 3rd Royal Tank Regiment, arrived soon afterwards and they briefed them on the German dispositions and the location of Cochenhausen's command post. The vital target was the Ferme de Mahenne, because if that were neutralized the Kampfgruppe Böhm would be separated from Cochenhausen's force. The baron then went to see the 29th Brigade's artillery commander, begging him to spare the great church at Foy-Notre-Dame, which the gunners managed to do when shelling the village taken over by Böhm's Kampfgruppe.

Hitler was exultant when he heard that the forward elements of the 2nd Panzer-Division were now only seven kilometres from Dinant.

He passed on his warmest congratulations to Lüttwitz and Lauchert, the divisional commander. Both men must have winced, knowing how precarious their position was, with little chance of supplies getting through. Lüttwitz, who had commanded the 2nd Panzer in the doomed Avranches counter-attack in August, recommended to Manteuffel that they should start to withdraw the division from the tip of the whole German salient. But he knew that Hitler would never contemplate such a move.

On the left flank of the 2nd Panzer, Bayerlein's Panzer Lehr had advanced from Saint-Hubert north to Rochefort, with General von Manteuffel accompanying them. Their artillery shelled the town in the afternoon. A patrol entered the edge of Rochefort and reported back that it was empty, but they had not looked carefully enough. A battalion from the 84th Infantry Division and a platoon of tank destroyers were concealed and waiting. The road into Rochefort ran along the L'Homme river in a rocky gorge, which made the German attack a risky enterprise. As night fell, Bayerlein gave a characteristic order: 'Right, let's go! Shut your eyes and in you go.'

Led by the 902nd Panzergrenadiers, commanded by Oberstleutnant Joachim Ritter von Poschinger, the charge was brought to a sudden halt under a massive fusillade at a major barricade in Rochefort. The fighting was ferocious and lasted through the night. The panzergrenadiers lost many men and a heavy Jagdpanzer was knocked out near the central square. The American defenders, heavily outnumbered, were eventually forced back. The survivors escaped north next day, to join up with the 2nd Armored Division.

Most of the townsfolk sought shelter in caves at the base of the cliffs surrounding Rochefort. They were to stay there for some time, since Rochefort now became a target for American artillery. During the worst of the shelling, Jeanne Ory and her younger sister asked their mother: 'Mummy, are we going to die?' She replied: 'Say your prayers, my children.' And everyone around would recite the rosary together. One man found a friend dead in the frozen street face down with a cat sitting serenely on his back, profiting from the last of the body's heat. The Trappist monks from the Abbaye de Saint-Remy took on the task of removing bodies.

That evening, President Roosevelt in Washington wrote to Josef Stalin. 'I wish to direct General Eisenhower to send to Moscow a fully qualified officer of his staff to discuss with you Eisenhower's situation on the Western Front and its relation to the Eastern Front, in order that all of us may have information essential to our coordination of effort . . . The situation in Belgium is not bad but it is time to talk of the next plan. In view of the emergency an early reply to this proposal is requested.' Stalin replied two days later to agree. The very mention of 'emergency' in the last sentence must have suggested to him that the Allies had their backs against the wall. Air Chief Marshal Tedder and General Bull were designated to confer with Stalin. They prepared to fly from France to Cairo and then on to Moscow, but because of long delays they would not see Stalin until 15 January, well after the crisis was over.

17
SUNDAY 24 DECEMBER

Sunday 24 December again produced bright sun and blue skies. Captain Mudgett, the 12th Army Group meteorologist in Luxembourg, was 'almost hysterical with his continued success in the weather. He looks proudly out over the blue sky that stretches way into Germany over the stone ramparts and the three spires of the cathedral.'

Bradley's Eagle Tac headquarters now had few fears about the defence of Bastogne, with the men of the 101st Airborne 'clinging stubbornly to their position like a wagon train in the pioneer days of the west'. But staff officers were well aware of the plight of the wounded in the town. McAuliffe had asked for four surgical teams to be dropped by parachute. Plans went ahead for them to be brought in by glider instead.

While Patton's III Corps with the 4th Armored Division was struggling to break through to Bastogne from the south against much heavier resistance than expected,

Hansen was amused by a bizarre report. 'Today a quartermaster soldier asked for the road to Luxembourg while passing through Arlon. He got on the wrong road, [and] drove up the road to Bastogne. When someone fired on him, he only got more frightened, pressed his accelerator and finally drove into the area of the 101st — the first person to make contact with them, and in a purely accidental manner.'

Confirmation of the tough fighting on the southern side of the perimeter came from a signals intercept. The 5th Fallschirmjäger-Division was clamouring for more Panzer-fausts and anti-tank guns to help in its battle against the 4th Armored Division. The Third Army commander appeared to have no doubts about the outcome. 'General Patton was in several times today,' Hansen noted. 'He is boisterous and noisy, feeling good in the middle of a fight.' But in fact Patton was concealing his embarrassment that the 4th Armored's advance was not going nearly as rapidly as he had predicted and was meeting tough opposition. The division had also found that VIII Corps engineers in the retreat to Bastogne 'blew everything in sight', so their progress 'was impeded not by the enemy but by demolitions and blown bridges caused by friendly engineers'.

The Luxembourgers were more confident. They were reassured by the endless convoys of Third Army troops streaming through the city, and believed that the Germans would not be coming back. Strangely, 12th Army Group intelligence suddenly increased their estimate of German tank and assault-gun strength from 345 to 905, which was rather more than the earlier estimated panzer total for the whole of the western front.

Despite the terrible cold which made men shiver uncontrollably in their foxholes, morale was high within the Bastogne perimeter. Although the paratroopers and 10th Armored looked forward to relief by Patton's forces, they rejected any idea that they needed to be saved. With another brilliant day of flying weather, they watched the sky fill with Allied planes of every description. They listened to bombs exploding and the clatter of machine guns, as fighters strafed the German columns. Dogfights against the few Focke-Wulfs and Messerschmitts provoked ferocious cheers and roars as if it were a deadly boxing match, and bitter cries broke out if an Allied transport dropping supplies was hit by ground fire.

Allied fighter-bombers during this period proved very effective in breaking up German attacks as they were assembling. They were directed on to targets by air controllers in Bastogne. A warning of the threat, with coordinates coming from a regimental command post or an artillery liaison plane, meant that 'it was usually only a matter of minutes until planes were striking the enemy forces'.

With priority on artillery ammunition in the airdrops, the food situation for troops barely improved. Many depended on the generosity of Belgian families sharing what they had. Both in Bastogne and on the northern shoulder, 'rations were frequently supplemented with beef, venison and rabbit when these animals set off the mines by running into the trip-wires'. Snipers shot hare and even boar, but the longing for wild pork was greatly reduced after hogs had been sighted eating the intestines of battle casualties.

The intense cold and deep snow caused more than discomfort. They greatly affected fighting performance. Those who did not keep a spare set of dry socks in their helmet-liner and change them frequently were the first to suffer from trench foot or frostbite. The newly arrived 11th Armored Division on the Meuse followed, perhaps unknowingly, the old practice of Russian armies for avoiding frostbite, by providing blanket strips to make foot bandages. Tank crewmen standing on metal in such conditions for hours on end, not moving their feet sufficiently, were particularly vulnerable. But at least those in armoured vehicles and truck drivers could dry out their footwear on engine exhausts.

Condoms were fitted over the sights of anti-tank guns, and also on radio and telephone mouthpieces, because breath condensation soon froze them up. The traverse mechanism on tanks and tank destroyers needed to be thawed out. Snow would get into weapons and ammunition clips and freeze solid. Machine guns were the most likely to jam. The heavy .50 machine gun was essential for shooting enemy marksmen out of trees and other hiding places. American soldiers soon discovered that German snipers waited for artillery or anti-aircraft fire before they pulled the trigger, so that their shot would not be heard.

Lessons learned in one sector were rapidly passed to other formations through 'combat observer' reports. German patrols would cut cables at night and run one of the severed ends into an ambush position, so that they could seize any linesman sent out to repair it. German soldiers sometimes fired a bullet through their own helmet in advance, so that if they were overrun they could play dead and then shoot one of their attackers in the back. They often mined or booby-trapped their own trenches just before withdrawing.

American patrols were advised that when encountering the enemy at night, 'fire at random, throw yourself into cover, then yell like mad as if you were going into the attack, and they will start firing', which would reveal their position. In defence, they should place dummies well to the front of their foxholes to prompt Germans to open fire prematurely. They should provide cover for the enemy in front, but bury mines under it; construct fake defences between strongpoints. Just before going into the attack, it helped to make digging noises to mislead the enemy. And when inside a house, they should never fire from the window, but keep it open and shoot from well back in the room.

The most respected and vital members of a company were the aid men. They were trusted with grain alcohol to prevent the water freezing in their canteens which they would offer to the wounded. 'The stimulating effect of the alcohol does no harm either,' the report added. Chaplains were also sent to the aid stations with alcohol to make a hot toddy for wounded men coming in. Countless men later acknowledged that they owed their lives to the dedication, courage and sometimes inventiveness of aid men. PFC Floyd Maquart, with the 101st, saved one soldier severely wounded in the face and neck by cutting open his throat with a parachute knife and inserting the hollow part of a fountain pen into his windpipe.

Conditions for more than 700 patients in the riding school and the chapel of the seminary in Bastogne continued to deteriorate, since the German capture of the field hospital meant that there was only one surgeon. The doctor from the 10th Armored was assisted by two trained Belgian nurses: Augusta Chiwy, a fearless young woman from the Congo, and Renée Lemaire, the fiancée of a Jew arrested in Brussels by the Gestapo earlier in the year. Those with serious head and stomach wounds were least likely to survive, and the piles of frozen corpses grew, stacked like cordwood under tarpaulins outside. A number of patients suffered from gas gangrene which gave off an appalling stench, and the stock of hydrogen peroxide to clean such wounds was almost all gone. The dwindling supply of plasma froze solid, and bags had to be thawed by being placed in somebody's armpit. For some operations, a slug of cognac had to replace anaesthetics. Sedatives were also in very short supply to deal with the increasing number of combat-fatigue casualties, who would sit up and suddenly start screaming. Men who had demonstrated great bravery in Normandy and in Holland had finally succumbed to stress and exhaustion. Cold and lack of proper food had accelerated the process.

As well as the setpiece assaults, which General major Kokott had been forced to launch, there were many more German attacks at night, often with four tanks and a hundred infantry. Their soldiers in snow suits were well camouflaged out in the snowfields, but when they were against a dark background of trees or buildings they stood out. Realizing this they took off the jacket, but the white legs still gave them away.

'Knocking out tanks is a matter of teamwork, mutual confidence and guts,' an VIII Corps report stated. 'The infantry stay in their foxholes and take care of the hostile infantry and the tank destroyers take care of the tanks.' Providing both elements did their job, the Germans were usually repulsed. Some paratroopers, however, clearly got a thrill out of stalking panzers with bazookas. The 101st claimed that altogether between 19 and 30 December it knocked out 151 tanks and assault guns and 25 half-tracks. These figures were almost certainly exaggerated, rather like the victories claimed by fighter pilots. Many targets were shared with the Sherman tanks of the 10th Armored and the Hellcats of Colonel Templeton's 705th Tank Destroyer Battalion.

The continuing fight against the 901st Panzergrenadiers around Marvie had become increasingly confused in the early hours of the morning. An American machine-gunner shot two glider infantrymen who appeared over a crest. The Americans were forced back from the village, but managed to hold the hill to the west. McAuliffe's headquarters in Bastogne re-examined their defences. The push into the town from Marvie had only just been stopped, but they were also vulnerable on the western side of the perimeter. It was decided to pull back from the Flamierge and Mande-Saint-Etienne salient, and withdraw from Senonchamps. Reducing the overall frontage would strengthen their lines, but they also reorganized their forces by attaching tanks and tank destroyers permanently to each regiment.

Generalmajor Kokott, meanwhile, was left in no doubt from both his corps commander Lüttwitz and Manteuffel that Bastogne must be crushed next day, before the 4th Armored Division broke through from the south. Kokott, while waiting for the 15th Panzer-grenadier-Division to deploy on the north-western sector, became increasingly concerned about the 5th Fallschirmjäger's defence line to the south. He thought it prudent to set up a southern security screen of 'emergency platoons' from his own supply personnel with a few anti-tank guns. The anti-aircraft battalion near Hompré was also told to be ready to switch to a ground role to take on American tanks. It was a comfort to know that at least the main road south to Arlon was covered by the 901st Panzer-grenadier-Regiment from the Panzer Lehr.

The 5th Fallschirmjäger-Division certainly appeared ill equipped for its task of defending the southern flank of the Fifth Panzer Army. Its much disliked commander General-major Ludwig Heilmann despised his Luft-

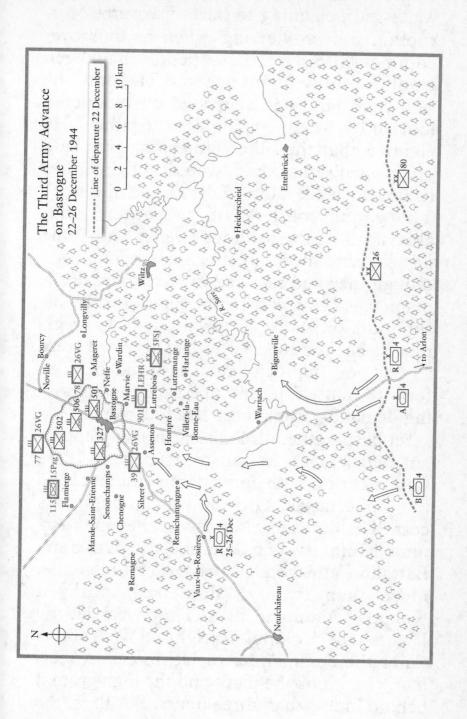

The Third Army Advance
on Bastogne
22–26 December 1944

------- Line of departure 22 December

0 2 4 6 8 10 km

N

waffe staff, claiming to have discovered 'corruption and profiteering' when he took over command. 'So far these people had been employed only in France and Holland,' he said later, 'and had vegetated on plundered loot and were all accomplices together.' He claimed that the older Unteroffizieren said quite openly that they 'would not dream of risking their life now at the end of the war'. The young soldiers, on the other hand, almost all of them under twenty and some just sixteen, 'made a better impression', even though they had received little training. Heilmann was being constantly questioned by his superiors on the exact positions of his regiments, but the reports he had received were so few and imprecise that he decided to go forward himself, if only to escape the 'harassing demands' from corps headquarters.

Yet despite the 5th Fallschirmjäger's apparent deficiencies, its mostly teenage soldiers were fighting with formidable resilience, as the 4th Armored Division was finding to its cost. That morning at dawn, the 53rd Armored Infantry Battalion and the 37th Tank Battalion attacked the village of Bigonville, more than twenty kilometres south of Kokott's command post. They were led by Lieutenant Colonel Creighton W. Abrams (later the commander of US forces in Vietnam), and took the place and the high ground behind in less than three hours. But then 'the enemy managed to infiltrate back into the town and more fighting was required to clear it'. To make matters worse, the American force was then bombed and strafed by P-47 Thunderbolts, which turned away only after coloured smoke grenades had been set off and snow brushed off identification panels. Securing Bigonville a second time took another three hours, and this village came at a heavy cost. Tank commanders, with their heads out of the turret, attracted the fire of German snipers, who 'accounted for nine in the 37th Tank Battalion, including the C Company commander'.

The 4th Armored Division was also suffering from the extreme weather. 'Our company commander was evacuated with pneumonia,' wrote a soldier with the 51st Armored Infantry Battalion, 'and we lost our platoon sergeant because his feet froze.' By the next day there was only one officer left in the company. Patton's hope of relieving Bastogne by Christmas was fading fast.

Kokott's forces like most German formations in the Ardennes were running short of ammunition, especially mortar rounds. Allied airstrikes on marshalling yards and forward supply lines were already having an effect. That afternoon, the Americans noticed that the German guns had fallen silent. The defenders guessed that they were conserving their ammunition for a major attack on

Christmas morning.

Some fifty kilometres to the north, the remnants of Kampfgruppe Peiper in La Gleize had prepared the destruction of their vehicles, prior to a breakout on foot across the River Amblève. At 03.00 on 24 December, the main group of some 800 men crossed the river and trudged up through the thick woods on the south side towards the ridge line. Peiper, just behind the point detachment, took Major McCown with him. Two hours later they heard explosions behind them and, down in the valley, the ruined village was lit by the flames from burning vehicles.

Peiper, unsure where the German lines lay, led them south parallel with the River Salm. McCown recounted later that they had nothing to eat but four dried biscuits and two gulps of cognac. An hour after dark they bumped into an American outpost, where a sentry opened fire. The panzergrenadiers were exhausted, especially the two dozen walking wounded. They blundered about in the dark, wading streams to avoid roads and villages. In the early hours of Christmas morning they ran into another American position north of Bergeval, triggering a formidable response with mortars and machine guns firing tracer. McCown escaped during the confusion, and rejoined the American lines where he identified himself to paratroopers of the 82nd Airborne. He was taken to General Jim Gavin's command post.

Peiper and his men withdrew down into the Salm valley and swam across the freezing river. The I SS Panzer Corps reported his arrival, apparently wounded, later on Christmas morning. This was at about the same time as the 30th Infantry Division crushed the other pocket of his men, trapped near Stavelot. Their resistance was fanatical, probably out of a belief that their opponents would not be taking prisoners. 'Attacking waves literally waded knee-deep through their own dead in their desperate assaults,' the after-action report stated. The divisional artillery commander estimated that there were more than a thousand German dead piled at one point, and the woods around Stavelot and La Gleize were strewn with corpses. The Americans estimated that 2,500 members of the Kampfgruppe had been killed and ninety-two tanks and assault guns destroyed.

Now that the only breakthrough by the Sixth Panzer Army had been thoroughly destroyed, the eyes of Hitler and the OKW were firmly on Manteuffel's panzer divisions to the west. The build-up against the northern shoulder line appeared overwhelming. After the 2nd SS Panzer-Division *Das Reich* had crushed the force at Baraque-de-Fraiture, it was reinforced by the advance guard of the 9th

Panzer-Division. The *Führer Begleit* Brigade was on its way to attack Hotton, and the 18th and 62nd Volksgrenadier-Divisions, supported by the 9th SS Panzer-Division *Hohenstaufen,* were attacking the 82nd Airborne on the Vielsalm sector, where General Ridgway insisted on holding a right-angled wedge.

General Bradley was outraged to hear that Montgomery had deployed Collins's VII Corps along the shoulder line rather than hold it back for a major counter-attack. (In fact it was Collins himself who had committed his divisions because there was no choice.) Once again it demonstrated how completely Bradley failed to understand what was really happening. With four panzer divisions attacking north and north-west, a defence line had to be secured before a counter-attack took place. First Army headquarters, which was considering a major withdrawal on the VII Corps front, even recorded that evening: 'Despite the air's magnificent performance today things tonight look, if anything, worse than before.' Concern about a breakthrough by the panzer divisions to the west even prompted First Army to consider pulling back all the heavy equipment of V Corps in case of a sudden retreat.

Ridgway was livid when Montgomery overruled him once more, on this occasion by ordering Gavin's 82nd Airborne to withdraw from Vielsalm to the base of the triangle from

Trois-Ponts to Manhay. The 82nd was coming under heavy pressure from the 9th SS Panzer-Division *Hohenstaufen,* the rest of the 1st SS Panzer-Division and the 18th and 62nd Volksgrenadier-Divisions. Yet Ridgway felt insulted by the idea that the United States Army should be ordered to give ground in this way. He attributed the move to Montgomery's obsession with 'tidying-up the battlefield', and protested vehemently to General Hodges, 'but apparently received little sympathy there', as Hansen later acknowledged. Bradley became obsessed with Montgomery's decision and harped on about it for some time to come.

Gavin, however, saw the point of the redeployment, and Montgomery was almost certainly right. The 82nd was already overstretched even before the next wave of German formations was due to arrive. Reducing their front from twenty-seven kilometres to sixteen meant a much stronger defence line. The withdrawal began that night, and 'morale in the 82nd was not materially affected'. Gavin's paratroopers soon had plenty of frozen German corpses to use as sandbags in their new positions, and they refused to allow Graves Registration personnel to take them away.

Task Force Kane and a regiment of the newly arrived 17th Airborne were positioned to defend the Manhay crossroads, against what First Army headquarters still believed to be an attempt to capture American supply bases in Liège. The untried 75th Infantry Division was on its way to support Rose's 3rd Armored Division as it attempted to extricate Task Force Hogan, surrounded at Marcouray.

The defenders at Manhay expected a fearsome attack by the *Das Reich,* but it advanced cautiously through the forests either side of the highway and occupied Odeigne. This was partly due to continuing fuel-supply problems, but mainly to avoid moving in the open on another day of brilliant sunshine. An armoured column in daylight would become easy prey for the fighter-bombers overhead, scouring the snowbound landscape for targets.

Brigadeführer Heinz Lammerding, the commander of the *Das Reich* responsible for the massacres of Tulle and Oradour-sur-Glane on their advance north to Normandy in June, was tall and arrogant with a pitted face. He was famous for his ruthlessness, like most of his officers. They even thought it funny that the *Das Reich* had murdered the inhabitants of the wrong Oradour. 'An SS-Führer told me with a laugh', Heydte was secretly recorded later as saying, 'that it had been the wrong village. "It was just too bad for them," [he said]. It turned out afterwards that there weren't any partisans in that village.'

As soon as dark fell and the Thunderbolt and Lightning fighter-bombers had departed, the tanks and half-tracks of the SS *Das Reich* emerged from the woods and drove north towards Manhay. The Germans employed their usual trick of placing a captured Sherman at the head of the column. The Americans held their fire, in case it was a task force from the 3rd Armored Division. But then the SS fired flares to blind the American tank gunners. Two panzergrenadier regiments attacked abreast at 21.00. By midnight, they had taken Manhay. The combat command of the 7th Armored lost nineteen tanks in the night battle, and its exhausted tank crews had to escape on foot. The *Das Reich* panzer regiment lost none.

Waldenburg's 116th Panzer-Division, having been sent round to the west of the River Ourthe, received orders to break through between Marche-en-Famenne and Hotton, then to swing west towards Ciney to protect the right flank of the 2nd Panzer-Division. But Bolling's 84th Infantry Division held a strong line south of the main Marche–Hotton road. The 116th managed to break through around the village of Verdenne, but the success did not last. This was just the start of what Waldenburg called 'bitter and ever-

'changing' battles. Houses and positions changed hands many times.

Marche itself was threatened. The twenty-one-year-old Henry Kissinger with the 84th's intelligence branch volunteered to stay behind under cover despite the added risk of being Jewish. But Bolling's men held firm and his artillery eventually inflicted terrible losses on Waldenburg's men. Field artillery battalions used the new Pozit fuse at high elevation, if necessary by digging down the trails, so as to achieve air bursts over the German positions. The American infantry watched the effect with savage glee, and reported back '*beaucoup* dead'.

Allied fighter-bombers also wheeled back and forth, dropping bombs and strafing. 'Of the German Luftwaffe nothing was to be seen or heard,' Waldenburg commented angrily. The closest his panzergrenadiers came to Marche was the treeline north-west of Champlon-Famenne overlooking the town, where they were constantly bombarded by American artillery. To this day the local landowner cannot sell timber from the forest because of the shards of metal buried deep in the massive conifers.

At the furthest tip of the German salient, the 2nd Panzer-Division had now lost three tanks in its clashes with the 3rd Royal Tank Regiment. Lieutenant Colonel Brown, concerned that the Germans were now so close to the bridge at Dinant, reinforced the approaches in case panzergrenadiers tried to slip through on foot. He had learned that the German fuel situation had become desperate. British artillery began to bombard 2nd Panzer positions around Celles, and plans were made to attack from Sorinnes the next day to crush Böhm's reconnaissance battalion in Foy-Notre-Dame. Brown did not yet know that the British 53rd Division was starting to cross the Meuse, so he would have strong support.

Major General Harmon, instantly recognizable from his barrel-chest, military moustache and gravelly voice, could scarcely control his impatience to be at the enemy. He had received orders from General Collins to hold back until the moment was ripe for a counter-attack, but Collins could not be reached as he was preoccupied with the dangerous situation on his east flank. Montgomery had even issued an instruction that, because of the threat from the 2nd Panzer and Panzer Lehr in the west, Collins's corps could, 'if forced', swing back to a line between Hotton and Andenne, some thirty kilometres north of Marche as the crow flies. This would have constituted a major retreat and, unlike the withdrawal of Gavin's 82nd Airborne, a huge mistake. But fortunately Montgomery had left Collins with the authority to take his own decisions.

Harmon suspected that there was a large panzer force around Celles, but had no confirmation until two P-51 Mustangs reported flak firing from near by. (No contact had yet been established with the British at Sorinnes.) Amid considerable confusion between First Army headquarters and VII Corps during Collins's absence, Harmon refused to wait any longer. He ordered his Combat Command B to join Combat Command A at Ciney, and sent forward two battalions of self-propelled artillery. When finally Collins spoke to Harmon by telephone that evening and gave him leave to attack next morning, Harmon apparently roared: 'The bastards are in the bag!' Montgomery backed Collins's decision to deploy the 2nd Armored Division, even though it now meant that his plan to hold back the VII Corps for a counter-attack had unravelled.

The Cochenhausen Kampfgruppe had taken up all-round defence in two pockets between Celles and Conneux, while awaiting promised reinforcements from the 9th Panzer-Division. But the 9th Panzer was in turn delayed, waiting to refuel. The 2nd Panzer's forward elements were also clamouring for ammunition and fuel, but the extended supply line was far from secure. This was made worse by renewed American attacks on the high ground south-west of Marche and the increasing numbers of Allied fighter-bombers overhead. Staff in the 2nd Panzer-Division headquarters south of Marche burned with frustration that this should happen when they were so close to their objective. An instruction from Generalfeldmarschall Model went out to Foy-Notre-Dame: 'If necessary, elements of the reconnaissance battalion were to capture the Dinant bridge on foot, in a coup de main,' just as Colonel Brown had imagined. But Böhm's Kampfgruppe was the hardest pressed of all, as British artillery ranged in on it.

Frustration soon turned to alarm in the 2nd Panzer-Division headquarters 'since both pockets reported that their supply of ammunition and fuel would not allow them to continue the battle much longer', Oberstleutnant Rüdiger Weiz recorded. 'And since the fuel available at the front was not sufficient for the withdrawal of the forces, the nearly unsolvable question arose how to bring help to the elements fighting in the front line.'

Lauchert decided to pull out the Kampfgruppe commanded by Major Friedrich Holtmeyer screening Marche. He ordered it to move west via Rochefort, and thrust towards Conneux to relieve the encircled forces there. This operation could be carried out only at night because of American air supremacy. Lüttwitz agreed with the plan, but permission first had to be obtained from

Fifth Panzer Army headquarters. Lauchert received authorization that afternoon, but the reconnaissance battalion was no longer responding on the radio. Holtmeyer's force set out that evening, but this difficult manoeuvre in the dark was further hindered by American groups attacking as they withdrew.

Ten kilometres south-east of Marche, the village of Bande stands on a hill above the N4 highway from Marche to Bastogne. As mentioned earlier, German SS troops had burned thirty-five houses along the N4 highway near the village during their retreat from the region in September as a reprisal for attacks by the Belgian Resistance. On 22 December, leading elements of the 2nd Panzer-Division had passed by, and on the following day some of their troops were billeted in the village. They behaved well. On Christmas Eve, a very different group, some thirty strong, appeared wearing grey SS uniforms. They had the badge of the Sicherheitsdienst — an SD in a lozenge — on the left sleeve. The majority of this Sondereinheitkommando 8 were not German, but French, Belgian and Dutch fascists led by a Swiss and attached to the Gestapo.

They stayed apart from the panzergrenadiers, and took over some wooden buildings near the main road. Christmas Eve happened to be a Sunday, so almost the whole village was at mass. As the doors opened afterwards and the congregation came out, every man of military age was seized, supposedly for an examination of identity papers. Altogether some seventy men were rounded up. Just under half — those aged between seventeen and thirty-one — were taken under guard down to a sawmill near the main road where they were locked up. Many of them were refugees from elsewhere, but they too were interrogated brutally about the attacks in the area on retreating German forces three and a half months before. One by one, they were taken out and shot.

There was just a single survivor, Léon Praile, a powerful and athletic twenty-one-year-old. He had tried to persuade others to join him in rushing their guards, but could find no volunteers. When his turn came — by then night was falling fast — he suddenly punched his escort hard in the face and took off, leaping a low stone wall and sprinting towards the stream. Shots were fired in his direction, but he escaped.

When the village was eventually liberated in January by British paratroopers from the 6th Airborne Division, the Abbé Musty and Léon Praile took them to where the thirty-four bodies, by now frozen stiff, had been concealed. 'After the deed was done,' stated the British report, 'the Germans half covered the bodies with earth and planks. Finally they wrote on a wall of the house "Revenging the honour of our German heroes, killed by the Belgians" . . . [the victims] show signs of having been beaten before being shot through the back of the head.'

The massacre seemed inexplicable to the villagers, and the shock produced a false rumour that Praile could have escaped death only by betraying his comrades. Over the years this idea became a fixation. Praile decided never to return to the region.

Generaloberst Guderian, the army chief of staff responsible for the eastern front, drove from Zossen, south of Berlin, to see Hitler at the Adlerhorst. It was quite clear to him that the Ardennes offensive had failed to achieve its goals and was not worth continuing. The point of maximum danger lay to the east, where the Red Army was preparing its great winter offensive. In his briefcase he had a rather more accurate assessment than usual from Generalmajor Reinhard Gehlen, the head of Fremde Heere Ost, the army intelligence department dealing with the eastern front. Gehlen had been wrong many times in the past, which did not help his arguments, but Guderian was convinced that his warnings were correct. Gehlen's department estimated that the Red Army had a superiority of eleven to one in infantry, seven to one in tanks and twenty to one in artillery. Soviet aviation also enjoyed almost total air supremacy, which prevented the Germans from carrying out photo-reconnaissance.

In the conference room, Guderian found himself facing Heinrich Himmler, the Reichsführer-SS, Generalfeldmarschall Keitel and Generaloberst Jodl. As he presented the intelligence estimates, Hitler stopped him. He declared that such estimates of Soviet strength were preposterous. Red Army tank corps had hardly any tanks and their rifle divisions were reduced to little more than 7,000 men each. 'It's the greatest imposture since Genghis Khan,' he shouted. 'Who is responsible for producing all this rubbish?'

Guderian's attempts to defend Gehlen's figures were treated with contempt, and Jodl, to his horror, argued that attacks in the west should continue. At dinner Himmler, a military ignoramus who had just been made commander-in-chief Army Group Upper Rhine, confidently told Guderian that the Soviet build-up was an enormous bluff. Guderian had no option but to return in despair to Zossen.

On the extreme right of Patton's two army corps, the 5th Infantry Division had begun to advance north-west from behind the 4th Infantry Division. Hemingway, recovered from flu and drinking his own urine, watched and joked on a hilltop with friends from his adopted division as the soldiers below proceeded in extended order wearing their bedsheet camouflage and firing aimlessly in front of them. There did not seem to be any Germans shooting back. On Christmas Eve he went to the 22nd Infantry's headquarters at Rodenbourg not knowing that the new commander, Colonel Ruggles, had also invited Hemingway's estranged wife. Ruggles had sent a Jeep to Luxembourg to fetch Martha Gellhorn, hoping it would be a pleasant surprise for both of them. The disengaged couple found themselves having to share a room.

The night before Christmas carried a special significance for soldiers on both sides. In Bastogne, the less seriously wounded received rations of brandy and listened to the endlessly repeated song 'White Christmas' on a salvaged civilian radio. North-east of the town in Foy, German soldiers packed into houses and farms to get warm. A young German soldier quietly told the Belgian family in whose house he was billeted that he intended to go home alive: three of his brothers had already been killed. On other parts of the perimeter American soldiers listened to their enemies singing 'Stille Nacht, Heilige Nacht'. They could only talk about Christmas at home, imagining their families in front of warm fires. Some of their luckier comrades to the rear attended a midnight mass, such as the one in the chapel of the Château de Rolley, packed with refugees and the family of the owners. In most cases, they also sang 'Silent Night', thinking of home. In Bastogne, about a hundred soldiers assembled for mass in front of an improvised altar lit by candles set in empty ration tins. The chaplain in his address to them offered simple advice. 'Do not plan, for God's plan will prevail.'

At Boisseilles, between Celles and Foy-Notre-Dame, German soldiers also joined the civilians sheltering in the chateau there. One panzergrenadier from the 2nd Panzer, perhaps inflamed by alcohol, declared that 'Tomorrow we will cross the Meuse!' Another, in a more realistic frame of mind, sighed, 'Poor Christmas.'

The advanced units of the 2nd Panzer were famished, if not starving. In Celles an Alsatian soldier knocked at a door and, when the family opened it cautiously, went down on his knees to beg for a little food. The condition of many of them was so pitiable that locals felt compelled to give their occupiers something to eat out of Christian charity. There were impressively few cases of 2nd Panzer soldiers seizing food at gunpoint, although some might order a farmer's wife to make them soup, or a pie from her store of preserved fruits in jars, as a Christmas gesture. Others forced local women to wash their socks or underclothes.

German soldiers, despite their intense hunger, were even more desperate to find drink to drown their sorrows on Christmas Eve. In Rochefort, a fourteen-year-old girl, Liliane Delhomme, saw a *Landser* smash the glass door of the Café Grégoire with his fist, cutting himself badly in the process, to get himself a bottle. Homesickness is worse at Christmas. Many soldiers gazed at photographs of their family and wept silently.

Infantrymen on both sides spent the night in their foxholes. The Americans had only frozen C-Rations to celebrate with, which was at any rate more than most Germans. One paratrooper described how he cut out chunks of frozen hash one by one to thaw them out in his mouth before being able to eat them. On the most northerly shoulder at Höfen, a soldier in the 99th Infantry Division wrote in his diary: 'The fellows are calling up and down the line wishing each other a Merry Christmas. It is a very pretty night with the ground covered with snow.' The fortunate ones were visited by an officer passing round a bottle.

Command posts and higher headquarters had Christmas trees, usually decorated with the strips of aluminium foil for radar-jamming. The higher the headquarters, the greater the opportunity for a proper celebration. The city of Luxembourg, still untouched by the war, now felt secure. And as snowflakes fell gently on the night of Christmas Eve, US Army chaplain Frederick A. McDonald was about to conduct the service in a candle-lit church. He had been warned that General Patton would be attending communion that night. The church was packed, but McDonald had no trouble recognizing 'this General of stern expression' standing alone and erect at the back. He went to welcome him and mentioned that, in the First World War, Kaiser Wilhelm II had come to services in this church. McDonald, no doubt aware of this general's desire to commune with history, asked: 'Would you, sir, like to sit in the Kaiser's pew?' Patton smiled. 'Lead me to it,' he said.

18
CHRISTMAS DAY

The short-lived silence of Christmas night in Bastogne was broken by a Luftwaffe bomber flying over the town dropping magnesium flares, followed by waves of Junkers 88. The Americans had come to regard the Luftwaffe as a spent force, and the effect was far more devastating than even the most intense artillery bombardment. The shock was still worse for the refugees and Bastognards packed into the cellars, when buildings collapsed above them.

McAuliffe's headquarters were hit. Walls vibrated as in an earthquake, and everyone was terrified they would be crushed by falling masonry. In the packed cellars of the Institut de Notre-Dame, people prayed or screamed in panic as clouds of dust descended. Several became completely crazed.

Captain Prior, the doctor with the 10th Armored aid station, had been sharing a Christmas bottle of champagne with several of his colleagues, including Augusta Chiwy, the Congolese nurse. They were all thrown to the ground by the force of a blast, and Prior suddenly feared that the aid post itself had been hit. Coated in dust, they struggled out into the street. The three-storey building had collapsed on top of their wounded patients and the ruins were on fire. Chiwy's fellow nurse Renée Lemaire was killed along with some twenty-five of the seriously wounded, burned to death in their beds. Soldiers rushed up to pull away debris to create an exit, but attempts to put out the fire with buckets of water were fruitless and soon abandoned. Some of the wounded, surrounded by flames, begged to be shot. The low-flying bombers machine-gunned the streets, prompting paratroopers to fire back with rifles. Bastogne had no anti-aircraft defences because the quadruple .50 half-tracks were all deployed to bolster the perimeter defences.

This attack, which was renewed several hours later, was clearly the opening salvo of the Germans' Christmas Day onslaught. The *Arko*, or senior artillery commander of the Fifth Panzer Army, had come on Manteuffel's instructions to supervise fire control. Kokott had moved his command post to Givry opposite the north-west flank. This sector had fewer woods and villages, which the Americans had used so effectively as strongpoints, and the open terrain presented obstacles no greater than small gullies covered with snow.

Even so, most of his volksgrenadiers dreaded the battle to come, and were not convinced by the exhortations and promises of their officers that this time they had overwhelming strength.

The double offensive from the north-west and the south-east was planned to break into Bastogne itself within five hours, but Kokott was dismayed to find that the 15th Panzergrenadier-Division was much weaker than he had expected. It had little more than a Kampfgruppe commanded by Oberstleutnant Wolfgang Maucke, with three battalions of panzergrenadiers, twenty tanks and assault guns, and two battalions of self-propelled artillery. A smaller force from the division had yet to catch up and would not be there until a day later.

The first assault was directed against the sector just in front of the village of Champs. At 05.00, Kokott's 77th Grenadier-Regiment stole up on American foxholes without a preparatory bombardment. Only then did German artillery begin firing against American gun positions. The village of Champs was 'taken, lost and re-taken' in furious fighting, Kokott observed. A company of paratroopers and two tank destroyers inflicted heavy casualties on his men. Their intensive training to 'strip and repair weapons under fire and in the dark' had certainly paid off. Stoppages on a jammed machine gun were cleared in moments, and the firing recommenced. Corporal Willis Fowler manning a machine gun on the west side of Champs managed to destroy a whole company of grenadiers while four German panzers hung back on the ridgeline behind them. American artillery was also extremely effective in breaking up attacks, and at 09.00 the warning cry of 'Jabos!' was heard in German ranks as American fighter-bombers dived in.

Kampfgruppe Maucke, meanwhile, had steamrollered the positions of the 401st Glider Infantry south-west of Champs and reached the hamlet of Hemroulle, less than three kilometres beyond. A group split off north to attack Champs, and a savage battle took place around the 502nd Parachute Infantry Regiment's command post and aid station. They were based in the Château de Rolley, an imposing eighteenth-century building next to a massive round tower which remained from the original medieval castle. A bridge leading to Rolley had been mined, but the extreme frost meant that the firing mechanism failed as the German panzers crossed. On that morning of plunging temperatures, when the wind whipped particles of snow off the frozen crust like sea-spray, paratroopers resorted to urinating on their machine guns to unfreeze the mechanism.

Every signaller, driver and cook in the chateau grabbed a rifle or bazooka to form a defence platoon. The doctor caring for the wounded on stretchers even had to hand a rifle to one of his patients, who became agitated at the thought of being caught unarmed. People shouted at the doctor to burn the book recording the dog-tag numbers of their dead, so that the enemy would not know how many paratroopers they had killed.

One member of the improvised defence group, Sergeant 'Sky' Jackson, managed to knock out several tanks. Another bazooka man was so carried away by excitement that he forgot to arm his round, so when it hit the tank there was just a loud clang. A Hellcat tank destroyer knocked out one more Panther. 'The Germans piled out of the tanks and they were mowed down,' another soldier recorded. 'It was just red blood on the snow.' Screams could be heard from inside one of the panzers.

A company of the 502nd Parachute Infantry Regiment sighted around 150 German infantry and four Mark IV panzers, which opened fire. The paratroop lieutenant pulled his men back to the line of a wood. He ordered his machine-gunners to keep the infantry down and the tanks 'buttoned up' by constant fire, while he and another bazooka team stalked them from around their flanks. They knocked out three tanks with their bazookas, and the neighbouring company got the fourth. The paratroopers had little to eat that day. Most had no more than half a cup of soup with white 'navy', or haricot, beans to keep them going.

In this all-out effort, Kampfgruppe Kunkel attacked again in the south-west near Senonchamps up towards Hemroulle. And on the far side of the perimeter, 'success seemed very close' by 10.00 as the 901st Panzergrenadiers fought their way in from the south-east. An assault group reached the road-fork at the entrance to Bastogne, and a German breakthrough appeared almost inevitable. In McAuliffe's makeshift headquarters staff officers prepared their weapons, and supply personnel collected any spare bazookas for a last-ditch defence.

'The Germans attacked our positions with tanks,' Corporal Jackson of the 502nd Parachute Infantry Regiment recorded. 'I was back at the C[ommand] P[ost] and we received word that more bazookas and bazooka ammunition were needed up front. I took a bazooka and all the ammunition I could carry. When I got to the front, I saw one tank retreating and one Mark IV, with nine men riding on it, out in a field. When the tank was about 40 yards away and broadside on, I jumped out and fired, hitting the tank in the side, just above the track. The rocket killed or stunned four of the men riding on the tank, and the tank immediately stopped and started to burn.' The crew and the remaining infantry were shot down as they tried to escape.

Even the snub-barrelled howitzers of a parachute field artillery battalion took on the panzers over open sights. Most destructive of all were the P-47 Thunderbolt fighter-bombers, dropping napalm 'blaze bombs' or strafing with their .50 machine guns. Local farms and their inhabitants were not spared in what American commanders saw as a fight to the finish.

The fire of Shermans, Hellcat tank destroyers and bazookas in the fighting around Champs, Rolley and Hemroulle inflicted heavy losses. By the afternoon, the 15th Panzergrenadier-Division reported that it hardly had a battle-worthy tank left. Another desperate assault was launched after dark, supported by the remaining Jagdpanzer tank destroyers from the reconnaissance battalion. Bazooka teams from the 502nd Parachute Infantry stalked and knocked out half of them at close range, including the commander's vehicle.

In the south-east, the assault group from the Panzer Lehr's 901st Panzergrenadiers were 'cut off and annihilated'. The regiment had no reserves left to reinforce or extricate them. Almost every man available had already been thrown into the battle. Kokott called off any further attacks. The 15th Panzer-grenadier-Division was practically wiped out, and his own division had suffered more than

800 casualties. Most companies now mustered fewer than twenty men, and a whole battalion in the 78th Grenadier-Regiment was reduced to forty. The worst losses were among the experienced officers and Unteroffizieren. 'We were 900 metres from the edge of Bastogne,' an officer in the 26th Volksgrenadier-Division complained bitterly, 'and couldn't get into the town.'

Kokott reported to corps headquarters that his forces were so reduced that any further attacks on Bastogne would be 'irresponsible and unfeasible'. Lüttwitz agreed that the encircling forces should simply hold their present positions until the arrival of Remer's *Führer Begleit* Brigade in the next forty-eight hours. But Kokott also heard that the 5th Fallschirmjäger was failing to hold the increasing attacks by Patton's forces coming from the south. All his volksgrenadiers could do was to lay minefields and prepare more anti-tank positions on the approach routes. The Ardennes offensive had failed, Kokott concluded. He wrote that the great operation had turned into a 'bloody, dubious and costly struggle for what was, in the final analysis, an unimportant village'. Evidently Führer headquarters was not prepared to accept the facts of the situation.

While the battle raged north and south-east of Bastogne, the pilot of a light observation plane, braving the flak, flew in a surgeon with supplies of penicillin. A P-38 Lightning also dropped maps, which were still in short supply, and a set of photo-reconnaissance prints of the whole area. That was all the defenders received that day, for bad visibility in England had prevented another major airdrop. To make matters worse, Patton's promised Christmas present of a breakthrough to Bastogne had not materialized. McAuliffe made his feelings clear by telephone to General Middleton, the VIII Corps commander. 'We have been let down,' he said.

Patton's III Corps was close. Around Lutrebois, just six kilometres south of the centre of Bastogne, the 134th Infantry Regiment of the 35th Division was closely supported by artillery and tank destroyers. German tanks had been spotted in the woods ahead, so the field artillery opened fire. Some Shermans, attracted by the firing, came up and joined in. Bazooka men had 'to lie in wait or sneak up just like stalking a moose'. They had been told to aim for the tracks on a Panther, as rounds simply bounced off its armour. In the end, out of twenty-seven German tanks, only three escaped.

The 4th Armored Division was battering the 5th Fallschirmjäger units south of Bastogne between the roads to Arlon and Neufchâteau. As the village of Assenois shook from the relentless explosions of shells, civilians could do little but hope and pray. 'We feel like we are in God's hand,' a woman wrote, 'and we surrender ourselves to it.' The Walloons were largely Catholic and deeply religious. Committing themselves to the hands of the Almighty was undoubtedly a comfort, when they had so little control over their own fate. Reciting the rosary together helped dull the pain of individual fear, and calm the nerves.

During the battle for Hemroulle, Model and Manteuffel had visited Lüttwitz's corps headquarters at the Château de Roumont near the highway to Marche. Lüttwitz was even more concerned about his old division stranded round Celles, and again urged that the 2nd Panzer must be saved by permitting its rapid withdrawal. Model and Manteuffel 'showed understanding', but they 'obviously were not authorized to decide the withdrawal of the 2nd Panzer-Division'. That order could come only from Hitler, and he was certainly not prepared to admit defeat.

Lüttwitz's worst fears for the Böhm and Cochenhausen Kampfgruppen were being realized as they spoke. The Allied counterattack had begun before dawn. The artillery with the 29th Armoured Brigade began to bombard Böhm's reconnaissance battalion in Foy-Notre-Dame, and fulfilled their promise of avoiding the seventeenth-century church.

American artillery batteries took up position in the fields around the villages of Haid and Chevetogne. When they had reached Haid the evening before they celebrated with the locals, who made galettes and hot chocolate: with milk from their own cows and melted Hershey bars. Afterwards, the American soldiers accompanied their new friends to midnight mass in the church. Only a couple of days before a sixteen-year-old Alsatian, who had been dragooned into the Wehrmacht, had broken down in tears, telling a farmer's wife about the horrors they had been through.

In Chevetogne, an officer went round the houses warning people to leave their windows open, or the blast from the guns would shatter them. Villagers watched an artillery spotter plane, which they called 'Petit Jules', circle over German positions. A little later, twin-tailed P-38 Lightning fighter-bombers appeared in force.

Combat Command A of Harmon's 2nd Armored Division advanced south to Buissonville a dozen kilometres to the east of the Cochenhausen Kampfgruppe, and clashed with a force from the Panzer Lehr which had advanced from Rochefort. They tracked one of the German columns to the farm of La Happe where fighting began. Most civilians in the area immediately took to their cellars, but a few climbed up to attics to watch the deadly firework display of a tank battle. Some twenty-nine Germans were killed and many more seriously wounded. The latter were carried to a barn and laid on the straw.

Combat Command B, meanwhile, coming from Ciney, split into two, with one task force heading for Conjoux and the other for Celles to surround the main Cochenhausen Kampfgruppe spread between the two villages. The Germans round Celles were sitting targets: they did not even have enough fuel for the *Feldlazarett*'s ambulance. In Celles itself, most of the inhabitants sheltered in the crypt of the church with the nuns and the priest. The straw laid during the September fighting was still there. Some farmworkers brought down a pail of milk for the children when there was a lull in the firing, and cooked a chicken which had been killed by an explosion. The rest crouched in cellars as the shells flew overhead. The Americans were using phosphorus shells, and naturally the locals feared for their farms.

The Shermans of the 3rd Royal Tank Regiment, supported by the American 82nd Reconnaissance Battalion and with P-38 Lightning fighters overhead, advanced from Sorinnes on Foy-Notre-Dame. It was retaken that afternoon, along with Major von Böhm and 148 of his men. Only a few managed to escape through the deep snow. Some families stayed hidden after the village had been liberated because they still heard firing, but this was due to a blazing half-track in a farmyard on which the ammunition continued to explode for a long time. For most, the first thing to do was to cut squares of cardboard as an emergency repair to their smashed windows. It was a great relief that this battle of the 'Tommies' and 'Sammies' against 'les gris' — the 'greys', or Germans — had finally come to an end.

A small girl among those being evacuated to Sorinnes had lost her shoes, so an American soldier from the 82nd Reconnaissance Battalion forced a German prisoner at gunpoint to take off his boots and give them to her. They were much too large, but she was just able to walk, while the German soldier faced frostbitten feet.

After American and British artillery had hammered the German positions round the farm of Mahenne between Foy-Notre-Dame and Celles, a local story grew up that SS officers had set fire to the place; but no SS were in the area and the destruction was entirely caused by shelling. Once again the black overalls and death's-head badge of the panzer arm appear to have been mistaken for the Waffen-SS.

Combat Command B of the 2nd Armored Division also entered Celles that afternoon. The famished and exhausted panzer troops, short of ammunition and out of fuel, could not resist for long. Mopping up continued for another two days. Some 2,500 Germans were killed or wounded and another 1,200 captured. In addition, eighty-two armoured fighting vehicles and eighty-two artillery pieces were taken or destroyed, as well as countless vehicles, many of which had been booty taken from American forces earlier. Most were out of fuel and ammunition.

Major von Cochenhausen, with some 600 of his men, managed to escape on foot across country after splitting up. Many were only too willing to give up. Around Celles, hidden Germans begged locals to find the Americans and tell them that they were ready to surrender. They were worried that if they appeared suddenly, even with their hands up, they might be shot. Some were afraid that, because they wore so many items of American uniform, they might be mistaken for members of the Skorzeny Kampfgruppe. In a few cases as a sign of goodwill they handed over their pistol to a Belgian civilian, who would then hand it over to the American soldiers. The locals did not realize until it was too late that they could have made a lot of money selling them instead. 'The Americans were mad to get their hands on one,' a farmer said. Many civilians were also afraid of holding on to items of German equipment in case the enemy returned yet again and found them in their houses.

Apart from the 2nd SS *Das Reich,* which still caused great concern to First Army in the fighting round Manhay and Grandménil, the other panzer divisions fared little better on the north-western flank of the Bulge. The 116th Panzer was still ordered to break through east of Marche, but as Generalmajor von Waldenburg recorded, the 'divisional units which fought in this battle were nearly completely wiped out', and Kampfgruppe Beyer of the 60th Panzergrenadiers was cut off. Only a few men and vehicles managed to escape.

That night Generalfeldmarschall von Rundstedt informed Hitler that the offensive had failed. He recommended a withdrawal from the salient before the bulk of Army Group B was trapped. Hitler rejected his advice angrily and insisted on more attacks against Bastogne, unaware that even more Allied reinforcements were arriving. The 17th Airborne Division was moving into position, although an VIII Corps staff officer thought that its paratroopers had 'a lot to learn'. The newly arrived 11th Armored Division also lacked experience, especially the drivers of their Shermans. 'Their tanks left a trail of uprooted trees and torn wire lines,' a report commented.

'A clear cold Christmas,' Patton wrote in his diary that day, 'lovely weather for killing Germans, which seems a bit queer, seeing Whose birthday it is.' Patton had moved his headquarters into the Industrial School in Luxembourg. He proudly showed off his lights, with the bulbs hanging in captured German helmets acting as lampshades.

But the festival brought little joy to the Belgian population of the Ardennes. In a village close to Elsenborn, where the fighting had died down, the Gronsfeld family decided to come out of their cellar to celebrate Christmas Day. The light was blinding with the sun reflecting off the snow as they sat at the kitchen table, father, mother and their young daughter, Elfriede. Suddenly, a German shell exploded near by, sending a sliver of shrapnel through the window. 'It cut deep into Elfriede Gronsfeld's neck. American medics came to her aid, but there was nothing they could do. The girl was buried on December 29. She was five years old. "What can one say to the mother?" one of the village's women mourned in her diary. "She cries and cannot understand." '

An American soldier on the Elsenborn ridge wrote to his wife that day: 'The bombers have fine, feathery white streams of vapor streaked across the sky and the fighters scrawl wavy designs as they try to murder each other.' They would keep their eye on Piper

Cub artillery spotters, often half dozen or more in the sky at once. When the aircraft suddenly kicked their tails straight up and dived towards the ground, 'we knew it was time to look for cover'. In another letter he wrote, 'We're getting strafed once or twice a day by our own planes.'

Profiting from clear skies again, American fighter-bombers 'like a swarm of wasps' roamed over St Vith as well. 'We prefer to walk instead of using a car on the main highway,' a German officer wrote in his diary. 'The American Jabos keep on attacking everything which moves on the roads . . . We walk across the fields from hedgerow to hedgerow.' But soon a much heavier droning sound of aircraft engines could be heard. Formations with seventy-six B-26 bombers had arrived and proceeded to flatten the remains of St Vith. The tactic was cynically known as 'putting the city in the street', that is to say filling the roads with rubble so that German supply convoys could not get through this key crossroads.

General Bradley, who had withdrawn into himself due to the shame of losing the bulk of his 12th Army Group to Montgomery, had barely involved himself in the advance of Patton's two corps. But on Christmas Day, at Montgomery's invitation, he flew to St Trond near 21st Army Group headquarters at Zonhoven accompanied by a fighter escort. He was determined to push Montgomery into launching an immediate counter-offensive. 'Monty was always expecting everybody to come to him,' Bradley complained later with justification. 'Ike insisted on my going up to see him. I don't know why in the hell I should.' Although Montgomery's headquarters looked 'very festive', with the walls covered in Christmas cards, Bradley claimed that he had only an apple for lunch.

Bradley's version of their encounter was so suffused with resentment that it is hard to take it literally. One can certainly imagine that Montgomery showed his habitual lack of tact and displayed an arrogant self-regard to the point of humiliating Bradley. He even harped on again about the single command of ground forces which should be given to him, and repeated his exasperating mantra that all their setbacks could have been avoided if only his strategy had been followed. But Bradley's accusation that 'Monty has dissipated the VII Corps' by putting it into the line rather than holding it back for a counter-attack again demonstrated his ignorance of events in the north-west. He even claimed to Patton on his return to Luxembourg that Montgomery had said that 'the First Army cannot attack for three months'. This is very hard to believe.

On the other hand, there is no doubt that

Montgomery was influenced by intelligence reports which said that the Germans intended to make another reinforced lunge for the Meuse. He therefore wanted to hold back until they had spent their strength. But his instruction the day before to Hodges's headquarters that Collins's VII Corps should be prepared to fall back in the west as far north as Andenne on the Meuse was an astonishing mistake which Collins had been absolutely right to disregard. So while Bradley had underestimated the German threat between Dinant and Marche, Montgomery had exaggerated it. Unlike American commanders, he did not sense that Christmas Day had marked the moment of maximum German effort.

Bradley had convinced himself that the field marshal was exploiting the situation for his own ends and was frightening SHAEF deliberately with his reports. He told Hansen later: 'I am sure [it was] Montgomery's alarms that were being reflected in Paris. Whether we realized it or not Paris was just hysterical.'* He

---

* SHAEF was hardly being duped by Montgomery. General Bedell Smith admitted later that the alarmist tone in cables back to Washington was a deliberate tactic. 'You know, we exploited the Ardennes crisis for all it was worth' to get resources and replacements which were otherwise going to the Pacific. 'We were short of men, so we yelled loud. We asked for everything we could get.'

then added: 'I am sure [the] Press in the US got all their information and panic from Versailles.' He felt that they should have a press section at 12th Army Group to counter the wrong impressions. British newspapers seemed to revel in stories of disaster, with headlines such as 'Months Added to War?' The next morning after his return, Bradley contacted SHAEF to demand that the First and Ninth Armies should be returned to his command, and he proposed to move his forward headquarters to Namur, close to the action on the northern flank. The war within the Allied camp was approaching a climax, and Montgomery had no inkling that he was playing a losing hand very badly indeed.

19
TUESDAY 26 DECEMBER

On Tuesday 26 December, Patton famously boasted to Bradley: 'The Kraut has stuck his head in the meat grinder and I've got the handle.' But this bravado concealed his lingering embarrassment that the advance to Bastogne had not gone as he had claimed it would. He was acutely aware of Eisenhower's disappointment and frustration.

After the brilliant redeployment of his formations between 19 and 22 December, Patton knew that his subsequent handling of the operation had not been his best. He had underestimated the weather, the terrain and the determined resistance of the German Seventh Army formations defending the southern flank of the salient. American intelligence had failed to identify the presence of the *Führer Grenadier* Brigade, another offshoot of the *Grossdeutschland* Division. And the 352nd Volksgrenadier-Division, based on the formation which had inflicted such heavy losses on Omaha beach, deployed next to the

5th Fallschirmjäger. At the same time, Patton had overestimated the capacity of his own troops, many of them replacements, especially in the weakened 26th Infantry Division in the centre. His favourite formation, the 4th Armored Division, was also handicapped by battle-weary tanks. The roads were so icy that the metal-tracked Shermans slid off them or crashed into each other, and the terrain, with woods and steep little valleys, was not good tank-country.

Patton's impatience had made things worse by demanding head-on attacks, which resulted in many casualties. On 24 December, he acknowledged in his diary: 'This has been a very bad Christmas Eve. All along our line we have received violent counter-attacks, one of which forced the 4th Armored back some miles with the loss of ten tanks. This was probably my fault, because I had been insisting on day and night attacks.' His men were weak from lack of rest. Things looked little better on the morning of 26 December. 'Today has been rather trying in spite of our efforts,' he wrote. 'We have failed to make contact with the defenders of Bastogne.'

The defenders could hear the battle going on a few kilometres to the south, but having been let down before, they did not expect Patton's forces to break through. In any case, they were fully occupied in other ways. Another attack on the north-west sector reached Hemroulle. It was fought off by the exhausted paratroopers supported by the fire of field artillery battalions, but the American guns were now down literally to their last few rounds. At least the clear, freezing weather continued so the fighter-bombers could act as flying artillery. In the town, fires still raged from the bombing. The Institut de Notre-Dame was ablaze. American engineers tried to blast firebreaks, and human chains of refugees, soldiers and nuns passed buckets of water to keep the flames at bay.

The clear skies also permitted the arrival of sorely needed medical assistance. Escorted by four P-47 Thunderbolts, a C-47 transport appeared towing a Waco glider, loaded with five surgeons, four surgical assistants and 600 pounds of equipment, instruments and dressings. The glider 'cut loose at 300 feet' as if for a perfect landing, but it overshot and skidded over the frozen snow towards the German front line. 'The medical personnel barreled out and ran back to American lines while the doughboys charged forward to rescue the glider which carried medical supplies.' Another ten gliders followed bringing urgently needed fuel, then more waves of C-47 transports appeared to drop parachute bundles with 320 tons of ammunition, rations and even cigarettes.

The surgeons wasted no time. They went straight to the improvised hospital in the barracks and began operating on the 150 most seriously wounded out of more than 700 patients. They operated all through the night and until noon on 27 December, on wounds that in some cases had gone for eight days without surgical attention. As a result they had to perform 'many amputations'. In the circumstances, it was a testament to their skill that there were only three post-operative deaths.

Generalmajor Kokott became increasingly concerned during the artillery battle on the southern side about the weight of guns supporting the 4th Armored Division. He heard alarming rumours about what was happening, but could obtain no details from the 5th Fallschirmjäger-Division. He knew that there had been heavy fighting round Remichampagne, then in the afternoon he heard that an American task force had taken Hompré. Assenois was now threatened, so Kokott had to start transferring his own forces south.

At 14.00, Patton received a call from the III Corps commander, who proposed a risky venture. Instead of attacking Sibret to widen the salient, he suggested a charge straight through Assenois north into Bastogne. Patton instantly gave the plan his blessing. Lieutenant Colonel Creighton Abrams, who commanded the 37th Tank Battalion from a Sherman named 'Thunderbolt', was told to go all the way. Abrams asked Captain William A. Dwight to lead a column of five Shermans and a half-track with infantry straight up the road. The corps artillery shelled Assenois and fighter-bombers dropped napalm, just before the Shermans in tight formation charged into the village firing every gun they had. The Germans who scattered on both sides of the road risked hitting each other if they fired back. Beyond Assenois, some volksgrenadiers hurriedly pushed some Teller mines on to the road. One blew up the half-track, but Dwight leaped down from his tank and threw the other mines aside to clear a path.

When Kokott heard from the commander of his 39th Regiment that American tanks had entered Assenois, he immediately knew that 'it was all over'. He gave orders for the road to be blocked, but, as he feared, they were too late. With the lead Sherman firing forward, and the others firing outwards, Dwight's little column blasted any resistance from the woods on either side of the road. At 16.45, soon after dusk, the lead Shermans of Abrams's tank battalion made contact with the 326th Airborne Engineers manning that sector. Troops and tanks from the rest of the 4th Armored Division rushed in to secure the slim corridor and protect a convoy of trucks with provisions, which raced in during the night. Major General Maxwell D. Taylor, the commander of the 101st Airborne, who had been in the United States, came in soon afterwards to take over from Brigadier General McAuliffe. The siege of Bastogne was over, but many feared that the main battle was about to begin.

The 5th Fallschirmjäger had been badly mauled. Major Frank, a battalion commander in the 13th Fallschirmjäger-Regiment who was captured that day and interrogated, was intensely proud of the way his youngsters had fought. Some of them were only fifteen. 'But what spirit!' he exclaimed later in prison camp. 'After we had been taken prisoner, when I was alone, had been beaten and was being led out, there were two of them standing there with their heads to the wall, just in their socks: "Heil Hitler, Herr Major!" [they said]. It makes your heart swell.'

Lüttwitz heard that the *Führer Begleit* Brigade was coming to help cut the corridor, but he and his staff did not believe it would arrive in time for an attack planned for the next morning. He then heard that they had run out of fuel. Lüttwitz observed acidly that 'the *Führer Begleit* Brigade under the command of Oberst Remer always had gasoline trouble'.

News of the 4th Armored's breakthrough spread rapidly and prompted exuberant rejoicing in American headquarters. The correspondents Martha Gellhorn and Leland

Stowe stopped by Bradley's headquarters that evening to obtain more information, as they wanted to cover the relief of Bastogne. So did almost every journalist on the continent. The story was on almost every front page in the western hemisphere. The 101st Airborne found itself famous, but press accounts overlooked the vital roles of Combat Command B of the 10th Armored Division, the 705th Tank Destroyer Battalion and the artillery battalions.

Around Celles and Conneux mopping up continued all day, with some fierce engagements. But since the Panthers and Mark IVs were out of fuel and armour-piercing rounds, the fight was certainly one sided. The forward air controller with the 3rd Royal Tank Regiment called in a 'cab-rank' of rocket-firing Typhoons. The target was indicated with red smoke canisters, but the Germans rapidly fired similar-coloured smoke canisters into American positions east of Celles. 'Fortunately the RAF were not deceived by this,' Colonel Brown recorded, 'and made their attack on the correct target.' The 29th Armoured Brigade, still in the area, heard that it was to be reinforced by the 6th Airborne Division.

The Kampfgruppe Holtmeyer, on its way from Rochefort in a vain attempt to help its comrades at Celles and Conneux, had been blocked at Grande Trussogne, a few kilometres short of its objective. It picked up exhausted men who had escaped the night before from the reconnaissance battalion overrun at Foy-Notre-Dame. At Grande Trussogne, these troops were attacked by an infantry battalion of the 2nd Armored Division supported by Shermans. An American Piper Cub spotter plane then called in British Typhoons whose rockets smashed the column mercilessly, killing Major Holtmeyer.

Manteuffel instructed the Kampfgruppe to withdraw to the bridgehead at Rochefort held by the Panzer Lehr. Lüttwitz's headquarters passed on the message immediately by radio. Holtmeyer's replacement gave the order to blow up the remaining vehicles. Next day, he and most of his men made their way on foot back towards Rochefort, concealed by falling snow. 'Luckily,' wrote Oberstleutnant Rüdiger Weiz, 'the enemy was slow in following up and did not attack the route of retreat in any way worth mentioning.' But American artillery did catch up and shell the bridge in Rochefort over the River L'Homme, causing a number of casualties. That night and the following day, some 600 men in small groups managed to rejoin the division.

Between Celles and Conneux, several Germans were captured in American uniform. They were not part of the Skorzeny Kampfgruppe, but were shot on the spot anyway.

These unfortunates, suffering from the cold and on the edge of starvation, had stripped the clothes from dead Americans. In their desperation to live they pleaded with their captors, showing their wedding rings and, producing photographs from home, talked desperately of their wives and children. Most Alsatians and Luxembourgers from the 2nd Panzer-Division wanted to surrender at the first opportunity, and even some Austrians had lost their enthusiasm for the fight. One of them murmured to an inhabitant of Rochefort: 'Moi, pas Allemand! Autrichien.' And he raised his hands in the air to show that he wanted to surrender.

American soldiers in Celles, believing that Germans were hiding in the Ferme de la Cour just by the church, attacked it with flamethrowers. There were no Germans, only livestock which burned to death. It was the second time this farm had been burned down during the war. The first was in 1940 during the previous German charge to the Meuse.

At Buissonville, between Celles and Marche, American medical personnel set up their first-aid post in the church. The local priest and the American Catholic chaplain communicated in Latin as they worked together. In the same village, a less Christian attitude was adopted when American soldiers in a half-track took two German prisoners into the woods and shot them. They explained to Belgians who had witnessed the scene that they had killed them in revenge for the American prisoners who perished near Malmédy.

Some American officers became rather carried away by the victory over the 2nd Panzer-Division. 'It was estimated that the division's strength just before this four-day period was approximately 8,000 men and 100 tanks,' claimed a senior officer at VII Corps. 'Of the personnel, 1,050 were captured and an estimated 2,000–2,500 killed. Materiel captured or destroyed included 55 tanks, 18 artillery pieces, 8 anti-tank guns, 5 assault guns, and 190 vehicles . . . The meeting of the US 2nd Armored Division and the German 2nd Panzer-Division was a fitting comparison of Allied and German might.' But this triumphalism rather overlooked the fact that the 2nd Panzer was out of fuel and low on ammunition, and the men were half starved.

After the battle, according to the Baron de Villenfagne, the countryside around Celles was 'a vast cemetery of vehicles, destroyed or abandoned, and of equipment half buried in the snow'. Teenagers, obsessed by the war, explored burned-out panzers and examined the carbonized bodies inside. A number indulged in dangerous war games. Some collected hand grenades, then threw them to blow up in abandoned half-tracks. A boy in

Foy-Notre-Dame died after playing with a Panzerfaust which exploded.

The setback before Dinant only seemed to increase German bitterness. When a woman in Jemelle had the courage to ask a German officer why his men had nearly destroyed their village, he retorted: 'We want to do in Belgium what was done to Aachen.'

West of Hotton, most of the 116th Panzer-Division's attempts to relieve its surrounded Kampfgruppe were crushed by American artillery fire. But eventually a feint attack to distract the Americans enabled the survivors to break out clinging to armoured vehicles, and throwing grenades as they crashed through American lines.

During the battle, the *Führer Begleit* Brigade had received orders to disengage and head to Bastogne to assist Kokott's attempts to close the corridor. Oberst Remer protested twice at the casualties that this would cost, but was overruled each time. Remer also complained that 'motor fuel was so scarce that almost half of the vehicles had to be towed', so it is hard to tell whether Lüttwitz's suspicions were justified.

East of Hotton, Rose's 3rd Armored Division faced attacks from the 560th Volksgrenadiers consisting mainly of 'four or five tanks with an infantry company or about twenty tanks with an infantry battalion'. These were supported by self-propelled assault guns and artillery. But the arrival of the 75th Infantry Division to strengthen Rose's task forces meant that the sector had a stronger defence, even though its untried units suffered badly in their counter-attacks to secure the Soy–Hotton road. The icy conditions were proving particularly difficult for Sherman tank crews, because the metal tracks were so narrow and had little grip. Urgent efforts were made to add track extensions and spike-like studs to cope with the problem.

Lammerding, the commander of the *Das Reich,* was still trying to turn his division west from Manhay and Grandménil to open the road to Hotton and attack the 3rd Armored Division from behind; but the 9th SS Panzer-Division *Hohenstaufen* had still not come up to protect his right flank. With thirteen American field artillery battalions on a ten-kilometre frontage to the north, such a manoeuvre was doubly dangerous; and the *Das Reich* was fast running out of ammunition and fuel. Local farmers were forced at gunpoint to take their horses and carts to the rear to fetch tank and artillery shells from German dumps.

On the morning of 26 December, the 3rd SS Panzergrenadier-Regiment *Deutschland* from the *Das Reich* Division again attacked west from Grandménil. But American artillery firing shells with Pozit fuses decimated its ranks, then a reinforced task force from the 3rd Armored Division attacked the village. One German battalion commander was killed and another badly wounded. The II Battalion was trapped in Grandménil, and the rest of the regiment was forced to withdraw towards Manhay. American tanks and artillery harried it all the way back.

General Hodges and Major General Ridgway, still mistakenly fearing an attack north towards Liège, had been furious at the loss of Manhay. They left Brigadier General Hasbrouck of the battered and exhausted 7th Armored under no doubt that he had to retake it at whatever cost. The division's assault on Christmas Day had been dogged by heavy losses, largely because of the number of trees which it had blasted down across the road in its retreat. But preceded by a fresh battalion of the 517th Parachute Infantry, Hasbrouck's force entered Manhay that night.

Fifty wounded from the II Battalion of the 3rd SS Panzergrenadier-Regiment could not be extricated from Grandménil. The Germans claimed that when they sent in ambulances well marked with the Red Cross, American tank crews shot them up. The regiment then attempted to send out an officer and an interpreter under a white flag of truce, and a doctor with a flag and armband, to see whether they could evacuate their wounded from Grandménil. But according to the German account, 'the enemy opened fire on the parliamentaries, so this attempt had to be abandoned'. The Germans did not seem to understand that after the Malmédy massacre the SS were unlikely to be accorded any honours of war. So, leaving a medical orderly with their wounded, the remnants of the battalion slipped back to a defence line with the *Der Führer* Regiment near Odeigne, which was shelled all day by American artillery.

German activity around the Elsenborn ridge had almost ceased, so patrols from the 99th Infantry Division went forward to destroy ten enemy tanks from the 3rd Panzergrenadiers which had been abandoned after being stuck in the mud. This was to forestall German recovery teams, which were tireless and often ingenious in their attempts to retrieve and repair armoured vehicles.

American salvage parties, often manned by those showing signs of combat fatigue to give them a bit of a break, were sent off to collect weapons and ammunition thrown away earlier in the battle. American commanders were appalled by the tendency of their men to discard equipment and expect the military cornucopia to replace them at will. 'If the soldier does not need it right then, he will get rid of it,' one report stated. 'A bazooka man must not have a rifle. He must be given a pistol instead for personal protection. Otherwise, he will discard the bazooka and its shells because they are cumbersome and heavy.' Winter clothing, on the other hand, was jealously guarded. In most battalions a man at the aid station was told to take the padded 'arctic' coats from wounded men so that these vital items of clothing would not be lost to the unit.

St Vith had suffered badly on Christmas Day. Civilians had stayed in their cellars thinking that the worst must now be over, but in the afternoon of 26 December the 'heavies' of RAF Bomber Command arrived overhead. Nearly 300 Lancasters and Halifaxes dropped 1,140 tons of high explosive and incendiary bombs.

The blast effect created shockwaves which could be felt in villages several kilometres away, and terrorized the townsfolk sheltering underground as buildings collapsed above them. According to one account, 'people were struggling against the asphyxiating smoke and soot when another bomb blew a hole in the cellar wall that made them catch their breaths again. Before long, however, burning phosphorus was seeping into the cellar. The malicious substance released poisonous fumes and in the larger rooms set mattresses on fire. With the help of German soldiers, the panic-stricken civilians clawed their way through the hole and into the pulverised street.'

In the St Josef Kloster the chapel collapsed, with blocks of stone and beams smashing through the floor and crushing those below. The incendiaries set fire to anything remotely combustible. They also turned the convent itself into a raging blaze, consuming the old and incapacitated trapped on the upper floors. 'Most of them were burned alive. Like a more liquid form of lava, hissing phosphorus poured into the cellars that remained standing. People with horrible burns, broken bones, and blown minds were pulled out through the few unobstructed air shafts. Among the last to leave the inferno were the convent's sisters, blankets tightly drawn over their heads and shoulders.'

'Saint-Vith is still burning,' a German officer outside the town recorded. 'The bomb carpets come close to our village. I have never seen anything like that in all my life. The whole countryside is covered by one big cloud of smoke and fire.' He returned to St Vith in the evening. 'All streets are burning . . . Cattle are howling, ammunition exploding, tires burst. There is a strong smell of burnt rubber.' Delayed-action bombs continued to detonate from time to time.

In purely military terms, the raid was effective. St Vith was no more than 'a giant heap of rubble'. All roads were blocked for three days at least and some for over a week, while

German engineers were forced to create bypasses round the town. But the cost in civilian lives and suffering was untold. Nobody knew exactly how many had taken shelter in St Vith, but some 250 are estimated to have died. The survivors fled to neighbouring villages where they were cared for and fed.

That same night and the next, medium bombers of the Ninth US Air Force attacked La Roche-en-Ardenne. Since La Roche was situated along a river in a narrow defile, it provided a much easier target and only 150 tons of bombs were needed to block the route.

'Things continued to look better all day today,' the First Army diarist recorded after a meeting between Montgomery and Hodges. Prisoner interviews suggested that the Germans were facing real supply problems. 'Although it is yet too early to be optimistic the picture tonight is certainly far rosier than on any other day since the counteroffensive began.' Bradley, however, was still obsessed with what he regarded as the premature deployment of Collins's VII Corps. He wrote to Hodges to complain of the 'stagnating conservatism of tactics there where Monty has dissipated his reserve'. Patton, heavily influenced by Bradley's view of the field marshal, wrote in his diary: 'Monty is a tired little fart. War requires the taking of risks and he won't take them.'

After a telephone call from Manteuffel, General Jodl summoned up the courage to tell Hitler, who had not moved from the Adlerhorst at Ziegenberg: '*Mein Führer,* we must face facts. We cannot force the Meuse.' Reichsmarschall Göring arrived at Ziegenberg the same evening and declared, 'The war is lost!' He suggested that they must seek a truce. Hitler, trembling with rage, warned him against trying to negotiate behind his back. 'If you go against my orders, I will have you shot!' Hitler made no further mention of Antwerp. Instead no effort was to be spared to take Bastogne. Just as he had focused on Stalingrad in September 1942, when victory in the Caucasus eluded him, the recapture of Bastogne now became his ersatz symbol of victory.

But while Hitler refused to face reality in public, in rare moments he acknowledged the hopelessness of their position. Late in the evening in the bunker at Ziegenberg, he spoke to his Luftwaffe adjutant, Oberst Nicolaus von Below, about taking his own life. He still blamed setbacks on the Luftwaffe and the 'traitors' in the German army. 'I know the war is lost,' he told Below. 'The enemy superiority is too great. I have been betrayed. After 20 July everything came out, things I had considered impossible. It was precisely those circles against me who had profited most from National Socialism. I pampered and decorated them, and that was all the thanks I got. My best course now is to put a bullet in my head. I lacked hard fighters . . . We will not capitulate, ever. We may go down, but we will take the world with us.'

20
PREPARING THE ALLIED COUNTER-OFFENSIVE

Even though the 4th Armored Division had broken through to Bastogne, the airdrop planned for 27 December still went ahead. This time, however, the Germans were better prepared. General McAuliffe's warning that the aircraft should approach by a different route never got through. The curtain of flak and machine-gun fire was formidable, but the C-47 transports towing the gliders held their course. Eighteen gliders out of fifty were shot down and many others were riddled with bullets. One glider exploded in a fireball as a direct hit from flak set off the ammunition it was carrying. Gasoline cans were also hit and began to leak, but miraculously none caught fire.

Altogether some 900 aircraft — both transport and escort fighters — took part in the operation, and twenty-three were shot down. Paratroopers on the ground rushed from their foxholes to rescue those who had baled out and gave them slugs of brandy, to dull the pain from burns and twisted limbs. The pilot of one heavily hit C-47 managed a belly landing in the snow, although it clipped a truck on the road and spun it round, to the terror of the driver who had not seen it coming in.

The forty trucks that had brought in supplies during the night turned south again, loaded with the less seriously wounded, some of the German prisoners of war and glider pilots. Together with seventy ambulances carrying the 150 most serious cases, they trundled south escorted by light tanks through the narrow corridor. Intensive fighting began around Bastogne's southern flank as the Americans tried to widen the gap, and the Germans did all they could to seal it.

On 28 December, General Bradley wrote a memo for Eisenhower, urging him to put pressure on Montgomery. 'With the enemy attack losing its momentum in the Ardennes,' he wrote, 'it is important that strong counter-attacks be launched while his stocks of supplies are depleted, his troops tired and before he has had time thoroughly to dig in and consolidate his gains. The object of the counter-attack would be to trap the maximum enemy troops in the salient and to put our forces in a favorable position for further offensive action . . . The counter-attack must be launched immediately. Reports have been received that the enemy is digging in along the shoulders of his salient.'* Bradley was wrong to think that 'further delay will permit the enemy to bring more troops into the salient'. That very day First Army noted that 'high intelligence channels [a euphemism for Ultra] report that German concerns over the Soviet advance in Hungary might prompt the transfer of troops from the Ardennes to the Balkan front'. And in fact the opposite to what Bradley feared was soon to happen as the Red Army prepared its major winter offensive.

That evening Bradley was at least able to divert himself when Leland Stowe and Martha Gellhorn, who had not managed to get to Bastogne, came to dinner at the Hôtel Alfa in Luxembourg. Bradley appeared to be 'much smitten with "Marty" Gellhorn', Hansen recorded. 'She's a reddish blonde woman with a cover girl figure, a bouncing manner and a brilliant studied wit where each comment seems to come out perfectly tailored and smartly cut to fit the occasion, yet losing none of the spontaneity that makes it good.' Hansen added that General Patton, also pres-

* It is worth noting that Generalmajor von Waldenburg of the 116th Panzer argued later that the Allied 'counter-attack started too early' and that this was what saved the German forces 'from total annihilation'.

ent, 'grew flirtatious in his own inimitable manner with Marty'.

While Bradley twitched with impatience, Eisenhower was keen to discuss the situation with the field marshal. To a certain degree, he shared Montgomery's concern that the Allies had not yet assembled strong enough forces to crush the German salient. The slowness of Patton's advance from the south did not bode well, rather as Montgomery had predicted five days before. But at the same time Eisenhower was all too aware of Montgomery's ingrained reluctance to move until he had overwhelming force. The crushing of the 2nd Panzer-Division had greatly encouraged him.

Montgomery, who had been overinfluenced by his impression that 'the Americans have taken the most awful "bloody nose" ', correspondingly underestimated the damage inflicted on their attackers. He refused to believe that First Army had recovered sufficiently to mount such an ambitious operation. And he certainly did not think that Patton in the south was capable of achieving what he so belligerently claimed. Montgomery also feared that the Germans, once surrounded, would fight with even more desperation, and inflict far more casualties on the Allies. He was convinced that, using their massive airpower and artillery, the Allies could cause greater damage from defensive positions than by advancing into a battle of attrition.

On 26 December, Bradley wrote to General Hodges, arguing that the Germans had suffered badly and that he did not view the situation 'in as grave a light as Marshal Montgomery'. He urged Hodges to consider pushing the enemy back 'as soon as the situation seems to warrant'. Hodges does not appear to have seen that moment coming as quickly as Bradley. In fact right up to the afternoon of Christmas Day Hodges and his chief of staff had been begging for reinforcements just to hold the line. And 'General Hodges', as his headquarters diarist noted, 'has had enough of exposed flanks for the last two weeks.'

In stark contrast Patton wanted to advance north from Luxembourg, with his earlier idea of cutting the German salient off at the base. This was ruled out by First Army because the road network south-east of the Elsenborn ridge would not support the massive armoured advance necessary. 'Lightning Joe' Collins accordingly prepared three plans of attack, and took them to First Army headquarters on 27 December. His preferred one was for his VII Corps to advance from Malmédy south-east to St Vith to join up with Patton's Third Army and cut the Germans off there. Hodges, however, clearly preferred 'the most conservative of the three plans'.

Montgomery also insisted on the shallower thrust, just heading for Houffalize. In his forthright way, Collins told Montgomery: 'You're going to push the Germans out of the bag, just like you did at Falaise.' But as far as Montgomery was concerned, this was not Normandy in the summer. A major encirclement in such terrain and in such weather was far too ambitious. He had a point. It would be fine for the Red Army, equipped for warfare in deepest winter. The broad tracks of its T-34 tanks could cope with the ice and snow, but Shermans had already shown how vulnerable they were in such conditions.

Eisenhower's planned meeting with Montgomery in Brussels had to be postponed until 28 December because the Luftwaffe destroyed his train in a bombing raid. Just before leaving, he heard that Montgomery was at last contemplating a general offensive. 'Praise God from Whom all blessings flow!' he exclaimed. To his exasperation, the Counter Intelligence Corps remained obsessed with his personal security, and because of fog and ice the meeting had to be switched to Hasselt, close to Montgomery's headquarters. 'The roads are a sheet of ice, following last night's snow and ice storm,' General Simpson of Ninth Army noted that day.

Just before his meeting with the Supreme Commander, Montgomery had called a conference at Zonhoven on 28 December at 09.45 with the northern army commanders — Hodges, Simpson, Dempsey and General Harry Crerar of the First Canadian Army. Montgomery reaffirmed his plan. His own intelligence chief, the G-2 at First Army and Major General Strong at SHAEF all pointed to a renewed German attack. He therefore proposed to let the Germans first exhaust themselves and their resources, battering against the northern line, while fighter-bombers dealt with their rear. He also expected 'some sort of engagement on the British or Ninth Army fronts, as a demonstration'. In fact, Hitler had already cancelled the Fifteenth Army offensive planned to the north.[*]

Montgomery would move the British XXX Corps in to take over the defence from Hotton to Dinant, so that Collins's VII Corps could reform ready to lead a counter-strike down to Houffalize. During the final phase of crushing the German salient, he intended to launch Operation Veritable, the planned

* Even Bradley's 12th Army Group headquarters seemed to believe in a renewed attack northwards towards Liège with 'from four to five panzer divisions', according to Hansen. Three days later Hansen made the unexpected remark: 'Americans are very poor on intelligence; we have to depend upon the British for almost everything we have.'

Canadian army offensive down the west bank of the lower Rhine.

That afternoon at 14.30, Eisenhower and Montgomery met in Hasselt station. This was their first encounter since the battle had begun, and Montgomery was irritated that the Supreme Commander had not replied to his daily signals outlining the course of events. Closeted under guard at Versailles, Eisenhower had not ventured out since the Verdun conference. And during the unfortunate meeting on Christmas Day, Bradley had been forced to admit that he had no idea what Eisenhower's plans were. Montgomery was scornful of what he saw as Eisenhower's total inaction.

Eisenhower agreed to Montgomery's plan to advance on Houffalize, rather than St Vith as Bradley wanted. But once again Montgomery could not contain himself. He said that Bradley had made a mess of the situation, and that if he, Montgomery, did not have full operational command of all the armies north of the Moselle, then the advance to the Rhine would fail. For form's sake he offered to serve under Bradley, but this was hardly sincere after what he had said about him.

Montgomery assumed that his bullying had worked and that Eisenhower had agreed to all his proposals. Back in London, however, Field Marshal Sir Alan Brooke was disturbed when he heard Montgomery's account of the meeting. 'It looks to me as if Monty with his usual lack of tact has been rubbing into Ike the results of not having listened to Monty's advice!! Too much "I told you so".'

Eisenhower's staff at SHAEF, including the British, were furious at what they heard of the meeting, but Montgomery was about to make things much worse. Afraid that Eisenhower might back off from what he thought had been agreed, the field marshal wrote a letter on 29 December, again insisting on a single field command and again claiming that the Allies would fail if his advice was not followed. Major General de Guingand, his chief of staff now back in Belgium, delivered it to Eisenhower next day. For Eisenhower, Montgomery's letter was the final straw. The field marshal even had the temerity to dictate what Eisenhower's order should say when giving him 'full operational direction, control and co-ordination' over Bradley's 12th Army Group in the attack on the Ruhr.

The arrival of Montgomery's letter happened to coincide with a cable from General Marshall in Washington. He had been shown articles in the British press claiming that Montgomery had saved the Americans in the Ardennes and that he should be appointed overall ground force commander. Marshall made his feelings very clear to Eisenhower. 'Under no circumstances make any concessions of any kind whatsoever. You not only have our complete confidence but there would be a terrific resentment in this country following such an action. I am not assuming that you had in mind such a concession. I just wish you to be certain of our attitude on this side. You are doing a grand job and go on and give them hell.'

Eisenhower replied to Montgomery in reasoned tones, but with an unmistakable ultimatum. 'In your latest letter you disturb me by predictions of "failure" unless your exact opinions in the matter of giving you command over Bradley are met in detail. I assure you that in this matter I can go no further . . . For my part I would deplore the development of such an unbridgeable gulf of convictions between us that we would have to present our differences to the CC/S [Combined Chiefs of Staff].' There was no doubt whom the Combined Chiefs would back in a showdown.

De Guingand, hearing that Eisenhower was writing to Marshall, begged him to wait; and, although quite seriously ill, he immediately flew back to Zonhoven and explained to Montgomery that he was heading straight for the rocks. At first Montgomery refused to believe that things could be so bad. In any case, who could replace him? Field Marshal Sir Harold Alexander, came the reply. Montgomery was shaken to the core when the truth finally sank in. He had confidently told Eisenhower on an earlier occasion that 'the British public would not stand for a change'. From what de Guingand was telling him, that no longer counted. The Americans were now definitely in charge. 'What shall I do, Freddie?' an utterly deflated Montgomery asked.

De Guingand produced from the pocket of his battledress the draft of a letter. 'Dear Ike,' it read. 'Have seen Freddie and understand you are greatly worried by many considerations in these difficult days. I have given you my frank views because I have felt you like this . . . Whatever your decision may be you can rely on me one hundred percent to make it work and I know Brad will do the same. Very distressed that my letter may have upset you and I would ask you to tear it up. Your very devoted subordinate, Monty.' He signed, and it was encyphered and transmitted by cable without delay. The estimable Freddie de Guingand had once again saved his chief from his insufferable self. He then went to 21st Army Group's rear headquarters in Brussels to speak to journalists. He emphasized that Montgomery's command over the two American armies was temporary, and that in the interests of Allied solidarity the clamour for him to be made ground commander and the veiled criticism of Eisenhower must stop. They promised to consult their editors. De Guingand then rang Bedell Smith in Versailles to assure him that the field marshal had backed down completely.

All that needed to be settled was the date of the northern offensive. Eisenhower had convinced himself that it would be New Year's Day. Montgomery had at first favoured 4 January, but now brought it forward by twenty-four hours to 3 January. But a ground-swell of hostile opinion lingered on. Many American senior officers regretted later that Eisenhower had not seized the opportunity to get rid of the field marshal. They wanted a strategic victory in the Ardennes, utterly destroying all German forces in the Bulge. Montgomery believed that this was impracticable, and felt that they just wanted to wipe out the embarrassment of having been caught napping. He was impatient to get on with Operation Veritable to clear the Reichswald before crossing the Rhine north of the Ruhr. Bradley and Patton, on the other hand, had no intention of waiting until 3 January. They planned to launch their counter-offensive from Bastogne on 31 December.

On the southern side of Bastogne, the 35th Infantry Division, which had been greatly weakened during the battles in Lorraine, arrived to fill the gap between the 4th Armored Division and the 26th Infantry Division. The 35th was to attack north-east towards Marvie and the Longvilly–Bastogne road while the rest of the 4th Armored helped clear the villages east of the Arlon road. The infantry, with sodden boots from fording streams, were suffering as many cases of frostbite and trench foot as battle casualties. 'It was so cold . . . that the water in our canteens froze right on our bodies,' an officer in the 51st Armored Infantry wrote in his diary. 'We ate snow or melted it down to drink or make coffee.' His battalion, which had been 600 strong, suffered 461 battle and non-battle casualties in three weeks.

To the west, the 9th Armored Division's Combat Command A advanced up the road from Neufchâteau which ran close to Sibret, an important American objective. German reinforcements also began to arrive as the fighting for Bastogne intensified. On Thursday 28 December the *Führer Begleit* took over the Sibret sector on the south-west side. Oberst Remer claimed that, on the way down from the northern front, their medical company was shot up during 'a fighter-bomber attack lasting 35 minutes, although all vehicles were painted white and bore the red cross'. Manteuffel believed that Remer's formation would make all the difference, and its Panthers and Mark IVs went straight into action against the 9th Armored's tanks, setting a number of them on fire.

Remer was angry and mortified to learn

that he was now under the orders of the greatly reduced 3rd Panzergrenadier-Division. The *Führer Begleit,* despite being less than half the size of a standard division, was heavily armed at a time when the 5th Fallschirmjäger-Division was left with little artillery support, and the 26th Volksgrenadier had no more armour-piercing shells. Remer, who had a battery of 105mm anti-aircraft guns, transferred them to Chenogne ready to take on Patton's tanks. His 88mm batteries were deployed five kilometres further north round Flamierge where they claimed to have shot down 'ten cargo-carrying gliders'. But the *Führer Begleit* was too late to save the key village of Sibret. After a heavy artillery bombardment, the Americans forced the Germans out that night. A shot-down glider pilot had been captured by the Germans near by. He hid in a potato bin when they withdrew, and found himself a free man again.

The loss of Sibret dismayed Manteuffel as well as Lüttwitz, for now their chances of re-establishing the encirclement of Bastogne were greatly reduced. Lüttwitz ordered Remer to recapture Sibret the next morning with help from a Kampfgruppe from the 3rd Panzergrenadier-Division. 'If this attack failed,' Lüttwitz wrote, 'the Corps believed that it would be necessary to begin the immediate withdrawal of the front salient.' But Hitler, refusing yet again to accept reality, announced the creation of a so-called 'Army Group Lüttwitz' to crush Bastogne. In theory, it included the 2nd Panzer-Division, the Panzer Lehr, the 9th Panzer-Division, the 3rd and the 15th Panzergrenadier-Divisions, the 1st SS Panzer-Division *Leibstandarte Adolf Hitler,* the 5th Fallschirmjäger-Division and the *Führer Begleit* Brigade. But, despite its typically Hitlerian appellation, most of the formations designated were little more than remnants.

During the early hours of Friday 29 December, the *Führer Begleit* Brigade assembled on the southern edge of the woods near Chenogne for its counter-attack against Sibret. But as soon as Remer's troops emerged from the trees they were greeted by a massive concentration of fire from the field artillery battalions brought up to crush this expected riposte. Flanking fire from Villeroux to the east, which the Americans had taken after a fierce fight on 28 December, also caused many casualties. The woods south-east of Chenogne changed hands several times. One of Remer's 105mm anti-aircraft guns knocked out several American tanks during the fighting, but eventually its crew, despite defending their gun as infantrymen in close-combat fighting, were overwhelmed. A Sherman tank crushed their gun under its tracks. That evening Remer reported that the *Führer Be-*

gleit was now too weak to attempt another attack against Sibret.

Luftwaffe bombers raided Bastogne on the night of Friday 29 December just as the weather turned, with snow and mist now coming down from Scandinavia. But at least the corridor was secure, so hundreds of trucks ferried in large quantities of supplies for the defenders of Bastogne as well as 400 replacements for the 101st Airborne. General Taylor visited his troops in the front line of the perimeter to congratulate them. Some found his manner irritating. 'His instructions before leaving us', recorded Major Dick Winters of the 506th, 'were "Watch those woods in front of you!" What the hell did he think we had been doing while he was in Washington?'

The paratroopers were dejected to find that, despite their heroic treatment in the press, they were not to be replaced and returned to Mourmelon-le-Grand. At least they had received their mail and Christmas packages from home. The contents were shared with other platoon members or Belgian civilians. And finally they had enough to eat, with their preferred 'ten-in-one' ration packs. Some paratroopers also managed to 'liberate' the store of spirits which VIII Corps headquarters had left behind: it had been revealed when one of the Luftwaffe bombs had blown down the wall of a building. But the bitter cold and the routine of deadly skirmishes and dangerous patrols at night continued. Their commanders still wanted intelligence on the enemy units opposite, so snatch squads had to go out to seize a 'tongue' for interrogation. (German officers had confiscated their men's paybooks because they revealed too much information about their unit.) But moving silently at night was impossible, since every step made a noise as each foot crunched through the hard crust on top of the snow. And their white capes, frozen stiff, crackled as they moved. Experiments with bleached fatigue suits for camouflage were not very successful. Paratroopers envied the Germans' reversible jacket with a white lining, which was far better.

Since it was common practice to set up dummies out in front of defensive positions to prompt an enemy patrol to open fire prematurely, paratroopers resorted to using frozen German corpses propped up in the snow. One was called 'Oscar' after the unit's puppet-like mascot, which parachuted with them. It also served as a directional marker for fire orders in the event of a surprise attack. Paratroopers had been surprised to find that the faces of men who died in that extreme cold did not have the usual grey tinge, but went a burgundy colour as the blood capillaries froze rapidly under the skin.

As well as trench foot and frostbite many

paratroopers, already filthy and bearded, were suffering from dysentery, largely due to the impossibility of cleaning mess kits properly. Temperatures as low as minus 20 Centigrade could make the cooling jackets of their heavy machine guns burst. These weapons could be seen by their muzzle flash from a great distance, while its German equivalent could not be spotted at over a hundred metres. Paratroopers were not alone in preferring to use captured German MG-42 machine guns. New replacements needed to learn to avoid firing too long a burst which gave away their position.

Many soldiers liked to debate the best way to throw a grenade: whether like a baseball, a shot-put or an overarm lob. The baseball throw was rejected by many as it was liable to wrench the arm and shoulder. To prevent the Germans catching it and throwing it back, experienced soldiers would pull the pin, count to two or three and then throw. Grenades were often carried with the lever hooked into buttonholes. Officers despaired, knowing that they would fall off and be lost when men lay down. Clueless replacements were also found attaching them to their equipment by the rings, which was a quick way of blowing yourself up. A spare canteen cover usually proved the best carrier.

On 30 December, General Patton entered

Bastogne wearing his famous pearl-handled revolvers. He congratulated officers and men in his curiously high-pitched voice, presented medals, had his photograph taken in many places, examined burned-out German tanks and visited the main battle sites. They included the Château de Rolley, where he slept for a few hours before continuing his tour. An artillery observation officer with the 327th Glider Infantry, already under fire on a ridge from German tanks, was infuriated to see a group walking up quite openly from behind to join him. He swore at them to get down only to find an imperturbable General Patton who had come to watch. Having ranged in with a single gun, the captain ordered 'fire for effect' from his field battalion on the panzers. One lucky round scored a direct hit on the turret, setting off the ammunition inside and blasting the tank to pieces. 'Now by God that is good firing!' a triumphant Patton exclaimed. It had clearly made his day.

While the *Führer Begleit* and the 3rd Panzergrenadiers attacked from the west, a Kampfgruppe from the 1st SS Panzer-Division together with the 14th Fallschirm-jäger-Regiment and the 167th Volksgrenadier-Division, newly arrived from Hungary, attacked from the east around Lutrebois. A battalion of the American 35th Infantry Division in Villers-la-Bonne-Eau was taken by surprise in the fog before dawn. Two companies were wiped out, but the field artillery once again played a major role in saving the situation. With divisional and corps guns firing shells with the new Pozit fuses, the 167th Volksgrenadiers were 'cut to pieces', in the words of their commander.

When Shermans and tank destroyers from the 4th Armored, drawn by the sound of battle, joined in this chaotic battle, the infantry passed on their sightings of German tanks in the woods. The 134th Infantry Regiment claimed that twenty-seven tanks had been knocked out and the estimates of other units brought the total to over fifty, but this was a gross exaggeration. Even so the *Leibstandarte Adolf Hitler* had suffered heavy losses, and blamed its failure on the 5th Fallschirmjäger-Division. According to its commander, Generalmajor Heilmann, 'The SS spread the rumor that [my] paratroopers sat down in peace with Americans in the cellar of a house in Villers-la-Bonne-Eau and made a toast to brotherhood.' The *Leibstandarte* commander Brigadeführer Wilhelm Mohnke wanted to court-martial the officers of the 14th Fallschirmjäger-Regiment for cowardice, and apparently said that a 'National Socialist leadership officer[*] should be

[*] The role of Nazionalsozialistischen Führungsoffizier, or National Socialist leadership officer, was instituted on Hitler's orders in imitation of the

set at the throat of the Fallschirmjäger division'.

The mutual dislike between the Waffen-SS and other Wehrmacht formations reached new depths. The SS Panzer formations demanded priority on every route, causing chaos. 'These road conditions reached their peak when SS formations arrived in the Bastogne combat sector,' wrote Generalmajor Kokott. 'These units — unduly boastful and arrogant anyway — with their total lack of discipline so typical of them, with their well-known ruthlessness combined with considerable lack of logic, had a downright devastating effect and in all cases proved a handicap for any systematic conduct of fighting.' This hatred of the SS did not exist solely at senior officer level. Feldwebel Rösner in Kokott's division described how the SS 'broke into houses in Luxembourg and out of vandalism destroyed everything'. They had also destroyed holy pictures in the German Eifel, because the region was very Catholic.

The most encouraging event for Patton's III Corps was the arrival of forward elements of the 6th Armored Division to take over from the exhausted 4th Armored. This formation was both at full strength and experi-

---

Soviet commissar, or political officer, to watch over the loyalty and determination of army officers.

enced, a rare combination at that time. Some of their Shermans had the new 76mm gun — based on the British 17-pounder — which could finally take on a Mark VI Tiger with confidence. Although one combat command was delayed on its approach by having to share the same road as the 11th Armored, the other one moved into position on the south-east of the perimeter near Neffe ready to attack Wardin the next day.

Not all mistaken attacks on American troops came from Thunderbolt and Lightning fighter-bombers. On 31 December Third Army reported that 'bombers from the Eighth Air Force unfortunately bombed the headquarters of 4th Armored Division, the town of Wecker, and that part of the 4th Infantry Division at Echternach'. An urgent meeting was called with the air force generals Doolittle and Spaatz to discuss accidental bombing of 'our own forces' and 'inversely the firing upon our own airplanes by our own antiaircraft guns'. The 'accidental bombing' was hushed up in order 'not to shake the faith of the troops'. Faults lay on both sides, but after several incidents many American troops reverted to the slogan from Normandy 'If it flies, it dies', and they frequently opened fire at any aircraft approaching whether in or out of range. The army was also openly sceptical about the air force's inflated estimates of the number of panzers it had destroyed. 'It is obvious that Air Corps claims must be exaggerated,' 12th Army Group observed, 'otherwise the Germans would be without tanks whereas our recon indicates plenty of them.'

The Luftwaffe still made night bombing raids on Bastogne. On 1 January, German prisoners of war under guard were clearing debris near Bastogne's central square when one of them stepped on a 'Butterfly' bomblet dropped in the previous night's raid. It exploded upward into his groin. He fell to the ground screaming. The scene was witnessed by soldiers from the 52nd Armored Infantry of the 9th Armored Division. One of their officers wrote later: 'You could hear laughter coming from the throats of our GIs in the trucks.'

On the First Army front to the north, Montgomery had now moved in the 53rd Welsh Division and the American 83rd Infantry Division to relieve the 2nd Armored in the west and the 84th Infantry Division round Marche. The 51st Highland Division became a First Army reserve. As more of Horrocks's XXX Corps arrived, the rest of Collins's VII Corps could pull back to redeploy ready for the counter-attack on 3 January.* The British

* Montgomery had in fact just sent his favourite corps commander home on enforced medical leave.

581

6th Airborne Division which moved in east of Celles tried to dig defensive positions, but the ground was frozen so hard that the men's spades were useless. They resorted instead to hammering hollow camouflet rods into the ground, and then filled them with explosive to blast holes. They soon found that dealing with Teller mines buried under the snow was a dangerous task.

All around the area of maximum German advance, starving and frozen stragglers were being rounded up. A farmer's son went to look after the horses near Ychippe. When he returned a German soldier, whom he had seen limping towards their house, knocked at the door. Pointing to his feet, he said: 'Kaput!' He had been sleeping in a barn. He sat down by their stove, put down his pistol and removed his boots. An American patrol arrived, and took the German prisoner before he had a chance to seize his pistol. Other German soldiers had been hiding in neighbouring houses and farm buildings. One of them refused to come out of a barn when they were surrounded. He was wearing

---

He feared that his judgement had become impaired through exhaustion. Horrocks had suddenly advocated that they should let the Germans cross the Meuse then defeat them on the battlefield of Waterloo just south of Brussels.

American uniform and feared being shot. Eventually he was persuaded to come out when the Americans threatened to burn the barn down. They forced him to strip off the items of American uniform and then took him away in a Jeep. The villagers had no idea what happened to him.

In a number of places, such as Conjoux, villagers watched with sadness as American tank drivers smashed down their little orchards and hedgerows. They were less anxious when they saw American infantry approaching with columns of men on both sides of the road in Indian file. The parsimonious existence of farming folk in the region meant that nothing could be wasted. They took whatever they could from abandoned German vehicles, since this was likely to be the only compensation they could hope for in exchange for the damage to their fields, barns and houses, as well as the loss of fodder, horses and carts seized by the Germans. A caterpillar-tracked motorcycle constituted a great prize. They siphoned fuel from abandoned vehicles and took tool kits, tinned rations, tyres and wheels, and stripped almost anything else which could be disassembled. A few took away grenades in the hope of some productive fishing in the summer.

Several farmers tried removing the wheels from field guns, hoping to make a cart, but they found that they were too heavy for a horse to pull. In a far more successful improvisation, a mechanically expert farmer managed to build his own tractor entirely from parts taken from a range of German armoured vehicles. The engine came from a half-track. One household even removed the front seats from a *Kübelwagen,* the Wehrmacht equivalent of a Jeep, and used them in their parlour for almost thirty years. At Ychippe, a dead German officer was left for many days slumped back in the front seat of another *Kübelwagen.* Seventeen-year-old Theóphile Solot was fascinated by the fact that his beard continued to grow after death.

Women were desperately anxious about the fate of sons and husbands. Those who had escaped across the Meuse were indeed fortunate, because the Germans had rounded up large numbers of the men and boys who had remained. They were made to clear snow from roads and haul supplies. Many did not have the right clothes for the snow and ice. Barely fed, certainly not enough for hard work, they were also ill equipped. Few had gloves or even spades. They were treated as prisoners, and locked in barns at night. In some cases, their guards fixed grenades to doors and windows so that they could not escape. Many were marched all the way back to Germany to work there and were not liberated until the closing stages of the war. A number were killed by Allied aircraft because the pilots could not distinguish between groups of German soldiers and Belgian civilians. They all looked like little black figures against the snow.

In the last days of December, the British XXX Corps extended its new positions between the Meuse and Hotton. An English civil affairs officer took a rather romantic view of their surroundings. 'The Ardennes has a pronounced Ruritanian atmosphere,' he wrote, 'as one imagines in the story of the Prisoner of Zenda. The chateaus give the added effect, together with the larger woods of fir trees, laden with snow.'

Once the weather closed in, air reconnaissance had become impossible. When the 53rd Welsh Division replaced the Americans at Marche-en-Famenne, the Allies needed to know how the Panzer Lehr and the remnants of the 2nd Panzer were redeploying after their withdrawal from Rochefort. The British 61st Reconnaissance Regiment attached to the 6th Airborne Division, as well as Belgian and French SAS forces, some 350 strong, was sent into the large area of forest and bog south of Rochefort and Marche to find out.

The French squadron headed for Saint-Hubert, and on 31 December a Belgian squadron from the 5th SAS Regiment located part of the Panzer Lehr at Bure ten kilometres south of Rochefort. In their Jeeps, armed only with twin Vickers machine guns, they could do little more than harass the panzer-grenadiers. Three of their best men were killed straight off by a German 88mm gun. The Germans were holding on desperately in this area because almost all the remnants from the 2nd and 9th Panzer-Divisions, as well as the Panzer Lehr, had been extricating themselves from Rochefort along this route. After most of the inhabitants had sought shelter in the cellars of the religious college, the Germans seized all their sheets for cam-ouflage. And while the villagers sheltering underground had nothing to eat but potatoes, the panzergrenadiers killed and ate their chickens.

German artillery now shelled Rochefort, and the townsfolk remained in the surround-ing caves. Only a few ventured out during lulls to fetch food. All were deeply grateful to Frère Jacques, 'with his beret and big black rubber gloves', who collected corpses to give them a Christian burial.

The Germans also continued to bombard Liège with V-1 bombs. On New Year's Eve, Lance-Sergeant Walker in the Middlesex Regiment, a veteran of North Africa, Sicily and Normandy, was on his way to attend mass in a church at Sur-le-Mont just south of the city. A V-1 flying bomb was passing overhead, and as he looked up, he saw it turn over and start to dive. 'A Belgian child was standing a few yards from him oblivious of the danger,' the citation for his medal stated. 'Lance-Sergeant Walker leaped to the child, pulled him down on the ground and shielded him with his own body. The bomb exploded a few yards from where they lay and severely wounded Lance-Sergeant Walker. The child was unhurt.' The Royal Army Medical Corps gave up on Walker because his wounds were so severe, but he survived because the Americans scooped him up and conducted pioneering flesh-graft surgery on him which was filmed and sent to other field surgical hospitals for instructional purposes.

American headquarters all organized their own parties for New Year's Eve. At Simpson's Ninth Army, they celebrated with highballs and turkey. At Hodges's First Army, dinners were always formal. 'In his mess every night,' one of his officers recorded, 'we dressed for dinner: jacket, necktie, combat boots.' Hodges usually had a bourbon and Dubonnet on the rocks with a dash of bitters, but that night he ordered that the case of champagne which Collins had given him after the capture of Cherbourg should be opened to toast the New Year. At midnight there was a panic when soldiers began 'indiscriminately firing their rifles. Hasty investigation showed that no attack was going on but that simple exuberance [was] having its day.'

Bradley's 12th Army Group headquarters

also had a party. According to Hansen, Martha Gellhorn 'talked passionately half the evening of the war in Spain . . . she is the original newspaperwoman who believes in the goodness of man, having seen so much of his worst, having seen it abased in the battlefronts of the entire world'. It seems the party atmosphere was slightly spoiled by nervousness that there might be an official inquiry into the intelligence failure to foresee the German offensive. General William Donovan, the founder of the Office of Strategic Services, had just arrived from Washington, and mentioned that there was 'talk of a congressional investigation to determine why we were lax'. Bradley was extremely nervous and defensive over his 'calculated risk' before the German attack, leaving only four divisions to defend the Ardennes.

In Berlin, the diarist Ursula von Kardorff, who was connected to the July plotters, entertained a few friends on New Year's Eve. 'At midnight all was still. We stood there with raised glasses, hardly daring to clink them together. A single bell tinkled in the distance for the passing of the year, and we heard shots, and heavy boots crunching on the splintered glass [in the street from broken windows]. It was eerie, as though a shadow were passing over us and touching us with its dark wings.' In the Ardennes, Germans, and also Belgians, braced themselves for the Allied counter-offensive and the fighting still to come. 'My prayer on the threshold of the new year', wrote a young Volksgrenadier officer near St Vith, 'is with the Führer's and our strength to end this war victoriously.' In the next few hours, the Germans struck again, both in the air and in Alsace.

21
THE DOUBLE SURPRISE

On New Year's Eve at midnight, American artillery all around the Ardennes fired salvoes to tell the Wehrmacht that the year of its final defeat had begun. But the Germans had New Year messages of their own. A few minutes before the old year was out, Army Group Upper Rhine commanded by Reichsführer-SS Heinrich Himmler launched an offensive called Operation *Nordwind* against the left flank of General Devers's 6th Army Group.

The day after Christmas, Seventh Army intelligence had warned that the Germans might attack in northern Alsace during the first few days of January. General Devers had flown to Versailles to see General Eisenhower. Their relationship had not improved since Eisenhower rebuffed his plan to seize a bridgehead across the Rhine. And because the struggle in the Ardennes was approaching its climax, SHAEF simply wanted the American and French divisions in the south to go on the defensive. With most of Patton's

Third Army deployed on the southern side of the salient, Devers's forces, stripped to the bone to strengthen the Ardennes, had been forced to extend their frontage to more than 300 kilometres.

Eisenhower wanted to shorten the line in Alsace by withdrawing to the Vosges mountains, and probably giving up Strasbourg in the process. Tedder warned him strongly against such a move. (Ironically, it was now the British who opposed giving up territory.) This was to lead to a major confrontation with the French, for whom Strasbourg had powerful significance.

The other attack was much more unexpected. Reichsmarschall Hermann Göring, stung by the bitter criticism of his Luftwaffe, had decided on his own lightning strike. His plan for a major surprise against the Allied air forces had first been mentioned on 6 November, when Generalmajor Christian told Hitler that 'The Reichsmarschall has ordered that all these new groups now standing by should be deployed in a single day — a day when the weather doesn't pose a problem — all together, in one strike.'

Hitler was dubious. 'I am just afraid that, when this day comes, the groups won't coordinate and that they won't find the enemy . . . The hope of decimating the enemy with a mass deployment is not realistic.' He was also very sceptical of Luftwaffe claims and figures of aircraft ratios, and was exasperated that his pilots had shot down so few Allied planes. He exclaimed: 'There are still tons of [Luftwaffe aircraft] being produced. They're only eating up labor and material.'

The Luftwaffe faced many problems, but also created its own. Few veteran pilots remained because of the wasteful system of failing to give them sufficient breaks from front-line duty, and of not using them to pass on their expertise to trainees. 'They are all young pilots now with no experience,' a Messerschmitt 109 pilot said. 'All the experienced ones have gone.' 'What sort of training have the newcomers had to-day?' said another. 'It's pitiful, appalling.' Mainly because of fuel shortages, they arrived at operational units after only a few hours of flying solo. No wonder American fighter pilots said that they would far prefer to take on four new pilots than one veteran.

Morale was bad. One captured officer detailed the number of excuses pilots used to avoid flying or engaging in combat. They included 'engine trouble', and 'undercarriage not retracting'. One pilot who went up, flew around and shot at nothing was arrested when he landed. More senior officers 'used to fly', said another veteran pilot, 'but all that is over now. They don't do a thing. They don't fancy a hero's death any longer, those days are past.' A profound cynicism spread to all ranks. 'In our Staffel [squadron] you were looked at in amazement if you hadn't got venereal disease,' a Feldwebel reported. 'At least 70% had gonorrhoea.'

The greatest cynicism was reserved for their commander-in-chief, the Reichsmarschall. He 'seems to have run the Luftwaffe with much the same methods as those used by the Queen of Hearts in *Alice in Wonderland*', a senior officer with the Oberkommando Luftwaffe remarked, 'and with much the same effectiveness . . . For him the Luftwaffe was just another toy.' One of the few senior officers who took part in the great New Year's Day attack recalled asking a superior, 'Well, what's our Reichsmarschall doing now, Herr General?' The general replied: 'The Reichsmarschall is dealing in diamonds at the moment. He hasn't any time for us.' On the other hand, General der Flieger Karl Koller, the chief of staff, blamed Hitler more than anyone. 'He had no understanding of the needs of the Luftwaffe, remaining an infantryman in outlook throughout his life.'

In any case, Göring felt that he had no option but to go all out. He 'practically cried' about the state of the Luftwaffe, according to an Oberstleutnant, and said that 'unless we gained mastery in the air quickly, then we have lost the war'. Göring's final gamble, a shadow of Hitler's whole Ardennes offensive, was to be called *Unternehmen Bodenplatte* —

Operation Baseplate. Practically every fighter that could fly would take off to attack Allied airfields and shoot up their aircraft on the ground.

Although Luftwaffe officers had known of the plan for several weeks, the operational order caused astonishment and horror when they were called for briefing on the afternoon of New Year's Eve. Pilots were forbidden to drink any alcohol that evening or stay up to celebrate the New Year. Many dreaded the prospect of the morrow, and what looked like a suicidal Japanese *banzai* charge. Flying personnel were at least allocated 'take-off' rations, with extra butter, eggs and white bread. They were promised that on return from the operation they would receive a slab of chocolate, real coffee and a full 'operations' meal.

Almost 1,000 German aircraft on thirty-eight airfields started their engines soon after dawn. Oberstleutnant Johann Kogler, due to lead Jagdgeschwader 6 against Volkel airfield in Holland, sat in the cockpit of his Focke-Wulf 190. Kogler had few illusions. General der Flieger Adolf Galland had 'poured out his troubles to me; it was pretty grim'. Kogler's chief was the useless General der Flieger Beppo Schmidt, who had so misled Göring as his intelligence chief in 1940 that Generaloberst Franz Halder remarked that Göring was 'the worst-informed officer in the whole Luftwaffe'. Schmidt, appalled by the loss of fighter commanders, had tried to keep them on the ground. Kogler objected to such an idea on principle. 'Herr General, if we must fly to give the enemy some fun, so that they have something to shoot at; and if we are just being put into the air for the sake of doing something, then I do request that I should be allowed to accompany [my pilots] every time.'

The commander of a Focke-Wulf 190 Staffel, in Jagdgeschwader 26, found the choice of their targets bitterly ironic. 'We had been stationed on these airfields ourselves. I had to take my own Staffel to shoot up the very airfield where I used to be based.' Far more depressing was Göring's order. 'Whoever [returns after failing] to attack the airfield properly, or fails to find it, must immediately take off again afterwards and attack it again.' This was to prove a disastrous idea. Each group was to be accompanied by an Me 262 jet whose pilot's role was to identify anyone who showed a lack of determination in the attack.

Some pilots at least seemed to revel in their mission, reminiscing about their exploits earlier in the war. 'What a smashing we gave them at the beginning!' remembered one who was due to attack the airfield near Ghent. 'Sixty aircraft took off in each Gruppe.' He was clearly exultant even at this stage at the impression of power which *Bodenplatte* gave.

'Now in our sortie on the 1st [January] — Oh my goodness! What there was up in the air. I myself was amazed. I no longer knew which Geschwader I belonged to. They flew about all over the place. The civilians stared at us. Afterwards we flew over the front [and] the soldiers stood and gazed. We all flew low.'

This very optimistic impression omitted another aspect of the chaos. Following Hitler's security precautions before the Ardennes offensive, Göring had refused to allow German flak defences to be warned of Operation *Bodenplatte* in advance. As a result the flak batteries assumed that these large formations, which they suddenly saw overhead, must be enemy. They opened fire. Apparently sixteen of their own aircraft fell victim to friendly fire on the way to their objectives.

Their simultaneous attacks at 09.20 hours had targeted twelve British airfields in Belgium and southern Holland, and four American bases in France. But due mainly to navigational errors, they hit thirteen British bases and only three American. The Germans achieved surprise, but not in every case. The Geschwader attacking the Sint-Denijs-Westrem airfield at Ghent bounced a Polish squadron of Spitfires just as it was landing, and very short of fuel. The attackers destroyed nine of them and another six on the ground. But they in turn were caught by the other two Polish squadrons of 131 Wing, which shot down eighteen of them and damaged another five for the loss of only one Spitfire. Among the captured Focke-Wulf pilots was the one who had rejoiced at the number of German aircraft in the air.

The Americans fared better than the British, because one group of attackers became totally lost and failed to find their target, and a patrol of P-47 Thunderbolts dived into the force aiming for Metz; but the Germans still managed to destroy twenty out of forty fighter-bombers on the ground there. The heaviest British losses were at Eindhoven, where the Germans were lucky enough to hit the first squadron of Typhoons just as they were taking off. The crashed aircraft blocked the runway, trapping the other squadrons behind. 'One frustrated Typhoon pilot stood on his brakes and applied power to lift his aircraft's tail, so he could shoot at the low-flying attackers from the ground.'

At Evere a Spitfire squadron was also caught taxiing to the runway and destroyed, but one pilot managed to get airborne. He shot up one of the 'bandits', but was brought down himself. The Americans became convinced that the aircraft of the British 2nd Tactical Air Force had all been caught out 'closely parked in formation'. This was true only at Eindhoven, a photo-reconnaissance base, where Spitfires were lined up on an old Luftwaffe runway because there was nowhere else to put them. Bases were certainly over-full because many squadrons had had to concentrate on the airfields with hard run-ways, which could be cleared of snow more easily. The news that Field Marshal Mont-gomery's personal aircraft had also been destroyed on the ground prompted a distinct atmosphere of schadenfreude in American circles. 'They caught the British with their pants down so badly', wrote the First Army diarist the next day, 'that General Mont-gomery's G-2 [intelligence chief] sent a pair of suspenders [braces] as [a] present to the G-2 of their Tac[tical] Air Force.' Eisenhower, with great generosity, immediately gave Montgomery his own aircraft.

Staff officers at Ninth Army headquarters went out to watch the air battles. 'Mid-morning saw many dogfights in the Maas-tricht area, with ack-ack shooting wildly at unseen planes in the low hanging clouds.' Al-together the Allies lost 150 combat aircraft destroyed and 111 damaged, as well as 17 non-combat aircraft. Pilot losses were merci-fully light, but more than a hundred ground personnel were killed.

Many German fighters were brought down by anti-aircraft fire, including Oberstleutnant Kogler who was captured. Near Brussels, bizarrely, one low-flying German pilot in a Focke-Wulf was brought down by a partridge 'which tore a large hole in his radiator so the coolant drained out stopping the engine'. But as Ninth Army headquarters recognized, 'Jerry made one big error in this surprise attack, which proved very costly. He stayed too long. Enjoying the fun of shooting the place up, he delayed so long that our fighters from rear bases had time to get into the air and caught him as he turned for home. He suffered extremely heavy losses as a result.'

Those pilots who, under Göring's order, were made to refuel, rearm and attack again, flew back to find Allied squadrons in overwhelming strength, determined to wipe them from the skies. Worst of all, German air defences were still kept in total ignorance, even after the attack. 'A catastrophe overtook the Luftwaffe's great operation on 1 January,' Hitler's adjutant Nicolaus von Below noted. 'On their return our aircraft flew into heavy and accurate fire from our own flak defences, which had never been informed of the operation on security grounds. Our formations suffered heavy losses which could never be made good. This was the last major effort of the Luftwaffe.'

It was not even a partial victory. The Luftwaffe lost 271 fighters destroyed and 65 damaged. Their air-crew casualties were disastrous. Altogether 143 pilots were dead or missing, another 70 were taken prisoner and a further 21 were wounded. The losses included three Kommodore, five Gruppenkommodore, or wing commanders, and fourteen Staffelkapitäne, or squadron leaders. They would be very hard to replace.

Germans could do little about their fate, so they just plodded on, stumbling through ruins after Allied bombing raids had knocked out tram and rail tracks, on their way to factories and offices, usually without windows or electricity. Hitler did not mention the Ardennes offensive in his New Year speech that day. As he rambled on, most of his audience realized that he had nothing new to offer.

Hitler also made no mention of *Unternehmen Nordwind* — Operation North Wind. He had thought up the idea of *Nordwind* on 21 December and gave the operation its name on Christmas Day. Although the official intent was to destroy the American VI Corps in northern Alsace by linking up with the Nineteenth Army holding the Colmar pocket, his real intentions were to upset Patton's advance in the Ardennes and to give the impression that he still retained the initiative. On 28 December, Hitler had summoned the divisional commanders to the Adlerhorst so that he could address them personally, as he had done before the Ardennes offensive.

When Devers had returned to his headquarters after meeting Eisenhower in Versailles on 26 December, he had ordered fall-back lines

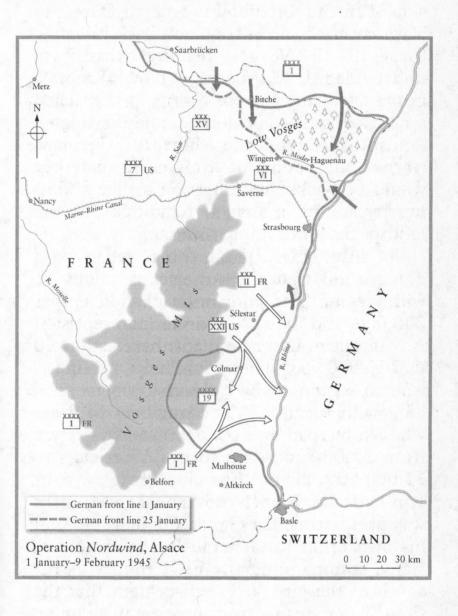

Saarbrücken
Metz
N
Bitche
XXXX
1
Low Vosges
XXX
XV
R. Saar
Wingen
R. Moder
Haguenau
XXXX
7 US
XXX
VI
Nancy
Marne–Rhine Canal
Saverne
Strasbourg
FRANCE
XXX
II FR
R. Moselle
Sélestat
XXX
XXI US
Colmar
Vosges Mts
XXXX
19
R. Rhine
GERMANY
XXXX
1 FR
XXX
I FR
Mulhouse
Belfort
Altkirch

German front line 1 January
German front line 25 January

Operation *Nordwind*, Alsace
1 January–9 February 1945

Basle
SWITZERLAND

0   10 20 30 km

to be studied in northern Alsace. After the German attack started on 1 January either side of Bitche, Eisenhower ordered Devers to leave covering forces, but pull back his main forces to the Vosges, leaving Strasbourg undefended. It was a serious blow to morale in the 6th Army Group. 'Spirits have reached a new low today,' a colonel wrote. Through a loudspeaker across the Rhine, the Germans warned the people of Strasbourg that they would be back. But American artillery, aiming by sound, managed to knock out the loudspeaker with impressive rapidity.

Not surprisingly, panic spread when word got around that the Americans might be withdrawing. The population of the city was 200,000, and many feared German reprisals. An American correspondent there estimated that 10,000 fled. 'They left mostly by train . . . women pushing baby carriages, wagons piled high with furniture.' The numbers of those who left by road over the next two days varied from 2,000 according to the Americans to 15,000 according to French sources.

In Paris, the French provisional government was up in arms. De Gaulle immediately sent his own order to General de Lattre de Tassigny, commanding the First French Army south of the city. 'It is self-evident that the French army can never agree to abandoning Strasbourg. In the eventuality of Allied forces withdrawing from their present positions to the north of the First French Army, I order you to take responsibility and ensure the defence of Strasbourg.' He then declared his position to Eisenhower and appealed to Churchill and Roosevelt to prevent an Allied withdrawal. SHAEF was warned that 100,000 people would have to be evacuated from the city, and another 300,000 more Alsatians risked German reprisals.

Next day General Alphonse Juin went to see Bedell Smith on de Gaulle's instruction, to say that the head of the provisional government would be coming to Versailles to see Eisenhower next day. Juin and Bedell Smith had fallen out before, and this was their stormiest meeting of all. Tensions had already arisen after General de Lattre had complained about the lack of equipment and supplies his First French Army had received, while the Americans had questioned the effectiveness of its attacks on the Colmar pocket. The French had suffered heavy casualties among their junior officers, and their replacements had trouble pushing their men forward.

Juin said that General de Gaulle would withdraw French troops from SHAEF command if American forces pulled back to the Vosges. According to Bedell Smith, he was extremely rude about Eisenhower's handling of the war. 'Juin said things to me', he told Eisenhower after the meeting, '[for] which, if he had been an American, I would have socked him in the jaw.'

On the morning of 3 January, before de Gaulle's visit, Eisenhower discussed the evacuation of Strasbourg with his staff. That afternoon, de Gaulle appeared with Juin. Winston Churchill, who was already on a visit to France, also appeared following de Gaulle's message. Eisenhower briefed the two heads of government on the dangerous position they faced. Then, in response to the French ultimatum of withdrawing their forces from SHAEF command, Eisenhower reminded de Gaulle that 'the French Army would get no ammunition, supplies, or food unless it obeyed my orders, and [I] pointedly told him that if the French Army had eliminated the Colmar Pocket this situation would not have arisen'. De Gaulle became extremely heated at this point.

'If we were involved in war games,' de Gaulle said, eventually controlling himself, 'I would agree with you. But I am forced to consider the affair from another point of view. The withdrawal in Alsace will hand French territory over to the enemy. On a strategic level, it would just be a manoeuvre. But for France it would be a national disaster, because Alsace is sacred to us. In any case, the Germans pretend that this province belongs to them, and so they will not miss the opportunity to take vengeance on the patriotism which its inhabitants have demonstrated.'

With Churchill's tacit support, de Gaulle won Eisenhower round. The Supreme Commander agreed to ring General Devers basically telling him to halt the withdrawal. 'This modification pleased de Gaulle very much,' Eisenhower wrote, 'and he left in a good humour.' He no longer had his offended expression, which Churchill once described as resembling a female llama surprised in her bath. After de Gaulle's departure, Churchill murmured to Eisenhower, 'I think we've done the wise and proper thing.'

De Gaulle was so exultant that he returned to dictate a communiqué to his *chef de cabinet* Gaston Palewski. Before issuing it, Palewski took it round to Duff Cooper, the British ambassador. It was so vainglorious that Cooper warned Palewski that it would hardly help matters. 'It suggested', wrote Cooper in his diary, 'that de Gaulle had summoned a military conference which the P[rime] M[inister] and Eisenhower had been allowed to attend.' In any case, Eisenhower justified his change of mind to President Roosevelt, whose opinion of the French leader had still not improved, on the grounds that if the provisional government collapsed, Allied armies might well face chaos in their rear areas.

The US VI Corps was 'in high spirits' when

'the order to withdraw to a line just east of the Vosges mountains was rescinded', wrote Colonel Heffner. 'It would have been a terrible blow to American prestige. We could never have lived it down. To be driven back is one thing and to give up without a fight is something else.'

French forces remained under SHAEF command as a result of Eisenhower's compromise, but headaches in dealing with the French authorities persisted. Eisenhower subsequently complained that the French 'next to the weather . . . have caused me more trouble in this war than any other single factor'. SHAEF decided to stop passing 'signal intelligence to First French Army' since it was 'not sufficiently secure'. On 7 January Devers warned General Patch, the commander of the Seventh Army in Alsace, that its telephone wires may be tapped. 'This presents a serious threat to Ultra security if reference should be made to Ultra intelligence by message or by disguised reference to a special form of intelligence. A few such references if pieced together by the enemy might be dangerously revealing.'

The German First Army's attack south was more or less held west of Bitche, where it was led by the 17th SS Panzergrenadier-Division *Götz von Berlichingen,* the 101st Airborne's opponent at Carentan in Normandy. The XV Corps had good positions and was supported by Leclerc's 2nd Armored Division, which once again showed its mettle. (According to the staff of 6th Army Group, Leclerc 'simply refused to fight under de Lattre', because Lattre had served in Pétain's Army of the Armistice.) But from Bitche to the Rhine two German army corps, attacking without an artillery bombardment and in heavy fog, managed to infiltrate past American positions in the forested areas. Advancing down towards the Saverne Gap, the German divisions forced back the overstretched American VI Corps spread across the Low Vosges and Rhine plain.

General Patch's Seventh Army was heavily outnumbered, and it fought well, with just a few exceptions due to panic in the rear or laziness at the front. Divisional commanders were angry to hear of troops 'surprised, captured or surrounded while bivouacked in or defending a town or village'. This was nearly always due to a lack of all-round security, or alertness. In Bannstein 'a unit was completely surprised. The men were sleeping and the Germans walked into the town unopposed and captured our troops, arms and a considerable number of vehicles.' In three other places, similar incidents took place, but most of the men were released when US troops came to their rescue.

Fighting conditions were made far worse by heavy snow and the twisting, ice-bound roads of the Low Vosges. By 5 January, the 6th SS Mountain Division, brought down from Scandinavia, had reached Wingen-sur-Moder twenty kilometres short of Saverne. Resisted strongly by the 45th Infantry Division, that was as far as they advanced on the western side. For the moment, the other three American infantry divisions held the line of the River Rothbach. But Himmler had obtained further divisions, including the 10th SS Panzer-Division *Frundsberg,* and prepared a fresh attack.

General Eisenhower may have rated the French as his biggest problem next to the weather, but he had also mentioned to General de Gaulle that Field Marshal Montgomery was not easy to deal with. He did not, however, foresee that the greatest crisis in Anglo-American relations was about to explode. On 5 January, Eisenhower heard that news in the States of Montgomery taking command of the Ninth and First US Armies had just broken, despite the fact that SHAEF had unwisely tried to suppress it. All of Air Chief Marshal Tedder's fears about the British press were realized. General de Guingand's plea to correspondents had failed: their newspapers again demanded that Montgomery should now be confirmed as ground forces commander in western Europe. The American press, not surprisingly, did not like the idea that a Briton, and especially Montgomery, should be in charge of two whole American armies. SHAEF was nevertheless forced to issue its own communiqué confirming the arrangement. Correspondents, both American and British, had become enraged by the inept and complacent treatment of the press by the military authorities at Versailles.

Bradley, already rattled by the prospect of a congressional investigation into why the US Army had been so unprepared for the Ardennes offensive, also feared how the news of Montgomery taking over two of his armies would be construed back home. And he deeply resented the fact that, in a poll for *Time* magazine's Man of the Year, Patton had been voted second to Eisenhower, while he had never even been considered. Deeply upset, he immediately suspected Montgomery of leaking the story about the change in command and regarded it as a deliberate 'attempt to discredit the Americans'. He rang Eisenhower to complain, but Eisenhower assured him that the story had broken in the States and had not been leaked from 21st Army Group headquarters.

According to Hansen, Bradley believed that 'the public clamor for this appointment is obviously officially inspired'. He remained convinced that Winston Churchill was scheming to have Montgomery named as overall ground forces commander. Clearly he still believed this to be a possibility, for he declared to Eisenhower that he 'wouldn't serve one day under Montgomery's command . . . General Patton has likewise indicated that he will not serve a single day under Montgomery. I intend to tell Montgomery this.' Eisenhower said that he would pass on his concerns to Churchill, but neither Churchill nor even Brooke was pushing for such a promotion. They were well aware of American views, and were privately appalled by the storm brewing. Churchill wrote to President Roosevelt, emphasizing British confidence in Eisenhower's leadership and praising the bravery of American divisions during the battle.

Bradley feared that the story would 'repudiate the efficacy of his Army Group command, undermine the confidence of his subordinate commanders and eventually [affect] the morale and confidence of the troops. Second, there is the equally evident picture that it may undermine public confidence in the States in his [Bradley's] command and indicate to our people there that it was necessary for us to resort in an emergency to British command in an effort to retrieve our "chestnuts from the fire".'

The British campaign to have Montgomery made field commander of the whole western front, Hansen wrote, implied that 'the German breakthrough would not have happened had Montgomery been in command to prevent it. The current inference of all news stories now is that the German attack succeeded because of the negligence of the American commander — namely Bradley . . . The effect has been a cataclysmic Roman holiday in the British press which has exulted over the announcement, and hailed it as an increase in the Montgomery command.' He went on: 'The troops are referred to as "Monty's troops" in a palavering gibberish that indicates a slavish hero devotion on the part of the British press . . . He is the symbol of success, the highly overrated and normally distorted picture of the British effort on our front.'

Bradley, wound up by his entourage, felt he was fighting for his career and reputation. He had just written to General Marshall, giving his view of the situation and justifying his 'calculated risk' in leaving the Ardennes front so weakly defended up to 16 December. 'At the same time,' he added, 'I don't want to apologize for what has happened.'

Montgomery telephoned Churchill to tell him that he planned to give a press conference to make a strong call for Allied unity and support for Eisenhower. Churchill replied that he thought it would be 'invaluable'. Field Marshal Brooke, on the other hand, was not so sure. He knew too well Montgomery's inability to control his bragging. So did several of Montgomery's senior staff officers.

Monty appeared at the press conference on 7 January wearing a new airborne maroon beret with double badge, having just been appointed colonel commandant of the Parachute Regiment. His chief of intelligence, the brilliant academic Brigadier Bill Williams, had read the draft of his speech and dreaded how it would be received, even though the text as it stood was relatively innocuous. The only provocative part was when he said: 'The battle has been most interesting — I think possibly one of the most interesting and tricky battles I have ever handled, with great issues at stake.' The rest of the text was a tribute to the American soldier and a declaration of loyalty to Eisenhower, and a plea for Allied solidarity from the press.

But then, having reached the end of his prepared statement, Montgomery proceeded to speak off the cuff. He gave a brief lecture on his 'military philosophy'. 'If he [the enemy] puts in a hard bang I have to be ready for him. That is terrifically important in the battle fighting. I learned it in Africa. You learn all these things by hard experience. When Rundstedt put in his hard blow and parted the American Army, it was automatic that the battle area must be untidy. Therefore the first thing I did when I was brought in and told to take over was to busy myself in getting the battle area tidy — getting it sorted out.'

Montgomery also greatly exaggerated the British contribution to the battle, almost making it sound as if the whole thing had been an Anglo-American operation.

In London the Cabinet Office commented later that 'although this statement, read in its entirety, was a handsome tribute to the American Army, its general tone and a certain smugness of delivery undoubtedly gave deep offence to many American officers at SHAEF and 12th Army Group'.

Many journalists present fumed or cringed, depending on their nationality, yet both the British and the American press concentrated on the positive aspects of what he had said. The next morning, however, a German radio station put out a fake broadcast on a BBC wavelength, with a commentary which deliberately set out to stir American anger, implying that Montgomery had sorted out a First US Army disaster. 'The Battle of the Ardennes', it concluded, 'can now be written off thanks to Field Marshal Montgomery.' This fake broadcast was taken as genuine by American troops and the wire services. And for some time afterwards, even when it had been revealed that it was a Nazi propaganda trick, many aggrieved Americans still believed the British were just trying to bolster their role because their international standing was failing fast.

Even before the Nazi broadcast, Bradley

was so angry that he rang Eisenhower to complain about Montgomery's statement, and expressed his fear that the Ninth Army would be left under British command. He begged Eisenhower to 'return it to me if it's only for twenty-four hours for the prestige of the American command'. He explained to Hansen that 'I wanted it back for prestige reasons, because the British had made so much of it.' Bradley still went on that day about Montgomery's order to the 82nd Airborne to withdraw.

Without warning Eisenhower, Bradley called his own press conference on 9 January. He wanted to justify the weakness of the American forces on the Ardennes front on 16 December and defend himself against accusations of being caught flat-footed; but also to emphasize that Montgomery's command of US forces was purely temporary. This prompted the *Daily Mail* to bang Montgomery's drum in the most provocative way, once more demanding that he be made land forces commander. The transatlantic press war began all over again with renewed ferocity.

Churchill was appalled. 'I fear great offence has been given to the American generals,' he wrote to his chief military assistant General Ismay on 10 January, 'not so much by Montgomery's speech as by the manner in which some of our papers seem to appropriate the whole credit for saving the battle to him.

Personally I thought his speech most unfortunate. It had a patronising tone and completely overlooked the fact that the United States have lost perhaps 80,000 men and we but 2,000 or 3,000 . . . Eisenhower told me that the anger of his generals was such that he would hardly dare to order any of them to serve under Montgomery.' Eisenhower late claimed that the whole episode caused hi more distress and worry than any other du ing the war.

While Eisenhower's emissaries, Air Cief Marshal Tedder and General Bull, were till struggling to get to Moscow, Churchil had been corresponding with Stalin about plans for the Red Army's great winter offnsive. On 6 January he had written to th Soviet leader, making clear that the Geman offensive in the Ardennes had been alted and the Allies were masters of the sitution. This did not stop Stalin (and Russia historians subsequently) from trying to claim that Churchill had been begging or help. Roosevelt's communication of 3 December, talking of an 'emergency', night have been seen in that light with rathr more justification, but Stalin liked to take every opportunity to make the western Allies feel guilty or beholden to him. And he would play the same card again at the Yalta conference in February.

Stalin pretended that the major offensives

westwards from the Vistula on 12 January and north into East Prussia the next day had been planned for 20 January, but that he had brought them forward to help the Allies in the Ardennes. The real reason was that meteorological reports had warned that a thaw would set in later in the month, and the Red Army needed the ground hard for its tanks. All of Guderian's fears about the German 'house of cards' collapsing in Poland and Silesia were to be proved justified. Hitler's Ardennes adventure had left the eastern front utterly vulnerable.

22
COUNTER-ATTACK

Patton's impatience to start the advance from round Bastogne was soon frustrated. Remer proclaimed the efforts of the *Führer Begleit* 'a defensive success on 31 December and estimated that they had destroyed thirty American tanks'. The Germans were left unmolested that night. This allowed them to form a new line of defence, which 'astonished us eastern front warriors very greatly'. Yet Remer acknowledged that the inexperienced American 87th Infantry Division had fought well. 'They were excellent fighters and had a number of commandos who spoke German and came behind our lines where they were able to knife many of our guards.' There is, however, little confirmation of such irregular tactics from American sources. But since Remer's tanks and assault guns were down to less than twenty kilometres' worth of fuel, he 'radioed Corps [headquarters] that we were fighting our last battle, and that they should send help'.

On the eastern flank, the 6th Armored Division passed through Bastogne on the morning of 1 January to attack Bizôry, Neffe and Mageret, where so many battles had been fought in the early days of the encirclement. The equally inexperienced 11th Armored Division, working with the 87th Infantry Division on the south-west side of Bastogne as part of Middleton's VIII Corps, was to advance towards Mande-Saint-Etienne, but came off badly in a clash with the 3rd Panzergrenadiers and the *Führer Begleit*. 'The 11th Armored is very green and took unnecessary casualties to no effect,' Patton recorded. The division was shaken by the shock of battle. Even its commander was thought to be close to cracking up under the strain, and officers seemed unable to control their men. After bitter fighting to take the ruins of Chenogne on 1 January, about sixty German prisoners were shot. 'There were some unfortunate incidents in the shooting of prisoners,' Patton wrote in his diary. 'I hope we can conceal this.' It would indeed have been embarrassing after all the American fulminations over the Malmédy–Baugnez massacre.

Tuesday 2 January was 'a bitter cold morning', with bright clear skies, but meteorologists warned that bad weather was on the way. Manteuffel appealed to Model to accept that Bastogne could no longer be taken. They

618

had to withdraw, but Model knew that Hitler would never agree. Lüttwitz also wanted to pull back east of the River Ourthe, as he recognized that the remnants of the 2nd Panzer-Division and the Panzer Lehr were dangerously exposed at Saint-Hubert and east of Rochefort. In the *Führer Begleit,* battalions were down to less than 150 men and their commanders were all casualties. Remer claimed that there was not even enough fuel to tow away the damaged tanks. The answer from the Adlerhorst was predictable. Hitler insisted on another attempt on 4 January, promising the 12th SS *Hitler Jugend* and a fresh Volksgrenadier division. He now justified his obstinacy on the grounds that, although his armies had failed to reach the Meuse, they had stopped Eisenhower from launching an offensive against the Ruhr.

The First Army and the British XXX Corps began the counteroffensive on 3 January as planned. Collins's VII Corps, led by the 2nd and 3rd Armored Divisions, attacked between Hotton and Manhay, with Ridgway's XVIII Airborne Corps on its eastern flank. But the advance was very slow. The weather conditions had worsened with snow, ice and now fog again. Shermans kept sliding off roads. No fighter-bombers could support the advance in the bad visibility. And the German divisions, although greatly reduced, fought back fiercely.

Although the 116th Panzer-Division was forced back from Hotton, German artillery, even while withdrawing, 'continued to pour destruction' on the town. The theatre, the school, the church, the sawmill, the Fanfare Royale café, the small shops on the main street, the houses and finally the Hôtel de la Paix were smashed. The only structure undamaged in Hotton was the bandstand on an island in the Ourthe river, and its roof was riddled by shell fragments.

On 4 January, Manteuffel launched a renewed assault on Bastogne as ordered, but this time his troops came in from the north and north-east led by the 9th SS *Hohenstaufen* and the SS *Hitler Jugend* supported by two Volksgrenadier divisions. In the north near Longchamps the 502nd Parachute Infantry, which had just fought a protracted battle, received a lucky break. A German panzergrenadier from the SS *Hohenstaufen* became lost in the snow-bound landscape. Seeing a soldier standing in a foxhole with his back to him, he assumed he was German, went up and tapped him on the shoulder to find out where he was. The paratrooper, although taken by surprise, managed to knock him down and overpower him. During interrogation, it transpired that the German prisoner was a company runner, carrying all the details of the attack planned for the fol-

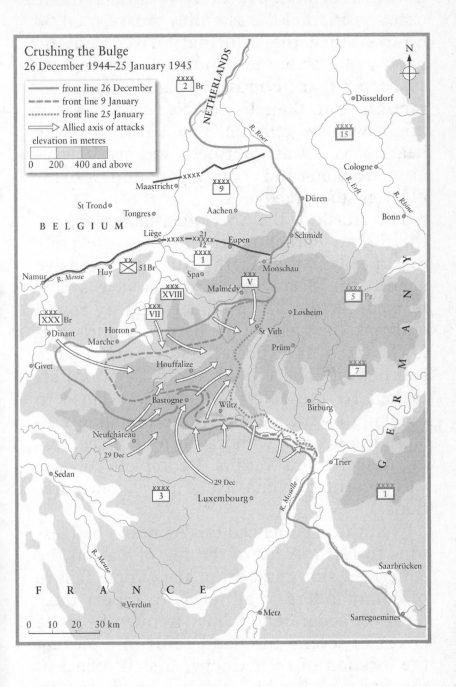

Crushing the Bulge
26 December 1944–25 January 1945

Legend:
- front line 26 December
- front line 9 January
- front line 25 January
- Allied axis of attacks

elevation in metres

| 0 | 200 | 400 and above |

N

NETHERLANDS

2 Br

Düsseldorf

R. Roer

15

Maastricht

9

Cologne

St Trond

Tongres

Aachen

Düren

R. Erft

R. Rhine

Bonn

BELGIUM

Liège

21
12

Eupen

Schmidt

Namur

R. Meuse

Huy

51Br

1

Spa

Monschau

5 Pz

Malmédy

V

Losheim

XXX Br

Dinant

XVIII

VII

Hotton

Marche

St Vith

Prüm

7

Givet

Houffalize

Bastogne

Wiltz

Birburg

GERMANY

Neufchâteau

29 Dec

29 Dec

Trier

Sedan

3

Luxembourg

1

R. Moselle

R. Meuse

F R A N C E

Saarbrücken

0   10   20   30 km

Verdun

Metz

Sarreguemines

lowing morning. He even volunteered the exact position of the assembly areas for 04.00 hours. Since the information seemed too good to be true, the regimental interrogator suspected that he must be planting disinformation, but then began to realize that it might well be genuine. The 101st Airborne headquarters was informed, and every available field artillery battalion and mortar platoon stood ready.

The attack of the SS *Hohenstaufen* against the 502nd Parachute Infantry was severely disrupted in the north. But the offensive against the Bastogne pocket, as it was now termed, hit the 327th Glider Infantry round Champs, the scene of the battle on Christmas Day, and was especially ferocious in the south-west. The 6th Armored Division, attacked by the *Hitler Jugend,* was close to breaking point; and after one battalion collapsed, a general withdrawal took place, losing Mageret and Wardin. A complete collapse was prevented by massive artillery concentrations.

Even the experienced 6th Armored had lessons to learn. A lot of the fog of war on the American side came from the simple failure of commanders at all levels to report their position accurately. 'Units frequently make errors of several thousand yards in reporting the location of their troops,' a staff officer at the division's headquarters observed. And on a more general perspective he wrote that American divisions were 'too sensitive to their flanks . . . they often do not move unless someone else is protecting their flanks when they are quite capable of furnishing the necessary protection themselves'. 'If you enter a village and you see no civilians,' another 6th Armored officer advised, 'be very very cautious. It means that they have gone to ground in their cellars expecting a battle, because they know German soldiers are around.'

Many soldiers closed their minds to the suffering of the Belgians as they focused on the priority of killing the enemy. Those who did care were marked for life by the horrors that they witnessed. Villages, the principal targets for artillery, were totally destroyed. Farms and barns blazed. Women and children, forced out into the snow by the Germans, were in many cases maimed or killed by mines or artillery from both sides, or simply gunned down by fighter-bombers because dark figures against the snow were frequently mistaken for the enemy. GIs found wounded livestock bellowing in pain, and starving dogs chewing at the flesh of lacerated cows and horses even before they were dead. Water sources were poisoned by white phosphorus. The Americans did what they could to evacuate civilians to safety, but all too often it was impossible in the middle of a battle.

West of Bastogne, the 17th Airborne Division took over from the 11th Armored Division on 3 January. The 11th Armored had advanced just ten kilometres in four days, at the cost of 661 battle casualties and fifty-four tanks. The newly arrived paratroopers appeared to fare little better in their first action. 'The 17th Airborne, which attacked this morning,' Patton wrote in his diary on 4 January, 'got a very bloody nose and reported the loss of 40% in some of its battalions. This is, of course, hysterical.'

The 17th Airborne, fighting towards Flamierge and Flamizoulle on the western edge of the Bastogne perimeter, was up against the far more experienced *Führer Begleit* and the 3rd Panzergrenadier-Division. 'We have had replacements who would flop down with the first burst of enemy fire and would not shoot even to protect others advancing,' an officer complained.

American advice came thick and fast. 'The German follows a fixed form. He sends over a barrage followed by tanks, followed by infantry. Never run, if you do you will surely get killed. Stick in your hole and let the barrage go over. Stick in your hole and let the tanks go by, then cut loose and mow the German infantry down.' 'Don't go to a white flag. Make the Germans come to you. Keep the Krauts covered.' Officers also found that their men must be trained what to do when shot in different parts of the body, so that they could look after themselves until a medic arrived. 'Each man takes care of himself until the medical men arrive. *No one* stops the fight to help another.' Yet badly wounded men left in the snow without help were unlikely to survive more than half an hour.

The 17th Airborne Division had a tank battalion manned entirely by African-American soldiers attached to it. 'Our men had great confidence in them,' a colonel reported. 'We used the tanks to protect our infantry moving forward. The tanks would come first with the doughboys riding on them and following in squad columns [behind them]. Selected men were in the last wave, tail end of the company, to knock off Jerries in snow capes. The Jerries in snow capes would let the tanks and bulk of the infantry pass, then rise up to shoot our infantry in the back, but our "tail enders" ended that.'

When they captured a position, they usually found that the ground was frozen so hard that it was impossible to dig in. The division decided that they needed to use their 155mm guns to blast shellholes on an objective or piece of ground to be occupied, so that foxholes could be prepared rapidly. With so much to learn against such hardened opponents, it was hardly surprising that the 17th Airborne had such a baptism of fire. 'The 17th has suffered a bloody nose,' 12th

Army Group noted, 'and in its first action lacks the élan of its airborne companions.' But there were also examples of outstanding heroism. Sergeant Isidore Jachman, from a Berlin Jewish family who had emigrated to the United States, seized a bazooka from another soldier who had been killed, and saved his company by fighting off two tanks. He was killed in the process and was awarded a posthumous Congressional Medal of Honor.

The 87th Infantry Division to the west was not making any better progress, having come up against a Kampfgruppe from the Panzer Lehr. There were constant complaints about soldiers being far too trigger-happy and wasting ammunition. A sergeant in the 87th Division described how he 'saw a rifleman shoot a German and then empty his gun and another clip into him although it was obvious that the first shot had done the job. A 57mm gun fired about forty rounds into a house suspected of having some Germans in it. Practically all were A[rmor] P[iercing] shells and fired into the upper floors. The Germans were in the basement and lower floor and stayed there until we attacked.'

The 87th Division, despite Remer's compliments on their fighting prowess, suffered all the usual faults of green troops. Men froze under mortar attack instead of running forward to escape it. And when soldiers were wounded, several would rush over to help them instead of leaving them to the aid men following on behind. Unused to winter warfare, the 87th and the 17th Airborne suffered many casualties from frostbite. Men were told to obtain footwear which was two sizes too big and then put on at least two pairs of socks, but it was a bit late for that once they were already in action.

Middleton was utterly dejected by the performance of the inexperienced divisions. Patton was furious: his reputation was at stake. He was even more convinced that the counter-attack should have been aimed at the eighty-kilometre base of the salient along the German frontier. He blamed Montgomery, but also Bradley who was 'all for putting new divisions in the Bastogne fight'. He was so disheartened that he wrote: 'We can still lose this war . . . the Germans are colder and hungrier than we are, but they fight better. I can never get over the stupidity of our green troops.' Patton refused to recognize that the lack of a good road network at the base of the salient, together with the terrain and the atrocious winter weather which frustrated Allied airpower, meant that his preferred option would probably have stood even less chance of rapid success.

The advance of the counter-offensive in the north fared only slightly better, even with the bulk of the German divisions switched to the Bastogne sector. There was nearly a metre of snow in the region and temperatures had dropped to minus 20 Centigrade. 'Roads were icy and tanks, despite the fact that gravel was laid, slipped off into the sides, destroying communication set-ups and slowing traffic.' The metal studs welded to the tracks for grip wore off in a very short time. In the freezing fog, artillery-spotting Cub planes could operate for only part of the day, and the fighter-bombers were grounded. The 2nd Armored Division found itself in an 'extremely heavy fight' with the remnants of the 2nd Panzer-Division. 'A lucky tree burst from an 88-mm shell knocked out between fifty and sixty of our armored infantry, the largest known number of casualties' from a single shell. But 'Trois Ponts was cleared as was Reharmont and by nightfall the line Hierlot–Amcomont–Dairmont–Bergeval was reached,' First Army noted. The 82nd Airborne Division took 500 prisoners.

Field Marshal Montgomery, who visited Hodges at 14.00, was 'greatly pleased with the progress made and kept remarking "Good show. Good show" '. He informed Hodges that two brigades of the British 53rd Division would attack at first light the next morning in the extreme west, to maintain contact with the flanks of the 2nd Armored Division. Yet the counter-attack was not proving nearly as easy as Bradley had assumed. Even 'the 2nd Armored Division of Bulldog Ernie Harmon is running into the same kind of resistance', wrote Hansen, 'finding it difficult to get an impetus in this difficult country with stern opposition'.

South of Rochefort, part of the British 6th Airborne Division advanced on Bure, which the Belgian SAS had reconnoitred four days before. The 13th (Lancashire) Battalion of the Parachute Regiment went into the attack at 13.00 hours. Heavy mortar fire from the Lehr's panzergrenadiers caused a number of casualties, but A Company made it into the village despite fire from six assault guns and automatic weapons. Panzergrenadiers supported by a Mark VI Tiger launched a counter-attack. Shermans from the Fife and Forfar Yeomanry arrived to help, but these tanks also had no control on the icy roads. The Germans were beaten off after dark, but during the night they attacked again and again, while tracer bullets set barns and farmhouses on fire.

The following day the paratroopers, under intense shellfire, managed to hold the village against another five attacks. The lone Tiger tank remained in the centre of the village, impervious to the anti-tank rounds fired by PIATs, the much less effective British counterpart to the American bazooka. Along with the German artillery, the Tiger accounted for sixteen Shermans from the Fife and Forfar. Houses shook and windows shattered every time the monster fired its 88mm main armament. Because the Tiger could control the main street with its machine guns, the wounded could not be evacuated. The firing was so intense that the only way the medical aid post was able to send more field dressings to paratroopers on the other side of the street was to tape them to rifle magazines and throw them across the road from one house to another through smashed windows. A company from the 2nd Battalion of the Oxfordshire and Buckinghamshire Light Infantry arrived to reinforce the paratroopers after so many losses. But late that evening another attack supported by two Tiger tanks forced the Ox and Bucks back from their section of the village.

On 5 January, in house-to-house combat with grenades and bayonets, the paratroopers began to clear the large village systematically. Belgians, sheltering in cellars and afraid of grenades being thrown down the stairs, cried out that they were civilians. Many villagers had sought shelter in the religious college, the Alumnat, where conditions became horrific from dysentery and people driven mad by the shelling. During the day the Panzer Lehr made more counter-attacks supported this time by four Tigers, but soon after nightfall the last German positions were eliminated. The battalion was ordered into reserve, having lost seven officers and 182 men. The 5th Battalion of the Parachute Regiment took its place and the 23rd Hussars replaced the Fife and Forfar.

The inhabitants had been forced to remain in their dark cellars while the battle raged overhead. Yvonne Louviaux, then fourteen years old, remembered her mother telling her children to squeeze up close to each other so that if they were killed, they would all die together. After three days, with only apples to eat, they were finally able to climb back to the ground floor. They found their sofa covered in blood from one of the wounded soldiers. The village itself was 70 per cent destroyed or seriously damaged, and most of the livestock killed. Telephone poles were smashed and wires and electric cables dangled dangerously on the blackened snow. Severed limbs from bodies blown apart in the fighting lay around. With a slightly sinister symmetry, two babies were born during the battle while two villagers were killed. Others died later from stepping on mines left from the battle.

One family returned to their house and found what at first sight seemed like a naked human corpse strung from the ceiling of their living room. On closer inspection they saw it was the carcass of their pig, which the Germans had started to butcher, but then evidently they had been interrupted by the arrival of the Allies. They were luckier than the majority, who had lost all their livestock, hams and preserves to German hunger, as well as their draught horses and forage to the Wehrmacht. There was so little food available that a large bull, which had survived, was butchered to feed the village. Everyone, including small children, gathered to watch.

Impatient optimism still seemed to get the better of 12th Army Group headquarters, perhaps because General Bradley could not wait for the moment when First Army and Third Army met up. This would mark the moment when the First Army would be returned to his command. But Hodges's diary keeper noted on 6 January that 'this headquarters thought laughable the suggestion made by General Siebert, G-2 of the 12th Army Group, that we should be on the alert for any "imminent German collapse" '. Even 'Lightning Joe' Collins thought the suggestion 'fairly ridiculous'. The very next day, Bradley called Patton to claim that the Germans were pulling all their armour and troops back from the Bastogne pocket. But according to Patton's staff the intelligence officers of all divisions and corps 'declare there's no evidence of this and in fact 6th Armored Division was fighting the strongest counterattack launched against them during the present campaign'.*

The advance of the British gave the Germans the excuse to begin their fighting withdrawal from round Jemelle. Sergeant G. O. Sanford of the Parachute Regiment was captured at the village of On next to Jemelle. Two panzergrenadiers led him off into a wood and shot him dead. At Forrières, when surrendering Germans emerged from a wood with their hands on their head, two British armoured cars positioned by the station opened fire and mowed them down. As a local observed: 'Undoubtedly the hard fighting in Bure had led these English to act in such a way.' Belgians expected British soldiers to be better behaved than those of other nations, and were shocked to witness lapses. One woman, on seeing a British paratrooper take a watch from the wrist of a dead German, remarked: 'they certainly did not seem to have that renowned English composure'.

In Jemelle on Monday 8 January, Sister Alexia Bruyère wrote in her diary: 'At 09.30

* This idea at 12th Army Group must have been based on speculation, since the first hint of withdrawal through Ultra intercepts did not come until late on 8 January when the 9th Panzer-Division revealed that it had pulled back to a line east of Rochefort and Marche, while the first indication of retreat around the Bastogne pocket came on 9 January.

we saw the Germans leave, keeping close to the walls, packs on their backs, heading towards the bridge at the railway station. The last ones were wearing white trousers (it is snowing), a bedsheet like a burnous and a cloth like a turban. One would have thought they were real Arabs.'

Refugees began to return with their remaining possessions piled on handcarts. One family entered their house in Rochefort and, on hearing little noises behind some heavy furniture, assumed that rats or mice had started a nest in their absence. But, on moving the furniture, they found a German soldier, hunched up in a ball and trembling with fear. He begged them not to give him up. He was an Austrian deserter. They reassured him that his unit had left, and he now could surrender to the Allies.

On the night of 5–6 January, ninety RAF Lancasters of Bomber Command flattened the town of Houffalize to block the key crossroads for German supply columns and the escape route for German forces. The place was impassable for three days.[*]

[*] General Patton, who unfortunately was drawn to writing verse, penned the following lines:

O little town of Houffalize,
How still we see thee lie;

Partly due to the bombing of Houffalize, the 116th Panzer-Division found that the roads became more and more congested during the gradual retreat, which at first averaged less than two kilometres a day. Most movements had to take place in daylight, but with the weather generally overcast until 10 January, there were few fighter-bomber attacks.

'Resistance never let up,' wrote an officer with the 83rd Infantry Division east of Manhay, 'and the brutality for which SS troops were notorious was brought home to us. A platoon of infantrymen from the 331st's 2nd Battalion became pinned down in an open field in drifting, waist-deep snow. With a hail of intense fire directed at them, they could only burrow deeper into the snow. Some were killed, and others were wounded. When the firing finally stopped, the platoon sergeant raised his head and saw two Germans approaching. They kicked each of the prostrate infantrymen, and if one groaned, he was shot

---

Above thy steep and battered streets
The aeroplanes sail by.

Yet in thy dark streets shineth
Not any Goddamned light;
The hopes and fears of all thy years
Were blown to hell last night.

in the head. After rifling the pockets of their victims, the Germans left. When darkness fell, the sergeant staggered back to safety, half frozen and half shocked out of his mind. Of 27 men in the platoon, he was the only one to come out alive. When kicked, he had played dead.'

German soldiers fought on even though many longed to be taken prisoner. 'Everyone thinks: "If only the time would come",' a German soldier called Friedl remarked, 'and then comes the officer, and you just carry out orders. That's what's tragic about the situation.' As American interrogators found from prisoners, German morale was suffering badly as the half-starved soldiers struggled to push vehicles and guns in freezing conditions, with the knowledge that the great offensive had failed. Nazi attempts to bludgeon their men into further efforts were based on orders which had been standard in Waffen-SS divisions since Normandy. 'Anyone taken prisoner without being wounded loses his honour and his dependants get no support.'

Waffen-SS prisoners were conspicuous by their rarity, either because of their determination to go down fighting, or from being shot on sight by their captors. One SS officer, however, attempted to justify his presence with unconvincing logic. He told his interrogator in a First Army cage: 'Do not get the impression that I am a coward because I have let myself become a prisoner of war. I would gladly have died a hero's death, but I thought it only fair and just to share the misfortune of my men.'

American divisions in the Third Army felt that prisoners should be treated differently according to circumstances. 'When the Germans are having success along a front,' the 6th Armored Division observed, 'prisoners taken are apt to be cocky and feel that though they were taken prisoner they just had an unlucky break. In the treatment of such PWs, they should not be fed, allowed to smoke, or given anything bordering on soft treatment until they have been questioned. On the other hand, prisoners taken when the Germans are suffering general reverses along the line are generally discouraged and disgusted with conditions in their lines and with their superiors. Many of these prisoners have voluntarily surrendered and are willing and eager to talk if well treated. If they are put at ease, allowed to sit down and smoke during questioning these men will unburden themselves, often volunteering information that has not been asked for.' This was true of both officers and ordinary soldiers.

In the case of captured SS, all depended on whether they saw themselves as Aryan supermen or whether they had been forced into the SS against their will, as was often the case with Poles and Alsatians. The latter could be treated as ordinary prisoners. 'The true "superman" requires stern treatment; it is all he has given anyone else and is what he expects. He has been in the habit of threatening physical violence and then carrying out his threat. For this reason he seems to be particularly susceptible to the threat of physical violence. It is not necessary to beat him up, but if he thinks he had better talk or else — he talks! To put it bluntly, we have found the best system is: for the humble and whipped prisoner, "A full stomach and an empty bladder"; for the arrogant and cocky, "A full bladder and an empty stomach".' The 35th Infantry Division, on the other hand, reported that the prisoners it had captured from the 1st SS Panzer-Division 'were more meek [than the volksgrenadiers], probably in anticipation of retribution', and they complained that their 'officers had withdrawn in time of danger, leaving them to hold their positions'.

The soldiers of the 28th Division did not believe in a dual approach. They objected to seeing rear-area troops giving German prisoners candy and cigarettes. Their own prisoners were all made to march back rather than ride in a truck, and they received only water until after they had been interrogated. 'Too good treatment of prisoners has a bad effect on our men. The way we handle them, our men distinctly have the idea that being a prisoner of war is not so good.' Another division was even tougher in its views. 'We have never been benefited by treating prisoners well . . . We are here to Kill Germans, not to baby them.' Some soldiers in the 30th Division exacted their own revenge when they captured Germans wearing American combat boots taken from the dead. They forced them at gunpoint to remove them and walk barefoot along the icy roads.

The US First Army noted that 'prisoners were beginning to complain of the lack of food and many told stories of long marches with heavy equipment owing to the lack of transportation'. On both the north and south sides of the salient, prisoner-of-war interrogations confirmed that German troops dreaded the air bursts from the new Pozit fuses on American artillery shells. 'The results of these new shells on German bodies and minds are very effective,' a First Army report on prisoner-of-war interrogations stated.

Around the Bastogne pocket, the fighting slackened a little after the battles of 3 and 4 January. The 5th Fallschirmjäger-Division now came under General der Panzertruppe Krüger's LVIII Panzer Corps. But when the paratroopers' commander Generalmajor Heilmann argued that it was futile to waste more lives in doomed attacks, Krüger retorted: 'If we want to win the war the 5th

Fallschirmjäger-Division has to take part in it too!'

On 6 January, Heilmann had received a secret order from Himmler which read: 'If there is any suspicion that a soldier has absented himself from his unit with a view to deserting and thus impairing the fighting strength of his unit one member of the soldier's family (wife) will be shot.' Presumably this had been prompted by a report from Brigadeführer Mohnke of the *Leibstandarte* to the SS-Reichsführer. Heilmann was sacked a few days later. Even in the more reliable 26th Volksgrenadier-Division men began to desert. 'Ten or twelve of the remnants of our company dressed in civilian clothes and hid,' a Feldwebel acknowledged in captivity.

As in all armies, it was not so much the fear of death as the fear of mutilation which preyed on minds. A German field hospital, or *Feldlazarett,* was little more than an amputation line. American doctors were horrified by the German army's tendency to cut off limbs without a moment's thought. A wounded American prisoner from the 401st Glider Infantry was appalled when taken into the operating room. 'I nearly gagged,' he wrote. 'There were half a dozen tables surrounded by doctors in white rubber aprons splattered with blood. All the tables were occupied with German wounded or men with frozen limbs. Buckets on the floor held toes, fingers and other appendages. The men on the tables had been given a local anesthetic, but were still screaming and groaning as the doctors worked.' When the buckets were left or emptied outside, local dogs soon helped themselves, as Belgians noted. The corpses of those who died under the knife were stacked outside, frozen solid, some with a coating of ice over their faces as if in a glass sarcophagus. Even those lucky enough to be evacuated to Germany had no idea of their destination or fate. 'The wounded are sent to wherever the hospital train happens to go,' a German doctor said. 'Nobody at the front knows the destination.'

American field hospitals could also be a grisly spectacle. A senior nurse with the Third Army described a ward known as the 'Chamber of Horrors', which stank of 'gore and sweat and human excretions'. She recounted a night shift, tending two soldiers who 'had been dying all day yesterday, and they were dying all night now . . . One, a private in the infantry, had lost both legs and one hand: he had a deep chest wound and his bowels were perforated by a shell fragment . . . The other patient was a corporal in a tank outfit. His spinal cord was severed and he was paralyzed from the waist down. His belly was open, and so was his chest.' Both boys were in a coma, breathing noisily. 'It's a good thing their mothers can't see them when they die,' she said.

Non-battle casualties were also mounting. In November and December losses to cold amounted to 23,000 men. Almost all were combat infantrymen, and since a division usually had 4,000 of them, this amounted to the equivalent of at least five and a half divisions. Neuropsychiatric cases, termed combat exhaustion, rose to nearly a quarter of all hospital admissions. The German army, which refused to recognize the condition, apparently suffered far fewer cases.

Combat exhaustion produced recognizable symptoms: 'nausea, crying, extreme nervousness and gastric conditions'. Some commanders felt that officer patients were returned to their unit too rapidly, because they often broke down again. The effect could also be infectious. 'When one man cracks, others will soon follow.' Yet isolation was the main problem. It was vital to get men out of their foxholes and mix with the others when not under shellfire. 'Tank fatigue' was due more to 'prolonged periods of continuous combat action'. It differed from the infantry version, even though symptoms were similar with 'upset stomach, nausea, dysentery, limpness and men crying in some cases in almost a state of hysteria'. The 2nd Armored Division blamed unhealthy eating, 'long hours of exposure' in extreme cold, as well as physical exhaustion. 'Cold C and K rations do not materially increase vitality and resistance, and in some cases cause upset stomachs.' Attempts to use captured German blowtorches to heat cans of food failed to resolve the problem. American doctors did not of course know then what the Germans had discovered after the battle of Stalingrad. The combination of stress, exhaustion, cold and malnourishment upsets the metabolism, and gravely reduces the body's capacity to absorb calories and vitamins.

'Even with hard and experienced troops, a soldier is only good for so long,' an officer with the 5th Infantry Division on Patton's right flank observed. 'I have seen some marvellous things done by some of my men and I have seen some of these men crack finally . . . Tired troops cannot do a job well. They'll go, but they lack smack. When you lack smack you start losing battles.'

On 8 January, the remnants of the 2nd and 9th Panzer-Divisions received the order to withdraw the next day. 'It is the coldest weather I've ever experienced,' a British civil affairs officer noted in his diary. 'The wind was just like a knife to the face . . . The roads are full of ditched vehicles with freezing drivers alongside them, waiting for whatever help can come.' Some people, however, thought it slightly ironic that the atrocious driving conditions greatly reduced the number of traffic accidents and deaths because the drivers were forced to proceed so carefully.

On 10 January, Generalfeldmarschall Model passed on an instruction from Hitler at the Adlerhorst. 'The Führer has ordered that I and II Panzer Corps, with the 1st, 2nd, 9th and 12th SS Panzer-Divisions, with immediate effect, are to assemble for rapid refitting behind Army Group B and placed at the disposal of Commander-in-Chief West in such a way that they no longer become involved in combat.' Army formations would once again feel angry that they would be expected to hold the line while Waffen-SS divisions were withdrawn to be rested and re-equipped.

The bitterness of defeat in the Ardennes was reflected among some German generals held prisoner in England. Having exulted in their material superiority earlier in the war, they now seemed to regard such advantages as unfair. Generalmajor Hans Bruhn, a divisional commander captured by the French in Alsace, was secretly recorded saying to his companions: 'It's the greatest mockery in the history of the world and at the same time the saddest part of it, that the flower of our manhood is being mowed down by the aircraft and the massed tanks of an army which has no real soldiers and which doesn't really want to fight.'

On Thursday 11 January, there were unmistakable signs that the Germans were pulling back. In the Houffalize–Bastogne area, their corridor was only thirteen kilometres wide and under heavy American artillery fire. The 30th Infantry Division told Ninth Army headquarters that bad visibility was allowing the Germans to escape. 'The Germans are pulling all their armor and heavy stuff entirely out of the Bulge in an orderly and leisurely withdrawal.' Also that day, the BBC announced that the broadcast on Montgomery's comments had been the product of German propaganda. The news did little to soften Bradley's feelings about his *bête noire.*

The next morning 12th Army Group received authorization to stockpile gas munitions in case the Germans resorted to chemical weapons in desperation, or on Hitler's orders. This had been prompted by a report from SHAEF to General Marshall's intelligence chief in Washington five days earlier. Major General Strong and his staff had been perturbed by five references to 'gas' found in Ultra decrypts.[*]

[*] 'We are aware of your views on this question but again wish to emphasize that this offensive is an all-out effort in which Hitler will employ any weapon. It has always been appreciated by you that Germany might initiate gas warfare to obtain a decisive result. The battle having gone badly, Hitler may regard

Friday 12 January was eventful in other ways. Göring, apparently forgiven for the disaster of Operation *Bodenplatte,* was summoned to the Führer's presence at the Adlerhorst to receive Hitler's congratulations on his fifty-second birthday. It was hardly an auspicious occasion. The date was far more important for other reasons. At 05.00 Moscow time, Marshal Ivan Konev's First Ukrainian Front attacked out of the Sandomierz bridgehead west of the River Vistula following a massive bombardment, which a panzergrenadier officer said was 'like the heavens falling down on earth'. Soviet tank armies advanced with slogans painted on their tank turrets declaring: 'Forward into the fascist lair!' and 'Revenge and death to the German occupiers!' The next day Marshal Georgy Zhukov's First Belorussian Front attacked from south of Warsaw, while two other Fronts assaulted East Prussia.

General Guderian had not exaggerated, but, like Cassandra's, his warnings had been

---

this as the moment. We should not overlook the chaos which would result among the civilian population in NW Europe on the possible employment of a gas warhead in V-1 and V-2 [missiles] . . . Would you please re-examine the matter in light of this further information and inform us of your views urgently.'

ignored. The Red Army had deployed 6.7 million men along the whole of the eastern front. He was almost speechless when he heard that Dietrich's Sixth Panzer Army, which was being withdrawn from the Ardennes, was to be transferred not to the Vistula or East Prussia but to Hungary to save the oilfields.

As soon as news of the great Soviet offensive reached 12th Army Group, Bradley immediately wanted to spread the impression that his forces' imminent victory in the Ardennes 'had enabled the Russian to attack with far greater numbers and more spectacular success than would otherwise have been possible'. He was right. There can be little doubt that the commitment and then grinding down of German forces in the Ardennes, especially the panzer divisions, had mortally weakened the Wehrmacht's capacity to defend the eastern front. But as another general in British captivity observed: 'The fear of Russia will keep Germany fighting to the bitter end.'

23
FLATTENING THE BULGE

Just as the final battle in the Ardennes commenced, the Germans threw more divisions into Operation *Nordwind*. On 5 January, after the initial attack had failed in its objectives, Himmler's Army Group *Oberrhein* finally began its supporting thrusts against the southern flank of the American VI Corps. The XIV SS Corps launched an attack across the Rhine north of Strasbourg, and two days later the Nineteenth Army advanced north from the Colmar pocket either side of the Rhône–Rhine Canal. The very survival of General Patch's VI Corps was threatened.

Devers, receiving no sympathy from Eisenhower, handed responsibility for the defence of Strasbourg to Lattre de Tassigny's First French Army, which now had to extend its front from the city to the Belfort Gap, a distance of 120 kilometres. But the point of greatest danger was round Gambsheim and Herrlisheim, where the XIV SS Corps had created a bridgehead south-east of Haguenau.

On 7 January, the 25th Panzergrenadier and the 21st Panzer-Division went into the attack. They reached the Haguenau Forest thirty kilometres north of Strasbourg, but were halted by the 14th Armored Division, Devers's last reserve. To the north in the Low Vosges, the 45th Infantry Division managed to hold back the 6th SS Mountain Division. One of the 45th Division's battalions was surrounded, and fought on for almost a week. Only two men escaped.

Hitler was still obsessed with Frederick the Great's dictum that he who throws in his last battalions wins the war. On 16 January, he sent in his final reserves, the 7th Fallschirmjäger-Division and the 10th SS Panzer-Division *Frundsberg*. Their attack along the Rhine as they tried to reach the Gambsheim bridgehead battered the inexperienced 12th Armored Division at Herrlisheim. This development provided the main subject for discussion at Eisenhower's morning briefing on 20 January. 'What gets me, Honest to God,' the Supreme Commander exclaimed, 'is that when two of their divisions are loose, we sit around and get scared.' Air Marshal Sir James Robb noted in his diary: 'The discussion which follows reveals a growing wonderment at the failure of our forces, whether divisions or corps, to achieve any real results compared to the immediate success of comparatively small German attacks.'

Faced with this unexpected advance, Devers was forced to retreat to a new line along the Rothbach, Moder and Zorn rivers. This withdrawal was well executed, and the new defensive positions held. The German offensive petered out around 25 January after General de Lattre's First Army, aided by the US XXI Corps on the northern side, began to crush the Colmar pocket, or what the Germans called Bridgehead Alsace. The American 3rd Infantry Division was supported by Cota's 28th Division, which one would have thought had suffered enough after the Hürtgen Forest and being crushed east of Bastogne. Fighting in the snow-covered forest of Riedwihr, the 3rd Infantry Division found itself under heavy counter-attacks, and Lieutenant Audie Murphy's astonishing bravery won him a Congressional Medal of Honor and a future career as a movie star in Hollywood. Once again, the Germans fought so doggedly in retreat, despite Allied superiority in aircraft and artillery, that more units from the Ardennes were diverted south. The Colmar pocket was not finally crushed until 9 February.

The 101st Airborne Division was one of the formations allocated to finish the fighting in Alsace, so its men were relieved to find that this time they were too late to take part.

Ten days before, on hearing that the 101st was to move to Alsace, Major Dick Winters had thought: 'My God, don't they have anybody else in this army to plug these gaps?' The division certainly needed a rest. During its last days at the northern end of the Bastogne pocket, Easy Company of the 506th Parachute Infantry had first been sent in to capture Foy. 'Every replacement that came into the platoon got killed in that town,' said a veteran of the company, 'and I don't know why.' The attack had started as a disaster, until the company commander was rapidly replaced. Then on 14 January, as temperatures dropped to minus 23 Centigrade and the snow deepened, the 506th advanced across open snowfields towards Noville where many of their comrades had died with Team Desobry at the very start of the battle.

Once Noville had been taken they were given another objective, the village of Rachamps just east of the route to Houffalize. Sergeant Earl Hale and Private Joseph Liebgott cornered six SS officers in a barn. They lined them up and warned them that they would shoot if they tried anything. A shell exploded outside, wounding Hale by the door, and instantly an SS officer whipped out a knife from his boot and slashed Hale's throat. Liebgott shot him dead, and then gunned down the others. A medic patched up Hale's throat. He was lucky — the oesophagus had been cut, but not the windpipe. Hale was evacuated by Jeep to Bastogne.[*]

Sergeant Robert Rader noticed an ordinary German soldier taken at Rachamps who looked as if he were grinning. An infuriated Rader raised his rifle to shoot him, but another paratrooper grabbed the barrel, shouting, 'Sarge, he has no lips or eyelids!' The German had lost them through frostbite on the eastern front. Rachamps was Easy Company's very last action in the battle for Bastogne. On 17 January, the 101st was relieved by the 17th Airborne. Packed into open trucks once again instead of aircraft, they were off to Alsace.

Resistance did not lessen in the salient, as the Fifth Panzer Army started to withdraw on 14 January towards Houffalize, which was still being bombed by the Allied air forces. The 2nd Panzer-Division and the Panzer Lehr covered the retreat in the usual German way of using assault guns and tanks with infantry to cover the withdrawal of their artil-

[*] Hale recovered, but with a crooked oesophagus. The doctor gave him a medical chit excusing him from wearing a tie. Hale was later confronted by an obsessive General Patton demanding to know why he was improperly dressed. The sergeant was able to produce his authorization, which apparently left Patton speechless.

lery regiments. Whenever American howitzers fired white phosphorus shells, it brought a 'violent enemy artillery reaction'.

Just as on the southern front, artillery pounded villages, setting houses and farms on fire. Often the shelling was so intense that German soldiers would seek shelter in the cellars, forcing the civilians aside. Pigs, horses and cows trapped in burning barns and byres stood little chance. In one village eleven people died from a single shell, which hit a stable in which twenty civilians were sheltering. Sometimes the old men, women and children could not stand the relentless shelling any longer, and would try to escape out into the snow. Mistaken for combatants, several were shot down. If those wounded were lucky, American ambulances or trucks would evacuate them to hospitals in the rear. Little, however, could be done for all those suffering from dysentery, pneumonia, diphtheria and a host of other serious ailments brought on by the filthy and freezing conditions of the last few weeks.

Moved by the fate of the luckless Belgians, American troops handed out rations, cigarettes, candy and chocolate. Only a few, brutalized by the war, went about looting and molesting women. To tell the compassionate from the brutal by outward appearances was impossible. Troops of all three nations by that stage looked like brigands, filthy, dishevelled and bearded. Villagers who had benefited earlier from American largesse were struck by the comparative poverty of British troops, who still shared what little they had. The Belgians did not much like the taste of either bully beef or British army-issue cigarettes, but were too polite to say so.

'Having visited villages recently cleared of the German Offensive,' a British civil affairs officer noted, 'it's good to see the joy of the people and their expressions of relief.' But in some places both British and American troops appalled their hosts by smashing up furniture for firewood. An officer in the 53rd Welsh Division noted that to escape the terrible cold, 'the troops have been over-enthusiastic in building up a roaring blaze in the old stone hearth, and consequently the chimney overheated, setting fire to part of the roof'. Almost every house occupied by Allied soldiers was left a squalid mess, with substantial damage. The British 6th Airborne Division appears to have provoked the greatest number of complaints.

The British XXX Corps pursued the Germans from the direction of La Roche-en-Ardenne, on the southern flank of Collins's VII Corps. 'The right wing of the 2nd Panzer-Division in the area of Nisramont had to face west,' wrote Generalmajor Lauchert. 'During this redeployment, a gap opened into which a British battalion advanced as far as Engreux.

The British attack behind the back of the defence line could only be halted by a feint attack. The divisional command post had to pull out back to Mont.' Like the American infantry, the British struggled badly in the deep snow. They were not helped by their sodden ammunition boots freezing rock hard. German jackboots were known to be more weather-resistant. The commanding officer of the 1st Gordons in the 51st Highland Division came across one of his sergeants in a wood, where he had strung up the corpse of a German soldier from a branch and had lit a fire under him. 'He was trying to thaw him out,' he wrote, 'in order to take off his boots.'

A Kampfgruppe of the 2nd Panzer-Division, with engineers, infantry, assault guns and tanks, set up a defence line in front of Houffalize. Hidden by the dark, its Panthers were able to take on American tanks at a range of 400–500 metres as they emerged from the woods because they showed up so clearly against the snow. 'Very soon an American tank burst into flames and provided such brightness that the American tanks were well lit and were easy to shoot. After a fire-fight lasting at most fifteen minutes, twenty-four American tanks went up in flames and a further ten were captured undamaged. The Germans lost only two tanks destroyed out of twenty-four.' As with most of these encounters, this account was probably both optimistic and boastful, but there can be little doubt that the Germans inflicted a number of bloody noses in the final stages of the battle.

On 15 January, the 30th Infantry Division attacking the village of Thirimont found that 'brick houses had been turned into veritable pill boxes, and heavy machineguns and other automatic weapons emplaced in them'. It required two battalions from the 120th Infantry Regiment, a tank battalion and a tank-destroyer battalion, as well as 'over 11,000 rounds of 105mm and 155mm ammunition', to take the place. The regiment suffered more than 450 casualties at the hands of the 3rd Fallschirmjäger-Division. Because of the deep snow and ice, 'ambulances couldn't get anywhere near the wounded', so the medical battalion borrowed horses and sledges from farmers to bring them back. Most of the Germans taken prisoner were suffering from frostbitten feet and could hardly walk.

Patton drove out in his Jeep to see the troops attacking Houffalize. 'At one point', he wrote, 'we came across a German machinegunner who had been killed and apparently instantly frozen as he was in a half-sitting position with his arms extended, holding a loaded belt of ammunition. I saw a lot of black objects sticking out of the snow and, on investigating, found that they were the toes of dead men.' He too was struck by the way the faces of men frozen rapidly on death turned 'a sort of claret color'. Patton regretted not having his camera with him to record this.

On 15 January, Hitler returned by train to Berlin, as Zhukov's and Konev's tank armies raced towards the line of the rivers Oder and Neisse. The industrial region of Silesia was about to be overrun. Apart from one sortie to an army headquarters on the Oder front, the Führer would never leave the capital again.

By nightfall on 15 January, both combat commands of the 2nd Armored Division had advanced to within a kilometre or so of Houffalize and consolidated for the night. Patrols were sent into the ruins of the town to discover enemy dispositions. They entered the town at 01.00 on 16 January but found little sign of the enemy. Patrols were also sent east to the River Ourthe where enemy positions had also been abandoned. 'Contact was established with Third Army patrols at 09.30 that day, marking the juncture of the First and Third Armies in the Ardennes offensive.'

The Ardennes offensive was almost at an end. A British regiment discovered that the Wehrmacht had run out of decorations for valour. Signed photographs of Generalfeldmarschall von Rundstedt were being offered in lieu. But a captured German communication to a corps headquarters stated: 'The

Division does not consider that this type of reward has any effect in encouraging the infantry to fight.'

As Eisenhower had decided, the US First Army reverted to the control of Bradley's 12th Army Group after the First and Third Armies had joined hands. This became official at midnight on 17 January. 'The situation is now restored,' Hansen recorded triumphantly. But Montgomery was not finished yet. Determined to retain control of the Ninth Army, he came up with a plan to give it priority over the proud First Army.

'At 10.30', General Simpson's diarist recorded on 15 January, 'the Field Marshal Monty [sic] arrived at our office for a conference with the C[ommanding] G[eneral] re the Ninth's taking over an additional sector. The FM tossed a bombshell. He requested the CG to prepare plans for the Ninth Army, of four Corps and 16 Divisions, to advance on Cologne and the Rhine river at the earliest practicable date . . . This would mean that the Ninth was to carry the ball for the western front drive — be the main effort, while the First Army would assume a holding mission on our south and, after the break-thru, protect the Ninth's south flank . . . 21st Army Group is now apparently considering such an operation quite seriously, and will submit our plan to SHAEF for approval.'

This was clearly a ploy by Montgomery, going behind the back of Bradley. But getting the Ninth Army to formulate its plans first was a clever move, especially since Simpson and his officers were thrilled with the idea of being given priority over the First Army, which would be forced into a subordinate role. 'That "protect the Ninth's flank" would be the greatest and most satisfying crack at the Grand Old Armie possible!' Simpson's diary recorded. 'How all here would love to see that in print!'

Montgomery believed that SHAEF had agreed with his plan, which he had shown only to Whiteley, the British deputy chief of operations. He did not know that Eisenhower considered Bradley stood a better chance of breaking through to the south, because the Germans would transfer their best formations to the north to protect the Ruhr. Above all, there was the general opposition among all American commanders, and voiced most passionately by Bradley on Tuesday 16 January, when he flew to Paris. Bradley landed at Villacoublay aerodrome, and drove to Versailles. The tensions of the last two weeks, and no doubt sleepless nights, had made him tired, but the flame of righteous indignation kept him going. Eisenhower was made to see that, after the recent row, there would be a storm of protest if Montgomery was allowed to command the main offensive with American forces under his command. It was Montgomery's own fault that political considerations and rivalries now dictated Allied strategy.

On 18 January, determined to repair fences, Churchill made a speech in the House of Commons to emphasize that 'the United States troops have done almost all the fighting and have suffered almost all the losses . . . Care must be taken in telling our proud tale not to claim for the British Army an undue share of what is undoubtedly the greatest American battle of the war and will, I believe, be regarded as an ever famous American victory.'

The same afternoon, Simpson rang Montgomery. 'I have just finished talking to Brad. He asked if it would be convenient for you to meet him here at my place [Maastricht] at 10.30 tomorrow morning.'

'I will be delighted,' Montgomery said. 'Where is Brad now?'

'He is with Courtney [Hodges].'

Simpson then rang Bradley straight away. Bradley said that he intended to get to Maastricht early so that he could talk to Simpson before Montgomery arrived. The purpose of the visit was to have a conference on 'future inter-group plans'. This presumably meant that he wanted to thwart Montgomery's arguments, which were based on the premise that 'First and Third US Armies in their present condition' would be incapable of continuing the counter-offensive in the Ardennes, which aimed to break through the Siegfried Line towards Prüm and Bonn. What Bradley said to Simpson drastically changed his previously positive attitude both to Montgomery and to his plan.

'Any future moves of the Ninth,' Simpson then wrote, 'in the light of present British publicity policy, will be [to] the greater glory of the FM himself, since he sees fit to assume all the glory and scarcely permits the mention of an Army Commander's name. Bitterness and real resentment is creeping in because of both the FM's and the British press's attitude in presenting British military accomplishments won with American blood, broadcast throughout Europe by the BBC.'

Bradley was finally getting his revenge for the way the field marshal had humiliated him on Christmas Day and afterwards. Montgomery was the one who would be sidelined once the Allied armies were across the Rhine. Bradley had said at the beginning of December that 'His forces are now relegated to a very minor and virtually unimportant role in this campaign where they are used simply to protect the flank of our giant steamroller.' Although not true then, it was about to become true now.

Montgomery was not 12th Army Group's only *bête noire*. Relations with SHAEF had continued to deteriorate. This was partly because Bradley could not forgive Eisenhower for having transferred First Army to Montgomery, and partly because Bedell Smith did not conceal his rather low opinion of Bradley's headquarters and Hodges. On 24 January, Bradley held a conference in his office after lunch, with Hodges, Patton and seven other generals. During this meeting Major General Whiteley called from SHAEF to say that several divisions would be withdrawn from his forthcoming offensive to create a strategic reserve and to strengthen Devers in Alsace.*

Bradley lost his temper and said for everyone in the room to hear: 'The reputation and the good will of the American soldiers and the American Army and its commanders are at stake. If you feel that way about it, then as far as I am concerned, you can take any goddam division and/or corps in the 12th Army Group, do with them as you see fit, and those of us that you leave back will sit on our ass until hell freezes over. I trust you do not think I am angry, but I want to impress upon you that I am goddam well incensed.' At this every officer in the room stood and clapped. Patton said in a voice loud enough to be

* The call from SHAEF in this account was said to be from Bedell Smith, but his biographer is certain that it was Major General Whiteley.

heard: 'Tell them to go to hell and all three of us [Bradley, Patton and Hodges] will resign. I will lead the procession.'

On 20 January, as the Americans approached St Vith, a German artillery officer wrote in his diary: 'The town is in ruins, but we will defend the ruins.' Attacking would not be easy with waist-deep snowdrifts. The next day he wrote: 'The noise of battle comes closer to the town . . . I'm sending back all my personal belongings. One never knows.' On 23 January, Combat Command B of the 7th Armored Division was given the honour of retaking the town which it had so bravely defended.

The fighters and fighter-bombers of the XIX Tactical Air Command and the Typhoons of 2nd Tactical Air Force continued to attack the retreating German vehicles. On 22 January XIX TAC claimed more than 1,100 motor vehicles destroyed and another 536 damaged. But such estimates were not confirmed by research later. 'The three tactical air forces claimed the destruction of a total of 413 enemy armoured vehicles,' the British official report stated. 'From a subsequent ground check carried out it appears that this figure is at least ten times too large.' The real contribution of Allied aircraft, it stated, came from 'the strafing and bombing of the supply-routes which prevented essential supplies from reaching the front'. German sources supported this conclusion. The Allied air forces 'did not play a decisive tactical part' in fighting at the front, Generalmajor von Waldenburg said later. 'The effect on the rear areas was stronger.'

On 23 January the 7th Armored Division secured St Vith. All survivors had fled, and the town was as silent as the grave. The only building of note left standing was the Büchel Tower. By 29 January the front line had been more or less restored to that of 15 December: it had taken a month and two weeks. Hansen wrote in his diary: 'The Third Army today regarded the battle of the salient as officially ended and started new attacks toward German objectives.'

In that last week of January, Bradley moved his Eagle Tac command post from Luxembourg to the provincial capital of Namur. Patton called on him to say goodbye. 'He is a good officer,' Patton wrote in his diary, 'but utterly lacks "it". Too bad.' The provincial governor was made to move out of the magnificent Palais de Namur, and Bradley established himself in vice-regal style. Simpson, visiting on 30 January, described it as 'a tremendous palace, replete with satin wall covers, velvet drapes, too many full-sized oils of the royal family, thick carpets and polished marble floors. The bedrooms, used as offices, are immense — as large as the ground floor of a good sized private home.'

For his private residence, Bradley took over the Château de Namur. It was in rather a forlorn state, so German prisoners of war were sent in to clean it up. Bradley's staff felt 'compelled to ransack the houses of collaborationists' for furniture. Even Hansen acknowledged that Eagle Tac was now being known as 'Eagle Took'. The chateau too had marble fireplaces and floors, according to Simpson, as well as large gardens and a magnificent view over the Meuse valley. Bradley insisted on having an ice-cream machine installed.

On Sunday 4 February, Montgomery was invited for a meeting and lunch. He arrived in his Rolls-Royce flying the Union Jack and escorted by outriders. According to Hansen, he made 'his customary slow, dramatic, deliberate hawk-like entrance'. Apparently he received a very cool reception from all the American officers. 'His ego, however, remained impervious to it and he joked, talked and gesticulated. He prevailed consistently and talked too loudly throughout the meal.'

In what appears to have been a deliberate snub, Bradley and Eisenhower simply left Montgomery at the table. They drove off through the rain to Bastogne to meet Patton. Soon after they had crossed the Meuse, they 'passed scarred and blackened hulks of enemy tanks as well as Shermans. There appeared remains of crashed C-47s and a lot of other abandoned impedimenta of war. Patton met us at the rear echelon headquarters of the VIII Corps in Bastogne. He consulted with Ike and Bradley in a small coal-stove room where the 101st Airborne sheltered its troops during the historic siege of the city.' The three generals then had their photographs taken together in the bombed centre of the town, climbed back into their vehicles and drove north up to Houffalize. They 'passed [numerous] Sherman tanks with scars of enemy artillery plainly imprinted on their armor'. From there, they carried on to meet General Hodges, who had moved his headquarters back to the town of Spa. It was a symbolic lap of honour which excluded the field marshal.

Belgium faced a crisis, to which SHAEF reacted slowly. Food shortages led to strikes in the mines, which in turn produced crippling coal shortages during that harsh winter. Government attempts to control rocketing prices were easily circumvented and the black market spread. In the countryside people reverted even more to barter, with much of the trade consisting of American and British troops exchanging tins of rations for fresh eggs.

An estimated 2,500 civilians had been killed in Belgium as a result of the Ardennes offensive, with another 500 non-combatants dead in the Grand Duchy of Luxembourg. It is thought that about a third had been killed by Allied air raids. If one adds in those who perished in V-weapon bombardments from at least 5,000 missiles during the whole winter from October to March, civilian casualties increase to more than 8,000 dead and missing and 23,584 wounded.

The destruction had been massive. Buildings, churches, farms, roads and railways had suffered terrible damage. So had sewers, water-pipes, telephone wires and electricity cables. Some 88,000 people were homeless. Those families returning with their few possessions on a handcart found that even houses which had not been hit by shells or bombs had no doors. Both Germans and Allies had ripped them out to provide overhead covering for foxholes and trenches. Bedding had also been seized in an attempt to provide a little warmth or camouflage. There was also a great shortage of warm clothing. A British civil affairs officer noted that a 'tremendous number of Belgian women are wearing coats made from Army blankets, and ski-suits from battledress, having just dyed them to black or brown and removed the pockets'.

In the Belgian provinces of Luxembourg and Namur, eighteen churches had been ruined and sixty-nine others badly damaged. In many cases, the shelling had also ploughed up graveyards, hurling ancient bones around.

In La Roche, which had been bombarded by both sides, 114 civilians had died and only four houses out of 639 remained habitable. The town was a mass of rubble. American bulldozers had to be called in to clear paths down the main streets. The following spring, locals noticed that swallows returning to nest became completely disorientated.

The Ardennes, which depended almost entirely on farming and forestry, had been dealt a body-blow. Few chickens were left, and some 50,000 farm animals had been killed in the fighting or taken by the Germans. The shelling had also filled trees with shards of shrapnel, reducing the value of timber and causing problems in sawmills for a long time afterwards. Only a small amount of the livestock slaughtered in the battle could be butchered for consumption. The vast majority had to be buried. Many of the surviving livestock died after drinking water from shell-holes, or other sources contaminated by rotting bodies or white phosphorus. There was also a food crisis in the Grand Duchy of Luxembourg from war-damage and because the Germans had stripped the north of the country.

One of the worst problems was how to deal with well over 100,000 mines buried by both sides, as well as booby-traps, unexploded shells and explosives abandoned all over the place. Some forty Belgians died in and around the former Bastogne perimeter after the fighting was over. In one incident ten British soldiers were maimed or badly wounded when one of their comrades stepped on a mine. The minefield must have been densely sown in a real 'devil's garden', because one after another fell victim trying to rescue the others.

Children were sent away to safe areas when the thaw came so that they would not step on a mine. But a number were hurt playing with munitions, especially when they emptied live shells to make their own fireworks. Allied troops did what they could in the short time before they were redeployed, but the main task fell upon the Belgian army, as well as volunteers and later conscripts brought in as *démineurs.* The squads dealing with unexploded shells and mines had to explode them in place. In villages and towns, they would warn the local inhabitants before the blast to open their windows, but some houses were so old that they could not be opened.

The rains which brought a rapid thaw in late January meant that carcasses and corpses, hidden by the snow, began to decompose rapidly. The stench was terrible, but the threat of disease, which might affect their own troops, prompted the American military authorities to send in army engineers with bulldozers. Moving German corpses was always dangerous as they might have been booby-trapped, so a rope had to be attached round the legs or hands, then the body towed a distance to make sure that a grenade had not been placed underneath. The Allied dead received individual graves, many of which were decorated with flowers by the local people. German bodies were simply dumped in mass pits like plague victims. Some corpses were so carbonized by phosphorus that their nationality was impossible to distinguish. Whether German or Allied, people hoped that death had come quickly for them.

24
CONCLUSIONS

The fatal crossroads at Baugnez–Malmédy had been retaken on 13 January. The next morning teams of engineers with mine detectors began to check whether SS panzergrenadiers had booby-trapped the bodies of those they had massacred. Then the Graves Registration teams and doctors began their work. The task was extremely difficult, for all the bodies were covered with at least half a metre of snow and frozen hard.

Most had multiple wounds, with bullet holes in foreheads, temples and the back of the head, presumably from when officers and panzergrenadiers went around delivering *coups de grâce.* Some were without eyes, which had probably been pecked out by crows. The empty sockets were filled with snow. A number of the dead still had their hands above their heads. The bodies were taken back to Malmédy to be defrosted in a railway building. Razors and knives had to be used to cut out pockets to retrieve personal items.

Evidence was assembled for a war crimes trial, and eventually the US Military Tribunal at Dachau sentenced seventy-three former members of the Kampfgruppe Peiper: forty-three of them to death; twenty-two to lifelong imprisonment; and eight to prison terms ranging from ten to twenty years. Another eleven were tried by a Belgian court in Liège in July 1948, where ten of them received sentences of between ten and fifteen years' hard labour. In the post-Nuremberg period of the nascent Cold War, all the death sentences handed out at Dachau were commuted, and the prisoners went home in the 1950s. Peiper was the last to be released. After serving eleven and a half years he went to live in obscurity in Traves, in the French department of Haute-Saône. Former members of the French Resistance killed him there on 13 July 1976. Peiper knew they were coming for him. Shortly before his death, he said that his former comrades would be waiting for him in Valhalla.

Fighting in the Ardennes had reached a degree of savagery unprecedented on the western front. The shooting of prisoners of war has always been a far more common practice than military historians in the past have been prepared to acknowledge, especially when writing of their own countrymen.

The Kampfgruppe Peiper's cold-blooded slaughter of prisoners in the Baugnez–Malmédy massacre was of course chilling, and its indiscriminate killing of civilians even more so. That American soldiers took revenge was hardly surprising, but it is surely shocking that a number of generals, from Bradley downwards, openly approved of the shooting of prisoners in retaliation. There are few details in the archives or in American accounts of the Chenogne massacre, where the ill-trained and badly bruised 11th Armored Division took out its rage on some sixty prisoners. Their vengeance was different from the cold-blooded executions perpetrated by the Waffen-SS at Baugnez–Malmédy, but it still reflects badly on their officers.

There were a few incidents of American soldiers killing Belgian or Luxembourg civilians, either by mistake or from suspicion that they might be fifth-columnists in an area where some of the German-speaking population still harboured sympathies for the Nazi regime. But on the whole American soldiers demonstrated great sympathy for civilians trapped in the battle, and US Army medical services did whatever they could to treat civilian casualties. The Waffen-SS and some Wehrmacht units, on the other hand, took out their anger at losing the war on innocent people. The worst, of course, were those obsessed with taking revenge on the Belgian

Resistance for its activities during the German retreat to the Siegfried Line in September. And one must not of course forget the other massacres of civilians at Noville and Bande, mainly by Sondereinheitkommando 8.

Historians, however, have often overlooked the terrible irony of twentieth-century warfare. After the bloodbath of the First World War, army commanders from western democracies were under great pressure at home to reduce their own casualties, so they relied on a massive use of artillery shells and bombs. As a result far more civilians died. White phosphorus especially was a weapon of terrible indiscrimination.

On 20 July 1945, a year to the day after the explosion of Stauffenberg's bomb at the Wolfsschanze, Generalfeldmarschall Keitel and Generaloberst Jodl were interrogated about the Ardennes offensive. Both the bombastic Keitel and the cold, calculating Jodl were fatalistic in their replies. They knew that they too would soon be facing a war crimes tribunal.

'The criticism', they said in a joint statement, 'whether it would have been better to have employed our available reserves in the East rather than in the West, we submit to the judgement of history. Whether it was a "crime" to prolong the war by this attack, we leave to the Allied courts. Our own judgement is unchanged and independent of them.' But they did acknowledge that 'with the Fifth and Sixth Panzer Armies committed in the Ardennes, the way was paved for the Russian offensive which was launched on 12 January from the Vistula bridgeheads'. Despite the reluctance of Russian historians to accept the fact, there can be no doubt that the success of the Red Army's advance from the Vistula to the Oder was in large part due to Hitler's offensive in the Ardennes.

It is impossible to assess how much Bradley's 'calculated risk' in leaving the Ardennes front so weakly defended aided the German breakthrough. In any case his deployment reflected Allied thinking at the time that the Germans were incapable of launching a strategic offensive. German misconceptions were much more serious. Not only Hitler and the OKW but most generals believed that the Americans would fall back in disorder to the Meuse and defend from there. They had not foreseen the resolute defence of the northern and southern shoulders, which cramped their movements and supply lines so disastrously on an inadequate road network in such bad weather. Also, as already mentioned, Hitler was convinced that Eisenhower would not be able to take quick decisions, because of the complications of coalition warfare.

'The promptness with which the Allies reacted did perhaps exceed our expectations,' Jodl acknowledged later. 'But above all it was the speed of our own movements which lagged far behind expectations.' Bradley had boasted with justification on Christmas Eve that 'no other army in the world could possibly have shifted forces as expertly and quickly as we have'. On the second day of the offensive, First Army moved 60,000 troops into the Ardennes in just twenty-four hours. The despised Com Z of General Lee had achieved miracles. It also managed to transport 85 per cent of ordnance stocks out of German reach. Between 17 and 26 December, 50,000 trucks and 248,000 men from quartermaster units shifted 2.8 million gallons of gasoline so that panzer spearheads could not refuel from captured dumps.

Although Hitler refused to face reality until it was far too late, German generals realized that the great offensive was doomed by the end of the first week. They may have achieved surprise, but they had failed to cause the collapse in American morale that they needed. It was German morale which began to suffer. 'Officers and men began to show more and more their loss of confidence in the German High Command,' wrote Generalmajor von Gersdorff. 'It was only the realization of the immediate danger of the homeland and its frontiers, which spurred the troops to increase their effort against an unmerciful enemy.'

Bayerlein of the Panzer Lehr despaired of the obstinacy of Hitler and the OKW after it had become obvious that German forces could not reach the Meuse. 'Every day that the troops waited and continued to hold the salient meant further losses in men and materiel which were disproportionate to the operational significance of the bulge for the German command.' He argued that the greatest mistake in the planning was to give the Sixth Panzer Army the main strength, when it was bound to face the strongest resistance. The only chance of reaching the Meuse lay with Manteuffel's Fifth Panzer Army, but even then the idea of reaching Antwerp was impossible given the balance of forces on the western front. Bayerlein described the Ardennes offensive as 'the last gasp of the collapsing Wehrmacht and the supreme command before its end'.

While undoubtedly an American triumph, the Ardennes campaign produced a political defeat for the British. Monty's disastrous press conference and the ill-considered clamour of the London press had stoked a rampant Anglophobia in the United States and especially among senior American officers in Europe. The row thwarted Churchill's hope that Field Marshal Alexander could replace Air Chief Marshal Tedder as deputy to Eisenhower. General Marshall firmly vetoed the idea because it might indicate that the British had won 'a major point in getting control of ground operations'. And as Churchill recognized, there was a much graver consequence. Montgomery would find himself sidelined once across the Rhine on the advance into Germany, and all British advice would be ignored. The country's influence in Allied councils was at an end. In fact, one cannot entirely rule out the possibility that President Eisenhower's anger at British perfidy during the Suez crisis just over eleven years later was partly conditioned by his experiences in January 1945.*

German and Allied casualties in the Ardennes fighting from 16 December 1944 to 29 January 1945 were fairly equal. Total German losses were around 80,000 dead, wounded and missing. The Americans suffered 75,482 casualties, with 8,407 killed. The British lost 1,408, of whom 200 were killed. The unfortunate 106th Infantry Division lost the most

* The rancour lasted for the rest of his life. When Cornelius Ryan asked about Montgomery some years after Suez and long after the war, Eisenhower exploded. 'He's a psychopath, don't forget that. He is such an egocentric . . . He has never made a mistake in his life.' Montgomery was trying 'to make sure that the Americans, and me in particular, had no credit, had nothing to do with this war. I just stopped communicating with him.'

men, 8,568, but many of them were prisoners of war. The 101st Airborne suffered the highest death rate with 535 killed in action.

In the Ardennes, front-line units manned entirely by African-American soldiers served for the first time in considerable numbers. Despite the fears and prejudices of many senior American officers they fought well, as the 17th Airborne testified. No fewer than nine of the field artillery battalions in VIII Corps had been black, as were four of the seven corps artillery units supporting the 106th Division. Two of them moved to Bastogne and played an important part in the defence of the perimeter. The 969th Field Artillery received the first Distinguished Unit Citation given to a black combat unit in the Second World War. There were also three tank-destroyer battalions and the 761st Tank Battalion, all with black soldiers, fighting in the Ardennes. Captain John Long, the officer commanding Company B of the 761st Tank Battalion, declared that he was fighting 'Not for God and country, but for me and my people'.

The unsung American victims of the Ardennes offensive were those captured by the enemy and condemned to spend the last months of the war in grim Stalag prison camps. Their journey to Germany was a series of long cold marches, interminable rail journeys packed into boxcars, being bombed and strafed by Allied aircraft and dogged by the debilitating squalor of dysentery.

Sergeant John Kline from the 106th Division described his ordeal in a diary. On 20 December, he and his fellow prisoners were made to march all day without food and with no water to drink. They resorted to handfuls of snow. At a little village 'the Germans made us take off our overshoes and give them to the civilians'. They saw German soldiers sitting in captured Jeeps eating what was supposed to have been their Christmas dinner. On 25 December, after German civilians threw stones at the column of prisoners of war, he wrote, 'No Christmas, except in our hearts.' Two days later they reached Koblenz in the afternoon, and were given some soup and bread from a portable kitchen. As they were marched on in groups of 500, a man in a business suit lunged into the street and hit him over the head with his briefcase. The German guard told him that the man must have been upset over the recent bombings.

As the fighting approached its end in April 1945, the Australian war correspondent Godfrey Blunden came across a group of young, half-starved American prisoners of war, presumably also from the 106th Infantry Division. He described them as having 'xylophone ribs', sunken cheeks, thin necks and 'gangling arms'. They were 'a little hysterical' in their joy at encountering fellow Anglo-Saxons. 'Some American prisoners whom I met this morning seemed to me to be the most pitiful of all I have seen,' Blunden wrote. 'They had arrived in Europe only last December, gone immediately into the front line and had received the full brunt of the German counter-offensive in the Ardennes that month. Since their capture they had been moved almost constantly from one place to another and they told stories of comrades clubbed to death by German guards merely for breaking line to grab sugar beets from fields. They were more pitiful because they were only boys drafted from nice homes in a nice country knowing nothing about Europe, not tough like Australians, or shrewd like the French or irreducibly stubborn like the English. They just didn't know what it was all about.' They at least were alive. A good number of their comrades had lacked the will to survive their imprisonment, like the original for Kurt Vonnegut's Billy Pilgrim, who acquired the '5,000 mile stare'. Reduced to blank apathy, they would not move or eat and died silently of starvation.

The surprise and ruthlessness of Hitler's Ardennes offensive had brought the terrifying brutality of the eastern front to the west. But, as with the Japanese invasion of China in 1937 and the Nazi invasion of the Soviet Union in 1941, the shock of total warfare did not achieve the universal panic and collapse expected. It provoked instead a critical mass of desperate resistance, a bloody-minded determination to fight on even when surrounded. When German formations attacked, screaming and whistling, isolated companies defended key villages against overwhelming odds. Their sacrifice bought the time needed to bring in reinforcements, and this was their vital contribution to the destruction of Hitler's dream. Perhaps the German leadership's greatest mistake in the Ardennes offensive was to have misjudged the soldiers of an army they had affected to despise.

ORDER OF BATTLE, ARDENNES OFFENSIVE

ALLIED

12th Army Group

Lieutenant General Omar N. Bradley

US First Army

Lieutenant General Courtney H. Hodges

V Corps

Major General Leonard T. Gerow

102nd Cavalry Group; 38th and 102nd Cavalry Reconnaissance Squadrons (attached)

613th Tank Destroyer Battalion

186th, 196th, 200th and 955th Field Artillery Battalions

187th Field Artillery Group (751st and 997th Field Artillery Battalions)

190th Field Artillery Group (62nd, 190th, 272nd and 268th Field Artillery Battalions)

406th Field Artillery Group (76th, 941st, 953rd and 987th Field Artillery Battalions)

1111th Engineer Combat Group (51st,

202nd, 291st and 296th Engineer Combat
Battalions)
1121st Engineer Combat Group (146th and
254th Engineer Combat Battalions)
1195th Engineer Combat Group
134th, 387th, 445th, 460th, 461st, 531st,
602nd, 639th and 863rd Anti-Aircraft Artillery Battalions

1st Infantry Division 'Big Red One'
Brigadier General Clift Andrus
16th, 18th and 26th Infantry Regiments
5th, 7th, 32nd and 33rd Field Artillery Battalions
745th Tank Battalion; 634th and 703rd Tank
Destroyer Battalions
1st Engineer Combat Battalion; 103rd Anti-
Aircraft Artillery Battalion

2nd Infantry Division 'Indianhead'
Major General Walter M. Robertson
9th, 23rd and 38th Infantry Regiments
12th, 15th, 37th and 38th Field Artillery Battalions
741st Tank Battalion; 612th and 644th Tank
Destroyer Battalions
2nd Engineer Combat Battalion; 462nd Anti-
Aircraft Artillery Battalion

9th Infantry Division 'Old Reliables'
Major General Louis A. Craig
39th, 47th and 60th Infantry Regiments

26th, 34th, 60th and 84th Field Artillery Battalions
15th Engineer Combat Battalion; 38th Cavalry Reconnaissance Squadron
746th Tank Battalion; 376th and 413th Anti-Aircraft Artillery Battalions

78th Infantry Division 'Lightning'
Major General Edwin P. Parker Jr
309th, 310th and 311th Infantry Regiments
307th, 308th, 309th and 903rd Field Artillery Battalions
709th Tank Battalion; 628th and 893rd Tank Destroyer Battalions
303rd Engineer Combat Battalion; 552nd Anti-Aircraft Artillery Battalion
Combat Command R, 5th Armored Division (attached); 2nd Ranger Battalion (attached)

99th Infantry Division 'Checkerboard'
Major General Walter E. Lauer
393rd, 394th and 395th Infantry Regiments
370th, 371st, 372nd and 924th Field Artillery Battalions
324th Engineer Combat Battalion; 801st Tank Destroyer Battalion
535th Anti-Aircraft Artillery Battalion

VII Corps
Major General Joseph Lawton Collins
4th Cavalry Group, Mechanized; 29th Infantry Regiment; 740th Tank Battalion

509th Parachute Infantry Battalion; 298th Engineer Combat Battalion

18th Field Artillery Group (188th, 666th and 981st Field Artillery Battalions)

142nd Field Artillery Group (195th and 266th Field Artillery Battalions)

188th Field Artillery Group (172nd, 951st and 980th Field Artillery Battalions)

18th, 83rd, 87th, 183rd, 193rd, 957th and 991st Field Artillery Battalions

Two French Light Infantry Battalions

2nd Armored Division 'Hell on Wheels'

Major General Ernest N. Harmon

CCA, CCB and CCR; 41st Armored Infantry Regiment; 66th and 67th Armored Regiments

14th, 78th and 92nd Armored Field Artillery Battalions

17th Armored Engineer Battalion; 82nd Armored Reconnaissance Battalion

702nd Tank Destroyer Battalion; 195th Anti-Aircraft Artillery Battalion

Elements of 738th Tank Battalion (special — mine clearing) attached

3rd Armored Division 'Spearhead'

Major General Maurice Rose

CCA, CCB and CCR; 36th Armored Infantry Regiment; 32nd and 33rd Armored Regiments

54th, 67th and 391st Armored Field Artillery

Battalions

23rd Armored Engineer Battalion; 83rd Reconnaissance Squadron

643rd and 703rd Tank Destroyer Battalions; 486th Anti-Aircraft Artillery Battalion

83rd Infantry Division 'Ohio'
Major General Robert C. Macon
329th, 330th and 331st Infantry Regiments
322nd, 323rd, 324th and 908th Field Artillery Battalions
308th Engineer Combat Battalion; 453rd Anti-Aircraft Artillery Battalion
774th Tank Battalion; 772nd Tank Destroyer Battalion

84th Infantry Division 'Railsplitters'
Brigadier General Alexander R. Bolling
333rd, 334th and 335th Infantry Regiments
325th, 326th, 327th and 909th Field Artillery Battalions
309th Engineer Combat Battalion
701st Tank Battalion, replaced by 771st Tank Battalion on 20 December
638th Tank Destroyer Battalion; 557th Anti-Aircraft Artillery Battalion

XVIII Airborne Corps
Major General Matthew B. Ridgway
14th Cavalry Group, Mechanized
254th, 275th, 400th and 460th Field Artillery Battalions

79th Field Artillery Group (153rd, 551st and
552nd Field Artillery Battalions)
179th Field Artillery Group (259th and
965th Field Artillery Battalions)
211th Field Artillery Group (240th and
264th Field Artillery Battalions)
401st Field Artillery Group (187th and 809th
Field Artillery Battalions)

7th Armored Division 'Lucky Seventh'
Brigadier General Robert W. Hasbrouck
CCA, CCB and CCR; 23rd, 38th and 48th
Armored Infantry Battalions
17th, 31st and 40th Tank Battalions; 87th
Reconnaissance Squadron
434th, 440th and 489th Armored Field Artillery Battalions
33rd Armored Engineer Battalion; 814th
Tank Destroyer Battalion
203rd Anti-Aircraft Artillery Battalion
820th Tank Destroyer Battalion (25–30 December)

30th Infantry Division 'Old Hickory'
Major General Leland S. Hobbs
117th, 119th and 120th Infantry Regiments
113th, 118th, 197th and 230th Field Artillery Battalions
517th Parachute Infantry Regiment attached;
105th Engineer Combat Battalion
743rd Tank Battalion; 823rd Tank Destroyer
Battalion

110th, 431st and 448th Anti-Aircraft Artillery Battalions

75th Infantry Division
Major General Fay B. Prickett
289th, 290th and 291st Infantry Regiments
730th, 897th, 898th and 899th Field Artillery Battalions
275th Engineer Combat Battalion; 440th Anti-Aircraft Artillery Battalion
750th Tank Battalion; 629th and 772nd Tank Destroyer Battalions

82nd Airborne Division 'All American'
Major General James M. Gavin
504th, 505th, 507th and 508th Parachute Infantry Regiments
325th Glider Infantry Regiment; 307th Airborne Engineer Battalion
319th and 320th Glider Field Artillery Battalions
376th and 456th Parachute Field Artillery Battalions; 80th Anti-Aircraft Artillery Battalion
551st Parachute Infantry Battalion; 628th Tank Destroyer Battalion (2–11 January)
740th Tank Battalion (30 December–11 January)
643rd Tank Destroyer Battalion (4–5 January)

106th Infantry Division 'Golden Lions'

Major General Alan W. Jones

422nd, 423rd and 424th Infantry Regiments

589th, 590th, 591st and 592nd Field Artillery Battalions

81st Engineer Combat Battalion; 820th Tank Destroyer Battalion

634th Anti-Aircraft Artillery Battalion (8–18 December)

440th Anti-Aircraft Artillery Battalion (8 December–4 January)

563rd Anti-Aircraft Artillery Battalion (9–18 December)

101st Airborne Division 'Screaming Eagles'

Brigadier General Anthony C. McAuliffe (Major General Maxwell D. Taylor)

501st, 502nd and 506th Parachute Infantry Regiments

327th Glider Infantry Regiment; 1st Battalion, 401st Glider Infantry

321st and 907th Glider Field Artillery Battalions

377th and 463rd Parachute Field Artillery Battalion

326th Airborne Engineer Battalion; 705th Tank Destroyer Battalion

81st Airborne Anti-Aircraft Artillery Battalion

US Third Army
Lieutenant General George S. Patton Jr
109th, 115th, 217th and 777th Anti-Aircraft
  Gun Battalions
456th, 465th, 550th and 565th Anti-Aircraft
  Artillery Battalions
280th Engineer Combat Battalion (later assigned to Ninth Army)

III Corps
Major General John Millikin
6th Cavalry Group, Mechanized; 179th,
  274th, 776th and 777th Field Artillery Battalions
193rd Field Artillery Group (177th, 253rd,
  696th, 776th and 949th Field Artillery Battalions)
203rd Field Artillery Group (278th, 742nd,
  762nd Field Artillery Battalions)
1137th Engineer Combat Group (145th,
  188th and 249th Engineer Combat Battalions)
183rd and 243rd Engineer Combat Battalions; 467th and 468th Anti-Aircraft Artillery Battalions

4th Armored Division
Major General Hugh J. Gaffey
CCA, CCB and CCR; 8th, 35th and 37th
  Tank Battalions
10th, 51st and 53rd Armored Infantry Bat-
  talions

691

22nd, 66th and 94th Armored Field Artillery Battalions

24th Armored Engineer Battalion; 25th Cavalry Reconnaissance Squadron

489th Anti-Aircraft Artillery Battalion; 704th Tank Destroyer Battalion

6th Armored Division 'Super Sixth'

Major General Robert W. Grow

CCA, CCB and CCR; 15th, 68th and 69th Tank Battalions

9th, 44th and 50th Armored Infantry Battalions

128th, 212th and 231st Armored Field Artillery Battalions

25th Armored Engineer Battalion; 86th Cavalry Reconnaissance Squadron

691st Tank Destroyer Battalion; 777th Anti-Aircraft Artillery Battalion

26th Infantry Division 'Yankee'

Major General Willard S. Paul

101st, 104th and 328th Infantry Regiments

101st, 102nd, 180th and 263rd Field Artillery Battalions

101st Engineer Combat Battalion; 735th Tank Battalion

818th Tank Destroyer Battalion; 390th Anti-Aircraft Artillery Battalion

35th Infantry Division 'Santa Fe'

Major General Paul W. Baade

134th, 137th and 320th Infantry Regiments
127th, 161st, 216th and 219th Field Artillery Battalions
60th Engineer Combat Battalion; 654th Tank Destroyer Battalion
448th Anti-Aircraft Artillery Battalion

90th Infantry Division 'Tough 'Ombres'
Major General James A. Van Fleet
357th, 358th and 359th Infantry Regiments
343rd, 344th, 345th and 915th Field Artillery Battalions
315th Engineer Combat Battalion; 773rd Tank Destroyer Battalion
774th Tank Destroyer Battalion (21 December–6 January)
537th Anti-Aircraft Artillery Battalion

VIII Corps
Major General Troy H. Middleton
174th Field Artillery Group (965th, 969th and 700th Field Artillery Battalions)
333rd Field Artillery Group (333rd and 771st Field Artillery Battalions)
402nd Field Artillery Group (559th, 561st and 740th Field Artillery Battalions)
422nd Field Artillery Group (81st and 174th Field Artillery Battalions)
687th Field Artillery Battalion; 178th and 249th Engineer Combat Battalions
1102nd Engineer Group (341st Engineer General Service Regiment)

693

1107th Engineer Combat Group (159th and 168th Engineer Combat Battalions)

1128th Engineer Combat Group (35th, 44th and 202nd Engineer Combat Battalions)

French Light Infantry (six Light Infantry Battalions from Metz region)

467th, 635th and 778th Anti-Aircraft Artillery Battalions

9th Armored Division 'Phantom'

Major General John W. Leonard

CCA, CCB and CCR; 27th, 52nd and 60th Armored Infantry Battalions

2nd, 14th and 19th Tank Battalions; 3rd, 16th and 73rd Armored Field Artillery Battalions

9th Armored Engineer Battalion; 89th Cavalry Squadron

811th Tank Destroyer Battalion; 482nd Anti-Aircraft Artillery Battalion

11th Armored Division 'Thunderbolt'

Brigadier General Charles S. Kilburn

CCA, CCB and CCR; 21st, 55th and 63rd Armored Infantry Battalions

22nd, 41st and 42nd Tank Battalions

490th, 491st and 492nd Armored Field Artillery Battalions

56th Armored Engineer Battalion; 602nd Tank Destroyer Battalion

41st Cavalry Squadron; 575th Anti-Aircraft Artillery Battalion

17th Airborne Division 'Golden Talons'
Major General William M. Miley
507th and 513th Parachute Infantry Regiments; 193rd and 194th Glider Infantry Regiments
680th and 681st Glider Field Artillery Battalions; 466th Parachute Field Artillery Battalion
139th Airborne Engineer Battalion; 155th Airborne Anti-Aircraft Artillery Battalion

28th Infantry Division 'Keystone'
Major General Norman D. Cota
109th, 110th and 112th Infantry Regiments
107th, 108th, 109th and 229th Field Artillery Battalions
103rd Engineer Combat Battalion; 447th Anti-Aircraft Artillery Battalion
707th Tank Battalion; 602nd and 630th Tank Destroyer Battalions

87th Infantry Division 'Golden Acorn'
Brigadier General Frank L. Culin Jr
345th, 346th and 347th Infantry Regiments
334th, 335th, 336th and 912th Field Artillery Battalions; 312th Engineer Combat Battalion
761st Tank Battalion; 549th Anti-Aircraft Artillery Battalion
610th Tank Destroyer Battalion (14–22 December)
691st Tank Destroyer Battalion (22–24 De-

cember and 8–26 January)
704th Tank Destroyer Battalion (17–19 December)

XII Corps
Major General Manton S. Eddy
2nd Cavalry Group, Mechanized
161st, 244th, 277th, 334th, 336th and 736th Field Artillery Battalions
177th Field Artillery Group (215th, 255th and 775th Field Artillery Battalions)
182nd Field Artillery Group (802nd, 945th and 974th Field Artillery Battalions)
183rd Field Artillery Group (695th and 776th Field Artillery Battalions)
404th Field Artillery Group (273rd, 512th and 752nd Field Artillery Battalions)

4th Infantry Division 'Ivy'
Major General Raymond O. Barton
8th, 12th and 22nd Infantry Regiments; 20th, 29th, 42nd and 44th Field Artillery Battalions
4th Engineer Combat Battalion; 70th Tank Battalion
802nd and 803rd Tank Destroyer Battalions; 377th Anti-Aircraft Artillery Battalion

5th Infantry Division 'Red Diamond'
Major General Stafford L. Irwin
2nd, 10th and 11th Infantry Regiments; 19th, 21st, 46th and 50th Field Artillery

Battalions

7th Engineer Combat Battalion; 737th Tank Battalion; 449th Anti-Aircraft Artillery Battalion

654th Tank Destroyer Battalion (22–25 December); 803rd Tank Destroyer Battalion (from 25 December)

807th Tank Destroyer Battalion (17–21 December); 818th Tank Destroyer Battalion (13 July–20 December)

10th Armored Division 'Tiger'

Major General William H. H. Morris Jr

CCA, CCB and CCR; 20th, 54th and 61st Armored Infantry Battalions

3rd, 11th and 21st Tank Battalions; 609th Tank Destroyer Battalion

419th, 420th and 423rd Armored Field Artillery Battalions

55th Armored Engineer Battalion; 90th Cavalry Reconnaissance Squadron

796th Anti-Aircraft Artillery Battalion

80th Infantry Division 'Blue Ridge'

Major General Horace L. McBride

317th, 318th and 319th Infantry Regiments

313th, 314th, 315th and 905th Field Artillery Battalions; 702nd Tank Battalion

305th Engineer Combat Battalion; 633rd Anti-Aircraft Artillery Battalion

610th Tank Destroyer Battalion (23 November–6 December and 21 December–

28 January)
808th Tank Destroyer Battalion (25 September–21 December)

XXX Corps
Lieutenant General Sir Brian Horrocks
2nd Household Cavalry Regiment; 11th Hussars
4th and 5th Regiments, Royal Horse Artillery; 27th Light Anti-Aircraft Regiment, Royal Artillery
7th, 64th and 84th Medium Regiments, Royal Artillery

6th Airborne Division
Major General Eric Bols
6th Airborne Armoured Reconnaissance Regiment, Royal Armoured Corps
249th Airborne Field Company, Royal Engineers; 3rd and 591st Parachute Squadrons, Royal Engineers; 3rd and 9th Airborne Squadrons, Royal Engineers; 53rd Light Regiment, Royal Artillery; 3rd and 4th Airlanding Anti-Tank Batteries, Royal Artillery
22nd Independent Parachute Company
3rd Parachute Brigade (8th Parachute Battalion; 9th Parachute Battalion; 1st Canadian Parachute Battalion)
5th Parachute Brigade (7th Parachute Battalion; 12th Parachute Battalion; 13th Parachute Battalion)
6th Airlanding Brigade (12th Battalion, Dev-

onshire Regiment; 2nd Battalion, Oxfordshire and Buckinghamshire Light Infantry;
1st Battalion, Royal Ulster Rifles)

51st (Highland) Infantry Division
Major General G. T. G. Rennie
2nd Derbyshire Yeomanry
126th, 127th and 128th Field Regiments,
   Royal Artillery; 61st Anti-Tank Regiment,
   Royal Artillery; 40th Light Anti-Aircraft
   Regiment, Royal Artillery
274th, 275th and 276th Field Companies,
   Royal Engineers
1/7 Machine-Gun Battalion, Middlesex Regiment
152nd Infantry Brigade (2nd Battalion, Seaforth Highlanders; 5th Battalion, Seaforth
   Highlanders; 5th Battalion, Queen's Own
   Cameron Highlanders)
153rd Infantry Brigade (5th Battalion, Black
   Watch; 1st Battalion, Gordon Highlanders;
   5/7th Battalion, Gordon Highlanders)
154th Infantry Brigade (1st Battalion, Black
   Watch; 7th Battalion, Black Watch; 7th Battalion, Argyll and Sutherland Highlanders)

53rd (Welsh) Infantry Division
Major General R. K. Ross
81st, 83rd and 133rd Field Regiments, Royal
   Artillery
53rd Reconnaissance Regiment, Royal Armoured Corps

71st Anti-Tank Regiment, Royal Artillery; 25th Light Anti-Aircraft Regiment, Royal Artillery

244th, 282nd and 555th Field Companies, Royal Engineers

71st Infantry Brigade (1st Battalion, Oxford and Buckinghamshire Light Infantry; 1st Battalion, Highland Light Infantry; 4th Battalion, Royal Welch Fusiliers)

158th Infantry Brigade (7th Battalion, Royal Welch Fusiliers; 1/5th Battalion, Welch Regiment; 1st Battalion, The East Lancashire Regiment)

160th Infantry Brigade (2nd Battalion, Monmouthshire Regiment; 1/5th Battalion, Welch Regiment; 6th Battalion, Royal Welch Fusiliers)

29th Armoured Brigade

Brigadier C. B. Harvey

23rd Hussars; 3rd Royal Tank Regiment; 2nd Fife and Forfar Yeomanry; 8th Battalion, Rifle Brigade

33rd Armoured Brigade

Brigadier H. B. Scott

144th Regiment, Royal Armoured Corps; 1st Northamptonshire Yeomanry; 1st East Riding Yeomanry

34th Army Tank Brigade

Brigadier W. S. Clarke

9th Royal Tank Regiment; 107th Regiment, Royal Armoured Corps; 147th Regiment, Royal Armoured Corps

Corps Reserve

Guards Armoured Division

50th (Northumbrian) Infantry Division

WEHRMACHT

Army Group B

Generalfeldmarschall Walter Model

Fifth Panzer Army

General der Panzertruppe Hasso von Manteuffel

19th Flak-Brigade; 207th and 600th Engineer Battalions

653rd Heavy Panzerjäger Battalion; 669th Ost (East) Battalion

638th, 1094th and 1095th Heavy Artillery Batteries

25th/975th Fortress Artillery Battery; 1099th, 1119th and 1121st Heavy Mortar Batteries

XLVII Panzer Corps

General der Panzertruppe Heinrich Freiherr von Lüttwitz

766th Volksartillerie Corps; 15th Volkswerfer-Brigade; 182nd Flak-Regiment

701

2nd Panzer-Division
Oberst Meinrad von Lauchert
3rd Panzer-Regiment; 2nd and 304th Panzergrenadier-Regiments
74th Artillery Regiment; 2nd Reconnaissance Battalion
38th Anti-Tank Battalion; 38th Engineer Battalion; 273rd Flak Battalion

9th Panzer-Division
Generalmajor Harald Freiherr von Elverfeldt
33rd Panzer-Regiment; 10th and 11th Panzergrenadier-Regiments
102nd Artillery Regiment; 9th Reconnaissance Battalion
50th Anti-Tank Battalion; 86th Engineer Battalion; 287th Flak Battalion
301st Heavy Panzer Battalion (attached)

Panzer Lehr Division
Generalleutnant Fritz Bayerlein
130th Panzer-Regiment; 901st and 902nd Panzergrenadier-Regiments
130th Artillery Regiment; 130th Reconnaissance Battalion
130th Anti-Tank Battalion; 130th Engineer Battalion; 311th Flak Battalion
559th Anti-Tank Battalion (attached); 243rd Assault Gun Brigade (attached)

26th Volksgrenadier-Division
Generalmajor Heinz Kokott
39th Fusilier Regiment; 77th and 78th Volksgrenadier-Regiments; 26th Artillery Regiment;
26th Reconnaissance Battalion; 26th Anti-Tank Battalion; 26th Engineer Battalion

Führer Begleit Brigade
Oberst Otto Remer
102nd Panzer Battalion; 100th Panzer-grenadier-Regiment; 120th Artillery Regiment
120th Reconnaissance Battalion; 120th Anti-Tank Battalion; 120th Engineer Battalion
828th Grenadier Battalion; 673rd Flak-Regiment

LXVI Corps
General der Artillerie Walter Lucht
16th Volkswerfer-Brigade (86th and 87th Werfer-Regiments)
244th Assault Gun Brigade; 460th Heavy Artillery Battalion

18th Volksgrenadier-Division
Oberst Günther Hoffmann-Schönborn
293rd, 294th and 295th Volksgrenadier-Regiments; 1818th Artillery Regiment
1818th Anti-Tank Battalion; 1818th Engineer Battalion

62nd Volksgrenadier-Division

Oberst Friedrich Kittel

164th, 190th and 193rd Volksgrenadier-Regiments; 162nd Artillery Regiment

162nd Anti-Tank Battalion; 162nd Engineer Battalion

LVIII Panzer Corps

General der Panzertruppe Walter Krüger

401st Volksartillerie Corps; 7th Volkswerfer-Brigade (84th and 85th Werfer-Regiments)

1st Flak-Regiment

116th Panzer-Division

Generalmajor Siegfried von Waldenburg

16th Panzer-Regiment; 60th and 156th Panzergrenadier-Regiments

146th Artillery Regiment; 146th Reconnaissance Battalion; 226th Anti-Tank Battalion

675th Engineer Battalion; 281st Flak Battalion

560th Volksgrenadier-Division

Oberst Rudolf Langhauser

1128th, 1129th and 1130th Volksgrenadier-Regiments; 1560th Artillery Regiment

1560th Anti-Tank Battalion; 1560th Engineer Battalion

XXXIX Panzer Corps

Generalleutnant Karl Decker

167th Volksgrenadier-Division
Generalleutnant Hans-Kurt Höcker
331st, 339th and 387th Volksgrenadier-
  Regiments; 167th Artillery Regiment
167th Anti-Tank Battalion; 167th Engineer
  Battalion

Sixth Panzer Army
SS-Oberstgruppenführer Josef Dietrich
506th Heavy Panzer Battalion; 683rd Heavy
  Anti-Tank Battalion
217th Assault Panzer Battalion; 394th, 667th
  and 902nd Assault Gun Battalions
741st Anti-Tank Battalion; 1098th, 1110th
  and 1120th Heavy Howitzer Batteries
428th Heavy Mortar Battery; 2nd Flak-
  Division (41st and 43rd Regiments)
Kampfgruppe Heydte

I SS Panzer Corps
SS-Gruppenführer Hermann Priess
14th, 51st, 53rd and 54th Werfer-Regiments;
  501st SS Artillery Battalion
388th Volksartillerie Corps; 402nd Volksartillerie Corps

*1st SS Panzer-Division Leibstandarte Adolf
Hitler*
SS-Brigadeführer Wilhelm Mohnke
1st SS Panzer-Regiment; 1st and 2nd SS
  Panzergrenadier-Regiments
1st SS Artillery Regiment; 1st SS Reconnais-

sance Battalion; 1st SS Anti-Tank Battalion
1st SS Engineer Battalion; 1st SS Flak Battalion; 501st SS Heavy Panzer Battalion (attached); 84th Luftwaffe Flak Battalion (attached)

3rd Fallschirmjäger-Division
Generalmajor Walther Wadehn
5th, 8th and 9th Fallschirmjäger-Regiments; 3rd Artillery Regiment;
3rd Reconnaissance Battalion; 3rd Anti-Tank Battalion; 3rd Engineer Battalion

12th SS Panzer-Division Hitler Jugend
SS-Standartenführer Hugo Kraas
12th SS Panzer-Regiment; 25th and 26th SS Panzergrenadier-Regiments
12th SS Artillery Regiment; 12th SS Reconnaissance Battalion
12th SS Anti-Tank Battalion; 12th SS Engineer Battalion; 12th SS Flak Battalion
560th Heavy Anti-Tank Battalion (attached)

12th Volksgrenadier-Division
Generalmajor Gerhard Engel
27th Fusilier Regiment; 48th and 89th Volksgrenadier-Regiments; 12th Fusilier Battalion
12th Artillery Regiment; 12th Anti-Tank Battalion; 12th Engineer Battalion

277th Volksgrenadier-Division
Oberst Wilhelm Viebig
289th, 990th and 991st Volksgrenadier-
  Regiments; 277th Artillery Regiment
277th Anti-Tank Battalion; 277th Engineer
  Battalion

150th Panzer-Brigade
SS-Obersturmbannführer Otto Skorzeny
Two Panzer companies; two Panzergrenadier
  companies; two anti-tank companies
A heavy mortar battalion (two batteries);
  600th SS Parachute Battalion Kampfgruppe 200

II SS Panzer Corps
SS-Obergruppenführer Willi Bittrich
410th Volksartillerie Corps; 502nd SS Heavy
  Artillery Battalion

2nd SS Panzer-Division Das Reich
SS-Brigadeführer Heinz Lammerding
2nd SS Panzer-Regiment; 3rd and 4th SS
  Panzergrenadier-Regiments; 2nd SS Artillery Regiment; 2nd SS Reconnaissance Battalion; 2nd SS Engineer Battalion; 2nd SS
  Flak Battalion

9th SS Panzer-Division Hohenstaufen
SS-Oberführer Sylvester Stadler
9th SS Panzer-Regiment; 19th and 20th SS
  Panzergrenadier-Regiments

9th SS Artillery Regiment; 9th SS Reconnaissance Battalion; 9th SS Anti-Tank Battalion

9th SS Engineer Battalion; 9th SS Flak Battalion; 519th Heavy Anti-Tank Battalion (attached)

LXVII Corps
Generalleutnant Otto Hitzfeld
17th Volkswerfer-Brigade (88th and 89th Werfer-Regiments)
405th Volksartillerie Corps; 1001st Heavy Assault Gun Company

3rd Panzergrenadier-Division
Generalmajor Walter Denkert
8th and 29th Panzergrenadier-Regiments; 103rd Panzer Battalion; 3rd Artillery Regiment
103rd Reconnaissance Battalion; 3rd Anti-Tank Battalion; 3rd Engineer Battalion 3rd Flak Battalion

246th Volksgrenadier-Division
Oberst Peter Körte
352nd, 404th and 689th Volksgrenadier-Regiments; 246th Artillery Regiment
246th Anti-Tank Battalion; 246th Engineer Battalion

272nd Volksgrenadier-Division
Generalmajor Eugen König
980th, 981st and 982nd Volksgrenadier-
Regiments; 272nd Artillery Regiment
272nd Anti-Tank Battalion; 272nd Engineer
Battalion

326th Volksgrenadier-Division
751st, 752nd and 753rd Volksgrenadier-
Regiments; 326th Artillery Regiment
326th Anti-Tank Battalion; 326th Engineer
Battalion

Seventh Army
General der Panzertruppe Erich Brandenberger
657th and 668th Heavy Anti-Tank Battalions;
501st Fortress Anti-Tank Battalion
47th Engineer Battalion; 1092nd, 1093rd,
1124th and 1125th Heavy Howitzer Batteries
660th Heavy Artillery Battery; 1029th,
1039th and 1122nd Heavy Mortar Batteries
999th Penal Battalion; 44th Machine-Gun
Battalion; 15th Flak-Regiment

LIII Corps
General der Kavallerie Edwin von Rothkirch

9th Volksgrenadier-Division
Oberst Werner Kolb
36th, 57th and 116th Volksgrenadier-Regiments; 9th Artillery Regiment
9th Anti-Tank Battalion; 9th Engineer Battalion

15th Panzergrenadier-Division
Oberst Hans Joachim Deckert
104th and 115th Panzergrenadier-Regiments; 115th Panzer Battalion; 115th Artillery Regiment
115th Reconnaissance Battalion; 33rd Anti-Tank Battalion; 33rd Engineer Battalion
33rd Flak Battalion

Führer Grenadier Brigade
Oberst Hans-Joachim Kahler
99th Panzergrenadier-Regiment; 101st Panzer Battalion; 911th Assault Gun Brigade
124th Anti-Tank Battalion; 124th Engineer Battalion; 124th Flak Battalion
124th Artillery Regiment

LXXX Corps
General der Infanterie Franz Beyer
408th Volksartillerie Corps; 8th Volkswerfer-Brigade; 2nd and *Lehr* Werfer-Regiments

212th Volksgrenadier-Division
Generalmajor Franz Sensfuss
316th, 320th and 423rd Volksgrenadier-

Regiments; 212th Artillery Regiment
212th Anti-Tank Battalion; 212th Engineer
Battalion

276th Volksgrenadier-Division
Generalmajor Kurt Möhring (later Oberst
Hugo Dempwolff)
986th, 987th and 988th Volksgrenadier-
Regiments; 276th Artillery Regiment;
276th Anti-Tank Battalion; 276th Engineer
Battalion

340th Volksgrenadier-Division
Oberst Theodor Tolsdorff
694th, 695th and 696th Volksgrenadier-
Regiments; 340th Artillery Regiment
340th Anti-Tank Battalion; 340th Engineer
Battalion

LXXXV Corps
General der Infanterie Baptist Kniess
406th Volksartillerie Corps; 18th Volkswerfer-
Brigade (21st and 22nd Werfer-Regiments)

5th Fallschirmjäger-Division
Generalmajor Ludwig Heilmann
13th, 14th and 15th Fallschirmjäger-
Regiments; 5th Artillery Regiment; 5th
Reconnaissance Battalion; 5th Engineer
Battalion; 5th Flak Battalion; 11th Assault
Gun Brigade

711

352nd Volksgrenadier-Division
Oberst Erich-Otto Schmidt
914th, 915th and 916th Volksgrenadier-Regiments; 352nd Artillery Regiment; 352nd Anti-Tank Battalion; 352nd Engineer Battalion

79th Volksgrenadier-Division
Oberst Alois Weber
208th, 212th and 226th Volksgrenadier-Regiments; 179th Artillery Regiment; 179th Anti-Tank Battalion; 179th Engineer Battalion

NOTES

ABBREVIATIONS

BA-MA   Bundesarchiv-Militärarchiv, Freiburg-im-Breisgau

BfZ-SS   Bibliothek für Zeitgeschichte, Sammlung Sterz, Stuttgart

CARL   Combined Arms Research Library, Fort Leavenworth, KS

CBHD   Chester B. Hansen Diaries, Chester B. Hansen Collection, Box 5, USAMHI

CBMP   Charles B. MacDonald Papers, USAMHI

CEOH   US Army Corps of Engineers, Office of History, Fort Belvoir, VA

CMH   Center of Military History, Fort McNair, Washington, DC

CMH *Ardennes*   Center of Military History, Hugh M. Cole, *United States Army in World War II: The European Theater of Operations: The Ardennes: Battle of the Bulge,* Washington, DC, 1988

CMH *Medical*   Center of Military History, Graham A. Cosmas and Albert E. Cowdrey,

United States Army in World War II: The European Theater of Operations: Medical Service in the European Theater of Operations, Washington, DC, 1992

CMH *SC* Center of Military History, Forrest C. Pogue, *United States Army in World War II: The European Theater of Operations: The Supreme Command,* Washington, DC, 1954

CSDIC Combined Services Detailed Interrogation Centre

CSI Combat Studies Institute, Fort Leavenworth, KS

DCD Duff Cooper Diaries (private collection)

DDE Lib Dwight D. Eisenhower Library, Abilene, KS

DRZW Das Deutsche Reich und der Zweiten Weltkrieg, vols. 6–10, Munich, 2004–8

ETHINT European Theater Historical Interrogations, 1945, OCMH, USAMHI

FCP *SC* Forrest C. Pogue, background interviews for *The Supreme Command,* USAMHI

FDRL MR Franklin Delano Roosevelt Library, Hyde Park, NY, Map Room documents

FMS Foreign Military Studies, USAMHI

GBP Godfrey Blunden Papers (private collection)

HLB Hitlers Lagebesprechungen: Die

Protokollfragmente seiner militärischen Konferenzen 1942–1945, Munich, 1984 (Helmut Heiber and David M. Glantz (eds.), *Hitler and his Generals: Military Conferences, 1942–1945,* London, 2002)

IWM   Documents Collection, Imperial War Museum, London

LHC-DP   Liddell Hart Centre — Dempsey Papers

LHCMA   Liddell Hart Centre of Military Archives, King's College London

MFF   MFF Armed Forces Oral Histories, LHCMA

NARA   National Archives and Records Administration, College Park, MD

OCMH   Office of the Chief of Military History, USAMHI

PDDE   *The Papers of Dwight David Eisenhower,* ed. Alfred D. Chandler, 21 vols., Baltimore, MA, 1970–2001

PP   *The Patton Papers,* ed. Martin Blumenson, New York, 1974

PWS   Papers of William Sylvan, OCMH, USAMHI

RWHP   Robert W. Hasbrouck Papers, USAMHI

SHD-DAT   Service Historique de la Défense, Département de l'Armée de Terre, Vincennes

SOOHP   Senior Officers Oral History Program, US Army War College, USAMHI

TBJG *Die Tagebücher von Joseph Goebbels,* ed. Elke Fröhlich, 29 vols., Munich, 1992– 2005

TNA The National Archives, Kew

USAMHI The United States Army Military History Institute at US Army Heritage and Education Center, Carlisle, PA

1 Victory Fever

'It's Sunday', Omar N. Bradley, *A Soldier's Story,* New York, 1964, 389–90; also Dwight D. Eisenhower, *Crusade in Europe,* New York, 1948, 325

'informal visit', NARA 407/427/24235

Gerow and Leclerc; 'continue on present mission', SHD-DAT 11 P 218; also NARA 407/427/24235

'a field of rubble', BA-MA RH19 IX/7 40, quoted Joachim Ludewig, *Rückzug: The German Retreat from France, 1944,* Lexington, KY, 2012, 133

'Pire que les boches', Forrest C. Pogue, *Pogue's War: Diaries of a WWII Combat Historian,* Lexington, KY, 2001, 214

'a show of force', 'to establish . . .', Eisenhower, *Crusade in Europe,* 326; and Bradley, 391

'From what I heard at SHAEF . . .', Arthur Tedder, *With Prejudice,* London, 1966, 586

28th Division in Paris, see Uzal W. Ent (ed.), *The First Century: A History of the 28th Infantry Division,* Harrisburg, PA, 1979, 165

'Une armée de mécanos', Jean Galtier-Boissière, *Mon journal pendant l'Occupation,* Paris, 1944, 288

'It was one of the most . . .', 1.2.45, CBHD

'The August battles . . .', CMH *SC,* 245

'The West Front is finished . . .', diary Oberstleutnant Fritz Fullriede, *Hermann Göring* Division, 2 September 1944, quoted Robert Kershaw, *It Never Snows in September,* London, 2008, 63

'We want peace . . .', prisoner-of-war interview, CSDIC, TNA WO 208/3616

Wehrmacht losses, Rüdiger Overmans, *Deutsche militärische Verluste im Zweiten Weltkrieg,* Munich, 2000, 238 and 278

For the German retreat from France see: Ludewig, 108/ff.; and David Wingeate Pike, 'Oberbefehl West: Armeegruppe G: Les Armées allemandes dans le Midi de la France', *Guerres Mondiales et Conflits Contemporains,* Nos. 152, 164, 174, 181

'You are fish', Generaloberst Student, CSDIC, TNA WO 208/4177

'a club of intellectuals', Generaloberst Halder, CSDIC, TNA WO 208/4366 GRGG 332

'Now I know why . . .', Albert Speer, *Inside the Third Reich,* London, 1971, 525

'There will be moments . . .', *HLB,* 466 and 468

'It is certain that the political conflicts . . .',

CMH *SC,* 249

'In the evening . . .', Kreipe diary, 31.8.44, FMS P-069

'By now a huge . . .', Traudl Junge, *Until the Final Hour: Hitler's Last Secretary,* London, 2002, 146

'an air landing . . .', 'unusual array', Generalmajor Otto Ernst Remer, *Führer Begleit Brigade,* FMS B-592

'typing out whole reams . . .', Junge, 144

For German civilian morale, see Richard J. Evans, *The Third Reich at War,* London, 2008, 650–3

'a military statesman . . .', Chester Wilmot, *The Struggle for Europe,* London, 1952, 496

'Ike said that Monty . . .', 'Ike did not thank . . .', *PP,* 533, 537

'what with champagne . . .', Brian Horrocks, *Corps Commander,* London, 1977, 79

'The captives sat on the straw . . .', Caroline Moorehead, *Martha Gellhorn,* London, 2003, 269

'You had barely crossed . . .', interrogation, General der Artillerie Walter Warlimont, Deputy Chief of the Wehrmachtführungsstab, CSDIC, TNA WO 208/3151

'We would let . . .', VII Corps, NARA RG 498 290/56/2/3, Box 1459

'with practically no maintenance', ibid.

'We employed . . .', VII Corps, ibid.

'The pace of the retreat . . .', Maurice Delvenne, 1.9.44, cited Jean-Michel Delvaux, *La*

Bataille des Ardennes autour de Rochefort, 2 vols., Hubaille, 2004–5, ii, 159–60

'Their looks are hard . . .', ibid.

'a sad platoon of Dutch . . .', Fullriede diary, 13 September 1944, quoted Kershaw, *It Never Snows in September,* 38

'a picture that is unworthy . . .', BA-MA RH24-89/10, quoted Ludewig, 191

'the world situation . . .', 'OKW Feldjäger' etc., Obergefreiter Gogl, Abt. V, Feldjäger Regiment (mot.) 3., OKW Streifendienst, TNA WO 208/3610

'malingerers and cowardly shirkers . . .', BA-MA RW4/vol. 494

'the only reinforcements . . .', NARA RG 498 290/56/2/3, Box 1466

'as much use to us . . .', Stephen Roskill, *Churchill and the Admirals,* London, 1977, 245, quoted Rick Atkinson, *The Guns at Last Light,* New York, 2013, 233

'Napoleon, no doubt . . .', Horrocks, 81

'Newspapers reported . . .', Pogue, *Pogue's War,* 208

2 Antwerp and the German Frontier

Montgomery and Rhine crossing at expense of Scheldt estuary, LHCMA, Alanbrooke 6/2/31

Montgomery to Brooke, 3.9.44; IWM LMD 62/12, Montgomery diary, 3.9.44; see John Buckley, *Monty's Men: The British Army and the Liberation of Europe,* London, 2013, 206

'In order to attack', *PP,* 538

'with [the] compliments . . .', Forrest C. Pogue, *Pogue's War: Diaries of a WWII Combat Historian,* Lexington, KY, 2001, 215–16

50,000 cases of champagne, Patton letter, *PP,* 549

'Even if all our allies . . .', Uffz. Alfred Lehmann, 11.9.44, BA-MA RH13/49, 5

Cancelled airborne operations, Headquarters Allied Airborne Army, NARA RG 498 290/56/2/3, Box 1466

'The damn airborne . . .', *PP,* 540

Versailles and Paris, Com Z, see Rick Atkinson, *The Guns at Last Light,* New York, 2013, 236

Letter of 21 September, CMH *SC,* 293

'The whole point . . .', CSDIC, TNA WO 208/4177

'narrow front', 'single knife-like drive . . .', CMH *SC,* 292

'dagger-thrust . . .', Patton diary, *PP,* 550

'The problem was . . .', Buckley, 203

'overwhelming egotism', Forrest C. Pogue, *George C. Marshall: Organizer of Victory,* New York, 1973, 475, quoted Atkinson, 304

'If you, as the . . .', 'You will hear . . .', *PDDE,* iii, 2224

'We took enough prisoners', XX Corps, NARA RG 498 290/56/2/3, Box 1465

'kept breaking down . . .', Obersturmbannführer Loenholdt, 17 SS PzGr-Div, CSDIC, TNA WO 208/4140 SRM 1254

'Relations between officers and men . . .', First Army report to the OKW, 1.10.44, BA-MA RH13/49, 9

'The war has reached . . .', O.Gefr. Ankenbeil, 22.9.44, BA-MA RH13/49, 10

'He doesn't attack . . .', O.Gefr. M. Kriebel, 18.9.44, BA-MA RH13/49, 11

'The American infantryman . . .', O.Gefr. Hans Büscher, 20.9.44, BA-MA RH13/49, 11

'Whoever has air . . .', O.Gefr. G. Riegler, 21.9.44, BA-MA RH13/49, 11

'Why sacrifice more and more . . .', O.Gefr. Hans Hoes, 15.9.44, BA-MA RH13/49, 12

'Führer interrupts Jodl . . .', diary of General der Flieger Kreipe, FMS P-069

'OKH [Army High Command] has serious doubts . . .', 18.9.44, ibid.

Rundstedt's drinking, CSDIC, TNA WO 208/4364 GRGG 208

'The [Nazi Party] Kreisleiter of Reutlingen . . .', Hauptmann Delica, II Battalion, 19th Fallschirmjäger-Regiment, CSDIC, TNA WO 208/4140 SRM 1227

'We have been lied to . . .', CSDIC, TNA WO 208/4139 SRM 968

3 The Battle for Aachen

'As we pass a pillbox . . .', PFC Richard Lowe Ballou, 117th Infantry, 30th Infantry

721

Division, MFF-7, C1-97 (3)

'The wounded come out . . .', V Corps, NARA RG 498 290/56/2/3, Box 1455

'When the doors . . .', MFF-7, C1-97(2)

'After a second charge of TNT . . .', ibid.

'The Führer wanted to defend . . .', Reichsmarschall Hermann Göring, ETHINT 30

'The sight of the Luftwaffe . . .', Generalmajor Rudolf Freiherr von Gersdorff, ETHINT 53

'We were reduced . . .', Gardner Botsford, *A Life of Privilege, Mostly,* New York, 2003, 47

Rumours of bacteriological weapons, CSDIC, TNA WO 208/4140 SRM 1245

'You should have seen . . .', CSDIC, TNA WO 208/4139 SRM 983

'And when the houses . . .', ibid.

Fear of foreign workers, CSDIC, TNA WO 208/4139 SRM 1103

'The Allied Forces serving . . .', CMH *SC,* 357

'American officers [are] using . . .', TNA WO 208/3654 PWIS H/LDC/ 631

'the troops were indignant . . .', ibid.

'former proud regiment . . .', letter of 26.9.44 to Hauptmann Knapp, NARA RG 498 290/56/5/3, Box 1463

'I had the most excellent . . .', CSDIC, TNA WO 208/4139 SRM 982

'a job that should have . . .', 'To make sure . . .', NARA RG 498 290/56/2/3, Box 1459 'resulted in a quick . . .', NARA RG 407 270/65/7/2 ML 248

'When attacked in this way . . .', V Corps, NARA RG 498 290/56/2/3, Box 1455

'The few assault guns . . .', CSDIC, TNA WO 208/4139 SRM 982

'no close-in bombing . . .', 'the flattened condition of the buildings . . .', NARA RG 498 290/56/2/3, Box 1459

'The operation was not unduly . . .', ibid.

'Numerous times we have had . . .', NARA RG 498 290/56/2, Box 1456

'the direct fire of the 155mm . . .', VII Corps, NARA RG 498 290/56/2/3, Box 1459

'Civilians must be . . .', Lt Col. Shaffer F. Jarrell, VII Corps, ibid.

'they held up all . . .', CSDIC, TNA WO 208/4156

'Eisenhower is attacking . . .', Victor Klemperer, *To the Bitter End: The Diaries of Victor Klemperer, 1942–45,* London, 2000, 462

'Every German homestead . . .', CSDIC, TNA WO 208/4140 SRM 1211

'Even the Führer's adjutant . . .', Wilck, CSDIC, TNA WO 208/4364 GRGG 216

'The civilian population . . .', Unterfeld-webel Kunz, 104th Infanterie-Regt, CSDIC, TNA WO 208/4164 SRX 2050

'the time gained at Aachen . . .', NARA RG 407 270/65/7/2, Box 19105 ML 258

'he would have been given . . .', CSDIC, TNA WO 208/5542 SIR 1548

'he has to watch . . .', FMS P-069

'Before the Generals or anyone . . .', CSDIC, TNA WO 208/4134 SRA 5610

'Fears in East Prussia . . .', FMS P-069

'Gumbinnen is on fire . . .', ibid.

4 Into the Winter of War

'The soldiers' behaviour today . . .', Stabartz Köllensperger, 8th Regiment, 3rd Fallschirmjäger-Division, TNA WO 311/54

'German propaganda urging . . .', CSDIC, TNA WO 208/3165

'You've no idea . . .', Luftwaffe Obergefreiter Hlavac, KG 51, TNA WO 208/4164 SRX 2117

'They called us prolongers . . .', Obergefreiter Marke, 16th Fallschirmjäger-Regiment, ibid.

'The mood there is shit . . .', CSDIC, TNA WO 208/4164 SRX 2084

'Versager-1', Nicholas Stargardt, *Witnesses of War: Children's Lives under the Nazis,* London, 2005, 262

'into a country . . .', quoted Martin Gilbert, *The Second World War,* London, 1989, 592

'every American soldier . . .', NARA RG 407 270/65/7/2, Box 19105 ML 258

'Well, it probably won't be . . .', 2.12.44, CBHD

'The German people must realize . . .', CMH *SC,* 342

'The power of Germany . . .', NARA RG

407 270/65/7/2, Box 19105 ML 258

'generally expected', ibid.

'Tommy and his Yankee pal . . .', 'while Americans . . .', TNA WO 171/4184

'German civilians don't know . . .', 24.11.44, NARA RG 407 270/65/7/2, Box 19105 ML 285

Nazi Party corruption, CSDIC, TNA WO 208/4139 SRM 902

'armed with a few . . .', 'suspicious civilians', 'intelligence missions of their own', NARA RG 407 270/65/7/2, Box 19105 ML 285

'Don't kick them around . . .', ibid.

Cologne and 'Edelweiss Pirates', CSDIC, TNA WO 208/4164 SRX 2074

'A Leutnant of ours . . .', Luftwaffe Unteroffizier Bock 3/JG 27, CSDIC, TNA WO 208/4164 SRX 2126

'What is cowardice?', 4.5.44, Victor Klemperer, *To the Bitter End: The Diaries of Victor Klemperer, 1942–45,* London, 2000, 383

'I am so accustomed now . . .', Marie 'Missie' Vassiltchikov, *The Berlin Diaries, 1940–1945,* London, 1987, 240

'Skin diseases . . .', CSDIC, TNA WO 208/3165 SIR 1573

Deserters in Berlin, CSDIC, TNA WO 208/4135 SRA 5727 13/1/45

'War is just like . . .', TNA WO 171/4184

10,000 executions, *DRZW,* 9/1 (Echternkamp), 48–50

'During the night of . . .', VI Corps, NARA RG 498 290/56/5/3, Box 1463

Black market in Berlin, CSDIC, TNA WO 208/4164 SRX 2074

Black-market coffee from Holland, CSDIC, TNA WO 208/4140 SRM 1189

'Greiser boasted . . .', TNA WO 311/54, 32

'Main meal without meat' ('Hauptgerichte einmal ohne Fleisch'), Branden-burgische Landeshauptarchiv, Pr. Br. Rep. 61A/11

'The prices rise . . .', NARA RG 407 270/ 65/7/2 ML 2279

'the over-heated soul . . .', Louis Simpson, *Selected Prose,* New York, 1989, 98

'according to his VD . . .', CMH *Medical,* 541

'Avenue de Salute', Forrest C. Pogue, *Pogue's War: Diaries of a WWII Combat Historian,* Lexington, KY, 2001, 230

'ardent and often . . .', NARA 711.51/3-945

Reaction of young woman, Antony Beevor and Artemis Cooper, *Paris after the Liberation, 1944–1949,* London, 1994, 129

'The French, cynical before . . .', Simpson, 143

US Army soldiers in black market, Allan B. Ecker, 'GI Racketeers in the Paris Black Market', *Yank,* 4.5.45

'extremely frigid . . .', 24.10.44, DCD

'there is absolutely no one . . .', NARA 851.00/9-745

'ardent admirers', Carlos Baker, *Ernest Hemingway: A Life Story,* New York, 1969, 564

For the political situation in Belgium, see CMH *SC,* 329–31

'We're still a . . .', V Corps, NARA RG 498 290/56/2/3, Box 1455

'Each morning . . .', Arthur S. Couch, 'An American Infantry Soldier in World War II Europe', unpublished memoir, private collection

'We couldn't get the new untrained . . .', NARA RG 498 290/56/2/3, Box 1465

'Sergeant Postalozzi . . .', Martha Gellhorn, *Point of No Return,* New York, 1989, 30

Hemingway, *Across the River and into the Trees,* New York, 1950, 255

'His chances seem at their . . .', Ralph Ingersoll, *Top Secret,* London, 1946, 185–6

'I was lucky . . .', Couch, 'An American Infantry Soldier in World War II Europe'

'The quality of replacements . . .', NARA RG 498 290/56/2/3, Box 1459

'Replacements have 13 weeks . . .', Tech. Sgt. Edward L. Brule, NARA RG 498 290/56/5/2, Box 3

'enemy weapons could . . .', 358th Infantry, NARA RG 498 290/56/2/3, Box 1465

'The worst fault I have . . .', V Corps, NARA RG 498 290/56/2/3, Box 1455

'Jerry puts mortar fire . . .', V Corps, ibid.

'We actually had . . .', NARA RG 498 290/

56/5/2, Box 3

'My first contact . . .', 358th Infantry, 90th Division, XX Corps, NARA RG 498 290/56/2/3, Box 1465

'one group of officer . . .', NARA RG 498 290/56/2/3, Box 1459

'Before entering combat . . .', Lt Col. J. E. Kelly, 3rd Battalion, 378th Infantry, NARA RG 498 290/56/2/3, Box 1465

5 The Hürtgen Forest

'In general it was believed . . .', Generalleutnant Hans Schmidt, 275th Infanterie-Division, FMS B-810

'This consisted . . .', Major Gen. Kenneth Strong, 02/14/2 3/25 — Intelligence Notes No. 33, IWM Documents 11656

'absolutely unfit . . .', Generalleutnant Hans Schmidt, 275th Infanterie-Division, FMS B-810

'almost the entire company . . .', ibid.

'the greatest demands . . .', ibid.

'cold rations at irregular intervals', ibid.

'It was like a drop of water . . .', ibid.

'without counting the great number . . .', ibid.

'The commitment of the old paterfamilias . . .', ibid.

'the German soldier shows . . .', 14.10.44, GBP

'I am returning . . .', VII Corps, NARA RG 498 290/56/2/3, Box 1459

'In dense woods . . .', ibid.

'One man kicked . . .', Charles B. MacDonald, *The Mighty Endeavour: The American War in Europe,* New York, 1992, 385

'Schu, Riegel, Teller . . .', NARA RG 498 290/56/2/3, Box 1459

'When mines are . . .', 5.11.44, V Corps, NARA RG 498 290/56/2/3, Box 1455

297th Engineer Combat Battalion, VII Corps, NARA RG 498 290/56/2/3, Box 1459

'The Germans are burying . . .', 22nd Infantry, 4th Inf. Div., ibid.

'The effective range . . .', VII Corps, ibid.

'Men over thirty . . .', ibid.

'It took guts . . .', Colonel Edwin M. Burnett, V Corps, NARA RG 498 290/56/2/3, Box 1455

'excellent', Rick Atkinson, *The Guns at Last Light,* New York, 2013, 317

'Certainly there will be . . .', Diary of General der Flieger Kreipe, FMS P-069, 43

'one big, old country . . .', V Corps, NARA RG 498 290/56/2/3, Box 1455

'When the driver . . .', Edward G. Miller, *A Dark and Bloody Ground: The Hürtgen Forest and the Roer River Dams, 1944–1945,* College Station, TX, 2008, 64

'after the effectiveness . . .', Generalmajor Rudolf Freiherr von Gersdorff, FMS A-892

'to prevent American troops from . . .', Gersdorff, FMS A-891

Lack of bazooka ammunition in Schmidt, Col. Nelson 112th Infantry, NARA RG 498 290/56/2/3, Box 1463

'General Eisenhower, General Bradley . . .', 8.11.44, PWS

'When the strength of an outfit . . .', Ralph Ingersoll, *Top Secret,* London, 1946, 185

'The surrounded American task force . . .', NARA RG 407 270/65/7/2, Box 19105 ML 258

'There was a stream . . .', Arthur S. Couch, 'An American Infantry Soldier in World War II Europe', unpublished memoir, private collection

'then blast hell . . .', VII Corps, NARA RG 498 290/56/2/3, Box 1459

4.2-inch mortars, NARA RG 407 270/65/7/2 ML 248

'The German artillery . . .', Couch, 'An American Infantry Soldier in World War II Europe'

'easier to defend . . .', Generalmajor Rudolf Freiherr von Gersdorff, ETHINT 53

'Just before dawn . . .', Couch, 'An American Infantry Soldier in World War II Europe'

275th Infanterie-Division, Generalleutnant Hans Schmidt, FMS B-373

Colonel Luckett, V Corps, NARA RG 498 290/56/2/3, Box 1455

'twelve to twenty men . . .', NARA RG 498 290/56/2/3, Box 1465

'In the daytime . . .', NARA RG 498 290/

56/2/3, Box 1464

'One time we didn't . . .', quoted John Ellis, *The Sharp End: The Fighting Man in World War II,* London, 1990, 152

'booby-trapped stretch . . .', Robert Sterling Rush, *Hell in Hürtgen Forest: The Ordeal and Triumph of an American Infantry Regiment,* Lawrence, KS, 2001, 139

1st Division avoiding trails, 18th Infantry, 1st Division, NARA RG 498 290/56/2/3, Box 1459

'A heavy snow . . .', Couch, 'An American Infantry Soldier in World War II Europe'

'Armistice Day and Georgie . . .', 11.11.44, CBHD

'The whole damn company . . .', Omar N. Bradley, *A Soldier's Story,* New York, 1964, 430–1

'fight to the last round', Generalmajor Ullersperger, CSDIC, TNA WO 208/4364 GRGG 237

'I am surprised that Himmler . . .', Generalmajor Vaterrodt, CSDIC, TNA WO 208/4177

'I've lost my unit', etc., ibid.

'Especially distressing . . .', Generalleutnant Straube, FMS A-891

'an open wound', FMS A-891

'death-mill', Gersdorff, FMS A-892

'Passchendaele with tree bursts', Ernest Hemingway, *Across the River and into the Trees,* New York, 1950, 249

'Old Ernie Hemorrhoid . . .', Carlos Baker, *Ernest Hemingway: A Life Story,* New York, 1969, 552

'an unoccupied foxhole', J. D. Salinger, 'Contributors', *Story,* No. 25 (November–December 1944), 1

'After five days . . .', Charles Whiting, *The Battle of Hürtgen Forest,* Stroud, 2007, 71

'The young battalion commanders . . .', Ingersoll, 184–5

'The men accept poor . . .', V Corps, NARA RG 498 290/56/2/3, Box 1455

'You drive by the surgical tents . . .', Ingersoll, 185

22nd Infantry casualties, Sterling Rush, 163

'keep control of . . .', FMS A-891

'Our men appear to have . . .', Sgt David Rothbart, 22nd Inf. Rgt, quoted Sterling Rush, 178

'would get up . . .', quoted Paul Fussell, *The Boys' Crusade,* New York, 2003, 91

'tree bursts that sent . . .', etc., Captain H. O. Sweet, US 908th Field Artillery, Attached to 331st Infantry, 83rd Division, IWM Documents 3415 95/33/1

8,000 psychological casualties, Peter Schrijvers, *The Crash of Ruin: American Combat Soldiers in Europe during World War II,* New York, 1998, 8

'There were few cases . . .', Generalarzt Schepukat, ETHINT 60

'In some cases . . .', Gersdorff, FMS A-892
'more than 5,000 battle . . .', 'The Ardennes', CSI Battlebook 10-A, May 1984

6 The Germans Prepare

'with the rather melancholy . . .', Traudl Junge, *Until the Final Hour: Hitler's Last Secretary,* London, 2002, 147

'He knew very well . . .', ibid.

'the column of cars . . .', ibid., 148

'Hitler had all day . . .', Generaloberst Alfred Jodl, ETHINT 50

'By remaining on the defensive . . .', ibid.

'another Dunkirk', CMH *Ardennes,* 18

'whisked away', General der Kavallerie Siegfried Westphal, ETHINT 79

'German divisions were gradually . . .', Generalmajor Rudolf Freiherr von Gersdorff, FMS A-892

'small solution' and conferences beginning November, CSDIC, TNA WO 208/4178 GRGG 330 (c)

'a snowplow effect', CMH *Ardennes,* 26

Hitler and American forces in front of Aachen, Generaloberst Alfred Jodl, ETHINT 50

Oberstleutnant Guderian, CSDIC, TNA WO 208/3653

'In our current . . .', *DRZW,* 6, 125

Manteuffel's fuel requests, Manteuffel, Fifth Panzer Army, ETHINT 45

'on principle, otherwise . . .', Generaloberst

Alfred Jodl, ETHINT 50

Preference for SS, General der Artillerie Walter Warlimont, CSDIC, TNA WO 208/3151

'There was a certain . . .', Generaloberst Alfred Jodl, ETHINT 51

'expressed his astonishment . . .', Jodl, TNA WO 231/30

'Not to be altered', 'to their subordinate . . .', CSDIC, TNA WO 208/4178 GRGG 330 (c)

'last gamble', TNA WO 231/30, 4

'final objective . . .', CSDIC, TNA WO 208/4178 GRGG 330 (c)

'Surprise, when it succeeds . . .', CSDIC, TNA WO 208/4178 GRGG 322

Security measures, CSDIC, TNA WO 208/4178 GRGG 330 (c)

'full to bursting point', Hauptmann Gaum, 3rd Bn, *Führer Begleit* Brigade, CSDIC, TNA WO 208/3611

Storch aircraft, TNA WO 231/30

Volksgrenadier divisions taking documents, CSDIC, TNA WO 208/4140 SRM 1140

'started a rumour . . .', Manteuffel, Fifth Panzer Army, ETHINT 46

'the political crisis in the . . .', Goebbels diaries, 1.12.44, *TBJG* II/14, 305

'We have all been . . .', SS Standartenführer Lingner, CSDIC, TNA WO 208/4140 SRM 1211

'The only thing . . .', Generalleutnant

Heim, CSDIC, TNA WO 208/4364 GRGG
220

'What a filthy trick!', CSDIC, TNA WO
208/4140 SRM 1210

'There were many comments . . .', Warlimont, CSDIC, TNA WO 208/3151

Dietrich refuses Kruse, CSDIC, TNA WO
208/4178 GRGG 330 (c)

'was not commanded as one formation . . .',
CSDIC, TNA WO 208/4178 GRGG 330 (c)

'Objectives, objectives! . . .', TNA WO
231/30

'a people's general', ibid.

Questionnaire after 20 July, CSDIC, TNA
WO 208/4140 SRM 1199

'and then give the English . . .', CSDIC,
TNA WO 208/5541 SIR 1425

'The Führer has ordered . . .', FMS B-823

'There was nothing but . . .', CSDIC, TNA
WO 208/4140 SRM 1187

'Germany's last reserves . . .', ibid.

'Only two pilots . . .', ibid.

'who was heavily . . .', 'Success or
failure . . .', CSDIC, TNA WO 208/3662

'the entire offensive had not more . . .',
Heydte, FMS B-823

'an old non-commissioned . . .', ibid.

'All that was known . . .', ibid.

'We'll annihilate them,' CSDIC, TNA WO
208/4140 SRM 1167

'a highly overstrung . . .', CSDIC, TNA WO
208/5541 SIR 1425

'Skorzeny, this next . . .', Skorzeny's account to his officers, NARA RG 407 ML 2279

'typical evil Nazi', Heydte to Leutnant von Trott zu Solz, CSDIC, TNA WO 208/4140 SRM 1182

'a real dirty dog . . .', CSDIC, TNA WO 208/4178 GRGG 301

'order from the Reichsführer', SS-Untersturmführer Schreiber, CSDIC, TNA WO 208/4140 SRM 1259

'Everything I know . . .', Mobile Field Interrogation Unit No. 1, NARA RG 407 ML 2279

'decisive effect on . . .', ibid.

Leutnant zur See Müntz, CSDIC, TNA WO 208/3619

'with the fork . . .', Mobile Field Interrogation Unit No. 1, NARA RG 407 ML 2279

'emphasized that the . . .', ibid.

'conspicuous friendship', Schreiber, CSDIC, TNA WO 208/4140 SRM 1259

'he was our pirate captain', Hans Post, *One Man in his Time,* Sydney, 2002, 167

'according to the German radio . . .', Leutnant Günther Schultz, captured Liège 19.12.44, Mobile Field Interrogation Unit No. 1, NARA RG 407 ML 2279

150th Panzer-Brigade, 'Ardennes Offensive', Obersturmbannführer Otto Skorzeny, ETHINT 12

Skorzeny and plans for Basle, CSDIC, TNA

WO 208/5543 SIR 1673

SHAEF and plan to go through Switzerland, NARA RG 407 270/65/7/2, Box 19124 ML 754

Trains needed for Ardennes offensive, TNA WO 231/30

'was already seeing in his mind's eye . . .', Nicolaus von Below, *Als Hitlers Adjutant, 1937–1945,* Mainz, 1980, 396

'Is your army ready?', SS-Oberstgruppenführer Sepp Dietrich, ETHINT 16

Hitler's speech, *HLB,* 535–40

'the worst prepared . . .', Dietrich, ETHINT 16.

Divisions remove insignia, 116th Panzer-Division, CSDIC, TNA WO 208/3628

Peiper's orders, 14.12.44, Obersturmbann-führer Joachim Peiper, ETHINT 10

'In twelve or fourteen . . .', Gefreiter Unruh, CSDIC, TNA WO 208/3611 SIR 1408

'an extraordinary optimism . . .', SS-Brigadeführer Heinz Harmel, 10th SS Panzer-Division *Frundsberg,* FMS P-109f

'the fighting spirit . . .', 2nd Panzer-Division, FMS P-109e

7 Intelligence Failure

'pathetically alone', etc., 6.12.44, CBHD, Box 5

'If we were fighting . . .', ibid.

'Victory or Siberia!', John S. D. Eisenhower, *The Bitter Woods,* New York, 1970, 200

'sledgehammer blows . . .', 7.12.44, CBHD

'Field Marshal Montgomery . . .', 'Notes of Meeting at Maastricht on 7.12.1944', Sidney H. Negrotto Papers, Box 4, USAMHI

'all operations north . . .', ibid.

'I think only Attila . . .', *PP,* 576

'This is General Patton . . .', James H. O'Neill, former Third Army chaplain, 'The True Story of the Patton Prayer', *Leadership,* No. 25

'Well, Padre . . .', ibid.

Eberbach conversation, CSDIC, TNA WO 208/4364 GRGG 220

'the big offensive . . .', Leutnant von der Goltz (St./Gren-Rgt 1039), CSDIC, TNA WO 208/4139 SRM 1083

German deserter, CMH *SC,* 363

'Germany's crippling shortage . . .', TNA CAB 106/1107

'the enemy's present practice . . .', CMH *SC,* 365

'aware of the danger', Strong, letter of 31.8.51, quoted ibid.

'as a Christmas present for the Führer', CMH *SC,* 370

'Hitler's orders for setting up . . .', 'Indications of the German Offensive of December 1944', dated 28.12.44, 'C' to Victor Cavendish-Bentinck, TNA HW 13/45

'as soon as replenishing . . .', BAY/XL 152,

TNA HW 13/45

'The GAF [Luftwaffe] evidence shows . . .', etc., 'Indications of the German Offensive of December 1944', 28.12.44, 'C' to Victor Cavendish-Bentinck, TNA HW 13/45

'a little startling . . .', 'Ever since . . .', ibid.

'quiet paradise . . .', 'The Ardennes', CSI Battlebook 10-A, May 1984

'The steady traffic . . .', Forrest C. Pogue, *Pogue's War: Diaries of a WWII Combat Historian,* Lexington, KY, 2001, 250

Evacuation of eastern cantons, Peter Schrijvers, *The Unknown Dead: Civilians in the Battle of the Bulge,* Lexington, KY, 2005, 12

Elections and *Rucksackdeutsche,* ibid., 7–8

'The bloody Heinies!', Louis Simpson, *Selected Prose,* New York, 1989, 117

'La Dietrich was bitching', 8.12.44, CBHD

'a good part of the afternoon', 13.12.44, PWS

'It is now certain that attrition . . .', TNA CAB 106/1107

12th Army Group short of 17,581 men, NARA RG 498 UD603, Box 3

'We think he is spread . . .', etc., 15.12.44, CBHD

'GI's in their zest . . .', Omar N. Bradley, *A Soldier's Story,* New York, 1964, 428

'German manpower . . .', John Buckley, *Monty's Men: The British Army and the Liberation of Europe,* London, 2013, 259

'My men were amazed . . .', Charles B. MacDonald, *Company Commander,* New York, 2002, 78

'It has been very quiet . . .', Colonel R. Ernest Dupuy, *St. Vith: Lion in the Way: The 106th Infantry Division in World War II,* Washington, DC, 1949, 15–16

'Dear Ruth . . .', captured letter translated 19 December, headquarters 1st Infantry Division, CBMP, Box 2

8 Saturday 16 December

German artillery targeting houses, V Corps, NARA RG 498 290/56/2/3, Box 1455

Manderfeld, Peter Schrijvers, *The Unknown Dead: Civilians in the Battle of the Bulge,* Lexington, KY, 2005, 14

'a World War I concept . . .', Manteuffel, Fifth Panzer Army, ETHINT 46

'a significant obstacle . . .', 'The Ardennes', CSI Battlebook 10-A, May 1984

'that surprise had been . . .', Generaloberst Alfred Jodl, ETHINT 51

'If in places . . .', Charles P. Roland, 99th Infantry Division, CBMP, Box 4

'They might at least . . .', John S. D. Eisenhower, *The Bitter Woods,* New York, 1970, 229

Lanzerath engagement, letter from Lieutenant Colonel Robert L. Kriz, 394th Infantry; and letter from Lyle J. Bouck, 19 January 1983, CBMP, Box 4

'Hold at all costs!', Eisenhower, *Bitter Woods,* 188

'to push through rapidly . . .', Obersturmbannführer Joachim Peiper, 1st SS Panzer-Regiment, ETHINT 10

'shouting that they were . . .', Adolf Schür, Lanzerath, CBMP, Box 6

'They might just as well . . .', Peiper, ETHINT 10

'We pulled our jeep . . .', FO, C Battery, 371st FA Bn, 99th Infantry Division, Richard H. Byers Papers, Box 1, USAMHI

'There were fellows . . .', Standartenführer Lingner, 17th SS Pzg-Div, CSDIC, TNA WO 208/4140 SRM 1205

'At 06.00 the Germans . . .', 'Defense of Höfen', *Infantry School Quarterly,* July 1948, CBMP, Box 4

'On the K Company front . . .', CBMP, Box 4

'We administered plasma . . .', Harry S. Arnold, E Company, 393rd Infantry, 99th Infantry Division, CBMP, Box 4

Nervous breakdown and self-inflicted injuries, Charles P. Roland, 99th Infantry Division, CBMP, Box 4

'The American Army never retreats!', Sidney Salins, CBMP, Box 4

Volksgrenadier divisions and artillery, General der Artillerie Kruse, CSDIC, TNA WO 208/4178 GRGG 330 (c)

'just a local diversion', NARA RG 407 270/

65/7/2 ML 2280

'05.15: Asleep in . . .', etc., Matt F. C. Konop, diary, 2nd Infantry Division, CBMP, Box 2

'local enemy action', ibid.

'They turned searchlights . . .', NARA RG 498 290/56/2/3, Box 1455

28th Infantry Division and artillery, NARA RG 498 290/56/2/3, Box 1463

'Ten Germans will be reported . . .', 28th Infantry Division, ibid.

'on the morning of the . . .', 112th Infantry Regiment, NARA RG 498 290/56/5/2, Box 3

'nearly destroyed', Generalmajor Siegfried von Waldenburg, 116th Panzer-Division, FMS A-873

'was the fact that . . .', Generalmajor Heinz Kokott, '26th Volksgrenadier Division in the Ardennes Offensive', FMS B-040

'willing but inept', etc., Major Frank, battalion commander, III/13th Fallschirmjäger, CSDIC, TNA WO 208/4140 SRM 1148, and WO 208/5540 SIR 1375

'a very ambitious, reckless soldier . . .', Heydte, CSDIC, TNA WO 208/5541 SIR 1425

'der Schlächter von Cassino', CSDIC, TNA WO 208/3611

Crossing the Our, 'Ardennes Offensive of Seventh Army', FMS A-876

'We are here!', 'The Ardennes', CSI Battlebook 10-A, May 1984

Lauterborn, ibid.

'It was the towns and road junctions . . .', ibid.

'God, I just want to see . . .', 16.12.44, CBHD

'The room, with two . . .', ibid.

'Tell him that Ike . . .', Eisenhower, *Bitter Woods*, 266

'That broke our hearts . . .', William R. Desobry Papers, USAMHI

'looks like the real thing', *PP*, 595

'It reminds me very much . . .', *PP*, 596

'Hodges [is] having a bit . . .', William H. Simpson Papers, Box 11, USAMHI

'very conscientious . . .', CSDIC, TNA WO 208/5541 SIR 1444

'new and nervous', ibid.

'an utter failure', CSDIC, TNA WO 208/3628

'pitifully small . . .', CSDIC, TNA WO 208/5541 SIR 1444

'German People, be confident!', TNA WO 171/4184

'We will win . . .', ibid.

'We heard a siren-like . . .', Arthur S. Couch, 'An American Infantry Soldier in World War II Europe', unpublished memoir, private collection

Order to 2nd Division, Major William F. Hancock, 1st Battalion, 9th Infantry, 2nd Infantry Division, CBMP, Box 2

'the decisive role . . .', Peiper, ETHINT 10

9 Sunday 17 December

'Say, Konop, I want you . . .', Matt F. C. Konop, diary, 2nd Infantry Division, CBMP, Box 2

'had had the hell knocked out . . .', Charles B. MacDonald, *Company Commander,* New York, 2002, 82–3

'The snow around . . .', ibid.

'Owing to the wretched condition . . .', General der Waffen-SS H. Priess, I SS Panzer Corps, FMS A-877

Peiper's Kampfgruppe in Honsfeld, Peter Schrijvers, *The Unknown Dead: Civilians in the Battle of the Bulge,* Lexington, KY, 2005, 35–6

Nazi civilian in Büllingen, ibid., 35

Fifty American prisoners shot at Büllingen, CMH *Ardennes,* 261

254th Engineer Battalion, V Corps, NARA RG 498 290/56/2/3, Box 1455

26th Infantry, CBMP, Box 2

'I think the war . . .', Gefreiter W.P., 17.12.44, BfZ-SS

'I will never move backwards . . .', etc., 17.12.44, CBHD

'the last air-raid . . .', Ralph Ingersoll, *Top Secret,* London, 1946, 194

'whether 12th Army Group . . .', First Army diary, quoted D. K. R. Crosswell, *Beetle: The Life of General Walter Bedell Smith,* Lexington, KY, 2010, 810

'The Army Group commander called . . .', Gaffey Papers, USAMHI

'a diversion for a larger . . .', 'everything depends . . .', 17.12.44, GBP

Kampfgruppe Heydte, Oberstleutnant von der Heydte, ETHINT 75

106th on 16–17 December, CMH *Ardennes,* 156–7

'great bear of a man', John S. D. Eisenhower, *The Bitter Woods,* New York, 1970, 280

'One futile effort', Royce L. Thompson, 'Air Resupply to Isolated Units, Ardennes Campaign', OCMH, Feb. 1951, typescript, CMH 2-3.7 AE P

Devine's combat fatigue, 'Report of Investigation, Action of 14th Cavalry Group on Occasion of German Attack Commencing on 16 Dec. 1944', 29.1.45, First Army IG NARA RG 338 290/62/05/1–2

'When I told him . . .', General der Panzertruppe Horst Stumpff, ETHINT 61

'I expected the right-hand . . .', NARA RG 407 270/65/7/2 ML 2280

'It was a case of . . .', Major Donald P. Boyer, 38th Armored Infantry Battalion, RWHP, Box 1

'panic stricken soldiers . . .', AAR, 7th AD Artillery, RWHP, Box 1

'the continuous stream of . . .', RWHP, Box 1

'The build-up of a defensive . . .', ibid.

'herded together . . .', 'Immediate publicity . . .', 17.12.44, PWS

'took the breath away from . . .', 18.12.44, CBHD

'What utter madness . . .', CSDIC, TNA WO 208/5516

Werbomont reprisals in September, Schrijvers, *Unknown Dead*, 40

Kampfgruppe Peiper at Stavelot, Obersturmbannführer Joachim Peiper, 1st SS Panzer-Regiment, ETHINT 10

Dogfight over Wahlerscheid, 3rd Battalion, 38th Infantry, CBMP, Box 2

'Against this demoralizing picture . . .', 1st Battalion, 9th Infantry, 2nd Infantry Division, CBMP, Box 2

'screaming among the enemy', ibid.

'In heavy and close combat . . .', 'The Ardennes', CSI Battlebook 10-A, May 1984

'One enemy soldier . . .', 3rd Battalion, 38th Infantry, CBMP, Box 2

'plunged through the thickly . . .', 'I felt like . . .', MacDonald, *Company Commander*, 97, 100

'The Germans had sent him . . .', 1st Battalion, 9th Infantry, 2nd Infantry Division, CBMP, Box 2

'the crews were picked off . . .', ibid.

'a mediocre division with no . . .', General der Infanterie Baptist Kniess, LXXXV Corps, ETHINT 40

'A group of men nearby . . .', 28th Infantry

Division, NARA RG 498 290/56/2/3, Box 1463

German infiltration of Clervaux, interview Joseph Maertz, Clervaux, 22.8.81, CBMP, Box 6

'sitting in his . . .', and defence of Clervaux, 'The Breakthrough to Bastogne', vol. ii, Clervaux, typescript, n.d., CMH, 8-3.1 AR

'If you're a Jewish . . .', Roger Cohen, 'The Lost Soldiers of Stalag IX-B', *New York Times Magazine,* 27.2.2005

Jean Servé, Clervaux, CBMP, Box 6

'rolled headlong . . .', 'The Ardennes', CSI Battlebook 10-A

'The G-2 estimate tonight', 17.12.44, PWS XLVII Panzer Corps, Lüttwitz, XLVII Panzer Corps, ETHINT 41

'to advance as rapidly . . .', Kniess, ETHINT 40

'All I know of the situation . . .', NARA RG 407 270/65/8/2 ML 130

'most of them, to hear them tell it . . .', Louis Simpson, *Selected Prose,* New York, 1989, 134

'As we walked through . . .', Walter Bedell Smith, *Eisenhower's Six Great Decisions,* London, 1956, 103

'There's been a complete . . .', Stanley Weintraub, *Eleven Days in December,* New York, 2006, 54–5 'yells, catcalls and many . . .', NARA RG 498, 290/56/5/2, Box 3

'cumbersome', etc., NARA RG 498 290/56/2/3, Box 1455

'tanks knocked out of action . . .', V Corps, NARA RG 498 290/56/2/3, Box 1455

'When the Battalion assembled . . .', CBMP, Box 2

'it was artillery . . .', 1st Battalion, 9th Infantry, 2nd Infantry Division, CBMP, Box 2

Battalion commander relieved, CO, 2nd Bn, 394th Inf., NARA RG 407, E 427-A (270/65/4/7)

'Trojan Horse trick', CBMP, Box 2

'A tank was observed . . .', V Corps, NARA RG 498 290/56/2/3, Box 1455

'The bayonet was . . .', 'gunners, drivers, assistant drivers . . .', ibid.

'saw a soldier silhouetted . . .', Charles B. MacDonald, *Company Commander,* New York, 2002, 103

'observed a Mark VI . . .', V Corps, NARA RG 498 290/56/2/3, Box 1455

'man from another outfit', ibid.

'None of them got away', 3rd Battalion, 38th Infantry, 2nd Division, CBMP, Box 2

'But I've a rendezvous . . .', FO, C Battery, 371st FA Bn, 99th Infantry Division, Richard Henry Byers, 'Battle of the Bulge', typescript, 1983

'It is dangerous at any time . . .', V Corps, NARA RG 498 290/56/2/3, Box 1455

Attack on Stavelot, Peiper, 1st SS Panzer-Regiment, ETHINT 10

Evacuation of fuel, CMH *Ardennes,* 667

'General, if you don't get out . . .', J. Lawton Collins, SOOHP, USAMHI

'The situation is rapidly deteriorating', 18.12.44, PWS

'He says that the situation . . .', William H. Simpson Papers, Box 11, USAMHI

'American flags, pictures of the President . . .', 21.12.44, PWS

'Hell, when this fight's over . . .', John S. D. Eisenhower, *The Bitter Woods,* New York, 1970, 303

'it would have been a simple . . .', Peiper, ETHINT 10

'in their winter clothing . . .', Louis Simpson, *Selected Prose,* New York, 1989, 134

'How many teams . . .', NARA RG 407 270/65/8/2 ML 130

Tensions in XLVII Panzer Corps, Kokott, FMS B-040

'The long resistance of Hosingen . . .', Generalmajor Heinz Kokott, 26th Volks-grenadier-Division, FMS B-040

'arrived too late . . .', Generalleutnant Fritz Bayerlein, Panzer Lehr Division, FMS A-942

The defence of Wiltz, 'The Breakthrough to Bastogne', typescript, n.d., CMH 8-3.1 AR

'Panzer Lehr, with their barrels . . .', Bayerlein, FMS A-942

Twenty-three Sherman tanks, Bayerlein, FMS A-941

'Noville is two towns up . . .', NARA RG 407 270/65/8/2 ML 130

'We could hear gunfire . . .', etc., William R. Desobry Papers, USAMHI

'There was a muffled explosion . . .', RWHP, Box 1

'*Führer Begleit* Brigade was involved . . .', 'pushing forward . . .', Hauptmann Gaum, 3rd Bn, CSDIC, TNA WO 208/3610

'declined to move in that . . .', General-major Otto Remer, ETHINT 80 and FMS B-592

'There's not the slightest . . .', 18.12.44, GBP

'I feel that you won't like . . .', *PP*, 596

'What the hell . . .', Omar N. Bradley, *A Soldier's Story,* New York, 1964, 469

'A very dangerous operation . . .', *PP*, 597

'the situation up there is . . .', ibid.

11 Skorzeny and Heydte

Leutnant Günther Schultz, Mobile Field Interrogation Unit No. 1, NARA RG 407 ML 2279

'may have a captured German officer . . .', 21.12.44, CBHD

Bradley security precautions, 22.12.44, CBHD

'Question the driver because . . .', 344/1/A

TNA WO 171/4184
'What is Sinatra's first name?', 21.12.44, PWS
'Only a kraut would . . .', quoted Danny S. Parker (ed.), *Hitler's Ardennes Offensive: The German View of the Battle of the Bulge,* London, 1997, 172
'I haven't the faintest idea . . .', David Niven, *The Moon's a Balloon,* London, 1994, 258
'General, if I were you . . .', Lord Tryon, conversation with author, 6.2.2013
Gerhardt Unger and Gunther Wertheim, Ernest Unger, conversation with author, 13.12.2012
'We were sentenced to death . . .', TNA WO 171/4184
Aywaille, NARA RG 407 E 427 (270/65/8-9/6-1) ML 7, Box 24201
Vichy Milice and the SS *Charlemagne* Division, TNA WO 171/4184
'the women sang in clear strong . . .', etc., 25.12.44, CBHD
'visibility was almost nil', Brigadier A. W. Brown, IWM Documents 13781 73/18/1
'swept up the bridge', 25.12.44, CBHD
150th Panzer-Brigade, 'Ardennes Offensive', Obersturmbannführer Otto Skorzeny, ETHINT 12
'hindering the operation of the corps . . .', SS-Oberstgruppenführer Sepp Dietrich, ETHINT 15

'amateurish, almost frivolous . . .', Heydte, FMS B-823

Kampfgruppe Heydte, CSDIC, TNA WO 208/5541 SIR 1444; also TNA WO 208/3628, TNA WO 208/3612

wire across road, NARA RG 498 290/56/2, Box 1456

'ambushed, captured and . . .', V Corps, NARA RG 498 290/56/2/3, Box 1455

'taken off believing . . .', 18.12.44, GBP; and V Corps, NARA RG 498 290/56/2/3, Box 1455

Failure to report parachutes found, NARA RG 498 290/56/2/3, Box 1459

Heydte Kampfgruppe casualties, ibid.

12 Tuesday 19 December

Peiper Kampfgruppe at Stoumont, Peiper, FMS C-004

Saint-Edouard sanatorium, Peter Schrijvers, *The Unknown Dead: Civilians in the Battle of the Bulge,* Lexington, KY, 2005, 54–6

'From his place of concealment . . .', V Corps, NARA RG 498 290/56/2/3, Box 1455

'Our battalion advanced . . .', TNA WO 311/54

'Some of them came along . . .', conversation with Obergefreiter Pompe of the 18th Volksgrenadier-Division, CSDIC, TNA WO 311/54

105th Engineer Battalion, NARA RG 407

290/56/5/1–3, Box 7

3rd Fallschirmjäger, Faymonville, Operations of the Sixth Panzer Army, FMS A-924

'poor physical specimens', etc., Kurt Vonnegut, C-Span, New Orleans, 30.5.95

'showers, warm beds . . .', NARA RG 407 E 427-A (270/65/4/7)

'Do not flee . . .', CBMP, Box 4

'the largest surrender . . .', Kurt Vonnegut, C-Span, New Orleans, 30.5.95

'inferred that the two . . .', Colonel Walter Stanton, deputy chief of staff VIII Corps, NARA RG 407 270/65/8/2 ML 299

'Endless columns of prisoners . . .', Diary of Oberleutnant Behman, Maurice Delaval Collection, Box 7, USAMHI

'licking its wounds', RWHP, Box 1

'the only Jerries we found . . .', etc., ibid.

'hysterical and a nervous wreck . . .', Hauptmann Gaum, 3rd Battalion *Führer Begleit* Brigade, CSDIC, TNA WO 208/3611

'lifted the man's head up . . .', Hans Post, *One Man in his Time,* Sydney, 2002, 170

'an ugly professional . . .', Ralph Ingersoll, *Top Secret,* London, 1946, 162

'fabulous Jeep . . .', 20.12.44, CBHD

'The present situation . . .', etc., Charles B. MacDonald, *A Time for Trumpets: The Untold Story of the Battle of the Bulge,* New York, 1984, 420; Dwight D. Eisenhower, *Crusade in Europe,* London, 1948, 371

'On the morning of December 21st . . .', D. K. R. Crosswell, *Beetle: The Life of General Walter Bedell Smith,* Lexington, KY, 2010, 812

Patton and date of counter-attack, *PP,* 599

'Every time I get a new star . . .', *PP,* 600

'fighting mad', 'I don't want to commit . . .', 19.12.44, CBHD

'Where are you going?', VIII Corps, NARA RG 407 270/65/8/2 ML 299

The fighting in Wiltz, 'The Breakthrough to Bastogne', typescript, n.d., CMH 8-3.1 AR

Scenes in Bastogne, Lieutenant Ed Shames, in Tim G. W. Holbert, 'Brothers at Bastogne — Easy Company's Toughest Task', *World War II Chronicles,* Winter 2004/5, 22–5

'a hod-carrying . . .', Louis Simpson, *Selected Prose,* New York, 1989, 121

'We have been wiped out', NARA RG 407 270/65/8/2 ML 130

'The surprise was complete', Generalmajor Heinz Kokott, 26th Volksgrenadier-Division, FMS B-040

'painful losses', ibid.

'The enemy had made . . .', ibid.

Panzer Lehr draining fuel tanks, Generalleutnant Fritz Bayerlein, FMS A-941

'day of surprises', ibid.

'not sufficiently coherent . . .', ibid.

'Ammunition and rations . . .', Kokott, FMS B-040

20th Armored Infantry at Noville, William R. Desobry Papers, USAMHI, and NARA RG 407 270/65/8/2 ML 130

'to go through the whole daggone . . .', NARA RG 407 270/65/8/2 ML 130

'They spread out . . .', William R. Desobry Papers, USAMHI

'You know those sound . . .', Holbert, 'Brothers at Bastogne — Easy Company's Toughest Task', 22–5

'Go on back . . .', quoted George E. Koskimaki, *The Battered Bastards of Bastogne: The 101st Airborne in the Battle of the Bulge*, New York, 2007, 113

Capture of 326th Field Hospital, CMH *Medical*, 409–14

Desobry's fortunes, William R. Desobry Papers, USAMHI

'laid in rows . . .', CMH *Medical*, 414

'We arrive at First Army HQ . . .', Carol Mather, *When the Grass Stops Growing*, Barnsley, 1997, 284–7

'got any bloody tanks . . .', ibid., 286

'oddly deserted countryside', 'He is considerably . . .', ibid., 287

'clearly alarmed', etc., ibid.

'Limey bastards', Crosswell, 814

'Certainly if Monty's were . . .', CMH *SC*, 378

'By God, Ike . . .', Kenneth Strong, *Intelligence at the Top*, London, 1970, 226 'absolutely livid . . . walked up and down . . .', Coningham, FCP *SC*

'Montgomery for a long time . . .', Bedell Smith, FCP *SC*

'as the personal inspiration . . .', Ingersoll, 205

'as a slam to me', Chester B. Hansen Collection, Box 42, S-25, USAMHI

13 Wednesday 20 December

'extremely delicate', Carol Mather, *When the Grass Stops Growing,* Barnsley, 1997, 287

'completely out of touch', Sir Carol Mather docs., IWM, 11/28/1 5

'On the important question . . .', ibid.

'Monty, we are in a bit . . .', Dempsey, FCP *SC*

'like Christ . . .', quoted Nigel Hamilton, *Monty: Master of the Battlefield 1942–1944,* London, 1984, 213

'What's the form?', 'It was a slight . . .', Mather, 288

'The General is now well located . . .', 23.12.44, PWS

'the weakest commander . . .', Bedell Smith, FCP *SC*

'whether we can hold . . .', 21.12.44, PWS

'We sandwiched the thermite grenades . . .', Ralph Ingersoll, *Top Secret,* London, 1946, 200

'The best way to handle . . .', 'The Ardennes', CSI Battlebook 10-A, May 1984 'four inside and eleven . . .', ibid.

'Schloss Hemingstein 1944', Carlos Baker, *Ernest Hemingway: A Life Story,* New York, 1969, 558

'caused a considerable waste . . .', Generalmajor Siegfried von Waldenburg, 116th Panzer-Division, FMS A-873

Easy Company, Lieutenant Ed Shames, in Tim G. W. Holbert, 'Brothers at Bastogne — Easy Company's Toughest Task', *World War II Chronicles,* Winter 2004/5, 22–5

Retreat from Noville, Charles B. MacDonald, *A Time for Trumpets: The Untold Story of the Battle of the Bulge,* New York, 1984, 499–500

'the fog up front . . .', 'Dead were lying . . .', quoted Peter Schrijvers, *Those Who Hold Bastogne,* New Haven, CN, 2014, 63

'The 2nd Panzer . . .', etc., Generalmajor Heinz Kokott, 26th Volksgrenadier-Division, FMS B-040

'considered Bastogne . . .', Generalleutnant Fritz Bayerlein, Panzer Lehr Division, FMS A-941

'Is Bastogne to be . . .', Kokott, FMS B-040.

'The Division dutifully . . .', ibid.

'the deep rumble . . .', ibid.

'with devastating . . .', ibid.

'seated negligently . . .', Louis Simpson, *Selected Prose,* New York, 1989, 137–8

Action at Cheneux, Charles B. MacDonald, *The Battle of the Bulge,* London, 1984, 448–9

'still very bad', etc., RWHP, Box 1

'We stressed to every . . .', Maj. Donald P. Boyer Jr, S-3, 'Narrative Account of Action of 38th Armored Infantry Battalion', n.d., RWHP, Box 1

Führer Begleit Brigade, Generalmajor Otto Remer, ETHINT 80

'neck-deep', etc., Mack Morriss, 'The Defense of Stavelot', *Yank,* 9.2.45

SS atrocities in Stavelot, NARA RG 407 290/56/5/1–3, Box 7

Fighting in Stavelot on 20 December, ibid.

'for the most part impassable . . .', Operations of the Sixth Panzer Army, FMS A-924

'under almost continuous . . .', V Corps, NARA RG 498 290/56/2/3, Box 1455

Items taken from Camp Elsenborn, Richard H. Byers, 'The Battle of the Bulge', Richard H. Byers Papers, Box 1, USAMHI

'Sherman Ecke', 'The concentrated . . .', 3rd Panzergrenadier-Division, FMS A-978

'Farmers learned to take . . .', Peter Schrijvers, *The Unknown Dead: Civilians in the Battle of the Bulge,* Lexington, KY, 2005, 30

'a ring of steel', MacDonald, *A Time for Trumpets,* 406

'Soon I noticed that . . .', Arthur S. Couch, 'An American Infantry Soldier in World War

II Europe', unpublished memoir, private collection

German casualties, MacDonald, *A Time for Trumpets,* 407

'That is precisely . . .', Martin Lindsay, *So Few Got Through,* Barnsley, 2000, 161

Movement order to XXX Corps, TNA WO 231/30

'bombed-up, tanked up . . .', J. W. Cunningham, IWM Documents 15439 06/126/1

'a small but steady . . .', Brigadier A. W. Brown, IWM Documents 13781 73/18/1

'I felt that we were all right . . .', Bedell Smith, FCP *SC*

'clamped down . . .', *Time,* 1.1.45

'Personally I would like to shoot . . .', 21.12.44, Hobart Gay Papers, USAMHI

'disastrous results . . .', Memo, R. H. C. Drummond-Wolff, chief, Liberated Territories Desk, PWD, 21.12.44, C. D. Jackson Papers, Box 3, DDE Lib

'The wholly unexpected . . .', Fritz Hockenjos, Kriegstagebuch, BA-MA, MsG2 4038

'You cannot imagine . . .', LHC-DP, No. 217, II, 5, quoted Ian Kershaw, *The End: Hitler's Germany 1944–45,* London, 2011, 156

'Be practical . . .', Antony Beevor, *Berlin: The Downfall 1945,* London, 2002, 1

'Just rumble forward . . .', CSDIC, TNA WO 208/4364 GRGG 235/6

'The old principle of tank warfare: "for-

ward, forward, forward!" . . .', ibid.
'This offensive is terrific!', ibid.
'That man will never . . .', ibid.
'It's Wednesday . . .', ibid.

14 Thursday 21 December

'pocketed without adequate supplies', Peiper, FMS C-004

Detilleux, Wanne and Refat, Peter Schrijvers, *The Unknown Dead: Civilians in the Battle of the Bulge,* Lexington, KY, 2005, 57–8

'duck shooting', NARA RG 407 290/56/5/1–3, Box 7

'After we saw . . .', Mack Morriss, 'The Defense of Stavelot', *Yank,* 9.2.45

'The prisoner bag is thus far small . . .', 21.12.44, PWS

'Prisoners from the 12th SS?', 24.12.44, CBHD

'caked in mud', 'The GIs looked . . .', 21.12.44, CBHD

'General Collins is full . . .', 21.12.44, PWS

'Monty would come . . .', J. Lawton Collins, SOOHP, Box 1, USAMHI

Hasbrouck and Clarke on Ridgway, Jonathan M. Soffer, *General Matthew B. Ridgway,* Westport, CN, 1998, 71

'dread Panzerfaust', etc., Major Donald P. Boyer Jr, RWHP, Box 1

'would prove to be . . .', ibid.

'Huge gashes . . .', etc., ibid.

'Reform. Save what vehicles . . .', RWHP, Box 1

St Vith and the St Josef Kloster; 'He took a chalice . . .', Schrijvers, *Unknown Dead,* 169

I&R Platoon, 423rd Infantry, 106th Division, Richard D. Sparks, 'A Walk through the Woods', 2003, http://www. ryansdom.com/theryans/sparks/ adobe/walk2.pdf

'a God-sent gift', etc., Generalmajor Siegfried von Waldenburg, 116th Panzer-Division, FMS A-873

'It was known . . .', 4th SS Panzergrenadier-Regiment *Der Führer,* FMS P-109b

'The troops began slowly . . .', Waldenburg, FMS A-873

Tenneville, NARA RG 407 270/65/8/2 ML 130

'Ike and [Major General] Bull . . .', *PP,* 603

Kokott and stragglers, NARA RG 407 270/65/8/2 ML 130

'It was like a tremendous . . .', Robert Harwick, 'Christmas for Real!', *The Magazine of the Gulf Companies,* November–December 1945, 70–1

'Two prisoners came back', ibid.

'One, terrified . . .', ibid.

The decision to send a negotiator to Bastogne, General der Panzertruppe Heinrich von Lüttwitz, XLVII Panzer Corps, FMS A-939

'After he was finished . . .', George E. Koskimaki, *The Battered Bastards of Bastogne:*

The 101st Airborne in the Battle of the Bulge,
New York, 2007, 148

15 Friday 22 December

'Your orders are . . .', Maurice Delaval Collection, Box 7, USAMHI

'We crawled wearily . . .', etc., I&R Platoon, 423rd Infantry, 106th Division, Richard D. Sparks, 'A Walk through the Woods', 2003, http://www. ryansdom.com/theryans/sparks/adobe/walk2.pdf

'As we crossed . . .', Sam Bordelon, ibid.

'I am throwing in . . .', 22.12.44, RWHP, Box 1

'You have accomplished . . .', Misc'l AG Records, NARA RG 407 E 427 2280, Box 2425

'The line troops vowed . . .', Sparks, 'A Walk through the Woods'

'broke the base plates . . .', Misc'l AG Records, NARA RG 407 E 427 2280, Box 2425

Withdrawal across the Salm, ibid.

'What the hell are you . . .', Maurice Delaval Collection, Box 7, USAMHI

Civilians in Bütgenbach, Peter Schrijvers, *The Unknown Dead: Civilians in the Battle of the Bulge,* Lexington, KY, 2005, 26–7

Stoumont and SS wounded, NARA RG 407 290/56/5/1–3, Box 7

'very grave', 'conspicuously marked', Peiper, ETHINT 10

'a single infantry division', Generalmajor Heinz Kokott, 26th Volksgrenadier-Division, FMS B-040

'In the course of . . .', ibid.

Two German soldiers in Mande-Saint-Etienne, André Meurisse, quoted George E. Koskimaki, *The Battered Bastards of Bastogne: The 101st Airborne in the Battle of the Bulge,* New York, 2007, 221–2

'I was never worried . . .', Bedell Smith interview, FCP *SC*

'The fog was sitting . . .', J. Lawton Collins, SOOHP, Box 1, USAMHI

'engaged in a fight . . .', John S. D. Eisenhower, *The Bitter Woods,* New York, 1970, 453

Advance on Marche, General der Panzertruppe Heinrich von Lüttwitz, XLVII Panzer Corps, FMS A-939

23rd Hussars report, William H. Simpson Papers, Box 11, USAMHI

High ground south-west of Marche, Oberstleutnant Rüdiger Weiz, 2nd Panzer-Division, FMS B-456

Change of route for 116th Panzer-Division, Generalmajor Siegfried von Waldenburg, FMS A-873

'a veritable postcard scene . . .', 22.12.44, CBHD

'acutely worried over . . .', ibid.

'The enemy is making . . .', Eisenhower, *Bitter Woods,* 422 'kept his head magnificently . . .', CMH *SC,* 381

'We learned that the . . .', Ralph Ingersoll, *Top Secret,* London, 1946, 201–4

16 Saturday 23 December

'visibility unlimited', CMH *Ardennes,* 468

'God damn! . . .', John S. D. Eisenhower, *The Bitter Woods,* New York, 1970, 424

'As soon as the enemy . . .', Generalleutnant Karl Thoholte, 'Army Group B Artillery in the Ardennes', FMS B-311

Jemelle repeater station, ETO Historical Division, NARA RG 498 290/57/17/6

Airdrops to Task Force Hogan, Royce L. Thompson, 'Air Resupply to Isolated Units, Ardennes Campaign', OCMH, Feb. 1951, typescript, CMH 2-3.7 AE P

'Position considerably worsened . . .', General der Waffen-SS H. Priess, I SS Panzer Corps, FMS A-877

'American troops are now refusing . . .', William H. Simpson Papers, Box 11, USAMHI

Civilians in Faymonville, Peter Schrijvers, *The Unknown Dead: Civilians in the Battle of the Bulge,* Lexington, KY, 2005, 27–8

'Manteuffel's report that he could not . . .', Major Herbert Büchs, ETHINT 34

'up to ten men . . .', Generalmajor Heinz Kokott, 26th Volksgrenadier-Division, FMS B-040

'The first enemy . . .', 'Towards noon . . .', ibid.

'Houses caught fire . . .', ibid.

'*Achtung!* Strong enemy . . .', ibid.

Pathfinders and drop, Thompson, 'Air Resupply to Isolated Units, Ardennes Campaign'

'The first thing you saw . . .', Martin Wolfe, *Green Light!*, Philadelphia, PA, 1989, 348

'cheering them wildly . . .', George E. Koskimaki, *The Battered Bastards of Bastogne: The 101st Airborne in the Battle of the Bulge,* New York, 2007, 257

'Watching those bundles . . .', ibid.

'but the bottles . . .', CMH *Medical,* 420

'Not a single German aircraft . . .', Kokott, FMS B-040

'From then on', Koskimaki, 147

'in this cold . . .', Louis Simpson, *Selected Prose,* New York, 1989, 138

'I peer down the slope . . .', ibid., 139

Allocation of air assets on 23.12.44, NARA RG 498 290/56/2/3, Box 1455

Friendly fire and 'Rules for Firing', V Corps, ibid.

'chipper and confident as usual', 22.12.44, PWS

'The German push . . .', A. J. Cowdery, Civil Affairs, IWM Documents 17395 10/18/1

'battle-weary Shermans', Derrick Jones,

IWM Documents 4309

'That's not a pig . . .', Henry Dubois, cited Jean-Michel Delvaux, *La Bataille des Ardennes autour de Rochefort,* 2 vols., Hubaille, 2004–5, i, 333

Chapois, Jean-Michel Delvaux, *La Bataille des Ardennes autour de Celles,* Hubaille, 2003, 38–9

'But the road is mined . . .', ibid., 81–2

'Right, let's go! . . .', CMH *Ardennes,* 437

Civilians in Rochefort, Delvaux, *Rochefort,* i, 238–9 and ii, 236

'I wish to direct . . .', 23.12.44, FDRL MR

17 Sunday 24 December

'almost hysterical with . . .', 24.12.44, CBHD

'clinging stubbornly . . .', ibid.

'Today a quartermaster soldier . . .', ibid.

'General Patton was in . . .', ibid.

'blew everything in sight', 'The Intervention of the Third Army: III Corps in the Attack', typescript, n.d., CMH 8-3.1 AR

'it was usually . . .', VIII Corps, Third Army, NARA RG 498 290/56/2/3, Box 1463

'rations were frequently . . .', VII Corps, NARA RG 498 290/56/2/3, Box 1459

German snipers, NARA RG 498, 290/56/5/2, Box 3

Combat observer reports, VIII Corps, Third Army, NARA RG 498 290/56/2/3, Box 1463

Aid men, ibid.

'Knocking out tanks . . .', ibid.

'corruption and profiteering', 'So far these people . . .', Generalmajor Ludwig Heilmann, 5th Fallschirmjäger-Division, FMS B-023

'the enemy managed . . .', Robert R. Summers et al., 'Armor at Bastogne', Armored School, Advanced Course, May 1949, CARL N-2146.71-2

'Our company commander . . .', 24.12.44, Diary of Robert Calvert Jr, Company C, 51st Armored Infantry Battalion, 4th Armored Division, *American Valor Quarterly,* Summer 2008, 22

'Attacking waves . . .', NARA RG 407 290/56/5/1–3, Box 7

'Despite the air's . . .', 24.12.44, PWS

'but apparently received little . . .', 8.1.45, CBHD

'morale in the 82nd . . .', John S. D. Eisenhower, *The Bitter Woods,* New York, 1970, 449

82nd Airborne keeping German corpses, William A. Carter, typescript, 1983, CEOH, Box V, 14, XII, 22

'An SS-Führer told me . . .', CSDIC, TNA WO 208/4140 SRM 1150

'bitter and ever-changing', Generalmajor Siegfried von Waldenburg, 116th Panzer-Division, FMS A-873

'*beaucoup* dead', VII Corps, NARA RG 498 290/56/2/3, Box 1459

'Of the German Luftwaffe . . .', Waldenburg, FMS A-873

3rd Royal Tank Regiment at Sorinnes, Brigadier A. W. Brown, IWM Documents 13781 73/18/1

'if forced', David W. Hogan Jr, *A Command Post at War: First Army Headquarters in Europe, 1943–1945,* Washington, DC, 2000, 223

'The bastards are in . . .', Eisenhower, *Bitter Woods,* 466

'If necessary, elements . . .', Oberstleutnant Rüdiger Weiz, 2nd Panzer-Division, FMS B-456

'since both pockets . . .', ibid.

Bande massacre and Léon Praile, see Jean-Michel Delvaux, *La Bataille des Ardennes autour de Rochefort,* 2 vols., Hubaille, 2004–5, i, 17–41

Sondereinheitkommando 8, A. J. Cowdery, Civil Affairs, IWM Documents 17395 10/18/1

'After the deed was done . . .', TNA WO 171/4184

'It's the greatest imposture . . .', Heinz Guderian, *Panzer Leader,* New York, 1996, 310–11

Hemingway and Gellhorn, Carlos Baker, *Ernest Hemingway: A Life Story,* New York, 1969, 558–9

Wounded in Bastogne, CMH *Medical,* 418

'Do not plan . . .', Stanley Weintraub, *Eleven Days in December,* New York, 2006, 137

'Tomorrow we will cross . . .', Simone Hesbois, quoted Delvaux, *Rochefort,* i, 328–9

Liliane Delhomme, Rochefort, Delvaux, *Rochefort,* ii, 240

Frozen C-Rations, Gerald Astor, *Battling Buzzards: The Odyssey of the 517th Parachute Regimental Combat Team 1943–1945,* New York, 1993, 300

'The fellows are calling . . .', PFC Warren Wilson, Coy I, 2nd Bn, 395th Inf., Weintraub, 125

'this General of stern expression . . .', Frederick A. McDonald, *Remembered Light: Glass Fragments from World War II,* San Francisco, 2007, 29

18 Christmas Day

The bombing of Bastogne, Peter Schrijvers, *Those Who Hold Bastogne,* New Haven, CN, 2014, 119–20

'taken, lost and re-taken', Generalmajor Heinz Kokott, 26th Volksgrenadier-Division, FMS B-040

'strip and repair weapons . . .', 502nd Parachute Infantry Regiment, VIII Corps, NARA RG 498 290/56/2/3, Box 1463

'The Germans piled out . . .', PFC Leonard Schwartz, George E. Koskimaki, *The Battered Bastards of Bastogne: The 101st Airborne in the Battle of the Bulge,* New York, 2007, 325 'buttoned up', 502nd Parachute Infantry Regiment, VIII Corps, NARA RG 498 290/56/2/3, Box 1463

'success seemed very close', Kokott, FMS B-040

'The Germans attacked our . . .', Cpl Jackson of the 502nd Parachute Infantry Regiment, VIII Corps, NARA RG 498 290/56/5/2, Box 3

'cut off and annihilated', Kokott, FMS B-040

'We were 900 metres . . .', TNA WO 311/54

'irresponsible and unfeasible', 'bloody, dubious and costly . . .', Kokott, FMS B-040

Airdrop on Christmas Day, Royce L. Thompson, 'Air Resupply to Isolated Units, Ardennes Campaign', OCMH, Feb. 1951, typescript, CMH 2-3.7 AE P

'We have been let down', NARA RG 407 270/65/8/2 ML 130

Lutrebois, 'to lie in wait . . .', NARA RG 498 290/56/5/2, Box 3

'We feel like we . . .', Denyse de Coune, 'Souvenirs de guerre: Assenois 1944–5', p. 125, quoted Peter Schrijvers, *The Unknown Dead: Civilians in the Battle of the Bulge*, Lexington, KY, 2005, p. xiii

'showed understanding', General der Panzertruppe Heinrich von Lüttwitz, XLVII Panzer Corps, FMS A-939

Haid, Jean-Michel Delvaux, *La Bataille des*

Ardennes autour de Rochefort, 2 vols., Hubaille, 2004–5, i, 341

Advance from Sorinnes, Brigadier A. W. Brown, IWM Documents 13781 73/18/1

Armoured vehicles at Celles, TNA WO 231/30

'The Americans were mad . . .', Jean-Michel Delvaux, *La Bataille des Ardennes autour de Celles,* Hubaille, 2003, 103

'divisional units which . . .', Generalmajor Siegfried von Waldenburg, 116th Panzer-Division, FMS A-873

'a lot to learn', VIII Corps, NARA RG 498 290/56/2/3, Box 1463

'Their tanks left . . .', VIII Corps, NARA RG 407 270/65/8/2 ML 299

'A clear cold Christmas . . .', *PP,* 606

'It cut deep . . .', Schrijvers, *Unknown Dead,* 31

'The bombers have fine . . .', Richard Henry Byers, 'Battle of the Bulge', typescript, 1983

'like a swarm of wasps', etc., Leutnant Martin Opitz, 295th Volksgrenadier-Division, NARA RG 407 290/56/5/1–3, Box 7

'Monty was always expecting . . .', etc., Chester B. Hansen Collection, Box 42, S-7, USAMHI

'the First Army cannot attack . . .', *PP,* 606

'I am sure . . .', Chester B. Hansen Collection, Box 42, S-7, USAMHI

'You know, we exploited . . .', Bedell Smith,

FCP *SC*
'Months Added to War?', *Daily Express,*
Stanley Weintraub, *Eleven Days in December,*
New York, 2006, 79

19 Tuesday 26 December
'The Kraut has stuck . . .', 26.12.44, CBHD
'This has been a very bad . . .', *PP,* 605
'Today has been rather . . .', *PP,* 607
The fires in Bastogne, Peter Schrijvers,
Those Who Hold Bastogne, New Haven, CN,
2014, 130
'cut loose at 300 feet', Royce L. Thompson, 'Air Resupply to Isolated Units, Ardennes Campaign', OCMH, Feb. 1951,
typescript, CMH 2-3.7 AE P
'The medical personnel . . .', 26.12.44,
CBHD
'many amputations', CMH *Medical,* 422
37th Tank Battalion, *American Valor Quarterly,* Summer 2008, 19
Assenois, NARA RG 407 270/65/8/2 ML
130
'it was all over', Generalmajor Rudolf
Freiherr von Gersdorff and Generalmajor
Heinz Kokott, ETHINT 44
'But what spirit!', Major Frank, commander
III/13th Fallschirmjäger, CSDIC, TNA WO
208/4140 SRM 1148
'the *Führer Begleit* Brigade . . .', General
der Panzertruppe Heinrich von Lüttwitz,
XLVII Panzer Corps, ETHINT 42

Martha Gellhorn and Leland Stowe, 26.12.44, CBHD

'Fortunately, the RAF were not . . .', Brigadier A. W. Brown, IWM Documents 13781 73/18/1

Order to Kampfgruppe Holtmeyer to withdraw, General der Panzertruppe Heinrich von Lüttwitz, XLVII Panzer Corps, FMS A-939

'Luckily the enemy was . . .', Oberstleutnant Rüdiger Weiz, 2nd Panzer-Division, FMS B-456

'Moi, pas Allemand! . . .', Jean-Michel Delvaux, *La Bataille des Ardennes autour de Rochefort,* 2 vols., Hubaille, 2004–5, i, 218

Buissonville, ibid., 304 and 308

'It was estimated that . . .', Colonel Shaffer F. Jarrell, VII Corps, NARA RG 498 290/56/2/3, Box 1459

'a vast cemetery . . .', Jean-Michel Delvaux, *La Bataille des Ardennes autour de Celles,* Hubaille, 2003, 94

'We want to do in Belgium . . .', diary of Sister Alexia Bruyère, 26.12.44, quoted Delvaux, *Rochefort,* i, 143

Surrounded Kampfgruppe of 116th Panzer-Division, Generalmajor Siegfried von Waldenburg, FMS A-873

'motor fuel was so scarce . . .', Generalmajor Otto Remer, ETHINT 80

'four or five tanks with . . .', CCA from 3rd Armored Division, TNA WO 231/30

3rd SS Panzergrenadier-Regiment and

Grandménil, FMS P-109

'the enemy opened fire . . .', Alfred Zerbel, 3rd SS Panzergrenadier-Regiment *Deutschland,* FMS P-109

'If the soldier does not need . . .', NARA RG 498 290/56/2/3, Box 1463

'people were struggling . . .', Peter Schrijvers, *The Unknown Dead: Civilians in the Battle of the Bulge,* Lexington, KY, 2005, 183

'Most of them were burned . . .', ibid., 184

'Saint-Vith is still burning . . .', Leutnant Martin Opitz, 295th Volksgrenadier-Division, NARA RG 407 290/56/5/1–3, Box 7

'a giant heap . . .', ibid.

Bombing campaign, La Roche, TNA WO 231/30

'Things continued to look . . .', 26.12.44, PWS

'stagnating conservatism . . .', 26.12.44, CBHD

'Monty is a tired . . .', 27.12.44, *PP,* 608

'*Mein Führer . . .*', etc., Samuel W. Mitcham Jr, *Panzers in Winter,* Mechanicsburg, PA, 2008, 153–4

'traitors', 'I know the war is lost . . .', Nicolaus von Below, *Als Hitlers Adjutant, 1937– 1945,* Mainz, 1980, 398

20 Preparing the Allied Counter-Offensive

Airdrop on Bastogne, 27 December, Royce L. Thompson, 'Air Resupply to Isolated Units, Ardennes Campaign', OCMH, Feb.

1951, typescript, CMH 2-3.7 AE P

Belly landing, George E. Koskimaki, *The Battered Bastards of Bastogne: The 101st Airborne in the Battle of the Bulge,* New York, 2007, 365–6

'With the enemy attack losing . . .', 'further delay will . . .', 12th Army Group, NARA RG 407 270/65/7/2 ML 209

'counter-attack started too early . . .', 'from total . . .', Generalmajor Siegfried von Waldenburg, 116th Panzer-Division, FMS B-038

'high intelligence channels . . .', 28.12.44, PWS

'much smitten with . . .', 28.12.44, CBHD

'the Americans have taken . . .', Montgomery letter to Mountbatten, 25.12.44, Nigel Hamilton, *Monty: The Field Marshal 1944–1976,* London, 1986, 238

'in as grave a light . . .', CMH *Ardennes,* 610

'General Hodges has had enough . . .', 27.12.44, PWS

'the most conservative . . .', ibid.

'You're going to push . . .', J. Lawton Collins, SOOHP, USAMHI

'Praise God from . . .', CMH *Ardennes,* 612

'The roads are a sheet of ice . . .', William H. Simpson Papers, Box 11, USAMHI

Montgomery's plan outlined at Zonhoven, Crerar diary, TNA CAB 106/1064

'from four to five panzer divisions',
31.12.44, CBHD

'Americans are very poor . . .', 2.1.45,
CBHD

'It looks to me as if . . .', Alanbrooke Diary,
30.12.44, LHCMA

'full operational direction . . .', quoted
Russell F. Weigley, *Eisenhower's Lieutenants*,
Bloomington, IN, 1990, 542–3

'Under no circumstances . . .', quoted
Hamilton, *Monty: The Field Marshal*, 275

'In your latest letter . . .', DDE Lib, Box 83

'the British public . . .', Eisenhower at
SHAEF meeting on 30.12.44, Air Chief
Marshal Sir James Robb's notes, NARA RG
319 270/19/5-6/7-1, Boxes 215–16 2-3.7 CB
8

'What shall I do . . .', F. de Guingand,
quoted Hamilton, *Monty: The Field Marshal*,
279

'Dear Ike . . .', DDE Lib, Box 83

'It was so cold . . .', diary of Robert Calvert
Jr, Company C, 51st Armored Infantry Bat-
talion, 4th Armored Division, *American Valor
Quarterly*, Summer 2008, 22

'a fighter-bomber attack . . .', Generalmajor
Otto Remer, ETHINT 80

'ten cargo-carrying . . .', ibid.

'If this attack failed . . .', General der Panzertruppe Heinrich von Lüttwitz, XLVII
Panzer Corps, FMS A-939

Fighting for Chenogne and Sibret, Remer,

ETHINT 80

'His instructions before . . .', Stephen E. Ambrose, *Band of Brothers*, New York, 2001, 194

'Oscar', Koskimaki, 393

'Now by God . . .', ibid., 391

35th Division, MFF-7, C1-107

'cut to pieces', CMH *Ardennes*, 626

Battle round Lutrebois, III Corps, NARA RG 498 290/56/5/2, Box 3

'The SS spread the rumor . . .', etc., Generalmajor Ludwig Heilmann, 5th Fallschirmjäger-Division, FMS B-023

'These road conditions . . .', Generalmajor Heinz Kokott, 26th Volksgrenadier-Division, FMS B-040

'broke into houses . . .', TNA WO 311/54

'bombers from the Eighth Air Force . . .', Third Army daily log, 31.12.44, Gaffey Papers, USAMHI

'It is obvious that . . .', 30.12.44, CBHD

'You could hear . . .', Letter, Eugene A. Watts, S-3, 52nd Armored Infantry Bn, 9th AD, 28.2.85, CBMP, Box 1

Horrocks on medical leave, Hamilton, *Monty: The Field Marshal*, 255–6

6th Airborne, Edward Horrell, IWM Documents 17408 10/4/1

Belgians and abandoned German equipment, Jean-Michel Delvaux, *La Bataille des Ardennes autour de Celles*, Hubaille, 2003, 40

Dead German officer, ibid., 36

'The Ardennes has a pronounced . . .', A. J. Cowdery, Civil Affairs, IWM Documents 17395 10/18/1

'with his beret and . . .', Liliane Delhomme, Jean-Michel Delvaux, *La Bataille des Ardennes autour de Rochefort,* 2 vols., Hubaille, 2004–5, ii, 241

Lance-Sergeant Walker, Letter to author from his son, Air Marshal Sir David Walker, 27.4.14

highballs and turkey, William H. Simpson Papers, Box 11, USAMHI

'In his mess every night . . .', G. Patrick Murray, 1973, SOOHP

'indiscriminately firing . . .', 31.12.44, PWS

'talked passionately . . .', etc., 31.12.44, CBHD

'At midnight all was still . . .', Ursula von Kardorff, *Diary of a Nightmare: Berlin 1942–1945,* London, 1965, 161

'My prayer . . .', Leutnant Martin Opitz, 295th Volksgrenadier-Division, NARA RG 407 290/56/ 5/1–3, Box 7

21 The Double Surprise

'The Reichsmarschall has . . .', *HLB,* 514, 517

'They are all young . . .', Fähnrich Schmid, CSDIC, TNA WO 208/4134 SRA 5615

'What sort of training . . .', Oberleutnant Hartigs, 4/JG 26, CSDIC, TNA WO 208/

4135 SRA 5767

'engine trouble', CSDIC, TNA WO 208/ 4134 SRA 5515

'used to fly . . .', Hartigs, CSDIC, TNA WO 208/4135 SRA 5764 20/1/45

'In our Staffel . . .', Feldwebel Halbritter, CSDIC, TNA WO 208/4134 SRA 5569

'seems to have run . . .', CSDIC, TNA WO 208/4135 SRA 5760 23/1/45

'Well, what's our Reichsmarschall . . .', CSDIC, TNA WO 208/4177

'He had no understanding . . .', CSDIC, TNA WO 208/4292 USAFE/M.72

'practically cried', 'unless we . . .', CSDIC, TNA WO 208/4164 SRX 21091

'take-off' rations, ibid.

'poured out his troubles . . .', Oberstleutnant Johann Kogler, CSDIC, TNA WO 208/4177

'the worst-informed . . .', CSDIC, TNA WO 208/4178

'Herr General . . .', CSDIC, TNA WO 208/ 4177

'We had been stationed . . .', Oberleutnant Hartigs, FW 190 4/JG 26, CSDIC, TNA WO 208/4164 SRX 2086

'Whoever [returns after failing] to attack . . .', ibid.

'What a smashing . . .', CSDIC, TNA WO 208/4164 SRX 2086

'One frustrated Typhoon pilot . . .', Sebastian Cox of the Air Historical Branch of the

Ministry of Defence, e-mail to author, 18.8.14. I am most grateful for his corrections and precise figures for aircraft losses on both sides

'closely parked in formation', 1.1.45, PWS

'They caught the British . . .', 2.1.45, PWS

'Mid-morning saw . . .', William H. Simpson Papers, Box 11, USAMHI

'which tore a large hole . . .', Sebastian Cox, e-mail to author, 18.8.14

'Jerry made one big error . . .', William H. Simpson Papers, Box 11, USAMHI

'A catastrophe overtook . . .', Nicolaus von Below, *Als Hitlers Adjutant, 1937–1945*, Mainz, 1980, 399

'Spirits have reached a new low . . .', letter to Colonel Waine Archer from Colonel Pete T. Heffner Jr, 3.1.45, NARA RG 498 290/56/5/3, Box 1463

Panic in Strasbourg, NARA RG 331, SHAEF records (290/715/2) E-240P, Box 38

'It is self-evident . . .', Charles de Gaulle, *Mémoires de Guerre: Le Salut, 1944–1946*, Paris, 1959, 145

'Juin said things . . .', James Robb diary, DDE Lib, Papers, Pre-Pres., Box 98

'the French Army would get . . .', Dwight D. Eisenhower, *Crusade in Europe*, London, 1948, 396

'If we were involved . . .', De Gaulle, *Mémoires de Guerre: Le Salut, 1944–1946*, 148

'This modification . . .', 'I think we've

done . . .', Eisenhower, *Crusade in Europe,* 396

'It suggested that . . .', 4.1.45, DCD

'in high spirits', letter to Colonel Waine Archer from Colonel Pete T. Heffner Jr, 5.1.45, NARA RG 498 290/56/5/3, Box 1463

'next to the weather . . .', *PDDE,* iv, 2491

'signal intelligence to . . .', 3.1.45, TNA HW 14/119

'This presents a serious . . .', ibid.

'simply refused . . .', Thomas E. Griess, 14.10.70, York County Heritage Trust, York, PA, Box 94

'surprised, captured or surrounded . . .', VI Corps, NARA RG 498 290/56/5/3, Box 1463

'attempt to discredit the Americans', Chester B. Hansen Collection, Box 42, S-28, USAMHI

'the public clamor . . .', 6.1.45, CBHD

'wouldn't serve one day . . .', 8.1.45, CBHD

'repudiate the efficacy . . .', ibid.

'the German breakthrough . . .', etc., 6.1.45, CBHD

'At the same time . . .', 5.1.45, CBHD

'invaluable', TNA CAB 106/1107

'The battle has been most interesting . . .', etc., TNA CAB 106/1107

'although this statement . . .', ibid.

'The Battle of the Ardennes . . .', ibid.

'return it to me . . .', 'I wanted it back . . .', 8.1.45, CBHD

'I fear great offence . . .', TNA CAB 106/1107

22 Counter-attack

'a defensive success . . .', etc., Generalmajor Otto Remer, ETHINT 80

'The 11th Armored is . . .', 4.1.45, *PP,* 615

'There were some unfortunate . . .', ibid.

'a bitter cold . . .', CBHD, Box 5

'continued to pour destruction', Ed Cunningham, 'The Cooks and Clerks', *Yank,* 16.3.45

'Units frequently make errors . . .', Lt Col. Glavin, G-3 6th Armored Division, VII Corps, NARA RG 498 290/56/2/3, Box 1459

'If you enter a village . . .', 6th Armored Division, NARA RG 498 290/56/5/2, Box 3

11th Armored Division, CMH *Ardennes,* 647

'The 17th Airborne, which attacked this . . .', 4.1.45, *PP,* 615

'We have had replacements . . .', 17th Airborne, NARA RG 498 290/56/5/2, Box 3

'The German follows a fixed form . . .', etc., ibid.

'Our men had great confidence . . .', Colonel J. R. Pierce, NARA RG 498 290/56/5/2, Box 3

Using artillery to dig foxholes, VII Corps, NARA RG 498 290/56/2/3, Box 1459

'The 17th has suffered . . .', 8.1.45, CBHD

Sergeant Isidore Jachman, Congressional

Medal of Honor Library, vol. i, 172–3, Peter Schrijvers, *Those Who Hold Bastogne*, New Haven, CN, 2014, 225

'saw a rifleman . . .', VIII Corps, NARA RG 498 290/56/2/3, Box 1463

'all for putting . . .', etc., *PP*, 615

'Roads were icy . . .', etc., 3.1.45, PWS

'A lucky tree burst . . .', William H. Simpson Papers, Box 11, USAMHI

'Trois Ponts was cleared . . .', 3.1.45, PWS

'greatly pleased with . . .', ibid.

'the 2nd Armored Division . . .', 4.1.45, CBHD

Fighting for Bure, War Diary, 13th Bn Parachute Regiment, TNA WO 171/1246

Yvonne Louviaux, in Jean-Michel Delvaux, *La Bataille des Ardennes autour de Rochefort*, 2 vols., Hubaille, 2004–5, ii, 123–4

'this headquarters thought . . .', 6.1.45, PWS

'declare there's no evidence . . .', 7.1.45, Hobart Gay Papers, USAMHI

'Undoubtedly the hard fighting . . .', José Cugnon, quoted Delvaux, *Rochefort*, ii, 28

'they certainly did not seem . . .', ibid., i, 232

'At 09.30, we saw . . .', diary of Sister Alexia Bruyère, quoted ibid., i, 143

'O little town of Houffalize . . .', *PP*, 632

'Resistance never let up . . .', Captain H. O. Sweet, IWM, 95/33/1

'Everyone thinks . . .', NARA RG 165,

Entry 178, Box 146353

'Anyone taken prisoner . . .', CSDIC, TNA WO 208/4157 SRN 4772 25/3/45

'Do not get the impression . . .', Major Gen. Kenneth Strong 02/14/2 3/25 — Intelligence Notes No. 33, IWM Documents 11656

'When the Germans are having . . .', etc., NARA RG 498 290/56/2/3, Box 1459

'were more meek . . .', MFF-7, C1-107

'Too good treatment . . .', VIII Corps, NARA RG 498 290/56/2/3, Box 1463

'We have never been . . .', NARA RG 498 290/56/2/3, Box 1466

Forcing German prisoners to walk barefoot, Gerald Astor, *A Blood-Dimmed Tide,* New York, 1992, 375

'prisoners were beginning . . .', TNA WO 231/30

Pozit fuses, V Corps, NARA RG 498 290/56/2/3, Box 1455

'The results of these . . .', VII Corps, NARA RG 498 290/56/2/3, Box 1459

'If we want to win the war . . .', Generalmajor Ludwig Heilmann, 5th Fallschirmjäger-Division, FMS B-023

'If there is any suspicion . . .', CSDIC, TNA WO 208/3616 SIR 1548

'Ten or twelve . . .', Feldwebel Rösner, 7th Battery, 26th Volksgrenadier-Division, TNA WO 311/54

'I nearly gagged . . .', Robert M. Bowen, *Fighting with the Screaming Eagles: With the*

101st Airborne from Normandy to Bastogne, London 2001, 204–5

'The wounded . . .', Assistant Arzt Dammann, CSDIC, TNA WO 208/3616 SIR 1573

'Chamber of Horrors', etc., 'Shock Nurse', Ernest O. Hauser, *Saturday Evening Post,* 10.3.45

Non-battle casualties, CMH *Medical,* 385–6

'nausea, crying . . .', VII Corps, NARA RG 498 290/56/2/3, Box 1459

'When one man cracks . . .', ibid.

'Tank fatigue', ibid.

'long hours of exposure', ibid.

'Even with hard and experienced . . .', 5th Infantry Division, XX Corps, NARA RG 498 290/56/2/3, Box 1465

2nd and 9th Panzer-Divisions, General der Panzertruppe Heinrich von Lüttwitz, XLVII Panzer Corps, FMS A-939

'It is the coldest weather . . .', 8.1.45, A. J. Cowdery, Civil Affairs, IWM Documents 17395 10/18/1

'The Führer has ordered . . .', *HLB,* 597

'It's the greatest mockery . . .', Generalmajor Hans Bruhn, 533rd Volksgrenadier-Division, CSDIC, TNA WO 208/4364 GRGG 240

'The Germans are pulling . . .', 11.1.45, William H. Simpson Papers, Box 11, USAMHI

'We are aware of your views . . .', to Major General Clayton Bissell, TNA WO 171/4184 'like the heavens . . .', Colonel Liebisch, *Art of War Symposium,* US Army War College, Carlisle, PA, 1986, 617

'Forward into the fascist . . .', *Velikaya Otechestvennaya Voina,* Moscow, 1999, iii, 26

'had enabled the Russian . . .', 15.1.45, CBHD

'The fear of Russia . . .', Generalleutnant von Heyking, 6th Fallschirmjäger-Division, TNA WO 171/4184

23 Flattening the Bulge

'What gets me . . .', quoted Air Marshal Sir James Robb, 'Higher Direction of War', typescript, 11.46, provided by his daughter

'My God, don't they have . . .', Stephen E. Ambrose, *Band of Brothers,* New York, 2001, 229

'Every replacement . . .', Tim G. W. Holbert, 'Brothers at Bastogne — Easy Company's Toughest Task', *World War II Chronicles,* Winter 2004/5, 22–5

2nd Battalion, 506th at Rachamps, Ambrose, *Band of Brothers,* 223–4

'violent enemy . . .', NARA RG 498 290/ 56/5/3, Box 1463

'Having visited villages . . .', 14.1.45, A. J. Cowdery, Civil Affairs, IWM Documents 17395 10/18/1

'the troops have been over-enthusiastic . . .', A. Fieber, 1st Bn, Manchester Rgt, in 53rd

(Welsh) Div., IWM Documents 4050 84/50/1

'The right wing . . .', 2nd Panzer-Division, FMS P-109e

'He was trying to thaw him out . . .', Martin Lindsay, *So Few Got Through,* Barnsley, 2000, 160

'Very soon an American . . .', 2nd Panzer-Division, FMS P-109e

'brick houses . . .', etc., MFF-7, C1-100/101

'At one point . . .', Patton, quoted Gerald Astor, *A Blood-Dimmed Tide,* NewYork, 1992, 366

'Contact was established . . .', Armored School, Fort Knox, General Instruction Dept, 16.4.48, CARL N-18000.127

'The Division does not . . .', quoted H. Essame, *The Battle for Germany,* London, 1970, 117

'The situation is now restored', 17.1.45, CBHD

'At 10.30 the Field Marshal . . .', William H. Simpson Papers, Box 11, USAMHI

'That "protect the Ninth's . . .', ibid.

'the United States troops . . .', TNA CAB 106/1107

Telephone transcript, William H. Simpson Papers, Box 11, USAMHI

'First and Third US Armies in . . .', Montgomery to Brooke, 14.1.45, Nigel Hamilton, *Monty: The Field Marshal 1944–1976,* London, 1986, 325

'Any future moves . . .', William H. Simpson Papers, Box 11, USAMHI

'His forces are now relegated . . .', 2.12.44, CBHD

Whiteley, not Bedell Smith, D. K. R. Crosswell, *Beetle: The Life of General Walter Bedell Smith,* Lexington, KY, 2010, 853

'The reputation and the good will . . .', 24.1.45, Hobart Gay Papers, USAMHI

'The town is in ruins . . .', NARA RG 407 E 427 2280, Box 2425

XIX TAC claims, CMH *SC,* 395 n. 111

'The three tactical air forces . . .', Joint Report No. 1 by Operational Research Section 2nd Tactical Air Force and No. 2 Operational Research Section, 21st Army Group, TNA WO 231/30

'did not play a decisive . . .', Generalmajor Siegfried von Waldenburg, 116th Panzer-Division, FMS B-038

'The Third Army today . . .', 29.1.45, CBHD

'He is a good officer . . .', *PP,* 630

'a tremendous palace . . .', William H. Simpson Papers, Box 11, USAMHI

'compelled to ransack . . .', 'Eagle Took', 16.1.45, CBHD

'his customary slow . . .', 4.2.45, CBHD

'passed scarred and . . .', ibid.

Belgian civilian casualties, CMH *SC,* 332

'tremendous number . . .', 25.1.45, A. J. Cowdery, Civil Affairs, IWM Documents

17395 10/18/1
Damage in La Roche, Peter Schrijvers, *The Unknown Dead: Civilians in the Battle of the Bulge,* Lexington, KY, 2005, 325

24 Conclusions
Trial of Kampfgruppe Peiper, FMS C-004
'The criticism whether it . . .', Interrogation of Generalfeldmarschall Keitel and Generaloberst Jodl, 20.7.45, TNA WO 231/30
Falling back to the Meuse, Seventh Army, FMS A-876
'The promptness with which . . .', Generaloberst Alfred Jodl, FMS A-928
'no other army in the world . . .', 24.12.44, CBHD
'Officers and men . . .', Generalmajor Rudolf Freiherr von Gersdorff, FMS A-933
'Every day that . . .', 'the last gasp . . .', Generalleutnant Fritz Bayerlein, Panzer Lehr Division, FMS A-941
'a major point . . .', quoted D. K. R. Crosswell, *Beetle: The Life of General Walter Bedell Smith,* Lexington, KY, 2010, 837
Churchill recognizing the graver consequence, Churchill to Ismay, 10.1.45, TNA PREM 3 4 31/2
'He's a psychopath . . .', Cornelius J. Ryan Collection, Ohio University, Box 43, file 7, typescript, n.d.
Allied casualties in the Ardennes, CMH *SC,* 396; and Royce L. Thompson, OCMH,

typescript, 28.4.52, CMH 2-3.7 AE P-15

'Not for God and country . . .', Gerald K. Johnson, 'The Black Soldiers in the Ardennes', *Soldiers,* February 1981, 16ff.

'the Germans made us take off . . .', etc., 'The Service Diary of German War Prisoner #315136', Sgt John P. Kline, Coy M, 3rd Battalion, 423rd Infantry Regiment, CBMP, Box 2

'xylophone ribs . . .', etc., 19.4.45, GBP

'5,000 mile stare', Vonnegut on C-Span, New Orleans, 30.5.95

SELECT BIBLIOGRAPHY

Ambrose, Stephen E., *Band of Brothers,* New York, 2001

Arend, Guy Franz, *Bastogne et la Bataille des Ardennes,* Bastogne, 1974

Astor, Gerald, *A Blood-Dimmed Tide,* New York, 1992

———— *Battling Buzzards: The Odyssey of the 517th Parachute Regimental Combat Team 1943–1945,* New York, 1993

Atkinson, Rick, *The Guns at Last Light,* New York, 2013

Baker, Carlos, *Ernest Hemingway: A Life Story,* New York, 1969

Bauer, Eddy, *L'Offensive des Ardennes,* Paris, 1983

Bedell Smith, Walter, *Eisenhower's Six Great Decisions,* London, 1956

Beevor, Antony, *Berlin: The Downfall 1945,* London, 2002

———— *The Second World War,* London, 2012

Beevor, Antony, and Cooper, Artemis, *Paris*

after the Liberation, 1944–1949, London, 1994

Belchem, David, *All in the Day's March,* London, 1978

Below, Nicolaus von, *Als Hitlers Adjutant, 1937–1945,* Mainz, 1980

Bennet, Ralph, *Ultra in the West,* New York, 1980

Boberach, Heinz (ed.), *Meldungen aus dem Reich: Die geheimen Lageberichte des Sicherheitsdienstes der SS 1938–1945,* 17 vols., Herrsching, 1984

Botsford, Gardner, *A Life of Privilege, Mostly,* New York, 2003

Bowen, Robert M., *Fighting with the Screaming Eagles: With the 101st Airborne from Normandy to Bastogne,* London 2001

Bradley, Omar N., *A Soldier's Story,* New York, 1964

Buckley, John, *Monty's Men: The British Army and the Liberation of Europe,* London, 2013

Cole, Hugh M., *United States Army in World War II: The European Theater of Operations: The Ardennes: Battle of the Bulge,* Washington, DC, 1988

Connell, J. Mark, *Ardennes: The Battle of the Bulge,* London, 2003

Couch, Arthur S., 'An American Infantry Soldier in World War II Europe', unpublished memoir, private collection

Crosswell, D. K. R., *Beetle: The Life of General Walter Bedell Smith*, Lexington, KY, 2010

D'Este, Carlo, *Eisenhower: Allied Supreme Commander*, London, 2002
De Gaulle, Charles, *Mémoires de Guerre: Le Salut, 1944–1946*, Paris, 1959
Delvaux, Jean-Michel, *La Bataille des Ardennes autour de Celles*, Hubaille, 2003
——— *La Bataille des Ardennes autour de Rochefort*, 2 vols., Hubaille, 2004–5
Domarus, Max (ed.), *Reden und Proklamationen 1932–1945*, Wiesbaden, 1973
Doubler, Michael D., *Closing with the Enemy: How GIs fought the War in Europe, 1944–1945*, Lawrence, KS, 1994
Dupuy, Colonel R. Ernest, *St. Vith: Lion in the Way: The 106th Infantry Division in World War II*, Washington, DC, 1949

Eisenhower, Dwight D., *Crusade in Europe*, London, 1948
Eisenhower, John S. D., *The Bitter Woods*, New York, 1970
Ellis, John, *The Sharp End: The Fighting Man in World War II*, London, 1990
Elstob, P., *Bastogne: La Bataille des Ardennes*, Paris, 1968
Ent, Uzal W. (ed.), *The First Century: A History of the 28th Infantry Division*, Harrisburg,

PA, 1979

Essame, H. *The Battle for Germany*, London, 1970

Evans, Richard J., *The Third Reich at War*, London, 2008

Ferguson, Niall, *The War of the World*, London, 2007

Forty, George, *The Reich's Last Gamble: The Ardennes Offensive, December 1944*, London, 2000

Friedrich, Jörg, *Der Brand: Deutschland im Bombenkrieg 1940–1945*, Berlin, 2002

Fussell, Paul, *The Boys' Crusade*, New York, 2003

Galtier-Boissière, Jean, *Mon journal pendant l'Occupation*, Paris, 1944

Gehlen, Reinhard, *The Gehlen Memoirs*, London, 1972

Gellhorn, Martha, *Point of No Return*, New York, 1989

Gilbert, Martin, *The Second World War*, London, 1989

Guderian, Heinz, *Panzer Leader*, New York, 1996

Hamilton, Nigel, *Monty: Master of the Battlefield 1942–1944*, London, 1984

——— *Monty: The Field Marshal 1944–1976*, London, 1986

Hastings, Max, *Armageddon: The Battle for Germany 1944–45*, London, 2004

――― *Finest Years: Churchill as Warlord, 1940–45*, London, 2009

Heiber, Helmut, and Glantz, David M. (eds.), *Hitler and his Generals: Military Conferences 1942–1945*, London, 2002; *Hitlers Lagebesprechungen: Die Protokollfragmente seiner militärischen Konferenzen 1942–1945*, Munich, 1984

Hemingway, Ernest, *Across the River and into the Trees*, New York, 1950

Henke, Klaus-Dietmar, *Die amerikanische Besetzung Deutschlands*, Munich, 1995

Hitchcock, William I., *Liberation: The Bitter Road to Freedom: Europe 1944–1945*, London, 2009

Hogan, David W., Jr, *A Command Post at War: First Army Headquarters in Europe, 1943–1945*, Washington, DC, 2000

Horrocks, Brian, *Corps Commander*, London, 1977

Hynes, Samuel, *The Soldiers' Tale: Bearing Witness to Modern War*, London, 1998

Ingersoll, Ralph, *Top Secret*, London, 1946

Isaacson, Walter, *Kissinger: A Biography*, London, 1992

Jordan, David, *The Battle of the Bulge: The First 24 Hours*, London, 2003

Jung, Hermann, *Die Ardennen-Offensive 1944/ 45: Ein Beispiel für die Kriegführung Hitlers,* Göttingen, 1971

Junge, Traudl, *Until the Final Hour: Hitler's Last Secretary,* London, 2002

Kardorff, Ursula von, *Diary of a Nightmare: Berlin 1942–1945,* London, 1965

Kershaw, Alex, *The Longest Winter,* New York, 2004

Kershaw, Ian, *Hitler 1936–1945: Nemesis,* London 2000

——— *The End: Hitler's Germany 1944–45,* London, 2011

Kershaw, Robert, *It Never Snows in September,* London, 2008

Klemperer, Victor, *To the Bitter End: The Diaries of Victor Klemperer, 1942–45,* London, 2000

Koskimaki, George E., *The Battered Bastards of Bastogne: The 101st Airborne in the Battle of the Bulge,* New York, 2007

Lacouture, Jean, *De Gaulle: Le Politique,* Paris, 1985

Lindsay, Martin, *So Few Got Through,* Barnsley, 2000

Ludewig, Joachim, *Rückzug: The German Retreat from France, 1944,* Lexington, KY, 2012

MacDonald, Charles B., *A Time for Trumpets: The Untold Story of the Battle of the Bulge,* New York, 1984; *The Battle of the Bulge,* London, 1984

———— *The Mighty Endeavour: The American War in Europe,* New York, 1992

———— *Company Commander,* New York, 2002

———— *The Battle of the Huertgen Forest,* Philadelphia, PA, 2003

McDonald, Frederick A., *Remembered Light: Glass Fragments from World War II,* San Francisco, 2007

Massu, Jacques, *Sept ans avec Leclerc,* Paris, 1974

Mather, Carol, *When the Grass Stops Growing,* Barnsley, 1997

Merriam, Robert E., *Dark December,* New York, 1947

———— *The Battle of the Bulge,* New York, 1991

Meyer, Hubert, *The 12th SS: The History of the Hitler Youth Panzer Division,* vol. ii, Mechanicsburg, PA, 2005

Miller, Edward G., *A Dark and Bloody Ground: The Hürtgen Forest and the Roer River Dams, 1944–1945,* College Station, TX, 2008

Mitcham, Samuel W., Jr, *Panzers in Winter,* Mechanicsburg, PA, 2008

Moorehead, Caroline, *Martha Gellhorn,* London, 2003

Mortimer Moore, William, *Free France's Lion: The Life of Philippe Leclerc,* Havertown, PA, 2011

Neillands, Robin, *The Battle for the Rhine 1944: Arnhem and the Ardennes,* London, 2006

Neitzel, Sönke, and Welzer, Harald, *Soldaten: On Fighting, Killing and Dying,* New York, 2012

Niven, David, *The Moon's a Balloon,* London, 1994

Nobécourt, Jacques, *Le Dernier Coup de dés de Hitler,* Paris, 1962

Overmans, Rüdiger, *Deutsche militärische Verluste im Zweiten Weltkrieg,* Munich, 2000

Parker, Danny S. (ed.), *Hitler's Ardennes Offensive: The German View of the Battle of the Bulge,* London, 1997

Pogue, Forrest C., *The Supreme Command,* Washington, DC, 1954

———— *George C. Marshall: Organizer of Victory,* New York, 1973

———— *Pogue's War: Diaries of a WWII Combat Historian,* Lexington, KY, 2001

Post, Hans, *One Man in his Time,* Sydney, 2002

Ritchie, Sebastian, *Arnhem: Myth and Reality: Airborne Warfare, Air Power and the Failure of Operation Market Garden*, London, 2011

Roberts, Andrew, *Masters and Commanders*, London, 2008

Roberts, Mary Louise, *Foreign Affairs: Sex, Power, and American G.I.s in France, 1944–1946*, Chicago, 2013

Schrijvers, Peter, *The Crash of Ruin: American Combat Soldiers in Europe during World War II*, New York, 1998

———— *The Unknown Dead: Civilians in the Battle of the Bulge*, Lexington, KY, 2005

———— *Liberators: The Allies and Belgian Society, 1944–1945*, Cambridge, 2009

———— *Those Who Hold Bastogne*, New Haven, CT, 2014

Sears, Stephen W., *The Battle of the Bulge*, New York, 2004

Simpson, Louis, *Selected Prose*, New York, 1989

Soffer, Jonathan M., *General Matthew B. Ridgway*, Westport, CT, 1998

Speer, Albert, *Inside the Third Reich*, London, 1971

Spoto, Donald, *Blue Angel: The Life of Marlene Dietrich*, New York, 1992

Stargardt, Nicholas, *Witnesses of War: Children's Lives under the Nazis*, London, 2005

Sterling Rush, Robert, *Hell in Hürtgen Forest:*

The Ordeal and Triumph of an American Infantry Regiment, Lawrence, KS, 2001

Strawson, John, *The Battle for the Ardennes,* London, 1972

Strong, Kenneth, *Intelligence at the Top,* London, 1970

Tedder, Arthur, *With Prejudice,* London, 1966

Van Creveld, Martin L., *Fighting Power: German and U.S. Army Performance, 1939–1945,* Westport, CT, 1982

Vassiltchikov, Marie 'Missie', *The Berlin Diaries, 1940–1945,* London, 1987

Weigley, Russell F., *Eisenhower's Lieutenants,* Bloomington, IN, 1990

Weinberg, Gerhard L., *A World at Arms: A Global History of World War II,* Cambridge, 1994

Weintraub, Stanley, *Eleven Days in December,* New York, 2006

Welch, David, *Propaganda and the German Cinema 1933–1945,* Oxford, 1983

Whiting, Charles, *The Battle of Hürtgen Forest,* Stroud, 2007

Wijers, Hans J. (ed.), *The Battle of the Bulge: The Losheim Gap, Doorway to the Meuse,* Brummen, 2001

Wilmot, Chester, *The Struggle for Europe,* London, 1952

Wingeate Pike, David, 'Oberbefehl West: Armeegruppe G: Les Armées allemandes dans le Midi de la France', *Guerres Mondiales et conflits contemporains,* Nos. 152, 164, 174, 181

Winton, Harold R., *Corps Commanders of the Bulge: Six American Generals and Victory in the Ardennes,* Lawrence, KS, 2007

Wolfe, Martin, *Green Light!,* Philadelphia, PA, 1989

Zimmermann, John, *Pflicht zum Untergang: Die deutsche Kriegführung im Westen des Reiches, 1944/45,* Paderborn, 2009

ACKNOWLEDGEMENTS

A book like this could not have been re-searched without an enormous amount of help from friends and strangers. I am above all deeply grateful to Rick Atkinson, who generously passed me all his research notes on the period. These proved an excellent guide, saving me much time in the early stages in the archives when one is apt to flounder.

I also owe a great deal to many others who deserve my heartfelt thanks. Le comte Hadelin de Liedekerke Beaufort, on whose estates round Celles the German spearhead of the 2nd Panzer-Division was smashed, not only invited me to stay. He also put me in touch with M. Jean-Michel Delvaux, the historian of civilian experiences in the region of Celles and Rochefort during the war, and whose own impressive work was a huge help. HSH le duc d'Arenberg, on whose estate the 116th Panzer-Division fought, kindly arranged for his steward, M. Paul Gobiet, to drive me

803

around to all the places of interest.

Sebastian Cox, the head of the Air Historical Branch at the Ministry of Defence, provided general advice on the use of airpower and was especially helpful on the details of Operation *Bodenplatte.* Orlando Figes put me in touch with his uncle Ernest Unger, who kindly related the story of Gerhardt Unger. Ron Schroer of the Australian War Memorial contacted Hans Post, who kindly provided his memoir and tapes of his interviews on his experiences in the SS during the campaign. Professor Tami Davis Biddle of the US Army War College, Sir Max Hastings, Dr Stefan Goebel and James Holland all helped with advice, material and books.

I am also indebted to Ronald Blunden, my publisher in France, for the papers of his father, Godfrey Blunden; Mrs Anne Induni, the daughter of Air Marshal Sir James Robb, the Deputy Chief of Staff (Air) at SHAEF, for her father's paper 'Higher Direction of War', written at Bentley Priory in November 1946; and Dr Arthur S. Couch for his unpublished memoir of the winter of 1944.

I naturally owe a great deal to the help and good advice of archivists, including William Spencer and his colleagues at The National Archives at Kew; Dr Conrad Crane, Dr Richard Sommers and all the staff at USAMHI, Carlisle, Pennsylvania; Dr Tim Nenninger and Richard Peuser at the NARA at College Park, Maryland; the staff at the Liddell Hart Centre for Military Archives at King's College London and the staff at the Imperial War Museum. Harland Evans helped me gather material at The National Archives, the IWM and the Liddell Hart Centre.

Finally I am forever grateful to my agent and friend Andrew Nurnberg, as well as Robin Straus in the United States, and also Eleo Gordon, my editor at Penguin in London, and Kathryn Court in New York. Peter James again proved to be the ideal copy-editor, but my greatest thanks as always go to my wife and editor of first resort, Artemis. The book is dedicated to our son Adam, who achieved a First in Modern History while I was writing some of the most complex chapters and thus spurred me on to greater effort.

ABOUT THE AUTHOR

Antony Beevor is the author of *Crete: The Battle and the Resistance* (winner of the Runciman Prize), *Stalingrad* (winner of the Samuel Johnson Prize, Wolfson Prize for History, and Hawthornden Prize for Literature), *Berlin: The Downfall*, *The Battle for Spain* (winner of Premio La Vanguardia), *D-Day: The Battle for Normandy* (winner of Prix Henry Malherbe and the Royal United Services Institute Westminster Medal), and *The Second World War*. His books have appeared in more than thirty languages and have sold more than six million copies. A former chairman of the Society of Authors, he has received honorary doctorates from the Universities of Kent, Bath, East Anglia and York. He is also a visiting professor at the University of Kent.

The employees of Thorndike Press hope you have enjoyed this Large Print book. All our Thorndike, Wheeler, and Kennebec Large Print titles are designed for easy reading, and all our books are made to last. Other Thorndike Press Large Print books are available at your library, through selected bookstores, or directly from us.

For information about titles, please call:
  (800) 223-1244

or visit our Web site at:
  http://gale.cengage.com/thorndike

To share your comments, please write:
  Publisher
  Thorndike Press
  10 Water St., Suite 310
  Waterville, ME 04901